PREFACE.

SOON after the appearance of the Second Edition (considerably enlarged) of the German original of these *Lectures*,[1] I received inquiries from various quarters, both in the United Kingdom and in America, as to my intention to promote their translation into English. These inquiries convinced me that, though calculated in the first instance to meet the special needs of thinking people in Germany, my work might yet prove useful, and supply a want that was sensibly felt elsewhere. Nothing, indeed, can be more evident than that there is everywhere in the present day a certain community of interests in the ranks both of Christianity and Unbelief,—no noteworthy production appearing anywhere now on either side without soon being made, by means of translations, the common property of like-minded readers in all languages. We all know too well how much injury German Rationalism and Infidelity have done to the cause of Christ in other lands. It seems, therefore, to be a special obligation resting on faithful orthodox theologians in Germany to endeavour to extend their influence beyond the limits of their own Fatherland, and to show to Christian students in other countries what weapons and tactics they have found most useful in repelling the assaults of Unbelief among themselves. In the present instance I had, moreover, peculiar motives for encouraging and aiding an English translation of my book. It is now ten years ago (the winter of 1863–4), that, being then pastor of the German congregation in Islington, I delivered (at the Albion Hall, London Wall) my first series of public lectures in defence of Christianity. These lectures were addressed to the educated Germans of London generally, and a portion of the groundwork of the present series was laid in that early

[1] *Moderne Zweifel am Christlichen Glauben.* Bonn : A. Marcus, 1870.

effort to set forth a systematic plan of Christian apologetics. I may say, therefore, that this translation does in a certain way carry back to England a production whose first beginnings took their rise in that country.

The three main sources of Modern Doubt in respect to the chief points of Christian belief and verity, may be found in some of the vaunted principles and assumed results of metaphysical philosophy, historical criticism, and natural science. With the first (Lect. I.–V.), and in part with the second of these sources (*e.g.* the modern critical theories of the gospel history and the *Origines* of early Christianity, Lect. VI.–VIII.), I have dealt in such a way that the whole argument is made to turn on one main central point, the Scriptural and Christian conceptions of the Divine Nature. It has been my chief endeavour, by treating first of the fundamental relations between Reason and Revelation (in Lect. II.), and discussing the non-scriptural conceptions of modern Speculative Theology (Lect. III.), to lead on the inquirer's mind to this one great central idea (as carefully developed in Lect. IV.), and then to avail myself of the positions so obtained in dealing with the question of miraculous agency (Lect. V.), and other points made matters of dispute by our modern negative historical criticism. In the lecture on Reason and Revelation I have purposely avoided entering on the subject of the Inspiration of Scripture. My motive for such abstinence was this. I believe the decided *separation* (and not mere *distinction*) now established between the idea of Revelation on the one hand, and that of Scriptural Inspiration on the other, to be a real gain for modern Dogmatic Theology, though by the popular mind the *terms* are still regarded as almost identical in meaning. Another motive for such omission was, that I have long determined, and still hope to be able, to deal with the general question of the Inspiration of Scripture and special points therewith connected (*e.g.* the *genesis* and credibility of particular books), as well as with the objections raised by the votaries of natural science to Scripture teaching on such points as the Creation, the Deluge, the Descent of Man, etc., in a second series of Apologetic Lectures. The preparation of such a course I have already undertaken, and its completion as soon as may be, in the midst of other arduous professional duties, I shall endeavour constantly to keep in view. The present English translation of this my first series differs from the second German edition of 1870, partly by the curtailment of various passages which seemed likely to be of less interest for English and American readers, and partly by some minor additions, and the mention of important works which have since appeared on either side.

It is now becoming more and more evident every day that Christian faith stands in need of a more extended line of defence, addressed in various suitable forms to the different sections of modern society. Whereas, when in former times objections were raised to the truths and facts of Christianity,—first in England, then in France, and finally in the German fatherland,—it was generally assumed that the challengers of Revelation ought to bear the burden of proof, the tables are now turned, and those who still believe *anything* are called on to justify their presumption in doing so. Experience, moreover, amply shows that countless as are the smaller apologetic writings composed for some special purpose or occasion, they are almost invariably short-lived, while more comprehensive works covering the whole ground are as yet by no means numerous. Popular works, moreover, in defence of Christianity, calculated to meet the needs of uncultured readers, however much good they may do in their own sphere, cannot satisfy the wants of the thoroughly educated, who, more intimately acquainted with the arguments on the other side, feel that a victory too easily won really leaves the battle unfought.

It is true that professed apologists, like Luthardt (whose lectures are well known by translations both in England and America), have addressed themselves in some respects to these higher needs. Still I have found many intelligent laymen who were far from being satisfied by a few remarks on certain cardinal questions, such as the relations between Reason and Revelation, the pantheistic and other philosophical conceptions of God, the possibility of the miraculous, etc., much to the point as those remarks might be; and from this I have been led to conclude that in some quarters a need was still felt of something beyond what had hitherto been effected by Christian apologists. This need I would fain meet by my treatment of these fundamental questions in the present work. Inclinations and wants differ greatly. Some—and these form the majority—wish to have everything compressed into the smallest possible compass, and *their* wants are already well attended to. But others—if not, perhaps, very many amongst the laity—are willing to expend time and trouble in studying the disputed points. To such I trust these lectures may prove of some service. They are not, it will be seen, intended to be "popular" in the broadest meaning of the word. They are primarily addressed, not to the great body of uncultured or half-cultured readers, but to earnest-minded inquirers among the really cultivated, who are accustomed to think logically, and whose mental powers I have accordingly in some passages pretty severely taxed. I have, however, throughout endeavoured to make myself widely intelligible, as well as to preserve the scientific character of the work; and I venture to hope that it may be of some use to students of divinity and other younger men at our universities generally, by conducting them to at least a preliminary acquaintance with the most important theological questions of the day. Infidelity is now, both in Germany and elsewhere, especially fond of vaunting itself as being "science" *par excellence;* and the influence exercised by the deluge of anti-Christian literature and journalism threatens to lead many from among our educated circles to ignore the fact that a Christian science and philosophy still exists to do battle for the claims of Christian faith. At such a time it is both our duty and our privilege to witness more particularly to men of thought and culture among us, and to give them clear and thorough proofs that in CHRIST are indeed "hidden all the treasures of wisdom and of knowledge;" that unbelief, in fighting against Christ, rejects the truth, and that in rejecting the truth it contradicts science. Doubly necessary must this be in an age which evinces more and more clearly that all the great intellectual, political, and social "questions" by which society is agitated, must finally be resolved into the one great problem of the truth of Christianity.

Towards the fulfilment of this ennobling apologetic task, I would fain contribute my own humble efforts. I have everywhere endeavoured to *acknowledge what is true in the views of my opponents;* and that the more, because I not unfrequently missed such acknowledgment in other apologetic works. Error is always assuredly a mixture of truth and falsehood, nor can be overcome so long as the elements of truth which it contains are unacknowledged, and not carefully separated from what is false. On the other hand, I have sought strictly to avoid unreal compromises—such as those attempted by a certain school in Germany—between Christianity and modern thought, believing, as I do, that they must invariably result in detriment to both sides; nor have I ever knowingly allowed myself to polish off the sharp angles of the One Corner-stone. Everywhere have I found it necessary fearlessly to indicate the fundamental conditions, both moral and religious, for the reception of our faith, and at the same time to maintain in its full force the distinction between "believers and unbelievers," which our opponents have of late attacked more boldly than ever. It is a sad token of religious laxity and indefiniteness that men should try to efface the clear line of demarcation here drawn by Scripture, and to change the decided colours into mere shades. If there be no essential difference in *this* matter, then there is none at all, and the whole strife has been waged in vain!

No genuine apologetic science can neglect this distinction; but for that very reason it cannot expect to succeed in bringing back at once the world as a whole to a belief in Christianity. Things moral and spiritual cannot be mathematically demonstrated, still less can divine truths. He who said, "My thoughts are not as your thoughts," has embodied in His words and actions a far higher logic than that whose principles Aristotle laid down. The acceptance of His truths cannot be forced on any by mere reasoning; least of all on those who have not the *will* to believe, and who therefore have never inquired earnestly as to the *way*. Even oral lectures in defence of Christianity, as far as my experience goes, are but rarely visited by persons of the latter class. The greater part by far of those who attend such lectures consists of professed believers and church-goers; and they, too, are the chief readers of apologetic works. In them they seek for armour against the attacks of infidelity, or for instruction which shall enable them to attain a clearer insight into the grounds of their belief. But even if such works should pass comparatively unnoticed by confirmed sceptics, yet should *furnish weapons to those who still hold to their faith,* strengthening their courage and enabling them to fight the good fight; this would be a full reward for the labour expended on them, and a good service rendered to the Church of Christ.

In conclusion, therefore, I would in all humility commend these feeble efforts to the Lord, that He would accompany them in their workings, both among friends and enemies, with His benediction. If what I have written should not avail to bring back many doubters to the faith, it may, nevertheless, instruct believers as to the certainty of the convictions which they have embraced, the stedfastness of the foundation on which they stand, and assure them of a complete and final victory. The Lord needs not us or our efforts in His cause. He who in His own person is the Truth itself, is at once Faith's argument, Faith's object, and Faith's pledge of ultimate triumph. Only His people must believe in that triumph if they would one day share in it, and that the more confidently when the course of this world seems to render it most improbable. Their faith, indeed, in Truth's final victory is already that Victory's inauguration!

THEODORE CHRISTLIEB.

BONN, *January* 1874.

CONTENTS.

FIRST LECTURE.

THE EXISTING BREACH BETWEEN MODERN CULTURE AND CHRISTIANITY.

SECOND LECTURE.

REASON AND REVELATION.

THIRD LECTURE.

MODERN NON-BIBLICAL CONCEPTIONS OF GOD.

FOURTH LECTURE.

THE THEOLOGY OF SCRIPTURE AND OF THE CHURCH.

FIFTH LECTURE.

THE MODERN NEGATION OF MIRACLES.

PAGE

SIXTH LECTURE.

MODERN ANTI-MIRACULOUS ACCOUNTS OF THE LIFE OF CHRIST

SEVENTH LECTURE.

MODERN DENIALS OF THE RESURRECTION.

EIGHTH LECTURE.

THE MODERN CRITICAL THEORY OF PRIMITIVE CHRISTIANITY.

MODERN DOUBT AND CHRISTIAN BELIEF.

FIRST LECTURE.

THE EXISTING BREACH BETWEEN MODERN CULTURE AND CHRISTIANITY.

OUR German forefathers had a grand old legend connected with the terrific battle of Chalons, at which, in the middle of the fifth century, the combined forces of Visigoths and Romans obtained a sanguinary triumph over the invading hordes of Attila. The bloody work of the sword was done, and the vast plain strewed with countless heaps of dead. But for three nights following—so ran the tale—the spirits of the slain might be discovered hovering over the scene of their late encounters, and continuing their ruthless conflicts in the air. The like has been the case with the age-long war still waged against the gospel, which, if at first conducted mainly with the sword, has now resolved itself into endless conflicts of opposing spirits. To give you some insight into the present condition of this world-wide struggle, more enduring and more significant than any material conflict, and lead you by the hand, as it were, to those parts of the battle-field where the hottest strife is raging, will be my endeavour in the following Lectures. And first, we must take a survey of the mighty field itself, or, in other words, make ourselves acquainted, so far as may be in a single view, with the full extent of the existing breach between our modern culture and Christianity.

That such a breach exists, needs surely no proof from me. Thousands of educated persons now feel themselves compelled, as by an essential requirement of modern intellectual culture, to assume a critical position towards the whole of Christianity, so far as it transcends the sphere of merely natural or rational religion, regarding it as an indubitable sign of defective cultivation or narrow-minded partisanship, when any one professes an unreserved adherence to all the articles of the Christian faith. Great masses of so-called "cultivated" persons in Germany may be said, indeed, to entertain a deep-seated mistrust of all that is positive in Christian faith, even though still acknowledging the truth and obligation of Christian morals. Such doctrines of the gospel as, for instance, the Trinity, the Incarnation, the Atonement, are quietly demurred to by these people, or put aside as mere anachronisms, about which the present generation hardly needs to trouble itself. Have they not read in numerous popular books and novels, papers and periodicals, and heard asserted in every educated circle, by how many social authorities these and the like doctrines are now openly impugned? The first discovery that it was so, and the assurance with which it was proclaimed, may indeed have startled some a little. But by degrees they got used to the current expression of sceptical opinions, and to appeals on their behalf to the imposing authority of great scientific and philosophic names, so as in the sequel, from fear of being laughed at in educated circles for their childlike credulity, to be found ready to surrender bit by bit the whole religious faith of their fathers. The first thing given up would of course be the personal existence of the Evil One; then (for the sake of Balaam's ass, or Joshua's address to the sun and moon, or the Mosaic history of creation) the authority of the Old Testament; then, one after another, single miracles of the New Testament; and finally, the doctrine of our Lord's divinity, His resurrection and ascension, and all the other revealed foundations on which Christian faith is built.

Serious and alarming as such a condition of things must be for every one who regards it in the light of past history and of the prophetic word, it will avail nothing to make these phenomena a mere subject of lamentation. We must have the courage to look them in the face, and endeavour to comprehend their true significance. Spinoza's word applies here: "Human things are neither to be laughed at nor wept over; our duty is to understand them." But this can only be accomplished in the present case by a careful investigation of the historical and other causes which have conspired to produce the present alienation of modern society from Christian faith.

We must inquire, therefore, first, What may be the historical and ethical factors by which the existing breach between Culture and Christianity has been gradually formed? and secondly, How wide and how deep this breach at present may be? A summary answer to these questions, which of course is all that could be attempted here, may nevertheless enable us, with our knowledge of the nature of Christianity and of Modern Culture, to suggest an answer to a third question, Whether at all, and how far, this breach can be closed?

I.—CAUSES OF THE BREACH.

These may be classed under the following heads: *Historical, Scientific, Ecclesiastical, Political, Social* and *Ethical,* to each of which we must now devote a brief attention.

a. And first, the *Historical.* Modern unbelief is only in part a new phenomenon. It stands in the closest connection with similar movements in all past times, of which it is the natural outcome and result. Christianity has never existed in the world without experiencing opposition, nor deceived itself by expecting it to be otherwise. "*This same is set for a sign that shall be spoken against,*" cried aged Simeon at the first contemplation of the child Jesus. And the history of the Acts of the Apostles closes with the witness of the Jews in Rome: "*Concerning this sect, we know that everywhere it is spoken against.*" To what a height the contradiction rose in the period embraced by this twofold testimony, may be seen in the histories of the Lord's passion, and of the persecutions of the early Church and His first disciples. Each apostle enters on his mission prepared for the extremest conflicts. "*We preach Christ crucified,*" exclaims St. Paul, "*to the Jews a stumbling-block, and to the Greeks foolishness.*" The first encounter between Christian truth and heathen culture is recorded in the seventeenth chapter of the Acts, which tells how fearlessly St. Paul proclaimed strange and unwelcome truths in the metropolis of classical refinement, and in the hearing of the leaders of the old systems of philosophy. From that moment the gospel was assailed, not only by the fanatical hatred of the Jew and the unscrupulous violence of Roman statecraft, but also by the intellectual weapons of Hellenic literature and science.

Cynics, Epicureans, and Neo-Platonists produce elaborate treatises in disproof of Christianity. Celsus attacks it with considerable acumen as an imposition. Lucian, a thorough unbeliever in all religious systems, pours out his scorn on Christianity as "the latest folly in the world's great madhouse," and ridicules its martyrs. Christian writers find it necessary to give their treatises in defence of the gospel a scientific shape, and a valuable apologetic literature is gradually formed among the Greek and Latin Fathers.

After three centuries of conflict, victory finally declares herself on the side of the new religion. Christianity triumphs in the Roman Empire, and gradually absorbing the remains of the old classic culture, derives therefrom a powerful impulse towards the production of a new Christian form of civilisation in the west. And even here the first beginnings of an occidental Christian philosophy are found to generate or foster doubts as to the proofs or evidences of some of the verities of Christian faith. The subtle doctors of medieval scholasticism are seen to move uneasily in the fetters of ecclesiastical dogma, and it ofttimes taxes the most strenuous efforts of a powerful hierarchy to conceal or cover over the yawning gulf between faith and science. The antagonists of revealed truth are henceforth to be found within the Christian camp itself, and their attacks become in consequence the more formidable.

The great Protestant Reformation, with all its added strength to the cause of faith, will be likewise found to have introduced fresh elements of danger. We now see the great religious principle of man's personal responsibility, though maintained by the Reformers in the strictest subordination to the supreme authority of the divine word, aiming more and more, under humanistic and other influences, at unlimited self-assertion, and gradually emancipating itself from every kind of authority, even upon fundamental articles of faith. The conditions of the conflict are now changed. Whereas in former times the various elements of the old classical culture and philosophy had opposed themselves to Christianity as something young and new, so now henceforth Christianity and its articles of faith are regarded as old and obsolescent by the advocates of modern cultivation and science. It is the children rising up in strife against an aged mother.

It was not, however, till towards the end of the seventeenth century that free modes of thought began to obtain any sensible influence with the common people. But now, the more cold and lifeless Church orthodoxy had become, and the more all sound theological inquiry was again degenerating into scholastic subtleties, the greater was the impulse felt to proceed with rapid strides from freedom of conscience to unrestrained free-thinking. Such thinkers as Descartes, Spinoza, Pufendorf, Thomasius, Bayle, Leibnitz, and Wolf, proceeded with more or less temerity to unsettle all traditional religious convictions, and in some cases to destroy their very foundations; while a new presumptuous popular philosophy of sound common sense (so called) began to develope an almost open hostility to the revealed doctrines of all churches.

In the fifteenth and sixteenth centuries, Italy had taken the lead in the development of free thought; in the seventeenth and eighteenth, England and France are the first to show the way. In England, from the middle of the seventeenth to that of the eighteenth century, one portion after another of the great body of Christian faith is dissolved in the crucible of a Hobbes or a Hume, or under the attacks of the long series of the English deists,—Herbert of Cherbury, Toland, Collins, Woolston, Shaftesbury, Tindal, Chubb, Bolingbroke, and others. Unitarians having begun with the denial of the Trinity and the Incarnation, these deists soon follow, first with the rejection of the prophecies and miracles of the Old Testament, and then of those of the New, as opposed to reason and the laws of nature; and finally, with the denial of a special Providence, or any possibility of a divine revelation. From about the year 1690 to the rise of Methodism, and the consequent revival of evangelical religion in the Church of England and among Protestant Dissenters, it might be said that in many a circle of English society the denial of all that was specifically Christian, or in excess of the axioms of natural religion, had come to be regarded as a sign of superior intelligence, and the maintenance of contrary opinions as a proof of being quite behind the progress of the times, as one so often hears remarked in a similar spirit in German circles now.

These results of English free-thinking were speedily introduced into France by Condillac and others. Jesuitism had in that country been slowly but surely undermining all the foundations of true religion and morality. Pascal, the man of conscience (a Protestant without knowing it), and Malebranche, were the last philosophers in France who reverenced Christianity. The *Grand Monarque,* whose influence formed the character of the whole century, based his supremacy in Europe on a culture which consciously derived its forms and principles, not from the spirit of the gospel, but from that of Greek and Roman civilisation. The general apostasy from Christian faith thus induced was for a time concealed (under the prevailing Jesuit influence) by the outward forms of a ceremonial religion, while secretly diffusing itself among the polished circles of Parisian society. Political interests, and not religious, were henceforth the motive powers in the public life of Europe, which became more and more secular and humanistic. Religious indifferentism, rapidly degenerating into selfish pleasure-seeking and grosser forms of immorality, became the prevalent temper in French social circles,—a phenomenon which is not wanting among those characteristic of our own time.

It was not, however, till the middle of the eighteenth century that all reverence for the teaching and witness of the Church was openly abandoned. Voltaire now appears upon the scene. Exercising almost absolute control, through the force of genius, over the intellect of Europe, and from the first directing inexhaustible stores of wit and raillery against religion, he did more than any other man of his age to promote the spread of unbelief among the people. The annihilation of positive Christianity Voltaire regarded as his great object in life. The heroes of the Bible were for him mere knaves and fools, and the Gospel history a tissue of fables, fit only for "cobblers and tailors." Luther, the Augustinian monk, opposed indulgences out of mere partisanship. "Had only Leo X. committed the sale to him and his order instead of the Dominicans, we should have had no Protestants!" Morality and progressive civilisation were to be regarded as much more indebted to classic paganism than to Christianity; and it is to ignorance of the gospel in the Chinese Empire that we may attribute the superiority of that people to ourselves in morals, philosophy, and general culture! Could only the Chinese religion of pure deism be adopted throughout Europe, it would put a speedy termination to all our miseries and disputes.[1] Notwithstanding all this wretched superficiality and perfidious perversion of historic truth, Voltaire succeeded in carrying the whole mind and spirit of his age along with him. Matters reached such a pass at length, that the most frivolous assailant of Christianity was more honoured and listened to than the most intelligent of its advocates. Doubts and arguments against the gospel were accepted without examination, while aught urged in its defence was condemned unheard: phenomena of which we have again a repetition in our own time. Take, for instance, among many other examples, the French Encyclopædists and Materialists; a Diderot with his axiom, "True religion is to have none at all;" a La Mettrie announcing to the world that it will never be happy till atheism becomes universal; the *Système de la Nature*, according to which man is no longer composed of body and spirit, but of mere material substances; and finally, the fatal convulsion of the French Revolution (the after-shocks of which are still felt in France and Europe), with its impudent assaults on the whole fabric of Christian faith and morals, down to the very existence of the Christian calendar,—take only these examples, and you will see how unbelief in the last century passed through the same stages and arrived at the same results as now: beginning with doubts and difficulties about Christian miracles and gospel mysteries, it ended with complete negation of the divine and spiritual, the very existence of God Himself, and of any moral and spiritual life in man. The laws of historical development are inexorable. The seed sown was Jesuitical morality and superstition: the harvest reaped was materialism and infidelity.

In Germany, the general influences of the spirit of the time were most profoundly felt. The mere name of Frederick the Great, "the philosopher of Sans Souci," friend and patron

[1] Compare especially, *Voltaire et son temps, Etudes sur le 18ième siècle*, par L. F. Bungener. Roman Catholics often complain that unbelief is a mere product of Protestantism. Quite lately Bishop Dupanloup, in his book *Atheism and the Social Danger*, says: "Protestantism began the work of unbelief in Europe." A comparison between the piety of Luther and the frivolity of Pope Leo, or the mere name of Voltaire, is enough for a refutation of this silly charge.

of Voltaire, is enough to indicate how great the influence must have been of French intellectual culture in our own land. And what the French literature of unbelief did for the general public, English literature accomplished among the learned. Rationalism, however, properly so called, *i.e.* the denial of all dogmas which seem incredible to the ordinary understanding, is an outgrowth of our own soil. The Leibnitz-Wolfian philosophy, which laid the foundation for a mechanical superficial treatment of Christian doctrines, contributed largely to the general alienation from Christian faith. A sort of natural religion began to be taught both in upper and lower schools, in which it was endeavoured to demonstrate the principles of Christian faith entirely by those of natural reason. Revealed religion, under this process, soon appeared to become a superfluity, and whatever in it could not be demonstrated by reason was quietly abandoned.

The most powerful attacks in Germany on the faith of the Church were made during the second half of the last century, when Rationalism had already gained the upper hand. The so-called *Wolfenbüttel Fragments*, published by Lessing, shook the faith of many in the truth of revelation, and especially in the cardinal doctrine of the resurrection of Christ, representing the whole of our Lord's life and teaching as mere human phenomena. The notorious Bahrdt, of sottish memory, first professor and finally publican (†1792), endeavoured, by an admixture of vulgar sentimentality, to convert our Lord's life into a kind of romance somewhat after the fashion of Renan. And finally, Nicolai, in his *Allgemeine Deutsche Bibliothek*, the most popular literary periodical of the time (1765–1805), made it his business to cast a reproach of superstition or suspicion of crypto-Jesuitism on all that went beyond the very baldest rationalistic morality. At such a time, when even ministers of the Church, conforming to the general taste, chose for the subjects of their sermons points of general morality or natural science, the pursuits of agriculture, or the benefits of vaccination, we cannot wonder at its becoming the general conviction that the breach between modern culture and Christianity was complete and final.

Such was the inheritance which the present century received from its predecessor. Can we wonder at its prevailing unbelief, even without the accession of other fresh causes of such alienation? Among these we proceed to mention—

b. Secondly, The *Modern Scientific* or *Philosophical.*

Several branches of modern science have received since the early years of the present century a very rapid and brilliant development, which has largely contributed to widen the breach between Modern Culture and Christianity. Of these we may mention Mental Science or Metaphysical Philosophy, the Historical Criticism of Scripture, and several branches of Natural Science.

The general, but at first indefinite, aim of the eighteenth century to resolve revealed religion into mere morality, and the cardinal articles of Christian faith into abstract ideas,—as of God, of freedom, of immortality, and the like,—received towards its close a definite expression and scientific form from one whose speculations constituted a fresh epoch in the history of philosophy—Immanuel Kant. This earnest thinker always spoke of the Bible and Christianity with the deepest reverence and respect. It was his honest endeavour to hold fast the faith in *God,* in *freedom,* and in *immortality* as indispensable requirements of "practical reason," and to limit the excesses of philosophical speculation by denying to "pure reason" (reason proper) the right or power of making positive determinations in things divine. Yet this notwithstanding, it cannot be denied that he contributed a powerful impulse to religious doubt, by laying down, and endeavouring with great force and subtlety to prove (in his *Critique of Pure Reason*), that those ideas, when practically applied, would lead only to erroneous and illogical consequences: that the idea of God, for instance, depends upon a chain of illogical conclusions, and that all received arguments for the existence of God are untenable. You will easily see what encouragement such speculations must have given to any floating doubts on the truth and certainty of positive religion.

With Kant's successors, Fichte and Schelling, these efforts of speculative reason were under much less restraint; and even the sacred triad of God, freedom, and immortality, which Kant had endeavoured to maintain by appeals to practical reason, was absorbed, along with the idea ot Divine Personality, in an all-confounding idealistic Pantheism. This last received from Hegel its final development, who maintained that the development of the universe consists in the inner logical process by which thought proceeds from consciousness to self-consciousness,—pure absolute unqualified Being having first to be developed into Nature before it can pass into its higher form of self-conscious Spirit.

But such metaphysical speculations, utterly unintelligible without profound study, would have had small influence on the general public, but for their reproduction in more genial and comprehensible forms in our classical literature. From Schiller, ardent student as he was of the Kantian philosophy, onwards to Heine (long an enthusiastic adherent of Hegelianism) and his English and American compeers, Carlyle and Emerson, we find innumerable views and utterances in the works of poets, orators, and historians which owe their origin to those philosophical systems. Hence in the present day we meet so many educated persons whose faith in the personal Deity has resolved itself into a belief in "the moral order of the universe," or in some universal "law" or "principle," from which there may not indeed be much to hope, but also —and that is something—very little to fear. Many who know nothing more of Kant or Fichte than one or two much-abused phrases, consider themselves raised by their philosophic insight above any necessity of submission to the dogmas of revealed religion.

But it is not so much philosophical speculation as historical criticism from which the present generation derives its unbelief. Truths which rest on plain facts of history are not in the long run to be successfully impugned by mere speculations. But assaults which threaten to shake the historical foundation on which they stand are much more formidable. And such have been those most frequently undertaken in our own times. The conflict is now removed from the field of mere speculative reasoning to that of historical criticism of the *Origines* of Christianity. Two Swabian celebrities, Strauss and Baur, here lead the way. Strauss, proceeding from a pantheistic point of view, and an absolute denial of the possibility of miracles, represented in his *Life of Jesus* (first published more than thirty years ago) the whole Gospel history as in all its essential portions a mere chain of myths, products of the inventive fancies of the first disciples and the early Church, and made special efforts to annihilate in detail the various miraculous accounts by a skilful combination of minute discrepancies in the Gospel narratives. A fresh revision, or rather the reproduction of the original work in a popular form, is that which has more recently appeared under the title of *The Life of Jesus for the German People.* Baur, on the other hand, starting from similar Hegelian views of the nature of historical developments, endeavoured in a series of acute and profoundly learned treatises to divest Christianity of its claims to any supernatural origin, by representing it as the natural product and combination of innumerable pre-Christian forms of thought, belief, and expectation. In his historical investigations concerning the New Testament, he arrived at the result that all its books, excepting only four epistles of St. Paul (Romans, 1 and 2 Corinthians, and Galatians), with the Revelation of St. John, are spurious productions of an age about a century later than that of the apostles and evangelists to whom they are assigned. The strenuous efforts now everywhere made to popularize such matters has brought at any rate the names of these and similar works by disciples of Strauss and Baur to the knowledge of almost every educated person in Germany; while Renan's (the French Strauss) *Vie de Jésus,* translated, as it has been, into all the languages of Europe, and everywhere disseminated in forms ridiculously cheap, has found hundreds of thousands of readers in the lowest grades of society.

Of the thorough and searching examination to which these works have been subjected in the replies of Neander, Tholuck, Ullmann, Ebrard, and many others, few except professed theologians seem to have even heard, and fewer still have given themselves the trouble to investigate the matter for themselves. Hence the assumption now so common among educated and half-educated people in Germany, that the mythical character of the Gospel narration, and the spuriousness of most of the books of the New Testament, are points no longer admitting of any serious question. Very few, indeed, in ordinary social circles would seem to be aware that the monstrously arbitrary assumptions of Strauss in his *Leben Jesu,* the weakness of his critical assaults on the historical sources of the Gospel narrative, and the scientifically untenable character of his much-vaunted results, have long ago been thoroughly exposed, and that the same work has been satisfactorily accomplished for Baur's elaborate theories of the nature and origin of primitive Christianity by a long series of orthodox historians and expositors.

But this is not all. To the afore-mentioned causes of our present unbelief you must add, further, the enormous influence of modern forms of that natural science to which, in preference to all others, the materialistic spirit of our age is so much inclined, the serious doubts raised by geology as to the truth of the scriptural narrative in reference to the Creation and Deluge, as well as to the age of the world and that of the human race; the objections raised on the score of astronomy to biblical representations of the creation of the heavenly bodies and the position of our earth in the starry universe; and the doubts, for which appeal is made to physiology and cognate sciences, as to the truth of the scriptural teaching concerning the derivation of all human races from a single pair. Putting all these doubts, objections, and assumptions together, and bearing in mind the boldness and assurance with which they are maintained, and the attitude assumed by modern science generally, with its claim even in its latest most infantine forms to summon all other teachers of truth before its bar, you will have a comprehensive though superficial view of the principal historical and scientific causes which have led to the existing breach between Modern Culture and Christianity.

But even these are not all. We must add to them—

c. Thirdly, *Causes Ecclesiastical.*—This deplorable breach, alas, is widened by the unhallowed labours, past and present, of the Church herself. And here you must suffer me awhile to pause and make a series of honest though painful confessions.

It is a phenomenon that meets us in the earliest history of the Christian Church, that the outbreak of heresies goes hand in hand with the loss of spiritual life in the Church at large; that the rise of doubts has often coincided with the prevalence of fruitless controversies; and that open opposition to, or separation from, the Church universal, has been the consequence of abuses and neglects in practice, or of one-sidedness and exaggeration in dogmatic teaching. How has the Church commonly acted in reference to such opposition, brought upon her so frequently by her own fault? Has she not, both in earlier and later times, been all too ready to condemn those who differed from her with stern anathemas, and to call in the aid of the secular arm to enforce obedience from the unconvinced and unwilling? And yet how much better would it have become her to have inquired, when opposition rose, what fault of her own might have given it occasion, and even some measure of right! How well would she have done in endeavouring to lay down from the very first a broad line of demarcation between undoubted and unchangeable Scripture truth and the human forms of ecclesiastical practice, which oftentimes not only admit of, but require modification, and in seeking to establish a clear distinction between what is the nucleus and centre of all Christian faith, the free grace of God in Christ, and doctrines which, belonging more to the circumference, do not immediately affect the foundations of the faith! How much distrust and painful doubt, how many a breach between progressive culture and retrogressive theology, between new discoveries of science and one-sided assertions of misapplied dogma, might have been thus avoided!

What was it in the middle ages that led so many nobler spirits into doubt as to the truth of Christianity itself, as well as to contempt of the existing Church system? Was it not, on the one hand, the growing moral corruptions of the Church, and on the other the enslavement of men's minds in the bondage of the letter? And so it came to pass that, under the shadow of an iron scholasticism, a scarcely disguised infidelity had gradually developed itself; and in the very metropolis of medieval Christianity, Rome itself, broke out occasionally into open mockery. I would on this point remind you merely of the characteristic saying attributed to Leo X. (1513–1521), 'All men know how much we and ours are indebted to the Christian fable" (showing that *Straussianer* existed long before Strauss), and of the decree of the Lateran Council, under the same Pope, that one must really believe in the immortality of the soul! So thoroughly at that time, in what was regarded as the very heart of Christendom, was the edifice of Christian faith shaken to its very foundations. The Church having lost all sense of spiritual freedom, her intellectual servitude was avenging itself by the rejection of every kind of restraint, and the surrender of all, even divine authority. Unbelief is often a mere reaction from superstition; and for the existence of the latter the Church itself is, in the first place, responsible.

Similar causes are still at work in the Roman Catholic Church in widening the breach between Culture and Christianity. On the one hand is the moral corruption of many priests and the practical abuses of the convent and the confessional; on the other, the retention of many points of medieval superstition, exposure of spurious relics on the Rhine, and periodical repetitions of miracles in Italy which no educated person can any longer seriously believe in. These things tend to make not only the Roman Catholic Church itself, but also our common Christianity, appear to many both odious and ludicrous, and a mere institute of obscurantism.

All this illustrates the important observation, that doubt and unbelief assail for the most part, not the pure essence, but the corrupted forms of Christianity. The corruptions of the Church and her dogmatic errors supply these enemies with their most formidable weapons of offence against her. They commit, indeed, the error of confounding the Church with Christianity; but this is one for which the Church herself must be held in large measure responsible, identifying, as she often does, herself, her institutions, and her customs with the very fundamentals of Christianity, so making it difficult for superficial observers to distinguish between the one and the other.

If from the Catholic Church we turn our eyes on the developments of Protestantism, we meet with the like phenomena, though in a less degree. What was it that in the last century prepared the way among ourselves for the prevalence of Rationalism? Was it not the petrification of evangelical faith in the dry forms of a dead orthodoxy, accompanied by an almost total cessation of all further efforts for the diffusion of the gospel? The sermons of that period were for the most part dry expositions of particular doctrines, accompanied by vehement attacks not only on other churches, but also on many in one's own church who happened to differ on some one point or other from the confessional standards, *e.g.* on Crypto-Calvinists, Syncretists, Synergists, Majorists, Antinomians, Osiandrians, Weigelians, and Arminians, etc. etc., making one's head swim with the bare enumeration of the various "isms" which the preacher felt himself called upon to denounce. At such a time, when a cold orthodoxy was almost everywhere being substituted for living faith, when slavish adherence to the Church's standards was put in the place of that free inquiry into the sense of Scripture which the first Reformers had pursued, and a fresh bondage of the letter was introduced, it became a simple necessity for energetic minds, like Lessing, to come to an open breach with traditional Protestantism, "which, however painful in the making, must nevertheless be regarded as providentially ordained." Rationalism was in a certain degree right in contending for simple morality in opposition to theoretic orthodoxy. Truth itself was divided; the orthodox retained one portion, their assailants another. The claims of "humanism," too long neglected on the one side, were now opposed by the other to those of "positive Christianity." Morality, too long unduly depreciated, was now exalted as unduly at the expense of faith. One extreme begat the other.

It must then be confessed that the Church theology of the last century deserves the chief blame for the general apostasy which then began from the ancient faith. And this defection was not only occasioned by the Church's own one-sidedness; it was adopted, cherished, and promoted by the Church itself. From the middle of the eighteenth to the end of the first third of the nineteenth century, the chief authorities in pulpit and university were promoters of Rationalism. If we have now so much reason to deplore the prevalence of this spirit in the educated circles of our town populations, and its spread among the lower ranks too, we have only ourselves to thank for it; we theologians reap that which ourselves have sown.

We often complain of our great poets, and our classical literature in general, that they exhibit such indifference, not to say hostility, to positive Christianity. Who is to blame for this? Once more—the Protestant Church amongst ourselves. How could it be otherwise, than that those great and leading spirits should, one after another, turn aside and separate themselves from her? What was it but the cold and stiff morality, the absence of all spiritual life and fervour, and the hard, unsympathetic deism of our preachers and theologians, which repelled ardent and poetic minds like Schiller, and made them turn, as he does in the *Gods of Greece,* to the beautiful forms of ancient paganism, in preference to the days of a degenerate Christianity? Such men are not to be regarded as the enemies of Christianity, but only of its rationalistic form as then presented to them. Schiller, in the poem referred to, is assailing not the religion of the gospel, but the vulgar Rationalism by which it was defaced. Perthes is perfectly right when he says: "It is the longing of a noble human heart which there finds utterance, pouring out its righteous indignation against formalists and mammon-worshippers, and striving after living communion with a real self-manifesting God. He only can mistake Schiller's true meaning who has no conception of the angry feelings which inspire the man who, never cheered by any true teaching as to the faith of Christians, cries out for help, and finds it denied him; desires intercourse with the living God, but receives from his age no other revelation than that of a dumb mechanical idol of the understanding, enthroned in mere astronomical sublimity above the subject world." Let us acknowledge, then, that true poetry thirsts for religion; that if our own great poets do occasionally seem to be in any measure cognisant and receptive of the spirit of the gospel, it is because they learned to find behind the mask of a degenerate Church the nucleus of life and truth which there lay hidden; and that such was indeed the case from Schiller onwards, with his profoundly Christian poem *The Song of the Bell,* to the pious Uhland, who thus pours forth the longings of his soul for "the Lost Church:"

"I wander through the wood alone,
No trodden path before me lies;
The world I leave is cold and dumb,
To God I lift my longing eyes.
I listen in the silent wild,
Till notes from heaven I seem to hear;
And as my longing swells, those notes
Seem to ring out more full and clear."

But all the heavier responsibility falls on the Church for having had no answer to such longings as these; all the more must we lament the misfortune that the development of our greatest poets and thinkers should belong to an age in which the Church had nothing to tell them of a true and living Christianity, and could only present them with its cold and lifeless skeleton.

But to come nearer to our own time, the Church of the present is also in this respect not free from blame. Even now in England, where for ages past faith has struck its strongest roots in the very heart of the common people, and still retains in great measure its hold upon them, doubts and sceptical theories are rapidly spreading. Resting on the so-called "evidences of Christianity," the Church of England in the last century had fallen, as we all know, into a deep slumber. From that slumber she has indeed long awakened, but it is now to contemplate with alarm her own impotence to withstand assaults from which the old "evidences" afford no longer adequate protection. She finds now that theological training has been too long neglected in her great universities, and the vast majority of her clergy quite inadequately furnished for encountering the attacks of modern criticism. Many will not acknowledge this to themselves, while others of a nobler temper rush in hot haste to translations from the German, in order to make themselves *au fait* in questions stirred by the Colenso and other "Broad Church" controversies. The want of experienced leaders through the thickest labyrinths of modern criticism is painfully felt; and many, in consequence, are seen heedlessly rushing on towards the most dangerous precipices of critical scepticism. Others, starting back in terror, seek in the communion of Rome a refuge from infidelity. Others, again,— and these naturally form the great majority, — still thoughtlessly cleave to the bare letter of Scripture and their Church formularies, and think to entrench themselves behind these paper fortifications in a vain security from the importations of German theology and critical science. By such persons a grossly exaggerated and thoroughly unevangelical view of the nature of inspiration is often made use of to decide off-hand on critical or scientific questions, which ought to be discussed on their own merits, and by no means interfere with the foundations of Christian faith. And so also, needless appeals to legal tribunals to decide on points where spiritual and intellectual weapons ought rather to be used, are calculated not to heal, but only to widen, the breach between Science and Christianity. To raise, moreover, mere questions of detail in the present controversies between natural science and theology into articles of faith, and give them an importance which is by no means assigned to them in Holy Scripture, is surely the very way to excite in many minds a not inexcusable indignation at such attempts at intellectual tyranny, but which is too apt itself to degenerate into total indifference towards any claims of divine revelation. The Church itself, and her one-sidedness, is here chiefly to blame.

Things are somewhat better in Germany. The Church here has certainly avoided some of these mistakes. She has not set herself in opposition to theological and scientific inquiry, perhaps has rather been too lax in duly limiting it. She has, on the whole, followed the maxim of meeting opponents on their own ground, and withstanding them with merely scientific weapons; and this course has resulted in a victorious advance of evangelical theology, despite the most formidable opposition, to a firmer, closer hold of the fundamental principles of the ancient faith. But here our commendation stops. The German Protestant Church has fallen into other faults and errors not less injurious than those of her English sister. She has favoured the advance of unbelief among her own people, by quietly looking on when she ought to have been up and doing. In the eyes of many, she has seemed to regard her own cause as lost. She has too long neglected a duty much better attended to in England,—that of encountering the sceptical popular literature of the day by popular religious journals, tracts, and magazines, in which assaults on Christianity were duly met and answered. It is only quite recently that our Church has seriously set herself, by a revived apologetic literature, to recover the ground thus lost.

The internal condition of our Church, moreover, in the last few decades affords in many respects a melancholy spectacle. How do we see her torn by endless strife about questions connected with the legal rights of the Prussian Union! How much ill-blood has been made among the laity, by the excessive and quite un-Lutheran and unevangelical claims put forth on behalf of the Church and the ministerial office! How much precious time wasted by theologians in useless controversies!

How much power and influence has the Church thereby been losing with the common people! With what bitterness do the three great parties into which we are now divided turn the one against the other!—the Extreme Left, on the one hand, inclining again to Rationalism, and the extreme Lutheran Right on the other, both equally hostile to the Evangelical Centre and its evangelical Church Congress; those of the Left summoning against it the Congress of German Protestants, and those of the Right the Lutheran Church Congress! Is it not enough to destroy the confidence of thousands in a Church which they see thus torn asunder by internal strife? And let me add one thing more: How many of our clergy are still addicted to the evil habit of using, parrot-like, a round of religious phrases which have lost for the most part their original force and meaning!—a habit than which nothing is more fitted to steel men's consciences against reception of the truth, and alienate all persons of thought and education.

Still greater is the hostility now excited in the minds of many against both Church and Christianity, by the position so perversely taken by some of our friends on questions of politics. The true position of the Church with regard to such questions is surely this: to exhort each one fearlessly and impartially to the performance of his duties to God and man; to bear witness before high and low alike on behalf of truth and right, and against all manner of wrong and injustice; and so to constitute herself the conscience, as it were, both of Government and people. How much real gratitude would the Church have earned from all right-thinking men had she really done this! But the contrary has too often been the case. Men of both the extreme parties have in several instances given just offence by one-sided and partisan action in politics, while the inactivity and seeming indifference of others has done hardly less harm. We cannot here, of course, enter into details, or presume to judge in individual cases; but one thing we may remark, that nothing is more likely to alienate popular confidence from the Church as a body, than when its representatives are seen to be wanting in impartiality in dealing with different ranks in the social system: when clergymen, for instance, are found bold and uncompromising in rebuking the sins of the common people, but timid or reticent with the great and powerful; and prepared to defend or advocate through thick and thin the line assumed by Government, whatever it may be. How often has it been remarked, with truth, that the feudal party in Prussia are only too ready to identify their cause with that of the gospel, and to range their own party principles under the sacred banner of the Cross! And have they not been greatly aided in this confusion of flesh and spirit by that portion of the clergy who, instead of maintaining the genuine impartiality which ought to characterize all teachers of truth, suffer themselves to be degraded into mere servants of a faction, and advocates of its prejudices? Christianity and the Christian Church cannot be incorporated with a single party, without subjecting itself to the liability of sharing all the odium and mortifications which in any political conflict that party may have to endure. Nor can we wonder that, under existing circumstances, the whole democratic section should be animated with a fanatical hatred to the Church, whose cause they see identified with that of the feudal aristocracy. Nothing has more powerfully contributed, since 1848, to the gradual and increasing alienation of the laity of the middle classes from the Church and its interests, than the belief that the clergy have entirely taken part with the upper classes against the interests of the people at large, and have no longer any heart for or sympathy with them in their endeavours to obtain redress even of the most crying abuses.

The other extreme party, that of the "Protestant" Congress, has fallen into the opposite mistake. Endeavouring to swim with the stream of political Liberalism, they not only oppose their brethren of the Conservative Church party with the utmost bitterness, but incur as much danger of truckling to the powers beneath as the others to those above them. Putting in the foreground the evangelical maxim of the universal priesthood of all Christians, they are apt to turn it into the maintenance of an ecclesiastical democracy, and an application to the Church of the theory of manhood suffrage. Proclaiming the great mass of the people just as it is to be truly Christian, and so, in fact, to constitute the Church, they remind one of the old watchword in the wilderness by which it was sought to overturn the government of Moses,—"You make too much of yourselves: the whole congregation is holy, and the Lord is among them,"—and seem quite to forget that it is not birth in a nominally Christian country, but the possession of Christ's spirit, which constitutes the Christian; and finally, by making common cause with the unscrupulous leaders of the party of progress, they give to their efforts a sort of ecclesiastical sanction, and drag down the Church as effectually as their opponents into the miry slough of political party warfare. The consequence of this is, that notwithstanding all their efforts to reconcile Christianity with modern culture and progress, inscribing as they do upon their banner, "Renovation of the Evangelical Church in unison with the general development of culture in our time," this so-called "Protestant" party does really contribute to the widening of the breach between such development and any positive form of Christianity. It works towards this end from the side of intellectual and social culture, even as the opposite extreme party from the side of a narrow-minded form of Christianity. It alienates the orthodox and devout portion of the community from the national cause and liberal interests, quite as surely as its opponents have alienated by their mistakes the national party from the cause of the Church. Adopting the tenets of the old rationalistic schools, it only confirms the already anti-religious liberalism of the time in its renunciation of all positive faith, betraying more and more clearly that the only reconciliation between the gospel and modern culture for which it has any heart, would consist in basing all the foundations of faith (so-called) on the dicta of that modern "consciousness" which aims as much as possible to dispense with any supernatural revelation. The natural consequence is, that many religious persons are rendered more and more mistrustful of anything calling itself culture or progress, and more opposed than ever to even the most moderate liberalism in Church or State; while not a few theologians, who in many principles might be inclined to coalesce with the members of the "Protestant Union," are deterred and disgusted by the excesses of their democratic radicalism.

Thousands also, it must be confessed, are alienated from the Church by the conduct of some so-called "pietists." To say that such are mere hypocrites is a crying injustice; but it must be allowed that one-sidedness of judgment and general narrowness of views does in many cases help to alienate men of culture from Christianity thus caricatured. When men see how shy and unfriendly our pietists (unlike so many good evangelical Christians in England and America) show themselves towards all national aspirations and endeavours; when they observe their narrow-minded withdrawal from what they call the world and all secular interests and pursuits; when they remark that, instead of being, as the Lord enjoins, a light to the world, and therefore especially to their own fellow-citizens, they prefer to let their light shine in the narrow bounds of a conventicle; when they hear them passing ignorant judgments on matters of art and science, or condemning everything as antichristian which does not wear the colour of their particular section, harping always on one string—the sinfulness and impotence of the natural man, or the prophetic announcements of the glory of the latter day,—as if these or the like were the whole of Christianity,—it is not to be wondered at that such narrowness of views in professed Christians should make Christianity itself an object of dislike or suspicion. The man of general cultivation is led to imagine that he must give up his clearer insight,—the patriot, that he must renounce his political aspirations,—if he would become what these people would alone recognise as an orthodox Christian; and this he is naturally not inclined to do.

What has been already said will be enough to show, that in our enumeration of the causes of the present breach between Culture and Christianity, we must add to those strictly ecclesiastical and found within the Church itself—

d. Fourthly, *Causes Political.*—Our modern political development and aspirations are largely felt to be antagonistic to, or at least to lie outside, the sphere of Christianity. And this constitutes what has been truly called "a profound internal discord in our life as a state and as a nation,"—namely, that the Christian and Church element on the one hand, the national and freedom-loving element on the other, should be so violently opposed, some regarding Christianity as in itself a reactionary principle opposed to all modern progress, and others fearing all advances towards political freedom and independence as necessarily inimical to Christianity, whereas all history teaches that freedom comes and perishes with religion, with faith, and that faith can only grow and flourish in conjunction with liberty. The two are, in the long run, inseparable.

"In many cases," says an English writer, "the true source of a man's irreligion will be found in his politics." With none is this more the case than with the German people. Whenever the Church sinks to a mere engine of the State, and advocate even of its errors and abuses, then the natural result is, that the opposition originally directed against the State is now turned against the Church and Christianity. Again, whenever the Church shows herself cold and indifferent, or even hostile to the legitimate aims and aspirations of the people, then also it will soon come to be generally regarded as a reactionary institution, and political dislike soon developes into infidelity. A striking example of this is now exhibited in the present relations of Italy and the Papacy. From the very beginning the latter has been wont to confound ecclesiastical and political interests, ofttimes making morality and religion subservient to its politics. The bitter fruits of these unhallowed confusions are now being reaped. The great spread of infidelity in Italy during the last decade is due to the hatred felt for the anti-national policy of the Papal See.

Experience shows that some systems of government are specially favourable to the growth of infidelity. Among these we may reckon especially despotism and bureaucracy. Church history proves clearly that the more freedom is granted to Christianity, the more it developes, the stronger it grows; the more the State interferes with its organization, and endeavours to direct its movements, the more sickly it becomes. It is not in the atmosphere of genuine freedom, but in the close and sultry air of bureaucratic government, that infidelity will be found to flourish most luxuriantly. The close atmosphere of red-tapist administration is for unbelief what a hothouse is for a plant. Look at France under the old *régime*. The despotism of Louis XIV. and XV. was a perfect hotbed of infidelity and free-thinking. Look at Germany. Nothing like the old bureaucratic system to produce and foster rationalism, which in the fresh air of the War of Independence began to wither. Patriotic, liberal, and religious impulses were then for a time harmoniously united, and the irresistible force of that great national movement grew out of that union, albeit an incomplete and immature one. But no sooner was the bureaucratic system re-established after the Congress of Vienna, than infidelity again raised its head and began to develope fresh energies. Since then, how many there have been and are who have sought to make up for cringing servility to the meanest representative of the State, by impudent self-assertion against God and religion! From that epoch onwards all political changes took a more and more unchristian character, till in 1848 the alienation of the German people from Christianity broke forth all at once and came to the light of day. And to what must we attribute this? Chiefly to that reaction, of which the secret poison slowly corrupted the whole spiritual life-blood of our people. "Rudely driven back from the threshold of political existence, and restricted to merely literary efforts," says a modern historian, "and deprived of every opportunity of exercising its energies in a public sphere of action, the younger generation has specially addicted itself to theological inquiries, and looks for triumphs in that sphere which are denied it in the field of action." This alone would go far to account for the spread of infidelity and rationalism among the masses of our population. The German Catholics and Friends of Light who made so great a stir in the fifth decade of this century, with their total rejection of all positive Christianity, were in many instances Liberal politicians driven from their natural sphere to wander after false lights of fancied liberty in the bypaths of rationalism.

The present generation has likewise been passing through a similar experience. The conservative reaction which speedily followed the revolutionary outbreaks of 1848 evoked in many quarters a spirit of yet more embittered and pronounced scepticism. Vogt, Moleschott, Büchner, and others came forward as the advocates of an impudent antichristian materialism, which hitherto had been unknown in Germany, but soon became popular in the circles of the opposition. Nor can we wonder at the vehement animosity of many Liberals to a Church which, starting back from the precipice before her, carried all her forces into the camp of their political adversaries. Conscience assured them that their aim to make a strong and united Germany was right and noble, and could not in itself be displeasing to God; while yet many were misled by this conviction to confound a carnal aversion from the truths of the gospel with zeal for liberal enlightenment and progress. It is now encouraging to note, that since the re-awakening of political life, the popular favour towards materialistic theories seems to have sensibly diminished.

e. But to these political we must add, Fifthly, various *social and ethical causes* for the present tendencies to scepticism and unbelief. Some of these we now see actively at work, especially in the artisan and labouring classes. What has Christianity done—what can it do for us? are questions frequently put among them, as they chafe under the inequalities of our social arrangements. And communism stands ready to give the answer, with its violent disruptions of existing ties and redistribution of land and property as the basis of a new political system. Our German sense of right and conscience still keeps these principles in check among us, but in many of our larger towns we find them already taking root, as likewise in England. In France, as we all know, communism prevails in large masses of the population, combined with the coarsest antichristian and atheistic materialism.

But, after all, it is to moral causes that we must assign a main influence in the present prevalence of unbelief. "Our systems of philosophy," said Fichte, "are very often but the reflex of our hearts and lives." You will, I am confident, accept this axiom as specially applicable to the subject now before us. Each man's position towards Christianity is ultimately determined by the inward condition of his heart and will. The gospel has from the first proclaimed that the only way of access to faith is by the path of practical obedience, combined with the ready ear that is ever open to the voice of truth. "If any man will do His will, he shall know of the doctrine, whether it be of God." "He that is of the truth heareth my voice." Action must go before knowledge, and a certain inward condition prepare the way for the gospel message. To understand the truth, we must first stand in it, or at least be willing to enter and submit to it.

Wherever there is a real alienation from the gospel, ethical causes have much to do with it. There is something humiliating in the first aspect of all Christian truth. It reminds us of personal responsibility, of personal shortcomings. It wounds our natural pride and self-sufficiency. And oh, how hard it is to many great and aspiring spirits to come down from their high estate and confess to guilt and error! For others, Christianity has too much that is alarming. It makes of human life so serious a thing; it warns so solemnly of the nearness of eternity and the certainty of future judgment; its sign of the Cross reminds us so awfully of the divine holiness and the hatefulness of sin. Too many, alas, are not prepared to fight their way through all these terrors to real and solid peace, and catch at the idlest doubts and shallowest surmises to escape from the pressure of unwelcome truths. What pride does for the former class, fear does for these, in deterring them from embracing the faith of the gospel. And as for both these classes the entrance of the way of life is found too strait, so for many others the way itself has proved too narrow. Their love of ease refuses to engage in the striving after holiness; their love of gain and worldly honour shrinks from the thorny path of humility and self-denial. With many, alas, sins of sensuality are either parents or offspring of unbelief; nay, every sin may be regarded as a step in that direction. The apostolic word is true of thousands in our day, as on the first preaching of the gospel: "The natural man receiveth not the things of the Spirit of God."

Ignorance with many is a cause of unbelief, superficiality with others. Many are so absorbed in the cares and turmoils of their earthly life, as to have neither time nor inclination to inquire into the grounds of Christian faith, and so fall an easy prey to the assaults of the shallowest scepticism. *Ars non habet osorem nisi ignorantem* is most true here. The most vehement opponents of gospel truth are ofttimes those who know least about it, and are not ashamed to exhibit the most astounding ignorance of both Catechism and Bible. Every close observer of the spirit of our times must be aware of its deep-seated aversion to any thorough inquiry as to the grounds or significance of any religious dogma. It would be a marvel in any age but ours that shallow pretentious books like Renan's *Vie de Jésus*, which set all sound criticism and historical investigation at defiance, should be so immensely popular, and go through so many editions. Who can wonder that an age so constituted should be driven about by every wind of doctrine,—

> "On its own axis turning restlessly,
> And never find the healing light of truth"?

And if there be so many various causes of alienation from Christian faith in the prevailing tendencies of our time, there are not a few which render the assumption of a sceptical temper pleasant and easy. Unbelief appeals mainly to the intellect, and lays no restraint on the waywardness of the heart. It flatters one of the favourite inclinations of the natural man to embrace and cherish doubt as to his own responsibility to any spiritual power placed above him. The first note of interrogation found in the Bible follows a doubt-injecting word of the demon-serpent to our first parents: *Hath God said?* and then came the flattering announcement which modern philosophy is so ready to repeat: *Ye shall be as gods;* of which the present improved version runs thus: Ye are yourselves God; that absolute Being whom ye once thought to be above you is in you and of you—your own spirit. What a welcome word to an unquiet conscience! There is no more eternity or judgment to come! How charming to the earthly mind of the votary of pleasure is the announcement that this world is everything, and the future nothing!

Let us ask our own consciences: Have we not here in these moral causes the deepest ground of our present unbelief, the fullest explanation of its ready acceptance? In divine and spiritual things, no one errs entirely without his own fault.

A due consideration of all these causes, old and new, which have co-operated in the production of our present forms of unbelief, will make intelligible the serious extent of the breach thus made between modern culture and Christianity. To this I must now invite your attention.

II.—THE PRESENT EXTENT OF THIS BREACH.

A look into our town churches shows at once the estrangement of the great majority of our educated classes from the Christian faith. Modern culture concentrates itself in our larger towns, and it is just there we find our emptiest churches, and, in comparison with the growing population, the fewest of them. Formerly the sceptic might say, with Faust,

> "I hear the doctrine,—what I want is faith;"

now, alas, too often the doctrine itself is no more heard. There are large parishes in Berlin and Hamburg where, according to recent statistics, only from one to two per cent. of the population are regular church-goers. Elsewhere it is somewhat better. But speaking of Germany in general, we may say that in our larger towns the proportion seldom exceeds nine or ten per cent., and in the majority of cases is far lower. And yet, in comparison with the days in which rationalism had possession of our pulpits, there is, in the matter of church attendance on the part of educated persons, considerable improvement. In country places things look far better. There, Christianity has still much greater hold on the mass of the population. But of these we do not now speak. Our agriculturists cannot yet boast of any high degree of culture. But in the towns, whether you visit the lecture-rooms of professors, or the council chambers of the municipality, or the barracks of the soldier, or the workshop of the artisan,—everywhere, in all places of private or public social gathering, you hear the same tale: The old faith is now obsolete; modern science renders all genuine belief in it now impossible; only ignoramuses and hypocrites profess to adhere to it any longer.

Still more is this the case among the educated and half-educated classes, *i.e.* among the town populations in Roman Catholic countries. France, the greatest of them, has never recovered from her radical breach with Christianity in 1793, when bishops and priests united in the abjuration of their former faith. It is well known that in Upper and Central Italy (in Naples the case is different) the great majority of educated persons have not only silently broken with their Church, but openly avow their unbelief. In Roman Catholic communities, infidel publications enjoy much more splendid triumphs than any which await them in the domains of Protestantism. For hundreds who read Strauss in Germany, tens of thousands in France and Italy have been seen devouring Renan. In Spain and Portugal the breach is not yet made so openly; but signs are not wanting that the hearts of a large number of the cultivated classes are alienated from their professed faith; that the hatred to the priests in many quarters is intense, especially since the last revolution; and that the religion of very many is limited to an occasional appearance in some processions. Even in Catholic Belgium there are many indications of a strong reaction against the Church, initiated by such societies as those of the *Affranchés*, the *Solidaires*, and the *Libres-Penseurs*. The members of the last-named society bind themselves to resist to the utmost all interference of the priesthood in the affairs of social and family life, and therefore (1) not to permit the visit of a priest in case of death, or his officiating at a funeral; (2) to take part in none but civil marriages; and (3) not to allow their children to be baptized, or go to first communion, or be confirmed. And tendencies of the same kind are manifesting themselves even in such thoroughly Romanized communities as the Spanish Republics of South America. Who, then, will deny that in Roman Catholic countries the breach between Culture and Christianity is already a very wide one? And it is one that is increasing every day.

But alas, all the factors of our modern intellectual life are largely influenced by a prevailing spirit of unbelief! Take first our universities and schools. Whereas amongst our theologians the old spirit of rationalism is in great measure overcome, it is quite otherwise among the teachers in our upper schools, and especially our mathematicians, whose training in the exact sciences disposes them to demand a proof for everything, to be strongly prejudiced in favour of "rational religion," to be too ready to forget how many incommensurable magnitudes exist in the moral world, and to seek for clearness of ideas at the expense of truth and life (Bengel). And so, also, the semi-cultured teachers in our popular schools are even more prone to succumb to the temptation of thinking themselves too enlightened and advanced to share the simple faith of the common people, or submit to its restraints. Hence the general outcry for the emancipation of the school from the control of the Church, the endeavour to abridge as much as possible the time given to religious instruction, and to banish it from the central position which it has hitherto occupied in popular education; while in many places, notwithstanding such frequent failures, the attempt is again and again renewed to establish undenominational schools, in which Catholics and Protestants may be educated together.

In our gymnasia and other grammar schools, religious instruction is, with some praiseworthy exceptions, relegated to a very inferior position. Boys and youths are often found to possess a remarkably good acquaintance with the details of other subjects, whose knowledge of Scripture history and Christian doctrine is of the most meagre description. Not long ago, it was discovered in a Prussian gymnasium that a secret society existed among the boys of from thirteen to fifteen years of age, with rules of a purely atheistic character, the first paragraph commencing with, "Any one believing in a God is thereby excluded from this society."

Such being the condition of our grammar schools, who can wonder that at the university few students but those reading theology should go to Church, while many lecturers allow themselves to hold such language on the subject as to lead their youthful audience to regard attendance on public worship as something quite beneath their dignity? The natural consequence is, that the large class of Government officials are for the most part indifferent, and in many cases even hostile, to Christianity, and that the mutual estrangement between Church and State increases every day.

A further glance at our modern literature will exhibit the almost abysmal profundity of the chasm which in this respect divides our present culture from our Christianity. Not many years ago, German infidelity was contented to appear in the courtly guise and with the aristocratic exclusiveness of science and philosophy; she now endeavours to clothe herself in forms in which every one may give her welcome. Unbelief is no longer a guarded secret among wits and scholars, or uttered in a language "not understanded of the people;" it is now commended in innumerable publications, tracts, novels, illustrated newspapers, to the attention of the working classes, and even of the peasantry.

The tendency to popularize all results of scientific investigation, which is so marked a feature of our time, is seen specially at work in this department, widening more and more the breach between modern popular thought and Christianity. A few decades back, the study of German philosophy required very severe application. Few then even read Hegel, and still fewer understood him. But the atheistic consequences drawn by Feuerbach and others from his speculations are found by many very piquant and agreeable reading now. Such philosophy every carpenter's apprentice can too readily understand. And so with Strauss. What thirty years ago he addressed to theologians, is now hashed up again and fitted to the palates of "the German people." Every writer now wishes to be popular. The old deductions of Hegelian philosophy paraded by Feuerbach and his compeers, that God is nothing more than one's own inward being made the object of self-contemplation, that prayer and adoration are in reality but forms of self-worship, —"signs," to use Emerson's language, "of infirmity of will:" these are now thrown broadcast by the labours of a hundred pens over the whole field of the popular mind; religion is to be no longer a seeking after God, but a resting on nature's bosom; no longer an obedience to a higher will, but the carrying out of one's own self-discovered system of morality. And hence, besides the general disbelief in the supernatural and miraculous characteristic of the popular mind in the present day, the multitude of empty unmeaning phrases which one hears in every social circle expressive of philosophical notions and deductions half understood, *e.g.* "the worship of genius," "religion of humanity," "moral order of the universe," "progress of the human race," etc. etc., while the use of any scriptural phrase or expression is regarded as a sign of narrow-mindedness or bad taste.

The same rationalistic, pantheistic, and materialistic influences pervade our modern æsthetic literature. Many of our would-be fine writers have come to regard Christianity as a direct hindrance to true Culture. So, for instance, Arnold Ruge, who will no longer call it by its name, but speaks of it as "*Asiatismus*," or Judaism: "This '*Asiatismus*' lies like a dead weight on all the departments of modern life, and holds us in the bondage of a refined (or unrefined) barbarism." Even Voltaire, Lessing, Göthe, Schiller, Kant, Fichte, and Hegel, with all their liberality, were unable to free themselves entirely from the yoke. And for such ludicrous outbursts of fanatical infidelity he is praised in a modern journal (the

Gartenlaube) as the ideal of a true German! Another sings the triumphs of natural science in such strains as these: "Brahma, Buddha, Jupiter, and Jehovah must now yield to worthier successors in reason and philanthropy."[1] A third, having weighed both Catholicism and Protestantism in the balances, and found them wanting, proceeds to instal the modern drama as the best teacher of true religion: "A great lie pervades the whole of modern society. Priests and laymen alike are liars against their will, and often without knowing it. When we let our children learn the Catechism without believing it ourselves, are we not making ourselves liars? What we want is a new Church. I am for a free stage. The theatre is my temple, where I would see inaugurated a new form of worship. The theatre should be regarded as a house of God, as it was among the ancient Greeks. Religion and the drama I would fain see identified." (Eckardt.)

To these signs of a literary and æsthetical alienation from Christianity we must add those of a more directly political character. Our daily press in far the largest number of instances takes up a perfectly indifferent, if not openly hostile, position. Witness the unmeasured scorn poured by a hundred of its organs on the efforts to promote home and foreign missions, and even on charitable associations if worked in a Christian spirit; and so likewise our political clubs and unions, nay, even those of a merely social character,—singing, rifle-shooting, athletic clubs, and trades-unions, such as that of the shawl weavers in Berlin,—often go out of their way to parade religious indifference and unbelief; and is it not in the memory of many of us how the great popular movements, some twenty years ago, for the political regeneration of our country were conducted in the spirit of the motto of the last named association:

"Consider, man, how great thou art—
Thy will is thy Redeemer;"

how the proposal to implore the divine blessing and assistance on the deliberations of the Frankfort Parliament was received with shouts of derisive laughter; and how in so many educationist meetings in later years the watchword most in favour

[1] Compare Wichern, *Die Verpflichtung der Kirche zum Kampf gegen die Widersacher des Glaubens*, p. 7 sq.

has been: The undenominational "Christianity of humanitarianism must henceforth be the religion of Germany"? Are not all these signs of the times, which exhibit the breach between our present Culture and true Christianity as most deplorably deep and wide?

It may then, I fear, be affirmed with truth, that the great mass of our educated, and yet more of our half-educated, classes in this our German Fatherland is alienated from all positive definite Christianity: our diplomatists almost without exception, and the great majority of our officers in the army, our Government officials, lawyers, doctors, teachers of all kinds but professed theologians, artists, manufacturers, merchants, shopkeepers, and artisans, stand on the basis of a merely rationalistic and nominal Christianity; while the lower middle class (always excepting the agriculturists and peasantry), carried away by the materialistic tendencies of the time, assume a more or less hostile position towards it.

But is not the condition of some other countries better than ours in this respect? It is so in England and America. There the mass of the people, especially the middle classes, still rest their faith on the old foundations; and England more especially still recognises with practical gratitude the inestimable blessings for which she is indebted to the gospel. But alas! the following statements are enough to show that even there the breach is of lamentable extent. It has been calculated that in the year 1851 more than 12,000,000 copies of infidel publications of various kinds issued from the London press,—640,000 purely atheistic, small pamphlets included, but without reckoning newspapers. These publications have an immense circulation among the working classes. To these must be added the enormous mass of immoral publications issued, according to a previous statement in the *Edinburgh Review*, at the rate of 29,000,000 copies a year,—making a larger aggregate than all the publications of the Bible, Tract, and many other religious societies put together. (Comp. *The Power of the Press*, published 1847, and Pearson's prize essay, *On Infidelity*, published in 1863.) The perusal of these works, and of the wretched penny papers dispersed in hundreds of thousands, must powerfully contribute to spread infidelity and immorality among the masses of the population. Turning to the upper classes, it must be noticed that the ardent pursuit of natural science has led many distinguished men to views widely different from those commonly received on the inspiration of Holy Scripture, or leading to the total rejection of its authority, and that these have been combated with considerable ability. The controversy is still proceeding.

"Secularism" so called,—the doctrine that the present life and world is everything, that men have only to live and care for what they see around them or in the immediate future,—a doctrine founded on the positivism of Auguste Comte,—has great attractions for the practical and somewhat materialistic English mind. Its apostle in England was Holyoake. If he has already of professed disciples not a few, the practical adherents of his system are everywhere multitudinous.

It is also well known that assaults more or less covert have been made on faith in England by professed theologians, nay, even by some who hold high places in the National Church. When we remember the eagerness with which the *Essays and Reviews*, and Bishop Colenso's attacks on the Pentateuch, were sought for and read by all classes of the English-speaking race, and even in its remotest colonies, we cannot but be sensible that the breach between culture and Christianity is for them likewise beginning seriously to widen.

So great and universal is the chasm which more or less in all countries of the civilised world is now dividing the spirit of the age and its most characteristic products from the faith, aspirations, and convictions of the Christian Church. That chasm is wider than most of us would willingly allow. Perhaps some of the statements, necessarily brief and superficial, which I have laid before you, may have astonished some of my most intelligent hearers. But being so, the duty is the more incumbent on us seriously to put the question, Is a reconciliation still possible? We must devote a somewhat careful investigation to our reply.

III.—CAN THIS BREACH BE FILLED UP?

If we are inclined to answer this question in the affirmative, we shall be very far from denying that between modern culture and Christianity there exist, in many respects, irreconcilable internal contradictions, and that it is no use for us to attempt to reconcile them. But there is another question: whether *true* culture and *genuine* Christianity mutually exclude one another; or whether, on the contrary, the latter does not naturally produce, or at any rate promote, the former; and whether the present time and our own countrymen are not peculiarly fitted to illustrate the real inward connection between the two, and so called upon to do their best in filling up this breach? In what follows, we desire to make an attempt to maintain this latter proposition.

However painful it may be to contemplate the assault which at the present day is made by innumerable adversaries with increasing bitterness on the structure of Christian faith, it nevertheless has, in some respects, a favourable aspect. If Christianity is that which from the very beginning it has professed to be, that is, absolute truth, which must prevail in the end, all these attacks upon it can only assist in advancing its ultimate victory, because they contribute to a deeper investigation of truth, and to a constant exhibition of fresh aspects of it. If it is true, as Christians believe, that all things, even the attacks of their enemies, take place under some higher guidance, then these attacks are never merely detrimental to Christianity, but from another point of view tend to further it. The open, honourable antagonism of an opponent, to say nothing of the victory over an error, always tends to intensify and enrich the treasure of truth possessed by the Church. The louder, therefore, the opposition of the present day, and the warmer the contest on all sides, the greater, after all, is the gain to be derived therefrom, and the nearer becomes the final, complete, and permanent victory. Nay, the numerous attacks made on Christian belief are even now a proof that Christianity is again beginning to become an important power in the life of nations. From all antiquity downwards, history tells us that the more powerful the development of Christianity, the stronger became the opposition to it. Unquestionably, at the present day, the opposition is great, and consequently Christianity must again have presented itself in a powerful form. Where there is much conflict, there is also much life. And perhaps the present time is just the very period when there is the least ground for despairing of the victory of the genuine Christian theory of the universe. If we survey the manifold bridges which are now being constructed, in order to facilitate the return of educated persons to Christian belief, and the increasing numbers of those who are beginning to find out this way of return, we are bound to say that, in the case of any one who examines the matter without prejudice, it is more easy now than in many previous periods to bring himself to a thorough reconciliation between culture and Christianity. Let us now more closely look into the main path to this end.

Who, then, are the chief exponents of modern culture? Are they not the Christian nations, and very especially those among whom the Holy Scriptures have free course, that is, Protestant nations? Is this fact to be taken as a mere accident? Does it not point to some internal connection between culture and Christianity? When, in the case of all other nations, we see civilisation, after flourishing for a brief period, decline and fall into complete decay, whilst in the case of Christian nations we see it, although amid interruptions, constantly increasing, is not the supposition a very obvious one, that just in their Christianity, and especially in the gospel, nations possess an inexhaustible source of culture, and a constant impulse and stimulus to progress? Nay, may we not entertain the supposition that, after all, Christianity and culture are so intimately connected, that they must increase or decay, stand or fall, *together?* This leads us to the perception that *Christianity is the source and exponent of all true culture.* And on this perception is based the possibility of putting an end to the dissension between modern culture and Christian belief, and of reconciling the two. This proposition may be proved to be in consonance both with *reason* and *history.* Allow me to state a few points with regard to both these sides of the question.

What, then, is the true idea, *the peculiar nature, of Christianity,* and what is the true idea of culture? On this point I must forthwith come into contact with many errors, some perhaps prevailing even among ourselves.

It is of the essence of Christianity not to be a mere complex of new doctrines; it is not, for instance, as Lessing asserted, "a practical teaching of personal immortality;" it began with *facts*, and its doctrines are only to be comprehended in connection with them. Immediately after its first word, "Repent!" attention is directed to a divine fact, "For the kingdom of heaven is at hand," which is rather a subject of spiritual than of intellectual apprehension. Christ therefore represents Himself to us in the gospel, not as a mere teacher, but rather as salvation and life made manifest; not as one who merely enunciates truths, but is Himself the *truth*. "I am the Truth and the Life."

Christianity is not, moreover, as Kant would have it, "the religion of a good life." To this many wise men have attained long before Christ preached, although not in so perfect a form. It is not a sum-total of moral precepts, as rationalists both of older and more recent times suppose, who assume that the main points in Christian faith are the general ideas of reverence for the Divine, honesty, charity, virtue, etc. etc. These ideas and moral precepts did not specifically constitute the new message which was delivered by Christ and the apostles: they were of course placed by Christianity in a new light, deepened, intensified, and widened; but they all had a previous existence, more especially in the Old Testament. (Compare the command of perfect love to God and our neighbour, Deut. vi. 5, Lev. xix. 2 and 18; and of love to our enemies, Ex. xxiii. 4, 5, *et al.*)

Let us cast a glance at the writings of the apostles. Do they put forward certain moral rules of life as the essence of their new doctrine? No; their exhortations to holiness, love, etc., appear everywhere as *accessory* to the chief matter which had been previously set forth, *the gospel of Jesus Christ*—His death, His resurrection, and the great salvation obtained through Him, and now proffered to the world. In the first place, they always preach and pray for grace and peace with God through Jesus Christ; and all the special exhortations and precepts that are subsequently added, are required by them to be fulfilled only as a consequence which at once results from this new revelation, and from the new relation of man to God which is thereby constituted; that is, they require these things as a fruit which is to grow out of the faith in Jesus Christ. Even John, the preacher of love, to whom some are very fond of appealing, sets forth, as the essential and new matter in his teaching, certainly not moral maxims, but that "*the Life was manifested*"—the Word which was from the beginning; "and we," he goes on to say, "have seen it, and bear witness, and show it unto you." He also, and he particularly, announces his message, not as a mere aggregate of truths and moral rules, but as a vital power, and as the revelation of a divinely established *matter of history*. And to what end? Is it merely in order that our moral conduct should be improved? No; something far more is intended. "That ye also may have fellowship with the Father, and His Son Jesus Christ" (1 John i. 3). Christianity has in view not merely to make man righteous, but also *to reconcile and unite him with God*, in the way opened out by the new revelation of Himself *in Christ*—"the Life made manifest." Unless the writings of the apostles are distorted to the very uttermost, taking as last that which is first, and as first that which is last, it is simply impossible to maintain that they set forth certain moral precepts as the essentials in their teaching.

But in favour of this view, may we not also appeal to the original teaching of Christ Himself? This is done, for instance by Baur, when, in allusion to the Sermon on the Mount, the parables, etc., he says, "The essence of Christianity is the doctrine of the kingdom of God, and the conditions requisite for a participation in this, so as to place man in a genuine moral relation to God;" also that the specific pre-eminence of Christianity over other religions is "its universally human and comprehensive nature,—the purely ethical character of its facts and doctrines." We have here, as a result from the same grounds, something too indefinite and one-sided. Christianity is concerned, not merely in bringing about a "genuine moral relation of man to God," but *in effecting a new relation through a distinct person,—that is, Christ.* Those discourses of Jesus formed only the starting-point of His teaching, the general ground-plan as it were, with which He sought, in the first place, to lay hold of the consciences of His hearers. But from this point He proceeds to further developments, gradually unveiling the significance of His own *personality* in reference to the kingdom of God, and His own position as the central point in the economy of salvation (for instance, that "He gave His life as a ransom for many," etc.; cf. Matt. xx.

28, and our Lord's discourses in the Gospel of St. John). It is therefore a perverse proceeding to confine attention to the mere starting-point; Baur himself being subsequently driven to confess that, after all, it is "the personality of its Founder on which depends the whole importance of Christianity in the history of the world."

We therefore arrive at the conclusion, that the essential in Christianity is *objectively* Christ Himself, and the redeeming work which has its source in His Person; *subjectively, faith in Him* as redemption manifested,—that is, the experience of this redeeming work in one's own heart. The object of Christianity is to lead men back to God and to their true destination, on the basis of the redemption and atonement which has taken place through Christ. This is the specific novelty in the teaching of Christ and the apostles. In every religion, man seeks in some way or other to draw nigh to God, to become well-pleasing to God, or to propitiate Him. But the means employed for this end are very various. In heathen religions, indeed in all religions not genuinely Christian, these means are some personal performances on the part of men,—sacrifices, penances, good works, and the like; or also, as rationalism and modern enlightenment maintain, moral principles and righteous living. Christianity stands out in opposition to all this: it denies that the goodwill of the holy God, whose desire is to see His children not merely outwardly righteous, but perfect as He is perfect (Matt. v. 48), can be attained by man *without grace*, or that the honour which men should have before God, and the righteousness which is of avail in God's sight, can be attained to by man without fellowship with Him who is alone perfectly righteous,—that is, with Christ. And it is therefore declared, that there is only one way which leads to the desired end, and that this way is *Christ*. "I am the way." The proper essence, therefore, of Christianity is the bringing back men to God, and their reunion with Him, by the one only way which is called, and is, Christ.

In respect to no idea is it more necessary to distinguish between the true and the false; no word is so mischievously misunderstood and misapplied, as this high-sounding watchword of our time—culture. Indeed, our century, before all others, seems to aspire to be the age of "culture." Nothing in the present day is so derogatory as to be considered "uneducated;" so that not a few even of our shoeblacks consider themselves "educated." How many are there, however, in our time, who are conscious of the points on which true culture really depends? Is it not a matter of fact, that a certain superficial refinement of manners, some acquaintance with the forms of good society, a little stock of ordinary phrases, and the fact of having seen or heard something of the best known products of literature, together with a fashionable style of dress, form, in the opinion of most persons, a sufficient claim to the possession of "culture"? But is that enough? Is it not then possible that a man, sunk in the lowest depths of moral rudeness and degradation, may appropriate some of this outward varnish of "culture," with very little reformation of his essential barbarism? Can we then, on this account, consider him as a really cultured man? We feel at once that true cultivation consists in real refinement of mind and spirit, and not in mere intellectual acquirements or outward accomplishments.

According to the sense of the word "*Bildung*" (culture), we call a thing "*gebildet*" (formed) when it is perfectly shaped, ready, and complete; when it is that which it is intended to be, and consequently completely fitted for its purpose. So, also, the truly formed or cultured man is he in whom all natural faculties are thoroughly developed, so as to enable him to fulfil the purpose for which he was created. The next question would therefore be, what this purpose is; and what the nature, extent, and destination of the faculties implanted in each individual, and what the end he has to aim at reaching. It is clear that, just as any one places a higher or lower estimate on this task,—that is, on the whole end and purpose of human life,—his ideas of culture must take either a higher or a lower form. But, in truth, what is this end and purpose? Nothing less than God Himself. God is the eternal prototype, in harmony with which man is to form himself; and *likeness to God* is the aim for which he is to strive, by perfectly cultivating and shaping all the powers implanted in him. His divine, psychico-moral faculties point him to nothing less than God. And so it stands in the fore-front of divine revelation, "God created man *in His own image, in the image of God* created He him." No poet who ever sang of the dignity of man, has conceived an idea of him more magnificent than this; and no sage ever before placed the destination of man on so immeasurably high a stage as is done by Christ, when He says, "Be ye therefore perfect, as your Father which is in heaven is perfect." Classical antiquity never attained to the sublimity of this view: in its ideas as to the destination of man, it had no one conception worthy of man; for it was without the idea of man's perfection and likeness to God. In the doctrine that man is created *after God's image*, and therefore *for* God, the *Holy Scriptures alone have given back to men the full idea of their own dignity, and have set forth the highest principle and aim of culture*, beyond which it is alike impossible either for philosophy or religion to pass. He who falls short of this, and is content with some lower aim, does an injury to his own dignity, and never becomes cultivated in the highest sense of the word.

This aim will likewise never be attained by him who, in respect to everything that belongs to the Divine image, and all the spiritual and moral capabilities implanted in him, fails to cultivate them *equally*, in harmony with God's purposes,—that is, by all the means which God has provided, and in conformity with the final aim which He has set before us. In an infinite number of cases, one capacity is thoroughly cultivated *at the cost of others*, especially the *intellect* at the expense of *heart* and *will*. The understanding and the memory are stored with all kinds of knowledge; and the external deportment is thus polished and refined, without any effort to render the heart and the conscience more tender and sensitive, the will more disciplined, and to lead it onwards by the path of obedience to true freedom and self-government. Hence it is that we frequently find inward rudeness combined with external polish.

And thus we get at the root of all *false culture*, and of all *inferior culture*. Man falls into this by a neglect of moral self-discipline; and even in Paradise had fallen into it. The first sin, as the Scriptures narrate its origin, was nothing more than an attempt to cultivate knowledge in a one-sided way, at the cost of the faculties of the heart and will. Man desired "to know good and evil," to increase in knowledge, without inquiring whether heart and will would be raised thereby to a higher stage of cultivation. Man desired to be "as God," but without endeavouring to approach God in the divinely prescribed path of obedience and moral self-discipline. Thus the new stage of cultivation was, in fact, a false development, which was increased by every sin that followed. For every sin tends to develope in a wrong direction the moral, and thereby also the intellectual, faculties of man. We are taught this plainly by experience, as well as by the word of God. This mis-development has through the universality of sin become a prevailing power, and henceforth man is no longer able to attain to God-likeness by the direct path, but only by a *return* from the *false* to the *true* course of development; that which the Scriptures understand by "conversion" being in reality nothing else than this return from mis-development, which makes us more and more unlike God, to a true, genuine, ethical, and religious culture, through which we once more attain to the Divine likeness.

We thus arrive at the result, that true moral culture, culture in the highest sense of the word, is nothing more than *reversion to the Divine image.* And how is this to be accomplished? Since the original character of man as the image of God has once for all been obscured in various ways by the misguiding power of sin, and, on the other hand, our eternal prototype—God—is invisible, it became necessary that God should again place before our eyes His holy image in a perfect shape, as a pattern and ideal, from which we might be able to recognise both Him and ourselves,—our true nature and destination, viz. to return to the Divine image. This was and is no longer possible without Christ, who is "the image of the invisible God" (Col. i. 15), and at the same time the pure, sinless, perfect Son of man, in whom, therefore, humanity was manifested in its most perfect likeness to God. Now, therefore, all true culture depends upon man forming himself anew, or rather allowing himself to be formed according to this pattern. He only who puts on the likeness of the All-perfect One, and on whom it is distinctly stamped, is, and will be more and more, completely educated, made like to God, and perfect; he alone will fulfil the purpose of his creation, and accomplish his true destiny.

Let us now see what we have ascertained. The aim of

Christianity is to lead man back to God by the Way which is called Christ; and culture in the highest sense is nothing else than a re-educating back to God, and to that Divine image which can only be attained through Christ. Where is there, then, any disagreement between culture and Christianity? The breach between them is filled up, and a bond of union formed: *aim and end are the same in both;* both desire to lead man back to God, and thus to the attainment of his destination. *Christianity is itself culture—the true, moral, and highest form of culture;* and culture in the highest sense of the word is impossible without Christianity.

Only look at a simple-minded man, not possessing much outward culture, but animated by the Spirit of Christ and by sound piety: what a sense of moral fitness, what correct tact, what sound judgment, especially as to the ethical value of any person or action, do we find gradually produced in him! In such a case, the educating influence of Christianity is frequently shown in a most surprising way.

Only a false, merely external, religionless, and Christless culture, unworthy of the name, because nothing more than mere outward training, is irreconcilably opposed to Christianity; just as it is only a false, one-sided Christianity which comes into conflict with genuine culture and science. When recognised in their true nature, both are seen to have a profound, internal unity; for, as Michael Angelo forcibly says, "Art is the imitation of God." All true culture and science has one tendency, to make human life more Godlike; and this is the very task of Christianity. Therefore, as regards the whole sphere of ancient and modern culture, all that truly cultivates and improves man, brings him nearer to truth and to God, and so far from opposing Christianity, prepares the way for it; whilst all that is genuinely Christian in Christian belief, all that is divinely true, so far from being a hindrance to true culture, is, on the contrary, its purest and richest source and worthiest exponent.

We may thus come to recognise the unity of culture and Christianity from the nature of both. But this point may be also proved *historically.*

Even in that first encounter between Christian truth and classical culture, when the Apostle Paul preached in the Areopagus at Athens (Acts xvii.), we see how the one points to the other. The apostle, in his discourse, quotes one of the Greek poets: "As certain also of your own poets have said, 'For we are also His offspring:'" taking it as a text for his argument. Compare also the quotation from Menander (1 Cor. xv. 33), and the hexameter of Epimenides (Tit. i. 12), both evincing St. Paul's acquaintance with classical literature. And we find the same thing occurring elsewhere. Wherever aught of Divine light and truth appears in Greek culture, we find points of connection for the preaching of the gospel; and Christianity, far from despising these elements of truth springing up on other ground, willingly adopted, amplified, deepened, and glorified them, and in this way proved its affinity to all that was true, and tended to real culture. All the real treasures of classical civilisation the Christian Church was enabled gradually to appropriate, and so to realize the innumerable helps afforded her by art and science for her own internal development, the deeper grounding of her faith, and its outward extension; whilst, on the other hand, a series of attempts was undertaken—though with much less success—by many cultivated heathen, to infuse new life into the timeworn Greek philosophies by the adoption of the substance of the Christian religion.

And truly this classical culture required the support of living exponents, if it was to be preserved from entire destruction. Wherever civilisation is not made to rest on the basis of moral and religious truth, it cannot attain to any permanent existence, and is incapable of preserving the nations possessed of it from spiritual starvation, to say nothing of political death. Greece and Rome were never more civilised, in the modern sense of the word, their culture had never become the common property of the people to so great an extent as when they began to decay. These are facts worthy of consideration by all who are of opinion that culture, that is, the public pursuit of art and science, can of itself afford an adequate guarantee for the future of a people, and who, alas, endeavour to persuade the German nation that their future depends on exchanging positive Christian religion for a *culture* and *religion of mere humanity!* What the fate of the German people would be in this case, we see clearly written upon the ruins of Greece. The polite culture of classical antiquity was deficient in any truly moral and religious basis. The whole system of life, all political, civil, and social duties, and all family relations, were in the last resort based on *selfishness*.[1] In consequence of this, those nations came to ruin. And for the same reason, all non-Christian civilised nations are even at the present day coming to ruin, caused by this fundamental error which their culture is unable to neutralize or overcome.

For the preservation of society, as well as of its culture, some new and counteracting basis of life was necessary,—that of *unselfish love*. And what else was there which could introduce this new principle into the world, save that religion, whose vital point is the belief in the love which sacrificed itself even unto death in behalf of man—the love of the Son of God and Man? Christianity alone could fulfil this great mission, and has in a measure fulfilled it, so that the heathen world has sometimes wonderingly exclaimed, "See how these Christians love one another!" But by the introduction of this principle, Christianity has for ever ensured the preservation of the genuine sentiment of humanity, and has thus become for all ages *the only sure and certain exponent, and the only inexhaustible source, of all true moral culture.*

It is already a matter of history that Christianity has in part fulfilled this vocation by absorbing into itself, on the breaking up of the system of ancient culture, all the valuable elements therein contained. When the irruption of the barbarian nations threatened the whole system of Græco-Roman culture with destruction, the Christian Church became the guardian and nurse of this culture, and carried the treasures of its genius through the storm into the middle ages. Christianity, in the next place, kindled in the nations of the West, one after another, the light of religious truth, and of a more elevated and permanent civilisation. How could it be otherwise, when the Church was teaching them to think of God as a *Spirit*, as the *Father* of man, as One who is *love*, and to regard mankind in the light of God's purpose of salvation in Christ, and of the moral duties thence resulting? And does it not at

[1] For the more precise proof of this, see C. Schmidt, *Die bürgerliche Gesellschaft in der altrömischen Welt und ihre Umgestaltung durch das Christenthum*, Leipzig 1857.

once become evident to us what germs and powers of culture for personal, domestic, civil, and political life were contained in this fundamental principle of Christianity, if, on the other hand, we compare the misguiding influence exercised by perverted views of God and man on the whole life of the heathen? From that time forward, most of these western nations began to take their place on the stage of history; they consequently owe the whole of their significance to having come in contact with Christianity. Now for the first time their languages become *written* languages, and new literatures begin to spring up. It is now that, on a Christian basis, under the fostering guidance of the Church, a new occidental civilisation is constructed, to which even the ancient classical culture is allowed to contribute many a useful stone. This new culture gradually assumed a somewhat different stamp in various lands, according to the varying national peculiarities which, as involving special powers of culture and special destinies, true Christianity seeks not to destroy, but only, with forbearing hand, to purify and refine. When the Church, by suffering the obscuration of God's Word, bid fair to lose the genuine principle of culture, and when the spirit of selfishness, with the immorality inseparable from it, was once more menacing the world with a relapse into heathen rudeness, then it was that the "*Reformation*," that is, the Christian conscience, recurred to the gospel, finding in it the solid *basis* of all true culture, the worship of God in spirit and in truth, and at the same time its strongest *motive*, the principle of liberty of conscience, and the right of free inquiry. And this principle, which could rest only on the ground of the gospel, has become the mainspring of the whole system of modern culture. Since its universal acknowledgment, it has not only given a fresh impulse to investigation in all fields of knowledge, so that the true age of civilisation seems to be but now beginning, but has also in the largest measure contributed to the diffusion of spiritual and moral culture *among the people*. The most comprehensive educational institution of modern times, the National or Elementary school, may be called the daughter of the Evangelical Church; and if on no other account, every philanthropist is bound to confess that, for the Christian education of the German people, no one acted more grandly and more vigorously than

Luther. The fact that in the present day we no longer have merely to speak of *individuals* or *classes*, but of *peoples* in the mass as educated, is pre-eminently due to these universal channels of education created by the Reformation. That since that era the breach between the learned and the lower classes has more and more vanished, that gradually the whole life of the people, public and civil, with the whole system of legislation, has assumed more and more the character of genuine humanity, is in the last instance a result of the giving back of the Holy Scriptures into the hands of the people; of the removal of the chasm once existing between priests and laity; of the restoration of the universal priesthood (1 Pet. ii. 9); and of the recognition (attained through the gospel) of the spiritual freedom and independence of each individual man.

Can it be supposed that all this should of a sudden have been changed? Can Christianity, after having been through whole centuries the exponent of all genuine educational development, suddenly have placed itself in hostile opposition to the culture which grew out of it, and for the most part sprang from its own impulses? Can it, then, have ceased to diffuse, along with the pulsations of its own inner life, the spirit of true culture and genuine humanity? What is it that at the present day, more now than at any former time, sheds the light of moral and religious culture into the darkness of *heathen* barbarism? Is it modern culture by itself, apart from Christianity? Is it the wandering natural philosopher or *savant*, who goes forth to make discoveries in distant lands in order to increase knowledge at home, but who gives neither time nor trouble to the object of contributing something lasting towards the moral elevation of the aborigines? Or is it the European merchant in the heathen world, whose main object has for the most part been to make a profit out of these lands, and who not only does not morally elevate the people that come in contact with him, but frequently leads them on to a still swifter ruin? Have there not existed for centuries mercantile settlements on many coasts, without any kind of educational institution on behalf of the aborigines having been established by the traders? The nearer to the coast, and the more the natives come in contact with the trade of the Christian world, the more degraded for the most part do we find the heathen,—a fact which affords a clear proof that culture in the mere service of selfishness, is nothing less than the greatest hindrance in the way of elevating the mental condition of any people.

No; it is not merely the contact with external culture, but contact with *the gospel* which *clears the path for civilisation* among the heathen. The Christian Church in modern times has again recognised and energetically taken up her missionary task: her emissaries, wherever they can find a footing, not only combat the darkness of heathenism by preaching and education—at the same time often rendering themselves the advocates of the oppressed heathen against the avarice and tyranny of the colonists (I only call attention to the names of a Thomas Coke, a Burchell, and a Knibb in the West Indies, a Van-der-Kemp at the Cape, etc.); but by the communication of more exact information as to lands, peoples, manners, traditions, and languages, hitherto little or not at all known, open out even for home circles new sources of culture, and enrich science in many branches. It is by their labours and the increasingly important progress of Christianity among the heathen, that we now see a number of barbarous peoples being gradually converted into cultivated nations, and beginning to make their appearance on the stage of the world's history. By means of the gospel their languages are reduced to writing; the commencement of their literature is the translation of the Bible. Through the influence of Christian morals and freedom, of Christian order and activity, all the resources of a land become available, its prosperity is raised, and all civil and social relations are ennobled.

If we confine our attention to our own *German culture* and science, it must certainly be confessed that for a long time past the Church has no longer been the exclusive exponent of them; we have indeed seen above in how many ways our modern culture has placed itself in direct opposition to Christianity. Nevertheless, it must be but a very superficial consideration of history which can fail to perceive that even *our German culture and science*—and in many branches they unquestionably take the lead of all—*are in all essential points a product of Christianity and of the gospel;* indeed that, even in those branches which manifest the greatest antagonism to

Christianity, they are involuntarily, consciously or unconsciously, indirectly or directly, assisted by the spirit of Christianity, and are to some extent either ruled or strongly influenced by Christian views.

At the very outset we find our *written language* shaped by the gospel, and its better elements interpenetrated by it. At the head of German literature, as its most ancient monument, we confessedly place the Gothic translation of the Bible by Bishop Ulfilas as "a prophecy of the vocation and tendency of the whole people." At the commencement of the New High German we have, as its nucleus and groundwork, the *translation of the Bible by Luther*, who thereby almost re-created our language, and that in a degree seldom reached by any other literary work.[1] This New High German which we still speak—for we have deviated but little, and that to the detriment of force and expression, from Luther's language—is both in body and spirit the Protestant dialect, mainly indebted to Luther and the gospel for its "freedom-breathing nature," its force, opulence, and beauty, as well as for its naturalization as the written language of the educated and learned classes (who previously always wrote in Latin).

Moreover, our German *poetical literature* does not disown the Christian soil from which it grew. In the works which mark the boundaries of the different periods of poetry, we see products of the Christian spirit which give a colour to the following literature. In our ancient German poetry, that grand Christian epic the Old-Saxon "*Heliand*" (*Heiland, Saviour*) stands prominently out as a remarkable proof how quickly and deeply Christianity made its way into the German blood and life. The first classical period of our literature, the time of our national epic poetry and minstrelsy in the middle ages, when it reached its acme and purest expression, bore the impress of "the most intimate blending of German nationality and Christian faith." At the beginning of the New High German, we find the *hymns of the Evangelical Church* laying hold with a sudden power on the hearts of the German people; and these hymns have ever since remained the living

[1] On this point, cf. Lübker, *Vorträge über Bildung und Christenthum*, Hamburg 1863, p. 202 ff., 267 ff.; R. v. Raumer, *Die Einwirkung des Christenthums auf die althochdeutsche Sprache*, Berlin 1845.

expression of their religious thought and feeling. How much have they contributed to the improvement and, in a Christian point of view, the refinement of popular song! And who was it that in the last century ushered in the day of our modern classical literature, not indeed as a sun, but as a bright morning star? Was it not Klopstock, who in his "Messiah" and his Odes blended ancient classical with German Christian elements, and thereby struck the key-note of all our modern poetry and art, which, however far they may in individual cases have severed themselves from specific Christian ideas, still, in their most beautiful and elevated creations, do not disown the influence of Christian views of the world and human life, and could never have become what they are, except amongst a *christianly* educated people? Or would it have been possible for an Euripides to have written an "Iphigenia" (to say nothing of a "Faust") such as that of Goethe?

The case is similar with regard to our other *arts and sciences.* It is true that in modern times they take their own course, frequently in opposition to Christianity. But if from German music, painting, sculpture, architecture, and from the most important branches of German science, we take away that which owes its origin and development to the influence of Christian ideas, we shall soon find that we have deprived them of their best, most spiritual, most ideal elements, which most tend to education and elevation; and we shall immediately recognise the impossibility of any such separation, just because Christianity is most intimately intertwined with our whole culture.

Or if, in the next place, we consider our civilised life in other points, both public and private, whence proceeds that earnest *assiduity in labour* which distinguishes us Germans beyond most other nations? It is an inestimable fruit of the gospel. Labour was considered by our heathen forefathers as a dishonour. And even in the present day, where the gospel has not free course, the stirring disposition, the assiduity, and the spirit of enterprise of the people is disproportionately less. The important difference between Protestant and Romanist countries in this respect affords everywhere, but especially in Germany and Switzerland, a whole series of irrefutable proofs of this fact.

Whence, again, come our views of *right* and *order*, of freedom and law; whence comes the humane spirit of our jurisprudence and of our civil institutions? For the most part, from what the gospel has taught us of the dignity of man, of true philanthropy, and of human rights and obligations. On merely heathen ground, no certain barrier can be raised against the most heartless despotism, or against the most shameful oppression and slavery. Even an Aristotle, the most cultivated heathen philosopher, thought that only a portion of mankind possessed a rational soul, and that the others had merely a higher kind of animal soul, and were therefore created for slavery! The only sure guarantee for spiritual and ultimately for civil freedom is contained in the gospel. Modern civilised states are indebted to the gospel for their liberal institutions.

Lastly, on what are founded the views we entertain at the present day as to *marriage* and *family life?* What is it that has aided the female sex in attaining the free and dignified position which it assumes among us? What is it that has taught us to treat children as if they were "little majesties"? It was and is the influence of the gospel, which teaches the equality of all men before God, and pays regard to every individual man on account of the Divine image in him, and his own eternal destiny. Allow me, at this point, to state to *you*, my lady hearers, that as regards position in society, none are so much indebted to Christianity as you. No one has so much to fear as you from any complete surrender of Christianity, and from the prevalence of unbelief. Your freedom and dignity stand and fall with Christianity. One glance at the civilised heathen nations, both of ancient and modern times, and the position that your sex assumes among them, will show you how little a culture without Christianity and without Christ is able to guard you against the most disgraceful servitude.

In fact, regarding our own civilised life at the present day from whatever side we please, we everywhere come in contact with Christianity as the spiritual power which supports and penetrates it. Even a Fichte, who certainly took up a very free position in regard to Christianity, was bound to confess, "We and our whole age are rooted in the soil of Christianity, and have sprung from it; it has exercised its influence in the most manifold ways on the whole of our culture, and we should be absolutely nothing of all that we are, if this mighty principle had not preceded us" (*Anweisung zum seligen Leben*).

These considerations apply to us Germans in a very special measure. No other nation has from the very first yielded itself so heartily to the influence of the gospel; no other possessed in its original purity of manners and force of character so great a predisposition to Christianity; no other nation in the world's history has become so deeply imbued with the Christian spirit or made itself to so great an extent its exponent. No nation, therefore, is less able to divorce itself and its culture from Christianity. It may be thought grand to disown or to decry the veritable sources of our present culture, but it certainly is not grateful. Even the most sceptical cannot withdraw himself from the influence of Christianity: he must derive his intellectual nourishment from the fruits of a culture which Christianity created; indeed, even in assailing it, he is compelled for the most part to derive his weapons from it, just as he who seeks to discover spots in the sun must for this purpose borrow the light of the sun itself.

Having thus recognised the historical unity of Christianity and culture, and the way in which they inwardly pervade and blend with one another, especially in our own nationality, it will be perfectly clear to us that nothing can be more perverse than to rend asunder things which both ideally and historically are so intimately connected. The fact already observed, that so many are labouring hard to widen this breach, and that the orthodox themselves have often been found working towards the same end, is the greatest misfortune of our time. "The deeply tragical contrast," as has been strikingly observed, "which pervades the whole of modern history, is that the idea of humanity, born and nurtured in the bosom of Christianity by the influence of the gospel for a thousand years, has been torn away from the root on which it grew, and should now be placed in conflict with Christianity as a power hostile to, and seeking to destroy it. It is desired to cherish culture without *true* culture, and civilisation without the root of all true morality; it is desired to have the system of laws built upon the idea of humanity without acknowledging the obligation of love and self-denial, in the absence of which, the free and joyous recognition of the rights of others, and also of society as a whole, cannot possibly last long. Let us openly confess the fact, that this contradiction constitutes the main root of all the conflicts and crises pregnant with evil, by which our time is agitated" (*Fabri, as above*).

If, in the face of this unhappy tendency, you still maintain the internal unity of culture and Christianity; if you are just enough not to forget all that we, either the so-called or really educated classes, owe as a matter of history to Christianity; then, as far as you are concerned, the great, although in point of fact unnatural and artificial, breach between culture and Christianity is filled up, or at least the way is made clear for their union.

And now, to bring the foregoing remarks to a *practical result*, before believing in any alleged contradiction between culture and Christianity, ask whether it be *true* culture and *true* Christianity, or distorted, falsified forms of either which are thus opposed. No truth, when dealt with by man, is safe against disfigurement, not even Christian truth; no mental possession safe against misuse. In every case, instead of regarding the *form* in which these opposing elements are made to appear, look to their true inward *nature*, and you will find affinity instead of contradiction. Is your attention drawn to some results of scientific inquiry, apparently irreconcilable with Scripture ? first ask the question—Are these real *results*, or, despite the confidence with which especially in popular works they are represented as perfectly reliable, are not the views of really scientific men so divided that the best course is to suspend your judgment; or even if this be not the case, might not after all a correct understanding and explanation of Scripture obviate all serious difficulties? Do the divisions and schisms of the Church offend you? then ask the question—Am I to lay this to the charge of Christianity, that is, to the charge of Christ Himself, His Word and Spirit ? Was it not His dying prayer, "that they may be one" ? Has not the primitive time left us as a testament the special article of faith, "I believe in One Holy Catholic Church" ? You will then be less ready to find fault with Christianity itself, though you may perceive much imperfection, and hence many differences, in the various Churches.

If you take offence at the ecclesiastical *onesidedness* and prejudice of many, who are of opinion that outside the limits of their own Church there is little else but error, you must recollect that true Christianity, that is, Christ Himself, says in opposition to these opinions, "Other sheep I have which are not of this fold," and *promises* that "there shall be one fold and one shepherd." If you take offence at the intolerance of many over-zealous representatives of orthodoxy, just inquire whether the rationalists of ancient and modern times were any better in this respect (the Swiss and Baden schools, for instance); and next, call to mind that Christianity, because it does not assert itself to be *a* truth, but *the* truth, the *absolute* truth, must come in conflict with, and denounce as error, everything which contradicts its spirit; but that in this conflict it admits of no kind of carnal weapons (2 Cor. x. 4); it is intolerant in the most tolerant way; it merely witnesses against everything antichristian in life and doctrine, but neither wishes nor is able to use compulsion. He who is the Truth is also the great Patience of the world, and once said to His disciples, when hastily refusing to tolerate one who was virtually if not formally associated with them: "Forbid him not; for he that is not against us is on our side;" and on another occasion, when they wished to rain down fire from heaven on those who rejected them, put them to shame by the inquiry, "Know ye not what manner of spirit ye are of?" Let us not then lay to the charge of Christ Himself, or of Christianity, the faults of His short-sighted, narrow-minded, or passionate disciples.

Or, if you are disgusted by the onesided *illiberal judgment* passed by many Christians on matters of art and science, do not ascribe this to the spirit of Christianity itself; but rather recollect how the apostle, casting a kingly glance at the immeasurable possessions of the Christian man, says, "All things are yours, both present and future;" and that into the Holy City "shall be brought the glory and honour of the nations." Or, when disposed to take offence at *churchmen* who timidly resist any freer political development, do not forget that the true Church maintains, in the words of the apostle, that "where the Spirit of the Lord is, there is liberty," and that Christianity furthers the cause of freedom everywhere on the one foundation of the

Truth which maketh free. So soon as you recognise the fact that the imperfection of the Church and of individual Christians is not a *consequence* but a *contradiction* of the genuine spirit of Christianity, and therefore is not by any means to be laid to its charge; that the obstructions often placed in the way of genuine culture and true progress are produced by those imperfections, and not by the *nature* of Christianity itself; that the tendency of both, when rightly understood, is essentially the same, viz. to help man to attain his divine destination; and that Christianity has proved itself to be even historically the richest source and the surest exponent of true culture,—then our scruples vanish, and the true method of reconciliation is discovered.

If we go on to inquire what, in the face of this position, is *our present task*, and especially that of our Theology and our Church, in endeavouring to facilitate the return to belief of our educated classes, it is first and foremost, not to under-estimate the depth of the yet existing breach, and not to proceed too rashly in bridging it over — a course which would result in rendering bad service to both sides. We may well rejoice if our theology, more now than at any previous time, aspires to a "reconciliation with the developments of modern culture," the very motto which the leaders of the "Protestant Union" inscribe on their banner. We wish for all this, and we are bound to wish for it. Faith, so far as it assumed a scientific character, has in all times been compelled to come to an understanding with the developments of culture, and to put itself in accord with them. But neither formerly nor now is this breach to be closed by any rationalistic methods, such as would tend to efface the essential difference between many views now in vogue and the fundamental doctrines of Christianity; surrendering, for instance, the miraculous element and other points of Christian faith which modern culture thinks itself to have outgrown, whilst the fundamental principle of Christianity, the belief in a supernatural revelation, is still unrecognised by the spirit of our age. A union on such terms can only be sought for by him who makes a merely secondary matter of the main point of all, the belief in Christ as the only-begotten Son of God, and as God incarnate, and utterly fails to recognise the true nature of Christianity as we have previously defined it. In such alliance, the culture of the present day would become a dangerous parasite, clinging round the great tree of Christianity, nourished on its juices, growing with its growth, but at the same time exhausting its vitality until it ceases to exist!

But neither does it help the matter to adhere to the forms in which the old faith has crystallized, and to try to force the intellectual convictions of them upon our time, in total disregard of the progress of science. By this course the breach can only be made wider. Our duty is rather to endeavour to penetrate more deeply into, and present more comprehensively, the old truths of faith by the aid of the growing light of science, especially that of scriptural investigation. It is better at once honourably to acknowledge as faulty anything which is evidently shown to be faulty in the mode in which it is comprehended or familiarized, *firmly maintaining,* however, *entire and undiminished,* the *fundamental points* of belief, which (as we shall subsequently see) neither science nor criticism can everthrow—for they come out of every contest more firmly and surely established,—I mean the great facts connected with our redemption through Christ. It cannot tend to peace if all the ideas which are moving society at the present day — those of freedom, progress, humanity, civilisation, etc.—are straightway branded by the Church as antichristian, as has recently been done by Rome: let the Church, rather, lovingly receive and acknowledge all the elements of truth contained therein; but let her, on the other hand, seek to purify and clear them from all that is false.

If the dissension is to be radically overcome, *we must allow to freedom that which belongs to freedom, and must leave to faith that which belongs to faith.* Let us at length learn to look beyond the many secondary matters dividing us in belief and practice; let us not bind the conscience where Christ has not bound it, and let us make a distinction between the essential and the non-essential. But, on the other hand, let us not treat main points, such as the divinity of Christ, His atoning death, His resurrection, etc., as secondary matters; let us not turn freedom into licence, nor ignore the doctrinal limits of our faith that are laid down in the Holy Scriptures by Christ and the apostles, limits without which faith must cease to exist. Let us not resolve historical, fundamental matters of fact (as, for instance, the resurrection of Christ) into mere mental conceptions and general vague ideas, whereby unspeakable confusion is produced, and absolutely no internal reconciliation between faith and the culture of the time is brought about; faith, on the contrary, being sacrificed to the repugnance to miracles exhibited in our time. So soon as we eliminate the cross of Christ from our belief, and thus chip off the angles of our corner-stone, throwing overboard all that comes in conflict with natural sense and understanding, there is no doubt that the union between faith and the spirit of the present day is easy enough: the offence of the cross ceases, but *Christian* faith as such is at the same time annihilated.

If any true reconciliation is to be effected, it must rather be accomplished: First, by a genuine apprehension of Christianity in this its "divine foolishness, which is wiser than men," *its divine nucleus and centre,* Christ Himself the eternal Son; and in its perfect purity, beauty, and truth, *bearing its own witness to every human heart,* and faithfully presented to the world: Secondly, by a genuine apprehension of the true nature and value of culture and science, their ennobling moral tendency in the formation of heart and character, and not merely of the intellect; and Thirdly, by the bringing home to the consciousness of men in general, *the inward affinity of this tendency with that of true Chrstianity.* The gospel, freed from the disfigurements inflicted upon it by the prejudice of friends and the misunderstanding of opponents, must again be brought home to the mind and conscience of our age as the only sure basis of all true popular culture, and once more made *intelligible to the genius of the nineteenth century,* so as to impart to the educated classes of the present day, with all their perverted and over-stimulated tastes, a feeling and an interest for divine truth. This result will not be effected by a paring down or total rejection of the germ of gospel truth, but by developing this germ, and by disclosing to men's hearts its inward spring of life.[1] Only let the Church hold fast

[1] It was one of Vinet's latest utterances, that, in the defence of Christian truth, "we must revert to the elementary, fundamental, and eternally unshaken points, if we desire that the new generation should again be fed with the bread of life."

Him who is her foundation and her end, Christ; *only let her proclaim Him not with the old merely, but also with new tongues.* Let her be mindful to present Him to the present age, with its needs of culture, not merely in His *divine glory*, but also in His *human beauty* and moral purity; and to exhibit the free grace and love of God manifested in Him not merely as *indispensable*, but also as *all-sufficient*, to a world feverishly agitated, and in every sphere of knowledge and action wearily excited, and as the only true source of peace and the only power which can permanently satisfy the deepest needs of human nature. These vital characteristics of the gospel have for many centuries wonderfully attracted hearts and minds, and the more purely and plainly it was set forth the greater was the power it exercised; and this attraction it will retain until the end of time.

The ultimate answer to all questions, the solution of all doubts, is contained in Him who is the mystery of all mysteries, the revelation of all revelations, that is, in Christ the Light of the world. If Christendom, now in so many ways Christless, is brought back to a *contemplation of Christ*, false prejudices will soon vanish, and the contradictions between knowledge and faith will begin to be solved, and from this light, beams will issue which will gradually illuminate even the darkest mysteries, or ensure the certainty of a future enlightenment. When that is the case, the inward schism of which we have spoken is already overcome, and the breach closes of itself.

We cannot, indeed, expect, and more especially if we accept the testimony of Holy Scripture, that the breach will speedily be healed in regard to *all*. No one, indeed, will wish to deny that in our modern culture there is much that is false, egotistic, and selfish; much that is misleading and exaggerated, and consequently opposed to true culture. Against these untrue elements of culture, Christianity will and must always take the field; it must not oppose progress, although it is at all times bound to show itself hostile to the *sins* of progress, just as from its very commencement it has always testified and striven against such sins. *Between Christless culture and Christianity, a bridge of accommodation can no more be built than between light and darkness;* and woe to him who undertakes this! But whatever in our modern culture is thoroughly *Christless*, and therefore Godless, is unworthy of the name, and can therefore claim from us no further consideration; it is mere naked rudeness and selfishness, ill-disguised by the gaudy rags of outward decency; a mere cherishing of the sensual nature, which, left to itself, would soon degenerate into monstrous barbarism, of which we already see many indications. See, for instance, how fearfully the thirst for gold unchristianizes and demoralizes men, and how much internal rudeness and want of moral discipline are thereby fostered in the face of all external and apparent culture! With moral failings of this kind, which are, alas! closely blended with the culture of the present day, the spirit of Christianity can never be reconciled. To overcome these failings, we need, as we have previously recognised, a high degree of moral resolution; and he who is not capable of this, will never be able to embrace even the purest form of Christianity; indeed, the more purely Christianity presents itself to such a one, the more direct will be the antagonism in which he finds himself placed towards it.

If, however, it is anywhere high time to undertake with earnest diligence the work of filling up this great breach in our modern civilised life, that duty methinks is incumbent upon us. *The Teutonic races have a special need and a special vocation to overcome this deep-seated contradiction* from which our age, and most of all *we Germans*, so greatly suffer. No nation has learnt to feel its internal disruptions so painfully as we. We are more truly than any other "a nation of contrarieties." Down to the latest period, in which, since the events of 1866, the German spirit has manifested itself as more and more essentially Protestant in church and school, science and politics, the opposing parties were very evenly balanced. This continuous tension of opposing forces of equal strength has been the cause of the paralysis of German power.

The difference, however, which in truth has been and is the greatest of all others, and before all others has laid hold of the heart and marrow of our people, is a religious one. Other countries are tinged with one prevailing colour in a religious point of view; they are either Protestant or Romanist. Down to a very recent period we were divided into two nearly equal parts; and this religious and ecclesiastical dualism has contributed and still contributes the greatest share to political division between North and South. Lately, indeed, in consequence of the mastery obtained by Jesuitism in the Roman Catholic Church, the breach between the two Churches has become more and more irreconcilable; and this growing breach is nowhere more painfully felt than among our people. Both camps are pervaded by this internal dissension between believers and unbelievers, between Christianity and modern ideas, and in public life neither tendency has hitherto held unlimited sway, while both parties are active and powerful. Elsewhere, a country developes either a predominant energy of faith, as, in a practical point of view, England, which is still on the whole Christian and evangelical, or a special energy of unbelief, as France, which perhaps to a greater degree than any other nation has been disintegrated by infidelity from the days of Voltaire down to the Comtes, Renans, Michelets, etc. *Germany* (and in a less measure Switzerland also) *furthers*, in a way peculiar to herself, *both belief and unbelief in almost equal proportions.* The believing Protestant theology of Germany, from the Reformers down to Schleiermacher, Neander, Tholuck, Dorner, etc., has rendered the greatest assistance towards the more profound comprehension, the scientific confirmation and vindication of our faith: by its intellectual products the Protestant theology of the whole world is still nourished. The Roman Catholic faith, likewise, as regards its scientific vindication, has found its chief supports in Germany, where alone any scientific Roman Catholic theology can be said really to exist, although latterly more and more oppressive fetters have been imposed upon it.

On the other hand, the negative and destructive productions of German theology have formed the groundwork in other countries of opinions hostile to Christian faith. Among all our opponents, it is German philosophers, critics, and theologians, who have made the most dangerous attacks on the framework of our Christian faith; and we find our foreign assailants standing shoulder to shoulder with our domestic enemies.

Thus among us, more than in other countries, we see the deepest antitheses maintaining a nearly equal balance. We are indeed a people of contrarieties, and *our need of reconciliation is consequently the greater.* The words which follow apply well to our time: "So long as a reconciliation between our religious and scientific culture is not attained by the greater number among us, that is, is not brought about in every sphere of our national education, in churches and schools, in our teaching and life, our age will be debilitated by this internal opposition, as by a secret ailment which threatens our moral and spiritual development with distortion and decay" (Gelzer). And all this is specially applicable to the German people. Its many internal differences will never be truly adjusted so long as the main cause of dissension, the religious difference, remains; and the matter still stands as it was put by a well-known historian in 1851: "Any one who desires to have a German empire must, in the first place, have a united and firmly-established German Church: German history for more than six centuries has taught this lesson!"

But for this very reason, the work of reconcilement is *our special vocation.* It is certainly the problem of our century, in the solution of which all are bound to join; but the "People of contrarieties" is called upon more than all others to do this for itself and for the world in general. It is fitted for this vocation both by internal *gifts* and also by its past *history.* Amid all its weaknesses and faults, the Teutonic genius more than any other combines a deep religious tendency with a peculiar power of speculative thought; high moral earnestness with the deepest and most comprehensive thirst for knowledge; peculiar energy for the most protracted and profound investigation, with humble submission to what is sacred and divine; an honest and enduring inspiration for all that is high and ideal, with peculiar sobriety, clearness, and acuteness of criticism. "The Nation of thinkers" is evidently at the same time a nation fitted for the service of Christ. And in many bitter trials it has maintained its public *conscience* more purely than has been the case with most other nations, and, in spite of all mortifications, has "never bartered away its ideal." By this moral attitude, and with the universality peculiar to it, it has been capable of containing within itself for so long a time, and even up to the present day, the above-mentioned evenly-balanced antitheses, for the mere toleration of which such an infinite tension and spiritual elasticity is requisite, that other nations would long ago have broken down in the attempt. It is this mental and moral tendency and attitude which capacitates the German people before all others for effecting the reconciliation of faith and science.

The genius of Germany has, however, already shown *historically* that it has recognised, and has begun to fulfil, this its vocation. When, at the close of the middle ages, in consequence of the degeneracy of the Church, culture and Christianity fell into a state of antagonism, it was the mind and conscience of the Teutonic races which sought and found the right way to unity. Together with the work of the Reformation, classical studies began to revive. In the Reformation we have Luther, the most German of Germans, the man of faith, standing side by side and hand in hand with the most profound adept in classical culture, Melancthon the Teacher of Germany,—a living and speaking proof how little faith and genuine science contradict, how nobly they supplement and further one another,—and both together showing to the world in the newly acquired gospel the way to escape out of the profound contradictions of the time, and to bring Christian faith once more into harmony with knowledge and conscience.

In later times the German people has indeed so powerfully furthered the unbelief which it received from others, that it bears a considerable share of the guilt incurred in its extension at the present day. For a long time past, the breach which it was their vocation to heal has been deepened and widened by them. But, however deeply entangled in unbelief, the German people is now beginning to make good the wrong committed against itself and others, and to direct its attention, both practically and scientifically, to the great religious task incumbent on it. German inquirers pre-eminently have followed out all doubts into their innermost grounds; and just as they have gone into them the more deeply, they have the more recognised the absolute irrefutableness of the fundamental articles of Christian faith, and shown anew to the world that belief and really thorough culture and science can exist together in the noblest union. And if in the future the breach is to be thoroughly healed, recourse must be had to all that German industry and German mental labour has done, and is still doing, in promoting the reconciliation of faith and knowledge. In these dissensions we have suffered, and are still suffering, not merely for ourselves, but, in a measure, for all; and some day others will be compelled to come to us—and many are now already coming —to ask us for the use of our weapons, and for the fruits of our victory.

As yet, this victory has been gained for a small number only. The greater proportion of educated persons still view the Christian faith with doubt and distrust. But must we therefore renounce all hope that this yawning breach will one day be filled up for the great body of our people? I think not. During the war of liberation, Christianity and German nationality solemnized an alliance, deficient indeed in depth and clearness (genuine Christianity being still obscured by the fog of rationalism), but from which, nevertheless, proceeded a new religious and moral impetus, which at the present day is still operative in various ways in our National Church. Many brave and earnest men are even now working at the bridging-over of this great gulf. For the last thirty years, in spite of all hostilities, a truly Christian science has begun victoriously to lead the way: by new and deeper exegetical researches; by historical investigation; by pointing out the remarkable harmony existing between many new archeological, ethnological, and even many scientific discoveries, and the utterances of Holy Scripture, it has vindicated the truth of the latter, and has confirmed the faith of many individuals. In the pulpits of by far the greater number of the German churches, and in the theological faculties of most of the universities, it has so completely driven unbelief out of the field, that the latter has been compelled to retire in a great measure into the divinity schools of adjacent countries (Switzerland, France, Holland, Hungary). When compared with these and other countries, Germany shows in various ways that unbelief has a greater tendency to insinuate itself into, and to make its permanent abode among, half-educated rather than thoroughly educated communities.

A great portion of the Church, moreover, has already turned away from fruitless controversies, and addressed itself to the practical work of Home and Foreign Missions, so as to exhibit to the world by dint of action what Christian faith and Christian love are able to effect; thus silencing many a scoffer. The commencement of a new apologetic and popular Christian literature, the interest of the people in Missions,—an interest increasing in spite of all invectives,—better attendance on the services of the Church, the highly necessary co-operation of the laity in Church organization, which has again begun, are all most significant intimations that even in German society *Christianity* and *nationality* may be brought to a more and more general *approximation.* We will not, therefore, be deprived of the hope that—

"The light will once again appear
To all our brethren, pure and clear,
Turning in penitence and love,
To the One Source which springs above!"

We may therefore be allowed, in view of these phenomena, to affirm that, our Christianity being such as it is, so deeply rooted in the popular life, and supported by an earnest and believing science, eliciting great respect even from abroad,—with an intellectual and moral power whose influence pervades the globe,—it will no longer do to pass by it with a supercilious shrug; the irresistible demand is laid upon every one who is desirous to escape the reproach of indifference, superficiality, or onesided partiality, and especially, therefore, on all "cultivated persons," that they should at least earnestly examine these claims.

The history of our people, both in ancient and modern times, proclaims the fact that the prosperity of its future depends on the energetic prosecution of this work of reconciliation between Christianity and culture. From the era of the middle ages, when our great German emperors appeared contemporaneously with the erection of our mighty cathedrals, down to the time of the wars of liberation, indeed down to the present day, it is clearly written on the face of our history that the periods of our national splendour were our periods of faith; *that apostasy from faith renders us weak and despised; return to it, strong and invincible!* If the former cost us an Austerlitz and a Jena, the latter gained a Leipsic and a Waterloo! Just as in former days, when Israel apostatized from the living God, it fell into political ignominy and bondage; so have we, on account of our scientific and religious vocation among nations, been compelled more palpably than others both to feel and suffer for it when we have fallen away from the faith of our fathers, and have become a prey to superstition and unbelief. To any one who has eyes to see it, our history will everywhere bring clearly before him the fact that belief in truth is the power and stronghold of our people, the inward moving spring of all its really great actions, the ultimate and surest means of protection against all our dangers both from within and without, and the crown of glory of our noblest heroes both in peace and war. And, although not in like measure, still in a similar way, the history of other nations confirms the fact that "all epochs in which faith prevailed have been the most heart-stirring and fruitful, both as regards contemporaries and posterity; whereas, on the other hand, all epochs in which unbelief obtains its miserable triumphs, even when they boast of some apparent brilliancy, are not less surely doomed to speedy oblivion." (Goethe, *Abhandlungen zum westöstlichen Divan.*)

If, in the recognition of these facts, parties desire to be made one in the *genuine* inheritance of their forefathers, and on the ground of the faith which includes and does not exclude culture; if, on the one hand, liberals and men of progress, now so commonly unbelievers, will only recognise with the ancient statesman, that "to obey God is freedom" (Seneca), and that "*a nation that desires to be free must believe, and a nation that will not believe must be in servitude;* that only despotism can dispense with faith, but not liberty;" if they would recognise the fact, that no institution, no idea, not even the humanitarianism so much bepraised, is a certain guarantee for the preservation of freedom, and that such guarantee is only to be found in the spirit of the gospel; if they would recognise the fact, that the bond of fellowship, so necessary between the various classes of the people and their different stages of culture, can only be restored by means of religion, and that, consequently, *in all liberal and national tendencies, resort must be had to Christianity;* and if, on the other hand, their opponents would be willing to comprehend that Christianity is not intended to hinder any free national development, but only to restrain and purify it, and that freedom does not hinder faith, which indeed springs up most vigorously in the free air of liberty; if both parties would but recognise the fact, that *their interests rightly understood do not sever, but really unite them,* and in this recognition would hold out to one another a helping hand: then would the breach which now separates us be already healed, and the main cause of our present paralysis be removed; no longer would one be hindering another in the reconstruction of Church or Commonwealth, all would joyously be working together; blessing and salvation would again descend from heaven; our protracted yearnings would be satisfied, our hope fulfilled, and seeking first the kingdom of God, we should find all other things added to us! And so at last would come the time of which one sings:

"Take down thy harp from the willow-tree,
  Thou nation of toil, thou nation of gloom;
Out of scorn and of cruel misery
  Shall eternal golden blessings bloom:—
The nations of the ransomed
  With joy approach Thy shrine;
Thyself our God's own heirdom,
  And all for ever Thine!"

. . . . . .

In a public place in ancient Rome, there once opened, in consequence of an earthquake, a deep chasm, which no amount of rubbish could fill up. The soothsayers were consulted, and answered, that "the most precious thing in Rome" must be cast into it. This was interpreted by a young hero as applying to manly energy and weapons; and courageous to the death and fully accoutred, he sprang into the yawning abyss, which immediately closed over him. I, too, have to lead you on to a deep gulf, which has been gradually formed by all kinds of storms and earthquakes in Church and State, Schools and Science. Nowhere else does it yawn so widely as among ourselves. Much has been already cast into it, but it will not close. Nor do I believe that this will happen, until that wherein we are strongest shall offer itself willingly for the glorious enterprise; until German science and German faith, arrayed in their respective panoplies of intellect and prayer—the former clad in its full equipment of critical acumen and the sense of truth, the latter in all the might derived from a heavenly presence and communion—step down into the depth, and there begin to build. No single man or generation will complete this work. It will be the work of many champions and of many years. But oh might it be granted me in the present lecture, to have cast into the gulf at least one stone!

SECOND LECTURE.

REASON AND REVELATION.

IN the great conflict between faith and unbelief, it is always the idea conceived of God that forms the inmost core and centre of every question, and in the case of each individual gives norm and shape to the whole of his religion, his theoretical convictions, and his practical rules of conduct. He who firmly holds that belief in the triune Deity, which from apostolic times has been recognised as constituting the basis of our Christian profession, has no longer any rational motive for impugning any essential portion of Christian truth, while one who has renounced such belief might find it difficult to maintain his adherence to a single dogma. Our entire position towards Christianity depends from first to last on this, whether we accept the scriptural and Christian idea of God or no.

Hence arises the necessity for our considering first among modern doubts respecting the articles of Christian faith, those which concern the fundamental Christian idea of God. And here starts up the preliminary question—*Whence is our knowledge of God derived?* Do we obtain it by the mere exertion of our natural faculties of reason from the contemplation of the world around us and its history, and of our own inward being and conscience? Are the foot-tracks of Deity thus laid down, and discoverable by us, adequate to enable us to form a just conception of what God is, and of the problem of our moral and religious being? Or do we need for this purpose a supernatural revelation on the part of God Himself, as to His own nature, will, and modes of dealing with us, such as is recorded in Holy Scripture? And if so, what relation does the Scripture Record bear to our knowledge of God obtained by the process of natural reason? Is reason in accord with revelation or not? or in the case of any discrepancy between them, must reason, as Deism and Rationalism maintain, take precedence of revelation as chief judge in questions of religious truth, so that nothing is to be received on the testimony of Scripture except that which is capable of rational demonstration? Or, on the other hand, is reason, as the orthodox view maintains, to be subordinated to revelation as to the highest and only certain source of divine knowledge, and that by which the intuitions of reason must be shaped and developed?

Such are the questions with which, in the first place, we have to deal. In attempting their solution, we must direct attention first to the rights, nature, and limits of reason, and to the witness of history as to its performances in comparison with the requirements of our religious nature, and more especially with reference to the contributions made by conscience to natural theology. Having done this, we must next examine the inner nature and laws of divine revelation, and attempt to ascertain its true worth, necessity, possibility, and recognisability by us, so as in the last place to draw conclusions as to the relation in which the one stands to the other.

Among these are certainly some rather dry and unattractive questions, in respect of which we must arm ourselves with patience; but they are all of the greatest practical importance. You meet a thousand times in life with those who in dealing with any religious question make at once their appeal to reason, and insist on forthwith rejecting aught that lies beyond its sphere, without however being able to render any clear account of the nature and proper limits of the knowledge thus derived, or of the relation in which such knowledge stands to the religious needs of man. I would invite you, therefore, to inquire seriously whether such persons are not really bowing down before an idol of the mind, which, while itself of very questionable worth, demands as much implicit faith from its worshippers as divine revelation itself.

We shall first, therefore, turn our attention to

I.—NATURAL THEOLOGY, OR THE KNOWLEDGE OF GOD DERIVED FROM NATURE AND REASON.

It is a reproach not seldom laid upon the faith of Christians by those who have ever on their lips—

"Science and Reason highest powers in man,"—

that it fails to recognise the rights and powers of reason and conscience as organs of divine knowledge, or at least does so very imperfectly; that it treats reason as an unformed, sickly child, and, subjecting it to an unbearable yoke, deprives it, in that crushed and slavish condition, of any healthy use of its faculties. Let us see whether there be any truth in this allegation.

And first as to the prerogatives which rightly belong to reason, it must be acknowledged that its incapacity has often been so grossly exaggerated by certain orthodox writers as to give some colour to this accusation. But here a distinction must be made between the exaggerations of individuals and the true doctrine of the Church and Holy Scripture. So little does the Bible demand a mere blind faith, that on the contrary it requires a spirit of examination in all things (1 Thess. v. 21; 1 Cor. x. 15; 1 John iv. 1 ff.). It often exhorts us to follow the Divine footsteps in the works of creation (Ps. civ.; Is. xl. 26 *et passim*); it affirms it to be the duty of all men, even of the heathen, *to seek the Lord if haply they might feel after Him, and find Him; because He is not far from any one of us, and we also are His offspring* (Acts xvii. 27-29, xiv. 17); it recognises the existence in man of *a spiritual eye*, by means of which he obtains and possesses light in respect to his relation to God (Matt. vi. 22, 23; Luke xi. 34–36); and it ascribes to the very heathen, and consequently to the human intellect *per se*, independently of the revelation contained in Scripture, a capacity for obtaining from creation and from conscience a certain amount of real knowledge as to the nature and will of God. On this point I would merely call your attention to Rom. i. 19, 20: *that which may be known of God is manifest in them* (the Gentiles); *for God* (Himself) *hath manifested it to them; since from the creation of the world His invisible attributes have through His works suffered themselves to be seen in the con-*

templation of reason, even His eternal power and Godhead; so that they are without excuse;—and to Rom. ii. 14, 15 (comp. Rom. i. 32): *these, having not the law* (once given to Israel), *are unto themselves a law; as showing the work of the law* (the conduct required by the law and will of God) *written in their hearts* (as for Israel it was written on the tables of stone), *their conscience bearing witness to it, etc.*

There is, therefore, according to Scripture, first, a natural knowledge of God which, since the creation, has been obtainable by man through a rational contemplation of His works, and which so obtrudes itself on man as to deprive of all means of exculpation those who reject it. Just as the outer world presents itself to the senses for external recognition, so God in and by the world presents Himself to reason for internal recognition. And this doctrine of the apostle of the Gentiles is not only almost literally repeated in so many words by Gentile philosophers,—as *e.g.* by Aristotle (*de Mundo*, c. 6): "Although invisible to every mortal nature, God is yet manifested by His works;" and by Cicero (*Tusc.* i. 29): "Thou seest not God, and yet thou knowest Him from His works,"—but also has its truth practically demonstrated by the various forms of religion, however imperfect, of all heathen nations.[1] And so again as to conscience: the law and will of God respecting human conduct, manifesting itself as a moral law and divine revelation in the hearts of all men, was equally well known to those who spoke of the conscience as, on the one hand, "irrefragable and immutable, recompensing every good action," and on the other, as "arrows of the gods penetrating the heart of the ungodly" (Cicero), who "night and day bear about within, their own accuser" (Juvenal); and again, as "a holy spirit settled in the inmost heart and watching over all actions, whether good or evil" (Seneca and the Laws of Menu).

It is then in accordance with the general conviction among all nations that Holy Scripture has thus assigned to reason a definite province in the domain of theology; a capacity, nay, an inward necessity for independent search after God, and the traces of His presence both in the material world without and the spiritual world within. The impulse towards and capacity

[1] On this and what follows, comp. Delitzsch's excellent work, *System der Christl. Apologetik*, Leipzig 1869, p. 63 ff.

for this search is the divine patent of nobility in the human spirit, and the Christian must not forego his inalienable right to claim it.

Even the Reformers, who so strongly (especially Luther) insisted at times on the incapacity of natural reason, by no means called this right in question. So, for instance, Luther himself in the *Disputation vom Menschen*: "It is a settled point that reason is among all things in the life of man the chiefest and the best, nay, something divine—a sun, and as it were a god placed over the government of things in this life. And this glory God has not withdrawn from reason since the Fall, but rather confirmed her in it." And in another place (the tract *Von den Klostergelübden*) he also writes: "Whatever is opposed to reason is certainly much more opposed to God. How should not that be contrary to truth divine which is opposed to human truth and right reason?" It cannot therefore be maintained that the Christian Church thinks lightly of reason.

But still the question remains, how far the province of reason extends. What are the limitations of that knowledge of which reason is the source? Or is there any such knowledge at all? To elucidate this question, we must first come to some understanding in respect to the difficult preliminary question, variously answered by the profoundest thinkers both in ancient and modern times, as to *the nature and idea of reason itself*. The attempt has constantly been made to elucidate the idea of *reason* by comparison or contrast with that of the *understanding*. But here we can hardly rest satisfied with Kant's mode of distinguishing the two, when he makes the understanding to be the faculty which contains the categories or logical forms of thought and judgment, and reason the faculty containing ideas or forms of conclusion. The distinction between these two activities of thought seems to us much too subtle for us to assign them to two distinct mental faculties. But the other distinction, which regards the understanding as the organ of logical notions, and reason that of ideas, is probably correct, and is generally accepted. The former gathers from the outer world of sense perceptions and presentments, which it proceeds to combine in general categories. The latter pursues the material presented to it by the senses and the understanding to its ultimate basis, in order, if possible, to apprehend it in its innermost ground and unity of being. Just then as *notions* are products of formal logical processes of thought, so are *ideas* the products of "real radical apprehension." Kant, however, in assuming that (excepting only the appetitive faculty with *its categorical imperative*) there is no proof of there being any real existence corresponding to the ideas of reason, seems to have overlooked the fact that the very (German) word *Vernehmen* (perceive or apprehend), from which *Vernunft* (reason) is derived, points to something real and actual, which presents itself to the apprehension of the reason; and that such apprehension may therefore be like the contemplation of the world of sense by the understanding, a genuine source of experimental certainty. This "real something" is the *Supersensuous*. Jacobi, therefore, was right in vindicating against Kant the true significance of the idea-constructing activity of reason, and defining it as the faculty which apprehends the supersensuous. Only, we must remember, that the activities of reason are not exclusively directed towards the supersensuous, but in general towards the central unity and essence of the object contemplated: the last basis or ground of each phenomenon. This impulse to seek after and discover the substantial unity in everything which is made an object of thought is characteristic of all the operations of this faculty. It is at once *analytical*, resolving phenomena into their ultimate grounds, and *synthetical*, combining these grounds so discovered into ideal unities.

And now, supposing reason by a like impulse to endeavour to combine all these ideas into one yet deeper absolute idea, and to pursue in thought the ultimate ground of all being, *i.e.* God; can it (we must ask) by its own innate power, and through contemplation of the external world and the witness of conscience, arrive at such knowledge and apprehension as to be able permanently to satisfy man's religious needs? Or must it for that end be stimulated and guided in its search after the only One and the True by supernatural revelations?

These questions bring us to the great fundamental antithesis between Holy Scripture and modern philosophy. Whereas Kant himself frankly denied the existence in reason of any power to arrive at certain knowledge in divine things, his successors maintained her absolute authority even in the highest sphere. Reason, they asserted, was able of herself, even without appeal to the testimony of the external universe and the witness of history, and *à fortiori* without the aid of revelation or Scripture, to solve by her own unaided faculties the world's enigma; to penetrate to the ground of all being, *i.e.* God Himself; and so to answer all moral and religious questions in respect to man's ultimate destiny and purpose. In this way all limitations being removed, the power of reason to attain to the knowledge of God was asserted in the most absolute terms.

Scripture, on the contrary, teaches thus: Reason, like every other faculty and every other talent, needs culture and education, such as God from the beginning has vouchsafed it; first, through the medium of the outer world (Gen. i. 28–30, ii. 15, 19, 20); and, secondly, by the imposition of a moral commandment. By the transgression of the latter, mankind entered on a perverted course of development, a mis-culture; so that their moral, and thereby also their intellectual faculties, experienced such a weakening and disturbance, that henceforth, for the knowledge of truth and of salvation, a special revelation of God to man became infinitely more a necessity than before; just as a sick child needs help much more than a healthy one (Matt. vi. 22, 23; John ix. 39–41). It is true, as we have been previously told by St. Paul, that reason, even in its present condition, possesses the power of apprehending in the conscience something of God; but this fragmentary natural knowledge of God has not had the practical effect of preventing those deprived of further *supernatural* revelation, that is, the heathen, from fundamental mistakes as to their moral and religious duty, and from seeking God in a perverted way (cf. Rom. i. 21–32). According to the Scriptures, therefore, *natural reason is insufficient for obtaining a right knowledge of God;* and a supernatural revelation of the nature and will of God is absolutely necessary as a light to the darkened reason and the weakened conscience, to prevent their falling into various aberrations.

We have here presented to us yet another important difference, which is closely connected with the previous one. Scripture distinguishes between *reason in itself,* as it was intended to be, and its *present condition, as disturbed* by sin. Philosophy and rationalism recognise no substantial importance in this distinction. They pronounce reason as it now is, adequate for obtaining a speculative and religious knowledge of God, and therefore subject all dogmas to its judgment; whereas Scripture not only lays down the necessity of the submission of finite reason to the infinite, but also pronounces the necessity of its enlightenment and correction by means of revelation (*e.g.* Ps. xviii. 29; Isa. xxv. 7, liii. 6; Luke ii. 32; John i. 9; Eph. i. 17, 18, *et al.*).

To this must be added, as a further difference, that philosophy assumes the *absolute* cognizability of God, and believes itself able to penetrate to the ultimate ground of things, and to place itself in the full possession of all truth; whereas Scripture teaches, "God dwelleth in a light that no man can approach unto; whom no man hath seen nor can see." It maintains, therefore, only a *partial* cognizability of God; teaching that in this life, even with the aid of revelation, we can attain only to "a knowing in part" in divine things, and not to anything whole and complete. According to Scripture, therefore, this rational knowledge has defined limits, drawn partly by the nature of reason itself, partly by the deteriorating influence of sin, and again by the infinite nature of the Object; philosophy, on the contrary, aims at demolishing all these restraining limits, and looks upon reason as self-sufficing for the recognition of truth. For which party shall we decide?

In order to support these claims of reason, some would ascribe to it innate ideas existing anterior to all experience—by means of which it can generate conceptions of every kind of existence. This view has recently and with good right been abandoned. It has been shown that there is, psychologically considered, nothing contained in reason which could become the property of man in any other way than by means of experience;[1] that reason is purely a mental faculty, without concrete contents; and that the logical and mathematical laws which we must assume to exist for all minds with which we hold intercourse, do not extend further than the production of

[1] Cf. also Lotze, *Medicinische Psychologie*, p. 474 ff., and Krauss and Delitzsch, *ut supra*.

general forms of thought. It has been recognised that the human mind is so constituted, that whenever it is set in action certain ideas develope themselves, to which it is from its nature predisposed; but that every concrete truth so arrived at is not a product of reason as an abstract faculty, but a result of its contact with the outward world, and consequently a product of the individual reason practically developed.

This preliminary question is therefore already decided, on philosophical grounds, against the claims of the older and later idealistic philosophy.

For our purpose we need not enter further into this question, but merely ask, *whether reason is to be regarded as a material source of knowledge, or as a mere faculty?* Evidently the latter, and the former only so far as, from the spiritual powers and qualities of human nature, a retrospective conclusion as to the divine Archetype is allowable and even necessary. But in general it must be regarded as a mere faculty of perception, by which the divine and supersensuous element in things is discerned. Is not reason essentially a receptive organ, whose function is to hear, to learn, and to embrace truths which come to it either from without or from above? Is it not, therefore, naturally predisposed to receive revelations, the word being taken in the most general sense? If then, according to the later idealistic philosophy, reason assumes to be able to comprehend by means of its innate notions and ideas the divine ground of all things, and to solve the enigma of the universe and its destinies, is it claiming more than to comprehend itself, and solve its own self-constituted enigmas? And is not this an internal contradiction? With equal truth and simplicity it has been objected against these claims: Philosophy has ever desired to solve the questions, What am I? Whence am I? and, Whither am I and the world going? But who is it puts these questions? Reason. But reason, we are told, is able to answer them. Is it able? *Would it persist in asking questions of which it knew the answer?* If reason, the organ of perception, refuses to *perceive,* it becomes *thereby* itself *irrational.*

But now arises a further question, whether reason, in order to attain to a right knowledge in divine things, has to exercise its perceptive function merely on the world without and conscience within—God's natural revelation of Himself,—or whether a supernatural revelation of God is also necessary? On these points, let the impartial judgment of history decide. Let us inquire of the history of religion and the history of philosophy how far natural reason apart from revelation has succeeded in its efforts. First, let us turn to those races of classical antiquity who were destitute of a special revelation. God suffered them "to follow their own ways," but He gave them the most intelligent minds, surrounded them with the noblest objects of nature, gave them a history full of the most illustrious proofs that He judges with a holy arm, and a period of several thousand years in which "they should seek the Lord, if haply they might feel after Him and find Him." With all these advantages, what knowledge of God did they attain to? To an obscure presentiment, breaking forth here and there, but not to the clear knowledge, much less to the practical assertion of the simplest truth of all, namely, that God is and can be only *One!* Neither in ancient nor in modern times has it been possible to find in the whole earth a nation which, without the revelation recorded in Scripture, and by its own powers of thought, has arrived at definite belief in one living personal God! Perhaps you will adduce India against me. "One God, and beside Him none other" (*Ek Brumho, dittyo nashti*), is an utterance which is in fact, even in the present day, to be heard from the lips of every Brahmin. Brahminism, at least in its most ancient elements, shows clear traces of a monotheism. But if even the thoughts of the old Hindoos did sometimes rise from the contemplation of various deified natural phenomena, such as the dawn, the lightnings, and the storms, etc., to that of the one primal cause of all things, this cause was regarded not as the One God, but as an impersonal undefined existence, of which all that could be said was, *that* it is not *what* it is; with which, therefore, any personal communion in prayer would be impossible. Monotheism in this case was attained by the surrender of the *living character* and *personality* of God, and so was essentially *pantheistic;* whilst the popular view, adhering to belief in personifications of divine power, lost thereby the divine unity in millions of gods derived from nature. The same thing occurred subsequently in Greece;[1] and Mahomet himself arrived at monotheism, not by means of his own reason, but through the influence of Judaism and Christianity.

Moreover, notwithstanding all the witness of conscience and history, the reason of the heathen world, when left to itself, never attained to those other fundamental truths, that God is and must be an *absolutely good* and *holy* being. It occasionally assigned to its heaven its own human beauty, but with it also its human shame. The gods of even the most cultivated heathen, Greeks, Romans, Hindoos, etc., suffer under the very same moral infirmities, indeed gross vices, as men. Truly, reason cannot boast much of her performances in a religious point of view; for can any genuine, moral, and religious knowledge of God be imagined, devoid of the two fundamental truths above-named? Are we then to conclude from this that revelation is, or is not needed as a guide to erring reason? But let us not be too precipitate!

The objection might be urged, that the Greek philosophers, for instance, did not share in the popular conceptions concerning the gods. This is quite correct. Some of them have emphatically opposed those immoral conceptions, and so approached nearer to the idea of monotheism. But not one completely attained to this idea. For them, the Divine Being was always losing Himself in nature, or some general idea. Even Plato did not make his way up to the idea of a divine, self-conscious, personal Being; nor ever distinctly propounded the question of the personality of God. It is true that Aristotle maintained more definitely than Plato that the Deity must be a personal Being. But even for him, it was not an absolute, free, creative power, but one limited by primordial matter; not the world's *Creator*, but only One who gave shape to the rude material, and so not truly absolute.

But now let us look more closely into the *history of philosophy* in general, and question the results of reason's efforts extending over thousands of years. Where are they? I could call your attention to many an honest confession on the part of philosophers,—to the complaint of Plato how hard it is to discover the Father of the Universe; to the utterances of

[1] Cf. also Gess and Riggenbach, *Apologetische Beiträge*, p. 50 ff., and Supplement No. 9.

Socrates, that he held it to be the greatest happiness to know the will of the gods, but did not believe this could be discovered by the conclusions of reason, and therefore recommended an appeal to the science of divination,—utterances which reveal to us what a profound longing after some special, divine revelation existed in the greatest philosophers of antiquity,—or to some of the impressive songs of the Indian *Rigveda,* in which the longing for a knowledge of the original source of life, and the pain of uncertainty on the part of the seeker, is expressed in the ever-recurring refrain,—

"Who is the God to whom our gifts belong?"

or to the way in which Fichte, after first combating revelation, confessed later on that reason stood in need of its assistance: "A Higher Being undertook the charge of the first members of our race, just as an old and venerable document containing the deepest and sublimest truths, represents Him to have done; *and to this testimony all philosophy must revert in the end.*"

Instead of further calling your attention to all this, I would only point out to you a single noteworthy matter of fact, that up to the present day, no one has been able to show to the world what the outcome of so long-continued a process of thought on the part of so many minds, and the certain gain in respect to moral and religious knowledge, actually amount to; in short, *what the generally acknowledged results of philosophy are.* In other sciences, after some time, certain truths can be collected as fixed results, from which advances can be made to further investigations. Why, then, has no one succeeded in finding and establishing such results of the long process of philosophical developments? (For what Schelling attempted in his *Positive Philosophy* remained an attempt which received only partial acceptance; and all he did beyond this was founded on the Christian view of things, and so became, what we are not here concerned with, a "Philosophy of Revelation.") Whence arises this surprising phenomenon? Simply from the fact, *that philosophy has arrived at no definite results in theology properly so called, and never laid down any principle as to the nature of God, which has not in its turn been assailed and upset.*

In saying all this, it is not our intention to deny absolutely the value of philosophy. The present generation, intoxicated by triumphs in the domain of natural science, must be summoned to rather than deterred from the study of philosophy (but it should be a *thorough* study). Most of the sciences, and theology above all, have very much to thank it for; without philosophy they would not be what they now are. But we maintain that no philosophy, which entirely rejected the aid of revelation, and sought to comprehend the world and God by mere efforts of reason, ever succeeded in attaining to any positive, lasting results. From Thales and Pythagoras, onward to Hegel and Herbart, not only has one system taken the place in due time of another, but also by its criticism has demolished the earlier one. In criticism and in negation, then, philosophy has made mighty strides; men have grown wiser in pulling down, but not in building up. The former is no doubt much the easier of the two. Down to our time, philosophers have come to no agreement even as to the basis from which philosophical speculation has to proceed; whether from some general principle or idea, or from matter; whether from the idea of pure being, or from human consciousness, etc.;—they are not yet agreed as to the relation between the real and the ideal, whether the former or the latter is that which truly is;—not yet agreed as to the idea and nature of God and His relation to the world, nor as to that of man, his reason, and his spirit;—they are not yet agreed as to the relation existing between body, soul, and spirit; nor as to our freedom of will and our accountability; nor, in short, as to any one fundamental question in speculative knowledge, morals, or religion. In whatever direction we turn, we find ourselves confronted by "open questions," unsolved problems, and views either diametrically opposed or importantly divergent.

We may therefore justly affirm, that philosophy in itself, *i.e.* abstract rational speculation, has not yet attained to positive results. When, as in modern times, it has pretended, without the guidance of experience, and by means of mere reflection, to attain to some positive result, and to construct reality out of its own ideas, the results have always had to be corrected by experience, and not seldom laid themselves open to ridicule or contempt. Hegel, for instance, believed that he had philosophically proved that there could not be more than eleven planets; and in his time there were not more than eleven known. Subsequently, however, more exact astronomical investigation has added several dozens to this number.

If, then, reason without experience thus fares in the province of nature, will it not meet with a similar fate, when, without the aid of revelation, it seeks to attain to a real knowledge of God, and to positive religious truth? Is not the Greek poet right when he says:

> "Except the gods themselves to thee unveil,
> Search as thou wilt the world, thou seek'st in vain"?

In fact, no great objection can be raised, if, in opposition to this boundless and yet ever changing assumption of reason, Christianity steps in and says: Philosophy is condemned by its own history: always imagining that in some particular system it has arrived at a conclusion; whilst nevertheless reason, both in individuals and in the whole race of man, is subjected to a continuous process of development; it is ever falling into the *error of looking upon reason as absolutely free, and failing to recognise the disturbing influence of sin.* No wonder, then, if, with these defects, philosophy never attains by its own powers to any absolute certainty or any complete knowledge of the truth, and the apostolic witness remains unshaken: "The world by its wisdom knew not God in His" (1 Cor. i. 21). Is not this witness confirmed by history? And if this be the case, we arrive at the conclusion, that reason by itself does not suffice for attaining to a true knowledge of God; that in fact it needs a light, to which it must be subordinate, a corrective against error; that is, *it needs the help of revelation.* "In Thy light shall we see light" (Ps. xxxvi. 9); we remain in darkness and uncertainty, so long as we are illuminated by nothing but the dim lamp of our own reason. This has been confessed by some even of the greatest philosophers, such as Fichte and Schelling, who, after manifold voyages and wanderings over the sea of rational speculation and contemplation of nature, have at last steered a more and more decided course for the haven which is found in a belief in revelation.

This conclusion will hardly be weakened by an appeal to the results of natural science in the present day, which, in direct antithesis to metaphysical philosophy, assigns to sensible experience as a source of knowledge the place which the other claims for reason. We will only ask: What has modern natural science, apart from revelation, done for moral and religious knowledge? It also has sought, in its own way, to solve the problem of the world's origin and of the life upon it; but in that attempt has involved itself in such absurdities, that, now-a-days, all sober naturalists, one after another, are openly proclaiming that their science can adopt no other basis than the proposition, "In the beginning God created the heaven and the earth," without involving itself in a cloud of windy hypotheses, so soon as it attempts in other ways to solve the riddle of the world's beginning. Can, then, natural science make any progress in its endeavours to explain the origin and formation of the outward universe, "without tacitly assuming the activity of some originating, adapting, and arranging power, indicated in those first words of Holy Scripture?"[1] In this case, also, we see *the need of revelation.* Natural science has also sought, by means of its own investigations, to solve the question as to the origin of man, and has arrived in the end at a total denial of the spiritual part in man, the destruction of his ethical personality, a doing away with all morality and religion, and the annihilation of all moral freedom in subjection to an absolute natural necessity. The materialism of the present day shows more clearly than any previous phenomenon, that *nature does not merely reveal but also conceals God.* Minute observations of natural phenomena have been brought to an unprecedented degree of perfection, and thereby unveiled more clearly than ever the depths of divine wisdom to the believers in revelation. But he who rejects the lamp of revelation, and stops short at mere material results, fails thereby to recognise the connection of the whole, and through the material, loses the sense of the immaterial, the spiritual, and the divine.

It happens, as Goethe predicts:

"Who of the living seeks to know and tell,
Strives first the living spirit to expel;
He has in hand the *separate parts* alone,
But lacks the spirit-bond that makes them one!"

---

[1] See the proof of this in Ulrici, *Gott und die Natur*, pp. 341-422. We revert to this again in Lect. III.

Let who will call this progress—any man with a just sense will soon note, that *moral and religious* knowledge (for we are not speaking here of what is gained by the separate branches of natural science as such) can only lose thereby and gain nothing; whilst, on the other hand, splendid results are obtained in favour of the deeper knowledge of the divine wisdom and love by an investigation of nature, so soon as it permits revelation to intensify its view of the "spiritual bond of union," of the One in the many, the eternal Cause and the eternal end and aim of the world.

Some have attempted lately to make of *conscience,* as the third factor of natural theology, the highest source of religious knowledge, and to represent revelation as dependent upon it. So they follow one after another. Reason having wearied herself in the attempt to solve the mysteries of God and the universe, nature tried her hand at the same problem; and now that a onesided contemplation of nature has led inquirers into the slough of materialism, they begin to interrogate conscience. In things divine it would seem as if men would question and attend to any witness rather than God Himself.

Of these three factors, conscience would certainly appear to be the most reliable. Nevertheless, the numerous researches which have been recently instituted by different theologians into the nature of conscience, are in their results just as divergent as the researches of philosophers into the nature of reason. On this point also we need not go beyond what is generally agreed on. That the word "conscience" is used in different senses, sometimes for a definite subjective knowledge, sometimes for that which is objectively known; that we speak not only of a religious and moral, but also of an ecclesiastical, a Christian, a scientific, an æsthetic, indeed even of a public conscience, etc., need not disturb us here, for all we are now inquiring after is the common fundamental notion represented by the word in all these uses of it.

Now conscience is confessedly that consciousness which testifies to the law of God implanted in us; that moral faculty whereby man discerns with inward certainty what is right and what is wrong in the sight of God (Rom. i. 32), and is conscious that the eye of God is turned upon him. It is "the moral heart-throb in man, testifying to the existence of a higher will by which it is implanted, and seeking to control, awakening, guiding, judging, all the movements of human life, so far as it pertains to the province of free-will." Therefore, *moral* convictions only are directly derived from the action of conscience. As being man's knowledge of the law written in his heart (συνείδησις), it produces, indirectly, a certain knowledge of the Lawgiver and His will, that is, of God, as a holy and righteous being, the moral consciousness being here identified with the religious. So far, in fact, conscience is, from a humanitarian point of view, a genuine source of natural theology.

Scripture, as we have already seen, not only recognises this, but also affirms that even with the heathen, conscience has not wholly lost its efficacy (Rom. ii. 14, 15). Even fallen man possesses in conscience a certain sense and moral appreciation of truth, which, if he follow, he is "of the truth," susceptible for higher divine truth (John xviii. 37). On the other hand, Scripture by no means supports the position "that conscience is the source and judge of the whole complex of Christian doctrine; that no dogma is to find place therein which cannot be referred to an utterance of conscience; that conscience must decide without appeal as to the divinity of Scripture as a whole or in detail."[1] According to this, conscience would be the chief if not the only source and highest rule of faith, as of our religion generally. And this is more or less the view of those who may often in the present day be heard to say, that in everything man need only follow his conscience; and that that is the best, nay, the only true religion. In all this, the assumption evidently is, that conscience is an ever reliable witness for the truth, a constant and immutable source of moral and religious knowledge. Scripture teaches otherwise, namely, that conscience may err, be defiled, become impure and weak (Tit. i. 15; 1 Cor. viii. 7–10, 12; 1 Tim. iv. 2); that as a matter of fact it has *become weakened and confused by sin;* that, in order to attain to perfect clearness and power, it needs enlightenment through God's word and Spirit (*e.g.* Rom. ix. 1), purification (Heb. ix. 14), and awakening by the revealed will of God. The oftentimes confused, though never perfectly extinguished, subjective revelation of God's will in the con-

[1] Cf. Schenkel, *Christliche Dogmatik vom Standpunkt des Gewissens*, 1858-59.

science, needs for its complement the pure and only constantly reliable objective revelation of God in His Word. It is not, therefore, revelation which is to be determined and ruled by conscience, but the latter by revelation, as its necessary accompaniment and indispensable guide.

Here also, therefore, we have essentially the same controversy as in the case of reason: are we to acknowledge, or not, that the conscience has been darkened and confused by sin? This question is practically answered in the negative, when conscience is made the source and arbiter of the whole body of faith. Which view is the right one? Whether conscience is the *judge* of revelation, is a point we cannot decide until we have considered what revelation itself is. On the other hand, the question we are dealing with is, whether conscience, either by itself or combined with reason and nature, is not an adequate *source* for attaining the knowledge of God—a source which renders revelation superfluous?

Is it so? We do not here go beyond the question as to what conscience objectively lays down. Is this always the same? By no means. We find, of course, in all men a conscience, and make the further observation that neither its witness nor its nature is dependent on human caprice. It bears its testimony with an authority independent of our will, and this is an essential characteristic of conscience as it exists in all men. But it is just as universally the case that conscience differs partially in each individual.[1] It bids and forbids, decides and judges of right and wrong, *according to the insight in each individual,* which is not absolutely common to all men, but in part at least very changeable and various. Hence the difference in the utterances of conscience in the case of men of different degrees of culture and of different religions, side by side with a certain fundamental similarity. Hence the peculiar deficiencies and *lacunæ* in the consciences of so many men. Evidently, therefore, conscience, like reason, is, "on the one hand, something *which has become,* on the other hand, something *which is becoming.*"

[1] Cf. Güder, *Erörterungen über die Lehre vom Gewissen nach der Schrift,* Krauss *ut supr.*, p. 134 ff., who, on account of its dissimilar purport, defines conscience as "the innate compulsion to have an ideal and to acknowledge it as judge over oneself." Besides also cf. R. Hofmann, *die Lehre vom Gewissen,* 1866; Kahler, *Lehre vom Gewissen,* 1864, and Delitzsch *ut supr.*, 71 ff., 161 ff.

What follows from all this? First of all, that Scripture is right when it speaks of the variations and confusions of conscience; that it is, therefore, a most questionable step, to make of the changeful utterances of conscience a main source of Christian dogma; nay, that it is no longer possible to derive a natural religion with truths *universally* valid, from the utterances of conscience *taken by itself,* apart from the influences which help to determine it. Not with *truth universally valid,* for every conscience, on account of its individual character, has real moral weight for its possessor only (cf. 1 Cor. x. 29); not from the utterances of conscience by itself, for every separate utterance of each individual conscience has its source in special circumstances, and is most commonly determined by the influence of some positive religion.

If all this already renders us somewhat cautious in the use of the conscience as a source of the knowledge of God, the testimony of *history* will make us still more cautious. Here also history, not abstract researches, must be suffered to decide. What, according to its testimony, has conscience accomplished for true theology apart from revelation? We have already heard the answer to this question: The heathen, notwithstanding all their listening to the voice of conscience, as it spoke in the very noblest spirits among them, did not attain to the knowledge of God as the personal, absolutely Holy One, but "changed the glory of the unchangeable God into an image like to perishable man and beasts" (Rom. i. 23).

Let us take a glance at the heathen world. One man aims at deliverance from sin by means of a bath; another (*e.g.* the North American Indians) thinks to purify his heart by the aid of an emetic; here another sets prayer mills in motion at the caprice of the wind; another pours out libations of wine or tea, sheds human blood, or offers his only child as the most acceptable sacrifice. Here a man can take no rest, until he has accomplished sanguinary vengeance on the man-slayer; there a fanatical Mussulman seeks to purchase paradise for himself by destroying as many Christians as possible, and the like. Are not all these just so many examples of an *erring conscience,* which is strong enough to insist on some kind of sacrifice or expiation, but is still too dark to apprehend the perversity of these ways and means? What a mistaken idea of God and the moral duty of man is presupposed in all this!

Is this mere spark of moral and religious knowledge to be supposed sufficient to enable men to solve the problem of moral duty? The fall of the noblest nations of antiquity—the moral corruption of heathen nations of the present day adding ever fresh confirmation to the fearful description of heathen vices in Rom. i. 21–32—answers with a thousand-tongued voice, No! Even the knowledge of God derived from conscience was not and is not sufficient to guard men against the most grievous moral errors and the wickedest religious abominations; nor has it been able to save any heathen nations from moral and religious, and, finally, even from material destruction.

But is it so? Must it not be allowed that the natural religion of conscience goes further than this? May we not turn from the dry tree of popular error to the green tree of philosophical speculation? Well, then, let us take one philosopher who approached more nearly than many others to a true knowledge of God, ascribing to Him goodness as His most essential attribute,—let us glance, for instance, at Plato's Republic. What do we find there? In his commonwealth, he desires to see introduced a community both of goods and wives; he desires that parents should not even know their children, to say nothing of educating them; that a man should look upon all children as his own, which, according to the time of their birth, might possibly have been his; that the mother should nourish sometimes one child and sometimes another, and among these children, only incidentally those which were born from her; that the rulers of the State should be permitted, without further question, to put to death weakly and unhealthy persons, and should prescribe for every one his vocation, etc.; in short, he sacrifices—and this, indeed, fully in conformity with the ancient idea of a commonwealth—the right, the freedom, and the property of individuals, in the very harshest way, to the good of the State. I now ask—According to all these details, have philosophers been able to keep themselves free from the clouded moral consciousness and erring conscience of their time? And what, then, is in this case the fundamental deficiency? The want here, as in the whole of heathenism, is the recognition of the *worth of each human personality.* This man only begins to see, when he knows the God of love, that is, by means of revelation. But if the heathen is deficient in a right knowledge of his own moral worth, and thus also of his moral duty, with his whole life bound up in the worship of the impulses of nature—a mere life of selfishness, how is it possible for his mind to rise to any clear knowledge and apprehension of God, as an absolutely holy and loving Will? But neglect of the divine law in the conscience must, the longer it exists, lead more and more to a misapprehension and neglect of the Lawgiver. The loss of the living God must then be made good by the creation of false gods of one's own. And as the creator, so his creatures. A people sunk in sensuality and cruelty, creates for itself sensual and cruel gods, and worships them with corresponding rites.

In fact, the history of heathenism is the history of the aberrations of conscience, and one long proof of the need of revealed religion for its enlightenment and purification. But this history is likewise a proof that conscience is never completely extinguished, and that it absolutely is not, as certain materialists seek to make us believe, a matter of arbitrary agreement and of conventional manners and customs, but is an original revelation of God in man, which forms a part of universal human essence and of our moral nature. For no sooner is God's true will as revealed in His word presented to the heathen mind, than conscience is awakened even in the cannibal, who reverting to his higher instincts, feels shame for his present conduct as inconsistent with them; and this alone were enough to prove that conscience, as a source of natural religion, has still a potential existence in every human mind, however much obscured by error and sin.

And is not the history of Christendom also replete with proofs that without the continual guidance and stimulus of revelation, the conscience soon becomes darkened? What, for instance, has brought so many to the stake? Very frequently nothing but the erring conscience which thought that thereby "it did God service" (John xvi. 2). Whence the darkening of the Christian conscience, such as that exhibited in so many ways in the moral history of the middle ages? The light of revelation was placed "under a bushel!" And what is it that has subsequently awakened the Christian conscience, so that it has again reverted to the worship of God in spirit and in truth? The light of God's word! Thus, therefore, as in the case of reason and nature, we again arrive at the old conclusion, that this factor of natural theology also *stands in need of revelation;* that conscience is practically exposed to such violent fluctuations, and so readily errs and is perplexed, that it cannot dispense with the continual enlightenment and fixed rule of the revealed word.

These facts are overlooked by many of those who now regard conscience as an adequate guide in matters of faith and religion, and believe that they can dispense with revelation.[1] Besides this, they disregard the fact, that *Christian* conscience can no longer be entirely dissevered from revelation; that its witness is *a priori* influenced by the spirit of Christianity, of which the strongest rationalists cannot wholly divest themselves, so that, although they desire to adopt a mere natural religion, they are, nevertheless, unable to dispense with the assistance of supernatural revelation. Finally, they overestimate the force and range of conscience and reason, *in respect to the satisfaction of our moral and religious need.*

An old mystic says somewhere, "God is an unutterable sigh in the innermost depths of the soul." With still greater justice, we may well reverse the proposition and say, the soul is a never-ending sigh after God; because she is from Him, she is also for Him, and tends to Him. In her deepest recesses there lives or slumbers, however hidden, an inextinguishable longing after God. She knows herself, by an inward sentiment, not merely to be *dependent* on Him, but at the same time drawn towards Him, and destined for a union with Him. Being essentially "reasonable," she reads God everywhere, both in and without herself, so that she is unable to free herself from His presence, however far removed from Him, as the voice of conscience shows. But the more she seeks and apprehends, the greater is her longing after Him. And the more we consider the nature of this longing, the more we discern that what it aims at, is not a mere intellectual apprehension of God, but a vital experience, enjoyment, and communion. The

[1] As F. Pécaut, in his late work *Le Christ et la conscience,* repeats with innumerable terms of expression, that the religious and moral life has merely God and individual conscience as its two factors.

religious need is essentially of a practical nature; it is an impulse to draw nigh to God, and to place one's self in personal fellowship with Him, proceeding from the presentiment that our spirit can find its abiding rest and satisfaction in nothing but this fellowship, and in the enjoyment of the love and peace of God. The question then stands finally thus: Whether natural religion, besides imparting a true knowledge, succeeds likewise in conducting the soul to a living communion with God, and so, in satisfying its deepest need?

But how completely incompetent in this respect is it shown to be if we seek God in nature? How little can we discern what He truly is, let alone the failure in revealing the *personal relations* between Him and us, which are required by our religious need! We feel that there is an infinite Being above us, by whose almighty power we are encompassed; but just when we feel the nearness of the Eternal One, the words and ideas are wanting, which might, as it were, clinch the impression made and fix it in the form of clear conceptions. Again and again, the Inexpressible One eludes our imagination, or, we only too readily confound Him with natural powers and phenomena, and so thrust into a dark and vanishing distance the Father of our spirits who is indeed so nigh!

Or if we seek God in the realm of thought, how little falls from the barren heights of speculation to cheer the longing heart and its burning spirit of inquiry! We look in vain even from those who are most advanced in such inquiries for testimony as to any real satisfaction derived therefrom. Socrates and Plato attained perhaps to a sense of the Divine, but still think of God as one who remains far from them. Prophets and apostles, on the other hand, speak of Him as One who is very nigh them, and whom to approach is their highest good (Ps. lxxiii. 28). The former deduce the notion of God in acute syllogisms; the latter are learning to know Him as He is, as the true Shepherd of their souls, as "the strength of their hearts, and their portion for ever." In the one case a religious need is satisfied, in the other it is not. In order to estimate the whole extent of this difference, compare, for instance, the 23d or the 73d Psalm with any one of Plato's dialogues. In the latter, there is perhaps an approximately correct answer given to the question of reason, What is God in Himself? But in the former we find a solution to the question of the heart, What is God *for me?* How can I *personally* become a partaker in Him? Nor till these questions are solved can the religious need be satisfied.

I am well aware that many will here object, that they feel their religious need to be fully satisfied by their rational religion, so that, in this case, natural religion does all that is required. They will further appeal to their own "good" conscience in proof of the inward satisfaction of their heart. But is there not here a fatal self-deception? I should like to ask these "good" consciences whether they can honestly maintain that their moral convictions and their practical conduct never disagree, and whether the former are actually sufficient to enable them to resist evil and to do good. As being the moral *impulse* in man, conscience should do both these things, and produce the knowledge of good and the power of doing it. But what are we taught by history and experience as to the relation between these two? Answer: *Action always falls short of knowledge*—even that is not done which man knows from his own conscience to be the will of God. So it was with the heathen. "When they knew God, they glorified Him not as God, neither were thankful" (Rom. i. 21). We see the truth of this in the confession of Marcus Aurelius, "I should have lived better than I have done, had I always followed the monitions of the gods."

The *knowledge* of the heathen, therefore, in divine things was greater and better than *its practical result.* Hence their sense of *guilt,* turning their good conscience into an evil, self-condemning one; or, in time, into a conscience which is erring and seared. Attention paid to conscience, so far from leading to the satisfaction of our religious needs, conducts to a kind of moral dualism, of which we find virtuous heathen making the same complaint[1] which Paul, in Rom. vii. 7–25, so impressively describes. Just as prophecy was the incorporated conscience

[1] Cf., for instance, the passage in Xenophon, *Cyr.* vi. 1–41: "I certainly have two souls, for if there were only one, it surely could not be at the same time good and bad, nor could it at the same time love good and base actions, and also at the same time wish the very same thing and not desire to put the wish into action; but evidently there are two souls, and if the good soul gets the upper hand, then good will be done, and if the evil, then shameful actions will be perpetrated" (Delitzsch *ut supr.*).

of Israel, so the conscience was "the prophet of the heathen," which was intended to awaken the longing for a divine redemption, by means of the sorrowful recognition of its own impotence.

And has it ever been otherwise, in the case of any one who has rejected the aid of revealed religion in his moral conflicts? Is not the saying of St. Paul again and again confirmed by every day's experience, "For to will is present with me; but how to perform that which is good I find not: for the good that I would I do not"? (Rom. vii. 18, 19.) Does not the practical conduct often fall short of the better knowledge and will? If we all are more or less compelled to acknowledge this,[1] what follows? Why, that our power for good, derived from conscience and natural religion, is so impaired that we can never keep ourselves wholly free from evil, nor get beyond a feeling of guilt which, in consequence of the contradiction existing between our knowledge and our actions, is ever asserting itself; and if we then seek a way of escape from such condemnation, and inquire how we may be reconciled with God, what further counsel can reason or conscience now afford us? None, or at least none that is satisfactory. Into what follies have the heathen fallen upon this point! This is the juncture at which natural religion either fails most miserably or utterly misleads; *it knows no way to peace or expiation of our guilt.* The more profoundly the knowledge of the Holy One penetrates the conscience, the purer is the heart's desire after atonement; but the more a man seeks to find comfort in false means of expiation, the more confused and darkened does his conscience become. If, with nothing but the religion of reason and the conscience, man cannot place himself in a right, normal, and peaceful relation to God; if experience teaches him that this religion cannot help him to get over the moral dualism, it follows that it is also absolutely inadequate to the satisfaction of his religious needs.

Here also the decisive question is, *whether or not evil be*

[1] That so much is allowed even by the most "free-thinking" theologians, we see *e.g.* from the *Predigten aus der Gegenwart,* by Dr. Schwarz of Gotha, III. *Samml.*: "Oh, do not tell me that to act uprightly, and to do one's duty, and to have a good conscience, are sufficient. I ask you, ye virtuous ones, who among us does his duty and has a good conscience in the highest sense of the word? Not one among us all. We all are, and remain, striving and struggling ones, who in manifold ways err, and stumble, and fall short."

acknowledged as an actually disturbing power, which darkens the conscience, separates us from God, and therefore requires an atonement. But if a man resolves sin into a mere venial weakness, and the divine precept of perfection into that of a mere external honesty and righteousness,—that is, if conscience be so weakened in him as no longer to produce any real self-condemnation (though, perhaps, retaining some measure of influence on his outward life), if a tendency of mind has been given him which no longer attacks sin in its innermost centre, —then he may readily consider his natural religion as adequate to the satisfaction of his inmost needs, and thereby assure us of his good conscience. But there is in this case a *darkened* and *enfeebled* conscience, and not a really good and pure one. The world is full of "good" consciences of this kind. Do not allow yourselves to be deceived by supposing that revelation can be dispensed with in attaining true peace with God. There is such a thing as a delusive peace, and a delusive satisfaction of one's religious need.

In contrast to these delusions, keep firmly to this view;—if natural religion is really to satisfy our spiritual need, it must be able to confer strength adequate to the resistance of evil and the performance of good; and, inasmuch as evil already exists, to indicate the way to real reconciliation with a righteous God. But *experience* teaches that natural religion, together with conscience, is not able to do either the one or the other; its inadequacy hence is evident. We are therefore, from the bare consideration of our religious need, driven to the necessity of some supernatural revelation. And this revelation must not only purify, enlighten, and regulate, but also *supplement our religious knowledge*, communicating *new* truths, to the assistance of natural religion, and attesting its special divine character by its redemptive energy in breaking down the power of evil. Does Christian revelation do this?

We have previously seen that its aim is to bring fallen man back to God, in the way which is called and is Christ. Its pith and centre is the doctrine of the Atonement. It therefore points out to our religious need a new mode of attaining satisfaction, *Christ*. And further still; it also confers the power of embracing it. It enlightens and enlarges knowledge, but not without first becoming a power in the *heart*, and an energy in the *will ;* it becomes, indeed, a man's own possession, not intellectually, but in a moral way, by the self-surrender of the heart and will. It can therefore once more reconcile knowledge and action by a restoration of the moral faculty and re-invigoration of the power for good. Hence it accomplishes both ends, shows the way of reconciliation, and imparts strength for future righteousness. And this is confirmed by the daily experience of all true-hearted Christians. Ask of them whether, in the salvation revealed, they do not find life and full satisfaction for their religious need ?

After all this, we can understand the statement of Scripture, that there can be no true insight in divine things without regeneration, without a new, higher life being implanted in us from above. Not until we are reconciled to Him can we again truly love the Divine Being, from whom we have been separated by sin, and be so intimately united with Him in love, that His glory shall be ever increasingly revealed to us. And we shall also be compelled to acknowledge the truth of that prophecy which represents all Gentile nations as shrouded in ignorance and error, till the true divine and saving knowledge manifests itself in the new covenant of the latter day : "The Lord of Hosts will destroy in this mountain the face of the covering cast over all peoples, and the veil that is spread over all nations" (Isa. xxv. 7).

This will appear still more clear to us, if we give a closer consideration to

II.—SUPERNATURAL THEOLOGY, OR THE KNOWLEDGE OF GOD DERIVED FROM REVELATION.

We take this last word in its *narrower* sense. In its more comprehensive sense, it signifies in general the whole divine energy of self-communication in creation, in the conscience, and in providence. In this revelation, as we have seen, even the heathen have a share. In the narrower sense, revelation denotes *a supernatural manifestation of divine grace influencing human knowledge for man's eternal good ;* an unveiling of mysteries which lie beyond the province of reason, and may therefore stand in a certain contrast to it. When, for instance, Christ says to Peter, "Flesh and blood hath not revealed this unto thee, but my Father which is in heaven;" or when St. Paul testifies that he had not received his gospel from any man, but "through the revelation of Jesus Christ," —these are revelations in this special sense. To the same category belongs all that Scripture tells us of God's self-communications, under both the old and the new covenant, whether made by immediate theophanies or through angelic and human instrumentality, through outward miracles or through inward spiritual manifestation, vision, and inspiration.

In respect to revelation, a distinction must be drawn between the divine action in itself and its influence on man, that is, between the outward *objective* self-manifestation of God, and the inward *subjective* illumination of the human intellect. Whatever manifestation of Himself God vouchsafes, He seeks at the same time to interpret to man by the Spirit, even as the manifestation of the divine glory in the universe is supplemented by the voice of the Divine Spirit in the conscience. Both together constitute revelation, properly so called. The crown and ultimate goal of all divine revelation is He in whom alone, according to the Scriptures, the perfection of divine knowledge dwelt, who alone on earth declared perfectly the divine will — the only-begotten Son, who could truly say of Himself: "He that hath seen me hath seen the Father" (John i. 18, vi. 46, xiv. 6-9). In Christ, therefore, both factors of revelation meet: He is at once the perfect manifestation of God, and the perfectly enlightened or inspired Man.

The object of divine revelation is *God Himself*, historically manifesting Himself in the character of Saviour; and Man needs no other object of revelation. God's self-revelation, therefore, is at the same time a special form of His work of redemption, and has human salvation for its end. The great miracle of revelation is historically developed in a threefold form:[1] sometimes God *appears*, sometimes He *speaks*, sometimes He *works miracles*. These forms are closely allied, and therefore, in the historical developments of revelation, often

[1] Cf. also in H. von der Goltz, *Gottes Offenbarung durch heilige Geschichte*, Basle 1868, the excellent section as to "the mode and form of divine revelation," pp. 84-107.

found together; the revelations being made either externally through the senses, as in angelic appearances, or internally through the workings of the human spirit, as in prophetic dreams or visions.

The announcement of this revelation, which, up to the "time of fulfilment," was confined to a particular branch of the human race, and, after Christ, became a common property of mankind, is contained in *Scripture;* and that which was previously communicated to special persons, in an extraordinary way, now comes to us all in an ordinary way, by the written or spoken word of human agents, along with the inward operation of the Holy Spirit; but even thus it presents itself to us as *supernatural* and divine truth. This, in all brevity, is the scriptural and Christian idea of revelation. Incomprehensible as it may at first appear, we must not overlook that revelation, despite its essentially supernatural character, has, and must have, a *natural side* also. In all divine manifestations, created existences are the *media* through which the presence and glory of God are revealed to men (Isa. vi.; Ezek. i., ix.; Rev. iv.). In all divine utterances, God condescends to the limits of human understanding, and adapts His revelation to the mental condition of its recipients; giving first milk, then strong meat (John xvi. 12; 1 Cor. iii. 1, 2; Heb. v. 12-14). And even divine miracles, as we shall see further on, have not unfrequently a *natural* basis. Revelation is never given without some previous preparation, in the historical developments of human thought and human needs.

Nor is this done in any irregular or arbitrary way: the developments of revelation follow fixed *internal laws* and a certain order, and are confined within definite limits; both Old and New Testament making manifest the divine purpose in the fourfold development of electing, calling, blessing, and taking into covenant. Even the superficial observer cannot fail to note the progressive developments of divine communications with man from the simple intercourse of a primeval time to the world-covenant made with Noah, and from thence onward to the covenant of promise established with Abraham, the covenant of the law made with Israel, and finally the covenant of grace in Christ with the whole world.

There is therefore a continuous progress—an ever clearer manifestation of the Divine Nature, and of its purposes of love for man, concluding with the mission of Christ and the Comforter (Heb. i. 1, 2).

There is also a certain progress in the *form* of revelation. At first, God revealed Himself in sensible manifestations, which were an inevitable accommodation to the needs of humanity while still in pupilage, just as every tutor has now to condescend to the capacity of the child. With Moses He spake "face to face, as a man talketh with his friend" (Ex. xxxiii. 11; Num. xii. 8). Then came miracles wrought by divine power, through human instrumentality; and in these we may note a certain internal educational progress from the material to the spiritual; the miracles of inspiration becoming gradually the more prevailing forms of divine manifestation, until, in the miracle of miracles, the person of Christ, the deepest spiritual mysteries of redemption were unfolded, and finally, through the outpouring of the Spirit and the inspired gospel records, revelation became abidingly an inward thing conveyed to us by the Word and Spirit.

Further, Scripture miracles are sparingly distributed, and after an ordered plan among various periods, and in very different measures, according to their differences of character. The most significant make their appearance at decisive *turning-points* in sacred history, *e.g.* the election of fresh agents of revelation, and the constitution of new forms of covenant. It was thus in the patriarchal age, and in those of Moses, of David, and of Christ and the Apostolic Church. In the periods between these epochs, miracles are not so frequent. When the point in question was more to maintain that which existed than to found something new, the Word, the most inward mode of revelation, remains the only form of it. We everywhere see a progressive preparation for the complete revelation of God in Christ; we see the sequel constantly linked on to that which precedes, and further developing it; we see also in Christ Himself a wise tutorial progress in making known the secret things of God down to the last and most profound, the doctrine of the Trinity, which not until He had His departure in view did He fully make known (Matt. xxviii. 19). Further, the lower forms of revelation, in which the chief point is some manifestation of Deity, always prepare the way for the more perfect forms of inward inspiration; and these, again, point onward further still to a final, all-completing manifestation in the second advent of Christ. Finally, we see the Divine Revealer keeping always one and the same end in view—man's eternal good, and thereby always adapting His revelations to the particular needs and capacity of their recipients.

But, more especially, divine revelation is something quite different in its mode of operation from what is called magic, and addresses itself to man in his ethical capacity; the moral condition of the recipient determines in the main its *measure* and its *limitations.* Although under special circumstances God may allow some sordid person like Balaam to be the medium of revelation, the rule nevertheless holds good, that God adopts as His instruments those who, through their moral and religious character, were peculiarly *capable of appreciating* divine things, such as Abraham, Moses, David, the prophets, the apostles, and, above all, Christ (Matt. xi. 25; Acts vii. 22, x. 35; Jas. iv. 8; Jer. xxix. 13). Everywhere we find that revelation is met on the part of man by a heart-seeking after God, after truth, and after sanctification. "If ye seek me with your whole heart, ye shall surely find me." This practical piety was, from Abraham to Christ, the constant medium of existing and progressive revelation, which varied in the clearness of its manifestations with the varying religious character of its exponents.

And so still the divine revelation contained in Scripture communicates itself as a full personal possession only to that heart which meets it with an honest seeking after truth. By indifference, or opposition to truth, the susceptibility for divine things is lost, and thus also the possibility of receiving any further revelations. In Nazareth, Christ "doeth not many miracles, on account of their unbelief." In revelation, as in other things, God deals with us as free, responsible creatures. His supernatural revelation is no more irregular and arbitrary than that through nature. On the contrary, everywhere we see measure, order, well-planned gradation, organic connection well-defined limits, and the operation of its own inward laws in all its self-impartations to man.

If we keep this in view, many rationalistic *objections* will refute themselves, raised as they are against the specific worth, necessity, possibility, and intelligibility of a supernatural revelation.

What Scripture tells of divine appearances, spiritual manifestations, visions, etc., is often compared with similar phenomena in heathen religions, and, consequently, the *specific value* of Christian revelation is denied.

Without comparing its moral and religious character with the pretended communications of heathen deities, it will here suffice us to point out the profound difference between the biblical and the whole heathen idea of revelation. The revelations of heathen gods invariably have reference to something isolated, external, and fortuitous; and even when they impart moral precepts, these have no real internal connection. In Scripture, on the other hand, revelation is one grand *systematic*, progressive *organism*, which from its very commencement goes on expanding, and so as to exhibit its smallest details in living connection with the whole, and its one great end, the moral and religious good of man.

We find nowhere else, in the whole course of the history of religion, a like conception of the end and purpose of divine revelations. The biblical view of revelation, apart from its sacred purport, is unique in its nature, and it is therefore *a priori* a mistake to force it down to the level of the heathen view. We must also note the important distinction, that in heathen legends it is always the *most ancient* times which abound in miracles, and that subsequently miracles gradually decrease; whereas in Scripture the grandest revelations and most striking miracles occur at *different* times, and, indeed, always at particular crises of sacred history, and without disappearing in the course of a history extending over four thousand years.

But if from the fact, that not Christianity and Judaism only, but many other religions also, advance a claim to revelation, any one is tempted to conclude that this claim is in no case trustworthy, and that we cannot know which is the true religion, seeing the "revealed" religions all contradict one another, and that therefore it is best to reject them *en masse*, he is excellently answered by A. Monod, in his *Lucile*: " If twenty persons at once set up along with you a claim to the inheritance of your cousin, could a just judgment nonsuiting you and all the rest be based on the assumption that there is *no* legal heir? A lie is only credible when it makes use of truth to back it up. Spurious money is not coined except where good money exists. Quack doctors obtain patronage only because there are true physicians and real remedies. *Instead of concluding that there is no true revelation because there are so many false ones, we should on the contrary conclude, that there are only so many false because there is one true.*" The other inference cannot be drawn, except by that indolent spirit which shirks the trouble of examining into the different claims of religious systems, a task which, at the present day, can hardly be very irksome. That can only be the true and perfect religion, which exercises the most wholesome influence on the moral life of individuals and of nations. " By their *fruits* ye shall know them." And who at the present day can stand in doubt on this point, if he compares Christian nations with heathen and Turks, or even with the Jews?

Against the *necessity* of revelation, the objection is generally made, from a rationalistic point of view, that if God was compelled from time to time to manifest Himself, then creation must have stood in need, as it were, of continuous " after-help." If animals can attain to their prescribed destiny by means of their natural powers, man can do the same by means of his reason. In opposition to these views, the rejoinder has justly been made, that if man and beast differ by means of reason, and consequently in their destination and in their means of attaining it, they may also well differ in the mode and way in which they realize their destiny.

But this whole theory of " after-help," by which God's original plan of creation is made to appear as having been incomplete, is absolutely inadmissible. Scripture represents the counsel of redemption as having been from the first co-existent in the Divine Mind with that of creation (Eph. i. 4; 1 Pet. i. 20). The fact of revelation, therefore, does not imply that God has been compelled by intervening circumstances, to wit, the genesis of sin, to resolve on affording such " after-help" to His own work; on the contrary, from the very beginning, due provision was made in the divine plan for such eventuality; and God's own free love is only carrying into effect, by means of revelation, that which from eternity He had determined and prepared for, in order to conduct the rational universe, spite of all disturbing influences, to its ultimate and glorious consummation. The very idea of any afterthought and alteration of the divine work or plan, is absolutely excluded by the very terms of the Scripture doctrine of revelation.

It is indeed the doctrine of Scripture, that man stands in need of divine assistance. A special revelation from God is a necessity for us, and that for two reasons: first, by reason of our natural *helplessness;* and secondly, on account of the Fall, and man's consequent *degeneracy.* For does not every child which is brought into the world need some "after-help"? And is it to be supposed that the first members of our race required no *education?* And who but God could have been their Educator? If their only teachers were the animals, whence came their gift of speech? Whence the development of their moral and spiritual faculties? Whence those purer religious ideas which are continually cropping up among the fragments of the oldest heathen religions? How can things of this kind be explained without presupposing a divine interposition and assistance? None but he who denies the necessity of any such education, can deny the necessity of some special intercourse between the first man and his Maker, or be offended at that paternal and quasi-human relation in which the first chapters of the Bible represent God as putting Himself with man. Our own little ones, feeling themselves their need of education, look for and submit to it. In doing this they exhibit more understanding than many adults.

But no sooner had sin entered the world, and with it an increasing radical disturbance of the very foundations of natural theology, and of the proper exercise of reason and conscience, than the necessity became manifest of further revelations on the part of God of Himself and of His plan for human redemption. When the unbelief of the natural man had developed into the various forms of pagan superstition, how was it any longer possible for man to find out for himself the highest absolute Good, the living and true personal God, without the aid of a new supernatural revelation? Here again our former position holds good: only he who denies the existence and power of *sin* can deny or dispute the necessity of some special revelation; but then let him also ask himself what he can make of the main facts of man's religious history, and of the clear proofs they give of the thorough incapacity of reason when left to itself? How natural and reasonable on the other hand, how conformable with the results of history and daily experience, is the teaching of Scripture as to the educating processes and progressive developments of divine revelation! For the first members of our race, regarded as children, revelation was a nurse who taught them to walk in leading-strings; for fallen man it became a task-master, as in the law of Moses; and finally, for those who had learned the need of redemption, it manifested itself as a freedom-giving law of the spirit of Christ and the gospel. Appeal, indeed, is often made to the perfection of the natural universe and its arrangements as not admitting of, much less requiring, any such divine manifestation or interference; but this is a point to which we shall have to recur when we come to a critique of Deism and to the question of miracles.

Of late, however, an attempt has been made, starting from this very assumption that there has been such a gradual progressive spiritual development of the human race, to deny the necessity of divine revelation, at least for us in our present stage of enlightenment. However necessary such revelation may have been at an earlier period, it is now maintained that "reason educated by Christianity, like a son who has attained his majority, can shift for itself." So speaks the spirit of our age, with its feverish longing for emancipation in every department of thought and action. The emancipation here, however, could be only a partial one. Reason by itself would be still inadequate for the task assigned it. Formed at first by Christian influences, it remains subject to such influences still. Previous revelations could not fail to operate still, and to exert at any rate an indirect influence on future developments.

How, we ask in the first place, is this result, the maturity of reason, to be maintained when divorced from its cause? Are those factors no longer in action which formerly rendered a revelation necessary? Does sin, then, no longer exist, whose power of obscuration in reason and conscience cannot, as we know from history and experience, be abidingly broken except by the redeeming influence of divine revelation? What other ultimate defence than Christian revelation have we against an immediate relapse into heathen barbarism—what that has not already historically shown itself to be a completely insufficient protection against moral, social, and national corruption? Is it our modern culture or our science? The main object of the theory under discussion is certainly to place these in opposition to Christianity, as the guiding stars of our future progress. But we have already in our former Lecture recognised the fact, that culture and science, apart from Christianity, have no abiding, moral, and spiritual efficiency. Modern civilisation is in every department dependent upon Christianity, and a severance from that which constitutes its groundwork would be nothing less than the initiative of a relapse into barbarism. Or has then reason, we would further ask, so manifestly attained her complete majority as to be now fully capable of "shifting for herself"? How many objections may be urged against such a position? The glance we lately took at philosophy showed us how little ground modern reason has to boast of its performances. On this point we would only ask one question: Are there not still many revealed truths (for instance, the doctrine of the atonement) indispensable for our religious needs, and yet not capable of rational demonstration? Finally, if we are now to believe that reason has outgrown the need of revelation, let it at least be shown that revelation, as a source of culture, is exhausted and used up, and can impart no more instruction. According to the Bible, God's revelation of Himself in Christ is perfect, inexhaustibly rich, sufficing for all ages and all needs, down to the consummation of all things. Is this so or not? On this point, one of our chief counter-authorities is Lessing, the great antagonist of revelation.

In his work *diė Erziehung des Menschengeschlechts* ("The Education of the Human Race"), Lessing had the merit of re-introducing into modern religious philosophy the idea of a divine education of man, referring to the Epistle to the Galatians, chap. iii. and iv., but without sounding the full depth of the scriptural idea of such education. Starting from this idea, he endeavoured to show that while the religion of the Old Testament was the childhood, and Christianity the youth, of mankind, a step was now to be made beyond them into full manhood; belief in revealed truths as motives of moral conduct being henceforth superseded by the spontaneous action of the human mind, following after goodness for its own sake, and *without reference to the doctrine of future rewards and punishments.*

We hear this thought reiterated on all sides in the present day, and in every possible form. Not long ago a literary journal in the Grand Duchy of Baden, discussing the propriety of teaching the ten commandments, propounded the opinion, that the fifth commandment was immoral because of the sanction attached to it, "that thy days may be long in the land, etc.," seeing that here a reward is held out as an inducement to obedience. So then, the "full age" to which humanity is now supposed to have attained consists in man's doing good purely for goodness' sake. Who sees not the hollowness of this bombastic talk? *That* man has yet to be born whose practice will be regulated by a theory so insipid.[1] For what is the idea of goodness *per se?* It must have *something* actually *good* as its substance. *The attainment of some end morally good,* either for himself or for others, must float before the mental vision of the man who acts morally—that is, he must have certain aims in view, which, again, react upon him as motives. And these aims must be distinctly conceived. The abstract idea of goodness is not an effectual motive for well-doing. An idea like this can only work effectually, and with living power, when prototypically realized in some actual *personality,* whereby it may lay hold of the heart of the individual man. No such perfectly good person-

[1] The original German is *dieser grauen Theorie*—"this grey theory," the reference being to Göthe's well-known words in *Faust*:—

"Grau, liebster Freund, ist alle Theorie,
Und grün des Lebens goldener Baum."

All theory, dearest friend, is pallid grey,
While life's fair golden tree is fresh and green.

ality is anywhere presented to us but by revelation; and in the person of Christ. Revelation, therefore, and the divine personality disclosed by it, remain a necessity so long as men are to do good as well as dream of goodness.

It is, moreover, a fundamental error to regard Christianity as in its essence a doctrine of *rewards and punishments.* This has long since been proved in reply to Lessing, and results from our own previous delineation of the true nature of Christianity. Neither Lessing himself, nor the later developments of rationalistic philosophy, have been able to reconcile or identify the actual, historical, supernatural basis of Christian revelation with that which they maintain to be its true and original substance. So both are driven to try to get beyond Christianity altogether, and to deny the continuous necessity of any revealed religion. And that is just what we might expect. For, if we eliminate from Christian faith its supernatural elements, the residuum will be so dry and soulless a skeleton, that, in fact, no reason will appear for tying down the spiritual development of humanity to such lifeless companionship. The only question, therefore, is, whether we recognise as matter of fact any supernatural element in Christianity; whether we allow or not the possibility of miracles—both points which we shall have to investigate more closely further on. If it be denied that God exercises any direct influence on human life, there can be no such thing as a divine education of mankind: man must have educated himself, because left to himself by God. But then comes the question: Could God, in accordance with His own nature, have thus treated man? and the answer depends on our conception of the idea itself of God. But if it be conceded that God did once begin to educate humanity, a twofold question thence arises: First, *Can this educating agency cease to operate* so long as God continues to be Ruler of the Universe, and before the final consummation of all things has set in?—can He leave man to himself, as having attained his "full age," so long as the continuing presence of sin puts him in constant danger of failing to attain his destination, in accordance with the divine idea? And next, Are the revelations made in past times by God, for the purpose of furthering our education, *already exhausted?*—is none of them any longer adequate to our present stage of culture?

We may as pupils get beyond a human teacher, but surely not a divine. Is there any one, for instance, who has but in some degree entered into a perception of the infinite beauty and glory of the character of Christ, and is yet bold enough to say that he has no more to learn concerning it? Where is the interpreter of Scripture to be found, worthy of the name, who would maintain that the interpretation of Scripture is now exhausted? We are, indeed, now further advanced than ever in this work of interpretation; but the more perfection we give to our exegetical appliances, the more plentifully, clearly, and transparently do the sources of divine knowledge flow, the more inexhaustible is their well-spring in the Scriptures shown to be. But the more profound the treasures of truth thus brought to light, the more full of blessing ought their influence to be on the moral and intellectual life of the present day, whether as regards the mass or the individual. Divine revelation, though culminating in Christ, is, even in this its last form, *not quiescent, but progressive; unfolding itself more and more richly* in word and spirit, and *constantly exercising, by ever fresh developments, a progressively educating influence on the humanity to which it has been given.* This truth was overlooked by Lessing. He who does not acknowledge the supernatural element, the deep things of God enshrined in revelation, must likewise fail to apprehend the inexhaustible fulness of the germs of human culture which are also contained within it.

Revelation, like mankind, has run its course of *childhood* and *youth.* The former, when God condescended to personal converse with Adam and the patriarchs; the latter, when He encompassed with the thorny hedge of the Law of Sinai the vigorous and aspiring but sensual and unruly people of Israel (or, looking at the heathen side, when the *Greek* world, from Achilles to Alexander, was stamping all its creations, both material and mental, with the impress of its youthful, cheerful, and ideal character). *But the manhood of the human race did not begin after the rise of Christianity, but together with it.* If riper knowledge and experience, more earnest and effective work, greater independence and firmness in will and action, constitute the pre-eminence of the man over the youth, these are the very characteristics which the influence of Christianity brought to maturity, both in nations and individuals. It was only through the gospel that men attained to a deeper knowledge of their moral and religious duty, and learned to make a pure unselfish love, self-renunciation, and self-denial the bases of their new and nobler life: it was the gospel that first taught men to strive and to suffer, with the manlike weapons of intellect and patience, for a more and more complete apprehension of truth, and to be more and more strenuous in labours for its propagation: it was not till the advent of Christianity that men became spiritually free and independent, and conscious of their individual and personal dignity. In fact, Christianity has ever been, in a way that no other agency has been able to approach, a nursing-school for true men, for heroes in thought, in action, and in suffering; and that because it presents to the world, and to every man's spiritual apprehension, the Hero of all heroes, the Sufferer of all sufferers, as leader and example. In view of what Christianity has done for individuals and the race during well-nigh two thousand years, we may confidently say: He whom the school of Christ does not make into a man will never learn true manliness in any other! If nations and individuals are to retain any power of further spiritual development, they can only do it by retaining a living sense of the truth and efficacy of the Christian revelation; once eliminate or weaken this source of strength, the freshness of spiritual life will soon wither away. Any step taken in supposed advance of Christianity would prove a transition, *not from youth to manhood, but from manhood to senility*,—*i.e.* to a mental condition of absolute indifference or doubt, a temper of the idlest, most self-sufficient hypercriticism, the shallowest subjectivity, and an all-disintegrating egotistical selfishness. Offensive practical proofs are no longer wanting of what the condition of things would be were mankind once to turn their backs on all positive Christian belief. And such facts afford, we think, the strongest arguments for the continuous necessity of revelation.

So long, however, as the ennobling influence of revealed Christian truth continues to operate, no one has a right to say that its mission has ended, or that the present generation has outgrown it. It is not that we are in advance of revelation, but that revelation ever keeps, and has kept, in advance of us;

raising men by just degrees to purer heights in the knowing and doing of goodness and truth, and imparting to all who honestly seek to apprehend it, the enjoyment of ever larger manifestations of its divine light. Our *human apprehension* of Christian truth, both the scientific and the practical, is not only susceptible of, but of necessity requires, constant enlargement; but this cannot be said of God's own revelation of Himself in Christ, which by its very idea must from the first have been absolutely perfect. Whatsoever the Spirit of Truth may have vouchsafed since the Lord's ascension to reveal, or shall still reveal to men, "He will take," says Christ, "of *mine* and will show it unto you;" thereby indicating that all true progress in religious knowledge has its only source in Christ, and that there is *no possibility of a perfecting of religion beyond Christianity*. It follows, therefore—and that is the element of truth in the above-mentioned objection—that no *fresh* revelation will be needed till the consummation of God's kingdom. But for that very reason the revelation already vouchsafed is not to be set aside, but remains for all time equally valid and necessary. And this must be remembered in all discussions of the views of the many who, in the present day, would retain Christianity as a general groundwork while desiring to dispense with its positive dogmas, who speak of "a religion of the future," or a "religion of humanity developed from the religion of Christ" (Strauss), and so destroy the very foundations on which they pretend to build. The very notion of a "religion of humanity" is a product of revelation;—what is it, indeed, but a mere abstract term expressing the fact that God has revealed to mankind things concerning their own nature of which they had themselves become oblivious?

One word more. Revelation must continue to be a *necessity* for human nature as long as the mind and heart of man remain in their created dependence upon God, and that even apart from the existence of sin. The inner life of the soul of man is, as we have seen, "an infinite longing after God." We find tokens of the existence of this longing everywhere, even among the heathen. They too seek to make approaches to what they believe to be divine; they neither can nor desire to get rid of the conviction that their divinities draw nigh, appear to, and communicate with them. And has this deep universal longing been implanted in man, never to be satisfied by a special revelation on the part of Him who implanted it; whereas both experience and history teach that his spiritual thirst can never more be stilled by draughts of a mere natural theology? Even though the fact of God's existence were made certain to us in other ways, should we not still, in the absence of a direct revelation, "feel astonishment and take offence at such complete immobility in a Being who is life itself, and such a hard and stubborn silence in Him who is infinite Wisdom and *Love?*" (Rougemont.) To questions like these, which ground the necessity of a divine revelation alike on the nature of God Himself and our own human needs, the only answer our opponents have to give, is found in a deistical conception which completely isolates Him from His own universe,—a conception which, further on, we shall have to consider more closely.

But we proceed to ask, is such a revelation of Himself by God *possible?* The answer to this question must ultimately depend on the conception we have formed of God and of man. He who believes in a *living personal God,* and in *the existence in man's nature of the divine image,* a capacity for perceiving God by reason and for recognising Him in the conscience, together with an inward longing for communications from Him, cannot but maintain from both these points of view the *possibility* of revelation. For all revelation is but the highest expression on the part of God Himself, of His actual personal relations to man as His creature and His child. If this our fundamental position be granted, the refutation of all objections made by opponents is easy. But if any dispute it, the argument must revert to a discussion of the fundamental conception of God, and of the possibility of miracles. Every act of divine revelation is indeed a *miracle;* and the acknowledgment of its possibility concedes the principle that miracles are possible. This part of the question we defer to a future lecture (Lect. v.). Here we take in view some special difficulties, by which the acceptance of the possibility of a supernatural revelation appears to be encumbered.

How—that is our first query—may the infinite *distance between God and man* be so bridged over that a personal communication between them shall become possible? Let us see what help we may find in Scripture towards answering this question. And in order not to anticipate what will have to be said in a future lecture on the doctrine of the Trinity, you will allow me to touch but briefly on the main points.

First of all, the distinction must be observed which exists in the Divine Nature itself, an aspect of self-concealment and one of self-manifestation. The latter is called in Scripture the Word, or Logos, which "in the beginning" "was with God," and by whom "all things were made;" "the only-begotten Son in the bosom of the Father," who alone has "declared Him." All revelations from creation to Pentecost, and from Pentecost to the end, have been and can be made only through Him. He is the eternal, hypostatic self-manifestation of God, and therefore called "the Light of the World." In Him, as in His other self, God can draw nigh to other beings also, having in Him, as it were, already become another. *It is in the internal distinctions of the Divine Essence that the possibility lies of divine external manifestation.* The second (and third) "Persons" in the Godhead form, so to speak, the bridge between God and creation. In Christ, as "the everlasting life and light of men," there has existed from eternity a bond between man and God. In Christ, God *can* draw nigh to us and hold communication with us. And here we may already see, what further on will be made more evident, that one who believes not in the Eternal Son of God can hardly recognise the possibility of any special divine revelation; the infinite exaltation of the Divine Being above all created things may well seem to such an one to interpose a gulf that nothing can bridge over. The only bridge possible, exists not for him.

Further, we find in all divine revelations recorded in Scripture a certain *self-limitation* on the part of God, either hiding His divine glory in angelic or human shape, or in that of some physical phenomenon—wind, cloud, or fire; or else only partially disclosing it so as even, while revealing Himself, to remain still the hidden, supramundane, and invisible One. So Moses, with whom the Almighty speaks "mouth to mouth," can only see Him from behind, and receives the admonition, "My face shall not be seen" (Ex. xxxiii. 18–23). And even when *He* appears in whom "the fulness of the Godhead dwelleth bodily," the Father still remains the supramundane and invisible One. The Infinite cannot communicate itself to the finite, except in a limited manner; the whole cannot possibly come into manifestation. Scripture, therefore, draws a distinction between "that which may be known of God" (Rom. i. 19), on the one hand, and His hidden, incomprehensible essence on the other; whereof it is said, "God dwelleth in the light which no man can approach, whom no man hath seen, nor can see" (1 Tim. vi. 16). And therefore in all revelations, God puts, as it were, a restraint upon Himself, communicates to man only so much light as he is able to bear, and with the wonted condescension of true love submits for our sakes to self-limitation.

So much, in brief, concerning the divine end of the bridge formed by revelation between God and man. Now for the other, the human end of it. And here we observe, that a peculiar fitness is predicated in Scripture of the *recipients of revelation.* They are all, as we have seen above, men endowed beforehand with a special capability and susceptibility in relation to the Divine, they are the elect ones of mankind,—an Abraham, a Moses, a David, an Isaiah, a Paul, a Peter, a John,—men already standing by their personal faith in a closer relation to God than others. And even these men, in receiving revelations, experience an emancipation from creaturely limitations corresponding to the voluntary condescension and self-limitation on the part of God. They are raised above their ordinary consciousness in a greater or a less degree; they are "in the Spirit," or a visionary trance, at the time when spiritual revelations are afforded them. This at least would seem to be more especially the case with the prophets and apostles; whilst in that of Moses, God's condescending limitation of Himself is made more prominent. The transfiguration of our Lord was a temporary emancipation of the same nature; and in the world to come we may anticipate that such liberation from the present condition of human intelligence will be fully vouchsafed to all saints: on it, indeed, depends the possibility of our knowing God hereafter, "even as also we ourselves are known" (1 Cor. xiii. 12).

Finally, yet another agency of mediation between God and man is found in the angels, who appear as heaven-sent messengers (and especially in manifestations of the divine glory), not only to Abraham and Moses (Acts vii. 30, 35,

53), to David and Zechariah under the Old Testament, but also in attendance on our blessed Lord (John i. 51), and in the New Testament generally. These glorious beings are represented as, on the one hand, allied by their creaturely nature to man, and, on the other, by their higher, spiritual, and sinless condition, as standing in closer affinity to God, and therefore as more capable than we of receiving direct communication from Him, and of being His ambassadors and representatives in the world. On this difficult question of angelic agency there remains, no doubt, as on that of miracles generally, many a knotty problem to be solved; but so much we fearlessly assert ourselves to have established, that there is no sufficient *a priori* ground in reason for precipitate rejection of the possibility, ay, and the necessity too, of a supernatural revelation of God to man.

For surely the considerations which we have now been urging get rid at once of some of the most common *objections to the possibility of revelation.* The objection, for instance, so often made, that the Absolute and Infinite cannot communicate itself to the finite, just because the latter is incapable of comprehending it, is perfectly correct. But where is it taught in Scripture that God, in any of His revelations, has made a complete communication of Himself to us ? The above-named scriptural distinction between the *self-revealing* side of the divine nature and the hidden and incomprehensible one is in this objection entirely overlooked. God still remains the supramundane and the infinite, even while communicating Himself in revelation to man. We do not comprehend Him fully, but only perceive "that which may be known of God," that which for salvation it is needful to know. The best knowledge is but imperfect here (1 Cor. xiii. 9); the perfect is reserved for the world to come.

This scriptural distinction is also overlooked by Strauss (*Christl. Glaubensl.*) when urging the *immutability* of the divine nature as rendering any special revelation impossible; because the assumption of such "an isolated act of God in time contradicts the idea of His unchangeableness:" an objection this somewhat unbecoming in a representative of Pantheism; for where is God represented as more subject to change than in the process of "becoming" to which the Pantheist would condemn Him? In like manner argues the otherwise very meritorious philologer Jacob Grimm; that the fact of God's once having spoken to a man would imply that He has subjected Himself to an historical process which the Uncreated and Immutable cannot do. Our answer is, that it is only in His *self-revealing* aspect that God appears under the conditions of time and historical development; in His inner nature He still remains the supramundane and immutable One. Revelation *is* a development, but not one to which the Divine Nature is itself subjected. In whatever measure God condescends to work upon and rule the world, He sets in motion there a course of gradual historical processes, pre-arranged in harmony with the needs and conduct of man; but His own eternal nature is never drawn into the ebb and flow of these developments. The Absolute and Eternal One cannot *become* anything other than Himself, but can only *be* and continue from everlasting to everlasting what He *is*. And so Scripture speaks of "becoming" or "happening," or of any distinctions of time, in reference only to creatures; of God it simply says that "He is what He is," "the same yesterday, to-day, and for ever" (Ex. iii. 14; Ps. cii. 28; Heb. xiii. 8). We may, indeed, turn the point of their own argument against our opponents and say: The divine immutability is realized and secured by divine acts of revelation. If God is to remain in Himself immutable, and, despite the abuse of human freedom of will, is to accomplish His own eternal counsels concerning the world and man, He must conduct by special act of revelation the universe of His creatures towards its eternally predetermined end and aim. God's immutability in essence and in purpose on the one hand, and special revelations of His purposes to man on the other, are necessary correlatives. He only who substitutes for the scriptural idea of a living personal God an abstract impersonal Order of the universe, is precluded from recognising the possibility of such special acts of divine self-manifestation, and loses at the same time the very idea of a moral order in the world around him.

Grimm's strange objection, that the notion of God speaking to man at all implies His possession of "a body and teeth," loses all force and application when we bear in mind the Scripture doctrine that His chief revelation is made in Christ the Incarnate Logos, and many others through angelic spirits, with their etherial corporeity. And in any other cases of apparent anthropomorphism we may surely apply the Scripture argument, "He that made the eye, shall He not see?" He that made the mouth, shall He not speak? *i.e.* shall He fail in methods for making known to us His will?

A like fear of seeming to degrade and materialize the idea of God, by admitting the possibility of special acts of self-manifestation, determines many minds in the present day to deny all revelation except by inward mental processes, and to relegate all external manifestations of the divine into the realm of fable. This sounds grand, and flatters the conceit of modern enlightenment. So, for instance, writes the rationalistic Schenkel: "When, in accordance with traditional theology, God is supposed to have revealed Himself through external natural phenomena, angelic agencies, and the like, men forget that God is a Spirit, and that every conception which degrades His self-manifestations, by mixing them up with the alternations of material phenomena, is radically untheological, and destructive of the true idea of God." But we have just seen that this is by no means the case; not the inner nature and essence, but only the self-revealing aspect of Deity, enters into any connection with material phenomena. And why should it not be able to do this? God is indeed a Spirit; but is the world then mere lifeless matter which the Spirit can never employ as its organ? Is it not rather upheld and pervaded in all its parts by divine powers, ideas, and purposes, by means of which it becomes a *cosmos*, an harmoniously articulated organism, wherein, as in a mirror, we discern the workings of the Divine Spirit? And if the world be already in itself a revelation of God, why should not He have been able to make it yet more so by means of special acts and manifestations? The consequences, moreover, in reference to the person of Christ, which are involved in the doctrine of a merely spiritual revelation, are not a little serious. Either the incarnation of the Divine Logos is impossible, or with that conceded, the self-manifestation of God in a material form is conceded also. But once degrade our Lord to a mere man, with whatever pretended illumination of the Spirit, you thereby deny all internal distinctions in the Divine Nature, and may as well at the same time deny the possibility of any kind of revelation. The bridge connecting God and His creatures is finally broken down.

Another argument against the possibility of revelation is sometimes drawn from the divine attributes of goodness and righteousness. How, it is argued, can the infinitely good and righteous One have attached salvation to the reception of revealed verities, of which the majority of mankind are ignorant without any fault of their own, and others are cognizant without deservings? This argument, strongly urged in former times by J. J. Rousseau, in his *Profession de foi du vicaire Savoyard,* is warmly echoed by many in the present day, and derives some countenance from the harshness and onesidedness of many Christian theologians. But Scripture nowhere teaches, that all who die without knowledge of the revelation of God in Christ are irretrievably and eternally lost. It is one thing innocently not to *know;* it is quite another wilfully to *reject.* The express doctrine of Scripture is that men will be judged hereafter "according to their works," and that the measure of such judgment will be the degree of revelation, supernatural or natural, vouchsafed them in the present life; and that hence from one man more, from another less, will be required, and that even among the lost it will go harder with some and be more tolerable for others (Matt. xi. 20–24, xii. 38–42; Luke xii. 47, 48; Rom. ii. 5, 12, v. 13). Nor are the Scriptures altogether without traces of the thought that the gospel was proffered, even after death, to those who had died in ignorance of the way of salvation (1 Pet. iii. 18–20, iv. 6). But to demand now, at once, an explanation why the divine counsels determine that some nations should receive the gospel earlier and others later, is a great act of presumption. It will not be till the final development and end of the world that it will be possible to survey the whole course of God's dealings with man, and so determine whether the way in which the knowledge of salvation has been spread among nations, and moulded their history, resulted from an absolutely wise and just and holy plan, or not. Finally, the divine attribute of goodness can be alleged as an argument against the probability of a special revelation only by one who *will* not see to how much nobler a degree of moral and spiritual elevation nations have attained with a revealed religion than without one, a fact the truth of which no reasonable persons ought to call in question.

But here another objection meets us from quite a different point of view. Granted the *possibility* of revelation in the abstract, how can we *know for certain that it has been vouchsafed?* how are we to learn to distinguish between an *objective* divine communication on the one hand, and the merely *subjective* operation of our own intellect on the other? This is the argument of Kant and Fichte. They allowed the possibility of a supernatural revelation, but denied that any one could determine with absolute certainty whether what seemed to him to be such was really divine, or merely the product of his own reason and conscience. Lessing (compare the "Dialogue between Lessing and Jacobi about Spinoza" in the *Letters to Mendelssohn,* and *The Christianity of Reason*) gave this objection a somewhat different turn, thus: Revealed truths must, he argued, translate themselves in due course into truths of pure reason. By a law of development proper to the human mind, the first form assumed by all religious convictions is that of an extraordinary divine revelation; it is only by degrees that man attains the consciousness that what has seemed to him a gift from without was really the product of his own mental powers. According to this, belief in any supernatural revelation is but a piece of self-deception on the part of the undeveloped human consciousness, which, on reaching maturity, recognises the sources of such supposed revelation as derived from within and not from without itself.

What is our answer to all this? In the first place, it may readily be observed that this objection proceeds from those whose views are narrowed by the assumptions of mere intellectualism, who decline to accept any religious truth, except by such a process of rational induction as we have already proved to be quite inadequate. Hence their efforts to make out that revelation must be strictly spiritual, the product of the internal workings of a man's own spirit. And this is the first untenable assumption. For Scripture plainly testifies that revelations were oftentimes vouchsafed of old externally, *i.e.* by appeals to the senses of sight and hearing, as in divine and angelic appearances. In such cases the revelation was not in the first place a new idea which presented itself to the consciousness, but a real external event. Are, then, all such narratives to be accounted *a priori* as myths and fables? If not, these external miraculous events were in themselves the most certain proof that, in each case of their occurrence, a supernatural communication from above had been vouchsafed. The miraculous element was in each revelation the most direct token of its divine character. The first recipients of such manifestations, under the forcible impression made by the accompanying phenomena, which in sundry cases smote them in terror to the earth, could not remain in doubt that it was an outward objective power that thus encountered them, and that the awful words so suddenly sounding in their ears could not be mere ideal products of their own minds; they must therefore have been well able to distinguish between their *human* consciousness on the one hand, and the divine revelation vouchsafed them on the other.

But if, diverting our attention from these outward manifestations, we direct it exclusively to those internal ones in which the element of inspiration prevails, we shall find that even with respect to these it cannot in every case be said that what was revealed were "mere rational conceptions concerning divine things;" an assumption which forms a second untenable hypothesis. How frequently, for instance, must the prophets have announced revelations, the depth of which they could not fathom, and delivered predictions whose range of application was still for them a veiled secret! Their own oracles were oftentimes as much objects of faith to themselves as to others. How often did they hear things which seemed to run counter to their own natural reason, and about which they ventured to interpose the liveliest expressions of doubt and remonstrance (*e.g.* Gen. xvii. 17; Jer. i. 6; Luke i. 18, 34; Acts x. 14)!—instances in which we clearly see *that the rational knowledge of the recipients was by no means always in accord with the revelation vouchsafed;* that the latter very often surpassed the former, and that the recipients were well aware of this distinction. But between the conclusions of their own reason and the truths revealed, what they could not even "rationally appropriate" could hardly have been a product of their own rational faculties. Only observe, for instance, how "the prophets *inquired* and *searched diligently*" (with their own natural faculties of reason) "what, or what manner of time the *Spirit* of Christ which was in them did signify" (1 Pet. i. 10, 11); and how clearly St. Paul had learned to distinguish between his own human knowledge and divine revelation when he wrote (1 Cor. vii. 12), "But to the rest speak I, *not the Lord;*" and afterwards (xi. 23), "I have received *of the Lord.*" Just as in the case of external manifestations, so also in the interior modes of revelation, we everywhere see it laid down in Scripture that the seers, in some way or other which doubtless imparted certainty to their own minds, were conscious of the fact that what was inwardly perceived or heard by them was not a figment of their own fancy, but a real revelation from God.

Furthermore, *prophecy*, which, both in its wider and its narrower sense, is revelation in the form of *word*, as contrasted with *miracle*, which is revelation in the form of divine *action*, is a second proof of the divine reality of revelation. Many prophecies, for instance, of the Old Testament give practical proof, by their punctual fulfilment centuries afterwards, that they were indeed revelations vouchsafed by God, far transcending the powers of any human calculation. This is more especially the case with some of the Messianic prophecies, which even the presumptuous criticism of the present day finds a difficulty in referring simply to historical events of the prophets' own time. So much at least may be said here, without at present going into further details; to which must be added, as a third argument, the testimony of the recipients of inspiration themselves to the reality of the communications vouchsafed them. Doubtless—and this is part of our reply to Lessing—that which in the first instance is a divine gift, received by faith, becomes by degrees the subject of rational apprehension ("*Credo ut intelligam*—I believe, and so come to understand"). Revelation has a constant tendency to become nature, that is, to transmute itself, as it were, into our human flesh and blood, and become part of our ordinary human intelligence. But even in this intellectual apprehension of revealed truth,—an apprehension, however, which is by no means merely intellectual, but far more practical and moral,—reason is so far from ignoring the supernatural origin of revelation, or from confounding it with any subjective products of its own, that, on the contrary, the longer it is exercised in this field, the more clearly does reason recognise the *divine* and transcendent character of revealed truth, as something supernaturally communicated to our human intelligence, and not self-produced; as something *to be* gradually *appropriated*, and not as an original possession. Belief, therefore, in the divine character of revelation is not a standpoint which reason has gradually to overcome, but one which, on the contrary, every increase of spiritual and moral insight has a constant tendency to illumine and corroborate.

These remarks apply equally to the intellectual apprehension of the original recipients of extraordinary revelations, and to our present knowledge of revealed truth as derived from Holy Scripture. With the preliminary question, whether the Bible really contains the records of a divine revelation, or is a mere product of human intelligence, we are not at present concerned. The only question we have to deal with here is, whether what we call the witness of the Spirit in our hearts—*i.e.* an inward consciousness of grace, of peace, and divine communion—may not after all be merely subjective, and have no producing cause beyond the operations of our own minds? "Whence canst thou know"—is the question now put to the Christian man—"that thine inward experiences and enlightenment are, in fact, the operations of the Divine Spirit, and so far supernatural revelations, and not merely derived from thine own mind? Is not thy whole faith, after all, nothing but self-deception?"

In answer to all this we reply, that Christian Revelation is ultimately based on *external matters of fact* and an objective history, and not on mere doctrinal truths. Christ Himself, as a historical personality, is the great fact and substance of His own revelation. But *Facts,* with which I become acquainted by testimony from without, as by hearing and reading, are quite different *sources of knowledge from the workings of my own mind;* and I can readily distinguish between the impression made by the former on my heart, and the effect of self-inspired ideas. My own reflection is sufficient to teach me that I need and long for something which shall make me inwardly free and happy. But the *sense* of this longing, and a *conscious-*

ness of its satisfaction, are two very different things: in the one case, I have an *idea;* in the other, a *fact of experience.* If, now, I feel my longings satisfied by the facts of the Christian Religion, whereas hitherto my heart has been kept in restless suspense, in spite of, nay, by reason of, all my meditation on the inherent ideas of the Good and the True, and if I suddenly receive from certain spiritual experiences a pledge of freedom and inward peace which no rational investigation could give me, then surely I must conclude that this new condition has been brought about by a Power from above, and is no mere creation of my own fancy. I have, consequently, a right to make a distinction between an objective divine revelation and the subjective action of my own mind.

If any one has once become conscious of revelation as a divine matter of fact in his own heart, he can but smile at the efforts of reason to deprive him of that fact. Any naturalist who, with hundreds of others, had long observed some phenomenon, would certainly laugh at the notion of any one proving to him dialectically that he had really seen nothing. We Christians claim to avail ourselves of the same right; for quite as groundless are the objections raised against the facts of our religious consciousness.

Nor shall we be disturbed in our position by the well-known objection raised by Lessing, primarily against the "demonstration of the Spirit and of power" (1 Cor. ii. 4), but in fact against the possibility of proof in the case of any special revelation whatsoever, arguing that "if no historical truth can be (absolutely) demonstrated, nothing can be demonstrated by means of historical truth," and as a corollary, that "incidental historical truths can never serve as a proof of necessary truths of reason." We do not desire to hold any long argument as to the doubtful sense and ambiguous wording of this often cited *dictum*,[1] nor will we inquire what may be the nature of these necessary truths of abstract reason, limitations of reason in the concrete. We would only point out that at the present day far more importance is attached to historical proof than was the case in Lessing's age of abstract philosophy. Everything must now be first demonstrated as historical reality, before it can put in a claim to be accepted

[1] Refer to the copious refutation of this in Krauss, *ut supr.* pp. 95–100.

as necessary truth. This is an axiom of all modern science, natural science especially establishing all its general principles by means of particular empirical facts. Why should not the same be permitted in the sphere of religion? Carefully examined, Lessing's utterance comes simply to this, that the Incidental cannot be alleged in proof of the Eternal. We submit that this argument, however incontestable, does not in the least affect the point here at issue, viz. the proof from history and inward experiences. For where will you find a Christian who considers God's revelations in history and the facts of his own spiritual experience as merely incidental, and not rather as the carrying out of eternal purposes? "Are not all His works known to God from the beginning of the world?" If, however, as is usually the case, the sense attributed to Lessing's words is, that no particular historical events can, in preference to any others, be regarded as the revelation of eternal truths; that God equally reveals Himself in all that happens according to eternal and immutable laws, which render any special interference a thing unimaginable, and that, consequently, single events are only of incidental importance,—we reply that this is simply the rationalistic view, the untenableness of which we shall presently exhibit in detail.

As in the experience of individuals, so in the entire history of the race, Revelation is most clearly *known by its fruits.* The final and surest proof of the actuality and divine origin of revelation, is its manifestation in individuals and nations, as a healing, sin-constraining power, diffusing everywhere light and life. This is in truth the case, and so evidently do the representatives of revealed religion excel all their contemporaries in moral and religious force and insight, as to furnish a weighty and indisputable argument against the rejecters of revelation. Let them explain to us how, *without* revelation, amidst the general obscuration of religious life, an Abraham could arise and shed abroad his light of faith; or the people of Israel, in the midst of heathen degradation, and surrounded by lascivious and cruel idolatries, discover and preserve such pure ideas of God, and so holy a moral law. Let them show further, how, in a period of universal corruption among both Jews and Gentiles, and without any supernatural interposition, Christ could arise as the Light of the world and give its whole development a new direction, even down to the present day, in the path of light and life! All, even the most painstaking recent attempts to prove a natural and human origin of these phenomena, have, as we shall see further on, turned out completely inadequate. The wondrous *uniqueness* of the facts themselves, and the blessings which have issued from them, will ever constitute an irrefragable proof of the divine origin of revelation.

Bearing this in mind, what shall we say to the bold assertion of Kant and his successors, that any revealed divine legislation, in addition to the law already recognised by reason and conscience, would be not merely unnecessary and, psychologically speaking, unverifiable, but even positively *injurious;* that free men, whose whole life should be guided by reason and conscience, would be reduced to moral slavery if "burdened" with a new law in addition to that already received? That this assertion contains nearly as many errors as words, is evident, we trust, from what has been already said as to the insufficiency of Natural Theology and the true character and need of Revelation. Only those who do not acknowledge the power of sin can thus speak. But how grievously, likewise, is the inner nature of Revelation here misunderstood? Why, it belongs to the very nature of Revelation not to appear as a *compulsory* law, but ever to appeal to human freedom! And is not its effect, when inwardly experienced, a *liberation from bondage rather than the imposition of a fresh yoke?* Revelation aids, purifies, and supplements Natural Theology, does not, as an alien element, hinder and oppose it, but rather links itself on to the whole circle of our other ideas. As it is, the Moral Law taken alone is found insufficient by Kant himself, who is fain to call in the aid of conceptions concerning God and His government of the world in order to its maintenance. How can he regard the influence of the divine Will on man as a burdening of the conscience, whilst elsewhere he makes it appear as a help? He confounds—a mistake that cannot be too strongly deprecated—certain ecclesiastical forms of Christianity with its living spirit and essence. The former may frequently be a burden, but not so the Spirit of the Lord, which is indeed a Spirit of liberty (2 Cor. iii. 17). He forgets that this Lord communicates and reveals Himself, not mechanically, or as a Lawgiver of the letter, but through the Spirit, which operates in our souls, liberating, purifying, enlightening, and stimulating all that is good in us, especially in the faculties of reason and conscience, but burdening and restricting only what is evil.

And thus, also, is refuted the objection made by Strauss, that Revelation, as "a direct action of God upon the human spirit, would leave the latter in a position of absolute passivity, God being, by His own nature, absolutely active; but the essence of the human spirit consisting in activity, it is not capable of becoming absolutely passive, and that, consequently, the very idea of revelation is impossible." This conclusion, too, is based on entirely false premises. In the first place, the above-named definition by no means exhaustively describes the essence of revelation. And where do we find taught in the Scriptures that there is any such direct influence of the divine activity on the recipient of revelation as would thus put a stop to his own, and merge it in absolute passivity? According to Scripture (as we have seen), God is not wont to work directly on man, but through some kind of medium. The recipients of revelation are of course *receptive,* but not absolutely *passive.* On the contrary, the very reception of divine communications, requiring a certain amount of activity, stimulates all their mental and moral energies to the highest degree. God, in drawing nigh to any individual man, has no desire to crush, but rather to awaken and carry onward him, and through him, others. Even divine commissions are not to be accepted and executed in a spirit of absolute passivity; and in the recipients of revelation (cf. Jer. i. 6 and Jonah i. 2, 3) their human freedom remains unfettered. How many opponents of revelation are still fighting against an idea which is not that of the Scriptures themselves!

The groundlessness of the various objections to Revelation having been thus shown, it remains for us now to take in review—

III.—THE RELATION BETWEEN REVEALED RELIGION AND NATURAL THEOLOGY.

Does the knowledge of God derived from Revelation stand in any way in contradiction to Natural Theology, so that one excludes the other? And if we allow that they agree, and indeed postulate each other, for which of these two factors must we claim precedence?

Reason and revelation have of late very often been placed in opposition to each other, because the existence of a corresponding *antithesis between faith and knowledge*[1] is taken for granted. The assumption of this antithesis is now so general, that there are not a few even among Christians who accept it. "With the head a heathen, at heart a Christian," as Jacobi has put it—this is the conclusion at which they would wish to stop, allotting to faith the feelings, to knowledge the understanding and reason, as their exclusive domain. It is high time that this *fundamental error*, the consequences of which are for the most part good-naturedly overlooked, should at last be recognised as such. In the first place, it is certainly psychologically impossible to sever feeling and understanding as opposed to one another. No one faculty of the soul can be brought into action separately without the others being at the same time exercised. In every act of the understanding, feeling and will are more or less involved; and feeling itself when perfected is one with understanding. We may well *distinguish* between the different functions of the soul, but we must not sever them from each other.

The same relation exists between faith and knowledge. The severance of the two, as mutually excluding opposites, indicates a superficial tone of thought. For *all knowledge is, in the last instance, conditioned by faith; and faith* (*i.e.* an act of belief) *is the preliminary and the medium of every act of intelligence.* Are you surprised at this proposition? The usual rationalistic axiom is certainly the reverse of it,—namely, that everything must first be proved and known before it can be believed. The superficiality of this axiom may, however, be

[1] On the following, cf. the excellent elucidation of the question in Fabri's *Briefe gegen den Materialismus*, 2d ed. pp. 164–190.

readily perceived. Is not every act of knowledge based upon an act of faith,—namely, the belief that we *are,* and that we *think?* This fact is always presupposed. But on what does its certainty depend? On our thinking? Can this possibly prove its own actuality? Would not this be to move in a circle, and presuppose that which is to be proved? The certainty of our thinking depends simply on an act of belief. Just as the eye never sees itself, but only the outward form of itself, so also the self-knowing of the mind is not a self-beholding, but "an ideal cognizance, a radical though mediated knowledge, *i.e. scire credendo*" (Delitzsch), a knowledge mediated by faith. It is by the direct testimony of our own minds that we are convinced of the fact that we exist, think, wake, and dream; and this fact neither needs nor is capable of proof; we merely *believe* it.

Or what is the case with learning? In every act of learning, must not a believing be presupposed, some belief in the authority of the teacher, and in the truth of that which is taught? He who does not start with this belief will never learn anything. And does not all philosophizing depend on faith? If a philosopher does not *believe* in the wisdom with which the world is filled, he cannot be a lover of wisdom. When a philosopher presumes to look down on faith, it is a proof that he does not know on what ground he himself is standing. And in every single act of cognition, does not belief form a connecting link necessary to its completion? In every cognition of a sensible object, the first decisive step is the sensuous perception; the second, often so momentary as to be scarcely perceptible, is the inward affirmation of this perception, the *belief in,* and acknowledgment of, the testimony of the senses; then, and not till then, follows the logical conclusion. It is just so with intellectual cognitions directed to the supersensuous. In this, also, the first point is an inward intellectual perception, the second an assent to or affirmation of it; whereupon follows the cognition properly so-called.

From this you see that faith is really a preliminary and a medium of all cognizance, and that all knowing is conditioned by an act of believing. *He who believes nothing, knows nothing.* "As its ultimate basis, even the most radical unbelief has one and the same principle of knowledge with Christianity and every other positive religion,—the principle of belief in given matters of fact, on the ground of the original and direct testimony of the human mind" (Fabri). He who believes this—and every one must do so—will find it a contradiction to reject the testimony of Christian and religious consciousness to the existence and the inward experience of some supersensuous world. The existence of this, as of the material world, can never be proved by mere reasoning; to this must be added an experience based on belief. If such testimony is allowed to be valid as regards the material world, why not as regards the supersensuous?

Our former remarks as to the certainty of an inwardly experienced fact of revelation are thus afresh corroborated. He who experiences in his own mind God's testimony of Himself as the living, holy, and gracious One, may take his stand upon this as a matter of fact, with as good a right as the naturalist on his experimental observations. For both attain their experimental knowledge on the same principle of belief.

A like view of the relation between faith and knowledge is found in Holy Scripture, which recognises no true knowledge except such as is grounded on belief. True faith, according to Scripture, conducts the human soul not only to peace and joy, but also to light and truth. It is the apprehension of divine truth which depends on one suffering himself to be apprehended; it is the saying "Yea and Amen" thereto, and is accomplished and perfected in the most intimate surrender of the heart, resulting, as does all perception and experience, in real knowledge. Peter says (John vi. 69), "*We have believed and are sure:*" *faith leads on to knowledge,* of which it is itself the first beginning. As an undoubting and assured conviction of the unseen (Heb. xi. 1), it is the organ for the immaterial world, and for our knowledge of it. *It is not therefore knowledge but unbelief which is opposed to faith;* that is, the resolve neither to accept nor to be convinced of the reality of the supersensuous and its influence on the world. For this postulate, the reality of the Invisible is the ultimate point at which faith and unbelief part company, and at which there is no alternative except either belief or unbelief. In religious things, therefore, the antithesis is *not that of faith and know-*

ledge, but that of faith and unbelief, or of religious knowledge and religious ignorance; or again, yet more often of religious belief and knowledge on the one hand, and irreligious belief and knowledge on the other.

From all this, we may now gather the right view of the relation between Revealed Religion and Natural Theology. *Revelation and reason, no more than faith and knowledge, can in principle contradict one another.* Reason cannot object if we derive our knowledge of God in a supernatural way, since, as we have seen, faith is the principle of knowledge in both cases. As far, however, as regards the substance of the knowledge thus arrived at, whether by means of Natural or Revealed Theology, we find as the result that the one postulates the other, and for this reason the two theologies cannot be considered as opposed. Reason, especially when under the influence of sin, shows, by the imperfection of its ideal products as exhibited in history, how much it stands in need of the guidance, regulation, and assistance of Divine Revelation. Reason and faith are, in the divine order of things, destined as it were to a spiritual wedlock, in which faith shall be the masculine and productive, reason the feminine and receptive power. Faith, from the invisible world in which it lives, must bring the truths unattainable by reason and impart them to her; while reason, thus fructified and invigorated, is enabled to search into the ultimate grounds and inner essence of the objects of religious knowledge, to connect, systematize, and duly arrange them. But if, without the aid of her lord and master, she endeavour to obtain for herself the materials of religious thought, we must, in view of all the independent efforts of merely rational theology in ancient and modern times, agree with the utterance of Matthias Claudius, that he "found it much more difficult to vindicate the wisdom of reason against faith, than that of faith against reason," or with the Scotch sceptic, when he says, that "the ultimate fruit of all philosophy is the observation of human ignorance and weakness" (Hume). In fine, might we not almost express the result of our investigation in the words of Hamann,—that "dark philosopher of the North," Kant's contemporary and fellow-townsman,—"As the law was given to the Jews, not to make them righteous, but to convict them of unrighteousness, so in the same way reason was given to our race, not to make us wise, but to convict us of our own ignorance; so that errors might thereby be multiplied as sin was strengthened by the law'" ?[1]

But, on the other hand, Revelation no less requires the co-operation of reason and conscience, with which, by its own inherent ethical laws and purposes, it is necessarily connected. Every particular revelation is based upon and fits into the universal and natural, the religious and moral elements of which it receives and adapts in order to give them further development, and impart to them a higher substance. If, for instance, Conscience is able of itself in some measure to recognise the justice of God, Revelation leads it to a comprehension of His absolute holiness. If in nature and in history we find some traces of a ruling providence, the observation is amplified by Revelation into the assurance that such a providence extends to all, even the most trivial-seeming circumstances of each individual life. When a consideration of the world and of ourselves has brought home to us the necessity of some divine assistance against the universal corruption of death, Revelation steps in and tells us of redemption accomplished, and of the way to salvation. By no means does it set aside Natural Theology as useless, nor does it desire—no matter how often the reproach may be made—*either to restrict or to suppress the operations of reason and conscience, but only, on the contrary, to elevate, enlarge, and render them more acute.* Revelation, it is true, would have reason "made captive to the obedience of Christ;" not, however, in order to render it blind, but to enable it to see more clearly, and to make it really serviceable and efficacious by liberating it from the bondage of error (John viii. 32). This submission only takes place to be followed by an exaltation; it is nothing but the transition to a knowledge all the higher and purer, and a use of reason all the more powerful. Hence the words of St. Paul, "When I am weak, then am I strong." *The act of submission brings with it the reception of light,* and the communication of a fuller moral and religious knowledge, thus producing sound and

[1] Collected Works, i. p. 405 ff. On the details of this, cf. the talented and instructive lecture of Grau, "*Ueber den Glauben als die höchste Vernunft*" (*Beweis des Glaubens*, 1865, p. 110 ff.).

enlightened views on all fundamental points, such as the doctrine of God, the world, the destination of man, sin and its cure;—views which must lead to a sound practical judgment, and a conformable course of life. *So far, therefore, from faith being unreason, it is in truth the highest form of reason,* and the only way to progressive perfection of the intellect. Innumerable instances might be adduced to prove this power of faith in thoroughly cultivating and infinitely raising our moral intuitions. The fact that the opponents of revelation so often reproach its defenders with "*obscurantism*," only goes to prove that they completely misapprehend the nature and the effects of faith.

And, as in the case of individuals, so also in that of the whole race and its Natural Theology, Revelation merely steps in to its aid, setting up, as it were, landmarks for necessary guidance in the region of moral and religious thought, and supplying a support for human infirmity in a few fundamental facts and truths; its purpose being to indicate to men, by a few master-strokes, their divine destiny and the way to its fulfilment; and that not in order to perplex, but to enlighten; not to bring into bondage, but to lead aright, to save from wandering in endless aimless labyrinths, and at the same time guide investigation of the traces of Divine Revelation in the world, in history, and in Scripture, and, in a word, assist the search after their underlying unity. Nor, in good sooth, does Reason forfeit aught of her dignity in thankfully accepting such assistance. If this assistance came from an inferior, Reason might find some excuse for despising it. But surely no creature need to be ashamed of help from its Creator; it does but honour itself in accepting it. "True Christianity," says Pascal, "consists in the submission as well as in the use of reason. It is Reason's last step to acknowledge that there is an infinity of things which transcend her powers. She remains weak till she comes to the acknowledgment of this her own insufficiency. Doubt and assert we all must at times, but must learn at proper times to submit also. He who cannot do this, knows not yet the true strength of Reason."

And that brings us to the right point of view from which to decide the last question,—To which of the two must we concede the superiority when Reason and Revelation diverge from one another? Although they are not, as we have seen, opposed in principle, still in certain cases the teachings of Revelation frequently lie so far beyond the scope of Reason as to make her slow to accept them. In this case, rationalism would make Reason the superior judge, and accept only that which can be logically demonstrated. Here we see a *growing* faculty that is ever changing, and constantly requires fresh material, without ever coming to maturity, put forward claims which would presuppose it *complete and perfect.* Instead of this, we gather from the preceding that the only true view is that which subordinates *reason to revelation.* Not, First understand and then accept, is the maxim to be adopted in seeking religious truth, but, First submit and accept the truth, then you will be able to obtain a thorough intellectual knowledge of it. Finite reason must submit itself to infinite; the never fully educated human understanding, limited as it is by time, matter, and individuality, must yield to the perfect truth which proceeds from God; a judgment which is subject to vacillations and disturbances, to one that is ever settled and abiding. "To improve religion by means of reason," exclaims Claudius on one occasion, "appears to me just as if I were to try to set the sun by my old wooden clock."

Let Reason ever remain mindful of her own limitations. Let her not summon everything before *her* judgment-seat alone, especially questions, the final decision of which belongs to the moral feelings and the will. Let her especially cease to confound that which is *above reason* with that which is *against reason:* an error fraught with evil consequences for so many. Those parts of revelation which it is beyond the power of Reason fully to comprehend—such as miraculous facts and the mysteries of faith—are presented to her not as *absurdities to be laughed at and rejected,* as is often done by intellectually slothful and superficial Unbelief, *but as deep and earnest problems,* which it is our solemn duty to investigate, although to master them a whole life-time, yea, eternities, were requisite. Mysteries like these, which in this life we cannot fully comprehend, need by no means fill us with mistrust of faith For "if all life has its mysteries, how much more the highest life! It all turns upon the question whether Reason recognises faith as *life*, and, indeed, the highest form of life," and has learnt to see that everywhere the higher life transcends the laws of the lower, and, so that *no higher form of being can be comprehended by the laws which regulate those beneath it* (see Lect. v., on Miracles). Let Reason therefore seek *in herself*, and not in faith or in revelation, as such, the cause of what is obscure and incomprehensible; and let her conclude, from that which she has learnt to see of revelation, as to the truth and excellence of that which still seems dark to her. Let her endeavour to bring light into this obscurity as far as possible, not, however, in a merely intellectual way, but first of all in that which revelation itself indicates as indispensable, the way of moral action and obedience (John v. 17). If, without pursuing this course, she seeks to appropriate supernatural truths, she will never attain her end. Only, let her not say that these truths are incredible and irrational, since she will not take the one possible way to understand and appropriate them.

If, on the contrary, Reason would only seek in the right way to penetrate into the mysteries of revelation, she would, with regard to much that might be new to her, and which she never could deduce from her own premises, be enabled, as it were, to follow the divine thought and sympathize with the divine intention; to recognise what was at first incomprehensible to her more and more in its wisdom and fitness, and, indeed, as the expression of the highest Reason, as the most certainly and absolutely True. In this way the objective facts of revelation would be ever growing more subjectively certain, and the original difference between the two would be tending more and more to disappear.

But what, in all conscience, gives Reason a right to reject historically attested matters of fact, merely because she is unable to derive and prove them directly from her own consciousness, or because she cannot forthwith understand them, while there are millions who testify that, in their case, the conviction of their truth only gradually dawned upon them? The same is the case with *Conscience*. Let him who would make conscience the criterion of revelation show us first of all—a much more difficult task than is generally supposed—what there is in the witness of conscience that is so special, independent, and immutable as to constitute it the measure of the truth of revelation. Let him show us, further, that those portions of revelation which conscience would reject are really of immoral tendency, and run counter to our inherent sense of right. If our previous delineation of the character of revelation has shown that this is impossible, and if history irrefutably proves that conscience in itself has no adequate guarantee against constant vacillations and errors, then surely it is sufficiently clear that *conscience must be subordinate to the revealed Word as its fixed rule and guiding-star.* Do we not perceive this in ourselves? Honestly speaking! must we not confess that our conscience is always clearer, tenderer, and more acute when we open it to the influence of revelation; and, on the other hand, that it is always duller, laxer, and more obscure when we withdraw it from that influence? Is not this again a proof that conscience must be guided and enlightened by revelation, and not *vice versa?* But clearly, whatever a thing is guided by, to that it must be subordinate.

True enough, it has been maintained, in order to claim for conscience greater fixedness of character, that it is the conscience of the whole *body of Christians,* and not that of individuals, which is to be the rule and measure of revelation. But who will show us this collective conscience? What differences would not present themselves on inquiry between the collective consciences of various Christian churches? And would not whatever they might hold in common be the fruit of the one revelation? Is the Christian conscience to sit in judgment on that from which it has virtually sprung? The truth is, that the conscience even of whole nations and churches is subject to great obscurations and disturbances, as we have previously hinted. How blinded, for instance, was the collective Christian conscience of the Southern States of North America with regard to the question of slavery? If revelation did not form the criterion of our belief, we should have no firm ground to stand upon. To make conscience the measure of our faith, is simply "to degrade the greatness of divine thoughts to the narrowness and smallness of human."

Revelation is for our theology what the telescope is for

our knowledge of the stars, and bears the same relation to reason and conscience as the telescope does to the naked eye. One in either case requires the other. The telescope enhances, sharpens, and extends the powers of the natural eye, but demands at the same time its full activity. Any one who should study astronomy without the use of the telescope would attain some slight degree of knowledge, but many thousand stars and beauties of the heavens would escape his observation. So he who would know God without the aid of revelation must suffer from the same poverty and insecurity in his religious knowledge. But just as the uncertain testimony of the naked eye is subordinate to the clearer testimony of the assisted vision, so should it be with natural knowledge in comparison with the witness of revelation. And if, on account of the imperfection of our thoughts as well as of our belief, the combined testimony of both leaves many lacunæ unfilled, yet these lacunæ are by no means contradictions. And even if Natural and Revealed Theology are now found in several respects to diverge from one another, *yet a day is certainly coming when their union will be complete.* Revelation and nature are developing towards one great goal at which they will coalesce. The perfecting of the one is that of the other. The fixed tendency of revelation to become nature, to make itself more and more a citizen on earth, in order to make earth the chosen place of divine revelation, this tendency is one day to be completely realized; *the consummated kingdom of God will combine both elements—the highest degree of revelation and the highest development of nature.*

It appears to me that the Holy Scriptures themselves explain very beautifully and profoundly the relation which natural and revealed religion bear to each other, and their close affinity in principle and purpose, in the *story of the Wise Men from the East.* They came to the Holy Land led by a supernatural revelation granted to them in connection with astronomy, the branch of natural learning which they pursued,—a comforting indication that *every earnest, honest search after light and truth leads to its discovery. The lower revelation, when rightly used, prepares for a higher one.* Not the law of Moses alone, but also the heathen philosophy and investigation of nature, was a preparation for the clear light of Truth which was to shine forth in Christ. It is only when superficially tasted—as Bacon well says—that philosophy leads us away from God; deeper draughts of a thorough and real philosophy bring us back to Him. And, we add, with a more modern natural philosopher (Oerstedt), "every thorough knowledge of nature leads to a knowledge of God." The true spirit of science, the only aim of which is truth, ever points and impels us towards the Centre of all knowledge and all truth; the One "in whom are hidden all the treasures of wisdom and of knowledge." To Him, not only the Scriptures with the ever-waxing light of their revelation, but heathen wisdom, too, amid its gropings for truth in the starry heavens, still point us; to attain to its salvation all history in its ruins, nature in her pangs, the heart in its grief, and the whole creation in its groaning and travailing for freedom (Rom. viii. 19–23) are ever striving.

The wise men come to Jerusalem; but they do not find the path to Bethlehem till enlightened by the prophetical word, —a hint that the light of Natural Revelation needs to be supplemented by that of Scripture. Their heathen knowledge, when aided even by the clearest light of Natural Revelation, brings them at best only *into the immediate neighbourhood of salvation;* fully attain to it they cannot, unless the Divine *Word* be vouchsafed as a key to the understanding of the Divine Works.

Lastly, they go from Jerusalem to Bethlehem, guided by the harmoniously blended light of the prophetic utterance and of the Star, which, through its means, has once more appeared to them,—a sign that no real contradictions exist between the two revelations in the Word and in nature, but that they are one both in their divine origin and in the end to which they point. We men may, perhaps, by our own fault, and owing to the imperfection of our knowledge, lose for a time the trace of a connection between the two; but he who deals faithfully with the measure of knowledge and revelation entrusted to him, and is obedient to the heavenly guidance, will be led step by step to the full knowledge of the truth. Such an one shall be more and more clearly and harmoniously enlightened by the different forms of God's revelation, until at last he sees how all their manifold beams converge in, and radiate from, the one Sun, which is the Brightness and the Heart of the Holy Scriptures, as well as the Light of the world and the Centre of its history,—from Him who, as the everlasting Word, unites in Himself at once eternal Reason and eternal Revelation.

THIRD LECTURE.

MODERN NON-BIBLICAL CONCEPTIONS OF GOD.

IT has been justly said, that religion is the first power upon earth. Any one who attentively considers the history of the world and its culture, in the light, not merely of surface events, but of the internal motives which determine its development, cannot fail to apprehend this truth.

Even Goethe, in his *Abhandlungen zum westöstlichen Divan*, acknowledges that "the only real and the deepest theme of the world's and of man's history, to which all other subjects are subordinate, is the conflict between faith and unbelief." As long as the religious question remains unsolved, there will always be plenty of external "questions" on the Tiber or the Rhine, in Constantinople or in Washington. Since the great French Revolution, however, the religious question has entered upon a fresh, and, if I am not mistaken, upon the last stage of its development. The issue, taken as a whole, no longer lies in isolated dogmatical differences between the various churches; even the controversy between Protestantism and Romanism has in public life become a secondary question. *The question now is, whether shall continue to exist at all —Christian belief.* The battle of centuries between belief and unbelief is in our days nearly tending to the point where the decisive question must be put, whether the Christian religion shall continue to be maintained as the basis and rule of our civilisation, or whether it must be wholly abandoned. "To be, or not to be; that is the question" now-a-days for the Christian faith; and this question, if any, must be the last, just as two thousand years ago it was the first.

Nothing shows this so clearly as the present position of the controversy about the *idea of God.* We have already remarked that, in the conflict between belief and unbelief, it is the idea of God which always forms the heart's core of the matter, the vital question, and which decides as to our view of Christianity generally, and of all particular dogmas. The present contest, too, as to the person of Christ, the gospel history, and the entire origin of Christianity, resolves itself into certain fundamental differences in the conception of God. The efforts of Strauss, Renan, and all the negative critics of this class, are, as we shall see, based upon a non-biblical—viz. the pantheistic—idea of God, and this they are seeking to introduce into the world. It is a non-biblical idea of God, the deistical, rationalistic idea, on which the "free-thinking" theology—that is, the theology which denies all that is supernatural—and all its products are based. Hegel's conception of God it really is which makes Baur and his school attempt to derive the entire origin of Christianity from merely natural sources. We shall therefore dwell rather longer on this cardinal point. For when we have once established the untenableness of these fundamental views, it will be all the easier to understand how weak is the criticism based upon them.

The controversy as to the idea of God is no longer the same as it was a hundred or two hundred years ago. At that time, if we except a few pantheists, the existence of a personal God was not generally called in question; and hence the only disputable point was God's action in the world, whether He could work miracles, whether His providence extended to all things, whether Christ was truly divine, and the like. In the present day, however, it is not merely this that is called in question, but also the existence of God at all, and consequently the existence of the human spirit as a distinct essence. Formerly the issue lay between Biblical Christianity and Deism: now it lies between Christianity and—nothing; between belief in God as the personal Spirit who is Love, and the denial of God, which must be the annihilation of man's spiritual and moral being. This you will see in the consideration of our next subject—*Atheism* and *Materialism.*

It would be an unprofitable and thankless undertaking were we to attempt in due order to refute all the non-biblical ideas of God which have ever presented themselves. Their number is incalculable. Almost every idea of reason, almost every imaginable conception of the universe, has, one time or another in the history of philosophy, been maintained as an idea of God. Reason restlessly moves from one fundamental principle to another, and, in its hasty progress towards something new, ultimately returns to that which is old, as in the present day Materialism has reverted to the principles of the older Ionic and Atomistic Philosophy. Under these circumstances, it is better to take in review only the *fundamental forms* under which all the non-biblical, philosophical, and scientific conceptions of God may be included; and in so doing, we shall, of course, give special attention to the ideas which prevail in our own time. We find that they diverge into *three main tendencies,* regarding the Absolute either as a universal *Material Substance,* or as an impersonal, unconsciously working *Anima Mundi,* or as *the Creator of the world*—personal indeed, but not exercising any direct influence on its present life. These are the distinguishing marks of the systems of MATERIALISM, PANTHEISM, and DEISM; but before considering them, we will first take a glance at ATHEISM as forming the most direct contrast to the biblical doctrine of God.

I.—ATHEISM.

This is the absolute denial of any kind of Θεός, that is, of any Divine Being, and therefore cannot be classed among the ideas of God above mentioned. This view, that there is absolutely no God at all, was so much detested by the ancient Greeks, that they considered Atheism synonymous with wickedness; and those who had the reputation of holding this opinion were more than once banished, and their names (as that of a Diagoras, a Bion, or a Lucian) stigmatized by history. We also find the principle of Atheism—although not strictly carried out—in Buddhism, inasmuch as it acknowledges as the Absolute, only the absolute Nothing from which everything springs and to which everything returns.

This view, after having for ages appeared only quite sporadically, first assumed the character of a system—if indeed it be worthy of the name—in the train of French Materialism. La Mettrie, for instance, pronounced the belief in the existence of a God to be as groundless as it was unprofitable. This tendency, as is well known, penetrated the mass of the French people during the "reign of terror" under the Convention, when the "Hebertists" laid it down as a principle, "that the King of Heaven must be dethroned just as the kings of the earth." Encouraged by the abjuration of Christianity on the part of the Bishop of Paris and his priests, they came before the Convention with a petition for the abrogation of Christianity, and the institution of a worship of Reason, presenting the wife of one of their colleagues as the Goddess of Reason. Clad in white garments and a sky-blue mantle, with the red cap on her head and a pike in her hand, they placed her on a fantastically ornamented car, and conducted her, surrounded by crowds of bacchanalian dancers, to the "Temple of Reason," as they were pleased to rename the Cathedral of Notre-Dame. There she was seated on the high altar, and, amidst profound obeisances, frantic speeches, and frivolous songs, divine honours were paid to her,—a scandal which was immediately imitated in several thousand churches in the country. Who does not see from this what abysses are opened before a nation when Atheism once gains ground in it!

Let no one imagine that such scenes cannot be repeated. Not many years ago, at a students' congress in Liège, some of the speakers declared, amidst universal applause, that "their aim was to do away with all religions, to destroy all churches, and to eradicate every thought of God from the consciousness of their fellow-men; and that in their opinion Atheism was the ultimate aim of all human science." Even amidst the bombastic perorations of a Geneva "Peace Congress," sentiments of this kind may now and then be distinctly recognised.

Quite recently all doubt as to the growing power of Atheism has been removed by the blasphemous "Manifestos" of the Commune[1] and the "International," as well as by the openly avowed tendency of many of our Socialist Unions.

Of late, too, some of our own literati and poets have been *un-German* enough to try to transplant this tendency into our

[1] Cf. what Gustave Flourens, the late leader of the Red Republican party in Paris, writes in his journal, *La libre Pensée*, for October 1870:—"Our enemy is God. Hatred of God is the beginning of wisdom. If mankind would make true progress, it must be in the basis of Atheism. Every trace of religion must be banished from the education of our children," etc. etc.

German soil. Ay, a well-known representative of the people has laid it down, as the task to be carried out, and to a great extent accomplished by the present age, "to educate in Atheism personal enemies of a personal God, especially amongst the class of German artisans." And was not, about twenty-five years since, Atheism publicly toasted at the banquet of a literary society? But philosophers also come forward as its advocates. Feuerbach pronounces, "There is no God; it is as clear as the sun and as evident as the day that there is no God, and still more, that there *can* be none. For if there were a God, then there *must be* one; He would be necessary. But now if *there is* no God, then there *can be* no God; therefore there is no God. There is no God, because there *cannot* be any." A pretty kind of logic, which saves us the trouble of any refutation! In a similar way, only in a more philosophical garb, another follower of Hegel, in his work, *Christenthum und Humanismus*, introduces his Atheism to the world by endeavouring to show that "because there is no God, there can also be no objective belief. Man has placed himself, in the shape of the ideal after which he strives, as a religious subject, outside and above his own consciousness, and worships the God whom he has thus set up." In fact the world, as one of his critics remarks, "is a great madhouse; by some inexplicable bewitchment man sees above him his own shadow, and takes it to be the real author of his existence."

If Atheism takes its stand on such arguments as these, we may fairly ask *whether those who proclaim it were themselves convinced of it?* It has been said, not without good reason, that Atheism never really existed as a full conviction in any human breast, and that there is always an underlying self-deception whenever any one professes to be a pure atheist. That one, in a fanatical over-estimation of reason, should imagine himself able to know and investigate everything, and curtly deny whatever is beyond his knowledge; or that, in the pride which declines to acknowledge either sin or its Avenger, he *should* believe himself all-sufficient, in base dependence on the world of sense, denying everything that does not belong to it, and thus persuading himself that no God exists,—this, after all, is conceivable enough. But that he should, consciously and conscientiously, make this idle notion his *per-*

manent conviction, and that he should not, when denying the Christian's God, venerate aught else as the Divine Power, this is difficult to believe, even apart from the fact that, notwithstanding all the trouble which atheists have taken to discover but one nation utterly devoid of religious consciousness, we have found, down to the present day, *in all nations*, even the most degraded, *some conception or other of a Higher Being*, and a feeling of dependence on supernatural powers, and consequently some kind of religious exercise. Cicero's question (*De Nat. Deorum*, i. 16) still holds good—"What people is there, or what race of men, which has not, even without traditional teaching, some presentiment of the existence of Gods?" Does not this indicate that the belief in some higher and more powerful Being by which he is conditioned, is both a *logical and a moral necessity* for man? Or must not that in which not merely many (which would prove nothing), but *all* agree, be grounded in the nature and essence of man himself?

Yes, human thought *must* recognise God *just* as certainly as itself and the world. As a modern apologist says: "We cannot, in any way, get rid of the idea."[1] We do not merely *believe* that there is a God, but we *know it in virtue of* an ideal cognition consisting in an immediate act of faith in human consciousness. And this very fact, that a direct *certainty of God* exists in our minds *per se*, is the most simple refutation of Atheism. It is not as if the idea of God were in its complete shape innate in our minds. We have seen above that there is no such thing as full-grown innate ideas. Rather, the idea of God developes itself (along with those of our own personality and the Cosmos) through contact with the outer world, *of necessity*, from the inward predisposition of our mental and moral constitution. Man, in becoming conscious of his own personality, becomes at the same time conscious of his state as a conditioned and limited being; from which follows, as a necessary corollary, the acknowledgment that there must be a Being who is absolute and unconditioned. "The perception of his own relativity leads man to the idea of some higher Being on whom his own existence

[1] Cf. the well-known and excellent *Apologetic Lectures* by Luthardt, of which a translation has been published by Messrs. Clark. Also, for what follows, *Delitzsch ut supr.*, pp. 66, 67.

depends, and this Being he can only conceive as one that is absolute—above himself and above nature—that is, God."[1]

Whether this higher Being must also be conceived as *personal,* we shall presently have to investigate, when considering the impersonal (pantheistic) idea of God. Here we have only to do with the idea of God as a necessary postulate of thought. And we see that the atheist can give no clear account of the inner elements and the extent of his own consciousness.

Even heathen thinkers have recognised the importance of this universal fact of ethnology and psychology as telling in favour of belief in God. That that "wherein all by nature agree must be true," is a conclusion rightly drawn by Cicero. Or could a man in his senses venture to tax the whole of mankind with an error in their consciousness? No lie can last for ever; only truth is eternal. If the consciousness of God were an error, it would, like any other error, have long ago vanished. But instead of this, we see it propagating itself with growing power through all the ages.

If, then, the existence of God be an inward necessity of thought, the denial of it can be nothing but an arbitrary act of our will; it is that we *will not acknowledge* this inward certainty. As an element of our consciousness, as a divine gift implanted in the heart, the idea of God precedes all other thought, and the only question is, whether we are *willing* to let it stand as truth or not. If we acknowledge it, the heart convinces the understanding, and not *vice versa.* Hence the belief in God is "not a science, but a virtue." If, however,

[1] *Delitzsch ut supr.* Taking this into consideration, we cannot deny that some weight is to be attached to the much reviled *ontological argument* for the existence of God. The way in which it is usually put is this—that the idea of the Most Perfect Being includes reality as one of His perfections, and that, consequently, the Most Perfect Being necessarily *exists,* which has been clearly shown by Kant to be a false conclusion. But is it not "an immediate certainty that the greatest, most beautiful, and most valuable object must be a reality, and not a mere matter of thought; for it would be utterly intolerable to believe our highest Ideal to be a mere conception of our intellect, without actual existence, power, or validity?" Even if we cannot, from the perfection of the absolutely Perfect, logically infer its actual existence, still *we distinctly feel the impossibility of its non-existence.* "If the Greatest *did not exist,* there would be no *Greatest;* and it is surely impossible that the Greatest of all imaginable beings should *not exist.*" Lotze, *Mikrokosmus,* iii. p. 557

we will not allow the idea of God, it is because the understanding is unwilling to be thus convinced by the heart, and this is an arbitrary act. It was therefore a perfectly correct instinct which led the Greeks to look upon Atheism as a *moral* fault. And every moral fault avenges itself. The refusal to acknowledge that which *is*, and absolutely is, and is directly certain to every heart, leads to the acceptance of that which is nothing but a deceptive shadow. Man must have a God. If he rejects the true God, he must make a God for himself, and this is of necessity a false one. "Man must believe in something. If he does not believe in the Eternal Reason, he believes in unreason; if he does not accept as the truth the living God, he believes in the idol of inanimate matter."

The pretensions of Atheism would seem to be supported by the rejection in modern times of the old arguments which had long obtained in favour of the existence of a God. We reserve the most important of these for our consideration of Pantheism, merely remarking that they are not, it is true, cogent. To one who does not believe in the foundation of all religion, that is, the reality of the supersensuous, they prove nothing; for the existence of the supersensuous can never be demonstrated by mere reasoning. But for one who has this belief, they do possess a certain force: they have the value of a "subjective assurance," since they make the existence of God in the highest degree probable to reason.

Granted, however, that the existence of a God cannot be proved, still less can His non-existence. This can be shown without difficulty. The denial of the existence of God involves a perfectly monstrous hypothesis; it is, when looked at more closely, an unconscionable assumption. Before one can say that the world is without a God, he must first have become thoroughly conversant with the whole world. He must have searched through the universe of suns and stars, as well as the history of all ages; he must have wandered through the whole realm of space and time in order to be able to assert with truth, "Nowhere has a trace of God been found!" He must be acquainted with every force in the whole universe; for should but one escape him, that very one might be God. He must be able to count up with certainty all the causes of existence; for were there *one* that he did not know, that one might be God. He must be in absolute possession of all the elements of truth, which form the whole body of our knowledge; for else the one factor which he did not possess might be *just the very* truth that there is a God. If he does not know and cannot explain everything that has happened in the course of ages, just the very point which he does not know, and is unable to explain, may involve the instrumentality of a God. In short, *to be able to affirm authoritatively that no God exists, a man must be omniscient and omnipresent, that is, he himself must be God;* and then after all there would be one. You see in this the monstrosity of the atheistic hypothesis, that it is possible to prove the non-existence of God. Atheism depends as much, and more, than Theism on *faith,* that is, on assumptions which cannot be proved.

Finally, we would ask, What advantage accrues to the solution of the world's enigma if we assume the non-existence of a God? None at all can we see. The atheist, just as the materialist and the pantheist, must suppose the world to be eternal. Is its existence in any way thus explained? It may, at the present day, be physically proved with tolerable certainty, that the first fact of which any trace is extant in the world's history is the appearance of light. This brings us, as a scientific naturalist remarks, "to the limit of our physical knowledge, and to the very end of what we can discover as regards the material world." If we inquire further, Whence this principle of light? Holy Scripture at once gives the answer: "God said, Let there be light;"—the atheist, the materialist, and the pantheist have no answer to give; they say that light, or the matter and force from which light is derived, has existed from everlasting. What does this explain? These sceptics may pronounce the idea of a God existing from all eternity incomprehensible, but they forget that their idea of eternal matter is at least equally unexplained. Where, then, is the advantage? For the rest, the arguments to be adduced against Materialism and Pantheism, especially those of a moral nature, apply also to Atheism.

II.—MATERIALISM.

Materialism is the twin brother of Atheism. They must necessarily be simultaneous; for he who denies the existence of God, is unable, as we shall see, to maintain the spiritual personality of man. Historically it invariably either proceeds or closely follows Atheism. The two play into one another's hands, and, in fact, amount to the same thing. For Atheism must ultimately believe in the eternity of matter, and, just like Materialism, must make it its God. Between Materialism and Pantheism, however, a distinction must be drawn. Pantheism considers God as the Soul of the world, and material nature as His body only. Materialism merges God in matter; for, according to it, *nothing at all exists but matter,—there is no such thing as a separate spiritual substance.* All that exists is material; and that which is called spirit, or spiritual life, is nothing but a function of the life of the body, a necessary product of sensuous perception, and of the nutritive matter absorbed by us, but pre-eminently of the action of the cerebral muscles. Materialism may well be called the gospel of the flesh; it is the absolute deification of matter and of the creature, traces of which pervade the whole history of mankind from Babel and Sodom onwards; nay, from the tasting of the forbidden fruit in Paradise down to our own days. Every false belief, and every act of unbelief, like that of Thomas, involves a disposition to sensualism and materialism. Every apostasy from the living God, who is a Spirit, necessitates a tendency in the opposite direction to the deification of the flesh, though it may not always go so far.

Hence unbelief has constantly from time to time landed in Materialism. We find it in the Buddhism of ancient India; in Greece, among the Atomists and the Sophists, the Epicureans and the Sceptics; we find it in the middle ages, when the Roman Church clearly betrayed her tendency to the worship of matter, and even at times among the occupants of the Papal throne, of whom, for instance, John XXIII. (d. 1419) and Paul III. (d. 1549) publicly denied the immortality of the soul; we find it in the seventeenth and eighteenth centuries, as the ultimate result of the long-protracted doubts as to revelation; and everywhere do we see it exercising the same pernicious effect on nations, everywhere rushing through the same circle till it attains its climax in despair of all knowledge of truth, giving the rein to all evil desires, and finally destroying its own existence.

In our days, the materialistic view has obtained a wide-spread acceptation, owing to the fact, that many natural philosophers assume the entirely material descent of mankind, and make out that the ancestors of our race, just like other mammals, especially apes, originally sprang from the primeval slime. In Germany, too, the influence of this school has been no slight one during the last decades. L. Feuerbach, C. Vogt, J. Moleschott, Büchner, Czolbe, and others, were, and still are, the chief heralds of this wisdom. "The soul," exclaims Vogt (*Physiologische Briefe*, 1846), "does not enter into the human fœtus like an evil spirit into one possessed, but is the product of the brain's development, just as muscular action is produced by the development of the muscles, and secretion by that of the glands.—To assume the existence of a soul which uses the brain as an instrument with which to work as it pleases, is utter nonsense. Physiology distinctly and categorically pronounces against any individual immortality, and against all ideas which are connected with the figment of a separate existence of the soul." "Man," says Moleschott (*der Kreislauf des Lebens, physiologische Antworten auf Liebig's chemische Briefe*, 4th Ed. 1863), "is produced from wind and ashes. The action of vegetable life called him into existence. Man is the sum of his parents and his wet-nurse, of time and place, of wind and weather, of sound and light, of food and clothing; his will is the necessary consequence of all these causes, governed by the laws of nature, just as the planet in its orbit, and the vegetable in its soil. Thought consists in the motion of matter, it is a translocation of the cerebral substance; without phosphorus there can be no thought; and consciousness itself is nothing but an attribute of matter." The watch-word of this school is, in short, *We are what we eat* (Feuerbach); in fact, man is nothing but a retort in which certain elements are chemically decomposed and combined, and certain gases generated; or as Czolbe expresses it (*Entstehung des Selbstbewusstseins*, 1856), "nothing more than a mosaic figure made up of different atoms and mechanically combined in an elaborate shape."

We need not delay to prove that this gospel of the flesh, the moral of which is to produce plenty of phosphorus by means of good eating and drinking, is diametrically opposed to the Holy Scriptures, which teach us to worship God as a Spirit, and in the spirit, and bid man, as the spiritual image of God, approach his Creator in the way of sanctification and subjection of the flesh to the spirit; which, from beginning to end, so often warn us against any deification of the creature, against the worship of the visible and the transient, against those "whose god is their belly," who say, "Let us eat and drink, for to-morrow we die." Surely this is a view *unworthy of refutation*; for oh! is it not a grievous and shameful thing that one should have to *prove* to men that they are something better than beasts? In opposition to such theories, an appeal to the self-consciousness of the soul and to its moral feelings should suffice. But since in our days Materialism, disguised under the garb of science, has impressed with the idea of its importance many who have not as yet gone so far as to adopt it in *theory*, but who do so all the more in *practice*, by exclusively directing all their energy towards gain and pleasure, it becomes a matter of necessity briefly to point out the *scientific weakness and groundlessness of this stand-point.*[1]

We might at once dismiss the "phosphorus theory" by simply denying the existence of phosphorus in the brain. And for a corroboration, we might appeal to the celebrated J. v. Liebig, who says: "The honour of the discovery that phosphorus exists in the brain belongs, not to me, but to Dr. Moleschott; and in my 'Chemical Letters' I have declared it to be a mistaken idea, not based on a single fact,"—an utterance which shows, at all events, how uncertain is the hypothesis upon which this theory is based. But it is not our business to pronounce an opinion on this controversy. We might ask

[1] Cf. on this subject, Fabri, *Briefe gegen den Materialismus*, 2d ed.; Ruete, *On the Existence of the Soul from the Stand-point of Natural Science*, Leipzig 1863; the History of Materialism in Böhner's *Naturforschung und Culturleben*, 2d ed. p. 101 ff.; and the works of Rud. Wagner, *Menschenschöpfung u. Seelensubstanz*, 1854; *der Kampf um die Seele*, 1857; *Vorstudien zu einer wissensch. Morphologie u. Physiologie des menschlichen Gehirns als Seelenorgan*, 1862.

those gentlemen who assert that thought is derived merely from the nerves and convolutions of the brain, to explain to us what is the specific *organ or acting medium of nervous activity*, and should thus not a little perplex them. For on this point physiologists are still most divided in their views. According to one, the nerves are like the strings of an instrument, the vibrations of which act upon the brain, and thence are reflected to the periphery. Another seeks to determine nervous action after the manner of the mechanical propagation of motion, *i.e.* as a concussion of minute globules. Others assume the presence in the nerves of an albuminous, or an acrid, or a sulphurous fluid, which, by means of a pressure at one end, produces a similar pressure at the other; and this nervous fluid is sometimes thought to be ether, sometimes luminous matter, sometimes caloric. Others, again, are of opinion that electricity and galvanism are the active principle of the nerves, etc. Whilst thus, as we see, nothing certain has yet been ascertained as to the *material* of the nervous functions, these people dare to attribute the mental functions, hitherto held by the whole world to be *immaterial*, to the nervous activity of the brain,—a totally unknown quantity, about which, forsooth, they claim to be able to set up hypotheses!

Let us, however, submit their main propositions to a closer examination. In order to eliminate the spirit from our nature, Materialism, both ancient and modern, adduces *two propositions:* first, *That sensuous perception is the source of all knowledge;* and second, *That all mental action is nothing more than the activity of matter, and therefore the soul itself is material and mortal.* Let us now consider the first proposition.

(*a*) Is it then a fact, that everything in the nature of thoughts, notions, and ideas which can be conceived by our understanding, our reason, or our memory, reaches us merely through the senses? Can it be that every idea of ours may be reduced to an original act of seeing, hearing, smelling, etc.? What right have we at all to assert the existence of a necessary mechanical relation between the perception of the senses and thought? The one process is separated from the other both temporally and locally; for, according to materialistic principles, thought is evolved by an irritation of the brain, and material perception by a function of the senses. Now Materialism, either thoughtlessly or sophistically, straightway asserts that there is a mechanically necessary mutual relation between the two,—an assertion what is contradicted by all experience. For is it not frequently a matter of fact, that one and the same material perception excites *different* thoughts even in the same individual, to say nothing of different persons? How, then, can we say with Vogt, "like causes, like results"? According to Vogt's law, similar sounds should produce similar thoughts. The two propositions, "There is a God," and "There is no God," sound very much alike, and differ only in two letters; how is it, then, that they call forth in us opposite and not similar thoughts?

Is it not further a matter of fact, that a perception of the senses does not by any means necessarily and in all cases call forth a thought? Cannot a man under the influence of violent irritation of the senses pursue a line of thought which stands in no kind of connection therewith? And are there not innumerable thoughts which arise completely independent of any external sensuous perception? Cannot I imagine something which I neither hear, see, nor smell, etc.? And how can the materialist explain dream-life, in which the functions of the five senses cease? Are dreams caused by nervous excitement; and if so, whence the excitement without any irritation of the senses? Or how can memory be explained? Since the substance of the body is being constantly renewed, the influence, for instance, of the journeys which we have taken in your youth ought gradually to fade away after about twelve years, because then the substance of the brain which originally received them has completely disappeared. Instead, however, of this, we find that many impressions and recollections lose nothing of their vividness even after the lapse of many decades. And then, to put isolated intellectual functions out of the question, we inquire: Whence the laws of thought themselves? And finally: Whence the idea of God, and all the moral ideas?

Material perception is therefore very far from forming the whole substance of our intellectual life, and hence cannot be the sole source of our knowledge. Indeed, the external influence does not even form the full substance of the material sensation that we are conscious of, but is only the outward incitement thereto. The individual acts of sensation are one thing, and the *capability* of perceiving light, colour, etc. is another. The capability itself cannot be looked upon as evolved in us solely by the exciting influences of waves of light and sound.

Instead of all this, we might inquire, if all thoughts arise merely from impressions which the senses are pleased to impart, why does not sensuous perception produce rational thought in *beasts* also? The fact that the latter do not really think, whilst their material perceptions are exceedingly acute, is a sufficient proof that a distinction must be drawn between thinking and material sensation, and that the former is something new and special as compared with the latter.[1] On the other hand, there are plenty of examples of human beings who are almost entirely deficient in the faculties of material perception, and who, nevertheless, exhibit a perfectly developed life of thought, and considerable mental acquirements. Laura Bridgman, born the 20th of December 1829, at Hanover, in New Hampshire, U.S., suffered up to the twentieth month of her age from convulsive fits; she then completely lost the senses of sight, hearing, and smell, and almost entirely that of taste,—the sense of touch being the only one left to her, without any recollection of the former possession of other faculties. Nevertheless, under the instruction of a skilful teacher of the deaf and dumb, she has succeeded in attaining an incredibly high development both in a physical, moral, and intellectual point of view: her understanding has developed just as in one possessed of all his senses; and, although four classes of material impressions are denied to her, still she is in perfect possession of all the elements of human reason. She is still (1863) living, and is happy and contented (see Ruete *ut supra*). In the face of facts like these, how can any one assert

[1] Cf. also the remarks which Liebig (*Chemische Briefe*, 1865, p. 38) makes, from a chemical stand-point, against the materialistic theory: "The strangest thing is, that many look upon the peculiarities of the self-conscious, thinking, and perceptive being in this habitation (the human body) as a simple consequence of its internal structure and the arrangement of its smallest particles, although chemistry supplies the indubitable proof that, as regards this extremely delicate combination which is almost beyond the perception of the senses, man is identical with the lowest animals." There is, therefore, every reason for the latter also being able to think.

that all rational knowledge is nothing but a product of the organs of sense?

(*b*) And how fares it with *the second axiom of Materialism, that mind is merely an activity and effect of matter?* This question turns upon the relation existing between the brain and thought. Hitherto the brain has been considered as the organ to which indeed thought was necessarily bound, but which the mind *freely* controlled. In order to subvert this view, the materialist must prove that a mechanical law governs the relation between a certain irritation of the brain and the excitation of a certain thought. All attempts, however, to supply this proof, lead only to the conclusion that a mutual relation subsists between the brain and thought, but do not demonstrate that this relation is a mechanically binding one. Many facts, indeed, directly contradict this. How does it come to pass that in many cases a morbid alteration of the brain, nay, even a partial loss of brain-matter (by wounds), does not weaken the mental life; or, conversely, that after long and vehement mental aberrations no alteration of the brain can be demonstrated? Whence, moreover, the absolutely inexhaustible fertility of the brain in the formation of thoughts, since a material structure of this sort, limited as to space, affords only a definite number of possibilities, and also since material perception is always of a limited nature? Besides, if thought be identical with the brain, and the soul with the body, it cannot rightly be understood why man should first have to make himself acquainted with his own body, a fact which is perfectly clear in the case of children. Does not the circumstance, that man must find out the locality of his own limbs by experience, indicate that the body is merely an instrument of the soul?

These are then indications of a *dualism* existing between nervous or cerebral activity and mental life; and this dualism is rendered still more probable by the comparison—so much in vogue at the present day—between our brain and that of the anthropoid apes. Modern anatomy has taught us that the brain, for instance, of the orang-outang only differs from that of man in an inferior intricacy of the convolutions, a somewhat greater protuberance of the cerebellum, as well as in a less delicate molecular composition (cf. the investigations of Perty,

Rougemont, and others). On the whole, however, the difference is not very important; in external size and weight, the two brains are pretty much alike. Anatomists have thus unwittingly supplied us with an excellent weapon for the vindication of the biblical view of man. The argument intended to support Materialism in fact refutes it. For we again ask, as in the case of sensuous perfections, if the *organ*, or, as materialists would say, the *substance* of thought, and to some extent the nourishment, are so similar in man and beast, why are not the products of thinking, that is, the ideas, also similar? *Why is it that the beast, with nearly the same development of brain as man, cannot succeed in producing nearly the same conceptions and ideas?* If this question cannot be answered satisfactorily, evidently the higher character of thought in man *cannot depend on the structure of his organs alone*,[1] and is not the product of merely material causes. For "the greater the number of organic similarities which are discovered between man and beast, the more evident is the different nature of the treasure which God has implanted in us" (G. Saint Hilaire), and has concealed under similar forms. It is thus perfectly clear that there is a *dualism* between the brain and the operations of thought, and that there must be a new factor which constitutes the latter in man.

In order to elude this simple conclusion, materialists have drawn special attention to the various phenomena in animal life which are analogous to the operations of the soul in man,—such as their prudence, their constructiveness, their memory, their expressions of joy, thankfulness, love, etc.,—as a proof that there is no specific difference, but only one of degree, between the mental life of man and that of beasts. Vogt, indeed, has but lately discovered "an ursine and feline morality," because bear cubs and kittens are growled at and cuffed by their parents, "just as our own dear little ones are when they make light of filial obedience." We do not object to consider such phenomena as *analogies* to the workings of the human soul. We would even go so far as to remind our opponents, if they have overlooked it, as a further argument in their favour, of

[1] For this reason, Moleschott has tacitly withdrawn, in the second edition of his above-named work, the attempt to prove the capability of thought in man from the structure of his brain.

the masterpiece of instinct in the case of the elephant, who at night-time escaped from his cage, and was found in the open fields, practising by moonlight the lesson which his keeper had been teaching him in the daytime.

But what do all such examples prove? Nothing but this: that animals possess, often in a high degree, the capability of sensuous cognition, and of making a judicious choice among the possible courses of action, as well as the faculty of memory. But what a wide difference there still remains between this lower form of consciousness in the beast, this mere force of impulse and instinct, and the self-conscious intellect of man, which forms conceptions and ideas! If these animal feats really indicated a tendency to rational thought, how could we explain the entire *want of progress* in the brute world? The swallow builds her nest, and the beaver his dam, exactly as they did in the time of Abraham. As they build, so they *must* build, and they neither need nor are able to learn their art from any one. Man must laboriously learn how to shape the creations of his industry; but he is compensated for this by the capability of infinite improvement, showing that the constitution of his mind is an infinite one given him by God. There is not much difference between the hands of men and apes. How is it, then, that man has made the whole of nature subject to him by means of this instrument, whilst the ape has not yet been able to make even a stone axe? The beast shows a certain gift of observation and memory; it can distinguish the succession of certain phenomena. But can it ever find out *the law* which governs these events? The beast has perceptions of pain and pleasure which are conveyed to it by the outward senses. But can it call up these feelings without a direct sensuous impression? Hence the beast has no *language*. The gorilla, for instance, is not deficient in the organs of voice. But why is it that, with a throat similar to that of man, he can only howl and whine, and that man, with a throat like the ape's, can speak and sing so delightfully?[1] The answer is, *that the beast cannot form an objective notion of his sensations and feelings*, and therefore is unable to reproduce them in language; it cannot distinguish between a personal *Ego* and the momentary sensation. It is the power

[1] Cf. also Rougemont, *Der Mensch und der Affe*, p. 47.

to do this, and not his organs of voice (for even the deaf and dumb make a language for themselves), which gives man the faculty of speech. It is this, the *self-conscious spirit,* in virtue of which he involuntarily feels himself, as compared with any other created being, of infinitely greater dignity and value.

And what shall we say of man's distinctive *moral and religious* disposition, and its development! Who can seriously speak of the moral attributes of beasts? Could any training ever bring a beast to a moral perception of good and evil? The dog is ashamed when he is caught thieving, that is, he is afraid of blows; the man is ashamed *of himself.* The beast sees and feels nothing but nature, the world of finite things. It has no knowledge of God; it perceives nothing of the divine government of the world; it sees and feels nothing of any higher purposes, aims, or ideals.

Does all this constitute merely a difference in point of degree, and not rather an immeasurable specific difference between the thoughts, feelings, and desires of men and those of beasts? In the latter, we see the consciousness of a soul unenlightened by any beam of the spirit, obscure and incapable of forming the conception of an Ego; in the former, real *self-consciousness.* In the latter, we have mere natural impulses, directed towards the satisfaction of material wants, and serving no other purpose than the maintenance of the *genus,* for which reason the individual beast as such has no value; in the former, we have the *moral* consciousness of a *person* who possesses in himself the purpose of his existence, and is therefore of infinite value and eternal significance. In short, in one case there is a living but irrational *soul;* in the other, the rational, God-like *spirit.* All these higher achievements on the part of beasts belong to the *soul*-life as distinguished from the spirit; because the illuminating centre of self-consciousness is wanting in them. The Holy Scriptures themselves attribute to beasts a soul as the vital principle of the corporal organism. The phenomena in the life of man, on the contrary, all point to some higher power, a substance that marks him as superior to all mere animal life, and gives to his intellect the self-conscious clearness and power, and to his actions a moral value; and this is the God-descended *spirit,* which is not only distinct from the soul, but can even be practically opposed to its inclinations, in virtue of its own higher law. Hence the scriptural doctrine, that man consists of body, soul, *and spirit.* (1 Thess. v. 23; Heb. iv. 12, *et al.*)

This Materialism completely ignores; hence its incapability to explain the fundamental difference between the merely animal and the human soul-life. If, however, this difference consists essentially in self-consciousness, there now arises a fresh and insuperable objection to the substantial unity of brain and thought, viz. *that no explanation can then be given as to the origin of self-consciousness in man.* Granted that the individual acts of our soul-life all resulted from nothing but chemico-physical causes, it can never be denied that these acts are all rooted in a certain fixed, permanent centre, in "the idea of the Ego as the basis of all thought;" that is, in self-consciousness. Whence then is this? This centre is *not identical with the individual acts of thought;* for it is not an isolated act, but a continuous condition. Materialism, it is true, would fain make it identical with thought, but again in opposition to all experience. For do we not clearly distinguish ourselves in self-consciousness from any definite act of thought? Are there not conditions in which correct reasoning is coexistent with perturbed consciousness? And *vice versa,* is there not sometimes a continuance of consciousness notwithstanding the cessation of intellectual activity? The materialist, who will hear of no operative factor except the individual agencies,—brain, muscles, nerves, etc.,—and who denies as an empty abstraction the bond which unites these separate agents, and preserves its own unity amid all the changes of thought and perception,—that is, the self-consciousness, or the personality as such,—makes out man to be a "purely mechanical lay-figure," or as Czolbe openly admits, "a piece of mosaic, mechanically constructed from various atoms,"—a theory which explains absolutely nothing of the practical phenomena of soul-life.

The whole foundation of materialism is thus shown to be simply an audacious sophism, the most arbitrary, because unproved and absolutely unprovable, of assumptions, which is contradicted at every turn by our own consciousness. "I do not wish," says Schleiden, in opposition to Materialism, "to puzzle these gentlemen with the task of unfolding to me in detail the process whereby, for instance, the feeling for beauty is actually secreted in the brain. All I want them to do is to prove to me the *possibility* that, some day at least, we may be able to recognise the very simplest idea, as for instance, tree, law, etc., as a chemical element present in the brain, or as a combination of such. But a naturalist who judges and decides as to the nature of things, the possibility of which (to say nothing of their reality) he is not in a position to demonstrate, appears in this respect not an exact investigator of nature, but merely a superficial talker." And these people, in their opposition to Christianity, are fond of talking of "ploughman's faith," although in truth more *faith in authority* is needed for the acceptance of their hypothesis than for believing all the miracles of the Bible!

We might conclude with this; but let us first glance at the *consequences* of the materialistic principles. First and foremost, it is clear that they do away with the immortality of the soul and all belief in another world. For he who does not acknowledge any immaterial principles in man, will not allow the existence of an absolute Spirit, *i.e.* of God, either in or above the world. The ideas of God as a Spirit and of the human spirit as a distinct substance are inseparable, and for this reason we were obliged carefully to investigate the latter question. Every one sees what questionable results follow from the negation of our immortality, even as regards *this life*, and the moral order of the present world. We will not now enter into the details of the well-known arguments for the immortality of the soul, the main purport of which is that God is a Spirit, and that man's soul is a breath of this Spirit, proceeding therefore from above and not from below; that it is an entity absolutely incomposite, indivisible, and immaterial; and that its immateriality becomes more and more evident the longer it is exposed to the impotent attempts made to degrade it to the level of mere matter. We would, however, point out in passing, that it is precisely the most exact modern research which increasingly tends to enhance and perfect the ancient arguments for immortality derived from nature, from the analogy of the spring, the grub, and butterfly, etc. Here is an example. It has been observed that the larva of the male stag-beetle, when it becomes a chrysalis, constructs a larger case than it needs to contain its curled-up body, in order that the horns, which will presently grow, may also find room. What does the larva know of its future form of existence? and yet it arranges its house with a view to it! Is it then to be supposed that the same Power, which created both the beetle and the man, "*instilled into the beetle a true instinct, and into man a lying faith,* which makes him arrange his *present* life with a view to a *future* one otherwise than he would were this not the case,—a faith which arises as naturally, and is as necessary for the development of mankind, as instinct in the larva?" (Ruete *ut supra*).

If there is no such thing as a soul, not only would a future life be done away with, and all religion be merged in the worship of this world,—we pastors becoming the most useless of all creatures,—but you will also perceive what revolutions must follow in the whole mode which has hitherto obtained of conducting our life, most of all in *education.* If thought is a secretion of the brain, produced from our nourishment by means of a kind of fermentation or filtration, or in some other way, we can breed youths at our pleasure to be warriors, philosophers, musicians, and the like; and the most important question for a teacher would always be, whether to feed his pupil to-day on roast veal or roast beef, on this or that kind of food and drink. Those who are slow of understanding ought to eat large quantities of peas, fish, eggs, and other phosphoric food, in order to increase and accelerate their powers of thought.

But we are left in no doubt whatever on the point, that everything which has hitherto been cherished and cultivated, as manners and morality, as freedom of the spirit and of the will, must sink into the grave of a fatalistic necessity. We see clearly how thoroughly and *with what shameless audacity Materialism would destroy all the moral faculties of our life,*—for instance, in the words of Moleschott, that "sin lies in the Unnatural, and not in the will to do evil. Speech and style, good and bad actions, courage, half-heartedness, and treachery, are all natural phenomena, and all of them stand in a direct relation to indispensable causes as their natural consequences, just as much as the revolutions of the globe." "The brain alters with the ages; and with the brain, custom, which is the standard of morals, is altered also." "Wickedness in individuals, like the whole man himself, is therefore only a natural phenomenon. And as the words, 'Thou shalt love thy neighbour as thyself,' form the pith of Christian morals, so the first maxim of the modern gospel should be, 'To understand everything is to tolerate everything'" (*ut supr.* p. 466). At the end of his book Moleschott vouchsafes to the world the sapient and delicate-minded advice, that the stationary churchyards, in which so much excellent manure remains useless, should be changed into moveable churchyards, in order that the dead may attain the only immortality which now remains open to them, and have the privilege of impregnating barren ground with ammonia, carbonic acid, etc., to help towards the production and nourishment of fresh men! Paine, one of the latest French materialists, pronounces man to be a beast in human (*sic*) shape, which is led by humour and instinct. "Humour and instinct proceed from the blood. Hence arises habit; necessity brandishes the whip, and the beast goes forward. But being full of pride and conceit, the beast fancies that it moves in accordance with its own will, and that there is no whip urging it forward. We fancy that we govern our passions, but in reality they govern us; and we ascribe to ourselves the actions which they have produced." Vogt, however, has, as he always does, expressed himself on this point most unequivocally and unconcernedly of all. "It is indeed true. Freewill does not exist, neither does any amenability or responsibility, such as morals and penal justice, and Heaven knows what else would impose upon us. At no moment are we our own masters any more than we can decree as to the secretions of our kidneys. The organism cannot govern itself; it is governed by the law of its material combination. It is impossible to demonstrate the admissibility of punishment, or to prove that there is any such thing as amenability or responsibility," etc.

Jurists, therefore, do not fare any better than we theologians. It is evident that there is no room for them in the world now. There is no right to punish, for there is no responsibility; everything takes place under an iron necessity. The man who robs and murders is no worse than the falling stone which crushes a man, nor, of course, any more valuable; both are involuntary slaves of the law of nature. Criminals should be sent into hospitals and asylums, not to prison. The judge must yield up his place to the physician! Who would not then begin to tremble for the safety of society? Who does not perceive the *moral danger involved in Materialism*, according to which all human action, even that of the mind and spirit, is subordinate to the law of nature, and man no longer does what he *ought to do*, but what he *must do*,—according to which, therefore, all the great and noble acts performed in the world's history are nothing but the necessary products of certain bodily impulses and conditions? But the whole matter assumes an exceedingly tragico-comical aspect when we find these people desirous to be thought the "squatters of advancing civilisation," without observing that they are its gravediggers; and see them swaggering as the *heralds of freedom and humanity*, whilst it does not occur to them that they are the *apostles of the most brutal tyranny*, and that the practical aim of their theory is that the best-organized beast, called man, should sit alone on the throne of unfettered self-deification and unchecked self-gratification. For if man is nothing but a beast without a future, and organized merely for the full enjoyment of his present existence, then all that we have hitherto stupidly considered to be virtue is only a sin against our destiny! Justice, duty, honour, self-sacrifice, compassion, etc., are morbid secretions of certain deranged lobes of the brain! What good is my fellow-man to me? To subject and tyrannize all others is the only aim which reasonable man can pursue! Such maxims carried into practice would render society a mere congeries of atoms.

In good sooth, the materialists are the *most dangerous enemies of progress* that the world has ever seen. For all progress in the last resort depends on the ideal of an Infinite Perfection, to which the God-derived spirit of man aspires. He who destroys this ideal destroys progress also. But this ideal *is* destroyed when health and sensual enjoyments are held up to our race as the sole aim of life, within which we are to move in an eternal circle!

In the face of these apparent consequences, we are in this case, too, really led to doubt whether these gentlemen themselves believe what they are trying to palm off upon us. Why do they seek to work upon the people by means of lectures and books ? The proper way to convert people to their opinions would be to make them eat the same food as they do! Just imagine a soulless professor, with the utmost ingenuity, demonstrating to soulless students from his professorial chair that they have no souls! Is not the wiseacre contradicted out of his own mouth by every word he utters, since every one of his words is addressed to the *souls* of his audience ? In fact, my honoured hearers, if any one among you has brought with him flesh, blood, bone, some phosphorus, *and nothing else*, I would make bold to intimate to him in a friendly way that all arguments, as far as he is concerned, are but lost time.

Doubtless, however, there is *something true* and justifiable in Materialism. All that exists has some right to its existence. We would not deny this. Materialism calls our attention more closely than in former days to the profound interpenetration of our soul-life and our bodily condition, and to the fact that the activity of our mind and will is partly determined by bodily functions,—the circulation of the blood, the action of the nerves, etc.; in a word, to the unquestionably very important influence exercised by material agents, both within and without us, on our mental condition. Materialism may thus teach a lesson, especially to those one-sided idealists whom we were before compelled to blame for looking upon their reason as something always absolutely free in its nature, without believing in their dependence on material influences. This one-sided spiritualism of necessity degenerates in time into its opposite, that is, into Materialism. The latter, then, forms a wholesome counterbalance to that system of philosophy in which the "idea" was all in all, and in which the inquirer was so taken up by speculations of pure reason as not to have time for any consideration of nature. Any future sound system of natural philosophy will have to seek the right course between these two extremes.

The Holy Scriptures, on the other hand, which observe an equal distance between these extremes, fully recognise this truth of the interpenetration of our soul-life with our bodily condition. They point out, with much emphasis, the predominance which, by means of sin, the flesh has attained over the spirit, the constant bondage and danger which the soul incurs from sensual inclinations,—in a word, "the law of sin in the members" (Rom. vii.); and in teaching our natural subjection to the power of sensuality, they bring clearly before our eyes the truth which is involved in the materialistic denial of freewill. But the Holy Scriptures do not lead us into a comfortless fatalism, but show us the way in which the spirit may again attain to predominance and freedom. But it is one thing to acknowledge these bodily influences and another to identify the soul with them,—to deny its separate existence, and thus to tread into the dust man's crown, the basis of all that is truly great and honourable, all that is high and God-like, in and above the world.

If theories of this kind appeared only among morally fickle and degraded nations, whose whole development, or rather misdevelopment, would naturally lead to them, we might, though with deep compassion, look on quietly. But the busy efforts of many, in modern times, to naturalize a materialistic popular philosophy, even on our German soil, must be characterized by every one who is aware of the profound ideality of the German mind, and of German Christian science and education, and who knows how for the last ten centuries Germans have done battle for the highest moral and spiritual treasures of life, *as an act of treason against the original and true nature of German research and science!* To similar opponents in his own time, Plato gave the counsel, "first to *reform*, so that then they might be capable of being taught." The Christian spirit of Germany, inheriting as it does the ideal impulses of the mind of ancient Greece, should give the same answer to the theories we have been considering.

III.—PANTHEISM.

Pantheism derives its name from the motto, ἓν καὶ πᾶν, *i.e.* One and All, which was first brought into vogue by the Greek philosopher Xenophanes. According to this view, God is the universe itself; *beyond* and *outside* the world He does not exist, but only *in* the world. He is the Soul, the Reason and the Spirit of the world, and all nature is His body. In reality, God is everything, and beside him there is nothing. Thus, making God the Soul of the world, Pantheism is distinguished, on the one hand, from Materialism, according to which God and nature are immediately identical; and, on the other hand, from Theism, that is, from the belief in a self-conscious, personal God, who created the world and guides even its most minute details. For the main point of pantheistic belief is that this Soul of the world is *not a personal, self-conscious* Being, who appears in his *totality* in any one phenomenon or at any one moment, so as to comprehend himself or become comprehensible for us, but that it is only the One ever same Essence which, filling everything and shaping everything, lives and moves in all existing things, and is revealed in all that is visible, yet is Itself never seen. Goethe has depicted it in the oft-quoted words:—

> "I rise and fall on the waves of life,
> I move to and fro in action's strife;
> Birth and the grave,—an eternal sea,—
> A web that changes alternately,—
> A life which must ever glow and burn,—
> On the whirring loom of life, in turn
> All these I weave, and the Godhead see
> Clad in a robe of vitality."

The fact that this view of the world is first met with among nations with polytheistic religions, such as the Hindus and Greeks, points to an internal *relationship between Polytheism and Pantheism which is often overlooked.* The two seem opposed; but, when accurately considered, they are in principle the same. Just as, *e.g.*, the ordinary Greeks believed that there was a nymph or a naiad in every tree and in every fountain, and, in addition to the Olympian gods, peopled all nature with innumerable demi-gods; so also, in every being and in every phenomenon the Greek pantheistic philosopher saw a manifestation of the Deity. Pantheism and Polytheism are but a higher and a lower form of one and the same view of the world. The former is the refined, the latter the vulgar mode of deifying nature; the former seeks after unity amid the individual phenomena, the latter stops short at and personifies them.

We have previously alluded to the fact that this One, All-inspiring, yet Unconscious, is characterized by Pantheism in various ways, as the Soul of the world, as universal Substance, as the Moral Order of the world, as Absolute Spirit, etc.[1] The father of occidental Pantheism in modern times was the Jew Spinoza (1632–1677). "I have," says he, "opinions as to God and nature entirely different from those which modern Christians are wont to vindicate. To my mind God is the immanent (that is, the intramundane), and not the transcendent (that is, the supramundane) Cause of all things; that is, the totality of finite objects is posited in the Essence of God, and not in His *Will.* Nature, considered *per se,* is one with the essence of God." According to Spinoza, God is the one universal Substance, in which all distinctions and all isolated qualifications are resolved into unity, to which *per se* we cannot therefore ascribe either understanding or will. He ridicules those who make out that God acts according to a purpose, and look upon the world as a product of the divine will or intellect. "God does not act in pursuance of a purpose, but only according to the *necessity* of His nature. Everything follows from nature with the same logical necessity as that by which the attributes of a thing follow from its idea, or from the nature of a triangle that its three angles are equal to two right angles." This expresses the fundamental view of every form of Pantheism. Even Hegel's conception of God, as the absolute Idea or the absolute Spirit which, in eternal self-movement, proceeds from itself and becomes nature, and then again reverting to Itself, becomes a self-conscious spirit, is, in truth, only another name for the same thing. For Spinoza himself distinguishes between nature "begetting" and "begotten" (*natura naturans et naturata*). The latter is the ever-varying phenomenal world, the "former" the intermittent bourne from which these phenomena take their rise, and into which they sink again.

From this we can already see how much falls to the ground if the personality of God be given up. In the first place, we can no longer acknowledge a creation of the world as a free

[1] There is even a form of Pantheism, or rather of semi-Pantheism, in which the personality of God is to some extent preserved, which looks upon the world *as an efflux from the Deity,* and hence as being of His essence, but not coextensive with Him. Thus, for instance, the doctrine of emanations in the Indian Vedas. But here, too, the personality of God is dangerously compromised by the necessity of the natural process in which these emanations take place. Since, however, this view has no representatives of importance in modern times, we shall confine our attention to the above-mentioned form of Pantheism.

act of the divine Will; since things are "posited in the nature of God, not in His will." Miracles and providence must fare in like manner, and especially the incarnation of God in Christ is left without any basis. It can no longer be looked upon as a fact which took place in this particular Individual, but only as a universal, everlasting and daily-renewed process. There is no longer any place for the freewill of man, and for the ordinary distinction between good and evil. If God has no liberty of action, but works "in accordance with the mere necessity of His nature," man fares no better; he is, indeed, nothing but one form of manifestation of the universal Soul; and the necessity under which the whole universe is developed must also be the standard for every individual thing. Everything is borne along by the one immutable stream of development; all that takes place is the consequence of an absolute necessity; and that which appears to be evil is only a necessary point of transition in the development of good, and therefore is not really evil at all. Finally, it is patent that the immortality of man, and the continuance of personal existence after death, are ideas which must henceforth be rejected. All personal life *must* again resolve itself into the impersonal primal Cause. *Religion itself can no longer be considered a reality.* For I can no more stand in any personal relation to this God than He can to me; I cannot address Him as "*thou*," for He is no personal *I;* I can neither pray to Him nor can I love and trust in Him, for He is only the One, the inflexible and unfeeling power of fate, in which I myself must one day be merged.

Clearly, we may call this an unbiblical idea of God. In the Scriptures God appears from the beginning as One who acts with self-consciousness, who creates and guides the world with definite purposes, whose essence, therefore, is clearly to be distinguished from His creation. He communicates Himself in special revelations, speaks of Himself in the first person, carries out an eternal counsel of love, and therefore cannot be imagined as any other than a personal Being. (Cf. Lect. iv.)

Pantheism is, however, not merely unbiblical, but, like every idea of God which denies His personality, also *scientifically untenable.* Allow me to prove this to you, by exhibiting its chief weaknesses from four different points of view, viz.: (*a*) from *logic,* (*b*) from a *consideration of the world,* (*c*) from *the history of religions,* and (*d*) from *moral and religious consciousness and life.*

(*a*) Let us first ask philosophy and logic. Just as *Atheism* depends on the monstrous assumption that we are acquainted with all the forces in the world; just as *Materialism* presupposes that the *matter of which the world is constituted* is eternal and has always existed;—so also Pantheism depends on *assumptions which are unproved and incapable of proof.* Let us take up Spinoza's *Ethics,* the classical text-book of modern pantheists, which to some extent forms the groundwork of all their systems. Its fundamental assumption is the existence of a universal substance. This substance, with its attributes—*i.e.,* in fact, this idea of God—is presupposed as a thing of course, and from this the further conclusions are deduced with mathematical precision. The thing itself is, however, simply presupposed or assumed to exist, and its acceptance therefore requires as much faith as the utterances of the Scriptures about God. Spinoza does not attempt to investigate whether this idea of God is in itself correct and true. Had he done so, he might have discovered that this universal substance, beside which nothing at all exists, which includes all actual objects as its individual qualifications, is in truth nothing but the highest logical *conception of universality,* in which all individual notions are blended into an undivided unity, and hence that it is merely a subjective idea, but not a real objective existence. But our philosopher immediately assumes, in the most uncritical manner, *that this merely subjective idea is an objective reality,* and that the merely imagined unity of notions in our consciousness is the actually existing unity of all things. Here, then, we see the same *confusion of thought with existence* which we meet with almost at every turn in modern philosophy. "Spinoza's whole system," says a modern critic, "depends on the postulate, that the logic form of the notion and its attributes is identical with the objective form of real existence."

Both Spinoza and all other pantheists are greatly at a loss how to answer the question as to the *origin of cosmical matter;* and on this point it is clearly evident that they ultimately depend on mere assumptions, and those illogical ones. They all of them reject the biblical doctrine, that God created the world, that is, from His own free, loving will called it into existence out of nothing. For, since they cannot conceive of God except in conjunction with the world, they cannot believe that He called it into existence out of its former nothingness; His activity is limited to shaping and organizing *matter already existing.* But if we go on to ask, whence this matter? we are either met with the reply, "it just exists," and are thus required to accept without demur their unproved assumption as a matter of fact; or, in the attempt to explain the origin of the actual world, we are expected to imagine such extraordinary things, that the biblical miracle of creation must appear to every unprejudiced person far more reasonable and conceivable. According to Spinoza, everything actual proceeds from the "begetting nature," which from eternity is incessantly begetting the mundane phenomena. But whence, then, its inexhaustible fulness of force and life? From what source is this vitality constantly renewed? The only reply is to this effect, that the forces of "begotten nature," by the mutual reaction in which they play upon one another, may effect reciprocal renewal; that the forces exhausted in begetting and bringing forth are constantly restored by the reactionary influence of that which is produced. But thus we make "begotten nature" the mother as well as the daughter of "begetting nature," and so are moving in a complete circle. If we demand the origin of the actual world, that is, of the "begotten nature," we are told that "begetting nature" is the ultimate cause; and if we demand the origin of the latter, we are again referred to the "begotten nature," that is, to the very fact of which we seek an explanation.[1] Granted, however, that these forces are constantly renewed by their harmonious mutual action, *must not this harmony be planned by some intelligence?* Is it to be supposed that unconscious nature working by *blind* necessity could have made a computation of this kind? Can our intellect feel satisfied with the idea, that from all eternity there exists a combined play of forces mutually exciting and renovating one another, blind indeed, yet computed with perfect wisdom? The absurdity of

[1] Cf. here also *Zur Verantwortung des christl. Glaubens,* No. II., *Natur oder Gott?* and Gess, *apologet. Beiträge.*

the assumption of an impersonal unconscious God here becomes clearly evident. That by which everything else is realized with absolute wisdom is supposed to be unable to realize itself in conscious thought! What a contradiction!

We do not fare much better under the guidance of Hegel. He teaches us to regard God as the *absolute Idea* which, from endless ages, realizes, inspires, and orders the whole phenomenal world: in other words, as the system of those conceptions on which all thought is necessarily based (*e.g.* being and becoming, force and effect, etc.), and which are supposed to possess reality, since without them all our thought would be null and void. But whence proceeds this absolute Idea? It is not conceived by a personal God, for none such exists. Neither can it conceive itself; for if it did, it would become self-conscious, and thus God would again become personal. How does Hegel get out of the difficulty? He says that the absolute Idea *posits itself* by means of the eternal position and organization of the world. If we inquire, Whence proceeds the world? we are met by the reply, It exists, and is continuously posited by the absolute Idea. And if we ask, Whence comes the absolute Idea, from what is it derived, and in what does its actuality consist? we are told, It is posited in and with the world, and has none but a mundane actuality. Do you see how we are being mocked with a shadow? The world is supposed to be posited by the absolute Idea, and yet the absolute Idea itself has an actual existence only in the world. How, then, can this absolute Idea posit itselt? and how can it be looked upon as the principle which posits the world if itself attains actuality only in the world?

Pantheism desires to realize the Infinite; but because the Infinite always has its actuality only in the Finite, the result is, that Pantheism constantly denies it in its endeavours to realize it. A close examination of this "self-positing" Idea clearly shows *that the pantheistic conception of God is one which destroys itself; for that only which is conscious of itself can posit itself*; but a being which is possessed of *self-consciousness* must also be possessed of *personality*. The impersonal idea of God, in fact, depends upon a hypothesis which on a more thorough consideration will be found to point beyond itself. The way, too, in which Hegel makes the Absolute develope itself is thoroughly illogical. First of all, in its *existence per se* it is a purely immaterial idea; next it emerges into *existence as distinct from itself*, and, distorting itself in time and space, becomes nature; then, from this self-alienation it reverts to itself, and in man attains to *self-existence*, and becomes self-knowing thought, or self-conscious spirit. In this process it is only the *existence per se*, and the existence as distinct from itself, in which the Idea *is* absolutely: *in its self-existence*, on the contrary, it is only in a *finite*, human-psychological form, although evidently the Absolute should include all three forms; that is, God, as a Spirit, must be His own *cause*, His own *object*, and the *subject* which comprehends, knows, and wills Himself.

Besides this, the pantheistic idea of God labours under two other great difficulties. In the first place, it cannot be understood how *personality* can proceed from an *impersonal* principle. We ourselves are persons, that is, we can conceive and determine ourselves; for in this personality consists. And although Spinoza denies the self-determination and freewill of man, still he does not deny his self-consciousness. Whence, then, is this self-consciousness supposed to proceed if the soul of the world, from which we ourselves have emanated, has no consciousness? Can God communicate that which He does not Himself possess, and create forms of existence which transcend His own? Can the effect contain anything which does not exist in the cause? To this one simple question no pantheist has as yet been able to give a satisfactory answer. Moreover, the idea of an *endless and aimless process of development* is illogical and self-contradictory. An endless development, an infinite process, which is for ever approaching its aim, but eternally remains infinitely far from it, is a contradiction with which our intellect cannot be satisfied.

The chief argument which pantheists bring forward against the existence of a personal God is, *that personality cannot be conceived without finite limitations.* Personality, they say, consists in the contraposition of self to another object, a non-ego which forms an insuperable limit to the ego; and hence the conception of absolute, limitless personality involves a direct contradiction. In short, the infinite greatness of God is supposed to be incompatible with His personality. To this we first reply by a question: Is it in our own case the limitation of self by the cosmical non-ego which is the *cause* of our consciousness reflecting upon itself, and thus becoming *self*-conscious or personal, so that without the non-ego our personality would cease to exist? No, this limitation is merely the *occasion;* the original cause of the self-reflection consists in the peculiar constitution of the human subject as a spirit, which points to a primal Spirit-subject as its Creator.

The root of personality in the ego lies in its nature *before* any contraposition to other objects. This contraposition, therefore, does not form the *essence* of the personality, but is only a *consequence* of its inherent nature. "Personality," says a well-known modern philosopher,[1] who has very tellingly answered this objection to the personality of God, "does not depend upon a past or present contraposition of the ego to the non-ego; but, conversely, it consists in an immediate *esse per se,* forms the necessary *prius* of this contraposition wherever it takes place." If, then, even in the finite subject self-consciousness is the result of *its own* action, based upon an *esse per se* which is not dependent on the world, how much less can the absolute Subject, God, by reason of His personality, be considered to be entirely dependent upon, and limited by, externals? Doubtless, in the case of the *finite* spirit as such, the development of personal consciousness can only take place under external influences proceeding from the non-ego; not, however, because it needed the contraposition to an alien object in order to be self-existent, but simply because it does not in this nor in any other respect possess in itself the conditions of its existence. But we do not meet with *this* limitation in the nature of the *Infinite.* "It alone, therefore, is capable of a self-existence, which needs neither initiation nor continuous development by means of anything which is alien to it, but maintains itself in an eternal movement within its own essence." And if we designate the inner personal life of the personal God, the current of His thought, feeling, and will, as one that is eternal and without beginning, never resting, and hence never excited into movement from any state of quiescence, "we do not impose a more difficult task

[1] Lotze, *Mikrokosmos*, i. p. 270 ff.; iii. pp. 565–576.

on the powers of imagination than does any pantheistic or materialistic theory."

And why should the idea of an eternal, absolute Personality be self-contradictory? For the very reason that we are finite, our personality is imperfect. To none but the Infinite *can* we ascribe perfect personality. But more than this, *we are compelled* to do so. Or is not a personality superior to an impersonal object? Is it not a matter of fact, that the greater and higher a being is, the more perfect is his personality? Do we not see the creation struggling towards personality, and mounting step by step through the preliminary stages of the vegetable and animal world, until in man it actually attains to individual personality, and becomes a self-conscious mind? "Whence this universal tendency of all that lives towards personality, if it be not the law of the world; and whence this law, if the Principle of the world is an impersonal one?" And if personality constitutes the pre-eminence of man over the inferior creation, can this pre-eminence be wanting in the highest Being of all? can God, the most perfect Being imaginable, be devoid of personality, the most perfect form of being? Is God indeed the absolute and entirely perfect One, if He be wanting in any one excellence? We do not assert that the most perfect Being as such necessarily *exists* (which was, as we saw, the false conclusion of the ontological argument. But we maintain that personality must belong to perfect *existence* as such (for the existence of God is acknowledged by Pantheism), because otherwise the most perfect form of existence would not have been attained. *So little, therefore, is the idea of God's personality contradicted by His infinite greatness and perfection, that, on the contrary, it is precisely by reason of them that He must be personal.* In fact, the Absolute can only be imagined as the absolute Subject, *i.e.* as the absolute Personality. If the Absolute is to be mere substance, *its idea remains incomplete;* because then the subjective spirit and the finite personality of man appear as something higher.

In support of this we can again appeal to the self-knowledge of man. We have already seen, in our arguments against Atheism, that, from the consciousness of his own conditionality and limitation, man derives the idea of an unconditioned absolute Being. If we now go a step further, and assert that this absolute Being must necessarily be conceived as a *personal* one, we are justified in so doing by the fact, that if man perceives that even a conditioned, relative being like himself is by its self-consciousness raised high above the level of mere nature, he cannot imagine the absolute Being, whom he regards as the creative Cause of himself and all conditioned existence, to be otherwise than possessed of absolute self-consciousness and freedom, *i.e.* as absolute Personality (Delitzsch *ut supra*, p. 69). That which man recognises in himself in a conditioned form, he must ascribe to his original Cause *absolutely*.

We here perceive the *fundamental weakness* of Pantheism,—*its absolute Being is not absolute at all*, just because It is deficient in the point of personality. The latter is not in the case of God, any more than of other beings, a defect, a restrictive limitation; but, on the contrary, a pre-eminence, a perfection, and consequently in the most perfect Being a necessity. Only we must not exaggerate the infinity of God, so as to make Him out to be something entirely colourless, abstract, and utterly devoid of attributes; but we must, notwithstanding all infinity, imagine Him at the same time as a definite Quantity, determined by Himself and not by others, whose self-posited unity is His own act, and in whom personality is the necessary form and determination (but not the limitation) of the infinite being. I say the *necessary* form; for how should that which has in itself no definite centre, and cannot even posit itself in thought and will, have power and stability to posit a world as distinct from itself, and to become the motive power of the universe? Indeed, how can that which in itself lacks all precision and definiteness ever be capable of shaping given cosmical matter into definite forms?

Lastly, the pantheist may object that a self-consciousness cannot most assuredly have an object; it requires *two* distinct subjects, such as are in fact presented to us in the Scriptures, in Father and Son. And further, it is clear that if *two* are required, God and the world cannot be *one*. Thus the above-mentioned objection, after all, recoils against its authors.

(*b*) The next set of arguments to show untenableness of the pantheistic conception of God are taken from a *cosmo-*

logical point of view; that is, from a *consideration of the world.* The well-known *cosmological* proof for the existence of a God is simply enough indicated in Scripture, viz. Heb. iii. 4: "For every house is builded by some man; but He that built all things is God." (Cf. Rom. i. 19–21.) It is sometimes argued from the effect to the cause, thus: All existence is the effect of some cause, which, in its turn, is the effect of another cause; and so on till we arrive at some first cause, which is not the effect of any other, but is itself the cause of its own existence (cf. the Aristotelian expression, "first mover," *πρῶτον κινοῦν*). At other times it is argued from the accidental to the necessary, thus: That there is no accidental—that is, what can be otherwise or not—without a corresponding necessary (used in this form by the school of Leibnitz and Wolff). Since the time of Kant it has been justly held that this argument only proves the existence of an unconditioned essence, eternal and self-subsisting, which forms the groundwork of everything else; but not that this essence must be an *unique and personal* Being.

Nevertheless, this argument should not be unconditionally rejected. That great man Sir Isaac Newton has said: "Although no actual step in this argumentation brings us directly to the knowledge of the First Cause, yet each one carries us constantly nearer to it." And how is this? Because the human spirit can believe of none but the *Spirit*, that it is a self-positing, unconditioned eternal Being. Of every other, that is, of every material existence, the mind asks, and must ask, Whence is it? and cannot rest satisfied with the mere thought that it has always existed. "We are no more able to believe of cosmical substance than, for instance, of the sun, that it is *per se* a necessary eternal being; for this cosmical substance possesses no understanding; it is not spirit" (Gess, *Apologet. Beiträge*, p. 190). If it be an assumption necessary to our intellectual being, that only the Spirit can posit itself and possesses eternal necessary being, it follows that we can only imagine as a *Spirit* that unconditioned Cause of all things, that absolute One, to whom we are led by the cosmological argument. That which is self-existent must also be self-conscious.

But the necessity of postulating self-consciousness as inherent in the Divine Nature is still more evident, if we consider the world not merely as matter, but as the *Cosmos;* that is, as a harmoniously proportioned and well-arranged organism. This brings us to the *teleological* argument, based upon the purpose or aim manifested in the universe, an argument which the results of modern science are rendering more and more important. It is based upon an idea of the creation, as a judiciously arranged whole, tending to a certain aim; and from the regularity and conformity to purpose exhibited in the universe, it argues that there must be an Intelligence which has ordered it according to a set purpose, and thus points us to a self-conscious, personal Spirit. In vain have endeavours been made to dispute the material premise of this argument, viz. that the world's course is arranged after a set purpose. It has been said that we know only a small portion of the universe, and must not therefore presuppose as a matter of course that the same order and wisdom prevail in all its spheres; and moreover, that the conformity to purpose shown in the earthly creation is by no means perfect, but that on the contrary there are many things in it which are purposeless or contrary to their true aim; for the world, human life, and history, form an exhibition of incompleteness and unsuitableness, as is proved by the many evils which exist. But, in the first place, if only a portion of the world be indubitably shown to be full of wisdom, the *whole* universe must be so also; because otherwise this portion would not for one moment be safe from being destroyed by the want of order in the remainder. And does not the fact that we need to meditate upon the world, and cannot help doing so, at once presuppose that the object of our thought must be a Reality full of wisdom? "A world of accident could not be an object of cogitation. If the world around us be not a system of thought, whence comes the need we feel for thinking about it? Why is not man satisfied with the use that beasts make of the world?" The very fact that we are compelled to think about this world is a proof that thoughts are inwrought in it.

With regard to the evil that is in the world, and the want of conformity to purpose shown in certain phenomena, we must first ask whether these incongruities form an intrinsic element of creation, or whether they are a later introduction.

According to Scripture, they are everywhere connected with sin, the destructive effects of which extend even to nature. This, however, by no means does away with the conformity to purpose which marks the universe as a *whole*. Indeed, the manner in which these temporary disturbances of the moral and physical order of the world are ultimately made serviceable to the divine aims is, the longer we consider it, the clearer proof of the greatest wisdom and conformity to plan. Thus the fundamental premise of the teleological argument for the existence of God remains unshaken.[1]

It may be said with more reason, that this argument has something incomplete about it, inasmuch as this conformity to purpose affects only the *form* and not the matter of the world, and that therefore we can derive from it only the idea of an *Architect*, not that of a *Creator*. But let us combine the result of this argument—that there must be a world-organizing intelligence—with that of the cosmological argument, that there must be an absolute Substance, which, on account of its eternity, we can imagine only as a *Spirit*, and we then have the cause in the one of the *matter*, in the other of the *form* of the world. If, then, the latter argument shows us the self-existent, all-creating nature of God, and the former His thinking intelligence which makes infinite plans and wisely carries them out, is there so very much wanting to constitute the idea of a personal Creator of the world? The only question that remains is, whether it is not in any way possible to derive the wisdom prevailing in the world from the agency of some blindly operating cause, some unconscious soul of the world?

In our inquiry after traces of the wisdom which so plentifully dwells and operates in creation, modern science furnishes us with a constantly increasing number of direct proofs, that everywhere a *foreseeing Wisdom, which must as such be conscious of itself and of its action, rules the world.* Indeed, these proofs

[1] The materialistic opponents of the "theory of adaptation to purpose" (Büchner, and others) frequently argue on the erroneous supposition, that theologians who believe in the Bible look upon the world in its present condition as absolutely perfect; and they seek, by various examples, to prove the contrary. If they would take the trouble to turn to Rom. viii. 19 ff., they might see that, long before their arguments, the imperfection of the world in its *present* condition was taught by Scripture.

have rendered Pantheism and Materialism, considered as hypotheses of natural science, simply absurd, and save us the trouble of refuting them from Scripture.[1] Listen, for instance, to what the great chemist, Liebig, says in opposition to these views: "There is no phenomenon in chemistry more wonderful, and none which so effectually strikes all human wisdom dumb, than that which is presented by the processes taking place in the soil of a field adapted for vegetable growth. During the filtration of rain-water through the soil, the earth does not surrender one particle of all the nutritive matter which it contains available for vegetable growth (such as potash, silicic acid, ammonia, etc.); the most unintermittent rain is unable to abstract from it (except by the mechanical action of floods) any of the chief requisites for its fertility. The particles of mould not only firmly retain all matter nutritive to vegetable growth, but also immediately absorb such as are contained in the rain-water (ammonia, potash, etc.). But only such substances are *completely* absorbed from the water as are *indispensable* requisites for vegetable growth; others remain either entirely or for the most part in a state of solution."[2] Thus every drop of rain is in its operation a miracle of conformity to purpose. No less wonderful are the well-known proportions in which oxygen and nitrogen are combined in the air, their continuous production and consumption, and the constant restoration of the due proportions amidst perpetual oscillations. And just as in these matters we see a previously unthought of "great scheme for the harmonious blending of forces," so, too, in modern astronomy. Here it has been demonstrated that those phenomena which were formerly called "disturbances" in the planetary orbits, and consequently appeared to point to some want of order, some little error on the part of the intelligence which arranged the universe, are in reality reciprocally compensating forces, and balance one another according to fixed laws,—thanks to a distribution of masses in our solar system, such as could only be contrived by the piercing mind of a heavenly Arithmetician, whose reckonings even a Lagrange was scarce able to follow.

And how many other facts are there in the world, in re-

[1] Cf. for what follows, Ulrici, *Gott und die Natur.*

[2] *Chemische Briefe*, 1865, p. 387 ff.

spect of which the truly profound natural philosopher must confess that they absolutely cannot be derived from blindly ruling forces of nature, but must point to some intelligence which guides everything according to wise and good purposes! How is it, for instance, that *drift-wood* is cast up on the coasts of Greenland—which stand in such need of it—and not upon those of England and France? How is it that the planets nearest to the sun have no moons, whilst those that are farther removed, and stand in more need of light, have several? How is it that iron is the metal which is found more frequently than any other? How is it that the trade-winds carry the clouds past one portion of America, so that they may gather round the summits of the Andes, and thence descend and moisten by mists and storms those provinces which would otherwise be arid? If it is said that these things are caused by certain natural laws which are hitherto unknown to us, the question still arises, whether every law does not presuppose a lawgiver?

In *organic* nature we meet with still clearer traces of intelligent forethought. Here we see each form of animal and vegetable life with a special function allotted to it, and provided with the requisite structure, but very often in such a way that the *organs make their appearance long before they are needed to exercise their functions.* Thus the leaf attached to the stamen of the lime-blossom remains motionless for months, until the pistil with the fruit, which has in the meantime ripened, becomes disengaged from the bough, and then by the help of this its leafy wing does not descend perpendicularly to the earth, but is carried in graceful spiral curves beyond the spreading roots of the parent trunk. The feathery crowns of the dandelion and the thistle, the teeth of the mammalia, and the wings of birds, all illustrate the same law. And the further we descend amongst the genera of the inferior animal creation, the more frequently are we confronted by phenomena which, to use the words of a Professor of Botany, "can scarcely be described otherwise than as the *predestined preparation for predestined future functions.*" Soo, too, with all the higher animals; the organs of the lungs, the eyes, and the ears are formed in the womb or in the egg long before there is any contact with the outer air, or any affection of the optical or aural nerves. (Notice, too, the complete refutation of Materialism involved in these facts.) And how exactly are these organs formed in respect of the purposes which they will have to fulfil! The eye of the fish is constructed in precise conformity with the laws that govern the refraction of light through water, whilst its gills are perfectly adapted to the nature of its vital element. The sole of the human foot and the palm of the hand are clothed, even in the womb, with a thicker skin than the remainder of the body. Indeed, the wise construction of the human hand has been not inaptly adduced as an irrefutable proof of the existence of God (by Sir Charles Bell in his *Bridgewater Treatise*).

And with what wonderful conformity to purpose is the life of the body carried on? It can only subsist by means of the continuous action of the blood, which in every limb absorbs and carries away all useless or noxious matter; and, on the other hand, brings to it all that is serviceable, by depositing phosphate of lime in the bones, nitrogen in the muscles, carbonic acid in the lungs, etc.,—every kind of matter in the right place, at the right time, and in the correct proportions. Surely, in the face of such clear facts, it is only the blindness of prejudice which can deny that a conformity to plan and purpose governs the various forces. The birth of all animals which live on any sort of food that is not always obtainable, takes place just at those periods of the year in which the food necessary for their young is to be had. Insects, too, do not emerge from the grub until the means of their subsistence are at hand; indeed, they conform to the irregularity of the seasons if the growth of the plants requisite for their food is delayed by bad weather.

How incomprehensible is all this, unless we assume the existence of Him "to whom all His works are known from the beginning of the world!" (Acts xv. 18). Is it not clear that the infinitely rich and yet united system of laws inherent in the whole of natural life—from the harmoniously circling heavenly bodies to the drops of dew upon the field, from the human body to the smallest blade of grass—can only be the work of a foreseeing and therefore self-conscious intelligence? If, however, from the systematic co-operation of all isolated natural forces towards one great *world-harmony*, the necessary deduction be the existence of some all-conditioning, all-governing and spiritual primal Power, then the utter untenableness of Pantheism is clearly evident. Logic proves that it cannot explain the origin of cosmical matter; and natural science reduces it to the utmost perplexity, by demanding an explanation of the cosmic harmony, and of the wondrously beautiful disposition of the component parts in the world's organism. In this matter its perplexity is twofold. First, it cannot point out *the origin of the individual forms of life* in the world. The origin of our own personality from the impersonal mundane Soul remains, as we showed above, a mystery; but the same remark applies to the origin of organic life generally. The natural science of the present day shows that at the earliest period nothing but inorganic life existed, and confesses its inability to conceive how organic life can be developed from inorganic matter. The pantheist, however, is, in accordance with his principles, compelled to maintain that this did take place. For if nature is the ultimate cause of everything, if everything is developed by necessity in an eternal circle, then no individual form of life can be isolated from all other entities by a special act of creation, or produced by a miracle; on the contrary, everything must form part of one firmly-linked chain of cause and effect. Therefore, the organic must take its origin spontaneously from the inorganic, and man must descend from some species of ape. Thus Pantheism stands in complete contradiction to all sound investigations of natural science.[1]

In the next place, Pantheism cannot explain the *connection* existing between the individual cosmical beings, *i.e.* the laws that govern them and combine them into a *Cosmos.* This marvel of wisdom and conformity to purpose, these predestined preparations for future activity, this magnificent scheme of harmonious adaptation of forces both in animated and inanimate nature,—all this has been produced, according to Pantheism, by an unconscious Wisdom, by a Soul of the world infinitely intelligent, it is true (for even Spinoza attributes thought to

[1] According to the latest observations of Pasteur, which are confirmed by the French Academy of Science, the assumption of a *generatio spontanea* or *æquivoca*, *i.e.* that organic life should spontaneously spring from inorganic matter, must henceforth be considered as scientifically disproved.

the universal Substance), but still impersonal. An *unconscious Wisdom!* An *infinite Intelligence devoid of self-consciousness!* Grasp who may such an idea! It is a *self-contradicting conception,* just as much as a wooden iron, or a quadrangular circle![1] For if, as infinite Intelligence, God knows everything, He must also know Himself, and must be a Person, since "the conception of the Ego is the root of all knowing."

The objection may, however, be raised, that the possibility of a wisdom devoid of consciousness is evident from the workings of *animal instinct* and the origin of human *language.* Many animals, such as the spider, the bee, the beaver, etc., do, indeed, without any clear consciousness, make structures eminently adapted to their purpose, and the genius of a people produces its own language, without any preconceived plan and any clear intention, and yet languages are replete with well-defined rules and laws. This objection is very plausible; nevertheless it proves nothing in favour of an absence of consciousness on the part of the mundane Soul. It cannot prove this, unless these wisely planned workings of animal instinct really proceed primarily from *the beast itself.* But this is not the case. On the contrary, instinct is *implanted* in the beast as a result of its organization, as *e.g.* the faculty of singing in the singing bird; and faculties of this kind are not produced by the animal itself, but are derived from some other source. In like manner, the peculiar features of a language arise from

[1] Hence, also, the contradictions in which pantheistic naturalists entangle themselves when endeavouring to explain the process of creation. Burmeister, for instance, has shown with praiseworthy pains that the creation of the various animal species always began with a type of the whole genus, which united in itself the qualities subsequently distributed among the different species. Hence he, too, acknowledges a "united plan, a definite law unalterably observed in the development of the animal world;" but at the same time he maintains that this law is only the result of the forces working in matter, and that as they altered, that which was produced by them assumed another form. But if these forces not only work, but also "alter" in conformity with "a united plan," so that they do not constantly produce similar formations, but such as are progressively more and more perfect; and if all this appears to be based upon some distinct universal conception, does it not evidently follow that it is not a number of forces *blindly* acting upon the matter with which they fortuitously meet, but only an intelligent and conscious Power operating according to *plan and conception,* which, by means of these natural forces and materials, has called forth the succession of animal species, and has guided the whole process of creation? Pantheism is here convicted from its own lips!

the bodily or mental constitution which the people has by nature; and this, too, is a gift conferred upon it. Hence, in reality, the wisdom which manifests itself in animal instinct and in the construction of languages is not derived from the beast itself, nor from the genius of the nation, "but from that Power to which both animals and men owe their organization. It is therefore impossible to argue, from the deficiency of self-consciousness in animal instinct, that the ultimate Cause which organizes every kind of life can operate unconsciously." A cleverly-constructed machine works well by itself, and produces things serviceable for the purpose intended; but this is a merit due, not to the machine, but to him who constructed it wisely, with a certain end in view. It works only with borrowed wisdom and forces implanted in it by man. Thus God implants in organic nature certain instincts and faculties, which then produce unconsciously things wondrously adapted for their purpose. But from this it by no means follows that the Creator, who conferred these gifts on animals or men, did so *unconsciously*.

No, it is a proposition clear and irrefutable as the axioms in mathematics, that the primal Reason, from which all that is rational in the world proceeds, cannot be blind, but must be self-conscious. "So long," says a prominent philosopher of the present day, "as the position of natural science allowed us to consider original matter to be a continuous substance extending into infinity, it was possible to take a pantheistic view of the spiritual Power governing it, as though this were inherent in matter, and formed it continually into the shapes which nature exhibits, *i.e.* as though it were merely the Soul or Spirit of the world. But since natural science has demonstrated that matter consists of an infinity of separate and different atoms, *it is scientifically impossible to cling to Pantheism as a theory of the world without betraying an utter want of reflection.*" If I shuffle promiscuously a thousand letters of the alphabet, is it likely that some happy accident will group them into a glorious poem, teeming in every line with intellect and beauty? You cannot believe this. Neither can you, then, believe that a *Cosmos*, such as presents itself to our eye, with more wisdom and beauty the longer we consider it, is the product of matter, of forces and atoms unconsciously meeting and combining with one another! At the present day the only choice left to us is between this extreme Materialism, which declares the origin of the world to be an accidentally fortunate combination of atoms, and the belief in the creative action of a spiritual, self-conscious, original Being, who governs according to purposes and ideas, that is, in the personal God. This, my honoured hearers, is the final dilemma put to you also: you must believe either in an accident which explains nothing at all, and puts a stop to all scientific investigations, or in a personal Creator!

The very same alternative is laid before you in respect to the whole *history of the world.* Its wonderful course is as much a proof for the existence of a wise and holy God who guides everything according to conscious aims and ends, as is the creation, for the existence of a wise and omnipotent God. "The wisely ordered march of history," says a modern apologist, "through the midst of all the turmoil brought about by the arbitrary conduct of so many millions of free men, can only be explained as resulting from the all-ruling providence of a personal God. It would be impossible, in the face of human freewill, for the unconscious wisdom of nature to retain the mastery over the course of events." Every individual personal being would possess in his freedom a power greater than all that of the impersonal mundane Soul, and could, by a single action, confound all the operations of the latter. *Nothing but a person can rule over and guide persons.* The rule of an impersonal power over personal beings is just as *impossible* for the one as it is *unworthy* for the other. We need not pursue this further, for it will suffice to refer each one to his own history. If God exists, then man, the being formed in His image, may demand that He should make Himself personally felt. And has He not already done so in our individual experience? With one who denies this, we cannot of course dispute further; but such an one will find his whole life one great unsolved enigma!

(*c*) This brings us to the *historical* arguments against Pantheism. These we will touch very shortly, and only from one point of view, viz. that of the *history of religions.* It is a matter of fact that, even in polytheistic religions, the presentiment of the One personal God has not entirely faded away. Only to take one instance, we should scarcely find even a Negro in Africa who denies the one God, the Creator of heaven and earth. The history of religions is making it more and more evident at the present day, that in the most ancient traditions of all nations there are to be found scattered traces and features, distorted but still recognisable, of a primitive revelation of the One personal God. But more than this, traces are not wanting that the growing darkness of superstition is sometimes painfully felt by the heathen as a *state of degradation* from the more elevated stage of that primitive revelation.[1] We do not consider this as a *direct* argument against Pantheism, but we take note of the fact that the testimony of Scripture respecting the original revelation of the One personal God is increasingly confirmed by the history of religion. But if Polytheism is shown to be an obscuration of the *original* revelation of God, then Pantheism, its reverse, must be the same. But the history of religions supplies us with a direct argument against Pantheism, in the fact that all religions show an *involuntary impulse towards forming a personal idea of their gods.* Nations cannot imagine their gods otherwise than as persons; and this is what Cicero means when he says: "All of us of every nation, following a necessity implanted in our nature, cannot ascribe to the gods any other shape than that of man." This religious feature is universal in the most ancient as well as in the most modern forms of heathenism. Even in the religions of nature the deified natural forces are invariably personified. The hymns and prayers addressed to them (cf. those of the Indian *Vedas*) presuppose their personality. Even the sacrifice intended to propitiate the fetish gives to it "a background of personality." So, too, the supreme God of the Chinese, who was subsequently worshipped by their philosophers as merely the impersonal soul of the world, was, according to modern investigations, not merely

[1] Cf. for instance (in Burckhardt's *Missionsbibliothek*, II. B., South Africa, p. 12), the confession of the Hottentots at the beginning of the 18th century, "that it had been related to them by their fathers how their ancestors had sinned so dreadfully against the great God that He had hardened the hearts of them and of their posterity, so that they could no longer know nor honour nor serve Him rightly." Also *Ergänzungsheft*, ii. 1868, p. 10. For what follows, cf. also Plath, *Die Relig. der alten Chinesen*, 1863, and Delitzsch *ut supra*, p. 53 ff.

originally imagined as a person, but is even at the present day practically personified as the Higher Emperor, Shang-Ti. All mythologies are based on the idea of personal historical intercourse between gods and men. Is not the conclusion a fair one, "that man *is inwardly compelled to think of the Godhead as a personal Being*, and that he cannot, at any stage of religious progress, get rid of this idea?" The objection that "it is a form of thought peculiar to the human mind to represent as persons all the unknown, secret causes of natural phenomena," in no way lessens the importance of this unique fact. For we clearly see that, following a necessary internal law which has been universally confirmed by history, man cannot look upon any of the beings which he ranks *above* himself, and with whom he stands in some religious connection, except as *personal* beings; because otherwise they would rank *under* him, and could not enter into reciprocal intercourse with him.

From these facts we draw the conclusion that, according to the unanimous testimony of religious history, Pantheism is nothing but an artificial system of philosophical abstractions, which keeps back, subtilizes, and generalizes the original and ever-recurring instinct that leads man to yearn after a personal God, and personal intercourse with Him. We now proceed to show that this internal law cannot be slighted without the infliction of a heavy injury on our moral and religious consciousness.

(*d*) This we do by means of the *moral and religious* arguments against the pantheistic idea of God. In the first place, we ask the pantheist, *Whence proceeds the conscience, the moral law implanted in us?* Whence this "categorical imperative" which makes itself directly felt and recognised in our soul? Does it not point to some absolute law-giving Will operating in us? Surely the *moral* law is something entirely different from the *natural* law. The latter is unconsciously carried out by nature; that is, it fulfils itself. But the law which lives in the conscience is not fulfilled until man has become conscious of it. And whilst the former law *must* be fulfilled, the latter, though requiring its fulfilment on the part of man, yet allows him *free* self-decision. The moral law cannot, therefore, be derived from nature; and if man discovers this law inherent in him, he cannot be a mere product of natural life. (This argument likewise holds good against Materialism.) Indeed this law may even contradict the natural law; for in some cases we feel ourselves bound to obey the moral law *in the teeth* of all our natural inclinations. If a man is hungry, and sees bread before him, the impulses of nature bid him appropriate it; but the moral law says, "Thou shalt not steal!" And if he disobeys the latter, he cannot avoid the painful feeling that he has thereby degraded himself. How is this? Why is this moral law permitted so frequently to contradict the laws of nature? And, lastly, *whence proceeds our religious consciousness*, which, as we have already seen [under the head (*c*)], demands fellowship with the personal God, and which, if the pantheistic idea of God were correct, would be mere self-contradiction, a lie, a mockery, and an eternally unappeased longing? No pantheist has as yet been able to give a satisfactory answer to these questions.

We are probably met with the reply, that "all this is connected with the *moral order of the world*;" which is supposed to be the origin, support, and end of moral consciousness in man. But this is a mere phrase, and does not explain anything. Whence does the moral order of the world proceed? Does it not, as much or still more than the conformity to law in external nature, presuppose a thinking, self-conscious Lawgiver, a free and holy Will, and a personal Creator and Ruler of the universe? Is our intellect again to acquiesce in the idea, that this moral order has arisen spontaneously, or has always existed? Supposing even it existed without any ordainer or lawgiver, would it by itself be able to implant the moral law in us, and to *maintain its authority?* We have already seen that the mere abstract idea of Goodness is no effective motive for doing good, and that it cannot operate with vital power unless it is seen realized in some *personality*, and thus takes hold of the heart. We ask: Is it possible that a mere law or universal order, an utter abstraction which it is difficult even to express, should draw forth a love from man which would prove an adequate motive for moral conduct, even in cases where such would require painful self-denial? Indeed, can such a law even exact the necessary respect from man's freewill? Practical experience answers this inquiry with a dear and unanimous—No. It teaches us that these effects can only follow when the law proceeds from, and is represented by, concrete personal beings. If, therefore, the moral ideas which man detects in his conscience are not to remain powerless and without effect, they must be derived from a personal Will; a living God must be their source and exponent, not a mere law. Where in all the world will a mere law obtain the respect due to it, unless it is supported by *persons* endowed with authority? And, in like manner, nobody would care for the moral law if it were supported by nothing but the "order of the universe," and not by the personality of a holy God. The same rule, as above, holds good here also, that only a personal will can rule persons; a free-will does not submit to the mere framework of a spontaneously generated mundane order.

We see that the *pantheistic idea of God* cannot afford any support to our moral life, inasmuch as *it is unable either to explain the moral law or enforce it.* It may, however, be shown still more simply that it *must lead even to the destruction of all morality;* and this is the last and heaviest charge which we bring forward against it.

The reason is this, that Pantheism (just as Materialism) is at last compelled, if consistent with its own principles, *to deny the freedom of man, his responsibility, and even the distinction between good and evil,* by which means all morality is done away with. According to the pantheistic view, the world is moving in a circle formed by an inexorably firm chain of cause and effects, one thing resulting from another with iron necessity. Man is no exception to this rule. He stands, according to Spinoza, as a link in the endless series of determining causes. In his spirit there is no such thing as free-will; for each act of his will is predetermined by some other cause, and this again by another, and so on *ad infinitum.* Whatever the will does, it cannot help doing. "Men believe that they are free agents, simply because they are conscious of their actions only, and not of the causes by which these actions are determined." The ideas of the distinction between good and evil are based upon an error. Nothing is in itself either good or evil; these are purely relative and subjective ideas, "mere prejudices, which arise from arbitrary conceptions formed by men of the standards at which things and actions are to aim, whilst in nature nothing really takes place which can be imputed to her as a fault." As soon as we turn our glance away from details and direct it towards the whole, we recognise that everything, even so-called evil, works together for the perfection and beauty of the whole. Truly, these utterances of Spinoza in his *Practical Philosophy* leave nothing to be desired as regards perspicuity. They completely destroy all morality. Whatever I do, I do it of necessity, and so it is right, seemly, and profitable for the whole!

Other pantheists, it is true, may not have admitted these awful conclusions quite so bluntly as Spinoza; but if they wish to be consistent with their principles, they are all inexorably compelled to do so, and hence in the case of each one of them they are more or less openly manifest. Theologians of the pantheistic school cannot do otherwise than represent the fall of man as a necessity, and with human freedom they must deny human guilt. Statesmen and national jurists of pantheistic opinions, if they remain faithful to their principles, must constantly allow the freedom of the individual to be merged in the mechanism of the commonwealth as a whole. The rights of the individual person can never be duly recognised by those who hold such opinions. Take *e.g.* Hegel's teachings as to law and government, and see how he utterly sacrifices the will of the individual to that of the commonwealth. The outcome of such doctrines is best described in Hegel's own words, when he says that "the world's history is the Golgotha of the Absolute Spirit; the fearfully tragic slaughter-house in which all individual life and happiness is sacrificed, in order that the universal ideal of humanity may progress." Under the dominion of a blindly ruling Soul of the universe, which is but another name for necessity itself, there is no room left for any being in the world to exercise freedom. Everything is swallowed up in the universal substance, and is ruled by the law of its development. The course of the world necessarily involves the life and death of all that we see. Everything has existed long since, and will again exist; everything remains as it always was, unaltered amidst all changes. Aimless and colourless, the current of the world's life eternally sweeps onward, and only to our short-sighted vision does it appear bright with different hues. And we, ourselves, mere specks that of necessity emerge only again to subside below this current, cannot in truth, either by our best or our worst actions, tinge the world's development by any difference or peculiarity of character, nor by any deed of abiding merit or demerit. *What a comfortless view of the world is this; how unworthy of man, how paralyzing, nay, destructive to all his moral powers!* Not only does it deprive us of any personal immortality, since the spirit after death is to be absorbed into the universal soul of the world, but, even in this life, when it deprives man of his freedom, it robs him of all joyfulness in action, of his responsibility, and hence of all moral value! This is the last and the heaviest accusation that we must bring against Pantheism, just as above against Materialism, that it destroys the whole ethical and spiritual dignity of man, and does away with all morality and all religion. Not only is it unable to satisfy the inmost need of our hearts, which long after personal intercourse with God, but it also robs our moral action of its last support. Pantheism, therefore, harmonizes neither with the world nor with ourselves; neither with the cosmical order nor with our reason; neither with the history of the world and religion nor with our conscience and the religious need implanted in our hearts. It is an evident contradiction of all these things.

Here, too, we see the great truth, that the *personality of God and the moral personality of man must stand or fall together.* If personality is not essential to the nature of God, it cannot be acknowledged in its full dignity in man; it is not a complete truth, for it is everywhere only transient in its character. Lessing says most justly, "If I am, God is also; He may be separated from me, but not I from Him." But for this very reason the converse holds good also. If God is not, then I am not; if He is no person, I can no longer maintain my personality. The man who denies the personality of God undermines the foundation of his own. Pantheism, in doing this, *swallows up God in man and man in God.* Well and truly may a modern philosopher say, "It is clearly evident that pantheistic and atheistical philosophy are alike based upon principles which are irrational and unphilosophical." A pious man, three thousand years ago, well knew this, though he expressed it somewhat more simply. "The *fool* hath said in his heart, There is no God" (Ps. xiv. 1).

Let me compress the result of all that I have said into a few words of advice. If you meet one who denies the personality of God, ask him the following questions: (1.) Whence does the cosmical substance proceed which you suppose to be shaped by the Soul of the universe? How can God produce this substance if He Himself is only produced and realized by it? Is not, therefore, its existence an unproved assumption? How is it possible that personality should proceed from the impersonal, and that God should create something which He Himself is devoid of? In fact, can the most perfect Being be deficient in anything that we His creatures possess? (2.) How is it conceivable that the Soul of the universe, which orders and guides everything with astonishing wisdom and according to evidently preconceived purposes, should form conceptions of everything else, but not of Itself? (3.) Why do all nations, both in ancient and modern times, always imagine their God or gods to be personal? (4.) If everything be a product of nature and the laws of nature, whence come our conscience, the moral law, and religious consciousness? And where is there any room left for my freedom of will and responsibility—for the dignity of my moral personality—if all things follow one another in an endless circle under the pressure of an internal necessity, and are connected in one firmly-linked chain of cause and effect? Until a pantheist can give you satisfactory answers to these questions—and you need not fear that this will be very readily done—you are perfectly justified in calling his stand-point *scientifically untenable.*

Unquestionably, however, there is *something true* even in Pantheism. There is something grand in the idea of the *unity of all being*, and of the connection of our life with the whole life of the universe. And this fundamental view is by no means entirely unjustifiable. The affinity between spirit and nature is a deeply seated one, and the laws of the two realms correspond to each other. They have one origin, and tend towards one goal of consummation. In man, too, the dualism between nature and spirit is to be done away with when he arrives at the condition of perfection. Hence a oneness of feature runs through the whole development of the physical and moral world, and the spirit in a thousand ways recognises itself and its laws in the objective reason which it meets with in nature. But the wrong lies in stopping short at this one universal life, just as if *it* were the origin of all things, that is, God Himself, instead of raising our minds to the recognition of that absolute Reason which must at the same time be absolute Will and Self-consciousness, *i.e.* to the One to whom this unity of being and becoming in the world directly points us as the origin and the goal of everything.

Further, it is the special effort of Pantheism to refer everything which exists and occurs to the direct agency of God, and to show its dependence on Him. It cannot imagine anything which is not an efflux of divine power, and therefore finds God in everything. And this, too, contains a great truth, viz., that it is utterly impossible to imagine the life of the world, its origin and continuance, both as a whole and in its smallest details, as severed from God, seeing that He must needs be *omnipresent* and *everywhere active.* This much may be learned from Pantheism by deists, rationalists, and all those who at the present day would attribute to the world a life and self-development independent of God's direct influence. But the *will,* the *activity* of God, is one thing, and His very *essence* is another. Although the world, down to its very smallest particle, may be entirely dependent on the former, it does not follow that the latter should be merged in and coextensive with the world. On the contrary, true and rational as is the first proposition, it is just as irrational to make out that God, the first Cause of the world, is Himself dependent on it, and only exists in the totality of the world's being; in other words, to deny His supramundane existence, and therefore His personality, just as if the Being who is the Cause of all things must not for this very reason be something different from the things caused!

Another truth expressed by Pantheism is this, that even evil is not to be thought of as entirely without the pale of God's government. There can be no power whatever which is not subject to Him or entirely independent of His control and guidance. He foresees evil and allows it; indeed, when it is once in existence, He makes use of it for His own purposes in the government of the world. But it is an error on this account to attribute the authorship of evil to the will of

God, as if the absolutely existent and eternal Being must not at the same time be the absolutely good and holy One. It is also wrong, by thus referring the origin of evil to the Divine Will, to do away with the freedom of man and to efface the distinction between good and evil, just as if the indelible self-certainty of man in respect to his moral freedom and responsibility, as well as his feeling of guilt, could be a lie.

Finally, there is something true in the pantheistic view, that the conception of personality is too limited and finite to be applied to God; for we cannot conceive of God *only as a single Person.* The fulness of His Being overflows the limits of this conception. But it is wrong, on this account, entirely to give up the idea of personality. There is a conception of God which leaves room for the infinite fulness of life in Him, and yet maintains the infinite prerogative of personality. This, as we shall see, is accomplished by the Christian doctrine of the *triune* personality of God. The true conception of God must as decidedly acknowledge and embrace these elements of truth as exclude the false inferences drawn from them. And such we shall show to be the case with the teaching of the Christian faith.

There now remains for our consideration one more conception of God which acknowledges His personality, and yet, from a scriptural point of view, must be rejected.

IV.—DEISM AND RATIONALISM.

This is in many respects the antithesis of Pantheism. According to Pantheism, God exists only *in* the world as its soul; according to Deism, He exists only *above* the world as a personal Spirit: by Pantheism, God and the world are regarded as absolutely inseparable; by Deism, as absolutely severed, and as not merely different, but divided one from the other. God is for the deist a *personal* Being, who, after creating the world by His will, now acts towards it like an artificer with a finished machine, which mechanically pursues its natural course according to the laws laid down for it, and no longer requires the immediate assistance or interference of its maker. The master shipbuilder has completed and launched his ship, and now leaves her to herself and her own crew. The clockmaker has completed and wound up his clock, which now goes of itself without any more need of him.

The being, personality, and supramundane nature of the Deity (hence the vague and awkward term "Deism"), and the creation of the world by Him, are thus acknowledged; while, on the other hand, any *continuous active presence of God in the world, and any living interposition in its affairs, are denied.* The world has outgrown its leading-strings, and, emancipated from divine control, is now left to itself. There is no special *providence: miracles* are an impossibility. Everything takes place in harmony with natural laws which are implanted in the universe, and suffer no alteration whatsoever. This is the chief characteristic of the deistical theory. For the pantheist, God is too near to seem to be above him; for the deist, too far off to be recognised as exercising any direct rule over the world which He has made. Relegating God, as it were, to the outermost confines of being, he seeks to keep Him as far off as possible, in order to follow the light of natural reason, unmolested by the cross-lights of a higher revelation. The first and immediate consequence of this is, that every special *manifestation of God,* no matter what, must be denied, all supernatural elements in the Christian belief, even those involved in the Person and Work of Christ, must be excluded, and anything in Scripture bearing on these points must be explained away by a reference to natural causes.

In all essentials, then, Deism coincides entirely with that which was formerly denominated *Naturalism*;[1] for it pronounces the laws of nature to be adequate to the continuous existence of the world, and natural religion to be the only essential form of belief, even in connection with Christianity. It likewise agrees in principle with what is called *Rationalism,* the essence of which consists in the position that Reason is not merely the formal, but also the material, principle of

[1] At the present day, in Germany, "Naturalism" and "Materialism" are used almost as synonymous terms for the theory which derives from the operation of the laws of nature only, not merely the continuance, but the very existence and even the origin of the world; whilst in England, for instance, "Naturalism" still retains its original meaning, and is defined as "the denial of any divine rule and providence extending to individuals" (cf., for instance, *Pearson on Infidelity*).

religion, and supreme arbiter over the whole substance of the Christian faith (cf. Lect. II. sec. 1 and 3).

This theory is, however, by no means new. We meet with something like it even in Greek philosophy, both in the mechanical interpretations of nature given by the *atomists* and Anaxagoras' notion of a world-forming intelligence absolutely separated from all matter, as well as in the teaching of Epicurus, that the gods can take no interest in human affairs. But it was first reduced to a real system in the seventeenth and eighteenth centuries by the English (and Dutch) "free-thinkers," "minute philosophers," and "deists," whose common principle might be described as the elevation of natural religion, on the basis of free thought and inquiry, to the position of supreme arbiter of all religion that claimed to be positive, as a denial of any special divine providence, of miracles, and generally of every direct interposition by God in the course of the world. Thus, for instance, Chubb taught that God held Himself aloof from human concerns; and that whatever happens to man is only the dependent result of second causes. In like manner, Bolingbroke maintained that God regards the universe as a whole, and not its individual parts; and that there is no divine intervention as to details either in nature or morals. In the Germany of the last generation, these rationalistic tendencies were prevalent among theologians and educated persons generally; but in such various shades and modifications as to the views taken of Divine Providence, and the chief of all miracles, the Person of our Lord, that we must be on our guard against comprehending them all in one category. While some of those speculations were not far removed from the Christian and scriptural ideas of God and Providence, others approximated very closely to Pantheism. But in general, it is a characteristic principle of Rationalism not to recognise any special divine interposition in the course of this world or the concerns of men, to explain in a manner comprehensible to natural reason everything in Scripture which implies such interposition, all miracles and special revelations, and so to eliminate the supernatural element generally.

At the present time, both in German and English theology, this principle has but few representatives, but reckons a proportionately larger number among Swiss (Zurich), French (Strasburg), and Dutch (Leyden and Gröningen) theologians, while the great body of educated laymen, and especially of the students of modern natural science, are confessedly under its influence. In spite of all the attempts which Rationalism has made, and is still making, to find for its theories a scriptural basis, we scarcely need any justification if we class its theological conceptions among the *non-biblical.* In every page, indeed, the Bible teaches a direct divine agency in the world, a providence extending to the minutest details (the very hairs of our head being all numbered), and a constant dependence of the world on God for its existence and guidance; points which, in the next lecture on the Scriptural Idea of God, will come before us in more detail.

But we affirm that this rationalistic conception of God is not merely unscriptural, but also impossible and false; and we maintain *the untenableness of its positions from a scientific point of view,*—in a word, the irrationality of Rationalism. In proof of these assertions, we may pursue a like course to that we followed in the case of Pantheism, and consider in succession the main arguments which can be adduced from a consideration of the nature of *God,* the *world,* and man's *moral* condition, against the fundamental positions of Deism and Rationalism. Having previously become acquainted to some extent with the weakness of Rationalism in its denial of revelation as such, and having also to submit hereafter the general question as to the possibility of miracles to a separate discussion, we need not now do more than take a brief view of its general principle as to the position it assigns to God in the world.

Deism, falsely named as it is, is also in its principle *an unnatural combination of conflicting elements,* adopting some things even from Atheism, when it regards the world, as now constituted, as existing without God or any divine influence, others from Materialism and Pantheism, when it seeks to derive all that takes place in the world from natural causes inherent in it, and to exclude all exercise of supernatural power on the part of God. So far, Deism shares in and suffers from the fundamental faults of the three other systems. *But it is itself more inconsistent than they,* attempting to make an essential distinction between the creation and that which followed it. During the creative process, the world, according to Deism, was not without God, but completely dependent on Him as its creating and shaping Principle; but ever since it has been left alone and independent. While creation was going on, God was interested in the work down to its smallest details, but has since withdrawn Himself into His own solitude, and has henceforth had an eye for the whole only, and not for any of its parts. During creation, God wrought miracle after miracle, creation itself being the greatest of all miracles; but no sooner was creation finished, than He tied, as it were, His own hand, and made any subsequent act of miraculous power a thing impossible. He who could once call worlds into being cannot now, by an act of miraculous healing, restore to health the life of a single invalid. What do we gain by these evident inconsistencies? Only this, that the world's enigma assumes now for us *three* forms, each more puzzling than the other. We no longer ask merely, as in respect to the God of Holy Scripture, How was creation possible? but we have to put the further question, How was it possible that God, *having created, should leave the world thus created alone?* How is its present independent continuance possible? And, lastly, how is it possible that God *should maintain* towards the world now an attitude so entirely different from that which He took in the beginning? At this point the greatest difficulties arise, in respect both to the nature and action of God Himself and the world's position towards Him.

(*a*) Let us, in the first place, consider for a moment the difficulties connected with the nature of God Himself. Our main objection to Deism on this ground is, *that God is thereby made to forfeit His own divinity.* Is He not, we ask, as the most perfect Being, necessarily the one Being who is ever consistent with Himself? How can I assume in Him a distinction between action and rest, such as would divide His conduct towards the world into *two contradictory positions?* How could this harmonize with the doctrine of His eternal unity and perfection? Labour with Him is rest, and rest labour; that which to us is sundered, is in God one and the same. Even in the rest of the seventh day His action goes on, for "God," we read, "blessed the seventh day, and hallowed it." The whole of Scripture is pervaded by the view that God the Creator is still continuously at work (John v. 17). Any one who makes an absolute severance between the divine action and the divine rest, *draws down the infinite Godhead into the changing revolutions of the finite!*

How much is this the case in the system we are considering! How unworthy and how degrading in this respect are the conceptions which Deism and Rationalism form of God's relation to the world! After only "six days'" work, He gives Himself up to a *state of rest,* and so remains, without giving Himself any further trouble about its details, content to take an occasional glance, as if from a shrine on the confines of the universe, at that universe as a whole! Where else will you find an artificer who conducts himself with so much indifference towards his own finished work? It will hardly be objected that, as it is unworthy of a great ruler to trouble himself about the insignificant details of government, so it is unworthy of God to extend His direct guidance and providence to smaller matters. Just the contrary! A great ruler is in nothing greater than in his power of dealing with details that appear most trifling. It is only inferior magnates who affect importance by looking down upon small matters; the truly great neither despise nor are indifferent to anything.

If, however, it be asserted that God troubles Himself only with *moral* and not with *physical* details, it is forgotten surely that the two are most closely connected. How often does the most trivial matter, the most insignificant event in the natural world, become either the occasion or the means of bringing about something morally good or evil! If God regards the latter, He cannot fail to pay attention to the former; if He looks to the result, He cannot be indifferent to every factor which helps to accomplish it. And does not, then, all nature ultimately tend towards some *moral* aim? Was it not *moral* motives which moved God to frame the world exactly as He did, and not in any other way, and to assign to everything its proper place? In a true *cosmos,* that is, in an harmoniously developed organism, the smallest portion has a direct significance in the arrangement of the whole. If, then, the world, in the divine idea of it, is arranged on moral principles, as Rationalism is never weary of maintaining, then everything that takes place therein is of moral significance, and claims and needs some attention from God.

And this attention must be not merely passive, but active and lively. Are there now operating in the world not merely natural powers, but creatures endowed with moral *freedom*, who, through their action, may every moment disturb, and actually do disturb, the divine order and harmony of the whole, at least in isolated points, and can it be supposed that God should quietly look on without any counteraction on His part? If, as the Holy One, He must be conducting the world towards some kind of holiness as its consummation, and yet man is allowed the freedom of opposing this consummation with all his powers, if every moment it is being counteracted in some way by sin in the case of numberless individuals, can it be supposed that God is to remain unsympathetic and inactive? Does He not owe it to Himself and to the world to suffer nothing to remain exempt from His guidance, or to occur without His permission, by a holy rule of providence to set some limits to the misuse of human freedom, and to neutralize some of its pernicious workings by a wholesome counteraction? And will not such a providential government come in contact in a thousand ways with the processes of the physical universe, and necessarily react upon them, as indeed is the case with all human activity?

Human freedom and its correlative, the holiness of the divine will and law, render necessary a continual and active interposition on the part of Divine Providence in the course of the world's development. It may be said that, in the laws of the world's "moral order," we have an adequate security for the due maintenance of that order, and the gradual conducting of the universe to its final consummation. But that is the same error that we have previously censured in Pantheism, assuming that mere law, *i.e.* something impersonal, can control persons and counteract free-will. Either this law, this moral order, is so inflexible in its nature that it *cannot* be broken, in which case it is all up with human freedom and with the whole distinction between right and wrong, that is, with morality itself; or this moral order *can* be broken, and is, in fact, constantly threatened and opposed by the operation of creaturely free-will: in that case, how can it be maintained, except by constant interpositions on the part of God restoring it when impaired, or making preparations for the future removal of the disturbances introduced by sin? In other words, so far from a "moral order of the world" rendering the living activity of God in the world superfluous, some such interference is, on the contrary, rendered necessary by its very existence.

We see that the most fundamentally essential attribute of God, His holiness, is not compatible with the denial of a divine providence actively extended to every individual. But God would lose in like manner all His other attributes too, if condemned to a repose so unworthy of Him, in the face of the continuous developments of the universe. There lies the world with all its sins and sorrows, and God Himself may not stir a finger to come to its help! Where, in this case, are His *goodness* and *faithfulness*, His *mercy* and *pity?* How am I still to look on Him as *love*, when this love has long since ceased to reveal itself to its creatures? What is to become of His *omnipresence*, if He can never actively manifest it within the sphere of creation? What does His *wisdom* profit me, and how should His *omniscience* inspire me with dread, if my human life remains unaffected by either? In short, *the God of the rationalists ceases to be God;* in ceasing to be truly *good* and *living*, He has divested Himself generally of all divine attributes. For all life is activity, and the highest life is the highest activity. Hence, a God who reposes in inaction ceases to be a source of life—ceases, in fact, to be God.

(*b*) Objections of no less importance to deistical theology arise from the consideration *of the world in its relation to God.* Our second class of objections to Deism rest on the following position: *Just as God loses his Godhead, so also the creature loses its creaturely character*, when the deistical conception is received! The world did not create itself, and yet is supposed able to maintain itself without its Creator. This view is based upon a twofold hypothesis: first, that the world, by means of inherent laws, *can*, as it were, *from its own resources, proceed to further developments;* and next, that its organism, just as it is, is absolutely perfect, rendering unnecessary any further interference on the part of its Originator. Both these assumptions are but half truths. It is, of course, true that God has implanted in things themselves the laws of their nature and natural operation; but is complete repose thereby enforced upon Him? Does any reasonable man adjust his work in such a way that he completely binds his hands in future, and condemns himself to become a mere looker-on? What is that which men call "*the play of accident*," but an exercise of divine freedom within the settled course of nature? If God has subjected the *powers of nature* to the laws of nature, it does not follow that He subjects *Himself* to His own creation. How can God possibly be placed in opposition to His own laws? What are these laws? Are they things existing by themselves, and independent of the will of God? A law taken by itself is nothing more than a particular way or rule, in or by which a power works or a movement runs its course. Without this impelling power the law can effect and is nothing. Hence, it is an incorrect use of language when a mere law is described as a motive cause. And so the laws of nature, if devoid of any power and intelligence working in them and through them, are mere abstractions, which we gather from a series of observations resembling one another, but which are not in themselves enduring realities. But if, as Deism confesses, God made all things as they are in the world, then the power and the intelligence which operate in the laws of nature must be a divine power and a divine intelligence. How, then, can they be opposed to the divine will and action as independent and exclusive energies?

It is true that *modern natural science*, as a rule, maintains this doctrine. It talks so much about the laws of nature, that at the present time the latter, in the view of numberless laymen, are become independent divinities, each absolute lord in its own special domain, and repudiating all interference even from God Himself. The old heathen personified the forces of nature and made them demi-gods; we do the same, and call them laws. The heathen, however, were rational enough to place these individual lesser gods in subjection to the Most High; while we invest our laws of nature with sovereign power, in whose august presence the very hands of God Himself are tied and bound! In our time, therefore, *natural science has become the main support of the separation made by Deism between God and the world.* It has followed out all the processes of development in both organic and inorganic nature so much more profoundly than was ever done before, and in that way brought to light so many fresh laws of natural change, and it has so succeeded in reducing almost the whole world of phenomena to its registers and categories, that, in fact, the temptation is a very natural one to recognise nothing else but these laws themselves, and to regard any constantly operating or spontaneous intervention on the part of God as not merely useless but disturbing. But that when the law of any phenomenon has been discovered, the real mystery of its being *is still far from being cleared up*, and nothing thereby really explained, but only some assistance afforded to future observations; and that, therefore, every law should be traced back to its lawgiver, and to the motives that guided him, are points for the most part overlooked by the advocates of natural science.

And so it came to pass that *the further discoveries were pushed in natural science, the smaller became the province which was left remaining for the creative action of God.* Whilst the old Deism and Naturalism assigned to God a "six days' work," and not until the process of creation had come to an end sought to make the world independent of Him, our modern systems claim His services for nothing more than the mere production of the original matter. With the words, "In the beginning God created the heaven and the earth," the Bible of modern science begins and ends. Any further special divine action or revelation is unnecessary. And why? Modern natural science has taught Deism that the world is not only able to maintain itself in the state in which it was created, but that the forces and laws inherent in the original matter are also perfectly adequate to infinite development. First formed itself, in virtue of some internal necessary development, a primary cell or bladder; and this became the germ of the first organism; from this were developed, in the next place, forms of life more and more complete, species of vegetables and animals ever higher in their grade, until at last, from the most perfect specimen of ape, proceeded man! All this is supposed to have happened without any special operation on the part of God, and merely through the laws immanent in nature.

Any closer consideration of these theories, which supply so

much assistance to Rationalism, would enter on the question of the origin of man, which we cannot dwell upon now. All we can do here is to remind ourselves that, as already shown, the assumption that organic life can be produced by the inorganic, is rejected as untenable by science; and further, that the new Darwinian theory of the origin of species, finds its most important positions impugned on the basis of undeniable matters of fact. Why are not new species continually starting up in the present day? Why is it that individuals bred by an artificial system of crossing can never prolong their species for any length of time? Why does nature herself in every case place such limits to her various species, as clearly and sharply to divide the one from the other? Why do not the lower plants and animals at the present day gradually improve themselves into higher forms of life, and ultimately rise into man? How can so many of the very lowest organisms, in spite of their imperfection, maintain their position against those which are so much further advanced? Why, amongst the fossil vegetables and animals which we discover in the geological strata of the earth, do we never find those intermediate stages which once formed the transition between the species which now often differ so widely from one another? The geological strata show most clearly that new species arose and disappeared *without any internal connection in respect to their origin.* Would not any formation of separate species, by means of constant fresh alterations and combinations of unlimited progression, be an impossibility, and would not the world become a chaotic confusion of forms? And how does Darwin's theory consist with the teleology which governs nature, and with the impulse of formation which is directed towards something future and still invisible? Generally speaking, does not "the struggle for existence" leave innumerable peculiarities unexplained. Of what nature might "the struggle for existence" be in which the violet became blue and the rose red?

With these and other weighty arguments the most enlightened natural philosophers repel these theories.[1] If, however,

[1] Among the opponents of the transmutation theory it is here only necessary to mention Pictet, Buckland, Sedgwick, Owen, Hitchcock (*The Religion of Geology*), Agassiz (*Contributions to the Natural History of the United States, III.*).

the various species and families did not proceed spontaneously one from the other, it is clear that some kind of intervening creative activity on the part of God was necessary for the formation of species. "That new systems should arise out of old ones without the intervention of God's power is absurd" (Newton).

But here we must leave these questions. At the present day, on the ground of natural science only, the first hypothesis, that the world has inherent powers of self-development, is no longer found acceptable.

But next, how stands the case with the second hypothesis: that the constitution of the world, just as it is, is so absolutely *perfect*, that any interposition on the part of God would only disturb it? The older systems of Rationalism laid it down, that to maintain the imperfection of nature is to bring a charge against the Creator. But in this view, the distinction between the world *per se*, as it proceeded from the hand of God, and its present condition, is entirely overlooked. May there not in the latter be disturbances which arise from the fault of the creature, and, consequently, are not chargeable on the Creator? Is it not a truth that death was a consequence of sin? Is not this confirmed by experience? Are there not in the natural world perfect masses of physical evil? Have we not seen some professors of natural science taking pains to particularize the imperfections of nature, with a view, indeed, of denying the idea of divine providence? How strange it is to see maintained, on the one hand, the absolute perfection of the world's organism, and, on the other, its faultiness asserted as zealously! only both in like opposition to the idea of God authorized in Holy Scripture. Evidently in this case the truth lies between the two extremes; and that truth is, that the world is now only on the way to perfection, and therefore cannot as yet be perfected. Unquestionably an infinite wisdom is manifested in the general arrangements of the

Forbes, Falconer, Quatrefagues, Rougemont, Andreas, and Rud. Wagner (Agassiz' *Principien der Classifik. der organ. Kärper—mit Rücksicht auf Darwin's Ansichten*, 1860; *Zoologisch-anthropolog. Untersuchungen*, 1861, and others), Joh. Müller, Göppert, Heer, Röper, Czolbe, Giebel (*Der Mensch, sein Korperbau*, etc., 1868, in which Darwin's theory is designated "a chaos of incredibilities and foolhardy assumptions"): among older authorities, Cuvier, etc.

cosmos as a whole. But this does not exclude the possibility of disturbances and evils finding an entry into it. Such disturbances are plain matters of fact; and in the face of them to speak of the world's absolute perfection, is truly to make an idol of nature.

But apart from these disturbances of moral order, which render divine interpositions doubly necessary, let us only realize the position in which the world would stand in regard to God, if His continuous agency therein were henceforth to be considered unnecessary and impossible. A world so independent of its Creator *would cease to be a creature, and become itself a part of the Absolute, a manifestation of Deity!* But God never can release any created thing, however perfect, from its condition of creaturely dependence; how much less this present world of sorrow and imperfection! *Self-maintaining and self-perfecting on the part of the world are just as impossible as its self-creation.* Either the world is a created thing, and in that case is and remains dependent on God, and subject to His rule and action; or it is independent and self-developing, and in that case, must have been so from all eternity, and therefore the idea of God as its personal Creator must be given up. You see the *self-contradictions of Deism:* a living personal God is assumed who yet has no authority over His creatures; a world is supposed to have been created by Him, and yet to remain entirely independent! Science is compelled to press forwards beyond these contradictions, and either to accept a living God standing in a relation of continuous activity to the world of creatures (Theism), or, in order to maintain consistently the world's independence, to surrender the doctrine of the Divine Personality (Pantheism). Hence, even in the first years of the present century, philosophy began to turn her back on her former allies Deism and Rationalism, and in some cases somewhat rudely,[1] as now in our own time Strauss ridicules with trenchant criticism "the half-and-half ones," who stop short of his conclusions. The conflict hence-

[1] Cf., for instance, what Hegel says in his treatise *Glauben und Wissen*, in the *Critical Journal* of Schelling and Hegel, ii. p. 1: — "Since stupidity and meanness have presumed to call themselves sound human understanding and morality, there are no longer any limits to their worthlessness and shamelessness, and we cannot help considering this mere skin of morality as the very worst cloak in which conceited ignorance ever hid itself."

forth must turn almost exclusively on the question whether we are to believe in the God of the Bible, or acquiesce in the theories of a pantheistic Materialism.

(*c*) A single glance at the third aspect in which we proposed to contemplate Deism, its influence on human morals, will make this yet more evident. Our third objection to that system may be stated thus: As Deism deprives God of His divinity and the world of its creaturely character, so does it in like proportion tend to deprive *morality of its main support and standing-ground, religion of its mainspring and lever, and the history of mankind of the one key required to disclose its enigmas.* And all this simply because the God of Deism has ceased, as we have seen, to be the All-Holy and the All-Good, the living, self-revealing, and self-communicating Love, and the all-wise Providence which directs all things. What is to maintain order in the moral world, and to dispose and rule over creatures endowed with freedom, if God has ceased to concern Himself about individual acts and persons? One who believes in moral order at all must also believe in a Providence which interests itself in the smallest matters of detail. A very sparrow falling to the ground,—how much more any action on the part of a moral free agent!—might produce disorder in the whole, if it could take place without the cognizance of the Father in heaven.

And if you say it is unworthy of man as a free agent to be in everything so strictly watched, and limited on all sides by the hand of God, you say what no doubt is very natural; in the desire to emancipate oneself from the inconvenient supervision and guidance of the Just and Holy One, lies probably the deepest and most influential motive of Deism, though I would not say that such must be the case in every instance. But, from another point of view, we may surely notice what comfortless results, as regards the whole of our moral and religious strivings, are involved in the denial of a special providence! Everything that takes place around us has some influence on our life. If God does not trouble Himself about everything, our wellbeing is but little dear to Him. In the eyes of a human father, even the pebble with which his child is playing is not without its importance; and yet God is supposed to remain unsympathetic in regard to anything which has reference to the life of His children! And if such a constantly attentive sympathy is not due to Himself and to His absolute perfection, still it is due to *us,* and to the special needs of our immortal spirit. Whosoever asserts that God looks on indifferently at the course of the world, can have no real conception *of the infinite worth of a human soul,* and of the importance which attaches to it and its actions in the sight of God.

But further, if God does not trouble Himself about me as regards anything that I do or suffer, the inference seems a just one, that He *cannot require me to trouble myself much about Him in like respects.* In other words, the inmost mainspring is removed from my moral and religious life and consciousness. For if God be no longer the ever-near One whose eyes watch over me, and whose love illumines my life, but infinitely far away, then the thought of Him can no longer be any encouragement in good, any comfort in affliction, any guard against evil, or any refuge in the hour of need; and so, neither fear of God, nor confidence in Him, can remain in any measure the guiding principle of my life. Then I no longer know whether He hears my prayers and heeds my aspirations; I no longer make my complaints to Him; I can no longer demand anything of Him; indeed, I cannot even justly hope for any future reward, for this would presuppose that God pays strict attention to minute details. *Of what profit to me is a God of this kind?* I cannot make any use of Him! For, as Luther says, "A God is One from whom we expect to receive every good thing, and in whom we may find a shelter in every hour of distress." If I cannot place this confidence in God, He is of little help to me, and the inmost impulse of my religious feeling must be stunted!

In fact, he who believes that prayer is heard, must also believe in a special Providence. But is not all history full of instances of particular answers to prayer, of deliverances out of trouble, vouchsafed to God's children by means of special dispensations of Providence, and of special judicial visitations for particular acts of wickedness? After all, is not the existence of the Christian Church on earth, and the maintenance of its position amid a thousand storms, a sufficient proof of a special Providence? Even at the present day, does not the daily life of the Christian afford a sufficient practical proof of God's merciful and judicial rule, not only *over*, but *in*, the world, that is, in the midst of men? Could not even some from among you, my honoured hearers, stand forth as living witnesses of this? Will it be desired to relegate to the realms of fancy, as a matter of course, all the most precious experiences of the children of God of His nearness and help, and, in the face of the moral grandeur of the ancient heroes of the faith, to hold it to be possible, that, as regards this point, fanciful conceptions and continuous self-deceptions should exist together with the clear light of their spiritual knowledge? Well, if it be so, we shall soon enough have to recognise the fact, that we have lost the key which would enable us to understand the world and its history, and the conduct of life in every individual! Without the providence of God guiding everything, and with a holy arm leading on the course of the world to its ultimate aim, the world and its history, both as a whole and in detail, presents itself, both to the pantheist (as before remarked), and also to the deist and the rationalist, as one great unsolved enigma, which the longer it is pondered over, becomes the more dark and perplexed! But even then, in dealing with him who would sever God from the world, we might at least refer him to his *conscience*, and say: In it thou hearest God's warning voice, in it God's will is laid down—the will of a God not infinitely distant, as thou thinkest, but dwelling in the midst of the world, and of that which is taking place in it, and in the inmost recesses of thine own heart! For "He is not far from every one of us: for in Him we live, and move, and have our being."

Nor is there, finally, much gain for Rationalism, when, in its latest form, it seeks to extend and diversify the possibility of divine influence in the world by teaching that God works upon us through the threefold agencies of the economy of nature, the moral order of the world, and the spiritual order of His kingdom, but through these only.[1] For, after all, it makes no great difference whether God's action is confined within the narrow scheme of one or three immutable ordinances. His own divine life and freedom, and with them the

[1] Cf. particularly, A. Schweizer, *Christl. Glaubenslehre nach protestant. Grundsätzen.*

moral and religious life of man, are, in any case, limited and endangered to the uttermost. What does it profit to allow God the free use of these three fingers—the Economy of Nature, of Moral Order, and of His own Spiritual Kingdom—by which to touch us, if, as to the rest, His hands are to continue bound? What does it profit to show that, in the great musical clock, so to speak, of the world's course, not one or two, but three different cylinders are fixed, if in the movement of even these three no alteration is henceforth to be made in time and harmony? No; if God is the living, the holy, the merciful, and the faithful One, He must have reserved to Himself free and unencumbered movement in the world He has created. If God be Master in His own house, He cannot, as it were, have walled in Himself within immutable ordinances, by which His action as regards every detail of the world's development has been prescribed from all eternity. Nay, we must believe that He rules the world *according to men's moral conduct, and constantly adapts the course of nature to express His judgment concerning that conduct.* Were it not the case, man himself would not be really free, and all his actions, his good as well as his evil conduct, would form but items in a predetermined order; his very fall and all his acts of sin being included in it, as, indeed, some rationalists are very apt to allow. We are thus landed in an inflexible determinism, which destroys the worth or worthlessness of all our actions.

Nor does it fare better, on this theory, with our religious than with our moral life If God be connected with man through those three Economies alone, then must they also be the only bridge whereby man can reach to God. But such provision would be inadequate to his religious need. Man needs a *personal* immediate union with God, and not merely that effected by these inflexible Economies. In religion, especially in the Christian form of it—childlike communion with the Father of spirits—man makes a personal and immediate surrender of himself, and desires therefore also to receive, no less immediately from God Himself, that which he requires for his personal needs. His "soul is athirst for God, for the *living* God," who works and communicates Himself in living, unfettered action, in accordance with laws not *outside* Himself, but *inherent in* His own nature.

In brief, this system assumes that God is a living Person, and yet unable to move or give any signs of free life; that God is love, and yet unable to communicate His love; that He is holy, and yet unable to act against evil either as a whole or in detail; that we must believe in some future and eternal retribution, and yet deny that everything takes place under God's immediate supervision and guidance; that the world was made by Him, but is now independent, and gets on well without Him; that God created man in His own image, but cannot conduct his education by any immediate action from Himself; that He has given to man desires after personal communion which He cannot meet half-way or assist; that I am to pray to God though He cannot hear me, or at least can vouchsafe me no special answer; that, because the harmonious interworking of God's universal operation and of His special action in regard to individuals involves, as undoubtedly it does, a yet unfathomed mystery, I am simply to deny the latter, though all history and my own personal experience are full of its traces, and perfectly unintelligible without the assumption of some special interpositions; that, in order therefore to evade *one* enigma, we are to create a thousand others; that the mighty miracle of the world's creation is never to be followed by any others; that we men are no longer to believe in ought miraculous, though man himself be a miracle, of which no interpretation can be found in the mere laws of nature! Is not all this the *very irrationality of Rationalism*, the *unreason of the faith of reason?*

In fact, honoured hearers, I need only ask you which of the two stands higher, and must do so in our innermost convictions,—which of the two thinks and feels more nobly, more truly, more religiously: the man who seats the Creator outside the doors of His own house, and will not suffer Him to exercise any kind of special intervention therein; *or* he whose soul is so deeply pervaded by a sense of the divine nearness and ever-present activity, that he sees or feels the finger of God in everything that happens, and traces his hand of love in every gift and blessing, and, overcome by the thought of such infinite condescension to each individual soul, cries out, "What is man, that Thou art mindful of him? and the son of man, that Thou visitest him?" "Put Thou my tears into Thy bottle;

are they not all numbered in Thy book?" "Behold, He that keepeth Israel neither slumbereth nor sleepeth"? Compare these two together, and let your hearts decide the controversy.

There is, however, after all, *some amount of truth* even in the deistic and rationalist theory. We must not deny this. It acknowledges the Divine Personality, and God as the Creator; it insists, in opposition to Pantheism, on His supramundane character. Only it overstrains the separation between the world and God, and makes it a complete severance, whereby God ceases to be a living God, and the world ceases to be a creature dependent on Him.

Nor must we ignore the points of truth contained even in the deistical denial of any Divine Interpositions. In the first place, no divine interposition can ever be a merely *arbitrary* one. God ever works by plan and rule, and in accordance with His own internal laws. But these laws are *internal*, self-imposed by the necessity of His own divine nature and all-holy will, not imposed upon Him as limitations from without. He remains therefore always, these laws notwithstanding, free and unfettered.

Moreover, it is true that, in His rule and operation, God neither can nor will *disturb* the sacred Economies which He has Himself established. Nor does Holy Scripture ever make Him do this. The God of the Bible is, and continues to be, a God of order. But precisely because He is this, He cannot persevere in the quiescence of indifference, but is compelled to interpose; not to break the world's *order*, but to repair *its disorder* by His own holy and curative influence. This will be shown more fully in our consideration of miracles. It is, moreover, true that, as a rule, God exercises His rule and providence, not in extraordinary ways, by means of constant miraculous interpositions, but through the laws and forces implanted in His creatures, and that in doing this He makes use of both circumstances and men. But for that very reason His omnipresence and universal activity and His special providence are all the more necessary. Nor does it follow that He is restricted to these inferior agencies from employing other ways and means of exercising influence on the world.

Lastly, it is true that God has vouchsafed a certain relative independence to the various spheres of created existence through the laws and forces implanted in them, in accordance with which they pursue their constant course; but these forces and laws are nevertheless *nothing but a constant outflow of the divine will*, and cease as soon as the latter is altered; hence the subsistence of the world is every moment unconditionally dependent upon God. It is likewise true, in respect to the rational creation, that God has imposed upon His operations a *limitation of His powers*, so as duly to maintain the freedom of man, and therefore that, in fact, for a long while He does not interpose, but quiescently looks on and waits, allowing us to dispose of matters just as if we were completely "our own masters." But all this is nothing more than His patience and long-suffering, His wise remission, in which, however, He *is never inactive*, but is only making His preparations in secret for a subsequent intervention. But from this attribute of God it does not follow that He does not trouble Himself about us, or that there is no special providence on His part, but only that our freedom is a fact, and not a sham!

Hence, when Deism one-sidedly overstrains the points of truth contained in it, by condemning God to inaction as regards the world, and by utterly severing the world from God, Pantheism, on the other hand, maintains against it its special truth, that God is omnipresent, and constantly active everywhere in the world; just as, conversely, against the one-sidedness of Pantheism, which would blend Him entirely with the world, Deism justly maintains its theory of a separation of God, as a personal Being and Will, from the world. Pantheism and Deism bear, therefore, such a relation to one another, that what is false and one-sided in either system is annihilated by the other, and what is true has its deficiencies supplied. Let us abandon the false and cleave to the true. If we adopt from Pantheism the doctrine of the divine activity and immanence within the world, and from Deism that of God's supramundane position and separate Personality, we shall have a near approach to the teaching of Holy Scripture.

LECTURE IV.

THE THEOLOGY OF SCRIPTURE AND OF THE CHURCH.

HITHERTO we have followed out one by one the various non-scriptural conceptions of the divine nature, and endeavoured to exhibit their untenableness from a scientific point of view, without at the same time closing our eyes to the scattered elements of truth which are nevertheless enshrined within them. We now turn to the Biblico-Christian conception as to that which alone is fundamentally true and scientifically tenable. In order to present it, we have only to gather up the various threads of our previous argument. The truth of the scriptural conception of the nature of God is evident from this, that *while it excludes all that in those other conceptions we have recognised as false and negative, it combines in a living unity all their* scattered *elements of positive truth.* In doing this we shall have to solve a twofold problem: first, to exhibit in general terms the fundamental scriptural conception of the divine nature, *i.e.* Biblical Theism, and establish the truth of its various Principles; and then to justify its full development in the Christian doctrine of the Trinity as the deepest, highest, perfectest presentation of the Idea of God.

I.—BIBLICAL THEISM.

The teaching of Scripture concerning God is based on the theistic conception, that, namely, which holds fast at once His supramundane and His intramundane character; the one in virtue of His nature and essence, the other of His will and power. For while Theism, on the one hand, regards the *Theos* (God) as a personal Being, and so as essentially distinct from the whole created universe and from man, it is no less careful, on the other hand, to present Him as the ever-living and working One in His immediate personal relationship to man and the universe by the doctrine of a universal Divine Providence. This view of the divine nature is virtually expressed in the first verse of the Bible: *In the beginning God created the heavens and the earth,* and in the fundamental article of the Apostles' Creed: *I believe in God, the Father Almighty, Maker of heaven and earth.* Let me now briefly endeavour to show you how this and other definitions of Holy Scripture exclude what is false in those conceptions of God and the universe which we have been examining.

And first, against *Atheism,* which we need scarcely mention, Scripture here, as everywhere, teaches an eternally existing unbeginning God, from whose creative activity heaven and earth and time itself took their beginning,—an absolute self-existent One, who saith, I AM THAT I AM, having in Himself the ground of His own being,—the unchangeable, ever-living One, who "hath life in Himself, and therefore hath given to the Son to have life in Himself" (St. John v. 26); "who is, and who was, and who is to come" (Rev. i. 4, 8).

Against *Materialism* we find a protest in the first sentence of the Bible. *Matter is not eternal.* It had a beginning along with time; heaven and earth were created in that beginning. Matter, therefore, cannot itself be God, but came into existence through an act of His will. And He is distinguished from it not only by priority of existence, but difference of nature. "*God is a Spirit*" (St. John iv. 24), that is, a *thinking Being: e.g.* "*Thy thoughts are very deep*" (Ps. xcii. 6); and "*of His wise thinking there is no end*" (literal rendering of Ps. cxlvii. 5).

In like manner we find in those first words of Scripture a protest against *Pantheism,* with its confusion of God and world, and its assumption of the identity of essence in both. God is both antemundane and supramundane, and as to His essence distinct and separate from the world, and existing independently of it: "*In the beginning God created—heaven and earth.*" God IS—is absolutely and without beginning; the world is brought into existence, and is dependent on its Creator, not He on it. Moreover, it comes into existence *through* Him, but not *from* Him. Every theory of emanation which would make the world, in whatever form, old Indian or modern pantheistic, an efflux from the Divine Essence, is from the first excluded by the word "created," which simply expresses the fact that the world's origin is derived not from the essence, but from the will of its Creator; that its production was not a necessity, but a free act on God's part, who is therefore to be distinguished and separated from the world as a living, thinking, willing, and *personal* Being. Throughout Scripture God speaks as a person—I—who does not, as Hegel thought, attain to self-consciousness in the human spirit, but has possessed it independently from the beginning. So little, according to Scripture, is God from us, that we are rather from Him. He is not a mere Idea, but Personality itself, absolute Freedom, and the highest Self-consciousness,—the prototype of all other Self-consciousness, all other Personality,—that which alone and eternally IS, which we are always becoming, who is before and above all, and from whom our own personality is derived (Gen. ii. 7; Eph. iv. 6). Whereas modern Pantheism affirms, in words which a well-known professor inscribed under his own portrait, "*Our God is an immanent God, and His true spirit is the human spirit*," the God of Holy Scripture says of Himself, "*My thoughts are not as your thoughts*" (Isa. lv. 8): His Spirit, therefore, is not our spirit. His Spirit searches out our spirit, His thoughts comprehend our thoughts: *Thou searchest me out and knowest me: Thou understandest my thoughts afar off* (Ps. cxxxix.). The Lord knoweth the thoughts of man (Ps. xciv. 11 *et passim*). He is fully conscious of all His own thoughts and works: "*I know the thoughts which I think toward you*," saith the Lord (Jer. xxix. 11). "*Known unto God are all His works from the beginning of the world*" (Acts xv. 18). Even in holding communion with man through His Spirit, He does not confound His Consciousness with ours: "The Spirit (of God) beareth witness to our spirit" (Rom. viii. 16).

Finally, against the false *deistic* and *rationalistic* separation between God and world, Holy Scripture makes like protest in that same opening sentence, which declares the dependence of the world in both its parts (heaven and earth) on the will of Him who called it into being. The same is also indicated in the divine names most commonly used in Scripture, expressive of divine power and might (*Elohim, El, Eloah*), as well as of lordship and dominion (*Adon, Adonai*), and indicating at once the essential unity of God in opposition to Polytheism (Deut. vi. 4) and His fulness of living energies: hence the plural form of the divine name *Elohim*, used ordinarily when reference is made to the Divine Activity in the creation, preservation, and providential government of the world in general. God (it tells us) makes Himself seen and felt by us, both in the universe as a whole and in its smallest details, as the absolutely simple and yet complex Life. He is, therefore, in the highest sense the living One and the living Agency, which not only created the world, but also continuously upholds and maintains it: who, "upholding all things by the word of His power" (Heb. i. 3), and in His omnipresence pervading everything, "giveth to all life, and breath, and all things" (Acts xvii. 25). So much, too, is He needed by the world at every moment of its existence, that all life would cease were His influence withdrawn: "Thou hidest Thy face, they are troubled: Thou takest away their breath, they die, and return to their dust" (Ps. civ. 29). Whereas Deism asserts that the Creator has withdrawn Himself from His work, and is now far removed from the world; the Scriptures say: "He is *not far* from every one of us: for in Him we live, and move, and have our being" (Acts xvii. 27, 28). He is not merely the Creator of *ourselves*, but also, in one point of view, of our actions (Ps. cxxxix. 5): He is the Ruler of hearts, who "worketh in us both to will and to do of His good pleasure" (Phil. ii. 13). Whereas the deist is of opinion that the providence of God extends to the world only as a whole, and to matters great and universal, the God of the Holy Scriptures, on the contrary, "beholdeth all the sons of men and considereth *all* their works" (Ps. xxxiii. 13, 15); He is the keeper of men, who neither slumbers nor sleeps, who marks every sigh, and numbers the hairs of our heads; nor permits even a sparrow to fall to the ground without the will of Him whose providence extends to the smallest things.

All these attributes follow still more clearly from the name "*Jehovah*."[1] Just as the general activity of God in the world

[1] In the Authorized Version, almost invariably rendered by "the LORD." The capitals serve to distinguish the translation of "Jehovah" from that of "Adonai," which is also rendered "Lord," but printed small.

is referred to *Elohim*, so almost without exception every divine action which relates to the theocratic revelation is ascribed to Jehovah. He is the covenant-God of Israel who reveals Himself specially to His people. In Ex. iii. 13–15, the name is explained: "I AM THAT I AM,"—the absolutely *independent and self-existing* One, who progressively shows and reveals Himself as God, in the constancy of His being, knowledge, will, and power,—who is the First and the Last throughout all epochs of revelation,—who was, and is, and is to come. He is, therefore, not merely the One who without beginning or end is all-sufficient in Himself, the *causa sui* who acts from His own freewill, and is absolutely self-controlled; but He also continues to be for His people that which from the beginning He showed Himself to be, and fulfils everything which He either promises or threatens. Hence He is the *faithful* and *true* God (Ps. xxxiii. 4; Num. xxiii. 19), who is a firm Defence and Rock to all that put their trust in Him (Ps. xviii. 2, 3; Isa. xxvi. 3, 4; Deut. vii. 9, 10; Josh. xxiii. 14, 16; 1 Kings viii. 56; 2 Kings x. 10). This eternally living, one Lord, though as "the *Holy* One of Israel" (Ps. lxxi. 22, lxxxix. 19; Isa. i. 4) He must necessarily be separate from all that is finite and impure, yet cannot and may not, in this very capacity, hold aloof from human affairs, or look on without concern at the development of the world. On the contrary, He guides it, both as a whole and in detail, according to His holy aims and purposes, and under the revealing aspect of His nature *Himself enters into* the growing development of things, in order to lead it on, by a free and independent, but ever consistent guidance, to the destiny which He has marked out.

Thus the mere name of *Jehovah* is in itself a refutation of Deism. The latter asserts that God worked on one occasion only,—in the creation,—and that since then the world has spontaneously followed its own course; but Christ says, "My Father *worketh hitherto*, and I work: the Son can do nothing of Himself, but what He seeth the Father do: for what things soever He doeth, these also doeth the Son likewise" (John v. 17, 19). Deism asserts in regard to its God, that miracles are a matter of impossibility to him; but the Scriptures say of the Christian's God, "With God nothing shall be impossible"

(Luke i. 37). Deism affirms that God cannot manifest and communicate Himself in special, supernatural modes; but the Scriptures, on the contrary, teach us that "God, who at sundry times, and in divers manners, spake in time past unto the fathers by the prophets, hath in these last days spoken unto us by His Son" (Heb. i. 1 ff.). The Scriptures represent God as One who is *love*, and must therefore continuously *communicate* Himself; who also has gradually revealed Himself more and more clearly and completely, till at length in Christ His entire fulness appeared; and who even now, by means of His Spirit, makes Himself recognised, felt, and enjoyed. In short, they tell of Him as One who in a thousand ways every moment places Himself in mutual relationship and active communication with man; who lives and rules not merely *above*, but *in* the world; from whose throne the current of life flows down to all creation, and lightnings, thunders, and voices go forth in every direction (Rev. iv. 5, xi. 19).

This is the living, personal, all-working God of the Holy Scriptures, whose active influence is omnipresent in the world, and yet, as the one free and independent Being, is enthroned in eternal majesty above it. From beginning to end—that is, from its origin in England in the 17th century down to its rationalistic scions of the present day—the whole tendency of Deism has been directed towards a *severance* between God and the world; in the Holy Scriptures, on the other hand, from first to last the holy God is represented as taking care to *connect* Himself in mercy and judgment more and more profoundly, pervadingly, and condescendingly, with the world and with man (Hos. ii. 19, 20). From the movement of the Spirit of God on the face of the primeval waters (Gen. i. 2), down to the dwelling of God amongst men in the new Jerusalem (Rev. xxi. 3 ff.), the life from God seeks to naturalize itself more and more completely on earth, and this is done through Him in whom an eternal, indissoluble, and personal bond of union between God and man has been cemented through Christ and His Holy Spirit.

From the foregoing it will be evident that we were thoroughly justified in applying the term *non-biblical* to those other conceptions of God; and likewise, that the false elements which we recognised in Pantheism and Deism,—viz. in the one, the blending together of God and the world; and in the other, their entire separation,—are excluded by the biblical conception of God.

Let us, however, now observe how the *scattered sparks of truth which scintillate amid the darkness of the other ideas of God, shine forth together as one clear light in the view taken of Him in the Bible.*

Atheism, which certainly is falsehood itself, and therefore does not contain one single spark of truth, rests upon the argument that nothing is to be seen of God. According to the Scriptures, God is really the invisible One (1 Tim. i. 17; John i. 18). So far, however, from this attribute diminishing the reality of His being, it is precisely that which certifies to His true, eternal existence; "for the things which are seen are temporal, but the things which are not seen are eternal" (2 Cor. iv. 18). The invisibility of God is not a defect, but a prerogative. For, in respect of His essence, God is so absolutely exalted above everything that is created and visible, that He *cannot manifest Himself directly* to the creature, but only in some shape which has a certain affinity to it.

Materialism identifies God with nature and with matter. It lays stress, as we saw above, not altogether unjustly, on the element in the being and working of the Spirit which is allied to, and interwoven with, nature. This aspect of the truth also receives its full due in the biblical view of God. According to it, although God is Spirit, He has nevertheless a *nature,* which we may term *substantial,* but not *material.* It is designated as light and fire: "We declare unto you, that God is light;" "Who coverest Thyself with light as with a garment," etc. (1 John i. 5; Rev. xxi. 23; Ps. civ. 2; 1 Tim. vi. 16); "Our God is a consuming fire;" "a fire goeth before Him," etc. (Deut. iv. 24, ix. 3; Heb. xii. 29; Isa x. 17; Ps. xcvii. 3; cf. also the visions of the prophets). However, this element of light in God's nature does not exclude its spirituality, but plainly indicates it.

The truth in *Pantheism* is the assertion that God is *omnipresent* and *universally active* in the world. We have already seen that these attributes are assigned to God by the Holy Scriptures everywhere, and with full emphasis. They entirely separate God from the world as regards His nature, but most closely connect Him with it as regards His will and His action. The Scriptures cannot at all imagine the life of the world without the animating presence of God in it. As an infinite Being, far exalted above all limits either of time or space, God is near to every being in every place, and that not as a mere idle looker-on, but quickening and maintaining, helping and directing it with His full power and activity (1 Kings viii. 27 ; Amos ix. 6 ; Isa. lxvi. 1 ; Jer. xxiii. 24 ; Ps. cxxxix. 7, 10, cv. 7 ; Matt. xxviii. 20 ; Eph. i. 23). But although *pervading* everything, and *in* everything, yet at the same time He is *above* everything (Eph. iv. 6). Biblical Monotheism does not, therefore, at all require the aid of Pantheism in order to maintain a constant, living relation between God and the world. The Bible teaches that God is the fulness of all life, and therefore recognises a veritable presence of God in all forms of the world's life ; so that as regards the fulness, multifariousness, and intimacy of the divine presence, it falls short neither of Pantheism nor of Polytheism. Further, Pantheism fears lest the idea of personality should involve a restriction in the being of God ; and, as we have previously seen, there is truth in this idea to the extent that God *cannot* be conceived as a *single Person.* He would thus be degraded to the level of other personalities. But Holy Scripture also considers Him not as a single Person, but as *absolute Personality,* which is neither limited nor restricted by anything else ; which is not a numerical *One* beside other single beings, but is both Unity and Plurality at once, *i.e.* a *triune* Being. Thus, as we shall subsequently see, room is left for the infinite fulness of life in God : and yet the great prerogative of personality is firmly maintained. Thus, moreover, full justice is done to the truth involved in *Polytheism,* viz. that plurality is an elementary form of being, and therefore must be derivable from God. Pantheism likewise demands, not without reason, that a self-conscious God must from all eternity have had an object which might reflect His consciousness back into itself ; but according to the biblico-Christian view, God has an object of this kind, existing from all eternity, in the distinction between the Persons of the Trinity in His own being,—an object which renders it superfluous to suppose that the world existed from everlasting. Because He is absolute Personality, He does not exist, or come into existence, in or through anything else, nor does He only receive His self-consciousness through something which encounters Him, and causes Him to revert upon Himself; but He derives it from Himself, and it flows to Him out of His own essence. For He is not merely *I*, but also constitutes Himself as *He;* hence He can say of Himself, "I am *He*" (Deut. xxxii. 39 ; Isa. xli. 4, xliii. 10, 13, 25, xlviii. 12). He is in Himself both subject and object.

The elements of truth contained in *Deism* and *Rationalism* we found to be that God is a personal Being, and, as the Creator of the world, must be conceived as separate from it; further, that His interposition in the world is not of an arbitrary character calculated to disturb its order, but avails itself of the forces and laws implanted therein ; also, that God, in His holy patience, even imposes upon Himself a certain self-limitation in respect of human freedom. These truths, likewise, have due importance accorded to them in the Holy Scriptures. For the all-guiding and all-watching God of the Bible, and none other, is a God of order (1 Cor. xiv. 33). The entire history of His holy rule over the world, as related to us in Scripture, is a proof of this. But this order not only does not render the providence of God in individual cases superfluous, but directly requires it. Again, even when Deism goes too far in exalting God above the world, in order not to degrade Him by mixing Him up with the finite and with the changes and chances of the world, this idea contains a twofold element of truth ;—first, the separation of God from all that is impure, His *holiness* and *incomparableness ;* and next, His eternal *immutability* and *constant conformity with Himself.* But what can set forth these attributes of God more prominently than do the Scriptures ? According to them, God is in His inmost nature *the only holy One,* who, being strictly severed from all that is impure, and unaffected by all the infirmities of finite beings, is supernaturally exalted above all their limitations. He is purity itself, and keeps far from Him everything that is opposed to His nature (Lev. xi. 44, 45, xix. 2 ; Ps. xxii. 4 ; Isa. vi. 3, liv. 5 ; John xvii. 11 ; Rev. xv. 4), because He is the incomparable One (Isa. xl. 25, xlvi. 5). And so, too, He is the immutable One. For whereas all the gods of polytheistic religions have a history full of personal events, changes, metamorphoses, and adventures, and the sacred writings of the heathen are mere collections of divine biographies, the God of the Bible has no biography and no personal adventures whatever, He is ever and unchangeably the same, because He is the only veritable *self-existent Being*, and not a being *brought into existence.* His peculiar nature also defines His relation to the world—"I am that I am;" "Thou art the same" (Ps. cii. 27); "I am the Lord; I change not" (Mal. iii. 6); "With whom is no variableness" (Jas. i. 17; cf. Heb. xiii. 8).

Thus, in the biblico-Christian conception of God, all the separate sparks of truth are concentrated, as it were, in a focus. It combines God's personality and independence, His connection with nature and capability of being known, His omnipresence and omnipotence, His invisibility, incomparableness, and immutability, His supramundane and yet intramundane existence; and, we may also add, everything which reason and conscience can, by means of natural knowledge, unveil of God's omnipotence, goodness, wisdom, and holiness, indeed, even all the *true* elements which are contained in the heathen conceptions of God, of His miracles and manifestations, His inspirations and incarnations. If one-sidedly maintained, these several elements of truth lead to a distorted and mistaken view of God; but if united, *each one checks any undue prominence of the other,* and so all contribute towards the perfect *truth, rationality, and beauty of the biblical conception of God.*

Allow me to lay this before you more in detail.

(*a*) The *intrinsic truth* of the biblical idea of God is shown by the fact that it alone affords the possibility of conceiving God as the *entirely perfect, the truly absolute Being.* No conception of God can be the true one which does not include every perfection. But in all the other ideas of God there is something essential wanting; at one time His spirituality (Materialism), or even His existence (Atheism), so again His consciousness (Pantheism), or His constant living activity (Deism). From the biblical point of view, however, God is made to possess all these attributes, and to possess them in the very highest degree—being and life, spirituality and omnipotence, consciousness and thought, will and freedom, and, in addition, a constant living and holy activity in the entire universe. Here alone He possesses both Himself and the world, and is *absolutely the Lord,* who rules everything according to His holy aims, and guides free spirits according to free moral laws; here alone does He possess every physical and moral perfection, and become "*God,*" that is, entirely and thoroughly *good,* as our Teutonic speech strikingly points out. *Therefore in this view only is the conception of the Absolute completely realized.* For God must needs determine and condition everything. But for this end it is necessary that He should be absolutely *good* and absolutely *free.* These two attributes are combined only in the God of Scripture,—the *holy,* and therefore also the free God, who does what pleases Him, whose will no one can gainsay (Rom. ix. 19); whereas the God of Pantheism is neither good nor free, and the God of Deism is at all events not free, and in reality not *perfectly* good.

Moreover, the true principle of all being can evidently be only that *from which everything that is may be derived.* Apart from the moral sphere, God must be the unity of all antitheses. This He is only according to the Christian conception, because this alone makes Him truly absolute. We can trace back to the almighty One all that is created, to the living One all that lives, to the self-conscious Spirit all the spiritually rational and personal life in the world. Here we see God as one, and yet containing in Himself the principle of multiplicity; pervading everything, and yet above all; capable of being known, and yet unsearchable; condescending to the lowest depths, and yet enthroned in unattainable sublimity; eternally near, and yet eternally far off.

Again, must not that be the truest idea of God which affords the deepest satisfaction to the *religious need* of man? This, as we have seen, tends to a complete union of the God-seeking soul with its Creator, and to its being pervaded, filled, and blessed by Him. This, according to Scripture, is the aim and conclusion of the whole revelation and world government of God and Christ, "that God may be all in all" (1 Cor. xv. 28). Once more, we must aver that this consummation of the world's development is unattainable except under the presupposition of the biblical idea of God. Neither the impersonal mundane soul of Pantheism, which destroys the higher self-conscious life as soon as it takes it back again into itself; nor yet the deistical God who abides outside the life of the world, and therefore does not communicate Himself to individual souls, can ever be "all in all," and thus fully satisfy the religious need of man. Only the God of Scripture can do this. And why? Because He is the perfect *Spirit* and perfect *love*, or, combining both attributes in one, *the Father*.

Here we have before us the most profound definition of Scripture as to the nature of God, *per se* definitions to the sublimity of which the presentiments and longings of no heathen people ever rose, although the truth of them directly forces itself on the reason and the conscience. God is *spirit* (Job iv. 24, not "a spirit"). Man *has* spirit, God *is* spirit. In Him the spirit does not form merely a portion of His being; but the whole substance of His nature, His peculiar self, is spirit. Here we have the idea of God in His *inner perfection*, just as the names Elohim and Jehovah tell us mainly His external position. As spirit, God is the eternal, self-dependent brightness and truth, absolute knowledge, the intelligent principle of all forces whose glance penetrates into everything, and produces light and truth in all directions. Spirit! how much food for thought does this one word give! Do we not feel as though it would cut asunder the hard knot which philosophy has placed before us with its conceptions of God, so laboriously wrought out, so artificially combined, and therefore often so difficult to understand? "God is spirit." Placing these simple words side by side with all the definitions of ancient and modern philosophers,—*e.g.* that God is the universal relative measure of the world's becoming (Heraclitus), or the indifference of the real and ideal (Schilling), etc.,—have we not even in the profound *simplicity* of the biblical doctrine a proof of its truth? The greatest truths are always those very ones which are the most surprisingly simple in their nature, whilst that which is artificial, contorted, and complicated, is in most cases only half true or entirely false.

How clear and intelligible, too, do all the other attributes ascribed to God in Scripture become, when considered in the light of this fundamental definition of spirituality! When once I know that God is spirit, I can much more readily conceive that He is the eternally living and personal One, and I can even forecast that this spiritual nature of fire and light may be the basis of His omnipresence, omniscience, and omnisapience, as well as of His omnipotence and glory. Nay, I can more readily comprehend those attributes, for it is only as spirit that they can appertain to Him. And conversely, when once the point is settled that He, as the most perfect Being, must possess all these, it follows that He must be spirit. This definition, therefore, is *not merely a truth, but a necessity,* which spontaneously results from the conception of the Absolute.

The same is made clear to us in the fundamental tenet of Scripture as to the *moral* nature of God, viz. that He is *holy love.* As spirituality is the vital foundation of His physical and intellectual perfections, so holy love is the internal basis of all His moral perfections, and a necessary deduction from the true idea of the Absolute. Benign, gracious, merciful, long-suffering, patient, faithful, true, just, and whatever other moral beauty may be ascribed to God in the Scriptures, all this He can only be because He is *holy* (cf. the passages above quoted), and because He is *love* (1 John iv. 8, 16). For the same reason He is also *light,* in which there is no darkness at all (1 John i. 5). Light is only the necessary effulgence of His intrinsically holy nature; for the moral and the natural are in God individually one. Truly has one said: "Holiness is the hidden glory, and glory the manifested holiness of God." As holy love, God has two attributes: He is distinctly *separated,* as we have seen, from all that is either internally or externally impure and base (the fundamental conception of holiness), and is therefore higher, more glorious, and more majestic than any creature; at the same time, He is full of the most tender *condescension* and—if I may so say—self-sacrifice; in infinite compassion imparting Himself to the world in order to eradicate from it sin and all impurity, and to render it a partaker in His perfect life and glory. "I am the Lord thy God," He exclaims to His people, "the *holy* One of Israel, thy *Saviour*" (Isa. xliii. 3, xlv. 15, liv. 5; John iii. 16; 1 Tim. iv. 10), etc.

What teaching about God can be more sublime or more adapted to the yearnings of our heart than this? Where do we find an idea of God which satisfies our religious need so abundantly as the truth that God is love? Does not every heart led by an involuntary bias say "Yea and amen" to this? Does not this idea force itself directly as the truth upon all, even unbelievers? Any man who, even in the smallest degree, acknowledges his deepest need, will lay hold on this truth with both hands, and cry out, "Yea, this is God; and He must be this, not merely on His own behalf, on behalf of His moral perfection and beauty, but *for my sake* also, if there is to be any hope for me; the God of *love* is the only God who can satisfy my needs."

No less comforting is the name of *Father*, as applied to God; and following from the twofold conception of spirit and love, God is thus called, sometimes in His character of universal originator (*e.g.* 1 Cor. viii. 6), sometimes in the special sense of begetting, as in the case of Christ (*e.g.* Ps. ii. 7) and the regenerate (*e.g.* Jas. i. 18), but specially because He exercises loving care, education, and providence. The former universal relationship is the groundwork of the latter more special one. This, however, we do not find only in the New Testament, but also in the Old (Deut. xxxii. 6; Ps. ciii. 13; Isa. lxiii. 16, lxiv. 8; Jer. iii. 4, 19, xxxi. 9; Mal. i. 6, ii. 10); although, it is true, the full depths of the divine Fatherhood are first revealed to us in the former, because the relation of God to men as Father was perfectly realized in Christ alone, and through Him was brought about for the whole world. This name points out His dignity no less than His accessibility and condescension, His holy prefiguration of us no less than His love and care, our own needy condition no less than our honour and dignity, as children created in our Father's image. What an encouragement and stimulus for a human heart,—how much that excites confidence, imposes awe, stimulates the conscience, and inspires love and hope,—what a sea of joy and bliss there is in that one name *Father!* "All our other knowledge of God contains nothing more than isolated letters and syllables of this one Name" (Tholuck). We Christians possess it and enjoy it in its fullest extent. In the whole range of heathen piety we find nothing but distant and obscure presentiments of the heart's-joy which overwhelms each one who, in the fulness of his soul, can cry, "Doubtless Thou art our Father and our Redeemer, from everlasting this is Thy name" (Isa. lxiii. 16); who can call upon his God by all the glorious names which the Scriptures apply to Him, — Physician, Stronghold, Rock of salvation, Refuge and Confidence, Shield and Buckler, Light and Consolation, Shepherd and Helper, Redeemer and Saviour.

Again, I ask, is there any idea of God which can more thoroughly satisfy the religious need of a human heart? Indeed, in view of this name of God, I may well venture to ask every one who rejects the biblical idea of Him, Hast thou ever earnestly considered its depths, in devout contemplation and active appropriation, without finding full satisfaction in it? Only we must never forget that the truth of the biblical idea of God must be recognised principally by *personal experience*. The true God must be found by a moral search. "The desire to attain to God, without God," says a philosopher, "is just such another feat as the tempter promised to teach our first parents · how, in opposition to God, and without Him, they might make themselves equal to Him" (Baader).

Or must not that be the true idea of God by which I, as a sinful being, am at once *bowed down and raised up*; by which I am made to feel the whole weight of my guilt, and yet not to despair, but to hope; by which I am shown the wide gulf which separates me from God, and also the way to a restoration of unity with Him? And what else in this respect can compare with the God of the Holy Scriptures, who in one breath says of Himself, "I dwell in the high and holy place, and with him who is of a contrite and humble spirit" (Isa. lvii. 15; comp. Ps. cxvii. 5–7), so as to make us feel at once His *holy distance* and His *comforting nearness*; or again, who, whilst asking sin-burdened Israel whether He ought not justly to make them like unto Sodom, immediately adds, "Mine heart is turned within me: my repentings are kindled together" (Hos. xi. 8)? And where shall we find the way to a restoration of union with God brought so lovingly before the fallen world as by Him who proclaims, "God so *loved* the world that He gave His only-begotten *Son*, that whosoever believeth in Him should *not perish*, but have *everlasting life*"?

And finally, must not that be the true idea of God which does the most to elevate man morally, to ennoble, to spiritualize him, and to render him like God? And from an *historical point of view* we ask, Where has there been any conception of God and religion which has so much elevated, educated, and enlightened both individuals and nations as the biblico-Christian conception? Whence may we expect a more powerful moral influence than from the worship of the God who, as spirit, desires to be worshipped only in spirit and in truth? Where is there a more forcible stimulus to purity, both of heart and life, than is found in the worship of Him of whom it is written, "Holy, holy, holy, Lord God of Sabaoth;" and, "Be ye holy, for I am holy"? And place side by side the fact, that other nations, who were acquainted with none but *unholy* gods, have, through their worship, sunk into an ever-deepening moral degradation, which could not be averted even through the influence of philosophy. "By their fruits ye shall know them." And indeed the truth of this conception of God is witnessed not merely by the Holy Scriptures, but also by our own heart and conscience, and the testimony of innumerable Christians, who have recognised it in their personal experience, and have given incontestable evidence of its moral fruits in their hearts and lives; and the whole history of the world and its civilisation confirms it!

(*b*) Nor does *reason* itself bear a less decided witness in favour of this view. Some one, perhaps, will say: It is all very well to heap together the greatest possible number of beautiful attributes; but the question is, whether it is rational to predicate all these *together* of God? Yes, I reply, the biblical conception of God is also the *most rational*, and the one that recommends itself most strongly to our understanding. It is true that His sublimities far transcend all the perceptions of reason. But they are not *unreasonable* because they are beyond the scope of reason. No reasonable man can expect that he as a finite being should entirely and perfectly comprehend the infinite God; to do this, he must himself be God. And it is therefore perfectly comprehensible to any discreet, temperate mind, which remains conscious of its limitations, that the Scriptures should reserve the perfect knowledge of God for the intuition of another life (1 Cor. xiii. 12; 2 Cor.

v. 7; 1 John iii. 2). The only question therefore is, whether this preliminary knowledge of God with which the Holy Scriptures furnish us, on the express understanding of its fragmentary nature, really recommends itself to our reason, and not merely to our hearts. And this it does infinitely more than any other conception.

Is it not, I ask in the first place, the most reasonable thing we can do to adopt that conception of God which renders the necessary divine perfections, and also the mystery of the world and our own being, more intelligible than does any other? Our idea of God fulfils all these requirements. We have already seen that the attributes of eternal vitality and personality, of omnipresence, omniscience, omnipotence, etc., which we are bound to attribute to the Absolute as such, are unintelligible, unless with the Bible we presuppose God to be spirit. Moreover, it is no longer a mystery to me that God should create worlds, notwithstanding the perfect self-sufficiency of His Being, if I know that He is Love, whose nature is to desire that other beings outside itself should rejoice in their existence. It is no longer a matter of wonder to me that, in every grain of dust and in every drop of water, traces of infinite wisdom obtrude themselves on my notice, when I think of God as the highest self-conscious Intelligence. I am no longer at a loss to account for the requirements of a law in my conscience which is altogether different to that which rules in nature, when I know that the holy God is thereby teaching me His holy will. Again, it appears to me in the highest degree reasonable that God should reveal Himself in the Scriptures step by step, gradually disclosing to man the depths of His own nature: first His power, goodness, and wisdom; then His holiness and justice; and last of all, in Christ, His world-subduing love. So soon as I form the idea that He is a Father who is educating man, I see why He communicates Himself to him in a special manner during childhood, and then places the earlier periods of man's existence under a law somewhat different from that which rules the later ones. Yes, in view of the moral freedom of man, it no longer seems inexplicable that God should have allowed him to sin, and thereby to bring such unutterable woes upon our race, if I can believe that the purpose and counsel of God from all eternity was to redeem man through Christ, and to bring him back into blessed fellowship with Himself. It no longer seems a strange chance that, in the course of the world's history, I should perceive so many traces of righteous justice and holy laws never to be infringed with impunity, when I know that a righteous God is in the seat of government, guiding everything according to His holy purposes. Nay, do not the mysteries of my own life's experience become closer and clearer when I illumine them with the light of the utterance, "I have loved thee with an everlasting love; therefore with loving-kindness have I drawn thee" (Jer. xxxi. 3); that is, with the belief in God as a Father, who in everything, be it love or be it severity, seeks to draw me to Himself? The inmost yearning of my soul after God only becomes intelligible to me, and is satisfied in its profoundest depths, when I know that God in His compassion meets me half way and imparts Himself to me, because He is love.

Once more I ask, is it not consonant with reason to accept an idea of God which furnishes me with *a key to the most important questions connected with the world and with my life*? If the other conceptions of God lead me only to an inexplicable *something*, at which my thoughts are to rest; and if, on the other hand, the biblical conception of God affords me, in respect to the ultimate cause of things, at least a notion, the substance of which I can in some measure comprehend, and which—even in practical life—solves many enigmas which must else remain unsolved; then surely the rationality of this conception of God must be greater than that of all others, and the words hold good, "The fear of the Lord," that is, the theoretical and practical observance of this idea, "is the beginning of wisdom."

(*c*) Finally, the biblical conception of God recommends itself by its *beauty* no less than in other ways; for in this respect, too, it far surpasses all other cognate ideas.

For the most part it would be hard to discover an aspect of beauty in the non-biblical conceptions of God. Philosophical definitions of the divine nature may tickle our intellectual palate; but abstract ideas of this kind will not touch our sense of beauty. And yet the God who formed the world, as a beautiful expression of His own mind (Gen. i. 31), and then made it over to man as His beautiful image, to impress upon it the divine brightness of His Spirit, and glorify it into His own likeness,—surely this God who is the most perfect Being must also be the most beautiful, and must, therefore, most forcibly arouse and attract to Himself the sense of beauty felt by His image—man. Both in His physical, His intellectual, and moral attributes, the God of the Holy Scriptures is a God of surpassing beauty. Not, indeed, His formless and invisible essence, but His overt action and self-manifestation, especially in Christ, have for this reason at all times been an inexhaustible mine of wealth for representative art, and have inspired it to its sublimest and most ideal productions.

All true beauty is the outward expression of something good. That which is perfectly good can only appear in perfect beauty. Hence the biblical doctrine as to the *glory* of God, and in connection with it the future transformation of the world. The holy and living God stands in the most effective relationship to His world. He is the glorious One, whose glory extends to the utmost limits of the universe, and is manifested by the creation, His own handiwork, in which He is all-present, and all-guiding. Even now "the heavens declare the glory of God," and "the whole earth is full of His glory" (Ps. xix. 2, xcvii. 6, cxiii. 4 ; Isa. vi. 3, *et al.*) ; and one day it shall be still more so when God's kingdom is consummated (Num. xiv. 21 ; Ps. lxxii. 19 ; Isa. xl. 5 ; Ezek. xxxviii. 23 ; Hab. ii. 14 ; Tit. ii. 13, *et al.*).

If we more closely consider the intrinsic substance and the apparent form of this divine glory, we find that the secret of God's beauty is primarily involved in His nature as light, which reflects the purity, holiness, grace, and gladness of His inner being, and radiates around Him this intrinsic beauty. Is there in nature anything more beautiful than light, and is there in the moral world anything more beautiful than holiness ? He is incomparable, both in His essence and in His actions (Ex. xv. 11 ; Ps. xxxv. 10, lxxi. 19, lxxxvi. 3, lxxxix. 9 ; Deut. iii. 24, etc.). What can we imagine more grand and majestic than the outward demonstrations of the glories of God, which are occasionally described in Scripture, from the manifestation on Sinai down to the glorious second advent of Christ ? What brilliant pictures are spread before us by the prophetic seers, describing the heavenly glories of

God and of Christ (Isa. vi.; Ezek. i.; Rev. i., iv.), and of the new world that is to come glorified in the light of God (Rev. xxi., xxii.; Isa. lxv. 17 ff.)! How plainly does the struggle for language show that words and figures were alike inadequate to express that which they intuitively perceived! Two names in particular which the Old Testament applies to God point to His majestic beauty and glory. The one is: "Jehovah that dwelleth between the cherubim" (1 Sam. iv. 4; 2 Sam. vi. 2; Ps. xcix. 1; Isa. xxxvii. 16); for the latter are simply the exponents of His glory and of his active presence in the world. The other name is still more frequently applied to God, viz. "Jehovah *Sabaoth*, the Lord of Hosts," that is, not only of the heavenly bodies, but especially of the heavenly spirits. Being the messengers of God and the instruments of His will (Ps. ciii. 20, and frequently), also the witnesses accompanying Jehovah when He Himself appears in His kingly and judicial glory (Deut. xxxiii. 2; Ps. lviii. 18), these spirits constitute, as it were, the "celestial Church," which heads "the antiphony of the universe" (Ps. cxlii. 2, cl. 1), offering adoration to God in the heavenly sanctuary, and celebrating both His mighty rule in nature (Ps. xxix. 19), and His miracles of mercy (Ps. lxxxix. 6 ff.). How grandly beautiful, how solely worthy of God are these views, and, in conjunction with them, how blessed the promise, "Thine eyes shall see the King in His beauty" (Isa. xxxiii. 17)!

But above all, what unique moral beauty is exhibited to us in "the Fairest among the children of men" (Ps. xlv. 3), who could say of Himself, "He that hath seen me, hath seen my Father also!" His countenance full of grace and truth, His actions full of infinite compassion, gentleness, and holy zeal, His sufferings full of priestly majesty, all place before our eyes a picture of perfect spiritual beauty and moral sublimity so absolutely harmonious and spotless, that the whole race of man has nothing which can be compared to it. And yet all this was nothing more than the reflection of the Father's glory shaded by an earthly and human incarnation (John i. 14; 1 Cor. ii. 8), in One who had divested Himself of His divine fulness, and had taken on Him the shape of a servant.

In the next place, if we transfer our attention from the revealed aspect of God to His internal nature, how beautiful is the intrinsic harmony of His Being, in all His attributes, both intellectual and moral! With what beautiful harmony do the fundamental principles of His nature flow one from the other —spirit, light, life, love! Or, if we distinguish these attributes one from another, how beautiful is their mutual correspondence! We may, for instance, distinguish, as above, between the attributes of God resulting from His vitality, and those flowing from His nature as light. On the one hand, there appertain to His vitality, His absence of beginning and all-sufficiency, His eternity and immutability, His omnipotence and omnipresence; on the other hand, to His nature as light, belong His invisibility, omnisapience, omniscience, love, justice, and holiness. How beautifully these two series of attributes correspond to and supplement each other!—in one, the all-sufficiency of God; in the other, His intrinsic life of love: in one, eternity and immutability; in the other, spirituality and invisibility: in one, omnipotence; in the other, omnisapience: in one, omnipresence; in the other, omniscience. Can there be a harmony more beautiful?

The beauty of God, as regards His action, further depends on the harmonious development of all His attributes in His overt manifestations. And with what perfect beauty does the God of the Bible unfold these attributes as *holy love,* in which idea the whole fulness of His essence and action is expressed! Can anything produce a more harmonious development than love? How beautifully does it unite such contrasts as sublimity and gentleness, as majesty and condescension! How beautifully does the fatherly guidance of God exhibit to us His holy wisdom and discipline, combined with a constant respect for our human freedom! With what wondrous and soothing beauty does God balance the awe with which His physical attributes inspire us by the trust and self-surrender which His moral attributes awaken in us—as, *e.g.*, in the text already quoted, "I dwell in the high and holy place, and with him also that is of a contrite and humble spirit!" How beautiful it is that His action ever awakens both veneration and love! And in what unequalled beauty shall this holy love stand before us at the end of the world's course, when old things have been done away with, and all things have become new! Then this love shall wipe away all tears from the eyes of the redeemed, and guide the thirsty to fountains of living water, and its pure beams shall illumine the heavenly city of God, in which He will dwell among His glorified people enthroned in everlasting glory (Rev. xxi., xxii.).

The poet might well complain of the deist's god, that under his sceptre life became so gloomy, and "the world deprived of deities" so soulless. When the world, "her leading-strings at length outgrown, free hovers and upholds herself,"—that is to say, when we accept the rationalist's idea of God,—this complaint is completely justified. But if, instead of this, the biblical idea of God, so glorious and yet so soothing, had been presented to the poet's eye, assuredly his soul would have embraced its living beauty with fervid aspirations.

Let us just for a moment compare the other conceptions of God with that of the Bible in point of beauty. In the one case we have an unconscious mundane soul, whose rule, in a moral point of view, is no better than that of animal instinct; in the other, a self-conscious, holy, all-wise intelligence: in the one case, a universal substance under the iron law of necessity, first begetting a world, and then again swallowing it up; in the other, a free, creative will which, in love to men, places itself in relation to them as free beings according to the moral laws: or again, in the one case, a Being who was once a Creator, but now rests in slothful inactivity, not troubling Himself about His creatures individually; in the other, a Father who "openeth His hand and filleth all things living with plenteousness," who also "clothes the lilies and the grass of the field," and "feeds the fowls of the air:" in the one case, a mere indifferent looker-on, who leaves the world entirely to itself, or at best observes it from some astronomical distance; in the other, "One who keepeth Israel, and neither slumbereth nor sleepeth," and guideth His people like a faithful shepherd. Listen, on the one hand, to a Lalande, who presumptuously exclaims, "For sixty years I have surveyed the heavens, and never as yet have I seen *Him!*" or to a La Place, who says, "In my heaven I can find no God;" and hear, on the other, the king of Israel, who, in holy awe, ejaculates, "Whither shall I flee from Thy presence?" "Behold, the heaven of heavens cannot contain Thee:" listen, on the one hand, to a Hegel, who looks upon the starry world as nothing better than "a luminous eruption, no more worthy of wonder than an eruption in man, or a swarm of flies;" and, on the other, to the pious psalmist, to whom "the heavens declare the glory of God." Compare, I pray you, these antagonistic views of God and the world, and then tell me candidly which is the more beautiful, the more sublime, and the more worthy of God and man?

On this point, however, the objection is very frequently raised, that, side by side with many exalted ideas of God, there are in the Bible, at least in the *Old Testament, many views unworthy of Him.* This widely-spread notion is in innumerable cases not merely a main item, but also the source of modern doubts as to the Christian faith. The Old Testament is not in harmony with the taste of the present day. Thus, for instance, a recent publication[1] expresses its opinion as to the God of the Old Testament in the following disgracefully blasphemous language: "The covenant of Jehovah is directed towards distinctly material and immoral aims. His agreement goes into the very smallest details, just as would any Jewish tradesman. He has to be incessantly reminded of His obligations; and in order to save His credit, He is compelled to incur considerable expense in furnishing manna and quails. The God of Moses is just such a person as the Jew likes to do business with. In paradise he takes His walk; travels to Sodom for the purpose of inspecting the property; dines with Abraham off roast veal and cakes; has a tussle with Jacob!!!" etc. Voices such as these might well be left to their own ignominy. But if we set aside the scurrility of expression, we find that they give vent to objections which go far to render the Old Testament repulsive to many. The chief stumbling-blocks in this case are the nature and mode of God's intercourse with man, His too human-like appearances and feelings, His wrath, vengeance, repentance, and the like. In the face of these objections,[2] of which we can here only consider the most important, I would recommend you to keep in view two things: *first,* the gradual progress of revelation, in which God must *educate* mankind

[1] *Die Juden und der deutsche Staat,* 5th ed., 1862.

[2] For further details, see Heintzeler *die Anstösse in der heil. Schrift,* Stuttgart, 1864.

(Deut. viii. 5), *dealing therefore with them at first as children,* and condescending to them in a way different from His bearing towards men; and, *second,* the circumstance that God Himself and the instruments of His manifestation, such as the angels in the case of Abraham and Jacob, are *not to be considered as absolutely identical.* In this way very many of the situations which are supposed to be unworthy of God lose their apparently offensive character.

God approaches the first sinners in Paradise "in the cool of the day," just as a father and tutor might do in a human or human-like shape. But if He sought to gain their confidence, could He converse with them in any other than human shape? Having once given a bodily form to the image of Himself in man, He manifests Himself so as to be recognised by his bodily senses. Man has now cut himself off from God; but God approaches man because He cannot and will not leave him. And for this purpose He chooses the evening, which in the east is the most pleasant hour, not in order to avoid being molested by the sun, but in order to give to the sinners one day more in which to present themselves to Him as penitent. "When the sun for the last time gilded with its rays the glory of Paradise," as Spurgeon exclaims, "when the evening dews dropped a tear over the sin of man, when all was so still that man was more easily led to think about himself and his offence, and the heaven above was resplendent with its lights, in order that man in now approaching darkness might still have hope," then the right moment had arrived, then He lets the guilty ones hear the rustling of His footsteps, so as to show them that man cannot hide himself from the face of God. And yet shallow mockers talk about "promenading in the cool of the evening!" This necessity for a human form of the divine manifestation, which has its true cause in His condescension to mankind, and its climax in the incarnation of God in Christ, it is not to be understood as if bodily shape formed part of the nature of God; for it is well known how strictly all images of God are forbidden in the Old Testament. But it explains to us what we read of divine communications and manifestations in the lives of our first parents and the patriarchs.

No words need be wasted on the scurrile objection to God's

covenant with Israel, as being an immoral Jewish business transaction. It is probably intended for a *jeu d' esprit,* but betrays a superficiality and triviality which are truly astounding. For where is there any human code of laws, or even any moral precept of a heathen philosopher, which can compare with the Mosaic law as regards the strictest requirements of the sublimest morality,—in other words, of holiness,—or in respect of the severe persecution and condemnation of sin, down to its innermost source in evil desire ?

We may deal in a similar way with the objection that has also often been raised, that it is unworthy of God for Him to appear, as He often does in the Old Testament, as "the particular God of a special nation," because He is often called "the Lord *thy* God," or because, *e.g.* in Ex. ix. 1, in speaking to Pharaoh, He calls Himself "the God of the Hebrews." But all this is mere superficial talk. For is not Monotheism,—*i.e.* the belief that there is only one true and living God in the whole world, and that this is the God of Israel,—is not this, I say, the groundwork of the Mosaic religion ? The phrase, "the Lord *thy* God," refers only to the *special covenant* of God with Israel; why should it be unworthy of God so to call Himself, thus reminding Israel of their covenant duties ? Surely none will attempt to deny that it was exceedingly wise, and even necessary, that the knowledge of the true divine revelation should be entrusted to one branch of the human race, and be continued in it until the time of fulfilment, when it might become a benefit common to all mankind! Even in this "particularism," have we not innumerable intimations of the fact, that the God of Israel was at the same time the God of the whole world, and that the gods of all other nations were but vain idols ? (Ps. xlvi. 5, xlv. 3, lxxxvi. 8, cxxxv. 5 ; Isa. ii. 18, xli. 29, xlv. 21, and frequently.) What can there be more universal than the one Creator and Lord of heaven and earth ? Or if the point of the objection is supposed to be, that the "special God of the Israelites," as such, ignored other nations, then we ask—must ask—Was it not God's purpose, in calling Abraham, in his seed to bless *all* the nations of the earth, although for a long time "He suffered all nations to walk in their own ways" ? (Acts xvi. 16.) Does, then, the Old Covenant contain no promises from the heathen? (cf. Isa. xix. 25, xlix. 6, lx. 3 ff.; Ps. lxxii. 10 ff., xcviii. 2 ff., and frequently.) How often is the *whole world* called upon to praise God! (Ps. xcvi., xcvii., xcviii., c., etc.) Or does the Old Testament, generally speaking, pay less consideration than it ought to other nations? What can we find more universal in its character than the history of mankind contained in the first ten chapters of the Bible? No people of antiquity ever attained even to the idea of an universal history of mankind; it is only possible on the ground of revelation; and there, it exists from the very beginning.

But did not the God of the Old Testament on one occasion incite to *robbery?* So we hear many indignantly ask, in view of the passage Ex. iii. 21, 22 (cf. xi. 2 ff., xii. 35 ff.). This reproach is based simply on a misunderstanding of the passage. Before its departure, Israel is told to demand from the Egyptians golden and silver vessels, and thus to "spoil the Egyptians" (as to the signification of the word, cf. 2 Chron. xx. 25). This command was subsequently carried out. But this "spoiling" is very different from secret theft, or from ostensibly borrowing (cf. xii. 36) without the intention to return. The Israelites from the outset *ask for* or *demand* these ornaments, without any intention of restoring them; and the Egyptians *give* (not "lend") them without hope of receiving them back. They were so overcome with terror, that they were glad enough to get rid of Israel on these terms. These gifts to which God inclined the hearts of the Egyptians were carried away by Israel as a booty, in token of the victory which God's omnipotence had granted to His weak people. The whole took place openly and fairly, and assuredly it was nothing more than equitable. How much valuable property in the shape of houses, lands, and utensils, must Israel have left behind in Egypt! And for how many centuries had Israel been robbed by the Egyptians, through unjust enslavement! The righteous God now takes care that Israel shall not remain unrewarded, or go away empty, after so long a period of severe labour; and so Israel is permitted to despoil his oppressors, but at the same time with their knowledge and consent,—"a prelude of the victory which the people of God, in their contest with the power of the world, shall always obtain" (Zech. xiv. 14).

Another stumbling-block for many lies in the divine command for the extirpation of the Canaanites (Deut. vii. 1 ff., xx. 16–18, etc.). Strange to say! For when we read elsewhere in history that a morally decrepit and enervated nation has been destroyed by some fresher people, then we talk about a *Nemesis*, a just fate, and the like. But in the present case, as soon as Jehovah steps forth in the place of this undefined power, these sentimentalists begin to shriek out about a bloodthirsty God. Nevertheless, not only in this, but in all similar cases, it is the same God who passes the sentence of extirpation, and makes use of certain nations as a scourge for others. Judgments of this kind are a universal law of history. The only distinction is this, that that which is accomplished by other nations unconsciously, though according to God's counsel, is to be done by Israel consciously and in name of his God. And can it be said that this condemnation was not a just one? Centuries before, God had said that He would allow the inhabitants of Canaan a respite until "their iniquity was full" (Gen. xv. 16). Now that measure of iniquity has been fulfilled. Not only the usual crimes of the heathen, but also special moral abominations, idolatry in its most frightful degeneracy, accompanied by the most unnatural sins of the flesh (Lev. xviii. 24 ff.; Deut. ix. 4, xii. 31, xviii. 12), were now to be judged, and, in addition to this, their hostile attitude towards Israel (Ex. xviii.; Num. xxi. 1 ff.; Deut. ii. and iii.) was to be punished. Just as the body forcibly ejects food which it cannot assimilate, so the land, defiled by the unnatural abominations of its inhabitants, forcibly vomited forth the Canaanites (Lev. xviii. 24, 25). In the world before the flood it was the water that carried out God's judgments, in Sodom it was fire, but now it was to be the sword of Israel (not, however, without exceptions; cf. Josh. vi. 25, Matt. i. 5, Josh. ix. 19 ff.). This visitation of divine wrath is not to be justified—as some have attempted to do—by bringing forward ancient rights of property dating from the patriarchal age, which Israel had the right to assert against the Canaanites (for this is contrary to Gen. xii. 6, xiii. 7). According to the Old Testament, the only ground on which Israel might take possession of the land of Canaan was the favour of God to whom the land belonged, who also conferred it upon His people; and the only ground for the extirpation of the Canaanitish tribes was the justice of God, whose long-suffering was at length exhausted, and who threatened Israel itself, in case it were guilty of the same sins, with the very same punishment (Lev. xviii. 28; Deut. viii. 19, 20; Josh. xxiii. 15, 16). But this sentence of extirpation was not merely a holy act of divine *penal justice*, it was also an act of divine *wisdom*. For by rooting out these tribes and their idolatry (Ex. xxxiv. 13 ff.), God desired to hold up to Israel and the surrounding nations which were spared a warning example; and especially by isolating Israel, to guard it from the danger of intermingling with the heathen (Ex. xxiii. 32 ff.; Lev. xx. 22–26). The fact that Israel did not fully carry out the divine command, but suffered many remnants of the Canaanites to remain in the land, which remnants soon became strong again, and were a snare to Israel, is an intimation to these sentimentalists that there is such a thing as *a false tolerance*. On the other hand, it is in a measure the prelude of that disobedience and fall of Israel, out of which, according to the wondrously wise and gracious providence of God, salvation was to accrue to the heathen world (Rom. xi. 11, 12).

After all, however, we must bear in mind that a certain distinction does exist between the avenging Judge of the Old Covenant and the God of mercy and love of the New Covenant. Not that God alters in His nature; He ever was and is unalterably holy in all His actions. But times and men certainly do alter. Hence in God's educatory dealings with man, everything has its wisely prescribed season. The truth that God is love could not be revealed in its full depth, until the law, by its penalties, had brought about the consciousness of sin and a longing for entire release from it.

These points should also be kept in view when considering those *Psalms* which contain *curses* or *prayers for vengeance* (cf. xxxv., lix., lxix., cix., cxxxvii.). Even believers in the Bible are sometimes offended by the manner in which the God of the Old Testament is appealed to in these psalms as a God of vengeance, and also, generally speaking, by the whole spirit expressed in those passages in which the poet invokes destruction on his enemies. Many look upon these passages as outbursts of a base thirst for vengeance, and as indicating that vindictive feelings, to a certain extent at least, are sanctioned by the Old Testament. This error ought to have been averted by a glance at the divine precept of love to one's enemies as contained in the Old Testament (Ex. xxiii. 4, 5; Prov. xxv. 21), also the divine prohibition of vindictive feeling (Lev. xix. 18), and the oft-expressed abhorrence of revenge and malignant pleasure in the misfortunes of others (*e.g.* Job xxxi. 29, 30; Ps. vii. 5; Prov. xx. 22, xxiv. 17, 18, 29; Ezek. xxxv. 15). Moreover, as regards David, the author of most of these psalms, objectors should first consider the generosity which he so often evinced towards his personal enemies, and also the fact that in moments of the highest religious inspiration, such as those in which the Psalms were composed, the impure fire of personal emotion could scarcely mingle with the holy fervour of love to God. The key to the right understanding of these psalms is contained in Ps. cxxxix. 19–21: "Surely Thou wilt slay the wicked, O God: depart from me, therefore, ye bloody men. For they speak against *Thee* wickedly, and Thine enemies take Thy name in vain. Do not I hate them, O Lord, that hate Thee? and am not I grieved with those that rise up against Thee?" According to this, the suffering servants of God see *in their own enemies the enemies of God Himself*, and their curses are directed against the latter. Hence they are not the expression of any *private* vengeance, on account of personal wrong experienced by them, but they are the outflow of a zealous wrath against the injury inflicted on the honour of God and the concerns of His kingdom. David, more especially in the face of his persecutors, feels himself to be the anointed of the Lord, and knows that on his fate hangs the future of Israel. Whoever persecutes him, sins also against Christ in him. "In this focus of self-contemplation, as an essential link in the history of redemption, the fire of his wrath is kindled." Frequently, too, the enemy whom the psalmist has in view, as well as the unjust persecutor, are not concrete, historical persons, but poetical personifications, pointing to the future victory over His enemies which the perfectly righteous One shall gain by His sufferings,—the curse in this case being addressed in general against the feeling of hostility to God. Where, however, the psalmist clearly refers to definite persons, it must be remembered that the vengeance of God on obstinate sinners is an act as *necessary* to His justice as wholesome for the consummation of the divine kingdom. Hence, even in the New Testament there are passages in which a curse is pronounced on irreclaimable enemies of God, and divine punishment is invoked upon them (Matt. xi. 20 ff., xxiii. 13 ff.; Acts viii. 20, xxiii. 3).

But at the same time we must acknowledge the *imperfection of the Old Testament standpoint* occupied by the sacred poets. The lively *impatience* of their longing for divine judgments on their enemies probably arose, in part, from a feeling of human *weakness* unable to cope with tribulation, and which is therefore in Rev. vi. 10, 11 exhorted to wait patiently. At that time, moreover, a dark veil permitted but dim glimpses of eternity, with heaven and hell; so that denunciations such as those in Ps. lxix. 28 could not have been understood by the poet in all their infinite depth. And finally, there had not yet been accomplished that world-embracing scheme of redemption ordained by divine love, from which alone could flow the love that would fain help *all* men, even her enemies. Hence the spirit of the New Covenant is in this respect a relatively different and a higher spirit. Not only were such utterances as sprang from the language and spirit of Sinai unsuited for the lips of Jesus, the meek Lamb of God, but even His disciples are not to emulate the spirit of wrath which inspired Elias (Luke ix. 54 et ss.), and which sometimes actuates the utterances of David (Ps. cix.). They are not permitted to wish that even their deadliest enemies should be everlastingly lost. Therefore when, in exceptional cases, the holy zeal of the New Testament seems to touch upon that of the Old, there is this barrier between them,—that the anathemas of the apostles apply only to the correction and temporal expulsion of enemies from the community, and not to their everlasting perdition (Acts viii. 22, cf. with ver. 20; 1 Cor. xvi. 22; Gal. i. 9, v. 12; 2 Tim. iv. 14). No one who believes in the necessity of a gradually progressive revelation can take offence at the form in which Old Testament piety occasionally presents itself to us,—a form which is incomplete enough when viewed from a Christian standpoint, although justifiable at its own peculiar stage. Indeed, it has been asserted, not without justice, that these psalms contain a very wholesome antidote against the mawkish religious sentimentality of our own days, which, in the case of many, is the chief source of all these difficulties, since they are alike incapable either of fervent love to that which is good, and of holy ardent hatred against that which is evil.

Having thus endeavoured to vindicate before the forum of modern consciousness the eternal truth of the general conception of God—that is, of His personality and special providence—as laid down in the Bible, we still feel that we have only accomplished the easier portion of our task. For the number of those who reject the general system of biblical Theism is, on the whole—and probably among my readers also—far less than that of those who entertain doubts as to the specific Christian, that is, the *Trinitarian*, conception of God. Now, therefore, we must give a closer consideration to the Christian *doctrine of the Trinity*. The subject, however, is so wide a one, that in respect of many questions which converge in this central point, we shall not be able to give more than mere hints, which may tend to remove the manifold offences that attach to this doctrine in particular.

II.—THE TRINITARIAN CONCEPTION OF THE DIVINE NATURE.

The doctrine of the Trinity set forth in its simplest form in the Apostles' (and Nicene) Creed, may be assumed as universally known. The so-called Apostles' Creed is, of course, not strictly speaking of apostolic authorship. Founded on our Lord's own baptismal formula (Matt. xxviii. 19), it grew by degrees into its present shape in the midst of the controversies of the first centuries of primitive Christianity. In accordance with this its origin, this Creed presents the doctrine of the Trinity in the simple form of a confession of personal faith in God the Father, in Jesus Christ His only-begotten Son, and in the Holy Spirit. But in the so-called Creed of St. Athanasius, which, in addition to the Apostles' and Nicene, is generally received in all divisions, Protestant as well as Roman Catholic, of the Western Church, we have the doctrine of the Trinity as formulated in the school of St.

Augustine in a much more developed shape. "*The Catholic faith*," according to this formula, "*is, that we worship one God in Trinity, and Trinity in Unity, neither confounding the Persons nor dividing the substance.*" The Persons, it proceeds to teach, are different, the substance one. Each of these divine Persons is uncreate, each is eternal, each almighty, etc. And yet there are not three Almighties or three Eternals, but one Almighty and one Eternal, etc.; and not three Gods or three Lords, but one Lord and one God. The Father is uncreate and unbegotten; the Son uncreate, but begotten of the Father; the Holy Ghost uncreate, but proceeding from the Father and the Son. And in this Trinity of divine Persons there is none before and none after, none higher and none less, but all three co-equal, etc.

This the faith of the Church universal, in respect to the divine nature, is regarded by many in the present day as an "*Aberglaube*," *i.e.* an "ultra-faith" or superstition; while others, without directly impugning the doctrine of the Trinity *per se*, regard this particular form in which it is enshrined as of doubtful validity, and some of its definitions as objectionable; whereas the Athanasian Creed itself declares with the utmost stringency, that "he who would be saved *must thus think* of the Trinity," and, indeed, rightly insists upon the doctrine as the necessary foundation of all Christian teaching. We will now, taking the definitions of this symbol as our starting-point, inquire as to the scriptural character of the doctrine thus formulated, and, faithful to our general principle, will endeavour frankly to acknowledge and concede where concession and acknowledgment may seem right and necessary.

And our first confession is this: That the scientific theology of the present day, and, indeed, that branch of it which most closely adheres to the teaching of Holy Scripture, professes to find (and not, I think, without some reason) sundry defects in the Athanasian definitions. The more closely one examines into what the Bible itself teaches concerning the Father, the Son, and the Holy Spirit, the more readily will he acknowledge that true and precious as the *nucleus* of its doctrine remains, there are nevertheless some points in the teaching of this Creed, concerning the relations of the divine

Persons, which are not in full accord with that of Scripture. And still less do they satisfy the questions and requirements of speculative theology. We confess with Nitzsch, that while the received doctrine of the Church enshrines the inestimable treasure of the truth itself, it does not always put it in a form acceptable or satisfactory to the philosophical inquirer. There is in the Athanasian formula, for instance, much that is hard and unnecessarily offensive, and even provocative of doubt and objection; nor can we be surprised if such objections are continually cropping up and appearing on the surface throughout the chequered course of Church History.

The Athanasian Creed is evidently too stiffly *arithmetical* in some of its definitions and antitheses, without attempt to reconcile their obvious contradictions. Thus each divine Person is said to be eternal, each uncreate, etc., and yet there are not three Eternals nor three uncreate, but one uncreate and one Eternal, etc. To these statements the objection is obvious, that they either destroy the Unity for the sake of the Trinity, or the Trinity in the interest of the Unity; nor is it quite easy with the doctrine so stated to rebut the charge alleged, not by Jews and Mahometans only, but also by many Christians, that Trinitarianism contradicts the fundamental article of all true religion, that there is only One living and true God. Hence the numerous attempts in ancient and modern times to remove this stumbling-block of the understanding, now in one way, now in another,—attempts in which the Trinity was naturally more frequently sacrificed than the Unity; as, for instance, by Socinians and Unitarians since the Reformation, who argue that inasmuch as Monotheism is evidently the fundamental doctrine of the Bible, it cannot teach the divinity of our Lord, and that Christ must be therefore a mere man, and the Holy Spirit merely a divine influence. Hence also the similar objections of modern Rationalism, that it contradicts the laws of thought, that a part should be equal to the whole, or a whole to its several parts,—that, for instance, $1=3$,—an objection the superficial character of which is obvious, and the answer to it easy. Mathematical axioms are out of place in metaphysical and ethical inquiries. Our minds must be carried into a higher sphere. Mathematically speaking, no doubt two persons are distinct entities. But of the persons of the Trinity, the Church has always taught their unity of substance and their absolute inseparability, and so lifted up the whole question into a region of transcendent thought and feeling, of which mathematical science is wholly ignorant. We must not confound the respective spheres.

The Church herself, however, is not quite free from blame in this respect, on account of the *arithmetical* character of some parts of her chief formulary. The objections stirred by these might have been avoided by anticipation, had a firm hold been taken from the first of the truth indicated by the Hebrew form of the divine name ELOHIM (as will be more fully shown presently), that in God unity and plurality consist as correlatives which mutually require one another; that, as we have already indicated, it is the essential characteristic of the true doctrine of the divine nature, in contradistinction to Polytheism on the one hand, and an abstract Monotheism on the other, that both elements of true Being, unicity and multiplicity, do in God meet and interpenetrate one another in a perfectly unique and transcendental way.

But now to come to the doctrine itself, and its basis in Holy Scripture. You are all aware that no such sentence as God is a triune God is to be found in the Bible. The well-known text, 1 John v. 7, *There are three that bear record in heaven, the Father, the Word, and the Holy Ghost, and these three are one*, is now universally recognised as an interpolation. The terms trinity, triunity, threefold personality, and even the word person itself, are not derived immediately from Scripture. It fares with these as with all attempts to express human conceptions concerning the Divine and Infinite—they are but imperfect, inadequate expressions which we accept and use for the want of better. The very term *persons* has something objectionable in it, suggesting at first the notion of distinct and separate individualities, which is perfectly inapplicable to the consubstantial, and therefore inseparable, *hypostases* of which the Bible speaks as Father, Son, and Holy Spirit.

Our Church formularies are undoubtedly right in laying stress on the unity of substance in these divine Persons; but it may be questioned whether they are also right in seeming to speak of the divine substance as if it were, in the first instance, something indefinite and universal, which was then resolved into three distinct hypostases. When we speak of "three persons in one divine substance," we use an expression which apparently implies that the substance is regarded as something abstract and impersonal, which assumes a threefold personality in the concrete forms of God the Father, God the Son, and God the Holy Ghost. Many earnest inquirers are sensible of a certain incongruity between this mode of speaking and the teaching of Scripture, and, we may add, the teaching also of the Apostles' and Nicene Creeds, as well as of the best and most authoritative Fathers of the Oriental Church. Holy Scripture and primitive theology undoubtedly regard the Divine Essence as in itself personal, naming it at once *God* and *Father*. They agree in speaking of the heavenly Father as (not the first member in a series of divine evolutions, but) Himself God, holding the fulness of the Godhead in Himself, *Fons totius Deitatis*, the spring and fountainhead of the whole Deity from which Son and Holy Spirit are evermore derived. This point is one of decisive significance in determining the relations between the divine Persons, and leads us at once into the midst of our present inquiry.

We propose therefore (A.) to examine the chief Scripture testimonies to the doctrine of the Trinity in general, viz. those concerning (*a*) The divine Father, (*b*) The Son, (*c*) The Holy Ghost, and (*d*) The mutual relations of the divine Persons. This done, we propose further (B.) to examine the results thus obtained by the light derived from the history of religious thought and from modern philosophical speculation, and to inquire as to what extraneous supports and testimonies may be thus afforded them.

A. *Scripture Testimonies to the Doctrine of the Trinity.*—Are then, according to the witness of Scripture, Father, Son, and Holy Ghost so one in essence that Son and Spirit are also God? And are they, notwithstanding this essential unity, three distinct though not separated subjects (or persons), having each His own knowledge and will? These are our first questions. The former point, the unity of the Son's essence with the Father, was denied by Paul of Samosata in the third, by the Arians in the fourth and following centuries, and in later times by Unitarians and Rationalists. The latter, the personal distinctions of the three divine hypostases, were disputed by the Sabellians as early as the third century. They taught that the one God, while manifesting Himself in a threefold relation to the world, now as Father, now as Son, and now as Holy Spirit, had nevertheless remained within Himself always one and the same; and that so, what we call the Persons of the Trinity were but different forms of divine manifestation;—a view which has often reappeared in various shapes in modern theology. The doctrine of Scripture stands in the midst between these two parties: it holds fast, on the one hand, the unity of substance, the consubstantiality of Son and Holy Spirit with the heavenly Father, and on the other, their personal distinctness: it combines, in reference to the doctrine of the Trinity (as we have seen to be the case in reference to other theories concerning the divine nature), all the various elements of truth which human systems are so prone to separate.

(*a*) And first, with regard to God the Father, He is the ultimate cause of all creation (1 Cor. viii. 6; Rom. xi. 36); to Him the whole development of the universe is due—*He worketh all in all* (1 Cor. xii. 6), and the goal toward which it is all tending—*that God may be all in all* (1 Cor. xi. 28). He is, therefore, the only Potentate and Lord of all (1 Tim. vi. 15); He is also the Author of all redemption, which, in accordance with His will, was determined from all eternity (Eph. i. 4; 2 Tim. i. 9, 10), and evolved in time. He is therefore designated simply by the title *Saviour* (Luke i. 47; 1 Tim. i. 1); by Him the Son is sent, and from Him the Paraclete proceeds (John iii. 16, xiv. 16). This divine Father, while not disdaining to enter His own world and make His dwelling in His saints (John xiv. 23; Acts xvii. 27), yet remains eternally unchangeable, in light unapproachable, the only deathless One (1 Tim. vi. 16); the only Wise, overruling and disposing all events by His holy will and providence (Rom. xvi. 27; Matt. xxiv. 36). No one disputes, indeed no one can deny, that deity and divine honour are in Scripture assigned to the Father. But how is it with the Son and the Spirit? Here the variety of teaching and opinion is manifold. We must consider the Scripture testimonies more in detail. And first let us examine: (*b*) The Scripture testimony to the consubstantiality of the Son with the Father. The very title which our Lord applies to Himself (John iii. 16, 18)—*Son*, and *only-begotten Son of God*—compared with the many passages in which He speaks of the Father in heaven as *His Father*, indicates a claim to stand in a peculiar filial relation to the Father such as no mere creature can aspire to. All attempts to deny this, and to make out that the Sonship claimed by our Lord is nothing more than the childlike relation which belongs to all believers (against which, compare John i. 12 with iv. 14 and 18), are plainly refuted by the observation, that He always makes a clear distinction in speaking to His disciples between *your Father* and *my Father*, *your God* and *my God;* that He never places Himself, so to speak, on the same line with them—never speaks of OUR *Father* (Matt. vi. 8, 32, xviii. 10, xvi. 17, xxvi. 53; John xx. 17)—(the first words of the Lord's Prayer are not in point (Matt. vi. 9), for Christ is there teaching His disciples to pray, and does not include Himself with them). Moreover, this specific filial relation to the Father is indicated in those places where our Lord speaks of Himself as sent by the Father, and coming into the world, as having come down from heaven, and as the Son of man who is in heaven (John iii. 13, comp. iv. 31, 32, vi. 33, 50, 58, viii. 23). He limits at the same time His own pre-existence: compare especially John viii. 58, *Before Abraham was, I am;* which is not, as we shall see more fully hereafter, to be understood in an ideal and impersonal, but in a strictly personal and realistic sense.

In accordance with this claim to a divine origin, we find our Lord assuming divine authority—(*But I say unto you*)—abrogating not merely Rabbinical but Sinaitic precepts (Matt. v. 19, 9)—declaring Himself greater than the temple, Lord of the Sabbath, more than Jonas and Solomon, and the dispenser of forgiveness (Matt. ix. 2, 6). It is only in virtue of His self-consciousness as God that He can regard Himself as a creditor to whom the sinner is indebted, and who, in His own name, vouchsafes remission (Luke vii. 41-50). God alone has the right to judge or to forgive the violation of His image in man by sin: were Christ not one with God, He would be guilty of blasphemy in assuming such power (Matt. ix. 2, 3). It is in virtue of the same claim to a divine character that our

Lord subordinates love to one's neighbour in His disciples to love towards Himself—*He that loveth father or mother more than me*, etc. (Matt. x. 37, which is virtually the same as John x. 30). And it is as being omniscient and pre-existent that He declares that He will hereafter come again as Judge (Matt. vii. 21-23, xxiv. 30, xxv. 31, etc.). It is as one with the omnipresent Father that He promises to be with His disciples everywhere and always to the world's end (Matt. xxviii. 20 compared with John xiv. 18). It will be observed that these proofs are in the first instance taken from the earlier Gospels, which modern criticism would fain separate by a wide gulf from that of St. John. How impossible it is to do so is evident from one example. Our Lord, in St. Matt. xi. 27, claims to stand in a position so unique to the heavenly Father that none can know the Father but Himself, or through His mediation, and none know Him but the Father only. The whole Gospel of St. John may be regarded as an illustration of this one utterance (cf. John iii. 35, xiv. 6, xvii. 25).

It is only like that knows like. It is only in virtue of unity of essence that the Son thus knows the Father, and is known only of Him. We need not, therefore, wonder to hear Him saying in the fourth Gospel: *I and my Father are one; I am in the Father, and the Father in me* (John x. 30, xiv. 11, 20, x. 38); *He that hath seen me hath seen the Father;* and claiming with the Father one undivided dignity, *that they all may honour* the Son *even as they honour the Father* (John v. 23, xiv. 13)—a claim refuting in the most complete way those who would deny adoration to be due to our Lord (compare Luke xxiv. 52). There is ONE WILL and ONE WORK (John v. 30, 19-21, xi. 41, etc.), as there is ONE LOVE (xiv. 21, xvii. 26) of the Father and the Son. And, therefore, the Son's return to the glory which *He had with the Father before the world was* (John xvii. 5), is a glorification *with the Father* such as no creature can attain to (John iii. 13, viii. 21, 23, xiii. 32, 33). He returns to a state in which He is the sender of the Spirit, even as the Father is (John xiv. 26, xv. 26; Luke xxiv. 49),—that Spirit who will take the substance of His witness from the things of the Son, and will glorify the Son (John xvi. 13-15) on earth, even as the Son once glorified the Father (xvii. 4) in His life here.

But if this witness of our Lord concerning Himself, and, indeed, the very terms Son of God and Only-begotten, justify the inference of His consubstantiality with the Father, they no less teach His derivation from, dependence on, and subordination to, the Father, albeit in co-equal Godhead. The Father hath, indeed, committed to the Son all that He hath; but one thing He could not impart, His own paternity, otherwise the Son would have ceased to be Son. The Father is the eternal unbeginning archetype, the Son the co-eternal perfect image of the Father. When it is said that "the Father hath given to the Son to have life in Himself," the meaning is, that the life of Godhead which the Son possesses is, as compared with the highest life among the creatures, original, creative, and archetypal; but as compared with the Father, it is still something given and received: "The Son can do nothing of Himself but what He seeth the Father do" (John v. 19); "My Father is greater than I" (John xiv. 28); "I ascend to my God and your God" (John xx. 17). Even in the heavenly glory the Father is still His God.

The apostolic testimonies in other parts of the New Testament conduct us to the same result as these utterances of our Lord contained in the Gospel. They establish both His consubstantiality with the Father and His filial subordination. We will refer to only one or two of the most important passages. First, then, our Lord's personal pre-existence is clearly taught by St. Paul (Col. i. 16, 17), "He is before all things" (compare His own I AM in John viii. 58); and His consubstantial dignity by the same apostle (Phil. ii. 6), *Being in the form of God;* where the reference is not to any manifestation of the Godhead in the days of His flesh (when "the form" which He took upon Him was that "of a servant"), but His position from eternity. And as a consequence of this, we find that even in His human nature God is immanent, that in Him "dwelt the fulness of the Godhead bodily" (Col. ii. 9; 2 Cor. v. 19; 1 Tim. iii. 16).

This unique and pre-existent unity of essence between the Father and the Son is wonderfully taught by St. John in the prologue of His Gospel: *In the beginning* (compare i. 1), *i.e.* before all created things, and when creation itself began, *was the Word,* the LOGOS, *i.e.* divine utterance or speech, and not merely divine inward thought or reason (λόγος προφορικός as well as λόγος ἐνδιαθετος). This Word was God's self-manifestation by which He was preparing to hold communion with His creatures. But before any of these came into existence this WORD was WITH God, or, more accurately, was *towards* God, *i.e.* resting in and clinging to Him by a natural tendency (compare the like remarkable expression in ver. 18, *the Only-begotten in*, or rather INTO, *the bosom of the Father*). From this it is evident that the Son in His pre-existent state was personally or hypostatically distinct from the Father. What follows shows not less clearly that He was consubstantial with Him: *And the Word was God, i.e.* of nature equal and one with the Father. And that explains how St. Paul could speak of Christ as not only more than man (Gal. i. 1), but also (as the best interpreters of Rom. ix. 5 allow) as "God over all" (comp. Tit. ii. 13, Heb. i. 8. 9, Eph. v. 5, John xx. 28, Luke xxiv. 52, and the adoration of the Lamb, Rev. v. 11, 12).

But the apostles no less clearly teach the filial subordination of the Son to the Father, both in His pre-existence before creation and in His glorification now (cf. Heb. i. 3, Acts vii. 55, Rom. viii. 34, Heb. x. 12), yea, and even in the consummation of an after eternity (1 Cor. xv. 28).

All this teaching is of great importance, from its bearing on the scriptural doctrine of the Trinity. Christ, it tells us, has occupied from eternity a relation of mediatorship between God and the universe. The very expression "only-begotten" indicates this. For if "begotten" refers to a transcendent process within the Godhead before all worlds, the "only" refers to the world of creatures which was to follow. The divine Word or Logos had not only an *inward tendency* (as explained above) towards the Godhead, but also an *outward* one towards the universe and the work of creation. Therefore St. John in his prologue goes on to say, "All things were made through Him, and without Him was made nothing" (chap. i. 4). The full apostolic teaching is, that creation is a work of the Father done *through* the Son (1 Cor. viii. 6; 2 Pet. iii. 5; Col. i. 16). The Son is not, *as such*, the final Cause, but the Divine co-equal Instrument of creation. He is also its Motive—the Heir of all things, because all things were made for Him, under whom, as its Head, the All is finally to be gathered (Heb. i. 2, 3; Eph. i. 10). As the immediate support of all life in the world of creatures, He is not Himself a creature, but yet "the First-born of all creation" (Col. i. 15, cf. Rev. iii. 14). This last expression—"First-born of" (or "before") "all creation," or "every creature"—teaches three things: His derivation from the Father, His essential unlikeness to all creatures (born, not made), and at the same time His mediatorial relation towards them. And so we see how, in the scriptural idea of the divine generation, it forms as it were a bridge to the work of creation. The eternal Son goes forth from the Father's bosom as the archetype of the world that is to be, and specially as the future Life and Light of man (John i. 4, viii. 12).

Moreover all these witnesses of Christ and the apostles prove no less clearly the distinct PERSONALITY of the Son of God. Unity with the Father is not identity with Him. The very word "with God" implies personal distinction. And it needs hardly to notice how in His earthly life our Lord, when most strongly asserting His oneness with the Father, yet never puts this personal distinction out of view: "I and my Father are one;" and yet, "My Father worketh hitherto, and I work." From His first utterance in the temple to His last upon the cross, He always speaks of the Father as a distinct person from Himself. And so also He speaks of the Holy Spirit as *another* Comforter, as His future representative in the world (John xiv. 16, xvi. 14, etc.), as sent by Him from the Father, and therefore as again a distinct person from Himself. And it is evident from every page of the Acts of the Apostles that these personal distinctions were not effaced by His return to glory.

One important result at which we arrive is plainly this: So surely as our Lord describes Himself as one with the Father, though yet personally distinct and derived from Him, so surely as He speaks of Himself as not only the teacher and pattern of divine love, but also as the Lord and Master of the hearts of all men,—so surely must His equality and unity with the Father, along with any personal distinction, be of an infinitely closer and more intimate kind than that between any creaturely offspring and its earthly parent. (Gess.)

And another result is, that if the well-known definition of the Athanasian Creed, "In this Trinity there is none before or after, nothing greater or less," must be regarded as a one-sided and inadequate statement of the truth, ignoring as it seems to do the filial subordination, so much more must we pronounce the teaching of Unitarianism and Rationalism as altogether antiscriptural in its denial of His co-equal consubstantial Godhead.

(*c*) A similar result would also follow from an investigation of the doctrine of Scripture concerning the Holy Spirit. Some ancient heretics regarded the Holy Spirit, as Rationalism does now, as a mere impersonal energy or virtue of the divine nature; others (like the Arians), as a created Being; some modern rationalists apply the term to the religious instinct of the existing Christian community. The Church teaches that the Holy Spirit is a divine person. To which of these forms of doctrine does Holy Scripture bear witness as the true?

None can deny that Scripture assigns to the Holy Ghost attributes and operations which are simply *divine*—omniscience (1 Cor. ii. 10), omnipresence (Ps. cxxxix. 7), creative energy (Ps. xxxiii. 6; Gen. i. 2). In Heb. ix. 2, He is called simply "the eternal Spirit;" in 1 Pet. iv. 14, "Spirit of God," and "Spirit of glory;" in 1 Cor. ii. 10, He is said to "search the deeps of God." There can be no doubt as to Scripture testimony to His Godhead, but how does the case stand as to Scripture teaching concerning His personality?

Now here it must be first observed, that as in the natural world the Spirit of God is represented as the quickening energy which imparts life and form and power of development to what before was dead and formless matter, so in the spiritual world He is the life-giving influence for the soul of man, and the imparter to it of spiritual life and true personality (Gen. ii. 7). This life He can at all times quicken and renew, and through Him it is that the believer becomes first a person and then a child of God. Is it not *à priori* probable that He from whom the principle of personality comes should be Himself a person?

Further, *personal* attributes are constantly assigned in Holy Scripture to the Holy Spirit—self-consciousness, knowledge will, self-determination, speech, and action. So, when the Spirit is spoken of as "searching all things," as "only knowing what is in God" (1 Cor. ii. 11), as the "other Comforter" who "convinces," "teaches," "brings to remembrance," "leads into all truth," "takes of the things of Jesus and shows them to believers," and so "glorifies Christ in them" (John xiv. 16, 28, xvi. 7, 8, 13–15); when it is said of Him that He aids our prayers by "making intercession for us with groanings that cannot be uttered" (Rom. viii. 26),—all this is unintelligible without assuming personal self-consciousness in the divine agent. And again, when He is said to be grieved (Eph. iv. 30), lied to (Acts v. 3), blasphemed (Matt. xii. 31), to be the Lord and Distributer of heavenly gifts, imparting to each man severally as He will (1 Cor. xii. 11), to speak and witness in the disciples (Matt. x. 20; Rom. viii. 16), and even to speak to them in the first person (Acts xiii. 2: "Separate me Barnabas and Saul"), personal feeling, will, and action are evidently attributed to Him.

It is, indeed, often noticed that the Holy Spirit is spoken of as a gift (Acts ii. 38; Heb. vi. 4), as "power from on high" (Luke xxiv. 49) with which the first disciples were to be endowed; and this, it is argued, is incompatible with personality. But so Christ Himself, we reply, is spoken of as the gift of God (John iii. 16, iv. 10); and the Distributer of heavenly gifts cannot Himself be a gift in a neutral or material, but only in a personal sense. It is only as being the personal principle of all the powers of the kingdom of God, and not merely as a single power or divine property, that the Spirit can be co-ordinated, as in 1 Cor. xii. 4–6, with the Father and the Son. It is only as a person distinct from the Father that He can make intercession in the hearts of believers (Rom. viii. 26).

A question is sometimes asked: If the Holy Spirit is poured out upon and imparted to so many thousands of believers, can it, in this distribution and manifold division, be one and the same person? The solution is found in the divine omnipresence of the Spirit. Is not our Lord Himself spoken of as dwelling in individual saints (2 Cor. xiii. 5; Gal. ii. 20), without any thought of denying His distinct personality? And when we consider that it belongs to the very idea of the Holy Spirit that He should be the principle of unity in the divine attributes, and that it is, as it were, the law of His being that He should be self-distributing and self-imparting, we see at once how *natural* it is for Him to dwell in a multitude of spiritual homes. And therefore He is represented, in this self-division and innate disposition to self-impartation, as "the seven Spirits before the throne of God," "sent out into all the earth" (Rev. i. 4, iv. 5). These "seven Spirits" are further said (Isa. xi. 1, 2) to "rest upon" "the rod of the stem of Jesse," as manifold and yet as One—the *Holy Spirit* of the New Testament which comes to us from Him as the Spirit of Jesus, through one and the same with the personal and consubstantial Spirit of the Father.

In heaven, then, the Holy Spirit appears as a person, the personal principle or unity of the divine powers; on earth He is manifested to us as a multiplicity of gifts (Acts ii. 38). But even these "gifts" have something "personal" in them. They dwell in us without being lost or confounded with our personality. The Spirit speaks to the heart of the believer, "bears witness with our spirit," and even speaks from us to the world without (Matt. x. 20).

But at the same time He is and remains very God, consubstantial with the Father and the Son. This is evident not only from what was said above, but also from the numerous passages of Scripture in which He is spoken of as the principle of the new birth and source of our sanctification (cf. 1 Thess. i. 5; 1 Cor. ii. 4, 5; John iii. 5 foll.; Rom. ii. 29, viii. 9, v. 5, xiv. 17; 1 Cor. xii. 3, 13; 1 John ii. 27, iii. 24; Acts vii. 51, xix. 2–5), even as the same is said of the Father and the Son. Those who are born of the Spirit are also born of God; those who lie to the Holy Ghost, lie also to God. Christ, too, identifies His own operation with that of the Spirit. The coming of the Paraclete is His coming likewise (John xiv. 16–18). That blasphemy against the Holy Ghost should be the only unpardonable sin is a clear proof that He cannot in dignity be less than God.

And thus we arrive at the like result with regard to the Holy Spirit to that which appeared to us the doctrine of Scripture in regard to the Son. Consubstantial with the Father and the Son, He is yet personally distinct from them, and in a certain way subordinate, from being from Both derived and from Both proceeding. "He speaks not of Himself, but that which He hears;" He takes of the fulness of Christ to impart to us (John xvi. 13, 14). His coming to us is dependent on the Lord's completion of the Lord's redeeming work and His entrance into glory (John vii. 39, xvi. 7). He is sent by Him from the Father. And as in the kingdom of grace, so in the natural and moral world He is the principle of communication between the *Creator* and the *creatures*—the breath of life from God in the world.

(*d*) We conclude this investigation with a brief review of a few passages of Scripture, in which the doctrine of the Trinity is contained as a whole, in which Father, Son, and Holy Ghost are spoken of together.

The received dogmatic theology of the Church distinguishes between an essential (immanent Ontological) Trinity of persons in the Godhead and an ECONOMICAL Trinity, *i.e.* a threefold manifestation or self-revelation of the one God to us. The Church believes in and affirms both. But many theologians in the present day, and among them not a few sincere believers in revelation, deny the scriptural authority of the former, while all receive and acknowledge the latter.

Leaving on one side for the present this point of controversy, we will first inquire how far the testimony of Scripture supports the essential features in the doctrine of the Church concerning the personal distinctness and yet real unity and consubstantiality of God the Father, the Son, and the Holy Spirit.

The fundamental scriptural authority for the whole doctrine is the formula of baptism (Matt. xxviii. 19): "Baptizing them in (or into) the name of the Father, and of the Son, and of the Holy Ghost." That what is here spoken of is a baptism into communion with Father, Son, and Spirit, all sound exegesis must allow. And therefrom must follow, in the first place, that by these terms cannot be meant three successive phases of development (Sabellianism), but three contemporaneous distinctions in the divine nature. And further, we are warranted in drawing a threefold conclusion: (1) That these three distinct manifestations must be *personal.* There is no instance in Scripture of an action being performed in the name of any abstract thing, but only of a personal subject.

Moreover, it would be impossible to enter into communion with any but a person. (2) That these three persons are co-equal and divine. They are named together on equal terms, and the same divine honour is accorded to each of them. (Especially significant is here the co-equal divine personality assigned to the Holy Spirit. No one will deny that Father and Son are terms properly applied only to distinct persons; but how with such could an impersonal power or virtue be associated in the way in which the Holy Spirit is here?) And (3) the singular term "*in the name*" indicates that these three persons are yet essentially one, not three different beings or separate individuals. The same divine name manifests itself as Father in the Father, as Son in the Son, as Holy Ghost in the Holy Spirit. Then is unity without singularity, consubstantiality along with personal distinctions, distinction without separation.

Another Trinitarian passage is 2 Cor. xiii. 13: "The grace of our Lord Jesus Christ, the love of God ("the God," *i.e.* God the Father), and the communion of the Holy Ghost be with you all." Compare this with 1 Cor. xii. 4–6, where manifold "gifts" are associated with "one Spirit," manifold "ministrations" with "one Lord" Christ (Eph. iv. 11), and manifold "operations" with "one God" (the Father) who worketh all in all; and with Eph. iv. 4–6, which speaks of one Spirit, one Lord, one God and Father of all. These passages compared together prove what we have already established by other considerations, that in the doctrine of Scripture God the Father is the source and well-spring of the whole Godhead (*Fons totius Deitatis*), of that of the Son, and of that of the Spirit, who are not separate existences, but in the Father and from Him. Compare also 1 Pet. i. 1, 2, where the foreknowledge and predetermination of the Father is represented as the source and mainspring of the whole work of grace. The same thing is taught in our original passage, 2 Cor. xiii. 13. The love of God the Father is the source of all grace, which manifests itself in the Son, our Lord Jesus Christ; and the product of this grace and love is the communion of the Holy Spirit.

And if with these and other Trinitarian passages of Scripture (such as Rev. i. 4, 5 and Rom. xi. 36) we compare the

Gospel narratives which have a specially Trinitarian character, —such as the Annunciation (Luke i. 35), and the Lord's Baptism, in which the sinless one, who had placed Himself in fellowship with sinners for their salvation, is raised, as it were, by the Father's voice, and introduced by the illapse of the Spirit into the "communion" of the Trinity,—we shall be in a condition to form a judgment in the controversy between those who regard the doctrine of the Trinity as expressing eternal and essential distinctions in the divine nature, and those who regard the divine persons as mere economical manifestations of the Holy One in His relation to ourselves.

Now, first of all, it is clear, and allowed on all sides, that the doctrine of the Trinity rests upon, and is derived from, great facts of divine revelation. It is because God has revealed Himself to us as Father, Son, and Holy Spirit, that we believe in a triune God. The very form of the Apostles' and Nicene Creed proves this. The divine name in the baptismal formula is a threefold name of revelation as to God's relation to us. And so the love of God (the Father) in 2 Cor. xiii. 13, in connection with the grace (of the Son) and the communion of the Spirit which follow, points in the first instance to the relation in which He reveals Himself as standing to the world. In all these ways we have undoubtedly a *trinity of revelation* (an economical trinity).

But it cannot, on the other hand, be denied that in Holy Scripture some passages may be found which point to the existence of real internal distinctions in the divine nature, that is, to a trinity of hypostatic existence (an Ontological Trinity). The uncreated Word or Logos is before all worlds "with" or "towards" (πρός) God, and sinking as it were into (εἰς) the Father's bosom. And the same inwardly directed tendency towards "the deeps of the Godhead" is predicated of the divine Spirit (1 Cor. ii. 10). The very names of Father, Son, and Holy Spirit, though in the first instance names of a trinity of revelation, do, if expressive of a real revelation, indicate real internal distinctions in the divine nature. And so also in our Lord's Baptism we have not only a divine revelation made to us, and a link in the chain of the works of redeeming love, but we also see the divine persons acting and reacting one on the other.

The conclusion at which we arrive is this: If the teaching of Scripture is in the main concerned with the divine relations to us, and its Trinity is therefore in the main a Trinity of revelation, it is yet going much too far to say that it does not contain expressive hints of a real internal ontological Trinity. And this latter has a very deep interest for Speculative Theology.

But we may surely ask further, Is it then necessary, or even rational, to make so broad a distinction between this external and this internal Trinity? If God reveal Himself to the world as Father, Son, and Holy Spirit, is it not because He IS what He reveals Himself as being? The Trinity of revelation points to a Trinity of inward being which it thus makes manifest. The one implies and presupposes the other. The eternal generation of the Son and procession of the Spirit involve a divine impulse from eternity to creation and redemption. And in like manner the Trinity of revelation has ontological elements. If love be the essence of the divine nature, the impulse to revelation is inherent in it. In other words: God's actions *without* imply *inward* workings and relations, and His inward actions and relations are the necessary premises and preparations for His outward working. In revelation God reveals *Himself,* and the impulse of self-manifestation belongs to His inmost being.

The *comparative* silence of Holy Scripture as to the ontological code of Trinitarian doctrine is easily accounted for by the considerations already offered, as to the self-hiding as well as the self-revealing characteristics of the divine nature. It is naturally the latter which are prominently presented to us in Holy Scripture.

But before we proceed to the final result of what has been said on this subject, we must briefly consider an objection which has seemed to many to militate against the doctrine of the Trinity. Why is nothing said, they ask, with regard to this truth in the Old Testament? Why did God withhold for 4000 years a self-revelation which is assumed to be so essential to the spiritual good of His creatures? And if this were indeed the case, if in the Old Testament, which professes to be a revelation of the true and living God, there were *no* traces of this truth, we might indeed be seriously shaken as to the very groundwork of Christian doctrine. But a closer examination shows that it is not so. If for good reasons God was pleased to withhold under the Old Covenant a full revelation of His triune nature, He gave at least manifold hints of it in the names and words and facts of the ancient Scriptures. We can only briefly hint at some of these.

Many passages of the Old Testament, for instance, teach the divinity of the future Messiah, as when He is called *the Son of God* (Ps. ii. 7; Prov. xxx. 4), the Branch of the Lord (Isa. iv. 2; Zech. iii. 8), the Lord (Ps. cx. compared with Matt. xxii. 44), God (Ps. xlv. 8), Mighty God (Isa. ix. 6 comp. x. 21); His pre-existence is hinted at (Mic. v. 1 comp. with Isa. xlviii. 16), and an eternal post-existence promised Him (Dan. vii. 14), an eternal kingdom and an eternal priesthood (Ps. cx. 4). And if with regard to the Holy Spirit many passages of the Old Testament do not go beyond the notion of a divine energy or influence, it cannot surely be denied that in others, activities are ascribed to Him which imply personal subsistence, as His striving (Gen. vi. 3), speaking (2 Sam. xxiii. 2), leading (Ps. cxliii. 10), His being made grieved and made angry (Isa. lxiii. 10), to which we have so many parallels in the New Testament. The Spirit of God, moreover, is represented in the Old Testament as resting on Messiah in His sevenfold eradiation (Isa. xi. 2), and as not only imparting Himself to individuals (Num. xi. 25–29; 1 Sam. xix. 23; 2 Kings ii. 9–15), but as outpoured on the whole people of the redeemed in Messianic times (Isa. xliv. 3); as the Spirit of vision and prophecy (Joel ii. 28), of inward renewal and sanctification (Ezek. xxxvi. 27, xxxix. 29), of grace and prayer (Zech. xii. 10).

These are only hints, but they are enough to show that the Old Testament attributes to the Messiah predicates which belong to no mere creature, and so teaches His true Godhead, while it ascribes a real independent activity to the Holy Spirit. And there are also numerous indications in the Old Testament of a certain plurality in the divine nature, an organized and complex unity, a mutual indwelling and co-operation of the three divine hypostases.

Such an indication may be found in in the Hebrew name for God, *Elohim*. The plural (as is well known) is commonly used with a singular verb. So in the very first words of Scripture (Gen. i. 1), which may be said to contain the first trace of the doctrine of the Trinity: "In the beginning Elohim" (plural) "created" (singular) "heaven and earth." This is hardly to be accounted for by the hypothesis of a *pluralis majestatis*, of the use of which there is no other clear evidence in Scripture. But even if it were so, the plural might still be regarded as indicating an internal divine plurality of powers and forms of being. The same may be said of the "Us" in Gen. i. 26 and iii. 22 (comp. Gen. xi. 7 and Isa. vi. 8). The hypothesis that God is here speaking of the angels as associated with Himself, is perfectly inadmissible, so far, at any rate, as the first two passages are concerned. It would contradict all other teachings of Scripture, which clearly ascribe to God the creation of mankind without any intervention of angelic agencies (Gen. ii. 7–22; Isa. xl. 13 foll., xliv. 24). We may say indeed of Gen. i. 1, that we have here an intimation of the divine plurality in unity, and unity in plurality; that all subsequent Trinitarian developments are but unfoldings of what is here presented in the germ.

Again, consider what is said in Scripture of God's creating all things by His Word (cf. John i. 1–3), and by His Spirit moving on the face of the waters (Gen. i. 2). Comp. Ps. xxxiii. 6, "The heavens were made by the Word of Jehovah, and all the host of them by the Spirit of His mouth;" to which "Word" and "Spirit" the "Us" of Gen. i. 26 must be referred, and not to an association of angels. An interpretation to which we are the more entitled, inasmuch as several places in the Old Testament refer unmistakeably to twofold and threefold self-distinctions in the divine essence, *e.g.*: "The Lord caused it to rain from the Lord out of heaven" (Gen. xix. 24); "I have filled Bezaleel with the Spirit of God" (Ex. xxxi. 3), where the Lord who speaks distinguishes between Himself and God (the Father) as well as (the Holy) Spirit; "The Lord" (God the Father) "said unto my Lord" (Messiah, son of David, who at the same time is David's Lord, Ps. cx. 1); "O God, hear for the Lord's sake" (Dan. ix. 17); and especially Isa. xlviii. 16: "From the time that it took place there am I (Messiah, the servant of the Lord), and now the Lord God hath sent me, and His Spirit." Compare also the Lord's

(Jehovah's) proclamation concerning the name of the Lord (Ex. xxxiv. 5–7).

Moreover the WORD is, in the Old Testament, Mediator in the Lord's redeeming work as well as in that of creation. "He sent forth His Word and healed them" (Ps. cvii. 20). To which, if we add the fore-cited passages wherein the future Messiah is designated as the Son of God, we have the New Testament doctrine of *the Word made flesh* in germ and early development. And this will be confirmed by observation of the divine agency in the history of the Exodus, the type of the redemption under the New Testament. There we see the Angel of Jehovah, sent by God, the Father of His people (Deut. xxxii. 6), to lead them through the wilderness, as the angelic and quasi-human organ of His presence (Ex. xxiii. 20, 21, xxxiii. 14); and His Spirit poured out upon their leaders, Moses, Aaron, the seventy elders, Joshua (Num. xi, 25, xxvii. 18; Neh. ix. 20). So that in after times Isaiah could describe the redemption from Egypt as the work of Jehovah, of His Angel, and His Spirit (Isa. lxiii. 8–10). *This is the trinity of the Old Testament.* "These three forms of divine manifestation dominate the whole of its history." (Delitzsch, *Apologetik*, pp. 314 foll., 411, 420.)

And further, these observations enable us to trace Trinitarian doctrine in the Levitical blessing (Num. vi. 24–27), the putting of the threefold sacred name on the children of Israel: "The Lord bless thee and keep thee" (God the Father, Maker, and Preserver); the Lord make His face to shine upon thee, and be gracious unto thee (God the Son, the Light of the world, full of grace and truth); the Lord lift up His countenance unto thee and give thee peace (God the Holy Ghost, who brings nearer and appropriates to us the divine grace and peace). You will observe how here we have an essential unity in the thrice repeated Lord (Jehovah) with diversity of operations.[1] And to this threefold name of blessing here on earth, corresponds the thrice-repeated Holy of the seraphim in the heavenly sanctuary (Isa. vi. 3). When throughout the Old Testament we find God calling Himself the God of Abraham, Isaac, and Jacob,—Abraham, the father

[1] This point has been more fully treated in the author's Sermons, entitled *Der Segen des Herrn.* London, 1860.

who was willing to offer up his only son; Isaac, the son who carried the wood of his sacrifice, and suffered himself to be laid thereon; and Jacob, the founder and prototype of a spiritual Israel,—have we not here a prophetic type of that divine manifestation in which God gives up His Son as a sacrifice for all, and sends forth His Spirit to form a spiritual people, and so reveals the sacred name of the Father, the Son, and the Holy Ghost?

After all this, we surely cannot deny that Holy Scripture from the very beginning exhibits germs of Trinitarian doctrine. But these germs are not the unfolded flower. A clear developed dogma of the Trinity is not to be found in the Old Testament, and that for good reasons. It was all-important under that dispensation, that, in the face of heathen Polytheism, the great fundamental truth of the divine unity should be impressed on the religious consciousness of God's ancient people: "Hear, O Israel; The Lord our God is one Lord." Too plain an utterance of Trinitarian doctrine would in such times have obscured the truth of the divine unity, and misled into Tritheism. And for the like *pædagogic* reasons our Lord did not at first reveal the triunity of the divine nature to His disciples. It was not till they had learned to believe in His divine Sonship, and in some measure to apprehend His unity with the Father and pre-existence, that He could speak to them of the divine person of the Second Comforter; nay, it was not till He had proved Himself to be the Fountain of eternal life by His own resurrection, and by His breathing on the apostles had kindled in their hearts the fire of the Holy Spirit, that He found them capable of receiving the divinest of mysteries, and therefore could leave behind Him as a precious heirloom to His Church—as the deepest revelation of the divine nature, as the one foundation of Christian faith, knowledge, and practice, and as the final seal and crown of all His teaching while here on earth—the great commission: "Go into all the world, and make disciples of all the nations, baptizing them into the Name of the Father, and of the Son, and of the Holy Ghost."

The objection, therefore, so often raised, that the doctrine of the Trinity is not even founded on Scripture, is itself baseless. From the first of its pages to the last, Scripture is full of indications of this mystery; from the description of the work of creation in Gen. i. to that of the New Jerusalem in the last chapter of the Apocalypse, where the living water (symbol of the Spirit, John vii. 38, 39) is seen issuing from the throne of God and of the Lamb. Everywhere we hear hints both of the personal distinctions and the unity of essence. A striking indication may be found of this in the observation, that whereas each divine hypostasis has a special work and mode of revelation assigned Him, the other two are throughout associated with Him in its discharge. The creation and preservation of the universe is, for instance, the special work and revelation of God the Father. But it is by *the Word* of His power that He makes and upholds all things, and by His *Spirit* that life and form are given to chaos, and the face of the earth continually renewed. The special work of the Son is redemption. But here, too, the Father sends and constantly co-operates and finally receives the finished sacrifice; and here, likewise, the Spirit is co-worker. It is by the Spirit that the eternal Word takes upon Him our nature, that the man Christ Jesus is anointed at His baptism and prepared for His ministry, that He offers Himself without spot to God the Father, and rises again from the dead; and finally, it is by the Spirit taking of the things of Christ that His redemption is applied to each believer. The special work of the Spirit is sanctification; but He is sent forth to that work by the Father and by the Son, and it is the Father's will and the Son's redemption by which He accomplishes it. No communion with one divine person is possible for man, without a like fellowship with the others. He that hath not the Spirit of Christ is none of His; he that denieth the Son hath not the Father (Rom. viii. 9; 1 John ii. 23). We might perhaps venture to express this unity and distinctness of the divine persons in their work and manifestations by three cognate predicates of our own Teutonic speech, and that almost as neatly in English as in German: The Father is *heilig*, the Holy One; the Son, *heilend*, the Healing One; the Spirit, *heiligend*, the Hallowing One.

And here we see—a remark of great importance in respect to the reproach of Tritheism so often brought against Trinitarian doctrine—that what we necessarily represent to our own minds, and to others, as a Trinitarian *process*, is really in its divine eternal ground the simultaneous co-working of three co-eternal divine hypostases. Speculatively overstepping the lines actually drawn in Scripture, we recognise the necessity of the conclusion that God could never have been Father without the Son, and that, therefore, the generation of the Son is not only before time, but co-eternal with the Godhead of the Father; and in the same way, that the procession of the Spirit is co-eternal too. We recognise also, that as there is but one God who manifests in one work the one eternal counsel of His love, and that by revealing Himself as Father, Son, and Spirit; so these three factors constitute by their mutual indwelling and co-working the self-consciousness of the Godhead, which is not to be thought of as a *fourth* producing them. The teaching of the Church has always insisted on the unity of the Godhead, and maintained that the Father is not only God, but the source also of the Godhead, of the Son and Holy Spirit (*Fons Deitatis*), and thereby has cut off all possible basis for a charge of *Tritheism*.

And now, to gather up the threads of the whole inquiry, the Trinitarian doctrine of Scripture is briefly this: The Father is simply God, the God, the divine subject, the source and well-spring of the Godhead of both Son and Holy Spirit; the Son is God, true God, in hypostatic distinction, though derived from the Father; and the Spirit is also truly God in a form which is predicated of the whole divine nature (for God is a Spirit, John iv. 24; and the Lord is the Spirit, 2 Cor. iii. 17), but also in hypostatic distinction from the Father and the Son, by whom He is sent, and from whom He proceeds. There is therefore at once the most essential unity and a threefold hypostatic distinction. The divine nature remains undivided; the whole Godhead (θεότης) is in the Son and in the Holy Spirit—in the Son (Logos) as God's own self-utterance, in the Spirit as the divine self-consciousness. And as the Son is the uttered thought of the Father concerning Himself, so it is again His office to speak out into the world the Father's thoughts of creation and redemption, and thus to stand to the creatures generally, and especially to mankind, in an original archetypal relation (John i. 4). And finally, as the Son is thus the archetypal and ideal principle of mediation between God and the world, of creation and of redemption, so the Holy Spirit is the real or efficient principle, effecting and individualizing all the creative and redeeming energies of the Father and the Son, applying, for instance, to each individual believer the justification *ideally* (*i.e.* in the idea or thought of God) accomplished by the Son, and so effecting a *real* sanctification and regeneration (Eph. ii. 18; 1 Cor. xii. 3): in which process He takes, indeed, everything from the Son, the real and actual having always the ideal and transcendent for its ultimate ground and condition.

And if from this point we now look back on those dogmatic statements of the Athanasian Creed from which we started, we shall find them confirmed in essentials by Holy Scripture; the Son and the Holy Spirit are with their immanence in the Father yet distinct persons, and with their distinct personality they continue immanent. Therefore, neither may we confound the three persons nor divide the one substance. And if the definitions of that formulary go somewhat beyond the teaching of Scripture and of the earlier Church, in the *absolute* equalization of the divine persons (none before or after, none greater or less), to the partial obscuration of the truth of the derivation and subordination of the Son and Holy Spirit in the co-equal Godhead, it must nevertheless be acknowledged that the Church possesses and guards in the Athanasian Creed an invaluable restraint and bulwark against speculative errors, whether of a tritheistic or deistic or pantheistic tendency.

At the same time, it must further be acknowledged that these definitions and distinctions are not sufficient to bridge over the chasm which still yawns between Faith and Reason. The old question is evermore recurring: How can the unity of one being or substance admit of a threefold self-consciousness? How can there be one substance in three distinct persons, and with three distinct personal activities? Eighteen centuries of toilsome thought have not succeeded in solving this enigma. The most recent efforts of Speculative Theology make us only feel more acutely that here we stand in presence of the mystery of all mysteries, and see only darkly as through a mirror of obscure reflection. "It is a truth" (to use the noble words of Hilary of Poitiers) "which lies beyond the domain of human language, beyond the scope of sense, beyond the comprehension of reason. The archangels know it not, the angels understand it not, the ages do not comprehend it, no prophet has discovered it, no apostle explored it, the Son Himself has not made it fully known." Divine mysteries cannot, and were never intended to be made perfectly plausible to human reason; they are, and must be, in the first instance, matters of faith.

On the other hand, it is no less certain that they must also present points of contact for our apprehension; the believing inquirer seeks for a reason for the faith that is in him, and to penetrate more and more with intelligent understanding into its depths (see above, Lect. II. 3). It is given to him not only to believe, but also to *know* the mysteries of the kingdom of heaven (Matt. xiii. 11). And this is the case with the fundamental doctrine of the holy Trinity. The revelations of Scripture on this subject, however inadequate may be the forms given to them in the systems of earlier and later theology, are not only of the last importance for our knowledge of God, of man, and of the universe; but also present so many aids to fruitful meditation, and are themselves in so many ways confirmed by the witness of history and the soundest results of rational speculation, that only the most indolent superficiality would pretend to reject them unexamined. So much has been effected in our own day for the illustration of this doctrine, in the departments of scriptural exegesis and philosophical speculation, as well as in that of dogmatic and historical theology, that we have already sufficient grounds of reason for our adherence to this the apostolic faith; which, not having its source in mere reason, is above but not against it. Only, he who would enter into this as into any other truth, must have his *standing in it* before he can *understand.* But whosoever, not in the carping, one-sided spirit of mere intellectual exercise, but in the practical way of both moral and intellectual self-surrender to the quickening and illuminating influences of the triune Godhead, seeks to apprehend this truth of the divine nature, to him an ever-widening field of rational inquiry will be revealed, and he will learn more and more to find in this mystery a key to the understanding of the deepest enigmas of his own nature and that of the world around him. This will be clear to us if, in conclusion, we proceed—

B. To examine the results just arrived at by the light of our present advances in thought and knowledge. We shall see how many *collateral supports may be derived from history and philosophy in support of this truth.* Supports they must be, not positive proofs; for such can never be alleged in respect of a divine mystery. We shall proceed to ask: (*a*) Whether the *history of religious* thought and development does not bear witness to our Trinitarian faith, and that both positively and negatively? (*b*) What *advantages* the Trinitarian conception affords in respect of our theological and cosmological knowledge? And then, what arguments of a *speculative* character in favour of the doctrine may be drawn (*c*) from a consideration of the *divine nature;* (*d*) from a study of *human nature* and the visible universe; and (*e*) from the testimony of *modern philosophy?*

(*a*) The history of the chief religions of the world itself affords so many collateral supports to our Trinitarian conception of God, as to have given rise to the assertion that primeval humanity must in some shape or other have possessed the knowledge of the triune God, which thence was transmitted in a distorted form to the heathen religions. For we find traces of it, not only here and there, but in the mythologies of all nations. In any case, it is certain that in a very early age men learned to look upon three as the perfect number, expressing absolute harmony, and uniting in itself beginning, middle, and end. Hence *a trinity of deities in common to all nations.*[1] We give a few instances. The Emperor of China offers once every year a sacrifice to the Spirit of Trinity and Unity. Lao-tse the great philosopher, to whom the Chinese pay almost divine honours (600 B.C.), says: Tao (*i.e.* the intelligent principle of all being) is by nature one: the first begat the second; both together brought forth the third; these three made all things. We are more familiar with the *Indian* Trimurti (Trinity), Brahma, Vishnu, and Shiva, who are also represented and worshipped as three persons, though the original divine principle, Brahm, is but one. One of the Purannas (their sacred writings) plainly declares that the great unity is to be distinctly recognised as

[1] Passages in verification of the statements here made, are quoted by Keerl in his work *Die Schöpfung u. die Lehre vom Paradies*, p. 159 et ss.

three Gods in one person. In a commentary on the Rigveda (a book of sacred hymns collected between 1300 and 600 B.C.) it is said: There are three Deities, but there is only one Godhead, the great soul. The so-called *Chaldæan Oracle* says: "The Unity brought forth the Duality which dwells with it and shines in intellectual light; from these proceeded the Trinity which shines through the whole world. The names of the Chaldæan Trinity are Anos, Illinos, Aos. In like manner we find a Divine Trinity among the *Babylonians* (witness the three images in the temple of Belus), the *Phœnicians* (Ulomus, Ulosuros, Eliun), and the *Egyptians* (Kneph or Ammun, Phthas, and Osiris). The divinities of *Greece* were grouped by mythologers both in a successive (Uranos, Chronos, Zeus) and a simultaneous Trinity (Zeus, Poseidon, Aidoneus). The coinage of the *Dalai Lama* (in Thibet) is stamped with a representation of a threefold divinity. A coin, supposed to be Tatarian, and preserved in the Imperial collection at St. Petersburg, bears the impress of a human figure with three heads, and on the reverse the inscription: "Glorious and holy picture of the Godhead, to be contemplated in three forms."

So, too, in the Keltic, Germanic, and Slavic mythology we find the same idea of a Divine Trinity; amongst the *Irish* (Kriosan, Biosena, Siva), the *Scandinavians* (Thor, Woden, Fricco), the ancient *Prussians* (Petrimpos, Perkunos, Pikullos), and the *Pomeranians* and *Wends* (whose God was named Triglav, *i.e.* the three-headed). The *Edda* teaches that the earth was created by Odin, Vile, and Ve, or by Odin, Thor, and Freya. And, finally, the ancient *Americans* worshipped the sun under three images, which they called Father, Son, and Brother Sun. One of their great idols was called Tangalanga, *i.e.* One in Three and Three in One. The three Gods who emanated from the original Spirit they called Trinimaaka, *i.e.* Trinity.

Do not all these coincidences serve as an indirect proof that we are justified in holding that Elohim, the oldest divine name in Scripture, contains an indication of the Trinity in its plural form? And does not this strange agreement compel us to acknowledge that Schelling was right when he said: "The philosophy of mythology proves that *a Trinity of Divine*

Potentialities is the root from which have grown the religious ideas of all nations of any importance that are known to us"? In a former passage we confronted Atheism with the fact, noticed even by heathens themselves, that all nations are agreed in worshipping some higher Being; and we regarded this as a proof that our consciousness of God does not deceive us. Now we may point those who deny the doctrine of the Trinity to this general agreement of all nations, as a proof for the truth of our Christian conception of God; while, by the *pre*-Christian origin of these mythologies, we are guarded against the objection that these Trinitarian ideas might have proceeded from the influence of Christian ideas upon the heathen legends. "This idea does not exist because there is such a thing as Christianity; on the contrary, Christianity exists because this idea is the most original of all" (Schelling).

But in addition to this positive argument in favour of Trinitarianism, the history of religions furnishes us with a no less important negative support in the example of those nations whose creed has remained an *abstract Monotheism*—the Jews and the Mohammedans. Here we see that the mere abstract unity of the Godhead, which does not include a multiplicity, soon leads to a cold and lifeless Deism; and as soon as it has reached this point, is forced to seek refreshment from the pantheistic religions of nature. After the Jews and Mohammedans had rejected the idea of a Son who is of the same divine essence with His Father as idolatry, they were fated *to find their absolutely monotheistic conception of God utterly empty and lifeless,* so that they yearned after the warm vitality of Pantheism. This is a phenomenon which is clearly evident from the history of the Jewish philosophers (especially Spinoza), as well as of the Indian and Persian pantheists. And so, too, it could not but happen that philosophical Pantheism should tread on the heels of German Deism and Rationalism. As long as Theism distinguishes only between God and the world, and not between God and God, it will always have a tendency to Pantheism, or to some other denial of absolute Being. "The abstract and absolutely monotheistic philosophers underwent just that fate which Schiller describes in *The Gods of Greece.* Fulness and vitality vanished with revelation; One has taken to Himself all life, and neutralizes all the vital fulness of nature. We no longer feel love or joy. There is but One, around whom all things move, and He is a cold, mathematical quantity, a point of pure abstraction. This, assuredly, is the meaning of Schiller's poem" (Nitzsch). Hence we can well understand his plaintive lament:—

"A desert chill around us lies,
Devoid of life and warmth divine;
Dim shadows flit before our eyes,
Where once a world of grace did shine.

"The blooms of ancient faiths must flit
Before a northern blast, that One,
Enriched by all their spoils, may sit
High on a barren, cheerless throne."

But if a Christian poet could thus sing, it is still more natural that non-Christian monotheists of this class should yearn after the freshness and fulness of nature's life. Backwards they could not go to the polytheistic religion of nature, since they had already attained to the conception of the divine unity, and hence they had no choice but to sink this unity in matter, and turn to Pantheism.

If, then, we put the question, *How is Monotheism to be preserved from sinking back again into the deification of nature?* the answer will be, *Only through belief in the Trinity.* Polytheism contains a bare contradiction (for the god who has other gods beside him is for that very reason not god, not the highest being, not almighty, etc.). The untenableness of Pantheism we have already seen. Abstract Monotheism has too little life-blood to offer an enduring resistance to the pantheistic deification of nature. What remains open to us but the doctrine of the Trinity? In it we have a Unity; not, however, unloving and lifeless, a cold numerical One, but a complex of living and loving energies,—a living Unity embracing a Plurality, and bearing the sacred name of Father, Son, and Spirit.

(*b*) This brings us to the great *advantages* derived from the Trinitarian conception, in respect to the knowledge of God in general, and His relation to the world and to man.

We have already remarked, that the fulness of God's being cannot be contained in an abstract Unity, and yet that His absolute personality must have unity for its fundamental attribute. Here we find both of these in vital interpenetration. God is One it is true, but at the same time He is the Living One, the organic fulness of power and love, and thus alone is the conception of a truly living God actually realized.

Furthermore, the conception of the triune God furnishes us with *the sole bridge that can fill up the breach between God and the world.* None but this can fill up the void which separates the transcendent unity of God from the rich and manifold organization of natural life. Here we see the possibility of the world's creation by the premundane Word of God and His Spirit, whose work it is to realize the divine thoughts. The Word is the image of the invisible God, and the first-born before all creatures, in which God sees as it were His *alter ego,* and stands in relation to Himself, and through which also He can place Himself in relation to other beings. This Word, which finally becomes incarnate in order to do and suffer for mankind, and the Spirit who by His power begets fresh life, both stand between God and the world as mediate causes, which not only render the creation of the world a possibility, but also guarantee the divine presence in it, and its return to God. Here, then, we have all the fulness and freshness of Pantheism combined with the truth of Monotheism, whilst the element in which the latter is wanting, viz. a real connecting link between God and the world, is here supplied to us. Philosophy has not been slow to recognise these advantages, and to turn them to account in her speculations, as we shall see hereafter.

Here, first of all, we have a connecting link between God and man in the person of the Incarnate Logos, who is the eternal Archetype of the whole creation, and especially of man,[1] and who, for all future æons, will be the head of the whole body. Here, too, the spiritual chasm which yawns between sinful man and the absolutely sinless God-man, is filled up by the regenerating and sanctifying influences of the Holy Spirit. Hence the doctrine of the Trinity affords the most important aids in determining our *practical* relation to God. We have seen that our religious need can only be fully

[1] By this we do not mean to affirm that the incarnation of the Logos was necessary *per se,* apart from the sin of man ; since, on the contrary, Scripture always represents it as ordained by the *free* mercy of God *on account of sin.*

satisfied by the idea of God as the eternal and all-holy love. The belief in this love must revert to the idea of the love which the Father bears to His only-begotten Son, and it can only be perfected practically as well as theoretically by a knowledge of the perfect and eternal object of the divine self-knowledge and self-love. So, too, a real belief in the self-communication of this love can only be vitalized and preserved from error by the Trinitarian doctrine of the Holy Spirit.

From all this it follows, that *the doctrine of the Trinity is the consummation and the only perfect protection of Theism.* We have already shown that the theistic conception of God is the only true one; and we may now add, that if this theistic conception is to be effectually guarded against Atheism, Polytheism, Pantheism, Dualism, and Deism, it must be expanded into the Trinitarian idea. No true Theism without the Trinity. The One absolute Personality as such can only be the triune God. Trinitarianism is no less true and necessary than Theism; and what we adduced as proofs for the latter, are mediate arguments for the former. also.

(*c*) In addition to this, *Speculative Theology* furnishes us with many collateral arguments in favour of the truth and the intrinsic necessity of the Trinitarian doctrine. Many attempts have been made by modern theologians to derive the Trinitarian view of God from a consideration of the Divine essence itself. Of course, they are but attempts, and not perfectly successful or adequate explanations. In all such speculations it behoves us to take great care that we do not pass from the difficult to the unintelligible; bearing this in mind, I would lay before you some of the most important of these tentative theories. They start partly from the *self-consciousness* of God, partly from the idea of the Absolute *Love*.

Nitzsch remarks that the Divine Ego, in order to have a really living personality, must not only view its second *other* self as an object, but also revert to itself by a further act as a *third* subject, as that it comprehends its *alter ego* as the real image of itself. "If God be conceived as the primal Ego, and from this basis begets an objective *alter Ego,* this thesis and antithesis still remain severed or incomplete until a third Ego proceeds from the Divine essence through the medium of the second, and thus the personality is fully consummated."

Modern religious philosophers have often reasoned thus: God must be personal, since He is the presupposition of *our* personality. The essence of personality is to comprehend itself, or to distinguish in itself the comprehending and the comprehended. The equality of these two elements must be developed into unity, but in such a way that they shall not coincide in absolute identity. This can only be brought about by their mutual union in a third factor. Hence three persons, I, thou, and he, are indispensable to self-comprehension. Thus the Three Persons of the Godhead presuppose each other; they are in one another, and yet distinct (not separate), so that each of the three Persons is I, Thou, and He, because personality includes the possibility and reality of self-transposition.[1]

Others argue thus: The Divine nature must be primarily conceived of as Being, as Necessity (Father), but at the same time as Action, as Freedom (Son); the mediation of both these factors being effected by Love (the Holy Spirit).

The interpretations drawn by Liebner, Sartorius, and others from the idea of *love* are clearer. The Trinity in Unity and absolute Personality, replete with truly moral and actually wrought out personal life, pertains to God, because He is Love, not because He is a self-conscious Spirit. For absolute Love demands a process of self-communication, which in its highest perfection must be trinitarian. Love is the transposition of *one's self* into *another person* as *his second self* (*alter ego*). God, who is Love, must therefore transpose Himself into *His second Self*, which as such is of the same Divine nature, since otherwise the act of self-transposition would not be perfect. No less necessary, however, is the conception of a third homogeneous Self, by which the infinite equality is mediated so as to produce harmonious unity in distinctions. This act it is which permanently fixes the divine personality; for mere self-transposition would be equal to infinite restlessness. Thus God is one person in three persons, each of which is only *in* and *through* the others; and this apparent contradiction, that several persons should be one, and have their full personality

[1] Cf. Mehring, "Die philosophisch-kritischen Grundsätze der Selbstveräusserung, oder die Religionsphilosophie," p. 91 et ss.; also the passage above quoted: "I am He."

only in this unity, is solved only by the principle of love (Liebner).

This idea is very beautifully worked out by Sartorius. "God is love—personal, primal love. What can He more delight to say than "My beloved"? God is the Father, the eternal Father. What is the Father's eternal and dearest Word other than Son, beloved Son (Matt. iii. 17)? Through the eternal Son, God is the eternal Father, the eternally loving and eternally loved One; the eternal I and the eternal Thou, as Christ addresses His Father in loving converse (John xvii. 24). And this Love is as ready to impart itself, as perfect and as great as God whose essence it is; and therefore the Son is not less than the Father, nor does He differ from Him either in essence or in origin. How small would be the Fatherhood were the Son but half God! We must distinguish between the love which *begets* the Son and that which *blesses* Him,—the love of the well-pleased Father, and again, the *answering* love on the Son's part. The breath of that blessing and answering love is the *Spirit*. But were He *only* breath, and not a person, the glorification of the Father and Son through the Spirit would be egoistical. This egoistical element is removed only if the Spirit who glorifies the Father and the Son is Himself a person."

The meaning of this sentiment is as follows: Love always includes delight in the object loved. If this object be an entirely separate person, the purity of my love is not sullied by my delight. But this is not the case with God. The object of His love is not a person outside of Him, but His second Self. Here, therefore, the delight in another is at the same time delight in Himself. In order, therefore, that this delight may not appear as self-seeking egotism, God has committed this delight in Himself to a third Person, which represents the mutual delight of Father and Son in each other; and this Person is the Holy Spirit. When the Father uttered Himself, He begat the Son, the eternal Word. But no speech can take place without breathing, and the breath of that spoken Word was hypostatized in the Spirit, which represents the delight of the Divine Love.

In a similar manner, Delitzsch has recently attempted to reconcile the trinitarian passages of Holy Scripture with the idea of God as contained in our reason. The triune God is—1. *Absolute Life*, the impulse of whose development is an act of will; in Him existence and will, necessity and freedom, interpenetrate each other. This Life is unfolded within the Divine Being without counteraction from the world; it is self-filled and self-consummated. But being such, it cannot be otherwise conceived than as a life of love. Hence the triune God is—2. *Absolute Love*. The object of this love cannot be the world,—since, then, God would not be love in Himself,—but only His *alter ego*, the Son; whereas the Holy Ghost consummates the mutual relationship between the Father and the Son, as it were, in a perfect circle of divine love. But both these conceptions of life and love point only to the personality of the Father and the Son, not to that of the Holy Ghost. Hence, finally, the triune God must be conceived of—3. As *Absolute Organism*, which unites in itself the essential characteristics of *nature* (substantial objectivity without self-consciousness) and *spirit* (self-consciousness without substantial objectivity). As the highest identity, it must combine these two factors, which in the world are separated; the latter raises it above created nature, the former above created spirit, so that it embraces both.—Delitzsch, *Apologetik*, p. 277 et ss.

Whatever objections may be raised against the force of such arguments, especially as regards the personality of the Spirit, yet thus much, at least, is clear and certain: *Because God is love, therefore there must be distinctions in Him, which, however, by love are again brought into unity.* The object of this (intra-divine) love can be nothing less important than God Himself, else this love would not be fully justified; nor can it be anything outside of God, else God's *intrinsic* nature would not be love. For both reasons this object cannot be the transitory world, but only the eternal Son, who is of the same essence with the Father. *How* this love preserves its equilibrium, or its unselfishness and purity through the Holy Ghost as the third Person, this must remain to us a mystery so long as the spirit of selfishness and sin is not overcome, and hinders even our self-knowledge, to say nothing of our knowledge of God, which is brought about by the surrender of ourselves to Him. The practical gist of this doctrine is simply this, *to proclaim that God is eternal and perfect love,* and that the historical revelation of His love in Christ corresponds to His eternal essence, in whose everlasting self-distinction and self-comprehension into unity the divine life is changelessly evolved.

(*d*) Another and more obvious series of collateral supports for the doctrine of the Trinity, may be found in a consideration of His image as reflected in our own *human nature,* and in creation generally. For if God be indeed Trinity in Unity, then there is every reason to suppose that the works of His hands should, in some degree at least, reflect His nature, and especially that man, who is created in the image of God should evince in His nature certain *analogies* which indicate a triune Creator.

And what an abundance of such indications meets our eye, so long as we do not forget that we cannot expect to find within the limits of created life analogies perfectly corresponding with that which is incomparable and unique! Christian thinkers, even in olden times, discovered traces of the Trinity in the life of the human spirit; and hence Augustine and others speak of a *human trinity,* consisting in the threefold function of feeling, thought, and will. And, indeed, these principal faculties of the spirit present us, as it were, with a threefold cord, the threads of which are distinct and yet one, and they give us some idea of the united and harmonious co-operation of the three Divine Persons. No single one of these three functions of feeling, thought, and will can be exercised without the simultaneous activity of the others. "Thus the spiritual life of man is, in fact, always *a multiplicity of intermingling actions.* In this intermingled action I see a picture of the threefold divine life, showing how every vital act of one Person calls forth and is necessarily accompanied by a corresponding act of both the others; so that the vital movements of any one Person posit those of the others" (Gess), just as we have seen in the work of creation, redemption, and sanctification. But just as with the soul, its three functions may be distinguished, but not separated, so, too, in the case of the three Persons who form the one Divine Being.

In like manner, the *process of our thought* will explain to us in some degree the pre-existence of the Son as the Logos or Word of the Father. In our human consciousness a certain thought always simultaneously produces the corresponding word; we can only think in conceptions and words, for our thought is inward speech. So, too, God's thought of Himself necessitates the utterance of the Word which represents this primal Thought; but the divine utterance is at the same time a real act, and hence this inner Word in God is a Being equal to Him. True, in our human self-consciousness we do not, by conceiving ourselves, produce a second self; we all the time have only one *ego*. But we are only creatures, not the creative source of life; and even our human consciousness is still imperfect. But the case is different with God, who is the eternal and almighty source of life and power. His self-consciousness is absolutely perfect, and hence the intellectual image of Himself, which He has conceived, may become a real substantial antitype of the Father. In any case, we have an analogy to the Trinity in the thought, its product the word, and the unity of both, the spirit. In addition to this argument for the personality of the Divine Word as drawn from our intellectual consciousness, we find that a similar argument for the personality of the Spirit may be drawn from our *religious* consciousness. Faith tells us that the Spirit is giving us true personality in the sight of God, and that without Him we cannot in any way attain to full, firm, Godlike personality. But, as we have already remarked, that which tends to promote true personality cannot in itself be impersonal.

Moreover, let us remember that *the fundamental form of all syntax*, which governs our thought and our speech, is a *triplicity* which contains a *unity*, or a unity which developes into triplicity. For every sentence consists of subject, predicate, and copula—three parts, which together express one thought. Indeed, every conception "has something of the trinity," since in it is the union of subject and predicate, which does away with their distinction. The fundamental schema of all spiritual development is always position, contraposition, higher unity of both (thesis, antithesis, synthesis). Everywhere three is the fundamental number of the self-reverting process.

As in the human spirit, so, too, in the *outward world of nature*, there are certain indications and reflections of the Trinity. This truth is not only revealed in Scripture, and confirmed by history and intellectual speculation, but it is, so to speak, omnipresent throughout the world. We constantly see one *life* in various *members;* in each one it acts in a special manner, yet in all it is one and the same. In the one *sun* we see *light* and *warmth* as different, and yet intermingling and co-operating forces. We have the one space divided into three dimensions of length, breadth, and height; time, similarly, into past, present, and future; all bodies into solid, liquid, and gaseous. In analogy with the three parts required to form a sentence, we find that the kingdom of sound is governed by the *triad,* as the basis of all chords; nor does this destroy the original unity of the key-note, but, on the contrary, makes it an organized unity embracing multiplicity. What remarkable analogies are shown by the laws of colour and of light! The three fundamental colours, red, yellow, and blue, dissolve into the unity of white light, so that an English naturalist (C. Woodward) might well call this white light a trinity in unity. But they coalesce in such a manner, "that each of the three rays preserves its distinctive attribute. Red is the caloric, yellow the luminous, blue the chemical (activic) ray."[1] God

[1] Cf. C. Woodward, *Familiar Introduction to the Study of Light.* If it is permissible to follow this analogy out further, we should say that the caloric ray evidently corresponds to the Father, the warm Source of life; the luminous ray to the Son, the Light of the world; and the chemical ray to the Spirit, which pierces into the innermost recesses of the heart, and imbues it with peculiar qualities and forces. One of the instances given by Woodward is very suggestive. Some plants (cucumbers and melons) were put under a glass which was so coloured as to absorb the blue (chemical) rays of light. The consequence was, that the plants grew with the greatest rapidity, and put forth luxuriant blossoms, but just as quickly they faded away again, without bringing fruit. Does not this look like a physical reflection of the Christian precept, "Quench not the Spirit," because without Him no real fruit can ripen? (1 Thess. v. 19; Gal. v. 22.) How mightily did men multiply before the flood! but because they utterly withdrew themselves from the influence of the Spirit, they only ripened, without fruit, for a sudden death. True, from a strictly scientific point of view we cannot attach much weight to such theosophical indications. Yet thus much we may affirm respecting certain fundamental principles (such as light, life, etc.) which occur in the region of intellect, physics, and morals,— that in them the whole enigma of the world and its history lies hid, and that by means of them we must endeavour to ascend from our discursive rational knowledge to a central intuition of the ultimate and universal Cause of all being. The man who has no presentiment of this is incapable of entering into any profound speculative philosophy. In this there lies a clue to the temple of knowledge, lost to man since his banishment from paradise, but of which scattered fragments at least may be found. To collect these, is the ultimate task of all science.

is Light; and, verily, natural light, the first of His creatures, bears the immediate impress of His triune Being!

No less does the number three govern the arrangement of Nature's *forces;* whether we adopt the classification of Ohm,[1] who divides the fundamental forces into those of "attraction, tension, and polarity," or the more general enumeration, *attraction, repulsion, equilibrium.* The whole of nature is ruled by the law of polarity, with its two magnetic poles and their equipoise. Positive and negative electricity are balanced by the electric spark. The entire development of the *vegetable* world takes place in a process of three degrees. First, the self-enclosed potential unity (seed, germinal cell, root), then the self-development into multiplicity (inward dilation and ramification of the germ, stem), and, finally, conclusion of the multiplicity in organized unity (leaf, fruit, return to the seed and germinal cell).

Is not the eternal Origin of life visible in all these things in a thousand pictures? Were we not right in saying that *the idea of the Trinity* was *omnipresent?* Not only do we bear it in our own spirit as the ruling law of all its vital functions; not only do we see it shine forth in the religions of all nations as a dark presentiment common to all: Nature herself reflects this truth "as in a thousand mirrors; everywhere we hear its harmony, we see its brightness, and feel it looking at us through a thousand eyes" (Delitzsch, *ubi sup.* pp. 282–286).

(*e*) No wonder that philosophy too—and that not only the old mystic theosophical speculation, but also modern idealism, with all the acuteness of its dialectics—has taken up the idea of a triune God, and endeavoured to comprehend and to prove it. True, they have often ended in proving the truth of an utterance once made by a profound divine in respect of the doctrine of the Trinity, and which I would beg my readers to lay to heart. "If we go too deeply, and yet not deeply enough into this matter, we shall be blinded by this sun." They have also confirmed our remarks as to the achievements of independent reason, which, with haughty self-sufficiency, despises the light of revelation, and therefore can attain to no sure and positive results. But still their efforts show us *that modern philosophy* (from Jacob Böhme onwards) *feels that this doctrine is the true*

[1] *Die Dreieinigkeit der Kraft*, Nürnberg, 1856.

solution of the world's enigma. Moreover, these philosophical investigations cast a strong light on the unconscionable superficiality and short-sightedness of those who most reject this fundamental doctrine of the Christian faith untested, without a notion of its deep religious, philosophical, and historical import.

Hegel calls the idea of the Trinity "the pivot of the world." According to him, the Father is God as self-existent, or as it were self-enclosed; He discloses Himself as the Son, and in this form takes upon Him the form of individual being, thereby compensating the contrariety between the Absolute and the Individual. The latter, however, is not the adequate form of absolute being; therefore it undergoes death, and rises again as the Spirit;—or, in other words, the Father is God in the abstract, mere universality; the Son is infinite particularity; the Spirit is phenomenality or individuality as such (*Religionsphilos.* iii.). True, the entire groundwork of this view is pantheistic, and the difference between it and the biblical doctrine is evident. For acccording to Hegel, Father, Son, and Spirit successively change into each other, whereas Scripture teaches that they exist simultaneously with and in each other. But in any case we see how deeply the conception of the Trinity is interwoven with Hegel's system.

Schelling has followed out this idea far more fully, and in his *Philosophie der Offenbarung* he approaches very closely to the Christian view. God is the perfect Spirit in three forms; proceeding from Himself, existing by Himself, and reverting to Himself. The Father is the Author of matter, the Son the Author of form, and the Spirit the ultimate Cause of the world as the unity of both. Hence the world is created by the Father, through the Son, to the Holy Ghost. A still greater affinity to the Christian doctrine is shown by the speculations of Baader (according to whom the divinity of the three Persons proceeds from the Father, their personality from the Son, and their spirituality from the Holy Spirit) and J. H. Fichte, who distinguishes between a real objective and an ideal subjective aspect of the Divine essence, combined in a third and higher principle, viz. that of volition or of love.

These instances will suffice to make us comprehend what a philosopher some years ago most truly remarked: "*The con-*

ceptions of speculative philosophy, where they are most profound, come nearest to the Christian doctrine; nor need we be anxious lest speculative philosophy should ever reach a height from which it may look down and say that the Christian element is left behind. No thought can transcend the Christian idea, for it is truth in itself" (Braniss).

Thus we are from all quarters forcibly referred to the idea of the Trinity; and should we ever be tempted to sacrifice the Trinity to the Unity, it will be well to remember that the scriptural and Christian conception of God is justified and proved, as far as a mystery can be, by history and science, by nature and philosophy.

We may apply to the doctrine of the Trinity the beautiful words uttered by Vinet, when speaking of love: "It is a mystery, the greatest of all mysteries, and the key of all mysteries, but itself has no key." The collateral arguments which we have adduced are by no means keys that can open this mystery, but they are handles for our intellect and imagination, which give us sufficient cause not to reject this doctrine as irrational. Indeed, they show that the idea of the Trinity is really *the key to a comprehension of the ultimate world-enigmas;* of the world's eternal pre-condition in God; of its creation, redemption, and consummation. Without this doctrine, Scripture is to us a sealed book; without it, we ourselves and the world's history are a dark riddle. For these reasons we ought thankfully to accept the revelation of this truth. True, this is a problem, the rational solution of which in this life is and must remain mere patchwork; but even this patchwork is far deeper and more valuable for our knowledge as a whole (to say nothing of our practical religion) than all that the cheap wisdom of the street can bring forward in objection. And so, too, the mere struggle to solve this problem, even though it should be without results, is of infinitely greater value than the ready rejection which we so often hear from the intellectual slothfulness of unbelief.

The conclusion already arrived at (Lect. II.) with regard to the relationship between reason and revelation, has there been perfectly confirmed, and that in the case of that very article of our belief which is most difficult for the intellect. We have seen that philosophy and faith, reason and revelation, are by no means natural enemies; on the contrary, if rightly used, they demand, they support, they supplement each other. More than this. We have seen that the darker the revelation the greater is the reward, both for faith and knowledge, which awaits those who gradually penetrate into it. Just because the doctrine of the Trinity is the most obscure and enigmatic revelation of God, therefore to him who penetrates into it with earnest searchings the profoundest depths of knowledge will be opened, and what is apparently self-contradictory will appear more and more in grand harmony and intrinsic necessity. At first it appears to be quite contrary to reason, afterwards reason is more and more in favour of it, and finally it cannot give it up, it becomes indispensable for her entire knowledge of God and the world.

We have seen that just the contrary is the case with the false non-biblical conceptions of God. At first they please our reason, and look as if they could give a simple solution of all enigmas. But the more deeply reason goes to work with them, the less satisfactory do they become; the more do enigmas, obscurities, aye, contradictions appear, till at length it is evident that the whole fabric rests on unproven and untenable assumptions, and that those conceptions really give none of those explanations which they at first promised.

But if by reason of this profound agreement between the testimony of Holy Scripture and the demands and discoveries of science, any one should adopt the Christian conception of God, let him not forget that in and with it he has essentially accepted the *entire* Christian faith. The Apostles' Creed shows that the Christian doctrines of creation, redemption, and sanctification, Christian faith and Christian morals, all centre in our belief in the triune God.

Does the choice still embarrass you? Then allow me, after the intellectual exertions which I could not dispense with, to put a question to your conscience. Supposing that eternity should show us that we were mistaken in our scriptural and Christian view of God, *what harm would it have done to us?* In this life, none at all. For our faith in the holy, personal and living God has proved to us a constant source of moral strength, and an enduring impulse to all that is good. Which of us would deny that, as often as we rose from our knees, or had been otherwise absorbed in this divine faith, we felt more capable and willing to do all that was good, more disinclined to all evil—more strong, more pure, and more divine? Nor could we hardly suffer harm in another life. For if we found no living, personal God there, our own personal existence would be at an end, and we could not even become conscious of our deception. But supposing, on the other hand, that we nourish our doubts, adopt a non-biblical conception of God, and then in another world find all that realized which here we had denied, *what would have been our gain* even in this life were our doubts able to inspire us with strength to do or to suffer? Did they not rather, in the depths of our soul, make us timid and undecided? Did they not exercise a paralyzing influence on our spiritual and moral life? For this life we should have gained nothing; but for the other life, when we have to meet the disregarded and dishonoured God, the Eternal King who is a consuming fire, how then?

"Give me *great* thoughts!" cried Herder on his death-bed. Yes; in death we all need great thoughts. This at least you will not deny. The greatest minds, princes in the realm of thought, grasp after them in their dying hour, and cling to them as a support amidst the great shipwreck in which the entire visible world is sinking before their eyes. But the greatest of all thoughts is God; the eternal, personal, holy God who is love. And in such moments He is the only great and enduring thought. All others vanish and dissolve before Him. Woe be to him who at that crisis lacks the eternal support of this thought; who only grasps it in earnest when he himself is being grasped by it!

See this exemplified in the case of a sceptic of the first rank during the last century, who was equalled by few in his persistent and life-long opposition to Christianity, by none in the endless floods of biting satire with which he deluged all scriptural belief; who gradually sank from Deism to Atheism, till at length he worshipped "the will of his sacred majesty, Chance:" I mean *Voltaire*. "All things considered," he writes to a lady who was in fear of death, "I am of opinion that one ought never to think of death. This thought is of no use whatever, save to embitter life. Death is a mere nothing. Those people who solemnly proclaim it are enemies of the human race; one must endeavour always to keep them off. Death is as like to sleep as one drop of water to another. It is merely the idea that we shall not wake up again which gives us pain." But when death, this despicable nothing, approached the man who thought that by his writings he had steeled himself, and half Europe besides, against the fear of another world, how did he then show himself? A reliable informant, Voltaire's own physician, writes to a friend as follows: "When I compare the death of a righteous man, which is like the close of a beautiful day, with that of Voltaire, I see the difference between bright, serene weather and a black thunderstorm. It was my lot that this man should die under my hands. Often did I tell him the truth, but, unhappily for him, I was the only person who did so. 'Yes, my friend,' he would often say to me, 'you are the only one who has given me good advice. Had I but followed it, I should not be in the horrible condition in which I now am. I have swallowed *nothing but smoke;* I have intoxicated myself with the incense that turned my head. You can do nothing more for me. Send me a mad-doctor! Have compassion on me, I am mad! I cannot think of it without shuddering.' . . . As soon as he saw that all the means which he had employed to increase his strength had just the opposite effect, death was constantly before his eyes. From this moment madness took possession of his soul. Think of the ravings of Orestes. He expired under the torments of the furies." [1]

Thus dies an apostle of unbelief! Worshipped by half the world, yet helpless and despairing; stupefied by the incense clouds of flattery, yet raving mad; beforehand mocking at death, now so convulsively clinging to life that he actually offers great sums of money (100 francs) for every minute of its prolongation; beforehand luxuriating in the sensation of having gained all his wishes, and triumphing over everything, now exclaiming in horror, "Nothing more can help me!"

Compare with such an one a witness for God and for Christ, *e.g.* a *St. Paul,* as he sees death approaching. See him then; not enveloped in clouds of incense, nor overwhelmed with marks of honour, but bearing in his body the scars of many wounds inflicted on him by the hatred of the world,

[1] Bungener, *Voltaire et son temps.*

the marks which he has received in the service of the Lord Jesus; in chains and degradation, under sentence of death, yet free and strong, quiet and joyful; not clinging to this poor life, but "forgetting the things that are behind, and pressing forward;" not in a condition of horrible agony, but desiring to depart and to be with Christ; looking backward in sweet peace on the past, and forward with blessed hope to the future. Hear his words in the Second Epistle to Timothy, his last legacy to the Church: "I am ready to be offered up, and the time of my departure is at hand. I have fought a good fight, I have finished my course, I have kept the faith: henceforth there is laid up for me a crown of righteousness;" not begging for help, but offering help to the world; witnessing for Christ till his last breath, and sealing his testimony with his blood;—*thus it is that an apostle of faith dies!*

"Choose you, therefore, this day whom ye will serve; . . . **but as for me, and my house, we will serve the Lord.**"

LECTURE V.

THE MODERN NEGATION OF MIRACLES.

I SCARCELY require a preliminary apology for still devoting a special discussion to the modern negation of miracles, after the examination of the objections to the biblical conception of God. True, when we have once proved the personality and freedom of God, and the necessity of His continued rule and operation in the world, we have also proved that miracles are possible. To this extent our present inquiry rests entirely on the previous one. But since *miracles are the greatest stumbling-block to the spirit of our age,*[1] the question of their possibility requires a special consideration. One of the first among its articles of faith is this: There is no such thing as a miracle, and never has been, since the supernatural is impossible. This unproved assertion, which is boldly put forward as a self-evident axiom, is the basis of the rationalistic dismemberment of the gospel history, and of those notorious attempts of Strauss and Renan to do away with the central miracle of history—the life of Jesus Christ—by reducing it to legend and poetry,—attempts which have made the question one of intense interest, especially among the laity. Upon the same axiom are based the efforts of Baur, to prove that Christianity is only the sum of the previously existing, scattered germs of culture, and that it is merely a link in the universal development of the world. The same presupposition, moreover, is the basis of the most important modern philosophical systems, as well as a maxim of most naturalists at the present day.

However much in other respects our opponents may differ, they all agree in the denial of miracles, and unitedly storm

[1] The chief offence which the old system of religion necessarily gives to the spirit of our age, is its superstitious belief in miracles.—STRAUSS, *Leben Jesu,* 1864, p. xviii.

this bulwark of the Christian faith; and in its defence we have to combat them all at once. But whence this unanimity? Because *with the truth of miracles the entire citadel of Christianity stands or falls.* For its beginning is a miracle, its Author is a miracle, its progress depends upon miracles, and they will hereafter be its consummation. If the principle of miracles be set aside, then all the heights of Christianity will be levelled with one stroke, and naught will remain but a heap of ruins. If we banish the supernatural from the Bible, there is nothing left us but the covers!

A glance at the *consequences* of the negation of miracles will at once reveal to us the momentous significance of the question. *The negation of miracles leads to the annihilation not merely of the Christian faith, but of all religion.* As a rule, anti-miraculists will not admit this. They imagine that miracles, and the doctrines resting upon them, merely belong to the outworks of Christianity, and that even if these fall, the essential, *i.e.* the moral, truths of Christianity will still remain. I have already sought to show how perverted this conception of Christianity is. Christianity, in its real essence, is not a definite quantity of moral truths or teachings, but a series of *facts*: it is Christ Himself, His person and work, the religion of the incarnation of God in Christ, and the redemption of the world therefrom resulting. In other words, Christianity is essentially miraculous: *its Founder*, in His personality as the God-man, is the *miracle of all miracles*, the miraculous goal towards which all foregoing miracles were tending, and of which all that follow are only an echo. Our Saviour's earthly life and work, from His sinless birth to His resurrection and ascension—all the chief facts of redemption—are nothing but miracles, and His entire teaching, as well as the law and the prophecies of the Old Testament, must be taken as the declaration of divine truths—as a supernatural revelation (John vii. 16; 2 Pet. i. 21), or in other words, as a miracle.

The Christian religion, however, does not show its miraculous character only in the facts and doctrines which constitute its beginnings, but it is to a certain extent a continuous and ever-present miracle in the *supernatural effects* which it produces on nations as well as on individuals, in its constant victories over the kingdoms of this world, and its experience in the heart of the believer. Whoever, therefore, seeks to exclude from Christianity all that is miraculous and supernatural, denies the entire Christian faith; he not merely plucks from the tree a few loose leaves, but fells the entire trunk, and cuts away all the roots. And if after this he still desires to retain the system of Christian morality, he is just as unreasonable as one who should first fell a tree, and then hope to continue in the enjoyment of its fruit.

But the denial of miracles leads to the annihilation, not only of Christianity, but also of *all religions whatever*. For every religion is based upon the supposition that certain superhuman powers extend their influence into the sphere [1] of our life. He who denies this immediate action of higher powers in the world, *i.e.* who does not believe in miracles, need no longer care for those powers. To him every religion, every divine service in which man with offerings and prayers, or by other means, approaches his deities and seeks their favour, must appear folly, since they can exert no special influence either for or against their suppliant. That this is the case with those who entertain pantheistic conceptions of God, as having no personal existence, is plainly evident. But even if, with the Deists, we grant Him personal existence, yet entirely separate Him from the world, and abandon the latter to its own laws, the same result follows. We need not care much for God, for neither does He care specially for us; nor have we much need of divine service and prayer, for God cannot really interfere with our life. He has no freedom of action in opposition to the course of nature, no true vitality, no continuous activity: He is only a sleeping, inactive, listless Something above the world, but without communication with it, like the dot over the i. Is such a Being a God worthy of worship, or indeed a God at all?

You see here the truth of the proposition uttered long since by Nitzsch, that the denial of miracles involves the *denial of the free, living, personal God*. Those who, like the Rationalists, deny the former and seek to maintain the latter, are guilty of illogical reasoning.

[1] An enemy of religion, at the Peace Congress in Berne, Aug. 1865, said very truly, "All religions, however diverse their creeds may be, have the miraculous element in common with each other."

The denial of the personality and living activity of God subverts not only all religion, but also the *moral personality of man* ; for both these, as we have seen, stand or fall together. By completely severing this world from a higher one, the denial of miracles confines us entirely to our present temporal existence, and leaves us without any safeguard against the worst Materialism. Only consider what an effect the extermination of miracles would have on our personal life! With regard to this, a recent advocate of miracles[1] strikingly says: "Didst thou believe that thou couldst trace the guiding hand of thy God at many a turning-point of thy history—fancies, pure junctures of nature, which neither know of thee nor inquire after thee? Thou beseechest God for the recovery of a child at the point of death—unnecessary trouble! from a blind, deaf process of nature thy trembling heart must await its destiny! Thou feelest at the coffin of a father, or a husband, that the bands of love cannot be sundered for ever—dreams! there is no resurrection. Thou sighest after divine help for the conquest of evil—in vain! the new birth itself would be an unnatural interruption of thy naturally sinful development. Sayest thou, that thou hast experienced this very miracle? They answer, Self-deception! Proud man, who hast dreamed of becoming perfect as thy Father in heaven is perfect, of a glory which was destined for thee before the world was, why wilt thou aspire to be something better than the entire universe? why wilt thou become holy and happy? 'Let us eat and drink, for to-morrow we die!' Such is the logical consequence of the denial of miracles. The same grave in which modern heathenism buries the miraculous, swallows up everything which gives to human existence an ideal character, a true value: the soul made in the divine image, faith and prayer, the holy person of the Redeemer, the entire system of Christian truth, the future world, the living God!" But, perchance, the world might be found too small, as well as the arm of the grave-diggers too weak, to bury all these together.

When we thus see how great the victory would be if our adversaries were able to banish miracles, and why they concentrate their attacks upon this point, we cannot wonder that

[1] Beyschlag, *Ueber die Bedeutung des Wunders im Christenthum.*

here the believing Christian should be determined not to yield an inch. To him there is nothing so firmly established as the miraculous; because, in the first place, faith itself is a miracle. What Hamann says is true: "Miracles cannot even be believed without a miracle." And so, to one who has experienced in his own heart through the power of Christ and His Spirit the miracle of regeneration, this miraculous power is the most certain of all things. Here, then, for more than two hundred years the contest has been hottest, against this foundation the universal assault has been directed, and from it all defence proceeds. Therefore this question deserves an especially careful consideration.

Such of you, my respected hearers, as still adhere to the biblical faith have now and then been somewhat perplexed at hearing everywhere, in the street and in the daily papers, attacks upon the miracles related in Holy Scripture. Against you stood the close phalanx of your adversaries: on the one side, the authority of the Scriptures, and a certain premonition that with the surrender of this article of our faith all would be lost; and on the other, so many distinguished scientific names! If, then, the judgment of many a one began to tremble, and still trembles in the balance, I would seek according to my ability to help him to attain a firm conviction, and will first afford him the consolation that, though the adversaries are many, there are not a few scientific defenders of the miraculous. If many rationalists, philosophers, critics, and naturalists are on the other side, there are on ours—to say nothing of the Prophets and Apostles—great philosophers and theosophists, from Jacob Böhme and Leibnitz down to Schelling in his later period; great naturalists, from Copernicus, Newton, and Kepler, to von Haller, Schubert, Cuvier, Marrel de Serres, Rougemont, Hugh Miller, Rudolphus, and Andrew Wagner, etc.; and besides these, the great majority of the representatives of our present scientific German Theology, among whom the contest is considered as essentially decided in favour of the faith, not only on dogmatical, but also on exegetical, historical, and speculative grounds.

We divide the questions which meet us here as follows: (1) After an exposition of the true *nature* of miracles, we shall consider the origin of their negation, and the presuppositions on which this negation is founded, so that we may be able to oppose to it a closer examination and proof of the *possibility* of the miraculous. Thence we proceed (2) to the positive counter-evidence for the *necessity* of miracles. To this end we must exhibit their internal aim, their indispensableness in the plan of redemption and the education of man, their *historical manifestation* and laws, the possibility of discerning their genuineness, and their foundation on fact. (3) In conclusion, we must briefly discuss the question of the *continuance of miracles* in our own times, in order to meet those objectors who ask why miracles are no longer performed.

I.—THE NATURE AND POSSIBILITY OF MIRACLES.

(*a*) *Nature of Miracles.*—In the use of the word miracle, as in that of revelation, we must discriminate between a *wider* and a *narrower sense.* In the wider sense, we often use it of all that is incomprehensible and extraordinary in nature and history, of which the origin is still concealed from us, or the existence of which excites our astonishment. So it occurs in the Holy Scriptures, where mention is made of God's miracles (or wonders) upon the sea, in the creation and guidance of man, and where man himself is called a wonder (Ps. cxxxix. 14). But in the narrower sense, miracles are (with the exception of the demoniacal miracles [1] occasionally mentioned in Scripture) unique and extraordinary manifestations of divine power, which influence nature in a manner incomprehensible to our empirical

[1] On this dark question, mostly disregarded by the apologists of the day, we will only remark, that the opinion held by many, that these are only to be considered as lying, or delusively imitated, but not as real miracles, is scarcely conformable to the sense of the passages, 2 Thess. ii. 9, Matt. xxiv. 24, Rev. xiii. 13. To be sure, St. Paul speaks of them as "lying wonders;" but if this were to be understood only in the sense of jugglery, could they in other passages properly be called "*great* signs and wonders"? They are lying, because they serve a lie, they proceed from a lie, and a lie is their goal, since their object is to obliterate the impression of the witnesses for the truth (Ex. vii. 12-22, viii. 7; 2 Tim. iii. 8);—"because they appear to attest the so-called gods as true gods; because the powers which their originators use are only stolen and abused; because they are the means of promoting error, falsehood, and destruction; because they pretend to be something else than they are, and to work good, while they further and promote evil" (Kurtz). It cannot be denied that heathenism, besides much fraud and superstition, has also exhibited facts which can only be explained as

knowledge, but always in accordance with some moral or spiritual end. Or, more exactly, they are creative acts of God, *i.e.* supernatural exertions of power upon certain points of Nature's domain, through which, by virtue of His own might already working in the course of nature, God, for the furtherance of His kingdom, brings forth some new thing which natural substances or causalities could not have produced by themselves, but which,—and this must not be overlooked,—as soon as they have taken place, range themselves in the natural course of things, without any disturbance arising on their account.

The *essential points in the conception of miracles, strictly so called*, are these :

1. They are *effects of God's power* in the domain of *Nature.* Miracles, in every case, are only performed through divine might: "Who alone doeth great wonders" (Ps. cxxxvi. 14). Man only performs them through God, and in unison with Him, *i.e.* he is permittted by divine authority, in the name of God (cf. the miracles of Moses) or of Christ (Acts iii. 6, iv. 10), to summon God's power, which pervades the creation, to a concentrated and intensified action at some definite point, and thus to bring forth extraordinary effects for definite holy ends. Christ, on account of His unique oneness with the Father, possessed this divine power in an extraordinary degree, not merely transiently like the prophets and apostles, but continually. Hence, although, on the one hand, He can "do nothing of Himself," but only the works "which the Father hath given Him" (John v. 19, 20, 36, x. 25, xi. 41), yet, on

the result of demoniacal influences. Hence the severity of the Mosaic enactments against all heathen magic, which cannot well be explained on the supposition that the whole was only an illusion. Demoniacal miracles are indeed servile imitations of the divine working, and thence they receive their seductive appearance and influence. But their full power to captivate the judgment lies in the fact that they are *really supernatural*, although their working is *not above the power of the creature.* But at the same time we maintain that even these miracles, and especially those still impending as the culminating point of Satanic working in the last decisive struggle between light and darkness (according to the previous passages), are, like all the powers of darkness, under God's direction and control. They are regulated and restricted by the divine government of the world, they appertain to the revelation of divine wrath, are not immediately decreed, but permitted and judicially inflicted in punishment for human frivolity and unbelief, 2 Thess. ii. 10–12 ; Matt. xxiv. 24. Cf. below, remarks on the discernibility of miracles.

the other, He reveals therein not only God's glory, but at the same time His own (John ii. 11 comp. with xi. 40), because His oneness with the Father extends to His power also (John v. 21, x. 28, 29). Not as if during His earthly course He were to be considered as "walking Omnipotence;" on the contrary, He was to unfold and work out the divine life dwelling within Him in growing communion with the Father, and therefore He regarded His miraculous acts as something done in virtue of a command received from the Father (John xi. 41, 42). But through the personal union of the world-creating Word with His human nature, through the fulness of the Godhead dwelling in Him bodily (Col. ii. 9), as well as through His perfect sinlessness, His dynamic relation to nature was entirely different to that of other men, so that He possessed an indwelling causality of working miracles, which needed only to be evoked from above. For this reason also He manifested *His own* glory in His miracles (comp. John ix. 33, x. 37). This is our stand-point in opposition not only to those who consider Him as pure Omnipotence, but also to those who would place Him on the same footing with other human workers of miracles. As operations of divine power, miracles are—

2. *Supernatural phenomena,* the effective causes of which cannot be found in the usual course of nature, nor in the spirit of man, but only in the immediate interposition of higher divine powers. Here, therefore, *all analogical conception ceases;* we cannot connect the miracle with our natural experience, but we can only say, "This is the finger of God" (Ex. viii. 19). So far the conception of miracles belongs to the critique of our knowledge.[1] We call that a miracle for which we can find no analogy whatever in that which has previously existed, *i.e.* in the established system of our empirical knowledge.[2] For the miracle is—

[1] Hence it has been truly said, "The word miracle is a critical designation, and a sign of the critically active spirit which measures that which now happens by that which has already happened."—MEHRING, *Religionsphilosophie,* S. 197 ff.

[2] By this I mean the totality of knowledge attainable by us as creatures. I do *not* refer merely to a lower degree of knowledge, according to which many things might seem to be miracles which on closer examination would prove to be natural events, for this would render the nature of miracles merely relative and subjective.

3. Always a beginning of *something new* (Ex. xxxiv. 10; Num. xvi. 30; Isa. lxv. 17; Jer. xxxi. 32), a creative act; partly an absolute calling into existence of new substances (as at the creation), partly a supernatural transformation, intensification, or increase of an already existing material. Miracles in the narrower sense belong, with the exception of the miracle of creation,

4. To the *preservation* and *government* of the *world*. They have become necessary because corruption has entered the world; they not only attest God's creative, but especially His *redeeming power*.

5. For this reason, finally, the object of miracles is one of moral *holiness* in mercy and judgment—a *redemptive object*. They tend to the furtherance of the divine kingdom, to the salvation and consummation of the world. In the present material creation, they are *isolated manifestations of a higher order of things*, effected by a special power from above.

The different expressions—"wonders, signs, mighty deeds" (or "powers")—which are used in the Old and New Testaments already indicate this. The *miracle* or *wonder* (τέρας, θαῦμα), in the first place, is meant to astonish; it is intended, as something striking and extraordinary, to work upon the moral consciousness, and to draw attention to itself. Further, it is intended to make us reflect; we are to perceive in it something of what God is doing, and is about to do. Thus it becomes a "sign" (σημεῖον) to direct us in the knowledge of the ways of God, and a pledge of His truth and faithfulness—an earnest of the future consummation of His kingdom. Through such reflections we finally arrive at the recognition of the higher supernatural "powers" (δυνάμεις), and of the "mighty deeds" of God, which are revealed in miracles; or if men work them, we recognise their divine mission. For miracles must everywhere reveal something of the omnipotent, just, and holy God, but especially of the merciful God, and of His work of redemption upon earth. Hence, although the miracle cannot be *comprehended*, because it is God's most especial act, yet it should be *apprehended* in its divine intention, as a sign for our faith.

The "*spiritual miracles*," *i.e.* the mighty workings of God and of His Spirit in the depths of the human soul, occupy, as it were, a middle position between miracles in the wider and those in the narrower sense. Here, too, God places Himself in immediate relation to a human creature, and brings forth in him effects which never could have been produced through natural forces or influences; effects such as spiritual enlightenment, conversion, regeneration, consolation, peace, etc. These may rightly be called miracles, for faith is always a kind of miracle; and these spiritual miracles are the necessary pre-condition of a genuine development of the Christian life—a pre-condition which is demanded by the very idea of religion. But they are not miracles in the strict sense, *i.e.* effects of God's working upon definite points of *Nature's* domain. As distinct from the latter, we must finally mention the special *miracles of inspiration.* By this we understand those peculiar workings of God upon individual men, through which He imparts to them, in an especial excitement of their spiritual and mental life, new religious truths, allows them to have a concrete and immediate vision of future developments in the plan of the world and of the divine kingdom, in order that under the influence of the Spirit they may testify of this before others. These miracles of inspiration and prophecy, as *extraordinary* spiritual processes, correspond still more directly than the last-named class to the conception of miracles, and will therefore be considered by many a separate kind, in which God partly *works* something new (manifestation), partly *says* something new (inspiration; comp. Isa. xlii. 9, xlviii. 6, 1 Cor. ii. 9, 10). We find both kinds, the external miraculous acts, and the internal miracles of inspiration, combined in the chief instruments of revelation, such as Moses, some of the Prophets, the Apostles, and to the highest degree in Christ.

The modern aversion to miracles, therefore, also extends to both kinds. We endeavoured to refute the objections against the miracles of *inspiration* in the chapter on Revelation; we now have to do with the attacks upon external miracles of *manifestation,* as miracles in the stricter sense. Whence their negation?

(*b*) *Origin of the Negation of Miracles.*—The negation of miracles is almost as old as miracles themselves. Moses, the first human worker of miracles mentioned in Scripture, is opposed by Pharaoh, the first denier of miracles, who, with his inward repugnance to the recognition of immediate divine working, stands before us as a prophecy and a warning. The generation, too, before the flood was one which denied miracles, which, while it resisted the inner striving of God's Spirit (Gen. vi. 3), was driven to consider God's mighty working in external nature as impossible. This points us to the true source of the negation of miracles, viz. that as a rule it rests not so much on external as on internal and moral grounds, from which, indeed, all estrangement from our faith usually proceeds. How hard it was even in the time of Christ for the learned Israelites to believe in His most manifest miracles, is plainly shown in the history of the man who was born blind (John ix.). Nevertheless the opposition at that time, as well as during the first centuries of Christianity, was not directed against the possibility of effects produced by supernatural causes. Jews and Gentiles both believed in this. Even the enemies of Christ did not deny His miracles (Matt. xxvii. 42; John xi. 47, 48; Acts iv. 16). It was rather the moral value and the divine origin of these mighty works which was doubted; the unbelieving Jews ascribing them to demoniacal powers ("He casteth out devils through Beelzebub, the chief of the devils"), and the heathen afterwards placing Christ in the same category as their pagan sorcerers and wonder-workers.

For the last two hundred years, however, men have begun absolutely to deny the possibility of miracles, and to reject every supernatural manifestation, from whatever quarter it may come, as being unhistorical, because impossible. This was first done by the English Deists. They gradually advanced from the negation of the Old Testament miracles to the denial of those in the New, and from the quest for historical impossibilities and internal contradictions in their narration to an utterly frivolous explanation of them. Chubb, *e.g.*, observes that if these miracles are to be considered as historical, they must have been base impositions. Renan has lately maintained substantially the same opinion in respect of the resurrection of Lazarus; but it had long since been pushed to the extreme by Voltaire, who pronounced the heroes of the Bible to be knaves and fools, and the gospel history in general a lie and a deception. Hume, in his *Essay on Miracles*, undertook a systematic refutation of their possibility, endeavouring to show that miracles are violations of the laws of nature, and that the doubtful testimony of a few for their authenticity cannot avail against the universal experience of the inviolability of these laws. We shall recur to this again. Before Hume, Spinoza had sought to get rid of miracles by appealing to the laws of nature. "The laws of nature," said he, "are the only realization of the divine will; if anything in nature could happen to contradict them, God would contradict Himself."

Notwithstanding the endeavours of the philosophy of Leibnitz and Wolff to defend the possibility of miracles, *Rationalism* continued to oppose them on the same grounds. In this particular our modern philosophy in general follows the lead of Spinoza and Hume; but it is now assisted in its attack on miracles especially by *New Testament Criticism and the Natural Sciences.* Each in its own way seeks to carry out the principle of the natural explanation of all phenomena in nature and history. All of them, especially the natural sciences, have already cleared up so many hitherto dark processes, and have made such progress in the knowledge of the universal laws of nature, that we must not be surprised to find them too hastily trying to establish the boundaries of the possible and the impossible, and utterly denying the incomprehensible, which must elude our natural understanding. In these endeavours opponents of the miraculous are supported by the universal tendency of our age, *not to endure any kind of monopoly.* This age is a universal leveller; it seeks everywhere to obliterate differences as much as possible, and has even proceeded, as we know, to the insane attempt to bridge over the gulf between man and beast. It endeavours to confine everything to universal fixed laws, and brooks no exceptions. But miracles are a kind of monopoly which the supernatural world has reserved for itself and its instruments. It is by virtue of an exception to the general rule that Christianity and Judaism occupy so prominent a position in history. He who attempts to degrade them from this peculiar position to the ordinary and natural course of things, and to deprive them of the monopoly of their divine origin, is doubtless consciously or unconsciously led by this universal impulse of our age to reduce everything to the same level. This impulse easily leads to the denial of the difference of dispensations in the divine methods of revelation and in the education of mankind, and finally, to the statement that what does not happen in these days never can have happened.

Many are averse to the miraculous through *fear of superstition.* They think that if they accept the miracles of Scripture, they cannot withhold their assent to a multitude of apocryphal miracles, nor, indeed, to the pretensions of all sorts of necromancers and wizards. In this, however, they overlook the sharp discrimination of Scripture between belief and superstition, between miraculous power and witchcraft. Whereas the heathen sorcerer pretends to make the supernatural powers subservient to *his person,* the prophet or apostle, if he performs a miracle, accounts himself only *the instrument of God.* Thus Peter says to the Jews (Acts iii.), after the healing of a lame man, "Why look ye so earnestly on us, as though by our own power or holiness we had made this man to walk? By the name of Jesus Christ of Nazareth doth this man stand before you whole" (Acts iv. 10). Whereas the sorcerer or magician seeks his own honour (*e.g.* Acts viii. 9) by means of his art, the workers of miracles in Holy Scripture ascribe all the glory to God, because it is not they who perform the miracles by virtue of any natural or artificial power of their own, nor by any secret charm or spell containing such power, but it is God alone who works. The Son Himself seeks, through His works, not His own honour, but that of the Father (John viii. 50, 54). Hence these God-sent workers cannot use the divine power arbitrarily, but only by virtue of the highest personal and spiritual communion with God, according to the teachings and purposes of His will. Only notice the noiseless unobtrusiveness of miracles in Holy Scripture, the chastity with which Christ sharply repels the vain curiosity and vulgar thirst of His age for wonders, and His frequent prohibition of their publication (Matt. xvi. 1–4, xii. 38–39; Mark viii. 11–13; Matt. ix. 30, xii. 16, xvi. 20; Mark i. 44, iii. 12, etc.). Compare with these features the sensational miracles in the Romish and Oriental churches,—images of saints who sweat blood, who nod the head, who roll the eyes,—or the Whitsuntide miracles among the Greeks and Armenians at

Jerusalem, when the Holy Ghost lights up candles, (but not hearts); and you will confess that such feats of legerdemain and jugglery betray, in their external pomp and straining after effect, anything but a divine origin. A glance at the internal evidences of truth in miracles, at their *moral and religious* character, which reflects and serves not only the power of God, but also His truth and holiness, and must prove pre-eminently their divine origin, will show that it is not a very difficult task for one to defend his belief in the biblical miracles against the charge of superstition.

It is a remarkable fact, however, that not the believers in miracles, but their deniers, fall most easily into superstition. How often one can observe their "half fearful, half prurient listening for the supposed higher powers of nature!" If there is a spiritual medium, a clairvoyante, or a fortune-teller, they are the first to consult this oracle. For unbelief and superstition are most intimately connected. "When men no longer believe in God, they begin to believe in ghosts. In truth, there has scarcely ever been an age in which men have snatched more greedily after the extravagant than our own, which derides the supernatural:"[1] a proof that only faith, and not unbelief, can fully overcome superstition.

And here we observe, that in the negative of miracles internal causes must co-operate with all the assumed historic or scientific reasons. As in the time of Moses, so in these times, there are many who have never confessed to the workings of divine power in their own hearts, and who are therefore inwardly compelled to dispute the external working of God in nature and history. And this the more, inasmuch as the divine miracles appeal far less to our merely logical sense than to our moral judgment. Only he who experiences and admits the spiritual miracles wrought by the finger of God in his own experience, can readily raise his mind to the idea of an especial working of God's power in external nature. Only that man can believe in miracles (which are throughout designed for the moral and religious training of mankind) who can testify from the depths of his own experience the reality of such a training.

c. The *Theoretical Presupposition* in the negation of the

[1] Schenkel, *Was ist Wahrheit?* S. 22.

miraculous, is partly a *false naturalistic conception of God,* partly a *mechanical conception of the world.* The former of these conceptions impels Pantheism, the latter impels Deism and Rationalism, to deny the possibility of miracles. If God has no personal existence apart from nature, and if He is merely the unconscious fettered Soul of the Universe, then He is entirely bound by the laws of nature, and nothing remains but to adopt Spinoza's principle. This one-sided conception of the divine *immanence* in the world must annihilate all miracles. On the other hand, we may start with the supposition that God is actually separated from the world; that the world, having been left to itself after the creation, has become independent, and continues its course mechanically; nor does it need the special providence of God, since its laws and regulations are perfectly adequate for its further development. From this we must infer that no miraculous interference of God in the course of nature is possible, since only a disturbance of the universal order would result. In this case the one-sided conception of the divine *transcendence,* and the complete emancipation of the world from God's power, makes the miraculous impossible. These two hypotheses are, it is true, opposed to each other; for in the one God is entirely lost in nature, in the other He is absolutely separated from it. But they both agree in maintaining that the world, as it now exists, no longer needs a special divine influence, and that it must continue to develope itself unassisted according to its indwelling laws.

In addition to this, it is further presupposed that these mundane *laws are absolutely perfect,* that the present condition of the world is a normal one, and that therefore every interference, from whatever source it may come, can only occasion *a disturbance.*

In these presuppositions there lies a threefold *fundamental error.* First, the relation in which *God* is placed to the world is false and untenable. God is neither identical with the world, nor is He completely separated from it. We have recognised the former as the error of Pantheism, the latter as that of Deism. On the other hand, we have recognised this as the truth, that God works by His *will* in the world no less than He possesses His *essence* as distinct from it; that He is actually, vitally present in it no less than He is personally free from it. In the union of these two elements, the supramundane personality and freedom of God on the one hand, and His intramundane working on the other, we have the possibility of miracles. *He who believes in God as a free, personal Will, has settled for himself the possibility of miracles.* Our opponents, too, acknowledge that "if God be once conceived of as an extramundane Will, a manifestation of this Will in the world must also be admitted; but this manifestation, as the encroachment of a transcendental principle in the course of the world, can only be a supernatural fact, *i.e.* a miracle." (Zeller.) The *second fundamental error* lies in a *false conception of the world,* as though it were normal and perfect, and therefore had no further need of God's interference. But we see that, on the contrary, the development of the world is in many ways so abnormal, so disturbed, *that just on account* of this abnormity, caused by the breaking in of sin, a healing and restoring interference on the part of God evidently becomes necessary. This shows us the root of the *third fundamental error,* viz. the opinion that the supernatural *interference of God must derange* and break up the established order of nature. We hold the reverse, that it is the means of *healing* and *restoring the order* which has been destroyed through sin and death.

This is the position which we take up as against all the adversaries of miracles, and which we now proceed to justify in detail.

This we do by means of a closer examination into the *possibility of the miraculous,* and an enumeration of the positive arguments in favour of it.

Let me here begin, as I have throughout sought to do, with the recognition of that which is *just* in the objections of our opponents. The old supranaturalistic theology was decidedly defective in its conception and treatment of miracles, and is now severely punished by their universal negation. It considered miracles singly, instead of as forming coherent parts of a whole. Its followers valued every miracle *per se,* as a means of proving Christianity and the divine mission of the wonder-worker, whilst it really proved nothing; because its own veracity rested on that which it was supposed to prove, namely, the divinity of Christ, or the divine mission and mighty gifts of other wonder-workers, or on the divine truthfulness of the Scriptures. Thus the fact was overlooked, that single miracles were only accompaniments of the divine message; that they were intended to work as a whole in the entire organism of Revelation, in which each part mutually supports and is sustained by the others.

In addition to this, that school of theology took pleasure in pointing out the antagonism of miracles to the order of nature, and in the most trenchant manner maintained the interference of God's mighty will in the world, according to His own pleasure, in defiance of the laws of nature, and without reference either to the unchangeable and holy ends which exclude all arbitrariness, or to the internal conformity to law which appears in the miraculous. Such a procedure could not fail to provoke contradiction, and lend force to an emphatic enunciation of the claims of nature's law. It is legitimate that in opposition to such a one-sided view, the modern consciousness of our age should again insist above all things on the internal agreement of all the works and ways of God,—on the harmony of the moral and natural laws,—and should interdict all inner contradiction in the preservation and government of the world. In this we are agreed. We admit, what we have already previously recognised as a truth of Deism, that the created world, although upheld by God's mighty will, yet has a separate existence and a measure of independence. We find a hint of this in the repose of God after the creation, which indicates that from that time forward an independent existence of the world was possible. We do not, therefore, maintain that the law of nature is only the will of God, free to change at any time; but we acknowledge that He has established fixed laws and rules in the creation, which He employs in His *ordinary* administration of the world, and which are sufficient for that purpose. We even acknowledge that God employs these laws to such an extent, that to the perception of many He is entirely concealed behind events which seem merely natural, so that such men cease to perceive Him and His working in the special dispensations of providence.

But we do *not* admit the *complete independence* of these laws as sovereign powers existing separately, and as absolutely incapable of modification, which would form an absolute barrier for God if He willed to do anything extraordinary, and therefore we do not relinquish the possibility of miracles. Nor do we admit that the laws of nature are deranged by miracles. On the contrary, we maintain with the modern biblical theologians, who are now defending the miraculous with increasing confidence, the united harmonious working of God in nature. At the same time, we undertake the task of showing, in the midst of the apparent contradiction between miracles and the order of nature, the deeper harmony, in the breaking through of the usual course, the *higher order* of the ways of God, and the conformity to law which manifests itself therein, excluding all that is abnormal and arbitrary. And therefore we do not consider miracles as detached apologetic proofs, but "we place them all in the great historical organism of redemption, of which Christ is the living heart." We consider them only as effective vehicles of one and the same redemption, as radiations from one and the same central miracle, Christ; *i.e.* we no longer believe in Christ for the sake of miracles, but in miracles for the sake of Christ. Still, the inverted order has never yet lost, and never will lose, its significance for certain times and circumstances (John ix. 16, 32, and especially xiv. 11).

From a theistic conception of God, *i.e.* from the knowledge that He is a personal, free Being, and that He is omnipotent and continually active in the world, the objective *possibility* of the miraculous necessarily follows. "The question whether a miracle is possible, amounts to the query, whether there is a living God who has created the world,"[1] and who preserves it. He who believes in a living God must logically believe in miracles; for God is the miracle of all miracles. As soon as we understand the declaration, "My Father worketh hitherto," and recognise that the world depends for its very existence upon the mighty will of God; that the living God, who "rolls up the heavens" and "renews the earth," rules in the whole world; when we remember that He has not withdrawn from His work, but continually directs it; that He *thus has kept open an entrance for Himself to every point of nature's harmony;* then we have in this *intramundane working of God a basis for the possibility of the miraculous.* The objection that miracles are beyond the *power* of God, at once falls to the ground.

[1] Auberlen.

If God could perform miracle upon miracle at the creation of the world, why not afterwards? There can be nothing more illogical than to admit, as Rationalism does, the miracle of creation, and at the same time to deny the possibility of other miracles. What God has once done He must always be able to do, otherwise He would cease to be God.

But here we are met by the objection that miracles are an outrage upon the degree of independent life due to the world—a *violation of the laws of nature.* They are said to be a breach of that fixed order, the irreversible authority of which is the only guarantee for the continual existence of the world,—that order which coheres so closely, that the slightest derangement must occasion confusion in the whole; in short, a miracle, as Strauss has lately expressed it, is a "*rent in the world,*" or, more exactly, a "rent in nature's harmony." Let us dwell somewhat on this chief objection.

First of all, we cannot admit that in the whole creation there exists, and always has existed, an uninterrupted chain of communication, or a fixed and universally binding connection of cause and effect. Where is the naturalist who could demonstrate its existence? *This chain,* the indestructibility of which is the ever-recurring premise in the negation of miracles, *in reality often enough breaks off in Nature's own domain.* The "rents" exist in the very nature of the creation. If we do not believe in the eternity of matter, but in the creation of the world by God, *i.e.* in its being called forth from non-existence into existence, the connecting chain is broken off at the very beginning. From the laws of the created world, the genesis of creation itself can never be deduced. The existence of the world, then, is a miracle, as well as the existence of God Himself. But putting this entirely aside, we meet with phenomena in the genetic process of nature itself at which that chain breaks off, with events which natural science never can explain from the laws and forces known to us. The original entrance of higher forms of life into the sphere hitherto filled up by lower ones, is one of the most striking phenomena of this kind. *How did the first living organism originate?* Modern natural science has unquestionably demonstrated that life did not always exist on the earth. Long ago, Cuvier confidently maintained this to be the case, and that we could easily indicate the point of time when life began;[1] and it is confirmed by Liebig, who says: " Some philosophers have affirmed that life has existed from eternity. Natural science, however, has proved that at a certain period the earth's temperature was such that no organic life could exist, and that, therefore, it must have had a beginning."[2] In addition to this, natural science has of late years increasingly confirmed the position, that it is impossible to demonstrate the natural evolution of organic life from inorganic matter, even in the smallest degree. What Müller once said still remains true, " Only a miraculous interruption of the natural laws can form the living organism out of lifeless matter."[3] Here, at all events, we have a beginning, which we can only explain through a creative act, *i.e.* through a miracle. And how did Spirit first enter the world? how man, with the law of conscience which transcends all the laws of nature? With him, too, the chain breaks off. He appears as a new beginning, as a third miracle, which retains its miraculous character even to this day. For what is every new-born man, with his peculiar individuality, his special talents and powers, but a never fully explicable miracle?[4] There is not merely poetical imagery, but real truth, in the words of the poet Rückert:

[1] *Discours sur les révolutions du globe*, p. 24.

[2] *Augsburger Allgemeine Zeitung*, 1856, Nr. 24.

[3] It is instructive to witness the desperate efforts of Strauss in his last work, *The Old and the New Faith*, 1873, p. 169 *et seq.*, to show that modern natural scientists have discovered the missing link between the organic and unorganic kingdom. In the face of the express opinion of a scientific man like Virchow, who certainly does not favour positive Christianity, but declares "that all known facts go to disprove the truth of spontaneous generation during the present era," he can only quote the hypotheses built by Huxley on his discovery of the "Bathybius," and by Hæckel on the existence of what he styles "Moneren."

[4] It is therefore only logical for deniers of the miraculous, like Strauss, to banish it from nature, in order thoroughly to get rid of it; and for this reason, above all, to seek a natural explanation for the origin of man. Thus Strauss (in his *Christl. Glaubenslehre*, i. p. 206 ff.) once gave vent to the desperate conjecture, that if it were possible for the tape-worm to grow from heterogeneous matter to a considerable length in the human intestines, without having been sexually generated, he did not see why man should not at some time or other, when the earth was far richer in generative forces than now, have been formed out of some sort of terrestrial matter, however foreign to his present being. At the present day, after the impossibility of a *generatio æquivoca* has been demon-

"Man is a miracle begotten and conceived,
A miracle, he lives, is born and nursed,
A miracle, he grows, and sees, and feels,
A miracle, he thinks, and what he thinks,
A miracle, he stands, miracles environing,
Miracles precede and follow all his steps ;
To them is he so gradually, unconsciously
Inured, that they appear to him quite natural,
And unaccustom'd only seems miraculous to him,
Who Nature's wonders unastonish'd sees."

We thus see that there are divers "rents,"[1] not, it is true, in the world, but in the connection of Nature, supposed to be perfect—rents which can only be filled up by the miraculous power of God. Not Nature herself, but the false conception of Nature from which the denial of the miraculous proceeds, is violated by these facts.

And do not a multitude of analogies go to show that God can interfere supernaturally at any time in all natural exist-

strated, Strauss would scarcely venture to make such assertions. Many years ago, Alexander v. Humboldt remarked on these tendencies of his : "What I do not like in Strauss, is the scientific frivolity with which he finds no difficulty in accepting the generation of organic matter from unorganic ; or even the formation of man from some primeval Chaldæan slime" (*Letters to Varnhagen*, 4th ed. p. 117). We see from this, that whoever believes in the superiority of man's nature, must believe in miracles also.

Renan, too (in his work on the Apostles), is obliged, in order to get rid of the miraculous, to abandon the supernatural origin of man. "Nothing can be more offensive," he says, "nothing more senseless, than the formation of mankind, if we regard it as a sudden, momentary act. It enters the region of universal analogies, if we regard it as the result of a slow progress going on through incalculable periods." So the divine origin of man is "offensive," but his derivation from the primal egg or cell of some first organism,—through the medium, probably, of the monkey tribe,—or, to use Renan's euphemism, from "universal analogies," is not only inoffensive, but the only reasonable view! What an utter perversion of ideas!!

[1] And not only does the entrance of higher forms of life interrupt the chain of natural causes : for within the different grades of existence themselves, we see *the universal laws broken by exceptions in certain points.* The only exception to the law, that heat expands and cold contracts, is water, which is most dense and heavy at a temperature of 4° (Cent.), but expands and becomes lighter below this mark. For this reason, the heavy water of the temperature above mentioned remains below, otherwise a few cold days would turn all our waters into ice, and our countries would have the climate of the frigid zones. "Thus we see in the case of water how God breaks through an otherwise universal law of nature, in order to make a greater part of the earth's surface habitable." This speaks at the same time against the unconscious mundane soul of the pantheist ; for the laws of such a being would allow of no exceptions in favour of a higher aim.

ence? *Each higher form of life has its peculiar laws, which transcend those of the lower forms, and cannot be explained by them. Therefore each in a certain sense can perform miracles in the inferior grades of existence,* that is to say, it can interfere as a higher will, and bring forth results which could not proceed from the laws and forces of the lower orders, and yet this takes place without disturbing them in their continued existence. How wonderfully, *e.g.*, an animal can interfere in the vegetable kingdom, by his sudden ravages! Think how the human will can interfere in the lower orders of nature. The sum of human activity is almost solely expended in seeking to realize that which Nature of herself cannot produce. Why, then, should it not be possible for God to interfere with His higher Will in earthly nature and the human world? If He has granted to human freedom an influence on the world, He must have reserved the same right for Himself. When man works upon nature and transforms it, or when the mind controls and directs the organs of the body, the power of the will is manifest. The spiritual works upon the sensuous, and produces that which Nature alone could not produce without in some way disturbing the simultaneous working of her forces and laws. For the mind rules the body, and through the power of the will moves the limbs innumerable times, in opposition to the law of gravitation. This very law of gravitation—the corner-stone upon which the naturalistic view of the world is based—is in a special sense the law of death, because it reigns entirely and absolutely only where there is death: and it is interrupted continually by every motion of life, from the germ bursting its shell to the flying bird or the working man. And yet its validity is always unimpaired. Why, then, should not divine power also act immediately upon certain points in the domain of creation, and be able to produce in it something which the resources of Nature could never produce, and that without disturbing the continuously operating forces and laws of the world, or permanently "rending" them asunder?

Moreover, we often see things in nature, merely by contact with other natural forces, enter into processes and conditions which we could not at all have inferred from the powers and laws hitherto observed in them; as when, *e.g.*, iron, which before lay on the ground through the force of gravitation, is lifted by the magnet. Why should not earthly creatures also, by contact with divine power, be enabled to pass into conditions or develope forces which we were unable to infer from their former nature *per se?*

From this we make two deductions: *First,* that the interference of the higher forces is not excluded by the operation of the lower, and, therefore, that the interference of God is not excluded by the operation of the laws of nature. *The man who endeavours to make the laws of nature a ground of proof against miracles, simply begs the question, for he always presupposes what he desires to prove.* If he say that the existence of these laws renders a higher influence impossible, he clearly presupposes that these laws alone are valid always and everywhere, and that is precisely what must first be proved. *Second,* we see that by the interference of the higher orders with the lower, the laws of the latter are in no way disturbed or abolished, but still continue in force. The same also is true of the interference of God in the course of the world. *The laws of nature are in no way suspended thereby,* but continue to retain their validity. And why? Because the forces of nature, strictly speaking, do not participate at all in the actual miracles, and because *the products of the miracle,* with all their consequences, immediately *take their place in the ordinary course of nature.*

I say the forces of nature do not participate at all in the act itself. Not they, but a higher divine power performs the miracle. But we must here discriminate between *miracles in the absolute sense of the word,* which exclude all mediation of the creature, and those which are accomplished through an enhancement of the forces of nature, and are thus connected with the legitimate activity of the latter. To the first belong, *e.g.,* the conception of Christ, and the miracles of the loaves and fishes. Here we have a process similar to the creation of the world. God by His own immediate activity places something in the course of nature which did not exist there before. What He once did for the universe, He is surely able to do for an individual part of it. But the forces of nature are not partakers in this immediate act of God. The miraculous *act* in these instances lies entirely beyond the laws of nature. They merely receive its product, which directly subordinates itself to them. The miraculous *act* itself can never be perceived by the senses, only its effect. How can any one in such a case speak of a disturbance or a breach in the laws of nature? And how can men say that the object thus introduced into the course of nature must necessarily produce endless changes in the world? *As soon as it enters the world, it becomes subject to the laws of nature,* and obeys them in its further existence. Apart from its origin, it ceases with its entrance into the world to be a miracle, and becomes part of the natural and the actual.

The same thing occurs here as in grafting a noble scion upon a wild stock. It is something foreign to the nature of the latter, but is dependent for its future existence upon all the conditions of that nature. So Christ is the noble scion grafted upon the human stock, not by the will of man, but through a creative act of God (John i. 13). The order of creation in nature and history, which is indeed the divine order, is so far from being interrupted, that it is throughout respected as sacred. Thus the *law of historical development* is respected. The Destroyer of the Serpent does not appear before the specifically religious as well as the general human pre-conditions are fulfilled, and thus the human race is ready to receive Him. "When the *fulness of the time* was come, God sent forth His Son," Gal. iv. 4. The *order of nature,* too, is respected. We do not see a fantastic descent from heaven of one apparently thirty years of age, whose human form is a mere phantom; but from the moment when the seed of the woman is roused to conception by a creative act of God, He is subject to all the natural conditions of birth and individual life in its gradual development. And, finally, the *moral law* as well as the national law of Judaism is respected. Jesus is "made under the law," fulfils all righteousness, is subject to His parents. He proves His morality in the course of His life under constant temptation and trial: in obedience to His Father even unto death. I ask, "Can the glory of God accommodate itself more humbly to human nature and history than it has done in the life and death of Christ?"[1]

[1] Cf. *Die Tübinger historische Schule* in the *Zeitschrift für Protestantismus und Kirche,* Apr. 1864, p. 223 et seq., and Beyschlag, *ubi supra.*

What reasonable man can speak of a rent in the laws of nature, in a sphere where she originally had neither anything to *do* nor to *suffer?* The same is true of other absolute miracles or new creations. "The already existing harmony of nature is as little annihilated by the appearance of an absolute creative act of God in the world, as is humanity itself by the entrance of a new personality."[1]

But in those miracles in which God produces supernatural effects through an intensification of the legitimate activity of nature (*e.g.* in the deluge and several of the Mosaic miracles, which were connected with certain natural phenomena of those regions), the natural order is preserved. The miracle is here connected with the existing life of nature, the slow process of which is but temporarily suspended while the divine power substitutes a concentrated and potential plastic energy. In these cases, as we have already hinted, God does the same as man, though in an infinitely higher manner and sphere. By controlling and intensifying the forces of nature in art and industry, we produce effects which the course of nature left to itself would never bring about. But what man can do, God can also do, and that without limitation. He who has created nature and determined its course, to whom it is perfectly clear and transparent in all its parts, must surely best understand how to play on that gigantic instrument upon which we, in spite of all our progress in the natural sciences, are still but clumsy performers. And even though whole countries and nations should be dashed to the ground by its most powerful chords, not one of the many strings would break so as to disorder the framework of His laws. Is He not the skilful Master to whom all His works are known from the foundation of the world? He does not intermeddle with them like the novice who stops the harmonious working of a watch; but with holy wisdom for the salvation of the world, and at the right hour, He exerts His supernatural power. To this day the world quietly moves on in its course, and the laws of nature exist and work in full force; therefore they have not been rent asunder, and still less annulled, by previous miracles. And, therefore, the power which performed them cannot be one which disturbed order, but its interference must have maintained it.

[1] Schenkel, *Christl. Dogmat.* p. 258.

Those who find it difficult to believe in anything which surpasses the ordinary course of nature, ought to determine for us precisely how much is included in the natural, and show us *the boundary beyond which natural forces cannot be intensified by the supernatural.* Or, if they maintain that such an intensification can never take place at all, let them show us why the natural, which originally proceeds from the supernatural, should not always continue to be open to its influence. If the laws of nature originally proceed from God, is He to be the only one who is not Master in His own house? Are these laws to be, as it were, prison walls, within which God has confined Himself? "Shall we—to adopt the language of a natural philosopher—dare to allow no freedom to the primitive source of all freedom, and make a strait-waistcoat for Him of His own laws, which we, moreover, but imperfectly understand?" The course of God in the government of the world and of man is, and always has been, one of freedom; His is the free election of grace. He will not, and cannot, allow His hands to be bound by anything. Why should He not have reserved to Himself the power to interfere in special cases and in special extraordinary ways? just as in every household, in spite of the strictest rules which continue both before and after, special regulations are required for special cases.

Whence arises the proverb, "There is no rule without an exception"? Does it not come from a true feeling that the rules which we have discovered or made are not immutably and absolutely valid, but that they admit of modifications? Nothing can ever limit the Infinite and Boundless. If He as the Absolute has His limitations only in Himself, and not in anything outside of Him, then no order of nature can stop Him, be it never so fixed in its working. As Matthias Claudius strikingly says to the learned men who are always appealing to the "nexus rerum," *i.e.* the strict connection of all things, "The gates of Gaza with their two posts had a strong connection with the stone archway and the bolts. Yet Samson came, and, taking them out of this beautiful 'nexus,' carried them to the top of the hill before Hebron,—a violent proceeding which certainly no professor of natural history in Gaza would have considered possible." And must not such an absolutely free and sometimes extraordinary divine interference be all the more necessary in a world where God not only has to do with inanimate things and mechanical laws, but with free beings who can thwart His moral order every moment? Could we under such circumstances imagine a government of the world, in which God had not the freedom to interfere in details, in order to realize His holy will in the history of the world, amid the action and reaction of the struggle with His free creatures?[1] From all this we see clearly that no valid objection against miracles can result either from the contemplation of God or from that of the laws of nature; and the talk about a "rent in the world" is shown to emanate from a great rent in the logic of those who invent such empty catchwords, which are unfortunately adopted by many without judgment or examination.

But here a new objection meets us. If it cannot be denied that miracles are consistent with the power of God, yet at least they seem to be incompatible with His *omniscience*, which must have *foreseen* and suitably arranged everything, and which, therefore, renders an extraordinary interference in the course of the world superfluous. Such *after-help*, in special cases, can only be necessary where the original regulations are imperfect, but not in God's perfect universe. Renan, amongst others, appeals to this trivial argument. "Miracles," says he, "are special interpositions like those of a watchmaker, who, though he has made a very fine watch, yet is compelled to regulate it from time to time in order to compensate for the insufficiency of the mechanism." We have already seen how ill this conception of a compensating assistance corresponds to God's special government in the world. Not *God's order*, but *we* men, and especially *fallen* men, require divine aid for our entire condition, and above all for our perception of the being and power of God, which has been darkened through sin! Hence this objection rests entirely upon the indiscrimination of those men who overlook the *moral aim* of miracles. Renan does so. He entirely waives the main question, whether it is not possible that a disturbance has really entered the mechanism of our existence. He has no idea of the moral

[1] Compare with this p. 196 et seq., where the fact of man's freedom was shown to be an argument against the deistic conception of the divine government of the world.

aspect of our question, and cannot have, because the ethical element is entirely wanting in his view of the world.

If we fix our attention upon this side of the question, we shall find that the miraculous is justified from another point of view. We now recognise in the condition of the world as vitiated by sin, not only the possibility, but also the *necessity of miracles,* and can proceed to enter upon the line of positive counter-proofs in opposition to their negation.

II.—NECESSITY AND HISTORICAL MANIFESTATIONS OF THE MIRACULOUS.

It has rightly been observed, that miracles are necessary if it were only for the development of history. For whilst the process of natural life is a mere repetition,[1] the historical process is a continuous onward march, in which the new must ever have a place. The life of the spirit in history requires the new, and lives by it. "History is nourished by the new, *i.e.* by the miraculous; it would become stagnant without it."[2] Here, however, the reference is to miracles in the wider sense.

But as the miraculous in general is necessary to history, so miracles properly so called are necessary, in consequence of the moral condition of the world after the entrance of sin. We, too, are well aware of a rent in the world and a disturbance of its original laws, not caused, however, by God, but by man; not *provoked* by miracles, but rather to be *remedied* by them. Our opponents say that the world would go to ruin if God through His interference were to violate the order of nature. To this we reply, that, on the contrary, since sin has entered the world, it would immediately go to ruin if left to itself, and therefore it only exists to this day because God in every age has graciously interfered in its self-inflicted disorder. We shall easily be convinced of this if we fix our attention upon the *internal aim of miracles,* and compare it with the end and aim of the world. And here the objection of those who talk of a "rent in the world" appears in all its folly.

[1] As Lessing remarked, that he had already seen the earth put on its green dress thirty-eight times, and now for once he should like to see it in a red one.

[2] Mehring, *Religionsphilosophie,* p. 199.

As God is the Creator of the world, so He is also the End for which it was created. He Himself is the aim of its development. Therefore, although it was "very good," as created by Him, yet from the beginning it was destined for a still higher consummation. Above the visible order of things there existed a higher supernatural sphere of glorious spirits. To this the natural world was to become gradually conformed. But what happened? Did the world move in a direct path towards this her destiny by faithfully preserving the original divine order? Let us look around. Evil meets us at every step. We see all life springing only from death, and hastening thither again. Strife and murder stalk throughout the entire creation. We see the elements raging against the works of man's hands, and rising in rebellion against their divinely ordained master, often to his destruction. Is that the original order which God beheld, and, lo, "it was very good"? Natural science may affirm this as often as it pleases, since it knows no better. The Christian, who believes in an infinitely benevolent and holy Creator, will always deny it. He is compelled to recognise that a far-reaching disturbance has entered into the originally divine order—a disturbance from which all evil proceeds, in consequence of which the curse of death rests upon every creature, and the world is checked in its development towards its eternal goal, aye, which threatens the loss of that goal,—and this disturbance is *sin*. *If, then, the divine aim in the creation of the world was ever to be attained, God must needs interfere in order to nullify the disturbance which had entered, and to realize the consummation which was intended by Him; He must immediately overcome the powers of sin and death with new creative energy,* in order to deliver that which was in bondage to them, *i.e.* He must perform a miracle. And this interference could not take place only in the spiritual and moral sphere, but it must also touch upon the domain of nature, since, as every one can trace in his own body, corruption has also penetrated the material world. Hence there is a necessity for miracles in the strict sense of the word.

Here we see the necessity and the aim of the miraculous. The whole question turns upon this, whether men set out with the supposition that the world in its present state is normal and perfect, or whether they admit that a disturbance has entered its development through sin. Only in the latter case can men arrive at a belief in the miraculous, as in general they only attain to faith at all when they first see their misery, and look not at their good, but at their evil. He only who believes in the fatal ruin of man as a consequence of sin, and at the same time in a holy God, who is love, and as such cannot forsake His creatures although they have forsaken Him, will also consider a divine interference necessary for the removal of the ruin which has entered the world. We therefore maintain that the first breach in the divine order which entails infinitely important consequences was made by sin,—sin has made a "rent" in the world; but miracles only enter in for the removal of the already existing disturbance.[1] The abnormal sinful course of our free development *not only can bear God's saving interference, but imperatively demands it as a work of mercy.* Hence we read, "Who alone doeth great wonders (or miracles): *for His mercy endureth for ever*" (Ps. cxxxvi. 4).

If men call the salvation wrought by Christ a violent interference in our natural development, they should also consider the grafting of wild trees and the healing of the sick as contrary to nature. "*Miracles do not unnaturally break through nature, but supernaturally through the unnatural.*" For surely it is plainly contrary to the laws of nature, and of a truth most unnatural, that one should have eyes and not see, ears and not hear, organs of speech and not speak, or limbs without the power to use them; but not that a Saviour should come and loose his fetters! Assuredly it is unnatural that there should be so much misery in the world, but not that a Saviour should seek to remove it! It is unnatural that one people should be most cruelly enslaved and abused by another, but not that God should regard them and lead them out of the land of bondage "by signs and wonders, by a mighty hand and a stretched-out arm" (Deut. vii. 19)! It is unnatural that the wind and the waves should rise against a good human action, but not that the Lord should command them! It were indeed unnatural that the five thousand who had gone after the Word of life should starve in the wilderness, but not that the bountiful hand of God should open and

[1] At present we are putting the miracle of the creation out of the question.

make much out of little, as it once made the universe out of nothing! It was contrary to nature that ruthless death should sever the bands of love, which God Himself has knit, between mother and son, between brother and sister; but not that a young man of Nain, or a Lazarus, should be released from the fetters of death through a mighty word! And that was the climax of the unnatural, that the world should nail the only righteous One to the cross; but not that the holy Bearer of that cross should conquer undeserved death, should rise and victoriously enter into His glory![1]

In every one of these cases the unnatural is removed by means of the miraculous, and the original laws of nature are re-established. *Here the supernatural is shown to be truly in accordance with nature. That which takes place here is so far from being a disturbance or a breach in real nature, that it is rather a healing and re-establishing of the original and genuine order.* The laws of nature, instead of being abolished, are confirmed and set up again in their full force. In the same way the healing of the sick is not a violation but a re-establishment of the laws of nature; and when the laws of the natural life of the soul are interrupted by the new birth, one does not feel in any wise a violation of the mind and spirit, but rather a replacement of the same in their sound, normal, and vigorous condition.

After having thus recognised the aim of miracles, their entire significance becomes clear to us. They presuppose man estranged from God, and a depraved course of nature, and they *aim at the restoration, salvation, and consummation of the world.* They only break through the laws of nature in order to raise her from her imperfection and bondage to the freedom and glory which was her original aim. They are isolated manifestations of a new creative activity of the divine will, infusions of a reorganizing power into the life of nature, whereby it is agitated and excited. This holy purpose lies, without exception, at the foundation of all true miracles, and in this especially consists the difference between the scriptural and apocryphal miracles. Hence miracles in Scripture are so often called *signs*, as we saw above. They are always signs of the divine intention which aims at the salvation of the world; tokens

[1] Beyschlag.

that God has not abandoned the high destiny for which He created it; pledges that He is bringing it nearer and nearer to this destiny in spite of all hindrances, and that He will at length redeem His word, "Behold, I make all things new" (Rev. xxi. 5). They are the first strokes of God's hammer, which is to break the great prison of nature and of the human world, and to loose the chains of corruption and death. Like single beams of the ruddy morn, they prophesy *the day of the final consummation*, when Christ will crown the deliverance of the soul by that of the body; they are the first-fruits of that future order of things wherein there is to be no more death, neither sorrow, nor any more pain—no further contradiction between spirit and matter. They point to that consummation of the world *in which glorified nature shall immediately obey the spirit*, and therefore miracles will no longer be the exception, but the rule. For "miracles upon earth are nature in heaven," as Jean Paul Richter has truly said.

But, it may be asked, is all this true of miracles in general, and not merely of the miracles of healing? Let us consider how far the *domain of the miraculous extends*. It embraces the whole region of the moral and religious life, and of the special providence of God. It is the domain of biblical history, the theatre of the divine. Miracles are the inseparable attendants of revelation, and are therefore manifested in a certain portion of humanity to which God has placed Himself in a special historical relation, and whose history without such special divine activity is entirely incomprehensible. Miracles can only be understood if considered in connection with the history of redemption. And in this their holy aim appears. "It is God's will, by means of the miraculous, to reveal Himself to men who are blinded by their sins."[1] So He did to Pharaoh and to the children of Israel in the time of Moses and the prophets, and subsequently in the time of Christ. The revelation for which the course of nature no longer sufficed, must take place through facts which lie outside of the course of nature. While miracles make the incredible visible, they serve to make the invisible credible. In them God always causes His holy being to shine forth in goodness and judgment. From the deluge and the destruction

[1] Rothe.

of Sodom to the future conflagration of the world, all the judicial miracles are designed perceptibly and palpably to reveal the holy justice of God to men, who otherwise could not be aroused. And from the deliverance out of Egypt, and the manna in the wilderness, down to the healing miracles of Christ and the outpouring of the Spirit in the New Testament, all the miracles of grace make the endless love of God to man no less palpably evident. Hence their purpose in the scheme of redemption is likewise an *educational* one.

Miracles are also intended to confirm the divine mission of those who perform them, and to add to the weight of their testimony. Christ Himself appeals to His miracles as tokens of His Messianic destiny (Matt. xi. 4–6 ; Isa. xxxv. 5, 6), of His divine mission and Sonship (John v. 36, x. 25, 37, xx. 31). And lastly, they serve (especially the healings recorded in the New Testament) to illustrate the internal miracles which take place in the souls of those who are spiritually blind, deaf, dumb, lame, and dead. Yet their evidence or inherent power of conviction is not irresistible (John xii. 37). It is not so great that contradiction is impossible; nor should it be. Faith in Jesus must never be made so easy that it would cease to be a matter of free determination, and become a necessity in which no other choice were possible. Therefore the proof from miracles is not sufficient in itself, but should always be united with the still more powerful proof from the entire substance and spirit of the teaching of Christ. His miracles should only work in harmony with the impression of His entire personality. Hence our Lord always refused the demand prompted by the fleshly lust of that age for wonders, and even rebuked those who attached too great importance to His miracles. Hence, too, His caution against their dissemination by those who did not comprehend the entire significance of His work, and who would thereby only have given an impetus to the carnal Messianic expectation of the people (Matt. ix. 30, xii. 16, xvi. 20; Mark i. 44, iii. 12, etc.). "The Lord prefers a faith which believes without seeing signs and wonders. But on account of the dull perception of man, which cleaves to the sensuous, God quickens and arouses him by sensuous means, in order to lead him to a faith which sees not and yet believes."[1] In the life and works of the apostles, miracles likewise appear only as accompaniments of their preaching, never as of primary importance. The Lord "*confirming the word,* with signs following" (Mark xvi. 20).

Hence, too, the modest proportion of the miracles performed by Christ and His apostles as compared with the deeds which a wonder-seeking fancy might imagine, or with the "signs from heaven" which the Jews expected of the Messiah (Matt. xvi. 1 ff., xii. 38 ff.). They did not even regard the acts of Jesus as proper miracles or Messianic signs. Although the Scriptures abound in miracles, yet the proportion of the miraculous for which they demand belief is really less than in any other religion. How much more incredible things, *e.g.*, does the Koran[2] record, to say nothing of pagan myths!

Miraculous manifestations occur throughout, only so far as is necessary in order to make God's love or righteousness more palpably evident through sensuous impressions upon the perception of man, which has been blunted by sin. Or they are intended to prepare him for a spiritual influence, to arouse his attention, and to facilitate his believing acceptance of the truths of salvation. The entire series of miracles perceptible to the senses, from the time of Abraham and Moses down to that of Christ, has accompanied every step of *the divine revelation, in order either to confirm it or to prepare the way for it.* Whenever revelation takes a step in advance, it is preceded by specially powerful miracles. They are only the reflections in nature of the progressive spiritual development, which have their legitimate foundation in the connection between nature and spirit. And in each case they are necessary from an educational point of view, in order to open men's eyes by means of sensuous signs to the spiritual revelation of salvation, and to the greater spiritual miracles which accompany them. Moses could not have made the power, truth, and majesty of God evident to the rude, sensual people whom he led out of Egypt, if God had not Himself done it in His

[1] Köstlin.

[2] *E.g.* when Mahomet is said to have caused darkness at noon, whereupon the moon flew to him, bowed before him, and slipped into his right sleeve, coming out again at his left, etc.—Comp. Tholuck, *Verm. Schr.* i. 1–27.

saving miracles in the sea and the wilderness, and in His thunderings and lightnings from Sinai. Elijah, the sole champion of Jehovah, could not have held out against an entire apostate kingdom and people, had he not been able to summon miraculous divine power to his aid, when the nation was to choose between Baal and Jehovah. And could Christ, when He became one of a race which felt its external far more than its internal misery, have opened the hearts of men for the divine love and grace, if He had not caused its beams to fall sensibly and palpably upon earthly distress, sickness, and death?

Every miracle, therefore, serves the purpose of salvation; on the one hand, in a subjective educational way, by preparing the heart for greater spiritual wonders, and affording a tangible proof of the divine love and righteousness; on the other hand, by counteracting sin and the ruin caused by death, and by preparing the way for the future consummation. God could not, and would not, magically obtrude redemption upon us. It was His will in manifold ways through a miraculous history to work gradually towards the goal of the world's renewal.

If we fix our attention more closely upon the *gradual historical manifestations of the miraculous, we shall see that Christ is the centre of this development, and the second great miracle after the creation.* With Him the beginning of a new era is inaugurated, which will attain its consummation when "all things have become new." In Him the power exists for the regeneration of the world, and from Him it goes forth to every creature; in His acts He appears as the divine Liberator of all physical and spiritual life from the thraldom of sin; His resurrection is the foundation and beginning of the glorified world, of that new order of things to which the creation is at length destined to be raised. He is the divine Miracle of love, which was demanded on the one hand by the redeeming love of God, and on the other by the actual condition and the destiny of man. But this takes place in such wise, that in Him "the miraculous appears as His true nature, as a human life of love, leading us through itself to its internal divine source."[1] Hence the resurrection, the greatest miracle

[1] Dorner.

which was accomplished in the person of Jesus, appears entirely natural, and is plainly demanded by His own being; it was not possible that this Holy One should see corruption (Acts ii. 27 ff.). And that which in consequence of His natural moral being is worked in Him through the power of God, is at the same time the object of His own will, which is one with, and mighty through, God. He Himself takes His own life again as He had laid it down (John x. 17, 18).

The entire *history of miracles* is grouped around this central miracle, and stands in internal connection with it, either as a prophecy or as an echo of that which is begun in Him. A glance at this confirms the result just before attained respecting the aim and significance of the miraculous, which we had hinted at in our remarks on the gradual progress of revelation (see p. 97). Before the time of Moses, God performs many miracles, but as yet without human agency. The patriarchs are endowed with the gift of inspiration, but not with that of miracles; on the other hand, visions and theophanies are frequent during this period. Moses is the first who has not only the gift of inspiration, but that of miracles, as a manifestation of his divine mission. Under him, and immediately after him, miracles are frequent, but the theophanies gradually disappear. Again, the judges appear under the influence of inspiration as prophets in deeds, though not in words. In Samuel, David, and Solomon, we see inspiration progressing towards the actual realization of the theocratic Church. With the encroaching sway of heathenism, miracles again appear more conspicuously. They are as necessary for the re-establishment of the law as they were at its foundation. Elijah often inflicts destructive blows; Elisha works in a milder, more beneficent manner. The later prophets are pre-eminently men of words, of inspiration, until finally both the gift of miracles and that of inspiration cease. Again, the forerunner of Christ, John the Baptist, appears as inspired, but without miraculous power, so that the miracles of Christ might make a deeper impression (John x. 41). The miracles of Christ, which are almost without exception beneficent miracles of grace, break forth with unparalleled splendour, yet in such a way that on some occasions He performs many signs, which at other times He omits, as we have seen before, because of unbelief, or because He foresees that they will be without result, and wishes to check the fleshly desire for wonders. To the apostles it is given to work "the signs of an apostle." Then this gift gradually disappears, and a free course is left for the *Spirit* of Christianity during a period characterized by spiritual miracles.[1]

Miracles, therefore, like revelation in general, belong to those *crises in which the divine kingdom is to make an important advance.* They are connected with certain periods and persons, namely, with the chief promoters of God's kingdom. The time of the foundation and re-establishment of the law by Moses and Elijah, the time of the founding and the first promulgation of the gospel by Christ and His apostles, were decisive epochs of this kind. In the intermediate ages miracles fall into the background. With this the prediction of Scripture exactly agrees, that at the end of time, when the last decisive struggle is being waged between the kingdom of God and the anti-christian power of this world, and when Christ returns, there will again be a period of miracles (Luke xxi. 25 ff.).

We need not be surprised that extraordinary forces work in such crises. Analogies from natural life sufficiently show that the moments in which a new creature is born into the world are not subject to the ordinary laws of development, but evince a plenitude of peculiar impulses, forces, and forms, which, after the fully accomplished birth, give place to the customary activity of the usual laws of life. It is known, *e.g.*, that the organic functions in the formation of the fœtus proceed according to other laws than those of the perfect organism. The same is true of the birth-hour of the Christian Church. This, as well as every other birth-hour, is subject to other laws than those of the ordinary course. The man who makes ordinary human development the standard for the extraordinary fulness of the Spirit, which appears in that most important epoch of human history, in order to exclude the miraculous, falls into the same error as he who makes the laws of the present

[1] With regard to the continuance of miracles after the apostolic age, we have testimonies not only from Tertullian and Origen, who tell us that many in their time were convinced against their will of the truth of Christianity by miraculous visions, but also much later from Theodore of Mopsueste († 429). The latter says: "Many heathen amongst us are being healed by Christians from whatever sicknesses they may have; so abundant are miracles in our midst."

course of nature a standard for the period of the creation. He is guilty of a ὕστερον πρότερον: he places that which is later before that which is earlier, and forgets that the laws of primary development are altogether different from those working in that which already exists.

From this history of the miraculous, and the holy purpose constantly manifested in it, we see *in how strict a manner it is governed by divine laws,* which render the mere thought of an arbitrary interference impossible. Miracles never have an anomalous disconnected[1] character. They are connected with each other, and with the central miracle, Christ; and they belong as necessary members to the entire organism of revelation, working together towards one great end, the salvation and consummation of the world. We neither see the boy Jesus play at miracles with childish caprice, as several of the apocryphal gospels relate, nor does the man Jesus ever arbitrarily or selfishly exert His miraculous power on His own behalf (comp. the history of the temptation). He employs it throughout only in the service of God, as proof of His divine mission, to relieve human need, and for redemptive ends. We may therefore expect miracles to a greater or less extent, according as they are needful, where the condition of the world and of God's kingdom demands them, and where unbelief sets no limits to the divine working (Matt. xiii. 58).

A further rule for the operation of the miraculous is this, that as it is often connected with natural phenomena, so its product takes its place in the existing order of nature without any disturbance of the laws hitherto obtaining; and as respects the form of its appearance, that it is as quiet as possible, without noise or pomp. The internal law for the human workers of miracles is this: their external miraculous power must be connected with inward and spiritual miracles taking place in their hearts. By means of the latter they must be raised into a specially close communion with God, and they may not seek their own honour, but only that of God and Christ. The

[1] Strauss (*Leben Jesu,* S. 148) is of opinion that a God who should now and then work a miracle, sometimes exerting, sometimes discontinuing a certain kind of activity, would be subject to the succession of events in time, and consequently no absolute Being. This purely external and superficial objection completely overlooks the internal connection of miracles with revelation, and the historical development of the divine kingdom

internal law for men, in whom the miracles of salvation take place, is faith. Faith is the medium of the divine operation; through it man surrenders himself to its effects. On this account such miracles can never be considered as unnatural, nor as contrary to nature. And so it is, too, with the internal miracles of conversion and regeneration. For the recipients of revelation, who are spectators of the miraculous, the law obtains, that though it may facilitate their faith, yet it must never absolutely compel them to believe. Here, also, God respects human freedom. Therefore He never intensifies His miraculous working to such a degree that all objections of a hardened heart would be for ever destroyed. He who *will* doubt, always *can* doubt. And finally, for the historical development of the miraculous the law is generally binding, that in proportion as the divine revelation dispenses with sensuous media, its miracles become more spiritual.

Strauss says, "If the friends of the miraculous would explain to us its working laws as clearly as we know the laws which govern the action of steam, we should then consider their arguments as something more than mere talk." So our opponents wish to know the laws which govern the miraculous. Well, its internal moral laws are those which we have just stated, and they exactly correspond to what we before ascertained to be the internal laws of revelation. But if Strauss means to demand a demonstration of the *physical* laws which govern the actions of miraculous forces, we answer that this is simply a contradiction in itself. For precisely that which gives the miracle its distinctive character is, that we cannot point out the *natural* laws and forces working in it, because they are *not* of a physical or mathematical kind, but supernatural. To exhibit the physical laws of the working of miracles would be to divest them of their miraculous character.

This confirms to us what we have already hinted to be the *true distinguishing mark of genuine miracles* from those which are either fictitious and apocryphal, or demoniacal. The divine origin of any miracle is apparent, not so much from the extraordinary power manifested in it, as from its moral and religious character,—from the spiritual power and moral truth which are reflected in it and promoted by it. Truly divine miracles appeal not merely to our logical faculty, but to our moral judgment, to our recognition of the divine in its supramundane character, to our transcendental knowledge, not to our physical acquaintance with the forces of nature. Therefore it has very rightly been said that it requires much more intelligence to believe miracles, than understanding to deny them (Schenkel). Miracles approve themselves to our moral sense of truth through their connection with the plan of redemption and their relation to Christ. They are performed in confirmation of a divine testimony. They must either be accomplished through the believing invocation of the name of God or of Christ (Acts iii. 16), or they must serve to awaken and confirm belief in Him (John ii. 11, xx. 31). A true miracle, further, should either make a new disclosure as to some saving truth, or it should tend to the deliverance of man, or finally, should contribute in some way to the furtherance of God's kingdom, and to the destruction of the powers of darkness. When such a purpose and connection cannot be traced, then it is not only our right, but our duty, to be distrustful and reserved.

Vulgar infidelity completely overlooks the existence of this moral tribunal in the soul, before which alone the miraculous and the laws of its manifestation are to be judged. For this reason we so often hear men say that they cannot believe in the possibility of a miracle until one has been authenticated by competent judges, such as professors of medicine or physics, etc. Renan, too, is superficial enough to fall into the same strain: "Miracles are not performed in the places where they ought to be. One single miracle performed in Paris before competent judges[1] would for ever settle so many doubts! But alas! none has ever taken place. No miracle was ever performed before the people who need to be converted,—I mean, before unbelievers. The *conditio sine qua non* of the miraculous is the credulity of the witnesses. No miracle was ever performed before those who could thoroughly discuss the matter, and decide in regard to it" ("Les Apôtres:" Introduction). If Renan would lay to heart why "not many mighty

[1] Perhaps before the French Academy? We would remind those who felt inclined to submit to its decision as infallible, that this body in former times rejected (1) the use of quinine, (2) vaccination, (3) lightning conductors, (4) the existence of meteorolites, (5) the steam engine.

works" were done in Nazareth (Matt. xiii. 58), perhaps he might soon find out why now-a-days still fewer are done in Paris. Certainly no miracle has ever yet been performed, nor ever will be, in order to tickle the curiosity of a professor, or to remind him of the limits of human knowledge. He who thinks that God ought to condescend to perform miracles before "competent judges," in order to prove His omnipotence, and for ever to silence all doubts, has no idea of the saving purpose of miracles, nor of the inviolable laws of the divine government, which, if faith is to remain faith, must ever leave a possibility for doubt. But difficult indeed it is to understand how one who has read, *e.g.*, the history of Christ healing the man who was born blind (John ix.), one who has observed what investigations the really *not very credulous* Pharisees instituted, can assert that a miracle was never performed before unbelievers, but always before credulous witnesses. The man who calmly affirms that no miracle has appeared before those who were capable of criticising it, and who thus declares the entire Jewish and Roman world, with all their learned and wise men, amongst whom Christ and the apostles did so many signs, to have been utterly incapable of forming a true judgment in regard to them,—such a man simply gives vent to the presumptuous self-esteem of the nineteenth century, which in so many questions arrogates to itself the monopoly of "competent" criticism.

Leaning upon these hollow arguments, Renan proceeds to contest the actuality of all the scriptural miracles, maintaining that no miracle has ever been established as such, and that "all supposed miraculous facts which we have been in a position to examine, have proved to be delusions or deceptions." This result, of course, is attained in a most facile manner, by simply changing the facts, which are too stubborn to evaporate into delusions, into myths and legends. Further on we shall see how M. Renan and the other deniers of the miraculous conduct their business. We will not here enter into a closer examination of the gospel histories. Every unprejudiced person can perceive that the source of these temperate, artless, true-hearted narrations, is neither unbridled oriental fancy nor intentional poetical invention, but simply historic events. Why, we ask, were no miracles attributed to John the Baptist, whom all men, even the adversaries of Jesus, considered to be a prophet? Simply because none were performed by him. Does it not follow that miracles were ascribed to Jesus because they *were* done by Him? One point more we would urge with confidence against our opponents, in favour of the reality and actuality of the scriptural miracles (as before in favour of Revelation): I mean the unique appearance of *Israel* and of the *Christian Church* in religious history. Look at Israel, with its pure conception of God in the midst of the deep degradation of heathenism,—with its ancient prophecies and their wonderful fulfilment, which, in spite of all the attempted deductions of historic criticism, cannot be explained away,—with its stern moral and religious spirit aroused in *opposition* to the natural propensity of the people, and yet sustained with wondrous clearness and vigour, because constantly quickened from above. Surely such a nation *is and remains an inexplicable phenomenon, unless supernatural divine revelations were vouchsafed to it, i.e. unless miracles sometimes interfered in its history!*[1] Once more: look at the *Christian Church,* founded and built upon the belief in the resurrection of Christ, arising and making its way in the midst of universal darkness and corruption, with new powers of truth for the conquest of the world, and new powers of life for its renewal. This Church *is and remains in its origin and victorious development an utterly inexplicable riddle, if we take away Christ the central miracle,* or the miraculous facts of His divine Sonship and resurrection! The actual existence of the Christian Church and of the Christian faith is the simplest and most irrefutable proof for the actuality of the New Testament miracles.

The results of these investigations leave little more to be said in answer to the *philosophical objections* against the miraculous to which we before alluded. Those foundation-stones for the denial of all miracles which were laid by Spinoza and Hume, and on which the critics of the present day still take a

[1] Diestel (among others) has very clearly shown that the Monotheism, as well as the entire moral and religious spirit of Israel, can by no means be derived from a universal tendency of the Semitic race in that direction, as Renan would have us believe (cf. *Jahrb. für deutsche Theol.* 1860, iv., "der Monotheismus des ältesten Heidenthums").

defiant stand, have crumbled away piecemeal before our eyes. Spinoza's axiom, that "the laws of nature are the only realization of the divine will," stands or falls with his pantheistic conception of the Deity—a conception which is not only unworthy of God and of man, but also contrary to reason. The Source of all freedom is supposed to have no freedom, but to be immured in His own laws! And to this Spinoza adds the conclusion: "If anything could take place in nature contrary to its laws, God would thereby contradict Himself." We have seen that just the converse is true, namely, that *if God performed no miracles*, and left the world to itself, *He would contradict Himself*; that He must perform miracles in order to maintain the end for which the world was created, and to bring it to the destiny which was originally intended. His miraculous action contradicts, not nature and its laws, but the unnatural which has entered the world through sin, and counteracts its destructive consequences in order to restore the life of the world to holy order. Only those who, like Spinoza, deny the reality of sin, and its destructive power, can question the necessity of the miraculous. The present condition not only of the human world, but also of nature, gives such opinions the lie at every step!

Hume, in like manner, bases his attack against the miraculous on a series of false assumptions: First, "Miracles are violations of the laws of nature." This is false, since miracles, far from violating, serve to re-establish the already violated order of the world, and do not injure the laws of nature. Second, "But we learn from experience that the laws of nature are never violated." This is false, because we ourselves immediately interfere with our higher will in the laws of nature, and interrupt them without their being violated. Third, "For miracles we have the questionable testimony of a few persons." This is false, because the entire Scriptures are full of miracles; and the historical testimony for them is unquestionable, since the appearance of Israel and of the Christian Church is perfectly incomprehensible without miracles. "But," he goes on, "against them we have universal experience; therefore this stronger testimony nullifies the weaker and more questionable." The pith of Hume's argument, then, is simply this: Because according to universal experience no miracles now take place, therefore none can ever have occurred. This proposition, in the first place, involves a begging of the question, since it is not at all certain that no miracles are performed now-a-days (on which point we are soon to speak); and second, it ignores the fact that different periods are subject to different laws, and with their very varied wants may demand varied kinds of revelatory action on the part of God. Certainly the negro who should affirm that there is no snow, because in his country according to "universal experience" it never snows, would be committing an absurdity. And no less illegitimate is it to measure all time by the universal (?) experience or non-experience of some particular period. Finally, Hume goes on to demand as a condition for the credibility of miracles, that they must be attested by an adequate number of sufficiently educated and honest persons, who could not be suspected of intentional deception, and that they should be done in so frequented a spot that the detection of the illusion would be inevitable. We shall see further on (in Lects. VI. and VII.) that these conditions were all essentially fulfilled in the case of the New Testament miracles. And yet, in spite of the evident weakness of Hume's argument, Strauss would have us believe that "Hume's *Essay on Miracles* is so universally convincing, that he may be said to have settled the question" (*Leben Jesu*, p. 148)! The author of *The Life of Christ* forgets to mention that Hume has long since been refuted in detail by the earlier and later English apologists,[1] to say nothing of the Germans; but then he knows that a very small proportion of his readers is aware of this fact.

To these objections not even our most modern philosophers have been able to add really new ones; and as against them all we may confidently maintain the following truths as the *result* of our investigation. The possibility of the miraculous rests upon the uninterrupted activity of a living God in the world. Its necessity arises on the one hand from the divine end and aim of the world, and on the other from the disturbance introduced into its development through sin. Therefore, although miracles are supernatural, they are not unnatural. Far from violating the conditions of life, of nature,

[1] *E.g.* by Campbell, Adam, Hey Price, Douglass, Paley, Whately, Dwight Alexander, Wardlaw, and Pearson.

or of humanity, they re-establish the life of the world which has already been deranged, and initiate the higher order of things for which the universe was created. "Thus the natural and spiritual miracles of the sacred narrative are only the notes of a higher harmony which resound throughout the discords of earthly history. To our dull sense, indeed, they may seem disconnected; but the more we listen the more we perceive a connected law of higher euphony now presaging, and finally bringing about, the solution of all dissonance into an eternal harmony. Surely, then, a believer may look down with pity upon the spirit of the age, and its declaration that the harmony of the Kosmos is destroyed by the miracles of the Bible" (Beyschlag), as well as on its blind belief in the immutability of natural laws. The old truth remains: "Neither are your ways my ways, saith the Lord. For as the heavens are higher than the earth, *so are my ways higher than your ways,* and my thoughts than your thoughts!"

Even a free-thinker like Rousseau says: "Seriously to raise this question (whether God can perform miracles) would be impious, if it were not absurd; and we should be doing the man who answered it in the negative too much honour by punishing him for it; it would be sufficient to keep him in custody" (*Lettres de la Montagne,* iii.). And Richard Rothe, a no less acute than liberal thinker of our times, remarks: "I will frankly confess that up to this hour I have never been able to discover any stumbling-block for my intellect in the conception of a miracle."

He who denies the miraculous, denies God and His revelation, since revelation is miraculous. All that we before adduced in proof of the possibility and necessity of a supernatural revelation, and of the existence of a personal God (*vide* Lects. II. and III.), thus turns into a justification of miracles. We have already demanded of those who deny the existence of a God (p. 144), *and we now demand of those who reject the miraculous, that they should explain to us from natural causes all phenomena in nature and history.* If they cannot do this, they have no right to contest the possibility and the historical nature of the miraculous. And we shall show more fully in the following lectures that in numberless cases unbelief has yet to find a satisfactory explanation for the most important facts in history. The more thoroughly it investigates, the less it can conceal this. It meets with phenomena in the sacred history for which even a Baur can find no sufficient ground of explanation (*e.g.* the belief in the resurrection of Christ, the conversion of Paul, etc.). And what is then the last resort for the deniers of the miraculous? When the connecting links in nature no longer suffice, they are fain to recur to *chance*, and (*e.g.* in the restorative miracles of Christ) to speak of "good luck," as Rationalism often does. But to take refuge in chance, is the death of all scientific investigation. Here again we see that the boasted scientific method very often results in an unscientific abandonment of the attempt to solve the riddle. As in the case of Pantheism (p. 181), so in that of the miraculous, we finally see ourselves placed before the dilemma of *believing either in miracles or in chance.*

But we must not close without considering one other very obvious objection frequently raised against miracles: *Why are miraculous manifestations no longer vouchsafed at the present day?* and this question we would now proceed briefly to discuss.

III.—ARE MIRACULOUS MANIFESTATIONS STILL VOUCHSAFED?

If miracles are directed, as we have seen, not against the world's order, but against its disorder, why do we not find them happening in every place where misery and death still prevail? Sin and evil exist to this day; misery and disorder still abound in the world; why should not God continue miraculously to interfere for the removal of all these, and for the re-establishment of the original order?

To this we answer, first of all: Are miracles (strictly so called) the only means through which God counteracts sin and evil? Does He not first employ the internal influences of His Word and Spirit? And this has not ceased as yet. Sin, it is true, still exists; but so does Christ, the great Physician for the maladies of the whole world, and His influence is ever becoming more powerful and more extended. Are new miracles then required, while *the old ones are still in active operation?* Let us beware of an idle longing after the miraculous. Luther's remarks on this subject are no less humble than true: "The world continually gapes after prodigies; it many a time mistakes chalk for cheese, and gladly believes in apparitions; believers keep to the Word, and follow it. I have very often prayed my God that I might not see any vision or miracle, nor be informed in dreams, since *I have enough to learn in His Word.*"

We have seen that the great mass of those who are averse to the miraculous usually argue thus: Miracles do not happen now-a-days; therefore, they never happened at all. This is in the first place a flagrant transgression of the logical rule, that one cannot argue from the majority to the whole. But we, on our part, cannot even admit the assumption that no miracles are now performed, without further consideration, and must therefore proceed to investigate the question, *whether miraculous manifestations are still vouchsafed.*

First of all, we must admit that miracles in these days have fallen into the background, having either almost or else entirely ceased. We do not live in a miraculous period such as that of Moses or of our Lord. But can we find no reasons for this? We have already recognised that miracles belong to the divine *education* of the human race. Now it is self-evident that a means of education must be differently applied at different times. The schoolmaster's ferule is as little adapted to every age as the miraculous rod in the hand of Moses. But we can by no means argue that because a certain means of education is not required at a definite period, it can never be needed. We have already seen from the history of the miraculous, that according to the Holy Scriptures miracles are more prominent in some periods and less so in others, and that the former periods are always crises in which the eyes of men are to be opened to the fact that the kingdom of God is on the eve of a momentous advance. If, then, our modern times are comparatively inferior in this respect to many of the earlier ages; if they have more of an intermediate character, as preparatory for great events which may be expected in the divine kingdom, it is simply in accordance with the laws hitherto recognised, that few or no miracles should occur in them.

The apostolic age required miracles, because it was the

epoch *in which the Church was first founded;* the present period, during which the Church is only *maintained,* no longer requires them to the same extent. If that period had miracles as the means of supporting its faith, ours has the testimony of history: we have before us the effects of the words and acts of Christ in the history of the world and its renewal; we see the Christian Church overcome the world and survive it, and thereby fulfil a great part of the predictions of Christ and the prophets. All this, together with the constant inner working of the Word and the Spirit of Christ, is a sufficient external support for our faith. In the last epoch of the consummation of the Church, however, she will again require for her final decisive struggle with the powers of darkness, the miraculous interference of her risen Lord, and hence the Scriptures lead us to expect miracles once more for this period.

Our age, however, is still characterized by the establishment of new churches. The work of missions is, outwardly at least, more extended than it ever was before. In this region, therefore, according to our former rule, miracles should not be entirely wanting. Nor are they. We cannot, therefore, fully admit the proposition that no more miracles are performed in our day. *In the history of modern missions we find many wonderful occurrences which unmistakeably remind us of the apostolic age.* In both periods there are similar hindrances to be overcome in the heathen world, and similar palpable confirmations of the Word are needed to convince the dull sense of men. We may, therefore, *expect* miracles in this case. And now read, *e.g.*, the history of Hans Egede, the first evangelical missionary in Greenland. He had given the Esquimaux a pictorial representation of the miracles of Christ before he had mastered their language. His hearers, who, like many in the time of Christ, had a perception only for bodily relief, urge him to prove the power of this Redeemer of the world upon their sick people. With many sighs and prayers he ventures to lay his hands upon several, prays over them, and, lo, he makes them whole in the name of Jesus Christ! The Lord could not reveal Himself plainly enough to this mentally blunted and degraded race by merely spiritual means, and therefore bodily signs were needed. In such cases, and in dealing with such men, miracles may not have been entirely wanting in the work of evangelization amongst other nations and in other ages, and we should not, therefore, absolutely reject all that is miraculous in the old legends as mere fables, though their statements must be received with great caution.

Let me mention another incident from the life of the Moravian missionaries Spangenberg and Zeisberger. On their way to the Indian tribes in the endless forests and wilds of North America, tormented with hunger, weary and exhausted, they came to a brook. Here Spangenberg begged his companion to bring out the fishing tackle. He did so without hope, since the water was clear and shallow, and at that time of the year the fish were known to remain in the deep water. But, encouraged by Spangenberg's faith, he obediently cast the net, and in a few moments Peter's miraculous draught of fishes was repeated.

The history of Missions at the present time affords many similar instances. At a Rhenish mission station in South Africa in 1858, an earnest native Christian saw an old friend who had become lame in both legs. Impressed with a peculiar sense of believing confidence, he went into the bushes to pray, and then came straight up to the cripple, and said, "The same Jesus who made the lame to walk can do so still; I say to thee, in the name of Jesus, Rise up and walk!" The lame man, with kindred faith, raised himself on his staff and walked, to the astonishment of all who knew him (*vide* the *Memoir of Kleinschmidt*, Barmen 1866, p. 58 ff.).

In view of the temperate and conscientious character of such messengers of the gospel, we have no right to doubt these reports of theirs, to which many similar ones could be added. But those who nevertheless persist in doubting them, we would point to *the people of Israel as a perennial living historical miracle.* The continued existence of this nation up to the present day, the preservation of its national peculiarities throughout thousands of years in spite of all dispersion and oppression, remains so unparalleled a phenomenon, that without the special providential preparation of God, and His constant interference and protection, it would be impossible for us to explain it. For where else is there a people over whom such judgments have passed, and yet not ended in destruction?

But even in modern times parallels are not entirely wanting

to some of the miraculous deliverances of Israel. Compare with theirs the history of the Waldenses, the Israel of the Alps. Read the history of the siege of the mountain fortress La Balsille; how the little band, having been surrounded by a French and Sardinian army throughout an entire summer, at length had to face the prospect of death by starvation, since the enemy was guarding every outlet of the valley. In midwinter they are driven by hunger to visit the snow-clad fields which they have been unable to harvest, and there under the deep snow they find the entire harvest still *uninjured.* Part of this was housed in good condition eighteen months after it had been sown. Read how in the following spring one breastwork of the small fortress after another sank under the enemy's cannonade, until finally the last intrenchment was demolished; how they then stood defenceless, at the mercy of a cruel foe, and could only cry to the Lord of Hosts; and how in their extremity a cloud of fog suddenly rolled down upon the valley, and enveloped it in so dense a darkness, that, although in the midst of their enemies, they were able to climb down the rocks unseen and effect their escape. This occurred on the 13th of May 1690. Does it not remind us of the God who once fed Israel so miraculously, and who covered them with the pillar of cloud as a defence against Pharaoh's army?[1]

Again, what a wonderful deliverance was experienced by

[1] Almost more wonderful deliverances are related in the history of the South African Missions. In one case "the terror of the Lord" suddenly fell on a triumphantly advancing enemy, who was about to set fire to the mission-house, so that the victory was turned into a sudden flight, and both friends and foes were compelled to confess that God had fought for His people. (*Vide Kleinschmidt, ubi supra*, pp. 73, 77; cf. Ps. xxxiv. 8, and 2 Kings vii. 6 ff.)

Another most remarkable instance occurred in the case of a missionary of the Rhenish Society, named Nommensen, working in Sumatra. On one occasion a heathen who had designs on his life managed secretly to mix a deadly poison in the rice which Nommensen was preparing for his dinner. Without suspicion the missionary ate the rice, and the heathen watched for him to fall down dead. Instead of this, however, the promise contained in Mark xvi. 18 was fulfilled, and he did not experience the slightest inconvenience. The heathen, by this palpable miraculous proof of the Christian God's power, became convinced of the truth, and was eventually converted: but not until his conscience had impelled him to confess his guilt to Nommensen, did the latter know from what danger he had been preserved. This incident is well attested (cf. V. Rohden, *Geschichte der rhein. Missionsgesellschaft*, 2d ed., p. 324), and the missionary still lives (1873).

the crew of the missionary ship *Harmony*, which every year visits the Moravian stations on the coast of Labrador, and supplies them with provisions! Some years ago an iceberg was one day perceived drifting rapidly towards the vessel. A moment more, and it would have inevitably been dashed to pieces. At a distance of only *one foot* from the ship, the monster suddenly stopped in its course, and drifted away again. I myself have heard the captain of the *Harmony* attest the truth of this incident, which the entire crew declared to be a miracle. Cases of this sort, especially as regards the marvellous deliverances of children, could be multiplied indefinitely, but they belong to miracles in the wider sense.

But even apart from the history of Missions, especially in the healing of the sick and in miraculous answers to prayer, our times offer resemblances at least to the apostolic age.

You all know with what victorious faith Luther once wrestled with God in prayer at the bedside of the dying Melanchthon, and how he then with firm confidence went up to the sick man, who felt that his last hour had come, and taking him by the hand, said, "Be of good cheer, Philip, you shall not die;" and how *from that hour* Melanchthon revived. Johann Albrecht Bengel, famous as the best interpreter of Holy Scripture in the last century, relates that a girl in a little town of South Germany,[1] who had been paralysed for twenty years, was suddenly healed by the prayer of faith. The case was examined and *publicly certified to be a miracle.* And surely the veracity of an informant like Bengel cannot be questioned.

Most of us are aware that wonderful things are related of the healing of the sick at the present day. Yet these are but weak analogies of that divine power of healing in the New Testament history, through which the severest and most chronic cases were instantly cured by a word. Our age, it is true, can show more cases of wonderful answers to prayer than many previous ones;[2] and assuredly all history as well as the present period abounds in wonders of the divine govern-

[1] Leonberg, near Stuttgart.

[2] I need only remind you of the humble origin and the grand development of so many Christian institutions and societies as related in the memoirs of A. H. Franke, J. Falk, Jung Stilling, J. Gossner, George Müller of Bristol, Theodor Fliedner, L. Harms, J. Wichern, and others, whom Spurgeon designates "modern workers of miracles."

ment, and in sudden divine interpositions which are no less the workings of God's providence for being often brought about by circumstances or men, and thus concealed from us through the dimness of our spiritual vision. But these signs and wonders do not possess the same force and clearness as the biblical miracles.

On the other hand, we see the sceptics of the present day reject with scorn the appeal to the lives of God's children, and the clear proofs afforded by them, for every one who is not wilfully blind, of a special divine providence; and we find them presuming to derive from merely natural sources all the answers to prayer, and all the dearest experiences of the children of God, or representing them as self-deceptions.[1] This shows us clearly that it is the want of faith in our age which is the greatest hindrance to the stronger and more marked appearance of that miraculous power which is working here and there in quiet concealment. *Unbelief* is the final and the most important reason for the retrogression of miracles.

[1] We often see unbelievers greatly embarrassed by the countless and undeniable answers to prayer in the lives of many children of God; answers which it is ridiculous to attribute to chance. An instance of this may be seen in the desperate explanation attempted by Perty (in his work, *Die mystischen Erscheinungen der menschlichen Natur*, 1861). According to him, those results proceed, not from the influence of the suppliant upon God, but from the mystic working of one human soul upon another. The spiritual energy of the suppliant occasions disquietude in other souls until they have satisfied his needs. If this be so, then *men* and not *God* hear prayer. What a wild fancy is this! Indeed, it is an incomparably greater miracle than that God should answer prayer! In many cases help comes from a person whom the suppliant did not know—of whose existence he was unconscious; or it does not come through persons at all, but through things and circumstances. How, in these cases, is a psychical influence conceivable? We see how unbelief in its despair prefers to accept the purest impossibility rather than the simple truth of Scripture. In this respect it is still true that "professing themselves to be wise, they become fools!" (Cf. *Apologet. Beiträge von Gess und Riggenbach*, p. 187.) The *Gartenlaube* remarks in a similar strain with regard to George Müller's wonderful work: "The 'Lord' who went before Müller was merely another form for his own German energy, his simple, feeling heart, etc.,—a form dear to him and imposing to the English public." Whoever takes the pains to read in *The Lord's dealings with G. Müller* (1860, 6th ed.), and to learn how, *without ever applying to any one for a gift*, he received the means to build those great palaces near Bristol, in which he provides for 2000 orphans, *only through prayer*, will immediately realize the folly of such a judgment. If it is always men who do such things, and not God, why do not these enlightened gentlemen make use of their own "simple, feeling hearts," and some "imposing form," say that of Materialism, in order to perform like wonders?

But though these facts—being miracles in a wider sense only—may be no direct proof for the miraculous, strictly so called, still they plainly prove that the omnipotent God is everywhere present and active in the natural as well as in the spiritual world. But when this fact is once admitted, it follows that the miraculous is constantly possible, and that God need not disturb nor destroy anything when He performs a miracle properly so called, of which we have at least single examples in our own days.

These alone may not be sufficient to lead one to a belief in the truth of the biblical miracles. But there is a still more cogent consideration which I would finally seek to impress upon you, viz. that *by a denial of the miraculous we do not in the least escape miracles, but only have to believe in greater prodigies.*

We have already seen that he who believes in God must also believe in the miraculous. Though one may not believe in God, yet he must believe in the miracle of the world, which, through a miracle, must have existed from eternity, and must have developed and preserved itself up to its present condition by means of still greater miracles and riddles. If one does not believe in the miraculous creation of man, he must believe in his descent from the monkey, and further back in his generation, from the original slime—a wild supposition which is contradicted by all experience and moral consciousness. He who does not believe in the miraculous revelation of God in history, especially in Christ, must assume that a people like Israel, and a phenomenon like Christianity, could have arisen of their own accord; he must assume that the preaching of a few poor Galilean fishermen could have overcome the world, and have ruled it spiritually until now, without the co-operation of divine power. And would that not be a far greater miracle? He who does not believe in the continual government of God's providence has lost the key for understanding the entire history of the world, of the divine kingdom, and of his own life, and has no longer any safeguard against the thoughtless belief in chance, which explains nothing.

As the Bible is much more inexplicable if we suppose it uninspired than if we grant its inspiration, so, too, the natural and the moral world are infinitely more full of riddles without the belief in miracles than with it. Though the latter may still leave much that is incomprehensible, yet the many comprehensible things which we find in Holy Scripture should induce us to believe the incomprehensible too. This is how children learn. For the sake of what they already understand, they accept that which for a long time is still beyond their powers of comprehension; and this is precisely the way to make progress in learning. In this respect we have much to learn from children, and especially do we see in them the simple *beauty and naturalness of the belief in miracles.* Since they have no doubt whatever of the existence of a higher world with its heavenly powers of love, miracles seem just as natural to them as to the angels; since their hearts are still open, and their consciences but little burdened, they joyously believe in the influence and interference of these divine powers in our lives. Were our children to find in some quiet meadow a ladder reaching up to heaven, they would not be so greatly astonished, but would straightway ascend it, while we older people still stood below, engrossed in critical considerations. And which would be the wiser?

There are in our day many doubtful souls, who, if they meet with a miracle in the Holy Scriptures, swallow it as a bitter pill, or even allow it to spoil their delight in the Word of God. And why? Because they would fain measure the great ways of God by their own small ideas, which are not even adequate to the understanding of that which daily takes place around them.[1] Because they think far too highly of our human wisdom and knowledge, they have far too small conceptions of God and of His mighty power. This view must be reversed in order to lead us to a belief in the miraculous. Think very highly, I pray you, of the infinite God, and make a very lowly estimate of all human knowledge and actions, and then, my respected hearers, the Scripture miracles will prove to you no longer a cross, but a comfort; a source no longer of timid doubts, but of heartfelt joy and of stronger faith!

As is Christ Himself, so certainly are all miracles, a sign which may be spoken against (Luke ii. 34); clear and unmis-

[1] Lord Bacon truly says: "Animus ad amplitudinem mysteriorum pro modulo suo dilatetur, non mysteria ad angustias animi constringantur."

takeable enough for him who is willing to believe, but dark and uncertain enough for him who *means* to doubt. Nor should it be otherwise. For only those can or may penetrate into the secrets of the divine government who have experienced the miraculous spiritual power of God in their own hearts. To him only who sustains a living relation to Christ, the miracle of all miracles, and who recognises himself as a miracle,—not merely as a man, but still more as a child of God,—and to such an one, assuredly, the miraculous operation of God in the world, as well as in his own experience, will appear intelligible and necessary; and the supernatural will seem natural, because it is shaping his inmost life. The longer his experience, the more profoundly and clearly will he trace the finger of God even in a thousand small events, where the blind world sees only natural laws and chance, because he discerns that finger continually in himself in grace and discipline. And therefore no one can dispute his right to continue in that faith which the angel invited in his announcement of the greatest miracle, that "*with God nothing shall be impossible*" (Luke i. 37).

SIXTH LECTURE.

MODERN ANTI-MIRACULOUS ACCOUNTS OF THE LIFE OF CHRIST.

"If they shall say that no miracles have been wrought, they will thereby only turn the edge of their weapons against themselves. For that were the greatest miracle, that without signs and wonders twelve poor and unlearned men should have drawn the whole world into their net."—CHRYSOSTOMUS (*in Act. Ap.* Hom. I.).

"WHAT think ye of Christ? whose Son is He?" This question it is which once more agitates the world most deeply in our own day. Thus did our Lord in a decisive hour address the assembled Pharisees in one of His last public discourses. And whenever this question is addressed to a whole people or generation, it is a sign that the times are pregnant with solemn issues, and that a turning-point in its history is at hand. It is not *a* question, but *the* question, the innermost vital issue, the decision of which by individuals or nations now, as then in the case of Israel, pronounces the sentence of judgment on their future destiny.

The answer to this question touches the centre of our faith. And surely the fact that the assault upon Christian belief is now being concentrated more and more upon this its central bulwark, is a proof that our age is pressing on to a decision, and that the battle of well-nigh two thousand years, which the Christian faith has been waging with science and with life, is at length nearing its final issue. The spirit of our age, weary—and that not without good reason—of mere speculation, is in every department asking for realities and facts. The study of dogma has had to yield to that of history. Men no longer look to authoritative statements of Church doctrines or dogmatic treatises, but to historical investigations of the Gospel narratives and of primeval Christianity, for an answer to the question, Who was and is Jesus Christ?

This question, so decisive for our whole faith, is forced upon us, not only by the spirit of our age, but also by the progressive development of modern theology. As formerly the Reformers appealed from the Church to the Scriptures, so now our modern critics appeal "from the Scriptures to the actual history upon which they are based,"[1] and claim to make a distinction between the biblical narration of facts and the facts themselves. In order to attain to an historical comprehension of the origin of Christianity, modern criticism first began to investigate the apostolic and post-apostolic ages, seeking in the struggles which agitated these periods to discover the growing germs of the Church and her faith. For a time the critics hovered round the person of Christ with a cautious reserve. But soon it became evident that all criticism must eventually have recourse to this as the only reasonable way to account for the origin of Christianity. Thus investigations into the latter made way for inquiries after the person of Christ. As this was the chief religious problem for the scribes in Israel and the wise men of heathendom, so, too, it is once more the great question that occupies the theology of the day, and has attracted more general interest than any other. This question is addressed to us also. We may not evade it, and therefore we must seek a clear and concise answer. No one may remain undecided in the face of this issue; for on it depends our whole future, as individuals, as churches, and (witness the example of Israel) as nations.

If we inquire after the inner motives which have led our modern theology back to this old question, it is not difficult to see that chief among them is the *aversion to the miraculous* which characterizes the spirit of our age. We have seen that Jesus Christ is the central miracle of history. He who denies the miraculous cannot accept this chief miracle. For this reason the deists and the old school of rationalists exerted themselves to get rid of one miracle after another; but they soon discovered that all this was labour lost, so long as the supernatural, in the person of Christ, was bodily present in the world and its history. Since then our opponents have become wiser, and have transferred the conflict to the person of Christ. The foundations of all supernatural revelation cannot

[1] Cf. Luthardt, *Die modernen Darstellungen des Lebens Jesu.*

be considered as destroyed until this Jesus of Nazareth, with His unique life,—until all His doings and sayings, and even His peculiar religious consciousness, are naturally explained as the result of a merely human development. Here we have the reason for the most recent attempts at a purely natural solution of this enigma.

But there is another alternative. The result of our investigations may show that all these attempts, even the most unbridled and arbitrary of them, still leave an *inexplicable something*, which the most desperate efforts to divest the life of Christ of its divinity cannot do away with; and that they arrive at this something only by means of an abrupt leap, *i.e.* by giving up all natural connecting links,—a proceeding which must lead us to the conclusion that it was a supernatural agency which here interfered. Our investigations may show that the old Stone of stumbling, the person of the Crucified, still lies before us to this day as a Rock of offence which the stormy floods of human criticism can neither wash away nor crumble into ordinary shingle; nay, a Stone from which all the learned human masons cannot even grind away the sharp corners, which they must needs let alone in the unique grandeur of its origin and its effects. If such be the case, then we have a fresh argument for the possibility of miracles in addition to those already adduced, viz. the impossibility of removing the miraculous from the Bible, and from history in general, since its opponents are fain to let it stand in its central manifestation—Christ.

Not a device has been left untried in order to divest the life of our Lord of its supernatural character. The most clumsy method was, to accuse either Himself or the gospel writers of lying and fraud. This was the main point in the well-known *Wolfenbüttel Fragments*, by Reimarus (†1768), and long before, in the writings of Celsus, that heathen adversary of the Christian faith in the second century. The same method, too, was partially carried out by some of the English deists, but especially by Voltaire and the French *illuminati*. In our day there is no longer any difference of opinion as to this frivolous and morally revolting theory. It is condemned by a single question: How can He from whom the moral regeneration of the world proceeded have been an immoral deceiver?

Or how can it be conceived as possible that a number of fraudulent men should be able to invent the purest, grandest, and most exalted character, the mere idea of which far transcends the loveliest visions of poets, and the noblest speculations of philosophers?

For this reason the accusation of conscious fraud soon fell to the ground, and others set up the theory that Christ was the victim of *self-deception* and enthusiasm. We shall find that this supposition is, partially at least, accepted by Strauss and Renan, who, in their explanation of our Saviour's words and deeds towards the close of His life, are compelled to make use of it. But neither does this theory explain anything; on the contrary, it only multiplies enigmas. For all the sayings and doings of Christ which are recorded in the Gospels give an unprejudiced reader the impression of the most sober clearness of spirit, the calmest dignity, and the most prudent self-command, ever wondrously the same in all situations; and this accompanied by the glance of profound knowledge which penetrates through all outward show to the real essence, and the sure judgment which is never deceived, but constantly hits the nail upon the head. Is not all this directly opposed to enthusiastic imagination and self-deception?

Others, therefore, have attributed the errors and the self-deception to the *disciples,* whom they suppose to have formed a false conception of the deeds of Christ, in their superstitious prejudice making purely natural events into supernatural ones, and converting an extraordinary human being into a God-man. This is the creed of vulgar Rationalism. We are to believe that the fabrications and dreams of a few Galilean fishermen, imposed upon Jews and Greeks, conquered the world, morally regenerated it, and have since proved to be a ruling spiritual power and an inexhaustible source of culture and education! And is this the pass at which exalted reason has arrived?

Since this theory has been undermined, in part by the historical contradictions which it provoked, but especially by the intolerably arbitrary exegesis which it necessitated, a final and most recent attempt has been made to show that the miraculous history and the "deification" of Christ originated in the (unconscious) *legendary invention of the first Christian communities,* which surrounded and darkened the original history with an ever-thickening cloud of myths and legends. This is the standpoint of Strauss and Renan. In it they were greatly strengthened by the attempt made in another quarter to remove the Gospels and the Acts, as well as most of the Epistles, into a period subsequent to the apostolic age,—attempts which, if successful, would leave the time necessary for the gradual formation of these mythical legends.

From this we see that every possible method has been tried in order to eliminate the miraculous from the gospel history. For it is easy to see that all these hypotheses are only set up as a *means of getting rid of the miraculous at any cost;* and, indeed, as much is openly confessed. Take, for instance, what Strauss says:[1] "The miraculous is a foreign element in the gospel narratives of Christ which defies all historical treatment, and *the conception of the myth is the means which we shall use in order to eliminate this element from our subject.*" This "mythical hypothesis," then, belongs to the same class as all other attempts of ancient or modern Rationalism to explain away the miraculous. They are all one in their aim, and therefore we comprise them all under the one category of "*anti-miraculous* accounts of the life of Christ."

From what we have already said, it is evident that all these theories exhibit one and the same tendency in two fundamental forms, the *rationalistic* and the *mythical.* Under the former aspect the Gospels are *real,* but *merely natural history,* in which all seemingly miraculous events are to be naturally accounted for. According to the latter view, they do not, for the most part, contain history at all, but merely *fictions* or *legends.* Schenkel's *Sketch of the Character of Christ* we consider to belong to the former of these two classes: the chief representatives of the latter are, as is well known, Strauss and Renan. The works of these three men—in addition to the writings of Baur, which we reserve for future consideration—are doubtless the great authorities for the negative gospel criticism of the present day. It will therefore be our duty, after a short sketch and consideration of the old rationalistic view of the life of Christ, to subject the writings of these three men to a closer investigation and critique.

Before so doing, I would remark, that the attacks on the

[1] In his *Leben Jesu für das deutsche Volk,* 1864, p. 146.

resurrection (as constituting the chief miracle in the life of our Lord) will be considered separately in Lect. VII., and will therefore remain unnoticed in this chapter. The important question, too, as to the origin of the Gospels cannot be treated merely *en passant*, and I must therefore reserve its consideration to a later occasion, when I hope to treat, in connection, of the doctrine of Scripture, its inspiration, the canon of both Testaments, and the origin of the individual books. At present we are only considering the principles involved in the modern accounts of our Saviour's life, both rationalistic and mythical. So well, however, have the Gospels been defended in our days by many learned divines, that we cannot pretend to handle the subject in a new or original manner. We therefore simply confine ourselves to gleaning from those who have gone before.

I.—OLD RATIONALISTIC ACCOUNTS OF THE LIFE OF CHRIST.

According to the rationalistic school, the miraculous element in the life of Christ originated, not from the facts themselves, but from the superstitious light in which the biblical narrators viewed them. In their simplicity, they looked upon extraordinary medical cures as supernatural wonders, although they were perfectly natural occurrences; and that extraordinary man, Jesus of Nazareth, a prophet mighty in word and in deed before God and all the people, they believed to be God, though he was really nothing but a man. We find this same practice of reducing all that is divine to merely natural and human proportions, many centuries back, in some Greek philosophers —Euhemerus and others—who made their national gods into men, saying that Zeus, Apollo, and the rest had, indeed, actually existed, but only as men, whom their station, or their deeds, or their knowledge had rendered famous, and caused them to be worshipped by their posterity as superhuman beings. The very principle of this heathen school is applied by our rationalists to the Christian faith. They say, Jesus Christ is a real historical character, but nothing more than a man, who, for the sake of his extraordinary doings and sayings, gradually came to be adored as divine. Thus unbelief constantly retreads the old worn-out paths, affording a specially striking illustration of the truth that "there is nothing new under the sun."

After Eichhorn's application of these principles chiefly to the Old Testament, they were carried out to their full extent by Dr. Paulus of Heidelberg in his *Commentary on the Gospels* (1800) and his *Life of Christ* (1828). He declares that the occurrences related in the Gospels are facts, but merely natural ones. How can this be? Dr. Paulus tells us that the historical critic must distinguish between *facts* and *opinions*, between the actual occurrence and its mistaken acceptance as miraculous by the narrator or the actor. In the tradition of the first churches, facts and opinions had been promiscuously propagated and identified. This obscuration of real facts, by attributing them to unreal miraculous causes, is to be done away with; the natural kernel of the matter is to be separated from its supernatural shell, and thus the actual historical truth to be arrived at. By means of this operation the life of Christ is transformed into the life of a wise Rabbi, who did not, it is true, perform any miracles, but instead of that, from love to man, executed innumerable works of charity, with the help of medical skill and good fortune.

I cannot better illustrate the violence done to Scripture by the rationalistic school, in reducing all miraculous occurrences to merely natural events, than by giving some *gleanings from the rationalistic exegesis.* The bright light shining around the shepherds in the night of our Lord's birth was "probably a meteor," or perhaps "the rays of a lantern that happened to pass by." The changing of the water into wine at Cana was a "harmless wedding joke;" the disciples had got the wine beforehand, and the twilight helped to deceive the guests. That Christ walked *on* the lake is simply a misapprehension on the part of the reader or expositor; he really walked "on the shores of the lake," or *above* it, on "one of its high banks." The stilling of the storm on the lake is resolved into the fact that Jesus, through his calm and dignified bearing, quieted the frightened disciples, and that by a "happy coincidence" the raging elements ceased their fury just at the same time. The healing of the blind was accomplished by means of an "efficacious eye-salve," which little circumstance was overlooked by the wonder-seeking narrator. The direction of Christ to the blind man, "Go to the pool of Siloam and wash," refers only to "taking the waters" at some neighbouring medicinal springs. St. John did not intend this for a miracle at all. The great miracle of the loaves and fishes, which made such an impression upon the people that they said, "Surely this is the Prophet which should come into the world" (John vi. 14), was accomplished by means of secret stores which were in the neighbourhood, and through the provisions which the people had brought with them; Christ, by His words, producing so great an effect upon the more wealthy among the multitude, who were well supplied with food, that they forthwith shared their stores with the poorer. The daughter of Jairus, the young man of Nain, and Lazarus, were raised—from a death-like trance. The transfiguration of our Saviour on the mountain, and His converse with Moses and Elias, are equally easy to explain. The disciples saw Jesus in a morning mist on the mountain speaking with two men, and as the sun broke forth at the moment, they thought that Moses and Elias were standing with their Master, and that He was shining with celestial light. The struggle in Gethsemane is an "unexpected indisposition caused by the damp night air of the valley;" in fact, a sudden cold. The resurrection of Christ is the return to life, not of a dead man, but of one who was apparently dead, having been laid in the grave swooning from the effects of the crucifixion. The angels in the grave were "the white linen cloths," which were taken by the women for celestial beings. Other angelic appearances are reduced to lightnings or storms. Dr. Paulus especially makes the lightning "fly in a hundred forked flashes around the heads of the Jews, without singeing a hair of them." The ascension of our Lord, finally, was merely His disappearance in a mountain cloud which happened to come between Him and His disciples; or, according to Bahrdt's account, Christ disappeared behind a hill, and withdrew into the circle of His more intimate disciples, until later on, according to a pre-arranged plan, He suddenly appeared from behind a bush to St. Paul on his way to Damascus!!

You see that the miracle-fearing rationalists accomplish perfectly miraculous feats by means of exegetical devices. Of such interpreters Göthe (in his *Faust*) says:—

Slavish fidelity is out of date;
When exposition fails, interpolate.

Assuredly such attempts are not exposition, but imposition. They need but be mentioned to be condemned by every unprejudiced mind as utterly desperate *coups de force*. The whole method is one of boundless *arbitrariness*, which turns and twists, clips and maims the historical documents, until they say no more than they are wanted to say, *i.e.* nothing supernatural. One does not listen to the narrators in order to learn what has taken place, but he knows beforehand that events cannot have happened in the manner in which they are described. One does not want to be taught by them, but rather to teach these simple, superstitious narrators by taking the bandage from their eyes and showing them what they did and what they did not really see and hear. The fruits of this arrogance consist not only in boundless caprice, but also in positive *vulgarity* which utterly disgusts us. The fine-sounding term, "natural explanation," turns to bitter irony when we see that it is *most unnatural* in its efforts to do away with the supernatural. I have already pointed out the irrationality of "rational belief." Here you have the clearest proofs of it.

In order to make this naturalization of the supernatural more acceptable, especially as regards the miracles of healing, recourse has often been had to *magnetism*, and similar mysterious though natural forces. Christ Himself and the other workers of miracles are supposed to have possessed a special magnetic power; and their laying of hands on the sick was the same manipulation as that performed by mesmerists in our own days. The rationalists and semi-rationalists even of the present day do not despise this expedient, as, *e.g.*, Weisse and Hase. But what is gained thereby? Did not the cures often take place without any personal contact, and even in some cases, at a distance (*e.g.* the centurion's servant and the daughter of the Syro-Phœnician woman)? Recently, however, this expedient has been annihilated, for natural science has taught that these supposed effects of animal magnetism are for the most part fictitious. It cannot be denied that magnetic stroking often produces peculiar effects on the nervous system, and, through it, on adjacent parts of the human frame.

But it is a great question whether these effects are produced by any distinct and special force; and the most learned physicians assure us that *sudden cures* of any bodily ailment or infirmity are never effected by it. Still more is the healing by this means of such diseases as leprosy out of the question. The critical deniers of the miraculous are not then so very critical in this case. Having been critical where they should have believed, they are now fain to believe implicitly where criticism would be most fitting.

Others recognise that no person in his senses could find accounts of modern magnetic cures in the Gospels or the Acts, and therefore have recourse to *psychology*. They suppose that the immense psychological influence which Christ exerted on the souls of men, the faith and the confidence with which He knew how to inspire them, were sufficient to effect His miracles. And true it is that Christ demands faith of the sick who look for help. But if the faith alone, without any special exertion of power on the part of Christ, could perform miracles then, why not now? According to this view of the matter, a physician need but inspire his patient with the firm belief that he is or immediately will be well, and he would straightway become so! And what is gained by such explanations in the case of other miracles, which had nothing to do with healing?

But it is not only that these expository arts do not stand the test of isolated cases: they are *unsound in principle.* It is supposed that the Gospels confound facts and opinions, and that the kernel of facts must be extracted from the shell of the narrators' false apprehension. All this is simply an arbitrary supposition, proceeding from an aversion to the miraculous. The man who reads the Gospels in an unprejudiced spirit, will find in them nothing but the most simple, artless, and true-hearted collation of facts, with scarcely anywhere an *opinion* of the narrator about them. Indeed, we may say that *there probably never were historians who gave so little of their own opinions in the course of their accounts as the evangelists*, and the sacred writers in general. Never has any one written in such a terse style of pregnant shortness as they. What with others would have filled thick volumes, is by them related in a few pages. And this could only be accomplished by a plain enumeration of facts *without* many subjective views; a delineation of their main features in a few bold strokes. Dr. Paulus need not take so much trouble to get at the kernel of the matter; it stands before us clearer, more transparent and unadorned, than was ever fact related by any writer. This grand, though simple style, passes by in silence a thousand questions, which our curiosity were fain to ask: "And He entered into a ship; and He saw a man sitting at the receipt of custom; and the disciples of John came unto Him." Any unbiassed reader will see here a simple and often abrupt collation of facts, the chief object of which always is to give a short account of the main points; a style such as even tax-gatherers and fishermen could attain. It is only when the reader puts on the erroneous and misleading glasses of a determined *aversion to the miraculous,* that he sees in the gospel narrative no longer the simple substance of real events, but a history overlaid with myths and legends.

And according to what *standard* are we to distinguish between the husk and the kernel of a narrative? Are we to take for our canon the rule that the laws of nature and of general human development are the limits of historical possibility and of critical allowableness? This is nothing but the principle from which proceeds the denial of the miraculous,—a principle already shown by us to be false. It is merely an extraneous presupposition brought to bear on the investigation of these historical records; an axiom which does not result from them, but stands in direct contradiction to them. For by means of it anti-miraculous critics make that appear to be the husk which, in the estimation of the evangelists themselves, is *the true kernel* of the narrative, *i.e.* the miraculous element. This they seek to peel off by their criticism, in order that a merely natural occurrence may be left as the historical kernel. But why does an evangelist relate a miraculous event? Clearly *for the sake of the miracle.* This is to him the root and centre of the matter, the important part for the sake of which the event appears to him worthy of commemoration. If this be taken away, it is not the husk which has been separated from the fruit, but the true kernel which has disappeared, leaving in most cases a shell not worth preserving.

This arbitrary procedure, which acknowledges as historical

only what does not contradict our anti-miraculous prejudices, and throws all else overboard, is evidently not the method of objective science, but only that of subjective inclination. As against such arbitrariness Strauss is quite right when he says: "*Either* the Gospels are really historical records, and miracles cannot be banished from the life of Christ; *or* the miraculous is incompatible with true history, and then the Gospels cannot be historical records" (*Leben Jesu*, p. 18).

This is true not only of isolated narratives, but of the life of Christ, depicted in the Gospels, *as a whole.* Whoever wishes to retain the historical character of the Gospels cannot cut out the miracles without losing *all.* It is labour lost to chip and pare down isolated miracles, and to give them a natural instead of a supernatural purport. *Not merely this or that occurrence, but the whole foundation of the Gospel history,* i.e. *the person of Christ itself, is intrinsically miraculous from beginning to end.* His words and deeds are likewise miraculous: so, too, is that in Him which rationalists acknowledge as historical; for His is a more than human development, inexplicable without the influence of supernatural powers and revelations. In short, the miraculous is not a mere outward appendage, which as such might be separated from the gospel history; on the contrary, it is the indispensable basis on which the latter rests, and one of its most essential elements. We should therefore gain nothing even did we succeed in a natural explanation of all the individual miracles, and the whole rationalistic undertaking—apart from the falsity of its anti-miraculous basis—cannot lead to any real results. For what use is it to prune away the miraculous from the twigs and branches if the whole tree be supernatural?

If the miraculous be once denied, it is far more logical and honest no longer to regard the Gospels as historical, but, as Strauss does, to consider them a chain of legends and fictions, and then to abjure Christianity openly. For *the elimination of the miraculous element from the gospel history can never take place without a deeply penetrating injury, or even a total and destructive alteration of the entire substance of the Christian religion.* What good is it to us to know all about the linen of the swaddling clothes which the rationalistic exegete will describe so learnedly and vividly, if it is no longer a divine

Child that was wrapped in them? What is the use of depicting to us the cross, if it is merely an apparently dead man who is being lifted down from it; or of describing the grave, if the Prince of life do not come forth from it? The whole foundation of our Christian life is shattered.

Take away the miraculous element from the Gospels, and what remains? The threadbare story of a wise and virtuous Rabbi, who preached pure morality,[1] and, having resolved to make his appearance as the Messiah, managed by the help of a natural power of healing, which he employed with good luck, to persuade a small portion of the people that he was such. He would appear to have been persecuted by the Pharisees, because he chastised their hypocrisy, and finally to have suffered death,—that is to say, apparent death, from which, after a swoon of many hours on the cross, he recovered; "only daring, however, to show himself to a few, and afterwards in all probability slowly languishing away in some remote part of Galilee from the effects of his sufferings." And to this poverty-stricken story the development of humanity is supposed to be attached! These commonplace occurrences, which might similarly take place in the case of any man who should excel his age in knowledge and moral power, and then, opposing himself to its spirit, should die as a martyr to his noble efforts—these are supposed to have unhinged the world's history, and marked out for it a fresh path. These exceedingly clumsy and simple narrators, who in their fanaticism took such simple events for one series of miracles, who were not even gifted with ordinary common sense, were yet able to depict for the benefit of mankind a character the moral beauty and profound spirituality of which has for centuries irresistibly fascinated the noblest minds, and become their richest source of culture: they could succeed in "writing a history which puts to shame the productions of the proudest historians!" What a miracle do anti-miraculous critics expect us to believe! Nay, more than a miracle, an utter absurdity.

[1] So pure, indeed, that it is perfectly unique, and, if taken together with the religious consciousness of the man who could preach it, still points to a supernatural origin. Further on we shall recur more fully to this "divine remnant" in the life of Christ which is still left after all the subtractions of critics have been made.

These monstrosities and inner weaknesses soon brought discredit on the "natural" explanation of the gospel history. We have already[1] heard the hard sentence of Hegel on the "stupidity and meanness which arrogates to itself the title of common sense and morality." Schelling, too,[2] condemns it, saying that "nothing is more doleful than the occupation of all rationalists, who strive to make that rational which declares itself to be above all reason." For the scientific annihilation of this standpoint, however, we have to thank Strauss, who in this way has done us real service. Not only did he in his former *Life of Christ* confute Dr. Paulus step by step, but in his latest writings, and most of all in the pamphlet entitled *Die Halben und die Ganzen,* he chastises the rationalists of the present day, especially the Baden school, with a bitter irony, and often with a scathing sarcasm nearly approaching to abuse. Thus it is that one of our opponents often confutes the other.

All the more does it give us cause for wonder that a well-known theologian of the present day, notwithstanding the undoubted bankruptcy of Rationalism, and in contradiction to his own past history, should have fallen back to the old rationalistic standpoint. I mean Dr. Schenkel in his *Sketch of the Character of Christ,*[3] a book which scarcely corresponds to its title, as it is in reality nothing but a life of Christ.

II.—DR. SCHENKEL'S "SKETCH OF THE CHARACTER OF CHRIST."

We shall soon see that we have a right to place Schenkel in the immediate vicinity of the rationalists, although much that is in his book reminds us of Strauss and Renan, and still more of the "Tübingen school," so that in fact his book is varied with almost every hue of thought. Before doing so, however, let us cast a glance at his *treatment of the Gospels with respect to their historical value.*

Schenkel agrees with several others of the most modern critics in considering the Gospel of St. Mark to be the oldest

[1] In the critique of Deism in Lect. III., p. 202.

[2] *Sämmtliche Werke,* Bd. ii., Abth. iv. p. 23.

[3] *Charakterbild Jesu.* We quote in the following from the 3d ed., 1864.

and most original, and he lays a stress upon the fact that his book "gives the first delineation of Christ from the standpoint of the second evangelist." This preference for the second Gospel may be the result of critical investigations, the correctness of which we cannot stop to examine here: certainly, however, it is connected with Dr. Schenkel's aversion for miracles; for, as he observes, "the second Gospel contains no trace of the 'Legend of the Infancy,' nor of the appearances of Christ after His resurrection;" and also, "many of its incidents are less embellished with miraculous paraphernalia than the corresponding ones in the first and third Gospels" (pp. 239, 240). But since even Mark relates much that is miraculous, Schenkel is forced to confess that the "miracle legends" had attained the preponderance even in this Gospel, notwithstanding its intimate connection with the reports of Peter, whose disciple Mark was. How, then, did the miraculous element penetrate into this comparatively trustworthy historical record? In the first place, "Peter himself, under the influence of Old Testament precedents, probably represented some of the gospel incidents in the light of miraculous workings;" second, "Mark treated the reports of Peter in a free manner, and doubtless wrote his Gospel under the influence of [other] oral tradition, and of the craving for the miraculous which was characteristic of the early churches;" and finally, we may suppose that the reviser of the "original Mark" (for the present Gospel is a revision of the original one) now and then imported later ideas into the older records. Thus, in order to explain the miraculous element in this Gospel, we are referred from Peter to Mark, from Mark to the oral tradition and the craving of the early churches for the miraculous, and thence to some later reviser of the original record; and all this evidently because Schenkel feels that none of these grounds of explanation really suffices. He who can represent purely natural occurrences "in the light of miraculous workings" places himself in a very doubtful light, even though he be an apostle. And the man who for the sake of his readers can make miracles out of events which were related to him by his teacher as perfectly natural, is surely ill fitted to be a credible narrator. More than this: how does this very free treatment of the records agree with what Dr.

Schenkel before stated, viz. that Mark wrote down the narrations of his teacher with great exactitude?

In whatever manner the miraculous element became introduced into this Gospel, the favoured record has to endure a very arbitrary treatment for its sake. At one time its clear testimony must go for nothing, *e.g.* in the healing of the palsied man (Mark ii. 10, 11), because, as Schenkel confesses, it contradicts his view of the case; at another time, the clear, unmistakeable sense of the words is arbitrarily distorted,—*e.g.* when Christ speaks of His coming again "in the glory of the Father with the holy angels" (Mark viii. 38), this is to be understood "figuratively of the Master's spiritual reappearance" (just as if a single one of our Lord's hearers would have thus received it). In chap. xiii. the second advent of Christ only means the epoch "at which the universal Christian Church began to exist;" but on account of His disciples' weak comprehension, Christ calls it the day of His second coming! In chap. xiv. 62, likewise, our Lord merely made use of "the figurative language familiar to the theocratic mind" (pp. 145, 259, 294). Probably it was because he was well acquainted with this figure of speech that the high priest rent his clothes, and condemned it as blasphemy!!

If the chief record is thus treated, it is not to be expected that the others should fare better. The whole history of the childhood of our Lord, as related by St. Luke, must of course be mythical, with the exception, however, of the story of Jesus at the age of twelve years in the temple. Why should this part merely be historical? Because in the other there is too much of the supernatural, which would not suit Schenkel's human picture of Jesus; this event is seemingly more natural (though, in truth, it points to a more than human development of the inquiring boy). The Sermon on the Mount appears to Schenkel suitable. It must, therefore, be brought over from St. Matthew's Gospel, with the excuse that in the present revision of St. Mark it was doubtless "overlooked," not "intentionally omitted" (p. 70). But our critic is not pleased with all that is contained in it; thus the declaration (Matt. v. 17), that heaven and earth shall pass away rather than the smallest fraction of the law remain unfulfilled, is an entire misunderstanding: this was really a saying of the Pharisees which was controverted by Jesus, and put into His mouth by some strange mistake (p. 271).

The worst treatment, however, is accorded to the fourth Gospel; and here we see the most flagrant instances of arbitrary treatment of the records. According to Schenkel, St. John occupies the last place among the gospel narrators, because, in his record, "there is no trace of a gradual development of the religious and Messianic consciousness in Christ, no perceptible growth or progress of his inner life" (p. 17); but, on the contrary, his earthly work is placed in connection with a pre-existent condition. We cannot help remembering that, six years before the publication of his *Sketch*, Schenkel conceded to St. John the first place amongst the evangelical historians, just "because he testifies most decidedly to the immediate and unconditional agreement of the self-consciousness of Christ with that of God." But since the substance of this Gospel is "not directly historical," there can be no hesitation, if necessary, in doing away with its testimony. St. John may tell us that Jesus, when hanging on the cross, committed His mother to the care of His beloved disciple; but Schenkel knows better, that Mary was not able "to bear the sight even from a distance." St. John, therefore, invented the circumstance in order to represent "this admirable endurance of motherly love, as an expiation for her former strange coldness towards the gospel;" although, in another place, he tells us that Mary *expected* a miracle at the wedding in Cana, and was therefore by no means indifferent to the gospel. Elsewhere, too, in the history of the passion, St. John shows himself to be an undependable narrator: he purposely omits to mention the institution of the Lord's Supper, and brings his farewell repast into connection with the washing of the disciples' feet, an ordinance "which was as plainly calculated to humble all priestly pride, as afterwards the Lord's Supper became the chief support of this sentiment." For this reason, therefore, it must be historically correct that Christ washed His disciples' feet, because this anti-hierarchical incident is excellently adapted to the purpose of Schenkel's *Sketch*. In the conversation of Christ with the woman of Samaria, St. John has misstated time and place, and has erroneously represented him as omniscient; nevertheless, the narrative must be based on some historical event, in order that "the grandest of all speeches in defence of tolerance," the "exalted wide-heartedness" shown in what Jesus says about the nature of worship, may not be wanting to the Sketch of Christ's character.

Indeed, such genuinely human features in the character of Christ are frequently recurring in the fourth Gospel. Schenkel is often fain to give the preference to this unhistorical, speculative record, as against the other Gospels, and even to correct his favourite St. Mark according to its statements. The discourse on the bread from heaven in chap. vi. betrays to us the origin of the legend of the loaves and fishes, and is therefore more credible than what the other evangelists relate in respect of this. The discourses of Christ as to His coming again, are more faithfully reproduced by St. John (chap. xiii.-xvii.) than in the three first Gospels. St. John alone is the true narrator in this case, although Schenkel informs us that Jesus could not possibly have held such long discourses on the last evening. And why? Because the reference to the Comforter whom He would send shows that, when Jesus spoke of His second coming, He did not refer to a personal and bodily reappearance, but only to an advent "in spirit" (186 et seq.).

From this you see *in what an arbitrary spirit Schenkel handles the gospel records.* His method is far more *self-contradictory* than even that of the old rationalists. Whatever can be explained as opposition to "High Churchism" or "orthodoxy," whatever may be strained to serve his well-known democratic church tendencies, whatever is calculated to make Jesus appear as a natural man, bounded by human limitations and imperfection,—all this is always a "genuine historical trait" (pp. 40, 149, 208, etc. etc.), whether it come from the Synoptics or from the fourth Gospel. But wherever the Gospels speak of the necessity of church discipline, and above all of the superhuman dignity and power of Christ, of His *divine* nature and self-consciousness, be their language never so distinct, and the occurrence of such sentiments never so frequent, this is not history, but some misunderstanding of a later reviser, or a legendary addition, no matter in which Gospel the passage occurs. Whoever pleases, may call this science and historical criticism; in truth, it is nothing but subjective inclination. Hence the best critics have already shown his self-contradictory treatment of the historical records to be a fault which vitiates the whole of Dr. Schenkel's work.[1]

We can easily guess of what description the sketch of Christ's character will be, which is produced by such a procedure. Let us look at it more closely.

Like the rationalists with their denial of the miraculous, so, too, Schenkel approaches the gospel history with a presupposition that decides everything beforehand, viz. the *denial of the Godhead of Christ.* On the first page of his book he declares that the teaching of the Church as to the person of Christ is an ancient absurdity, a remnant of Roman Catholicism in the Protestant Church; a doctrine imported into the Church by the Gentile Christian party, for the Jewish Christians always considered Christ to be a mere man. "The statement, that Jesus once lived among men, and still lives as very man and very God, must necessarily call forth the most weighty scruples" (p. 2). He was rather "a child of the people," the real son of Joseph and Mary; "his father was a man of the people, one who belonged to the working class, a carpenter" (p. 26).[2] The lad of twelve years old "calls God his Father, as any pious Jewish child might do" (pp. 259, 27). Jesus experienced an early "development of strong feeling, which temporarily repressed his filial piety" (p. 28). He doubtless "learned from the book of Nature, beneath the smiling skies of Galilee"[3] (p. 28). He was baptized by John, but there was never any intimate relationship between them, far less a declaration of Christ's divine sonship on the part of John (p. 30 et seq.). In baptism Jesus receives divine enlightenment "like a silver glance" from above, teaching him that henceforth not the law, but "the mild and gentle spirit of humility and love, symbolized by the dove, is to effect a moral regeneration of the people" (p. 35).

[1] Cf. Weiss: "Dr. Schenkel's *Charakterbild Jesu,* besonders von Seiten der Quellenbenutzung u. geschichtlichen Behandlungsweise beleuchtet;" in *Studien u. Kritiken* for 1865, Heft ii. p. 277 et seq. Also, Uhlhorn's valuable little book, *Die modernen Darstellungen des Lebens Jesu,* p. 39 et seq.

[2] And yet Dr. Schenkel *denied* this at the General Synod for Baden (18th May 1867), stating that his book merely contained a reference "to the parents of Jesus," but not that Jesus was the son of the carpenter! Cf. this statement with the above cited page of his book.

[3] Cf. further on, the description by Renan.

It is certain that Christ attributed to Himself an unexampled clearness in His consciousness of God, and, in consequence of it, a most intimate and indissoluble communion with God; also, that He designated this personal character of His as an inexhaustible source of revelation and life for the whole of humanity. But it does not follow that He attributed to Himself *divine* power or dignity, nor did He co-equalize the "Son" as the second person of the Godhead, with the "Father" as the first (pp. 121, 175). Schenkel actually endeavours to prove this by quoting Matt. xi. 29, where Christ calls Himself "meek and lowly;" indicating that He "sometimes had to struggle with anger" (p. 122)! Is not this genuine Rationalism, importing a meaning into the text instead of extracting one from it? for in the passage quoted our Lord says, if anything, directly the contrary to what Schenkel infers. Christ applies to Himself the designation "Son of God," in no other sense than "that in which the people of Israel or the theocratic king might be so called" (p. 177). "The fourth Gospel even, if we examine it closely, contains nothing about the God-equal dignity of Christ" (pp. 178, 150). But how about the many passages which indubitably apply to the divine power and dignity of the Son,—*e.g.*, "Whatsoever the Father doeth, that doeth the Son likewise;" "that they all may honour the Son even as they honour the Father;" the co-ordination of Father and Son in the baptismal command, and many others? These are partly passed over in silence, probably because they appear unnecessary (and at all events unsuitable) for the Sketch of Christ's character; partly they are disposed of—as *e.g.* the declaration, "All things are given unto me by my Father"—with a remark such as this, that "without the necessary limitation these words would be meaningless" (p. 120). When Jesus said, "I and the Father are one," He referred not to oneness of essence, but to oneness of will (p. 150). We have already shown that these oft-renewed attempts to deprive our Lord of His personal and conscious divinity are exegetically untenable.

"From His earliest youth a partaker in the sorrows and joys of the people," Christ soon felt "that His work must be devoted to them" (pp. 33, 41). "*Men from the people were the men of the future Christian Church*" (pp. 60, 44),—from amongst their number He chose His apostles. At the time of His first public appearance Jesus was not yet fully clear as to His calling, far less did He at once claim to be the Messiah. After the temptation in the wilderness "He is gifted with a preliminary insight into His vocation" (p. 40). He had seen from the example of John the Baptist that the old Jewish theocracy was possessed of no specific for the moral regeneration of the people, and that a new path must be struck out in order to attain to this end. Thence proceeded His proclamation: The time is fulfilled; the kingdom of God is come near —*i.e.* "the old age of ceremonial minority and traditional schooling of the people" has passed away. At that time, therefore, Christ did not make His appearance "as the Messiah promised by the prophets, but only as the founder of a new age, of a fresh communion of pious Israelites with God, which should be independent of theocratic conditions" (p. 43), which communion He sought to realize in the circle of His first disciples. It was the healing, *i.e.* quieting, by means of a consolatory assurance, of one whom the people thought possessed, which gave the first impulse to the spread of the opinion that Jesus worked miracles.

The opposition of the hierarchical party, the "orthodox school-theologians," the "High-Churchmen," *alias* the Scribes and Pharisees, who took violent offence especially at His breach of the Sabbath, convinced Jesus "with ever-increasing clearness, that it was the aim of His life to remove the yoke of the dead letter from His tormented people, to put bounds to the empty scholasticism and arrogant rule of the priesthood, and to elevate the neglected and forsaken community of laymen to moral and religious freedom" (p. 64). Henceforth He represents "the true dignity and the eternal rights of man" as against the school-theology of the priests and the spirit-killing letter of their traditions (pp. 64 et s., pp. 36 et s.), and seeks "to liberate the consciousness of God from all forms and limits" (p. 121). He proclaims the freedom of worship; for, in truth, "liberty of conscience and of faith were the starting-point as well as the leading ideas in His whole purpose and work" (p. 127). He wishes to introduce the religion of a universal love of man; that is to say, "of a universal charity, purified from all prejudices of confession, of social standing or of nationality: this He distinctly testifies to be the way to everlasting life" (p. 127). This "religion of unqualified humanity" He pronounced sacred in the parable of the good Samaritan (p. 127).

In virtue of these ideas, Jesus wished to proclaim Himself, not yet as Messiah, but as the Saviour of His people. He seeks to spread them by sending out the twelve, and thus to make the original nucleus of God-fearing Israelites outgrow its dimensions. He even makes a practical use of these ideas in the regions of Tyre and Zidon, etc., *i.e.* at the boundary of the Gentile world, in order to test the readiness of the heathen to receive the new doctrine.

When Peter, on His return from thence, solemnly confessed, "Thou art the Messiah," this was "a motto to hold His followers together; thus He unfolded His banner, and took up a definite position against the hierarchy. It would seem as if Jesus scarcely expected the decisive word to issue from the mouth of a disciple" (p. 99). Well knowing that, according to the Old Testament, the office of Messiah was one quite different from the work He had set before Himself, He did not approve of this opinion. But He could not help Himself; He must of necessity lay claim to be the Messiah, since this "was the sole means by which He could penetrate a portion at least of the nation with His ideas, and thus attain the object of His vocation" (p. 98).

It was, however, necessary that His Messiahship should be consecrated by suffering. His entry into Jerusalem, an open avowal of His claims, and the subsequent cleansing of the temple—a symbol of the approaching destruction of the outward temple-service—supplied His opponents with the weapons necessary for His accusation and sentence of death. He was amenable to the letter of the law. He "sacrifices Himself to the killing commandment, in order by His death to destroy it in principle for ever, as the most fearful hindrance of true religion and morality" (p. 199). His death was "the victory of liberty and love." The heartless law was accused by compassionate love; the hierarchy was condemned, and thenceforth became the object of detestation. This was the substance of Christ's redemption and reconciliation. Through the belief in His resurrection, arising "from a condition of ecstasy, the effect of deeply shaken feminine soul-life" (p. 226), the deceased Messiah was glorified as the ever-living One. He lives in all to whom His words are spirit and life. "The living Christ is the Spirit of the Church" (p. 234).

These are the salient points in the picture of Christ as drawn by Schenkel. The first thing that strikes us is the facile and matter-of-course way in which he (in common with all other anti-miraculous writers on the life of Christ) passes over the question as to the descent of our Lord; just as if the whole foundation of our faith were not destroyed by changing the "only-begotten Son of God, conceived of the Holy Ghost, born of the Virgin Mary," into the (illegitimate?) son of Joseph and Mary! In this and in other respects we recognise in the *Sketch* the same old, scrupulous, highly enlightened people's friend of the rationalistic age. Dr. Schenkel has only trimmed his garments after a more modern fashion, in order, for his own reasons, to set Him up in opposition to all true Churchmanship, either new or old. We need waste no words in proving that the Christ of the *Sketch* does not correspond in the remotest degree to Him whom St. Mark portrays. But we cannot help feeling surprised that Dr. Schenkel should reproach others, *e.g.* Renan, with "repeating in many respects the mistakes of the old rationalists." That he himself does this more than any one is especially evident from the manner in which he treats the *miracles of Christ.*

Schenkel distinguishes between two classes of miracles in the gospel history. First, the *miracles of healing*, which "are still approximately explicable by the laws of psychology, as the influence of a personality gifted with the highest spiritual talents and the rarest moral powers, met by an unqualified confidence on the part of those who sought help from him." Second, "the *works of absolute omnipotence*," occurring during the latter part of Christ's ministry, "in which all the laws of nature are simply suspended" (*e.g.* quieting of the storm, feeding the multitude, raising the dead). Since these latter break through the bounds of human finity, within which Christ is supposed to be confined throughout the first three Gospels, they are to be accounted as the products of legends and fancies. They reveal the "unconscious worship of an enthusiastic religious fancy, proceeding from the deeply excited consciences and hearts of the first disciples and churches, who thus gave a hyperbolical expression to the glow of their pious feelings, and to their admiration, love, and reverence for the departed hero,—an expression which, naturally enough, was scarcely in accordance with the standards of sober historical criticism" (pp. 15, 16). Dr. Schenkel appeals to the thoroughly rationalistic maxim, "that we must keep not to the shell but to the kernel of the gospel history;" and he lays stress on the absence of "an undisturbed power of perception, in the case even of the most immediate witnesses," who for that reason could not form a correct judgment (p. 105). Here we have the same distinction between facts and opinions as in the case of the rationalists. The only difference between them and Schenkel is, that the latter finds far more of legend in the miracles. For "the picture of the Redeemer's life, soon after His earthly departure, was surrounded by a rich stream of legends" (p. 16).

Dr. Schenkel is thus possessed of two means to get rid of the supernatural: the enthusiastic, exaggerating fancy of the disciples, and the legendary element. True, he himself speaks of a miraculous gift possessed by Christ, but only in the sence of a specially "intensified gift of human nature." For "if we were to consider the miraculous gift of Christ as the result of indwelling omnipotence, or as the shining forth of His divine nature, we should no longer be able to apply any human standards to His operation" (p. 48). As if miracle-workers before the time of Jesus had, as such, ceased to be men! But Schenkel's picture of Christ must not at any price exceed the limits of the purely natural.

"During His retirement in the desert, Jesus began to feel within Himself the workings of that mysterious power which we must believe to be the source of His miracles" (p. 39). And in what did it consist? Jesus had the "psychical power of calming troubled souls." His assurance, *e.g.*, of the forgiveness of sins, could thrill through the soul like an electric current, and communicate itself to the paralysed nerves of the sick man, thus producing bodily effects (p. 57). This was the case with the palsied man in Mark ii. 1–12. If so, however, why did not the sick man spring up immediately after the assurance, "Thy sins are forgiven thee," instead of waiting to hear the words, "Rise up and take thy bed," etc. ? In the synagogue at Capernaum (Mark i. 21 et s.), Christ merely quieted the convulsive fit of a highly excited madman (48, 49)—who, however, according to ver. 26, is most of all convulsed by the first words of the Saviour. Other sick people were cured "in consequence of undergoing spiritual suspense, and through passing incitements" (p. 89). The healing of the woman with an issue of blood is effected by "religious excitement in her soul" (p. 82), though the evangelist tells us that she was healed *before* Jesus turned round and spoke to her (Mark v. 30). In the case of the centurion's servant, "the chief cause of his recovery was the extraordinary spiritual excitement of the sick man, and his invincible faith in the healing power of Christ" (p. 74): yet the passage in question says not a word about the faith of the *servant*, but only about that of the centurion! Those who were sick of fever, Jesus quieted by a "loving grasp of the hand, probably accompanied by comforting and refreshing assurances" (p. 49). The leper "was probably cured in the main before he came to Christ" (p. 53)!

The miraculous power of Christ did not extend beyond (at best doubtful) results of this kind.

Are these not the old worn-out paths and threadbare arts of natural explanation ? is not this the same old rationalistic caprice which clips and pares the historical matter, till it no longer belies the axiom that there is no such thing as a miracle? According to Isaiah (iv. 6), Christ's name is "Wonderful;" according to Messrs. Schenkel & Co., "an entirely natural man." And yet this same Dr. Schenkel some twelve years since most truly remarked, "Few men only are wise enough to perceive that much more intellect is necessary to the believing of a miracle than cleverness to its denial!"

Yet we may find even in the "historical" remains left us by this violent exegesis enough to shatter the natural explanation of these incidents. When, *e.g.*, we read that the inhabitants of Capernaum bring all their sick folk to Jesus (p. 49), we should like Dr. Schenkel to explain how it was that the people *expected* this Rabbi, on His *first* appearance, to heal the sick ? Surely more must have happened than merely the quieting of a woman sick of fever, for the people to think Him a man of miracles who would heal all their sick. Indeed we may put the question in a general form: *If no miracles ever took place, how came the people constantly to expect them?* Schenkel, Strauss, and Renan all confess that that generation did expect them; indeed they employ this fact in support of their negation of the miraculous, arguing that the miracle-seeking propensities of that age were the chief source of miraculous narratives.[1] In the last resort this weapon may be used against our adversaries. It is perfectly true that an inordinate craving for the miraculous may invent miracles; and that later on it did so, is sufficiently proved by the apocryphal Gospels. But just as in later ages a "miracle-mania" created false miracles, so *in the first instance real and true miracles created the miracle-mania of later times.* It would never have occurred to men to coin false money, if there had not first been real money (cf. p. 112)! *How,* we ask, *did mankind ever arrive at the conception of a miracle, if not through witnessing workings of the Divine Omnipotence,* which were utterly beyond the reach of human comprehension? We are still waiting for an answer to this question from the critics who deny the miraculous.

Hitherto we have been considering Dr. Schenkel's treatment of the first class of miracles—those of healing. The second class, our Saviour's *works of omnipotence,* are disposed of either by similar violence, or else by their transposition into the realm of fable. The feeding of five thousand in the wilderness dwindles down to the fact that Christ satisfied them "with the heavenly bread of life," by "reverently consecrating the provisions which they had brought with them, or which they hastily procured in the neighbourhood," and then distributing them through His disciples (p. 86). The daughter of Jairus was still alive; for Christ Himself says, "She is not dead, but sleepeth." The narrative of the transfiguration "underwent a legendary transformation in the subsequent tradition" (p. 105). In like manner the legends of both the miracles on the lake arose from the simple fact, that during a storm Christ exhibited greater courage than frightened though experienced mariners, notwithstanding the despair of the helms-

[1] We shall see, however, in our consideration of Strauss' work, that the Jewish nation, as such, by no means had a proclivity for the miraculous.

man, and that He thereby inspirited all surrounders. This Dr. Schenkel considers to be "much grander and more stirring" than the quieting of the storm as related by the evangelists (pp. 79, 80)! On the other occasion Jesus walked in the dark of night, not on the water, but "along the shore," and this appeared to the disciples like a threatening apparition (p. 88). The raising of Lazarus is a myth which perhaps originated from the parable of Lazarus the beggar (p. 277). The later legends in general were not satisfied with the unadorned simplicity of the original narratives. The additions made by them give us many an instructive insight into the formation of miraculous narratives (p. 208). So, *e.g.*, with the bloody sweat in Gethsemane, which is "an unmistakeable exaggeration."[1]

Thus Dr. Schenkel, in contradistinction to the former attempts to explain away the miracles of Christ, which were either simply rationalistic or purely mythical, combines all methods—the natural, the mythical, the allegorical, the prosaic or sentimental rationalistic—to suit his own convenience.[2] Just as much violence is done to the *discourses of Christ* when they do not fit into Schenkel's portrait of Him, even though they may occur in the Gospel by St. Mark. Thus it is with the prophecies of Christ in regard to His second coming. These were all meant by Jesus to be taken impersonally; but the misapprehension of a later age converted them into predictions of a personal advent (p. 104). If we ask how such a misunderstanding was possible, we are told that Jesus spoke figuratively, because His disciples could not yet raise their minds to the idea of an impersonal advent; and these figures of speech originated the idea that Christ would appear again personally (p. 184 et s.). The mere inner grounds against such a view show it to be utterly impossible that Christ should have predicted of Himself a personal and corporal second advent in the splendour of heavenly glory, and accompanied by the angelic hosts for the purpose of erecting an earthly kingdom. He who came to found a spiritual kingdom of truth, justice, and love, could not possibly have designated

[1] The possibility of the formation of myths will be more closely examined in the consideration of Strauss' book.

[2] Cf. in Lecture VII. his theory as to the resurrection of Christ.

outward splendour, earthly power, and dazzling glory as the last aim of it (p. 104). We ask in amazement: Has the idea never dawned upon Dr. Schenkel that "corporality is the end of God's ways," and must be so? Does he not see that the kingdom of truth and justice, which in this world is being built up invisibly and in quiet concealment, must, in order to celebrate its full triumph, one day appear visibly; and that therefore Christ might point out both aspects of His kingdom—its present inward nature, and its future outward and visible incorporation? The deeper reason why Dr. Schenkel will not acknowledge these discourses as genuine, is simply his aversion to confess the Godhead of Him who is King of heaven and earth, and the future Judge of the world; who, therefore, in these discourses places His person far above all merely natural humanity.

The clearest view of the insufficiency and futility of this whole attempt to explain the life and person of Christ will accrue if we consider its central point, and ask for an answer to the question, how the man Jesus arrived at His *Messianic consciousness?* According to Schenkel, this came on Him gradually against His will, and indeed, in the first instance, against His better knowledge. We have already heard Schenkel tell us that Jesus was "not yet fully clear" as to His Redeemer's vocation on the occasion of His first public appearance at Nazareth. Even at the time that He preached in Nazareth (Luke iv. 16 et s.) He "was not convinced that, as a 'prophet' in a new and higher sense, He was to be the fulfiller of the still imperfect Old Testament prophecies of the Messiah" (pp. 14, 40, et s.). "Still imperfect?" Yes; because they aimed only at a restoration of Israel's ancient power and dominion, and at the extension of an outward theocracy over the whole earth, and that not only according to the then condition of Messianic expectations, but also according to the true meaning of the prophetical writings themselves (?). For this reason Christ was at first "unwilling to undertake the task assigned to the Messiah by the prophets" (p. 97). He only wished to become the Saviour of His nation—the founder of a new God-fearing community. But how if the nation expected its salvation and regeneration from none else than the Messiah? In this case He could not attain

His ends without laying claim to the Messiahship. He therefore "assumed the title and dignity of Messiah only in consequence of an unavoidable accommodation to the ideas and expectations of His contemporaries and co-patriots" (p. 199), because this was "the only means to attain the object of His vocation." And so when Peter had, to the surprise of Christ Himself, uttered the decisive "watchword," He could no longer help Himself, but was obliged to "permit" the application of Messianic ideas to His work and person.

But how could He in this case assume to be the Fulfiller of the Messianic prophecies, if they represented the Messiah as acting quite differently to what He had, according to His better knowledge, resolved to do? "He probably looked on these promises as a series of figurative representations of the future, which were indispensable to a spiritually backward nation, and served the purpose of a bridge leading in later times to a purer and deeper comprehension of God's self-revelation to man" (p. 98). So Christ endeavoured to purify the Messianic prophecies from the spurious elements contained in them, and thus to fulfil their true substance. Only from this point of view could He suffer them to be applied to His person. True, He must not "for a moment conceal from Himself, that every appeal to Old Testament passages would be open to the gravest misunderstandings and wrong interpretations" (*ibid.*). But not only in this respect did Christ put another interpretation on the Messianic prophecies; for He soon became aware of the necessity that He should become a *suffering* Messiah, "an idea which to the Jews was self-contradictory, and unknown to the Old Testament" (notwithstanding Isaiah liii.?). This converted the difference between His purer idea of the Messiah and the expectations of His nation into a positive contradiction. Dr. Schenkel is forced to confess that "the fulfilment of the Old Testament in His person, was the non-fulfilment of all theocratic expectations. There was no longer anything in common between the hopes of His fellow-countrymen and His own conviction" (pp. 101, 102).

Here once more we ask in amazement: To whose Messianic ideas did Christ "accommodate" Himself? Clearly neither to those of the old prophets nor to those of the people. And what would be the object of allowing the people to apply to Him the title of Messiah, if He did not fulfil their expectations? How could Christ conscientiously accept a title which to His own mind conveyed a meaning precisely opposed to that which the people attached to it,—a title which was not the substance formerly concealed by spurious wrappings, but simply the deceptive veil of a new idea, used by Him in order to secure more easy access to the affections of the people? If Jesus ought not, on account of false Messianic expectations, to have appealed to the Old Testament with its imperfect promises, how is it that He constantly does so, and represents Himself as the Fulfiller of the old economy? (Cf. the Sermon on the Mount, the discourse at Nazareth, etc.) Were this the case, Christ would have been guilty of an apparent acquiescence in the Old Testament, while neglecting to fulfil its most important part, and secretly transmuting it into something entirely different. And would not this have betrayed a want of sincerity? or would not a serious lack of clearness, firmness, and consistency be evident from the original reluctancy to become the Messiah, followed so soon by the resolution to claim this office? If Christ from the time of His baptism and His sojourn in the wilderness clearly saw that there was no way open to Him other than "an inner rupture with the theocracy, and a preparation to fight for life or death," why could He not from the very beginning recognise that He must needs take up a definite position as against the current ideas about Messiah? Why should Peter have been the first to give Him a clear view as to His future course? How piteously dependent on His disciple does the Master thus appear, though Schenkel says, with truth, that "Jesus grew rather from within than from without!" And yet, on the other hand, how blind are these disciples! They stamp their Master as the Messiah, but they do not see that the fulfilment of the Old Testament in His person was "the non-fulfilment of all theocratic hopes," and continue to cleave to them with their whole soul (Acts i. 8).

We see from these, and many other questions and contradictions, *how ill Dr. Schenkel has succeeded in solving the enigma of Christ's Messianic consciousness.* Instead of bringing light into the question, he has confused it on all hands. With unbounded caprice he treats the prophecies of the old Testament as intended to be fulfilled, but as incapable of fulfilment on account of their imperfection. He places Christ in a thoroughly false position as regards both the ancient prophets, His nation, and His disciples; thus heaping up one exegetical, psychological, or historical riddle on another. But this always will and must be the case when men will not listen to the plain voice of Scripture.

Of a truth, no! The Messianic consciousness of Christ was *not gradually* developed amid constant fluctuations. It was not after half His career was past that He at length forced Himself to appear as the Messiah under the pressure of outward circumstances and human ideas. *From the very beginning of His public ministry He knew that He was the Messiah,* and that from His own deepest convictions, which long preceded any confession by the disciples. All the Gospels clearly testify to this. They tell us that the Messianic consciousness of Christ, of which there was a presentiment in the lad of twelve, who lived in such close communion with His Father, broke forth at the baptism in Jordan. What a series of testimonies in word and deed to this effect do we find long before the confession of Peter! The history of the temptation; the first sermon in Nazareth, representing the Messianic passage (Isa. lxi. 1) as fulfilled in Himself; His first miracle in Capernaum, where the demon, without any contradiction on His part, declares Him to be the Holy One of God; the first adoration on the part of the disciples (John i. 45), who rejoice that they have found the Messiah; the Sermon on the Mount, in which He lays claim to be the Fulfiller of the law and the prophets (Matt. v. 17), and attributes to Himself the power of excluding from or admitting into the Messianic kingdom (vii. 21–23); the question of the Baptist, "Art Thou He that should come? aye, even the designations, "Son of man" and "Bridegroom," which the most recent investigations have proved to have a Messianic import; the series of parables in which He represents the kingdom of God as come through Him;—are not all these direct proofs of His distinct Messianic consciousness? We can very well understand why, for self-evident educational purposes, our Saviour endeavoured to rouse the faith of the people by His doings and sayings, instead of at once declaring, "I am the Messiah." The confession of

Peter is pleasing to Him,—not so much because it contains the acknowledgment of His Messiahship, as because it shows that the same "hard sayings" which had offended the mass of the people had only produced a firmer faith, and one born from inward experience, in the hearts of His disciples. This is clearly shown by John vi. 66–69.

Even Keim, in his *History of Jesus of Nazara*, acknowledges that He was "convinced of His Messianic vocation from His very first public appearance;" and in the face of this strong conviction, as well as of many other facts, he is "forced decidedly to reject the theories of Strauss and Schenkel, who hold that the Messianic idea was not formed until later on."[1] It should never be forgotten "that thirty years of tranquil development preceded this ministry of scarce three years, and that He who made His appearance so late, and yet so decidedly, must have formed a clear opinion as to Himself and His work; and finally, let all objectors remember, that no transitional turning-point in the life of Christ, no breaking forth of His Messianic consciousness, such as the Gospels describe at the opening of His ministry, can be either pointed out or imagined later on."[2]

Another defect, extending not only to this portion, but to the whole of Dr. Schenkel's *Sketch*, is the *mania*, which of late years has become perfectly morbid, *for discovering signs of development in the character of Christ.* We have already seen how this tendency sacrifices the Godhead of our Lord to His manhood, and misinterprets or rejects as spurious all the passages which testify to the former. True, if we accept the false axiom on which these attempts are based, there is something justifiable in them. Every real man must develope; and we confess the true manhood of Christ, as the Church in all ages has done, though it may not always have had its due rights conceded. But the question is, during which period did this

[1] Keim, *Geschichte Jesu von Nazara*, vol. i. pp. 453, 454. He goes on to remark, "At first, it is true, Jesus concealed this dignity, and did not make use of the terms, 'Messiah,' 'Christ,' or 'Son of God,' until a later period. Still there can be no doubt that from the very beginning He laid claim to the highest authority. In His opening discourses He proclaims His Messiahship in terms more or less distinct; but apart from these, all the Gospels agree that during the first period of His ministry He bore the title of the 'Son of man,' which was confessedly and indubitably indicative of the Messianic dignity."

[2] Cf. Beyschlag, *Die Christologie des neuen Testaments*, p. 37.

inner development of Christ take place? The anti-miraculous accounts of His life invariably date it *too late,* since they suppose it to result from the appearance of John the Baptist and the religious excitement thereby produced. The religious development of our Lord did not begin so late as this, for we find traces of it even in the child Jesus; and when the religious excitement broke out amongst His people, the purposes of Christ were nearly matured. In other words, *His inner development essentially took place, not during the period of His public ministry, but during the quiet of the preceding thirty years.* Whoever will consider the beginnings of Christ's ministry, as related in the Gospels, with an unbiassed mind, will at once be struck with the admirable certainty and firmness of His conduct, and will receive the impression that the new Prophet was perfectly clear as to His redemptory vocation, and His entire relation to the past, present, and future of Israel, the world, and the kingdom of God. Do not the purity, truth, and holy chastity of His intellect and will, which shine with such overpowering beauty in all His deeds and words,—do not these demand of us the belief that He never could have presented Himself to His own nation and to all mankind as their Redeemer, before, in virtue of His constant communion with God, becoming perfectly certain that "the fulness of time was come"? After this epoch, we must contemplate His life not so much under the aspect of inward *development* (though, of course, this is not to be excluded[1]), as under that of a moral *testing* of what He had inwardly attained by means of a struggle with the world and obedience to His heavenly Father even unto death. In the main, it is not Christ but His contemporaries who develope. As He offers them the fruits of His mature spiritual growth in word and deed, so they are forced to take up a more and more decided position towards this new divine Revelation; and this necessitates a corresponding behaviour on His part.

Apart from His Messianic consciousness, it is not easy to give proofs of development in Christ analogous to that of ordinary men during the time of His public ministry. Sup-

[1] Cf., *e.g.*, Luke ix. 31 with xii. 59. Still there are distinct traces of a recognition that it was needful for Him to suffer even during the earliest period of His ministry. Cf. Luke ix. 22, Matt. x. 16–25, v. 10, 11, Luke vii. 22 ff., and ii. 34, 35.

pose, *e.g.*, that we consider Him as an orator. Even the most gifted of human orators gradually attain the climax of their eloquence; but so soon as Christ opens His lips, we hear the *perfect Master* of divine speech. Do not the very first sentences of the Sermon on the Mount show the absolute incomparableness of the most gracious yet most thrilling Preacher? The same is the case with His actions, from the outset so holy and decided; with His look, which pierces the depth of the heart; with His ever sure and correct judgment; with His perfect wisdom in dealing with all men, combining a majesty which must command respect with a condescension that should win the hearts of all men.[1]

This mania for everywhere pointing out development in the life of Christ, is often rightly punished by an inability to discover any true development whatever. This is the case with Schenkel. In his book everything turns on the opposition to the "orthodox" Pharisees. This appears to be the mainspring which moves the drama of Christ's life, and brings about

[1] On the grounds above enumerated, we take exception to the above-quoted work of Keim's, *Geschichte Jesu von Nazara* (as well as to his previously published lectures on "the human development of Christ," "the historical dignity of Christ," and "the historical Christ"), because, in the constant endeavour to attain a historical comprehension of everything, he leaves no room for the divinity of our Saviour. This book far excels the work of Schenkel in well-conceived delineations, in scientific value, in purity of language, in real historical perception, and especially in a warm respect for all that is holy. On account, however, of its being written for the theological world, and not for the public at large, we have not taken it into consideration above. Keim's earlier writings we cannot reckon directly amongst the number of the anti-miraculous accounts of the life of Christ, especially as he emphatically defends the bodily resurrection of our Lord. Still, all these writings are closely allied to the rationalistic and mythical accounts; for Keim considers Christ to be *only a man*, although at the same time he calls Him a "mystery," and acknowledges that He applied to Himself "overwhelming names and titles, before which all human categories seem to sink into silence" (*Historical Dignity*, pp. 26 and 29). We would just devote a few words to one aspect of these writings.

According to Keim, Jesus "*resolved*" to be the Messiah. "Amidst conflicts and struggles, there was developed the wondrous world-transforming, primary thought of His life, to be the Son of God, and as such the Saviour of the world. Yes, this was the deed of His life, to offer Himself to the world as the true Messiah sent by God; yea, as the obedient Son of God Himself." "The greatest spiritual acquisition of His life was His *resolution to be the Messiah*" (*Historical Christ*, 3d ed. pp. 27, 76, et s.; cf. *Hist. Dignity*, pp. 12 et s.; *Jesu von Naz.*, pp. 543 et s.). Granted the premise that Jesus was a mere man, there is no escaping the conclusion that His Messiahship was a free inward resolve, whether

one important decision after another. But according to Dr. Schenkel, Christ is from the very commencement quite decided as to His behaviour towards the Pharisees; as early as His baptism, He sees that "they are possessed of no specific for the regeneration of their nation." In the wilderness He sees that there is no way open to Him but to "declare enmity against the Pharisees, and wage war to the knife." He "purposely" makes His disciples "break the Sabbath." In the Sermon on the Mount He abjures "all connection with the Jewish hierarchy and theocracy," etc. etc. But whence, then, is any further "development" to proceed? How can Schenkel afterwards say that "*now* the breach was inevitable," that Jesus was *now* "assuming the offensive," since all this had taken place *from the very beginning?*

True, there is *one* sacrifice by means of which we may purchase a purely human development in the life of Christ,—we mean the surrender of His sinlessness, as in Renan's work. This, however, to his honour be it said, is studiously avoided

it resulted from "the process of a lifetime" (*ubi sup.*) or was first formed at the baptism in Jordan, up to which Jesus "had by no means attained to a certainty as to His vocation, or a conviction of His Messiahship" (*Jesu von Naz.*, p. 543). But how could Christ, if He were a mere man, present Himself to the people as the "God-sent, true Messiah;" whereas the true Messiah, *i.e.* He who was promised in the Old Testament, was to be no mere man, but "the Branch of the Lord," whose "goings out are from everlasting to everlasting"? We have here a plain dilemma. *Either Jesus was the true Messiah, and that according to the preparation and foreknowledge of God, in which case He had no need to "resolve" to be so, but only to acknowledge and fulfil the task assigned to Him by God; or He was nothing of the kind, in which case no resolve, were it never so heroic, could make Him Messiah,*—at most it could but enable Him to play the part. Is it, indeed, in any way possible to resolve *to be* one thing or another? But even though this might be meant in the sense of becoming (or voluntarily undertaking the office of) Messiah, we must remember that such a "becoming" is, according to Scripture, only possible in consequence of a divinely-granted "Being," *i.e.* the divine Sonship, which cannot be dependent on the good pleasure of a man. A resolution cannot originate a new existence; it can only carry out the work belonging to that existence. True it is that the whole of Christ's work for our redemption, from His first appearance to the acceptance of the cup of suffering, was voluntary, and took place amid unceasing conflicts and assaults. Indeed, we believe that the free resolve of Christ extended still further than Keim would allow,—even His coming into the world was subject to it. Thus His "resolution to be the Messiah" was made, not in this world, at Jordan, but in a pre-existent life. But when He had once appeared in the flesh, it no longer depended upon His free will whether to be the Messiah or not; He could not act otherwise, according to the necessity of His nature. As, in the actions of God, liberty and necessity coalesce in a higher unity, so, too, by Dr. Schenkel as far as may be. Nevertheless, this same mania for development compels even him every now and then *to place the moral dignity of Christ in a dubious light.* Accordingly, in such passages he generally speaks with an indecision and vagueness which must of itself arouse suspicion. He does not look upon the baptism of Christ as His Messianic consecration, but as a ceremonial purification. Jesus being seized by the force of the great religious and moral movement of the people, "places Himself in their ranks" without pride or self-righteousness, but yet without "classing Himself amongst common sinners" (pp. 33, 35). He classed Himself "with the better portion of the people." Thus He prayed with His disciples: "Forgive *us our* debts" (p. 29), as if our Lord had not put this prayer into the mouths of *His disciples,* and thus spoken, placing Himself in *their* position; "After this manner, therefore, pray *ye*" (Matt. vi. 9); "When *ye* pray, say" (Luke xi. 2). Further, Christ allows Himself to be proclaimed as the Messiah for the sake of the people, and in order to attain His

in the work of Christ *we may not separate human liberty from divine necessity.* The latter, and, in fact, *the entire divine aspect of Christ's redeeming work clearly does not receive its due importance,* if we accept the theory of a "resolution to be Messiah and Son of God." However delicate may be the historical and psychological analysis by means of which Keim seeks to explain to us this process, and however much moral praise he may bestow on "the noble achievement of the Messianic resolve" (*Hist. Dign.* pp. 12 et. s.), nevertheless his whole theory detracts far too seriously from the *divine* preparation and execution of the redemption. Although Keim declares that *divine Providence* so ordered circumstances to work together that this resolve was suggested to our Lord, yet surely it would never have been consonant with the almighty rule of divine love and mercy to trust the most important turning-point in the history of mankind to the subjective decision of any mere human being, were he never so excellent. *Where there is a world to be renewed, God is far more actively present* than it would appear from Keim's theory. Keim himself seems to feel this, for his historical conscience compels him presently to confess that "the fibres of the spiritual process taking place in the Baptist and in Jesus did not run merely through the circuit of an earthly consciousness; they were connected with a higher world. They could not have dared to believe what they did, without being sure of the divine will. All their discourses, especially those of Jesus, constantly recur to this divine Counsellor and Helper. Our historical conscience forces us to confess that divine dispensations and instructions were introduced into the world on the banks of Jordan, and that the influence of the divine government must have accompanied the greatest deed and the greatest turning-point in the history of man" (*Jesu von Naz.*, p. 549). If Keim would but trace out those fibres, connecting with a higher world One "before whom all human categories sink into silence," surely he would see in Him, no longer a mere man, but the only-begotten Son of God.

object. What shall we say to this? If Christ really were "He that should come," then the title of Messiah ought not to have been repugnant to His feelings, notwithstanding any popular fallacies as to the idea; but if He was not that promised One, it was wrong in Him to let Himself be proclaimed as such without a standing protest. And the same with His healing works. If they were not miraculous, and yet Christ saw that they were held to be so, He ought to have loudly witnessed to the contrary; otherwise His sincerity would be open to suspicion.

Furthermore, Christ was liable to err; He made a mistake in His estimate of Judas, although this mistake proceeded from the purest motives (p. 194). He had often felt the allurements of temptation, and was well acquainted with the sinful inward emotions of flesh and blood (pp. 150, 207) For "only a man who has to struggle with anger can call himself 'meek,' and only a man who has been tempted by pride can call himself 'humble'" (p. 122)! Therefore He rejected the title "good" when applied to Himself, and this rejection "is a most valid testimony to His deep and earnest conviction that He was not in any way entitled to this attribute" (pp 140–150).[1] Keeping in mind His own natural weakness, He judged the moral corruption of men much more mildly than does the dogmatic theology of any age; indeed the great fail-

[1] This passage, so fondly quoted by all deniers of the Godhead of Christ, is differently given in the first Gospel and in the two following. In Matt. xix 16 ff., the true reading is not "Good Master," but simply "Master;" and further on, not "Why callest thou me good?" but "Why askest thou me about that which is good? none is good, save One," etc.,—*i.e.* God is the only source of goodness; and if thou wilt attain to Him as goodness in unity, thou must first be in earnest in keeping His commandments as goodness in multiplicity. This passage, therefore, does not apply to the person of Christ, and cannot be used by Schenkel. The two other Synoptics, however, have the reading to which Schenkel appeals (Mark x. 17 et s.; Luke xviii. 18 et s.); still they do not bear out his views. They show, in the first place, that our Lord wished to humble the questioner who used the word "good" so lightly, and who had too high an opinion of himself, by reminding him what true goodness was. Second, we see that Jesus, who was still being made "perfect through sufferings" (Heb. ii. 10), points out to the scribe the absolute meaning of the predicate "good," which He reserves for His Father only, since He Himself is still in the midst of His humiliation. But Christ could never have mean "that He was not *in any way* entitled to this attribute," else how could He have *invited one who was inquiring after perfection to follow Him?* (Ver. 21.)

ing of mankind in general, He found to be merely their natural weakness (208 et s.).

These are some of the shadows which Dr. Schenkel cannot help introducing into his *Sketch of Christ's Character*, because *the denial of our Saviour's Godhead ever impels men to deny His sinlessness.* But if this latter be denied, or only made uncertain, it follows of necessity that the moral corruption of mankind, as a whole, will appear in a more favourable light as mere "natural weakness." If the divine dignity of Christ be lost sight of, our own human nature will be unduly exalted. The school of Arius mostly lies hard by that of Pelagius.

But how can one who no longer thoroughly acknowledges the sinlessness of Christ, still see in Him the "Saviour" and "*Redeemer*"? True, Schenkel remarks that those who hold his views are perfectly justified in calling Jesus the "Redeemer," because He "released mankind from the errors of Judaism and heathenism." Against this evasion Strauss well remarks: "When was a man ever called 'Redeemer' because he released those who lived with and after him from certain errors? This expression proceeds from the idea of the sin-offering; it could never have resulted from Schenkel's rationalistic theory, and if he employs it notwithstanding, he is guilty of *double-dealing in the use of words.*[1] Most true! If Jesus was in truth the Redeemer, He could only be so in virtue of His sacrifice for the sin of humanity; but this He could only present if He were perfectly sinless. On the other hand, if we consider Schenkel's persistent, though futile, endeavour to represent Christ as sinless, the question at once arises, *How could He be sinless if He were a mere man?* Why should absolutely no one else have been so? We here stand

[1] *Die Halben u. die Ganzen*, pp. 48, 49. This is not the only instance in which Schenkel has done so. *E.g.*, in speaking of the satisfaction of God's justice through the sacrifice of love, he says that reconciliation with God consists in the recognition of His forgiving love, and that the follower of Jesus shows himself to be worthy of this love by sacrificing himself (pp. 88, 114, 198 et s., 218 et s.); and again (in the *Allgemeine Kirchl. Zeitschrift*, vol. vi., part 4, p. 234), that Christ "revealed the eternal essence of the Godhead, Its holy love, by means of the greatest sacrifice recorded in history." Here again, under cover of the term "sacrifice," he smuggles in a conception quite foreign to that of the Scriptures,—a conception in which the central truth of the biblical doctrine, the *vicarious atonement* of Christ, is quite ignored.

before the simple, incontrovertible conclusion, that if Jesus was a mere man, He was subjected to all the limitations of human nature and development, and by universal analogy could not have been sinless; if He was not sinless, He was not fitted to be the Redeemer of the world; if He was not fitted to be the Redeemer, He cannot have been or become such. But now, if He was *not* the Redeemer, in the name of fairness, let our opponents be open and honourable enough to drop the title since they have repudiated the true idea, instead of continuing to adulterate biblical conceptions, by using the same words while substituting an utterly different meaning! The same remarks apply to other predicates which Schenkel in his *Sketch* applies to Christ. If Jesus was a mere man, how could He be the "great Pattern" for all ages, or the "Light of the world"? In this case, however prominent, He could not be more than *one amongst others,* and not unique for all ages. If He was entirely borne along by the current of human development, He might "still mark a great epoch in our history, but not its climax and culminating point,"[1] as Strauss has clearly shown.

Finally, we ask, how can any man with so doubtful a view of Christ's moral dignity give us *any conception of His unique religious consciousness,*—that clear unsullied mirror of the purest union and communion with God, into which the astonished world has been gazing for eighteen centuries, but never without feeling how great the contrast between itself and Him? What other key have we to the explanation of this phenomenon, than the belief that in Christ there lived an original higher consciousness, which sprang from His unique relation to God, and was continually strengthened by perfect and sinless obedience to His Father?

This is *the most important element* (to speak figuratively) *of that sediment which no critical solution of the life of Christ has ever yet been able to dissolve, and which will baffle all such efforts to the end of time.* The fundamental hypothesis of Schenkel's whole sketch—that Jesus was a mere man—is here seen to be false, because it will not suffice to explain the *facts* of history; above all, it leaves in darkness the central feature of Christ's character, His *peculiar consciousness.*

[1] Uhlhorn, *ubi supra,* p. 58. The details of Strauss' argument, see below.

Before closing this notice of Dr. Schenkel's work, we cannot help alluding to one feature of it, which is particularly repulsive,—we mean the ultra-radical *party spirit* so glaringly manifested in its intemperate language and in its whole tendency. This is painfully evident to the German reader on nearly every page; but those of our English readers who wish to verify our remarks, we would refer to such passages as pp. 33, 41, 44, 58 et s., 76, 77, 92, 202, 234. All these and many others give this book the character of a violent party attack on all orthodox Christian belief and Church government,—an attack which invidiously imports descriptions and even epithets of ecclesiastical phenomena from the present day into the history of the past, thus taking away well-nigh all its value as a historical work. We cannot wonder that these defects, combined with its undecided, semi-rationalistic, semi-mythical character, have procured for the book a condemnation from critics of well-nigh all shades;[1] and we may safely predict, that ere long its influence will have died away.

These remarks do not apply to the book which it is now our turn to consider,—a book which is to a considerable extent the pattern of Dr. Schenkel's work, but which greatly excels it in strictness of logic and delicacy of delineation,—we mean *The Life of Christ* by Strauss. The name of David Friedrich Strauss brings us to the *mythical theory*, and, as this is one of the chief defences of modern scepticism, we must devote a little more time to it than to the others.

III.—STRAUSS' "LIFE OF CHRIST."

First of all, let us see *what was the origin of this standpoint.* Long before Strauss, men had begun to compare heathen mythologies with biblical narratives, and to conjecture that there might be some truths contained in the mythological fables, and some fables in the biblical history. Schelling discovered that all primitive history, proceeding from a time when writing was as yet unknown, especially if it contain

[1] Cf. Luthardt, *Die modernen Darstellungen des Lebens Jesu*, p. 46; and Uhlhorn, *ubi sup.*, p. 67.

miraculous elements, must be a myth, *i.e.* a legend or fiction. It was especially De Wette who proceeded to apply this principle to the Old Testament, and who promulgated the general rule, that where any record relates inconceivable things in good faith, it is to be considered not as historical, but as mythical. Others soon began by the light of this maxim to investigate New Testament history, impelled, too, by newly-arisen critical doubts as to the genuineness of the Gospels. The inward motive of these researches was the rationalistic axiom that the miraculous is impossible. This was accompanied by the influence of recent philosophy, which dissolved the person of our Lord into a universal principle, and evaporated His incarnation, death, and resurrection into a number of universal, eternal, and spiritual truths. Thus, in their subjective idealistic view of the world, these systems calmly sail away over all historical testimonies, and regard the biblical history as a sacred mythology sprung from active religious fancy.

This is the view represented by Grohmann, who wrote in 1799 on "Revelation and Mythology." He maintains that the ideas current among the Jews had long beforehand settled what Christ, *i.e.* the Messiah, was to do. But Jesus Christ, as a historical individual, did not correspond to the expectations of the Jews. Not even that, in which all accounts agree, is a matter of fact; the people's contributions formed a popular idea of His life, and from this popular idea His history was made. Here we have *the whole theory of Strauss and his followers enunciated thirty-six years before the first edition of Strauss'* Life of Christ *appeared.*

The principle of these critics is, that *the Gospels in the main consist of unintentional fictions as to the person of Christ, produced by the imagination of the first Christian churches, mostly in accordance with former Jewish predictions and expectations of the Messiah.* Christ Himself, they say, gave people the impression of His Messiahship through the power of His word and spirit only, without yielding to their craving for miracles. And thus the apostles and the primitive Church regarded and preached Him. It was not until His life lay far behind them that the following generations, from a want of historical feeling, though on the whole in good faith, began involuntarily to form legends, relating such outward wonders as were expected of Messiah, and to *apply* them to Christ. These legends were received without suspicion by our evangelists, who were men of the second century, and by them incorporated in the gospel narrative.

We now see the distinction between the principle of Rationalism and that of Mythicism. The former left a historical remainder after eliminating the miraculous element from the gospel narratives. This remainder is, for the most part, given up by the mythical treatment, and the Gospels are considered as productions of the religious imagination, clothing religious ideas in a quasi-historical, though really legendary garb. Of course, a certain amount of original fact is conceded even by this theory, and in this respect there is only a difference of degree between it and Rationalism, since its negations go a step further. Both agree entirely as regards the denial of the miraculous. But the mythical theory does not labour to give a natural explanation of the miracles. It acknowledges that no straightforward exposition can remove them from the gospel history, because the New Testament writers themselves believed in them; therefore it simply relegates them to the realm of legend; as Strauss[1] puts it: "We leave the writers in undisturbed enjoyment of their miracles; but we ourselves regard them as mere myths."

The first edition of Strauss' *Life of Christ* appeared in 1835 in 2 vols., and was written for the learned world. Its novelty consisted in the universal application of the mythical principle to the *whole* gospel history, and not merely the miracles of Christ, thus giving the finishing stroke to this theory by carrying it out to its last consequences.

We will now follow Strauss in his explanation of the origin of these myths. Without further inquiry, he states that during the reigns of Augustus and Tiberias certain *Messianic expectations* were rife amongst the people of Israel, who imagined that their Messiah would be a political liberator, and expected Him to perform still greater miracles than those related in the Old Testament. And what happened? In the reign of Tiberias there appeared an ascetic named John, who preached repentance, and baptized those who professed it

[1] *Leben Jesu*, edition of 1864, p. 146; cf. p. 23.

(sec. 45). Amongst his disciples there was a Galilean Jew, named Jesus, who was baptized amongst the rest (sec. 49); and when John had been put into prison, this man continued and developed his work. He conceived the idea of effecting a moral regeneration of the people by means of his teaching, and hoped for a supernatural interference on the part of God, by means of which the old kingdom of David should be again restored (i. 520). This perfectly corresponded to the long-cherished Messianic ideas of the people (p. 521), and thus it occurred to his followers, that he himself was probably the Messiah. At first he was alarmed at this idea (p. 497), but he gradually raised himself to believe it (p. 503). The hatred of the ruling priestly party, however, brought him to the cross.

This is, in short, the historical account of the life of Christ, as Strauss gives it in his book of 1835. This was the nucleus which was gradually encrusted by the present mass of legends and fictions in the following manner. After the first shock of Christ's death had passed away, the disciples felt the psychological need of reconciling the contradiction between the last fate of their master and their former Messianic hopes. On searching in the Old Testament, they found many passages which spoke of servants of God who were tormented to death, and these, by dint of their bad exegesis, they applied to the sufferings of Messiah. Thus the belief gained ground in them, that Jesus was fore-ordained to suffer and die *in this very capacity of Messiah;* they were enabled to retain their former opinion of him, and "the shamefully killed Christ was not lost, but left to them" (ii. p. 638). Christ, according to their idea, had now entered into his glory. "But how could he neglect to send thence a message to his followers? How well can we conceive that in the case of certain individuals, and especially of women, these feelings should have been subjectively excited so as to produce real visions; or, on the other hand, in the case of whole assemblies, that some visible or audible object, perchance the aspect of an unknown person, should produce the impression of an appearance of Christ!" Thus originated the legend of Christ's *resurrection.*

This was the impulse for the formation of further myths. Since the disciples preached that Christ had risen from the dead, the Jews asked whether he had done any *miracles*, as this was a necessary attribute of the Messiah. The more the disciples became convinced of this necessity, the more they made themselves believe that Jesus must have performed miracles, only they could not have seen them rightly. And so, in their enthusiastic fancy, without intending to deceive, they began to adorn the simple picture of Christ with a rich garland of miraculous tales, especially applying to him all the characteristics of the Messiah who was predicted and hoped for, till at length the real history was entirely covered, and, in fact, destroyed by these "parasitic plants" (second edit., p. 621). Many sayings of Christ were converted into miracles. "There was no rest for a word or a figure of speech in primitive Christian tradition, until, if possible, it had been developed into the story of a miracle" (p. 514). When Jesus said that he would make his disciples fishers of men, tradition transformed this into the miraculous draught of fishes (sec. 70 et ss.). When he declared that an unfruitful tree should be cut down, this became in course of tradition the story of the withered fig-tree (sec. 104). Especially did this restlessly inventive tradition apply all the miraculous features which could be discovered in *Moses and the prophets* in a magnified form to the life of Christ. Because the hand of Moses and likewise his sister Miriam had been leprous and become clean again, and because Elisha had healed a leper, therefore Christ must also have healed lepers (ii. 52). Because Moses changed water into blood, Christ must improve it into wine (i. 220). Because the former fed the people with manna in the wilderness, Jesus must have fed the people in the wilderness too; and because Elisha fed one hundred people with twenty loaves (1 Kings iv. 42–44), the proportion must be enhanced in the case of Christ, and hence five loaves for five thousand people (ii. 205). Because Elisha made one man see, and many others blind (2 Kings vi.), it was thought probable that Christ should have healed the blind (ii. 2). Because Elisha healed Naaman without being present at his washing, it was necessary that the Messiah should not do less (ii. 111 et ss.): hence the legends about the centurion of Capernaum, and the Syro-Phœnician woman, both of them cures effected at a distance. The Jews believed in a co-operation of the

Holy Ghost in the begetting of important men, and the first Christians literally interpreted Psalm ii. 7: "Thou art my Son: this day have I begotten Thee," as well as a number of passages in Isaiah: hence the myth that Christ was the Son of God, supernaturally conceived without sin. This is very similar to the belief of the heathen, that their great men were sons of the gods; as, too, their legends relate miraculous stories about the birth of Romulus, Hercules, and other of their heroes.

When the analogies of Jewish tradition are insufficient, such instances from heathen mythology are often appealed to. Thus, *e.g.*, to explain the darkening of the sun at the death of Christ, Strauss says: "This was in fashion then; did not the sun do the same, in the Roman legend, when Cæsar was murdered, and before Augustus died?" (p. 587.)

In this manner Strauss goes through every feature of the life of Christ, and explains them one after another as the products of tradition, which was taken either from Old Testament miracles by combining their different traits, or from Messianic hopes then current, or from analogous heathen legends. All these myths, however, are supposed to have been formed unconsciously and involuntarily. But we see at once that Strauss must presuppose a great deal of *reflective mental action* in the formation of each single myth, and hence that this could only take place *intentionally;* for this reason Strauss of late years has spoken more of "invention with a purpose" (*Tendenzerfindung*). From the rich material of these legends, which were often very different in different places, our four Gospels were composed, not, however, by the apostles, but in the second century.

So much for the principles and the method of Strauss' *Life of Christ*, a work which doubtless owes its world-wide fame in great measure to its polished style and æsthetic finish.

When this work appeared in 1835, it seemed as though the last balance had been struck in the criticism of the gospel history, and the result was—bankruptcy. An electric shock vibrated through the whole German theology. The theological world had not been in such excitement since the days of the *Wolfenbüttel Fragments.* Soon, however, the most notable divines came forward against Strauss, among them Steudel,

Tholuck, Neander, Ullmann, Dorner, and Ebrard; whilst others, such as Weisse, Gfrörer, Bruno Baur, endeavoured to carry out the mythical hypothesis in their own way. For a time, Strauss defended himself; but after some years he seemed to have spoken his last word, and the controversy was apparently settled. Ullmann, especially, had in his mild but clear way exposed Strauss' weak points.

But in 1864 the book once more appeared; this time, however, with a new address: "For the German People."[1] The times were changed. The principle of publicity had obtained more and more in every department. The public at large was beginning to demand an insight into the doings of the learned world. Formerly Strauss might boast, "Did I try to deprive the people of their faith by means of a popular book?"[2] Now, on the contrary, he thought himself justified in doing this. And why? "Since the great majority of theologians will not hear us, we must speak to the people" (Preface, p. xii). Here, then, he must speak more openly, and we are obliged to him for doing so.

He does not for a moment leave us in doubt as to the *fundamental tendency* of this new edition. "If we wish," says he, "to make progress in religious matters, then those theologians who stand above the prejudices and interests of the profession must go hand in hand with the thinking laymen in the Church. As soon as ever the best among the people have made progress enough to refuse what the clergy still for the most part offer them, these latter will think better of it. When Christianity has ceased to be miraculous, they will cease to be the miracle-men which they have hitherto set themselves up for. They will no longer be able to pronounce blessings, but only to impart instruction; but it is well known that the latter of these occupations is as difficult and thankless as the former is easy and profitable" (p. xii). Therefore, "a pressure must be brought to bear on them by public opinion. But (and this is the only italicised sentence in the whole book) *whoever wishes to do away with parsons in the Church, must first do away with the miracles in religion*" (p. xix).

[1] We quote from the first edition of 1864.
[2] *Streitschrift gegen Steudel*, I. p. 20.

So this work, also, is but the means to a demagogue's ends, though not quite in the same manner as that of Schenkel. "Our ultimate aim is not to ascertain the history of the past, but rather to help the human spirit in future to liberate itself from an oppressive yoke of belief" (p. xiv). Strauss' aim is "not in the past, but in the future" (p. xv). He lays the axe at the root of the miraculous New Testament history, in order that, when this is done away with, the parsons may be abolished too. It is his wish to establish a free Church commonwealth, and to dissolve the different confessions into one great religion of humanity. We scarcely need to point out that this is only the effect of his old grudge against the theologians, who formerly, by their unanimous verdict against him, spoilt his career, and reduced him to the occupation of a literary man (cf. p. xiii). We see that this grudge has rather increased than decreased from the select names, such as "field-mice," "rabble," "vermin," which he bestows upon us biblical theologians (p. 162). Moreover, he declares that it is not worth his while "to fight with such a rabble" as the recent apologists, because "the conservative theology of the present day is wearying itself with the strangest contortions and the most venturesome caprioles," and "its paper battlements do not deserve a real siege;" but yet he promises, "for the sake of the joke, not entirely to give up doing so." In all this, however, he forgets that *haughty contempt for the opponents* is everywhere the worst way to victory.

Attacks of this kind are probably intended as a piquant kind of spice to make the book more popular. But for all this, it is *not popular.* There will be but few readers who are able to peruse it without great omissions. Notwithstanding his promise to leave out learned details (p. xiii), Strauss' book still contains a mass of these details, which are fatiguing enough to go into. Strauss does not possess the same art of writing for the people as his French colleague. He gives too much and too little; too much for the people, even those who are educated, and too little for the professional theologian.

Moreover, the *arrangement* of the matter in this second edition is far too prolix to be interesting, going as it does *twice* through the whole subject. In the first edition, Strauss, after dissolving the life of Christ into a series of myths, merely gave a few positive hints as to what remained of Christianity according to his view; in the second edition, he begins with a positive account of the probable historical nucleus of the life of Christ. Thus the first part contains "a historical sketch of the life of Christ," and the second part, "origin and development of the mythical history of Christ;" first the tree, and then the creepers. But since both are followed out from end to end, there are of necessity many repetitions and constant references backwards and forwards, whilst numerous portions which belong together are separated.

The *first part* rests upon the axiom, that "*we now know for certain at least what Jesus was not and did not do, viz. nothing superhuman nor supernatural.* We shall thus probably be enabled to follow out the hints given in the Gospels as to his natural and human characteristics far enough to obtain an approximately correct outline of what he was and what he wanted" (p. 160 et s.). Strauss leaves as historical only what is in accordance with the course of nature at the present day, what would seem necessarily to result from the relations of Jewish and Gentile humanity at that time, and that in which all the evangelists strictly agree. All else is rejected, or at least impugned. Thus negations form the chief element even of this "positive" part. It can easily be imagined how little remains that is historical; much the same as in the former edition. Jesus, the son of a carpenter, was born in Nazareth, and not in Bethlehem, whither Luke transports him by means of "special machinery."[1] "He was induced by what he

[1] Pp. 323, 335, et ss.,—meaning, of course, the taxation in Luke ii. 1 et ss. It was an absolute necessity for the son of David somehow to be born in Bethlehem. As the writer of St. Luke's Gospel "was cudgelling his brains for an expedient which should bring the parents of Christ to Bethlehem, in order that he might be born there, this taxation occurred to him" (p. 336). But in adding, "When Cyrenius (*i.e.* Quirinus) was governor of Syria," he made a blunder of some six or seven years, for Quirinus did not become proconsul till so many years later on; and thus the unhistorical character of his narrative is betrayed. Strauss assures us that since 1835 he has "corrected and supplemented his results, according to the fruits of further investigations both by himself and by others" (p. xiii). Does he, then, know nothing of the fact that the investigations made as to this imperial taxation under Augustus have proved that Quirinus was *twice* proconsul? As early as 1854, Dr. Zumpt (in his work *Commentationum epigraphic. ad antiquit. Rom. pertinentium*, vol. ii.) showed from profane sources that Quirinus was proconsul in Syria not only from the year 6 A.D., but

heard of the Baptist to resort to Jordan, for he, too, was dissatisfied with the existing religious institutions" (p. 195); and he probably remained for some time amongst the followers of John. The silence of the Gospels is no proof against this (!), since they sought to avoid even a transitory subordination of Christ to the Baptist for dogmatic reasons. "Both of them aimed at the moral elevation of their people, and at the creation of a people's church, which should be worthy to receive the coming Messiah in its midst" (p. 196). John, however, "chiefly employed sharp denunciation and threats of divine judgment," whilst Jesus used only love. "For the highest religious sentiment which existed in his consciousness was that love which embraces all, and overcomes evil itself only with good, and this he transferred to God as the chief attribute of His Being" (p. 207). Hence His precepts in the Sermon on the Mount respecting tolerance, love to brethren and to enemies. "If any saying of the New Testament proceeded from the mouth of Christ, assuredly Matt. v. 45 did so ('He maketh His sun to rise on the evil and on the good,' etc.). This is a fundamental trait in the piety of Christ: he felt and conceived his heavenly Father as indiscriminate Goodness" (p. 206). Inasmuch as Christ, in this temper of humane love, felt Himself to be united with His heavenly Father, all His happiness sprang therefrom. "By developing in himself this cheerful frame of soul, at peace with God and in love with all men as brothers, Christ had realized the prophetic ideal of the

also once before, from the year 4 B.C. (It is well known that the precise year of our Lord's birth is uncertain; probably it is really some years earlier than our account makes it.) The last work of Zumpt (*das Geburtsjahr Christi; geschichtl. chronolog. Untersuchungen*, 1869) is a brilliant testimony to his learning, and arrives at the same conclusion as historically indubitable (pp. 43, 71). St. Luke himself only says that Christ was born at the time of that taxation, which was *the first under Quirinus*, in contradistinction to other similar ones; and he gives us the occasion of it, which consisted in an imperial edict issued long before. "The record of Luke gains full historical probability from the fact that the *second* taxation (of which Josephus tells) applied only to *property*, which according to Jewish law should necessarily be completed by a taxation of *persons* (or poll-tax), and that no fitter time can be fixed upon for this than the first proconsulate of Quirinus." The murder of the innocents at Bethlehem is also historical (p. 227 ff.). In Luke iii. 1, "the fifteenth year of Tiberius" is reckoned from his appointment to the co-regency of the provinces and armies, as was often done. "Thus all contradictions between the data of St. Luke and other writers are removed."

new covenant, with the law of God written in the heart; he had received the Deity into his will, and therefore for him the Deity had descended from Its eternal throne. This cheerful and unbroken spirit, acting out of the gladness and joy of a beautiful soul, we may call the Hellenic element in Christ. The pure spirituality and strict morality of his own heart's impulses, and of his idea of God, was a legacy of the Jewish national spirit; the result of his bringing up in the law, and his education in the prophets" (pp. 207, 208).

Strauss rightly rejects the opinion that Jesus merely accommodated Himself to the Messianic idea of the Jews. "In this case there can be no question of accommodation or of playing a part; in such a person every inch must have been conviction." For this reason he approves of Schleiermacher's saying, that "Christ must have been convinced from the depths of his inward consciousness that no one else but he was referred to in the Messianic prophecies contained in the sacred writings of his people" (p. 229). But Christ never represented himself to be the son of God in a unique superhuman sense.[1] In contradistinction to the Messiah as Son of God, Christ especially loved to call himself the son of man, a term which pointed to his natural humanity (p. 228). The fourth Gospel contains the fewest genuine traces of the religious consciousness of Christ. For "no man with a sound head and heart, whoever he were, could have spoken of himself in the way that does the Jesus of this Gospel" (p. 201). It is, however, certain that Christ connected the epoch of the world's consummation with a miraculous change to be produced by God, and that He spoke of His second coming in glory to judge the world. But in this respect "he appears to us not only as an enthusiast, but as guilty of undue self-exaltation" (pp. 241, 242).

As for *miracles*, not only did Christ never perform any, but neither did He ever say that He had. In Matt. xi. 5 only the *spiritually* blind and lame, etc. are referred to (p. 265; and yet even Strauss confesses that "the works of Christ," ver. 2, refer to His miracles). "However, it was little use for Jesus to refuse to do corporal miracles: according to the idea of his contemporaries and co-patriots, he must needs per-

[1] Cf. our refutation of this statement in Lect. IV. pp. 245-251.

form them *nolens volens.*" As a prophet, He was expected to possess miraculous power. When sufferers everywhere (?) tried to touch His garments, because they expected healing from Him, "it would have been strange if there had not been some cases of real cure or momentary alleviation, resulting from the intense impression, partly sensuous and partly spiritual, on an excited imagination; and these cures were, of course, ascribed to the miraculous power of Christ" (p. 226). Cures of this kind, through excitement of the imagination, were especially possible in the case of a sickness "which itself greatly depended on the imagination, and which was fashionable amongst the Jews at that time, viz. demoniacal possession." Relapses, of course, could not fail to appear in "fancy cures" such as these. At these miracles Strauss draws the boundary line of the historical region, and entirely banishes all the greater miracles, such as increasing the bread, changing the water into wine, raising the dead, into the realm of legend; because here "all conceivableness according to the laws of nature is at an end" (p. 267). Clearly this is a distinction between miracles of healing (as naturally explicable doings) and works of absolute omnipotence, similar to that of Schenkel (p. 362). Yet Strauss says (p. 33): "It is not permissible to make a distinction amongst miracles, and to accept those which show an analogy with natural occurrences, while rejecting others as magical, for every miracle is magical." How can he speak so, seeing that those who thus distinguish, like Strauss himself, do not consider the former class as miracles strictly speaking? What right has he to be so indignant at the rationalistic explanation of miracles practised by Schenkel and others, when he himself uses the old rationalistic arts of explaining away miracles by means of "excited imagination," and so forth?

Strauss has a very poor opinion of the disciples. Their dreams about a restoration of the kingdom of Israel (Luke xxiv. 21 and Acts i. 6) "give us a very small idea of their powers of comprehension." Their stubborn prejudice against the admission of Gentiles into the Messianic kingdom, shows us "that they were incapable of drawing conclusions from their master's principles." The one genuine writing of a disciple in the New Testament, the Revelation of St. John, "gives us a melancholy impression of the imperfect way in which Christ was understood by his most intimate disciple. . . . . The importance given to the subsequent appearance of Paul proves that there was no one amongst the immediate disciples of Christ who was fitted to be his representative, and capable of further developing the ideas of his master in accordance with the wants of the age" (p. 276).

Accompanied by His Galilean followers, Jesus goes to Jerusalem, cleanses the temple, attacks the ruling priestly party most sharply in public speeches, and exhorts the people to turn away from them. Of course all these steps could not but arouse the anxiety of the hierarchs, and move them to get rid of so dangerous an opponent by any means (p. 279). The scene in Gethsemane is certainly "strongly adorned with mythical traits." We cannot imagine that Jesus knew of His death beforehand with exactitude and certainty. Nevertheless during His last days, the thought of a violent end probably became more and more familiar to Him, and cast dark shadows on His soul. His death on the cross was real, and not merely apparent (p. 283 ff.). His burial by Joseph of Arimathea is uncertain on account of differences in the narratives; possibly he "was hastily interred in some dishonourable burying-place" (p. 287). According to traditional Jewish ideas, Christ had lost all claim to the title of Messiah by His death upon the cross. Now, however, "the disciples altered their old Jewish ideas in accordance with this fact, by including the attribute of a vicarious suffering, and of violent death as a redeeming sacrifice, in their conception of the Messiah" (p. 575). We have no testimonies of an eye-witness as to an appearance of the risen Christ (p. 291). Both the appearance of Christ to Saul on his way to Damascus, and all others, "were simply inward occurrences which might well affect the persons in question as outward and objective perceptions, but which we have to conceive of as visions produced by an excited condition of the mind" (cf. Lect. VII.).

This is the "historical kernel" of the life of Christ which Strauss leaves us. We should prefer to call it the shell from which the kernel has been extracted.

The *second part* of his book shows us how the various myths, as it were, crystallize around this nucleus. Along with the belief in the resurrection of Christ, we see the idea of Him "placed in a temperature which could not but result in a luxuriant growth, producing numerous unhistorical shoots, each one more miraculous than the last. The divinely inspired son of David now becomes the son of God, begotten without a father; the son of God developes into the incarnate creative Logos. The philanthropic miraculous physician becomes a raiser of the dead, the unlimited Lord of nature and her laws. The wise teacher of the people, the prophet who saw into men's hearts, now becomes the omniscient *alter Ego* of God. He who after his resurrection returned to God, came from Him before his birth" (p. 161). Thus one layer formed on another, each one being, as it were, the precipitate of the ideas current at a certain time, and in certain circles, till at length the fourth Gospel reached the climax of Christ's deification and spiritualization. Strauss then goes through the whole history of Christ in all its features, representing each one (just as in his former work) as the product of inventive legends. These he supposes to have gathered their materials from the histories of David, Moses, Samuel, and others, or from the writings of the prophets, many of whose sayings they uncritically applied to Christ, or even from the heathen mythology.[1] One cannot help wondering how so stunted a historical shrub could nourish so many mythological parasites.

Thus we see that the standpoint of this edition of the *Life of Christ* is essentially the same as that of the first one, only that now Strauss supposes far more *intentional invention* than formerly in place of the unconscious fabrication of myths. He himself says: "In this new work, I have, chiefly in consequence of Baur's investigations, used the supposition of conscious and intentional invention far more freely than before" (p. 159). At the same time he applies the term "myth" equally to the products of conscious and unconscious invention. *And yet the theories of Strauss and Baur do evi-*

[1] *E.g.* Strauss can find no parallel in the Old Testament to the visit of Jesus as a boy in the temple. He therefore proceeds to drag in by the head and shoulders a legend mentioned by Suetonius, that Augustus when a little child was once suddenly missed from his cradle, and found lying in the highest part of the house. And this he considers an analogy to Jesus remaining in the temple!!

dently exclude each other.[1] Strauss originally proceeds on the supposition of a simple inventive tradition, whilst Baur takes his stand on the relation of parties as at that day, and looks upon the writings of the New Testament as products of a distinct purpose. Strauss' theory assumes the utmost *naïveté* in the writers of the Gospel, Baur's the self-conscious purpose of the resolute partisan. It must make an exceedingly unpleasant impression on every impartial reader, to see how Strauss employs this art which he has learned from Baur by fathering upon narrators so simple and true-hearted as our evangelists such dogmatic presuppositions, conscious fictions, crafty intentions, ay, finely calculated lies.

The whole *style* of this book, except that of the preface, will disappoint the reader who considered Strauss to be a master of the art of delineation. Nowhere is there a life-like development, or an exciting progress, not even so much as in Schenkel's work. The various sections have no vital connection, even in the "positive" part; they stand side by side like abstract heads. They read like *so many critical treatises*, but not as a life-like delineation. The narrative is like a stuffed figure without flesh and blood: instead of being full of life, it is replete with marks of interrogation; instead of presenting a vivid and concrete reality, it merely leaves a few probabilities. Nowhere do we see—to say nothing of the Son of God—even the man Jesus, the Prophet of Nazareth as He walked and lived amongst men. A constant and wearisome sifting of the records only leaves us detached fragments of His person, His consciousness, His life, and His work. No sooner is a step made towards a description of actual history, no sooner have we entered on the oasis of some living reality, than straightway the ground beneath our feet again begins to rock, and we once more see before us the sad and sandy wastes of the mythical desert. Surely at that time, if ever, when the central figure of all history was walking upon earth, the pulse of history must have beat strongly. But instead of the fresh air of a world-renewing history, which breathes so sensibly in the Gospels, we have in this book the odours of a grave. Instead of the mighty hammers of an age that is being built up afresh,

[1] Though Zeller (in *Vorträge u. Abhandlungen geschichtl. Inhalts*, 1865) endeavours to combine them.

we hear only the monotonous creaking of the critical windmill, which, for the smallest differences, is grinding the gospel narratives into pieces against each other. We need not expect anything else, for the writer himself confesses that "the *negative* element is of primary importance." So that when we read a treatise on the "scene and duration of the ministry of Christ," the matter itself is described in a few sentences only; or when we read about "Christ's manner of teaching," we are told almost nothing about the doctrine itself, for even the parables of the first three Gospels are almost without exception crumbled away by criticism. Were we to eliminate the whole of the critical apparatus, there would be but few leaves of this thick volume left. And yet this is supposed to be a historical sketch "for the German nation!"

Strauss prefaces his work with a *critique of the Gospels* as records of the life of Christ, in which he comes to the conclusion that all our four Gospels are *spurious*. He makes a lengthy effort to support this assertion, but without doing justice to the present standpoint of criticism, for which reason our best authorities now condemn this performance as behind the age. Strauss simply accepts and argues from the positions of the Tübingen school. Unlike Schenkel, he considers the Gospel of St. Matthew, not indeed as the work of the apostle, but yet as the "most original and relatively credible" (p. 115) of the four, although it has probably undergone many revisions. St. Mark "made up" his Gospel from extracts taken out of Matthew and Luke, putting in here and there some fresh and vivid additions as a kind of "beauty spots" (p. 132). The Gospel of Luke was written between those of Matthew and Mark, *i.e.* before the year 135, but at a time "when it was scarcely possible that a companion of St. Paul should have been living and writing books." It only received Luke's name for the sake of the Acts (itself an unhistorical partisan fiction) (pp. 126, 127). The Gospel of John was composed far later in the course of the second century, and this in accordance with the conclusions of Baur, who regards it as a party production, without the slightest historical credibility. Strauss makes no secret of his contempt for this Gospel, nor indeed for the three others. He criticises them all, and especially the Gospel of St. John, with the most profane levity.

But with all this assumption of superiority, Strauss is some twenty-five *years behindhand* in his critical standpoint, and seems to feel this himself. He is so for this simple reason, that *the "Tübingen school,"* whose old theories he desperately clings to, *has in that time been compelled to make some very large concessions.* Baur himself first placed the Gospel of St. Matthew between the years 130 and 134, then in the year 115, and at last 105–110. According to C. R. Köstlin, this Gospel, in its present form, originated between 90 and 100; in its original form, between 70 and 80. According to Hilgenfeld, probably the most distinguished of Baur's disciples, it was composed in its present form certainly before the year 80; according to Holtzmann and Keim, before the destruction of Jerusalem, *i.e.* cir. A.D. 66. You see how the critical school has drawn back from its earlier positions. The Gospel of St. Mark has these various dates assigned to it: Köstlin, before 110; Keim, 100; Hilgenfeld, before 100; Volkmar, 73; Schenkel (in its original form), between 45 and 58. The Gospel of St Luke: Baur, 150; Zeller, 130; Hilgenfeld, before 120; Volkmar, 100; Köstlin (*vide* above), shortly before Matthew; Keim, 90; Holtzmann (with Mark), 75–80. Even as regards the Gospel of St. John, the critical school has had to retire step for step from Baur's calculation (160) to the beginning of the second century,[1] at which time John was probably still living. Amongst other distinguished men, Ewald sharply criticises the Tübingen school. He considers that Mark wrote soon after the death of Peter; the Gospel by Matthew was written before the destruction of Jerusalem (70); the Gospel by St. Luke, between 75 and 80. These are the results of criticism up to the present day. We would only stop to take exception to the statement made by Zeller and others, that the first churches would not feel the need of written records until after the apostolic generation had died out. Surely it is far more likely that this want should be felt while the apostles were still living, because they could

[1] Keim (*Jesu von Nazara*, p. 146) dates it from 100–117. Cf. against Keim and Scholten the excellent *Commentary on St. John* by Godet; also his work, *Prüfung der wichtigsten Kritischen Streitfragen über das vierte Evangelium* (1866); also Riggenbach, *Die Zeugnisse für das Ev. Johannis* (1866); van Oosterzee, *Das Johannisevangelium* (1867); and Leuschner, *Das Evang. St. Johannis u. seine neuesten Widersacher* (1873).

not be in all the churches at once to watch over the purity of tradition. But in the case of gospel records being written by others, we must always suppose them to have been directed and controlled by the apostles.

Thus we see that Strauss stands very much alone in his critical position, and that even the *most negative* portion of the critical school is shaking the ground under his feet. It is becoming more and more difficult for Strauss to maintain that his "myths" were formed during the post-apostolic age, since even the critical school itself acknowledges the existence of gospels, *i.e.* of extensive miraculous records, *in the apostolic age*, so that their writers, whoever they were, must have been contemporaries of friends and disciples of Jesus. In our day there is scarcely a single notable critic who would dare to deny that there were not numerous narratives of miracles performed by our Lord in circulation amongst the *first* Christians, which formed the basis of their testimony for His Messiahship, and that without contradiction from the apostles. Let us take note of this for the present. A hundred years after a man's death a legend about him may easily originate; but how, if his contemporaries relate it?

Having thus become acquainted with the work of Strauss in its general outlines, we will now proceed to *investigate* it: first, its *principles*, presuppositions, and method; then the *historical possibility of the formation of myths*; and last, its view of the *person and the self-testimony of Christ*.

In a recent pamphlet,[1] as in his former *Life of Christ*, Strauss has confessed with praiseworthy candour that his "former standpoint was that of the Hegelian philosophy." Nor is this otherwise now. The principle which governs the whole work is that of *Pantheism*. Strauss plainly enough indicates that he believes neither in a personal God, nor in the immortality of the soul, nor, of course, in retribution after death. To him the words apply, that "whosoever denieth the Son, the same hath not the Father" (1 John ii. 23). In the dedication at the beginning, he praises a deceased friend because he "never yielded to the temptation of deceiving himself by borrowing from another world" (p. 10). For his own part he renounces the hope of dying "happy," and only hopes to die "quietly"

[1] *Die Halben u. die Ganzen*, p. 42

(*ubi sup.*). For God is that "indiscriminate Goodness" which "rains upon the just and upon the unjust". (p. 206), before which the small distinctions that we make between good and evil are dissolved into one—all true signs of Pantheism.[1] Hence the pleasure which Strauss takes in those sayings of Christ which can be explained in this sense (p. 206 et s.), whilst he abhors the numerous passages which speak of a future retribution, or of Christ as Judge of the world (pp. 242, 276, 513, et s.). The former class of passages may stand as genuine and true; the latter must be either later additions springing from dogmatic presuppositions, or else serious tokens of fanaticism and self-exaltation in Christ. Thus Strauss explains the beatitudes which Christ promises for a *future* world, as applying to *this life.* In "transferring the realization of this blessedness to heaven, Jesus speaks according to the notions of his age and of his nation." In truth this blessedness simply means, that the new spiritual life which has been awakened in mankind is to shape the outward world in unison with itself, and this takes place naturally and little by little, though never perfectly, in *this* world, and is expected in the next as a wonderful compensation only by religious fancy (p. 205). The salvation of man is, "in more intelligible language, the possibility that he should fulfil his destiny, develope the powers implanted in him, and thus enjoy the corresponding measure of happiness" (p. 624). These sentiments will confirm what I have already remarked (p. 137), that the entire conflict in the present day as to the person of Christ springs from certain fundamental differences in the *idea of God*, and that the negative critics of the gospel history have in reality no other aim than to introduce into the Christian Church a new pantheistic conception of God. This is the "*forward* aim" of Strauss' book (p. xv). At the same time it is also evident that we were perfectly justified (p. 287) in representing the denial of the miraculous as leading to the destruction of all religion. For what profit is there in religion

[1] Compare the blasphemous way in which Strauss excuses the sins of Israel against Jehovah (p. 168): "After both of them had entered into a covenant, *either side soon had cause for complaint against the other;* there was not much to be felt of the special protection which Jehovah had promised to His Israel!!" etc. etc.

if there be no personal God, and no other world? This view of the world, it is true, would fain give itself the appearance of rendering man truly energetic by making him depend only on himself. But this is a lie. By depriving him of all supernatural help, it paralyses his powers and takes away his moral energy. Gœthe truly says, "*they who expect no other life, are for this life already dead.*"

The first consequence of these pantheistic principles of Strauss, is the *pre-established negation of all that is supernatural* either in the person or in the work of Christ. The sentiment above quoted, that "we know for certain at least what Christ was not and did not do, viz. nothing superhuman nor supernatural," decides the whole question, and settles the method of investigation beforehand. War is declared against everything in the works or words of Christ, which betrays a trace of God's special influence, or of His higher nature; all such elements must be got rid of at any price. This is the assumption with which Strauss sets to work. He so often speaks slightingly of "dogmatic presuppositions," and he himself *approaches his task with the largest presupposition of all*, with an axiom which decides the result of all his investigations beforehand. What is the real pivot of the entire controversy, if it be not the Godhead of Christ? If a man claim to write a life of Christ, the reader, and especially the "German people," may well demand that he should closely investigate this cardinal question. But what does Strauss do? He simply cuts short the whole matter by a bold assertion! *Just the most important point which ought to have been investigated and established is not examined into, but simply taken for granted.* Strauss knows for certain that it is so, and that is enough! And are we to accept this as criticism, as unbiassed historical investigation? "*We know for certain* that there was nothing supernatural in Christ:"—Strauss utters these words with an assurance which reminds us of the language of those who, when Christ was upon earth, thought they "knew for certain" that He was not from God. "We know that this man is a sinner." Strange, Strauss is especially fond of abusing the "priestly caste;" but it does not occur to him that in this self-contented "we know," he is speaking the language of the proudest "caste" that ever existed!

Strauss does make an effort, though an utterly unsuccessful one, to verify his opinion as to the spuriousness of our Gospels. But *in no place does he make a serious attempt to justify his denial of the supernatural or his aversion to the miraculous.* From the very beginning he professes his adherence to that view of the world which, "renouncing all supernatural sources of help, throws men on their own resources, and those of the natural order of things" (p. ix.). He proclaims his intention "to remove the delusive belief in miracles as the chief stumbling-block in the antique forms of religion" (p. xviii). When we inquire on what grounds he considers himself justified in so doing, we are merely told that one can "soon discover thus much about our Gospels, that neither one nor all of them possess sufficient historical certainty to compel our reason to give up its liberty so far as to believe in miracles" (p. xv.). "All philosophical systems which deserve the name, agree in one conclusion" [*i.e.* the negation of the miraculous (p. 147)]. This he boldly asserts, though surely well aware that many great philosophers and naturalists have defended, and still are defending, miracles (cf. p. 289). But Strauss is satisfied with his own assertions, and considers himself exempt from the trouble of further examining into his principles. For if, he urges, we allow of miracles in the times of primitive Christianity, we must concede that they are possible in any other religious region. Just as if there were not an immense intrinsic distinction between the two. Thus one problem only remains for Strauss, how the miraculous, this "foreign element which repels all historical treatment," may be removed from the gospel narratives? The only solution offered is the mythical hypothesis.

This therefore is merely a means for getting rid of the miraculous; as Strauss himself expresses it, "an apparatus for evaporating miracles into myths" (p. 159). All the labour expended on it becomes aimless and worthless, if the miraculous be—as we have seen in the last lecture—well grounded. All the more should this question have been thoroughly examined into by Strauss, instead of which he expects us simply to *presuppose* its impossibility.

We now see how Strauss' whole hypothesis, like all other pantheistic systems, *begs the question,* and postulates what most requires proof. This was the case, as we have seen, with Spinoza, and with those deniers of the miraculous who, like Strauss, have made the laws of nature an argument against the possibility of miracles. The fact that the Gospels contain so much that is miraculous, is for Strauss the fundamental proof of their mythical character. He is not driven to this conclusion by historical investigations, but simply by a naturalistic presupposition. He asks whether the Christian religion and its historical records are in agreement with our modern philosophy, or whether they are not rather proved to be unhistorical by their contradiction to it. It was the standpoint of the old world to regard as miraculous any unusual alterations in the world of nature and of man; but our modern age knows that all things are connected in one great chain of cause and effect, and that this chain cannot be broken without being destroyed. This it is which we have shown to be a complete delusion. The Jews are supposed to have had no historical consciousness, because they believed in the miraculous. *Either*, true historical perception, and no miracles; *or*, an acceptance of the miraculous, and unhistorical, simply dogmatic position—this is the fundamental dilemma which Strauss places before his readers. But what gives him any right to do so? Nothing but his own presupposition, his naturalistic bias which makes our ordinary everyday life the criterion of all reality! For in the last resort the cardinal question may prove to be, *whether the miracles themselves are not historical*, and their denial utterly unhistorical—a mere philosophical delusion. Is it, we ask, a sign of "historical consciousness" for a man not to give the old records a thorough and unbiassed examination according to their inward and outward credibility, but to approach them with the settled axiom, that there can be no such thing as a miracle: thus condemning beforehand all that does not agree with this axiom? By so doing, Strauss plainly shows *that he is no true historian*, which, indeed, no thorough-going disciple of Hegel ever can be. *He searches the records, not in order to find out what they are and what they contain, but in order to extract proofs from their miraculous narratives and individual discrepancies, that they are not what they profess to be, viz. not history, but myths; in other words, he goes to work in order to get proofs for his assumption.* On such a method even a critic like Schwegler remarks: The attempt to solve historical problems by means of philosophical categories must always fail; Strauss has sullied the purity of historical research by importing into the critique of the Gospels his presupposition as to the impossibility of the miraculous under the guise of a philosophical postulate. Hence it is that in the works both of Strauss and Schenkel we find the same *subjective caprice* in eliminating the spurious from the genuine, only that Strauss makes a more consistent use of the myth, as being the means which he has selected for this purpose.

This extreme caprice is palpably evident, as soon as we look at the *method* more closely. In the most paltry and exaggerated manner he scrapes together differences in the narratives of the evangelists, in order to show their legendary character, apparently proceeding from the assumption that the Gospels were intended to be exact chronological biographies, which is far from being the case. Small differences and omissions are magnified into great contradictions. *E.g.* the statement of St. John, that Nicodemus brings about 100 pounds of myrrh and aloes to embalm the body of Christ, and of the Synoptics, that the women buy spices, is held up as a great discrepancy and proof of the unhistorical nature of both accounts (p. 598 ff.), because the former quantity would have been more than enough. Just as if love would reckon in this strict way in the case of a dear one who was departed! On the other hand, great differences, which clearly show that two distinct events are referred to, are toned down into small shadings, in order to prove that the legend is relating the same matter in two different forms. Thus, for instance (in imitation of the feat first performed by Zeller), Lazarus of Bethany is identical with Lazarus in the parable, Luke xvi. (p. 479 et ss.); the anointing of Christ in Bethany (John xii.) is one with that in the house of Simon, Luke vii. (pp. 429 et ss.); so, too, the stilling of the storm and the walking on the sea (pp. 489 et ss.), and the two miracles of feeding (pp. 499 et ss.), etc.

In truth, Strauss is a master in the art of straining out gnats and swallowing camels. Repetitions of words are as suspicious to him as those of works, just as if it were not often necessary to repeat certain important truths several times, in order to impress them on the weak and slow comprehension of man. If an evangelist omits to mention some particular, he is put down as not knowing it, and this is adduced as proof of a myth. If one of them describes an incident exactly, this is a progress in the growth of the legend. If a narrative is simple and short, it is "entirely in conformity with the spirit of the original popular legend;" if it goes into details, this exactitude is the clearest proof of a mythical tendency. Poor evangelists! whatever they do is wrong!

The way in which an *intention is scented out* in the invention of the smallest and most trifling features of a story is often perfectly ridiculous. Thus, in the circumstance that John outruns Peter while both are hastening to the grave of Christ, Strauss detects an artfully contrived preferment of John to Peter, an exaltation of the spiritual Johannean Christianity above the Petrine carnality!! (p. 605.) We cannot be surprised at frivolity when a man looks through the spectacles of intentional invention in this manner. In several places Strauss has been unable to resist this temptation, as, *e.g.*, at p. 380, where, in connection with the flight of our Saviour into Egypt, he remarks, "Once more a correct impression as to the origin of the gospel narrative has led the ecclesiastical legend to bring in the *ass* from the Mosaic myth" (cf. pp. 409, 449, 455, 476, 513, 610).

It may be quite true that the events of the New Testament contain a reflection of what had gone before in the Old. But for all that, this constant derivation of the New Testament narratives, down to their smallest details, from incidents in the lives of Old Testament worthies, is simply a monstrous misapprehension of the wise and holy plan of the divine kingdom. Why should what is later have been invented or copied from what is earlier because it bears some resemblance to it? Why should not God be able to carry on His kingdom towards its consummation in a kind of rhythmic historical movement, in which certain events happening at different times and under different laws should yet distinctly correspond? It is just in this that we see the beauty and wisdom of His government, of which, it is true, Pantheism neither has nor can have any notion.

We now come to the principal question as to the *possibility of the formation of myths.* In this respect it is not difficult to point out *a number of historical and psychological impossibilities and internal contradictions* in Strauss' positions.

He will scarcely deny that the soil in which myths grow is the *childhood of nations.* How come myths to spring up so luxuriantly among the Jews at the time of Christ, destitute as their nationality was of all that is childlike, and well-nigh arrived at the hoary goal of its development? Are we to believe that after prophecy had so long been silent, and at a time when the chosen people and the world in general were in a state of spiritless languor, the poetic fancy of a few poor Jews should suddenly have made this mighty effort? The possibility of this is only conceivable on the supposition that there did exist some such personage as the Christ of the Gospels. But we will pursue the inquiry a little further. The childhood of nations is *their prehistoric age, and this age it is in which the formation of myths invariably takes place.*[1] It is before the contrast has been realized between the ideal and the actual worlds, when the spirit of man is still engrossed in the unconscious life of nature,—in a word, in its childhood,—that a nation dreams out its mythology. But as soon as reflection, reason, and conscience awake, the mythical world begins to vanish. See, *e.g.*, how Plato rejects or spiritualizes the Greek myths. In the clear daylight of historical consciousness the formation of myths comes to an end. Some fictitious anecdotes and legends may still attach themselves to the persons of a few great men, but the formation of a whole system of myths is inconceivable in a historic age. And if we contemplate the age in which our Gospels were composed, here assuredly *we find ourselves in a historic, and not a prehistoric period.* Reflection has long since awakened. Indeed, it is an age of great intellectual activity, and even of scepticism (cf. Pilate). Men have long since come to regard the Greek myths as the playful products of a poetic fancy. Is this a period favourable to the formation of myths?

Livy calls *writing* "the faithful guardian of history." And accordingly, we find myths only amongst nations *unacquainted with the art of writing, and consequently without either history*

[1] Cf. Hettinger, *Apologie des Christenthums*, i. 2, p. 236 ff.

or chronology. How different was the case in the apostolic age! Not only had Greece and Rome long possessed their great historians, and Egypt its Manetho, but even Palestine had its Flavius Josephus. Everywhere there was a lively historical, and literary activity, and a quick historical consciousness. How come myths to be formed in an age like this?

The improbability increases when we *compare the character of the gospel narratives with that of myths in other quarters.* Consider "the myths of Greece and Egypt, hovering as they do between memory and invention, between heaven and earth, between God and matter, between the natural and unnatural; consider the gigantic, bloody, monstrous fables concerning the fantastic gods of India; consider the dark, mist-woven forms of the old Germanic and Scandinavian mythology, without fixed outlines or clearly-defined personalities;" and contrast with these the clear, calm, holy, self-contained, self-consistent, and well-defined figure of Christ in the Gospels, and say *wherein lies the slightest resemblance between them?* There, we have the shadowy maze of prehistoric times; here, palpable bright reality on historical soil;—there, heathen deification of nature; here, a revelation of the one personal God;—there, the instinctive action of natural religion and natural life; here, holy and solemn works and words proceeding from a personal mind and will.

Moreover, as being a reflection of the life of nature, myths everywhere bear a *local* and *national* impress. According to the characteristics of people and country, they are differently developed in gladsome Greece, in arid India, and in the inhospitable North. The purport of the Gospels, on the other hand, is *universally human;* it is adaptable to every nation, every clime, every stage of time or cultivation. So little is it exclusively Jewish, that it constantly *contradicts* the prejudices of the nation from which it has originated. The portrait of Christ in the Gospels, instead of being that of a typical Jewish teacher, is *entirely opposed* to what such an one was considered to be.[1]

[1] Cf. Wiseman, *Zusammenhang zwischen Wissenschaft u. Offenbarung*, p. 228 (Connection between Science and Revealed Religion, London 1836, Lect. IV., pp. 255 et ss.). For a description of wise teachers in Israel at that time, *vide* Sepp, *Leben Christi*, ii. p. 47.

Further, it has been objected with truth, that myths know nothing of chronology; they are prone to mix up times, places, and persons. In the Gospels, on the contrary, from Luke i. 5 onwards, we find a series of exact data as to times, places, and persons, and a continuous reference to contemporaneous Roman and Jewish history. In the face of these historical relations, and of the inward opposition between mythical and gospel narratives, must it not, from the very beginning, be a vain undertaking to "evaporate" the latter into myths? But Strauss quietly passes by this important intrinsic distinction, with the remark that "the formation of Christian myths must be put on the same footing with the corresponding process in all other religions" (p. 153).

To all this we add another difficulty of considerable weight, viz. that the formation of myths is always a lengthy process, *requiring considerable time.* Homer's mythical account of the fall of Troy did not appear till some 200 years after the event. But the oldest of our Gospels appeared, as we have seen, before the fall of Jerusalem, *i.e.* hardly a generation after the death of Christ. Therefore a portion of these myths at least must have taken their rise amongst the disciples themselves; nor does Strauss deny that "the resurrection myth" in particular was believed and preached by the apostles themselves. Were these good people so utterly destitute of all historical sense and feeling? Had they not been taught by Christ Himself, in the Sermon on the Mount, in the discourses which Strauss acknowledges as genuine, to distinguish clearly between divine revelation in the law and the subsequent human additions,—between what had been said by them of old time and what is written as the truth of God? Was not this calculated to implant some historical feeling in the disciples, and to sharpen their perception of the difference between firmly established truths and human fictions? Or if the disciples were so simple and superstitious as not to be able to understand their Master, is it not incomprehensible how He came to choose such inefficient men, "who would have spoilt His work entirely if it had not luckily been saved by the unexpected conversion and activity of the Apostle Paul"? But what an unworthy idea does this give us of the progress of man's history, "if Christianity, the most powerful factor in the world's history, is made to depend on an unforeseen and incidental fact!"[1]

Or are we to suppose that the later evangelists are the chief culprits in this mythical and unhistorical introduction, or, in plain English, this lying cheat? To this we reply by the old question which we have already put to the rationalists, How can these biblical records, with their truthful spirit and pure morality, and the glorious ideal which they present to us, have their origin in mere lies? And how could these foolish writers, "who were so strongly biassed by their Jewish prejudices, draw a picture containing none of the *traditional* features common to great Jewish rabbis, but revealing a moral dignity and purity so great that centuries upon centuries have bowed down before it, and from its Original received their life?" "My friend," even Rousseau cried, full of admiration for the portrait of Christ in the Gospels, "such things cannot be invented! Never could Jewish writers have fabricated discourses and moral teachings such as these. The Gospel contains so great, so astonishing and perfectly inimitable traits of truth, that its inventor would be even more wonderful than its Hero."[1] Assuredly, I appeal with confidence to the unbiassed judgment of my readers. Is it possible or conceivable that *sinful* and imperfect men should beget the thought of so majestic and stainless a personage, of so holy and Godlike a life, and should carry it out in this vivid and lifelike manner, not having received it as an impression *from without?* This would be a miracle more perplexing and unheard of than any of those which Strauss rejects, and the whole issue would only be transferred from the person of Christ to that of His historian; in other words, we should by no means escape the miraculous. The old truth still stands; "the *portrait of Christ which is delivered to us;* the faultlessly perfect Original of God-filled humanity cannot have been invented, since that which has never

[1] Cf. Luthardt, *ubi sup.* p. 19.

[2] Rousseau, *Emile*, l. iv. pp. 109–111. Gœthe, too, in his *Gespräche mit Eckermann* (iii. p. 371), says: "I consider the Gospels decidedly genuine, for they are penetrated by the reflection of a *majesty* which proceeded from *the person of Christ;* and this is divine, if ever divinity appeared upon the earth." Cf. also Schaff, *Die Person Jesu Christi* (new edit., p. 302), and especially the remarkable series of testimonies from sceptics and opponents for the character of Christ, pp. 245–336 [English edition (Boston, 1865), pp. 251 et ss.].

entered into the heart of man as an impression cannot proceed from it as a lifelike fancy picture."[1] And does not the fragmentary character of the gospel records give us the impression that the narratives themselves were not capable of delineating this sublime Personage in an adequate manner, and that the reality must have gone far beyond what is told us? (cf. John xxi. 25.)

If the primitive Christian Church invented most of Christ's miracles, and made Him something quite different from what He really was, *why did not unbelievers on every hand protest against this?* Why did they not appeal to the surviving contemporaries of Jesus, or at least to their own immediate ancestors, many of whom must have seen Him, in disproof of all these miracles? Not even the most fanatical opponents of Christianity, such as the Pharisees, or later on, Celsus, Porphyry, Julian, and others, ever impugned the truth of the miracles related in the Gospels. Strauss tries to evade this very evident objection by asking how the unbelief of Israel is to be accounted for if Christ really did so many miracles? But he entirely overlooks the *moral* obstacles to faith. No miracles, nor any other works of God, ever absolutely compel man to believe; they are and they will be like our Lord Himself,—a sign which may be spoken against, clear enough for him who is willing to see, but dark enough for him who will not see nor believe. Else faith would cease to be a *moral* act,—a taking hold of the invisible: it would cease to be faith.

Again, we ask, is it not probable that those who joined the new doctrine, before they took this step, made some *examination* into these miraculous narratives? How could a man break off all connection with his past Judaism or heathenism, without having in some degree satisfied himself that he was not grasping after a shadow, but after living truth and historical reality? *Was it not in the interest of faith itself to know something certain about Christ,* in order to be able to say, "I know in whom I have believed"? (2 Tim. i. 12; cf. Luke i. 4, John xx. 31, 1 Cor. xi. 23, xv. 14–32.) And was not there a possibility of this, because the Christian Church gradually developed from a certain point without essential interruptions,

[1] Cf. Beyschlag, *Christologie*, p. 15; also Weiss, *Sechs Vorträge über die Person Christi.*

and thus it was *easy to trace the narratives of Christ to their source* and test them there? How could the Messiahship of Christ be proved to any one without first proving what He had done? The first thing in the vocation of the apostles surely was to testify of the works of Christ. Where, then, unless the apostles were intentional *deceivers*, is there room for the formation of myths?

And supposing that some myths had formed in the Church, must they not soon have been rejected by the apostles or their disciples, if we take account of the *intimate connection* which the Acts and the Epistles proved to have existed *amongst the primitive Churches?* Strauss prudently ignores this connection, and speaks as though every Church had remained isolated, and had continued to adorn the tradition of Christ in whatever way it pleased.

Strauss is constantly invoking the enthusiastic superstition of the primitive age as the source of myths. But why did not this enthusiastic superstition adorn other persons—*e.g.* the highly-esteemed Baptist—with miraculous garlands? It is by no means permissible to place the apostolic age on a level in this respect with the following period, which stands most palpably below it in spiritual, moral, and intellectual power. But that later *Judaism as such*—and Jewish Christians were the writers of the New Testament—*was not fond of miracles,* is clearly shown by their rare occurrence in the lives of the great prophets from Isaiah downwards. Only where Creator and creature are commingled—as in the case of heathenism—do we find a fertile soil for miracle mania. But where both are kept so entirely distinct as in Judaism, and "the human subject is penetrated with the feeling of God's greatness and its own nothingness, it cannot expect that miracles should take place every instant. It will look on them as something extraordinary, and expect them *seldom* to occur."

This is confirmed by the gospel history. Was not, *e.g.*, the strict examination of witnesses in the judicial inquiry respecting the man who was born blind (John ix.) a token of historical sense and sober inquiry? The age cannot, after all, have been so utterly destitute of these qualities; and should the Christian Church alone, of all other bodies, have been without members who were capable of such examination? Not even the Churches of the second century were entirely void of critical perception. Where there was a question as to the genuineness of certain writings, they could make very exact inquiries. Certain Fathers of the second century made journeys on purpose to get exact information from churches founded by the apostles about some disputed writings, in order afterwards to appeal confidently to this information in their discussions with heretics. A presbyter in Asia Minor who had composed an apocryphal book entitled, *Histories of Paul and Thekla,* was convicted, and confessed his fraud. The Church in Philippi wished to make a collection of the letters of Ignatius († 108), and for this purpose they wrote to Polycarp, Bishop of Smyrna, begging for his assistance, in order that the matter might be more certain.[1] Are not these proofs for the existence of a sober historical investigation in that age, and do they not at the same time witness favourably to the genuineness of our Gospels? And shall we not suppose that this spirit of critical investigation and inquiry was active as regards the oral tradition of the words and works of Christ in the Churches, especially in those of the first century, where such inquiry was considerably easier?

But the *historical* difficulty changes into a still greater *psychological* obstacle. *Must not the enthusiastic fancies of these primitive Christians,* we ask, *have been somewhat cooled down and sobered when the persecutions began? What motive could they have for holding to their delusion in the face of tribulation and death, and in exposing themselves to contumely, mockery, and hatred from Jews and Gentiles for the sake of their imaginary dreams?* But this supposition of extravagant enthusiasm amongst the primitive Christians is entirely incorrect. Beside the Old Testament, they received edification from certain of the apostolic epistles, especially those of St. Paul. But do these or any other of the New Testament epistles give us the impression that their writers were extravagant enthusiasts, or sharp-witted forgers? Does not the clear, simple, temperate, humble style of these writings make just the opposite impression on every unbiassed mind? Does the reading of them have an intoxicating or a sobering effect?

And what do these apostolical writings tell us? Let us look

[1] Cf. Stirm, *Apologie des Christenthums,* 2d ed., p. 25.

at some of them upon whose genuineness there has never rested the shadow of a doubt: the Epistles of St. Paul to the Romans and Corinthians. Does not St. Paul here speak of miraculous powers in the Church (1 Cor. xii. 10–30)? Does he not say of himself, that he brought the heathen into the obedience of faith "through mighty signs and wonders" (Rom. xv. 19), and that *amongst the Corinthians he accomplished the "signs of an apostle" with "wonders and mighty deeds"* (2 Cor. xii. 12; cf. Gal. iii. 5 and Heb. ii. 4),—doubtless, that is, miracles, especially of healing? These passages are a sore perplexity for the deniers of the miraculous, for here there is no time for the formation of myths intervening between the facts themselves and their confessedly genuine records; seeing that the miracles themselves are held up to the original witnesses of them at Corinth! The only resource left to Strauss is to touch on these important historical data as lightly as possible, and then to take a leaf out of the rationalist's book,[1] by reducing these miracles to "merely psychical, or even imaginary cures, which were the natural result of religious excitement in this circle" (p. 268). The visions of a man like St. Paul, who was in perfect spiritual health, and possessed of bodily vigour which could endure the greatest hardships, he accounts for by "convulsive, perhaps epileptic fits" (p. 302)! Such are the shifts to which anti-miraculous delineators of primitive Christianity are put.

We now see how greatly *the miraculous narratives in the Gospels are confirmed* by these sayings of an apostle. If signs and wonders were performed by an apostle in Corinth, may we not, nay, must we not, conclude that similar mighty deeds were likewise done by Christ, or rather that His life and work were accompanied by still greater and more numerous miracles? For the disciple is not above his Master; and as by the evangelists (Matt. x. 1, Luke ix. 1), so, too, by St. Paul (Rom. xv. 18), the apostolic authority and power is always traced back to Christ as its source. Even the belief of the apostles themselves, that they performed miracles, is utterly incomprehensible, unless they—and not only the later Churches—were

[1] So, too, does Baur; but still he confesses that even though Paul may have had an ecstatic element in his nature, yet this was kept so strictly in subjection by the clear rationality of his self-consciousness, that *it could never pass into extravagance.*

persuaded that He, the infinitely greater One, had preceded them in so doing.

Another important argument against the mythical hypothesis and its constant reference to the extravagant spirit of the primitive Christian age, lies in the simple, unadorned, and chaste character of the miracles themselves. *If the spirit of extravagant enthusiasm had woven a garland of myths around the life of Christ, it would have made Him perform miracles quite different from those which the Gospels relate of Him.* There would have appeared "signs from heaven" (Matt. xvi. 1 et ss.), changes in the heavenly bodies, and all other kinds of *fantastic* and *extravagant* portents, and in the end we should have had a *picture of Christ quite different* to that which the Gospels give. The case would have been the same as in some of the later apocryphal gospels, which really do make Christ, as a child, perform so many aimless and ridiculous miracles. Instead of this, look at the *modest measure* of the miracles performed by Christ and the apostles (mostly miracles of healing), their constant *holy purpose*, their *earnest* and *sober character*. This is not the impress of an extravagant fancy. Strauss is prudent enough from the very beginning to place the biblical miracles on a level with those of heathen mythology, magic, and jugglery [1] (pp. 147, 455, etc.), thus making the former fall before the same criticism as the latter. But this is (as we have already shown, cf. pp. 318 and 323) simply an act of violence which entirely ignores *the deep internal distinction between the biblical and the apocryphal miracles.*

And how are the difficulties multiplied when we consider the external and internal contradictions contained in Strauss' portrait of the *Person of Christ!* Here we are utterly at a loss to account for the formation of myths. Strauss' view of the incarnation of God in Christ is, as before, the pantheistic Hegelian. According to Scripture, "in Christ dwelleth all the fulness of the Godhead bodily" (Col. ii. 9); but according to Hegel, God, *i.e.* the "Absolute Idea," can never appear in

[1] Thus Strauss compares the healing of blind men by Christ with a juggling miracle performed by Vespasian before the populace in Alexandria (pp. 269, 429). But it has been proved by P. Cassel (in his pamphlet, *Le roi te touche*, 1864), that this performance of Vespasian's is to be attributed to his contact with Jewish thought; in other words, that it is an echo of Christ's miracles, and *a striking proof of the then wide-spread belief in the miracles of Christ.*

its entire fulness in a single individual, but only in the whole race. Therefore the incarnation of God does not take place in a single individual called Christ, but *universally* and continuously in Humanity as a whole. In a treatise with which he closed his former *Life of Christ*, Strauss characteristically remarks, "As the subject of the predicates which the Church applies to Christ we must posit an idea, but a real one, viz. the idea of the human race." This shows that he denies the specific divine Sonship of Christ. His teaching and His consciousness were but natural products of the preceding ages, the Hellenic and Jewish inheritance of which concentrated themselves in Him. The latter accounts for the purely spiritual and moral tendency of His religious views; the former, for His "spirit of humane love,"—the "cheerful, unbroken action proceeding from the joyous delight of a beautiful soul" (p. 207 ff.). We shall see in Lect. VIII. that these factors are by no means sufficient to explain the whole character of Christianity and its immense effects. But they are not even correctly stated. For the fundamental feature of His life and teaching is not the mild and cheerful Hellenic view of the world, but rather "a perfect concentration on the one highest aim, and an intense conviction that He was called to be a revealer of truth."[1] But according to Strauss, no unique position can be claimed for Christ. As a member in the development of the race, He only marks a special progress in the knowledge of the ideal man. "Every great moral character, every great thinker, has helped to develope the idea of human perfection." Christ stands in the first rank of those who have so done. "He introduced features into the ideal of humanity which before were wanting, or at least had remained undeveloped, the features of toleration, of charity, and of love to man" (p. 625 et ss.); but, on the other hand, his single life, his "merely passive relation to the state," his "visible repugnance" to all trade, his entire neglect of all "that belongs to art and the refinements of life," were "features which remained undeveloped in Christ, and leave marked deficiencies" (p. 626).[2]

[1] Cf. Weizsäcker, *Untersuchungen über die evangelische Geschichte* (p. 347).

[2] This is contradicted on p. 228, where Strauss says that "Jesus presented himself as the friend of men, who thought nothing human beneath his notice, *nothing human foreign to him*, who did not despise harmless human joys," etc.

Against this theory of a universal incarnation of God instead of the individual one, Ullmann (*ubi sup.*) has well argued that although the Revelation of God may progress through all nations and all ages, yet it must strive towards a centre and climax, such as appeared in Christ; and that the Church, in order to be an organism, must have a living Head. Furthermore, in the realm of art great geniuses from time to time appear, in whom the power and beauty of their art is concentrated, such as Homer, Raphael, Mozart. In them the fulness of the idea is to a great extent centred in one person, and so it must be still more entirely with the Godhead in Christ. And this is simply a necessity; for if God indeed be love, then a *perfect* self-revelation and self-communication on His part must take place within the human race which was created in His own image, and this can only be accomplished through Him who is at once the image and Son of God, the Redeemer, and *Head of mankind.* Only in such an One can the holy love of God be satisfied; only in Him can mankind have been the object of eternal predestination and future self-communication. "The idea and the reality of the Holy Son of God and man thus contains the exact opposite of that deprivation for the remainder of mankind, which Strauss and others make it out to be. The whole fulness of God is imparted to others only through Him." [1]

Here we see the fundamental deficiency in Strauss' view of the world; it *ignores the importance of a personality* in the life of history. In Hegel's philosophy all personalities are merely points at which the "ideas" converge, or masks through which the universal spirit looks. And so, too, in Strauss' view, mankind is but a mass of powerless atoms, which together make up a divine-human whole; but not a living *organism,* which, as such, has and must have its climax and its central organ.

Strauss wishes to substitute "*the ideal Christ—i.e.* the original type of man as he should be contained in our reason—*for the historical*" (p. 625); a proof, by the way, how little he cares for historical results from a religious point of view, and that his so-called historical criticism is only a means for the intro-

[1] Compare the article on "The Sinlessness of Christ," in Herzog's *Realencyclopädie,* vol. XXI, p. 210.

duction of his pantheistic principles. This is the way with all speculative philosophy; it invariably treats real history as a secondary matter. So, then, our "saving faith is to be transferred" from a palpable, living historical Person, to an intellectual conception. This is precisely the same *fundamental error* which we rejected in the case of Pantheism, as if an abstract idea which is not typically realized in some personality could of itself gain a hold on men's hearts; as if a mere principle, or even a moral law, could make itself respected and realize itself, unless certain persons endowed with power stood forth as its exponents. These are mere dreams, belied by the civil and religious history of all, and especially of Christian nations. The moral process going on in humanity is surely essentially calculated to develope personality, and is therefore also essentially dependent on the influence of notable moral personages. If the indispensable postulate, that moral goodness should be realized in this sinful world, is not to be given up, this realization must "proceed from an individual in whom goodness itself has become a human person." Our divine sonship can only proceed from the divine Son Himself.

As for what Strauss says in connection with this about a "development of Christ's religion into the religion of humanity," we can only repeat what we have already shown to be the case, that *Christ and His gospel alone* is the one sure and firm exponent, *the only inexhaustible source of all true culture and humanity;* this, and nothing else, not even Hellenicism. We repeat, that to go beyond Christ in the perfection of religion is an utter impossibility; and that to tear the idea of humanity away from the root which has borne it, would be—in spite of any outward varnish—not progress, but the surest retrogression into barbarism, into a dotage of scepticism, of entire subjectivity and selfishness. Christ is not one amongst others of those who have perfected the ideal of humanity; for what a spiritual and moral gulf is there between Him and even such men as Socrates or Moses! He is *Himself this Ideal;* for why else have centuries bowed down before His spiritual and moral dignity and stainless beauty, as before an ever-flowing spring of truth and holiness? That man only can discover "essential deficiencies in this portrait," who has from the beginning taken Him for a mere man instead of the divine Redeemer, and has thus made a false estimate of His character, His life's work, and His whole position in regard to human affairs.

Whereas Scripture subordinates the whole of humanity to Christ, Strauss subordinates Christ to humanity as a whole. According to Scripture, all humanity is gathered together under one Head, even Christ (Eph. i. 10, ἀνακεφαλαιώσασθαι τὰ πάντα ἐν τῷ Χριστῷ; cf. ver. 22 and Col. ii. 10); according to Strauss, this body remains ever headless, and over the unhappy trunk there hovers eternally distant—an ideal! I shall endeavour to show more at length in the last lecture, how all history is turned upside down by such attempts as these to derive Christianity from natural sources.

This entire view, then, runs counter to the representations of Scripture, which make Christ, not the almost accidental point of union for the previously existing germs of religious culture, but the creative centre of Christianity; and we cannot wonder if the picture of Christ drawn by its author is confused and insufficient. Hence the peculiar complaint of Strauss: "About few great men have we such insufficient information as about Christ; the figure of Socrates, though 400 years older, is incomparably more distinct" (p. 621). Indeed, this were passing strange. "No one ever made so great an impression upon mankind as he did; no one has ever left behind him such traces of his work as he; and yet of no man should we know so little as of him, though he belongs not to the dark days of hoary antiquity, but to the clear and open age of history!" (Luthardt, *ubi sup.*) To Strauss, only that which is purely human and imperfect appears clear. Because this evidently appears in the case of Socrates, therefore his figure is clear; but since it does not appear thus in Christ, His shape is indistinct.

In truth it cannot but become so, when men like Strauss and Schenkel are constantly *making historical difficulties,* and importing them into the narratives. According to Strauss, Christ performed *no miracles. But in this case how could the opinion take rise that He was the Messiah?* We are told that, as being a prophet, men attributed to Him miraculous power, and magnified natural cures or alleviations into miracles. But can this have been sufficient to produce that belief? Men expected the Messiah to perform the most extravagant things,

—works at least as great as those of Moses,—indeed, special "signs from heaven;" why, then, did they not rather attribute to Him Messianic signs of this description? And how is it that Jesus invariably refuses to show signs of this kind, when demanded from Him, in proof of His Messiahship (Matt. xvi. 1 et ss.; Mark viii. 11 et ss.; Luke xi. 16; John vi. 30 et ss.), and that He noiselessly performs signs of quite a different sort, and miracles of far more modest dimensions;[1] and yet this belief arises? How is it that He *combats* the carnal Messianic expectations of His disciples and hearers, and gives offence to them by declaring "the kingdom of God cometh not with outward show—it is within you;" and yet this opinion gains ground?

Furthermore, according to Strauss, certain prophetical designations of the Messiah, as "Son of David" and "Son of God," were then current. The first of these designations, however, Jesus never applied to Himself, and the second but seldom, and not without restriction (p. 224 et ss.); He preferred to call Himself by the humble title, "Son of man." Does not this make it all the more difficult to understand whence the belief in His Messiahship could arise, unless those greater miracles (loaves and fishes, raising of the dead, etc.) actually took place? These, we are told, were only gradually invented after the death of Christ, and it was not till then that the belief in His Messiahship began to spread in wider circles. But how did it arise in the disciples? If Jesus did no miracles, and yet was "evidently glad" when the belief in His Messiahship sprang up in the minds of Peter and His most intimate disciples, why did He not honestly disabuse them of the notion that the Messiah must do miracles? Or if He did so, how could the disciples after His death so soon fall back into their old miraculous delusion as to surround His life with such a garland of myths, and that in contradiction to their real experience? Or if they were obliged to do so in order to obtain a hearing from the people, why did they not

[1] According to the most recent investigations, the purport of the Messianic expectations of that age (which Strauss only examines superficially) consisted of miracles such as those of Moses. How far must the miracles of Christ have fallen short of such hopes! Witness, *e.g.*, the disproportion between the feeding of the five thousand and the manna in the wilderness, John vi. 30 et ss.

rather impute to their Master the tremendous miracles expected by the excited fancy of those times, and thus convince the mass of the unbelieving Jewish world of His Messiahship? On every hand this mythical hypothesis entangles us in enigmas.

One thing is perfectly clear, that Christ Himself must in some way or other have given an impulse to the fabrication of myths. Now, we have already seen how much is left of the historical Christ after all the myths are removed. We thus stand before the question, *How is it possible that the mere personal appearance of this simple Galilean Rabbi should have given so great an impulse? The greatest enigma of all is, that this poor skeleton of a life of Christ should ever have been enveloped in such a wealth of myths,* and that Christ, in contradiction to the universal belief in a miracle-working Messiah, should ever have been able to attain this dignity *without performing a single miracle.*[1]

The higher view of Jesus as the incarnate Son and the eternal Word of God, is, we are told, the "last layer in the process of the deification of Christ," and was not developed till the second century. But in the Book of Revelation, which Strauss acknowledges to have been written by St. John, we find Jesus already designated as "the Word of God" (xix. 13); as "the Alpha and Omega . . . . . the Lord which is, and which was, and which is to come, the Almighty" (i. 8). Can we conceive of a higher view of Christ's majesty and glory than that given in the descriptions of the Book of Revelation from beginning to end? If we search the Epistles of St.

[1] Schelling says: "As regards the hypothesis, that the life of Christ was adorned by myths, I suppose every one will admit that only such a life is glorified by myths or legends as has been already in some manner distinguished and moved into a higher region. Now the question is, How did this Jewish country rabbi Jesus become the object of such glorification? Was it in virtue of His teaching! The stones which they took up show how the Jews received this. What, then, is the presupposition which may render so extraordinary a glorification probable? *Only if we grant that Christ passed for what we have recognised Him to be,* is it conceivable that in consequence of this opinion certain 'myths' may have arisen. But if we grant this, we must presuppose the entire dignity of Christ, quite independently of the Gospels. It is not the Gospels which are necessary in order that we may recognise the majesty of Christ, but *it is the dignity of Christ which is necessary in order that we may be able to comprehend these Gospel narratives.*" ("Philosophie der Offenbarung," *Sämmtliche Werke,* Part II. vol. iv. p. 233.)

Paul, which Strauss himself accepts as genuine, we find that Christ is "the Lord of glory" (1 Cor. ii. 8), "the Lord from heaven" (1 Cor. xv. 47), "by whom are all things" (1 Cor. viii. 6), "the image of God" (2 Cor. iv. 4), who existed before His incarnation (1 Cor. x. 4). This higher view of Christ, then, dates from the first century, and from the apostolic circle. *How did the apostles arrive at this view, if Christ was a mere man?*

More than this. That higher view is found in *Christ's testimony respecting His own Person.* Strauss cannot help himself by drawing a line between the discourses of Christ in the fourth Gospel and those in the Synoptics. However much he may critically reject of the sayings of Christ, there will always be enough remaining even in the first three Gospels to confute his view. There will be passages where Christ calls God *His* Father in a perfectly unique sense; where He pronounces Himself to be greater than the temple, greater than Solomon, the Lord of the Sabbath, the Lord of the angels; where He makes Himself the Mediator and Dispenser of the forgiveness of sins; where He strictly distinguishes between His own undefiled conscience and our consciousness of sin; where He attaches to His own work and Person the highest, eternally valid authority in all matters of morals and religion; where He attributes to Himself, and His return in heavenly glory, the last judgment and the consummation of the world.[1] Do not such indubitable signs of Christ point to *a higher view of His Person contained in His own consciousness?* We cannot evade this conclusion by general phrases, such as that He called Himself Son of God "only in the acceptation of a purified Messianic idea," etc. No; He gave Himself, as Keim says, "overwhelming names and titles, before which all human categories must sink into silence." *What gave Christ the right to think thus of Himself if He was not truly the Son of God?* If we accept this self-testimony of Christ, then His Person stands so high above the world and the remainder of humanity,

[1] Cf. the proofs of this, pp. 245–249. With respect to Matt. xi. 27, "All things are delivered unto me of my Father," etc., Strauss confesses that the man who so speaks must place himself in an entirely unique relation to God, and that "this is the same as when the Johannean Christ says to his Father, 'All mine are Thine, and Thine are mine' (xvii. 10)."

that neither can His works be measured according to mere human and creature standards. But if we do not accept this testimony, we must necessarily accuse Christ of extravagance and undue self-exaltation; and then the crushing task remains, to reconcile these glaring defects with the light of truth and moral majesty, which otherwise shines so brightly in His words and works, and with the world-redeeming and regenerating influences that proceeded from Him.

And, in fact, Strauss finds himself compelled thus to reproach Christ. Considering Him as a mere man, and therefore imperfect, he does and must *undermine His sinlessness.* This is the worst, the fatal feature in his theory. "The notion that Christ was sinless, must be a death-blow to any historical treatment of his person" (*i.e.* any which denies His Godhead), "for even the best of men has constantly to accuse himself of some faults" (p. 195). "Humanity alone is sinless, inasmuch as its development is blameless, and impurity cleaves only to the individual!" Who that has an eye for the fearful corruption which is in the world through sin, can speak of a "sinless humanity"? Thus it is that the pantheistic creed turns everything upside down. Hitherto mankind was believed to be sinful and Christ sinless; now the former is supposed to be sinless, and the latter, because He is a mere individual, to be polluted, or at least imperfect. Mankind, however, gains little enough by the exchange. For if a sinless man be an impossibility, then sinfulness, moral weakness, and imperfection belong to the *idea of man* as an individual. Thus the idea of man is degraded by one who claims to have apprehended it more clearly. We see that to deny the sinlessness of Christ is to degrade the human race, because proceeding from too low an idea of man.

True, Strauss cannot conceal from himself the fact that the nature of Christ—"unlike those of a Paul, an Augustine, or a Luther, which were purified by means of a struggle and a violent rupture, and retained the scars of it ever after"—was uninterrupted and harmoniously unfolded, and that His "inner development took place without violent crises" (p. 208). This is, in point of fact, as much as to concede His sinlessness; for "the specific purport of the Old Testament is the recognition of God's *holiness* and man's *sin;* and on this soil an unbroken, harmonious nature could grow, only if the breach of God's will and the disharmony of sin were entirely foreign to it."[1] But Strauss contradicts himself by demanding that this unbroken development of Christ should be understood so as "not to exclude isolated fluctuations and faults which would necessitate continuous and earnest efforts for self-government" (*ubi sup.*).

These faults are supposed actually to have showed themselves towards the close of our Lord's life. At this period we see the depths of His divinity manifested more clearly than ever. All the more levers must be applied by anti-miraculous critics to obscure them; and when all other efforts fail, then they cast a moral slur on the only sinless One. Help what may; only His divinity must not be conceded! We will leave Strauss' frivolous remarks on the prayer of Christ at the grave of Lazarus[2] out of the question, because he considers the Christ of the fourth Gospel to be a fiction, and the whole narrative "an unhistorical creature of the primitive Christian imagination." But the remarks of Strauss on *Christ's discourses respecting His second coming* (*e.g.* Matt. xxv. 31 et ss.) leave no room for doubt. "Here we stand at a decisive point. For us, Christ exists either as a man only, or not at all. Such things as he predicts of himself here cannot be said of any man. If, notwithstanding, he did predict and expect these things, we must consider him a visionary, just as, had he said them without the full conviction of their truth, he would have been a bragging deceiver." So Strauss decides in favour of considering Him a visionary. "What offends us in all these discourses is only the one point, that Christ should have attached that miraculous change, the appearance of that ideal day of retribution, *to his own person*, and that he should have designated himself as the judge who would come in the clouds of heaven, accompanied by angels, to raise the dead and judge the world. The man who expects such things of himself is not only a visionary, he is guilty of *undue self-exaltation* in presuming to except himself from all others so far as to place himself above them as their future judge. In so doing, Jesus

[1] Beyschlag, *ubi supra*, p. 47.

[2] P. 476: "The Christ of this Gospel, thus praying out of accommodation ('because of the people'), looks like an actor, and, moreover, a clumsy actor, when he confesses that his prayer is a mere accommodation."

seems entirely to have forgotten how once he refused the predicate 'good' as belonging to God alone"[1] (p. 242).

In such sayings, then, we have extravagance and self-exaltation, spiritual and moral error. But what of the "beautiful nature," with the joyous Hellenic clearness of spirit, of which Strauss before spoke? He breaks off here, as though conscious that this is the most self-evidently *weak point of his whole historical construction.* Christ did speak those words. No criticism can remove from our Gospels the absolute divine consciousness which is expressed in the universal judicial function thus claimed by Him. Strauss himself acknowledges that these discourses are historical; and, indeed, they do form "a decisive point." In no part of his *Life of Christ* does he so twist and turn to get out of the difficulty, and in no part can he so ill hide the embarrassment of his "criticism." For either *Christ uttered these sentiments wrongly,* in extravagance and self-exaltation,—and then let any man reconcile them with His otherwise perfect moral majesty; let him explain how from this haughty enthusiast, from this religious leader who himself was subject to sin or error, there could proceed the religion of humility and love, and the kingdom of truth with its world-regenerating effects;—or, on the other hand, Christ was *right* in speaking these words, and did so with full clearness and truth; *but then He was more than a mere man.* From this we see that *though all the works of Christ should vanish into myths, yet His words remain as an irrefutable proof of His Messiahship and Godhead;* and so does His consciousness, with the views resulting therefrom of His person and dignity, as something incompatible with all mere human standards. This firm rock is to Strauss a *stone of stumbling which shatters his whole theory in pieces.* He is indignant that Jesus Christ should dare to bind the whole course of the world to His person, and should call all men, even Dr. Strauss, before His judgment throne;[2] and rather

[1] Cf. Beyschlag, *ubi sup.* p. 54. He rightly remarks, that by this last clause "Strauss reprehends his own abuse of the passage Mark x. 8 (cf. p. 376, note). Would not the simplest rule of interpretation have bound him to interpret this isolated passage so that it should *not contradict* so many indubitable sayings of Christ?"

[2] To show that we are not saying too much, it may be mentioned that Bruno Bauer, one of those who have developed the mythical hypothesis, feels himself

would he grasp after the crown of His sinlessness and freedom from error, to trample it in the dust, than bow down before His perfect and unique grandeur, and acknowledge before this holy mystery what poor piecework all our learning and investigation is. It is the old objection: "We will not have this man to reign over us" (Luke xix. 14; Ps. ii. 2 et ss.). Thence come mistakes which cannot be corrected by the best logic, theories whose upholders are not to be confuted by the clearest arguments.

The optical illusion of mythicism lies in the train of argument, that because in the Church herself the higher knowledge of Christ was gradually attained, therefore this higher knowledge was invented from the imagination of these primitive Christians, though, at the same time, we cannot understand how this idea should have occurred to them. From the angels' song in the first Christmas night, down to the words, "Simon, son of Jonas, lovest thou me?" coming from the lips of the risen One, the gospel history contains a series of pictures so beautiful and grand, so perfumed with heavenly grace, that innumerable features in it must be recognised as *uninventable.* Doubtless there is a *poetry* in them; but it is not that of arbitrary fiction, it is the result of holy and divinely ordered facts. Why should legends only invent what is beautiful? Why should not the finger of God in history trace out an objective beauty of facts which exceeds all that human fancy can invent? Instead of saying that it is too beautiful to be true, each man who believes in something more than our common everyday life should say, when looking at this page of history, "*It is too beautiful to be mere fiction,*" so beautiful that it must be true. There is an ideal perfection of beauty which is itself the highest reality; or, to use the words of Göthe,

> "The unattainable
> Is here accomplished;"

and this beauty it is which shines in the Gospels, above all, in the delineation which they give us of Christ.

Only if Christ really was what He was taken for, can we

"injured, offended, and angered" by the prominent dignity of Christ; "because one man is always set up as a model against the wickedness and stupidity of all the others!" (in his *Kritik der evang. Geschichte*, Preface.)

solve the enigma of primitive Christian faith, of the foundation, the spread, and the world-renewing power of the Christian Church. Christ could only live as the God-man in the hearts of His followers if He really was so. How else was it possible that so many Jews should have believed in One who was shamefully crucified (only think what a stumbling-block a crucified Messiah must have been to them!), and so many heathen should have accepted a crucified *Jew* as the Son of God? How is it conceivable that on this sandy, mythical foundation a *Church should have been built* up which possessed such *vitality and power of growth?* Whence did the Church, which is a Christian Church solely in virtue of her belief in Jesus as the only-begotten Son of God,—whence did the Church take her rise, if she were not formed by Christ in that capacity? *A myth cannot form*, cannot produce; it is itself only a product, a reflection of the popular mind, and that in prehistoric times: it cannot, therefore, have begotten the Christian Church; nay, it cannot even have helped to beget it. The establishment of the Church, this immense achievement, demands a *personal* Will, a creative power of the greatest energy; it cannot be accounted for by the empty pictures of imagination. And where else do we find this power, what else is a sufficient explanation, but the divine power of the crucified and risen One?

We look at the *enormous revolution in the world* accomplished through Christianity; we look at the *joyful heroism of its confessors*, braving death; and at the *purity of the primitive Christian Church*, which is born, grows, spreads, and finally conquers the world, though placed between a thoroughly corrupted Judaism on the one hand, and a no less thoroughly vitiated heathenism on the other; and having done so, we consider the attempt made to explain all this from the fact that *a certain Jew became convinced that he was the Messiah, whereupon his disciples after his death attributed to him all sorts of miracles, which they drew from their imagination;* and our final conclusion is, that *this explanation involves such an utter disproportion between cause and effect, that it is in itself the most inconceivable miracle, a pure historical impossibility.*

Strauss shares the fate of all anti-miraculists. Denying miracles, they are forced to substitute still greater enigmas for them, and yet are unable to explain real history. There stands Christ in the unique consciousness of His Godhead, His redeeming vocation, and His universal Kingship. There is the Church, there is Christianity with its world-regenerating effects,—all undeniable facts. All these *Strauss cannot explain*[1] by referring them to one who was not free from sin and error, or to the inventive, ay, deceptive, imagination of his followers. Here we see *the immense residuum which even Strauss cannot get rid of*, and which shows his whole hypothesis to be insufficient and wrong.

His hypothesis does not suit the clearness of that age, which was a *historical* and not a prehistoric one; it does not accord with the truth-breathing *spirit of the Gospels*, nor with their simple, clear, and temperate *style*; it does not accord with the personal greatness, the moral perfection, nor the self-consciousness and the self-testimony of Christ, for whom all human standards are insufficient; it suits neither the spiritual, conscientious, and honourable character of the *primitive Church*, nor the behaviour of its *opponents*, who raise no contradiction; it does not accord with the immense and ever beneficial moral *effects* of the Gospel, which cannot have proceeded from beautiful though unconscious fancies, nor from intentional deceptions; and finally, we boldly say, it does not accord with the *present age*, in which the Christ of the Gospels is still approving Himself to many thousand hearts and consciences as living power and truth, and not as legend.

It all comes to the dilemma: *Did Christ create the Church, or did the Church invent Christ?* The former of these propositions is supported by the entire analogy of history; the latter, as we have seen, is abnormal and inconceivable. The Christ of Strauss first called this wonderful Church into existence in a perfectly natural manner, and was then born again as a creature of her fancy. Is not this the old trick which Hegel tried to play, treating the world as posited by the "absolute Idea," whilst this "absolute Idea" is only realized in the world (*vide* p. 167)? No wonder that Nemesis appeared in the person of Bruno Bauer (not to be confounded

[1] Cf. Dorner, *History of Protestant Theology*, p. 838 (English edit., vol. ii. p. 372), and Schaff, *Die Person Jesu Christi* (Gotha, 1865), p. 110 et ss., English edition (Boston, 1865), pp. 187 et ss.

with Dr. Ferdinand Christian von Baur), who carried Strauss' hypothesis to its extreme, and said in effect: You derive everything from the idea of the Messiah which you suppose to have been already in existence; but, my friend, the existence of this idea itself is likewise a myth: neither Christ made the Church nor the Church Him, the Church made itself!! I will spare you any further delineation of this utter nonsense, which would make everything exist before it exists, and would engulf all historical development in an eternal progress from nothing to nothing.

"Simplex veri sigillum"—*Simplicity is the seal of the truth.* This wise motto of a great physician is applicable in all matters of history and of faith. Compare, my honoured hearers, this artificially invented, this laboriously and violently applied mythical hypothesis as to the life of Christ, with the simple and artless statements of the Gospels. Can you any longer doubt which bears the impress of truth?

IV.—RENAN'S "VIE DE JESUS."

After having thus fully discussed the mythical theory, it will suffice to give the *French Strauss* a shorter consideration than his German colleague. The standpoint of Ernest Renan in his *Vie de Jésus*[1] is essentially the same as that of Strauss, and is shattered to pieces on the same rock.

Goethe says somewhere: "A book which should explain to us Christ as a man glorified by the pure divine charm which surrounded him, would exercise an immense influence on Christianity." If the success of a book were any criterion of its intrinsic value, we might imagine that Renan had succeeded in solving this problem, and that Goethe's prophecy was fulfilled in him; although, to be sure, there is not much of the "pure divine charm" left us in his portrait of Christ. But we have every reason to believe that the unparalleled success of this book, which has been circulated by hundreds of thousands, especially in the Roman Catholic world (France and Italy), is primarily due to its graceful *form*.

[1] We quote from the edition of 1863.

Renan's work is an embodiment of the spirit of modern French infidelity. We see it here gracefully floating along in all its seductive elegance, labouring hard to compress much into brilliant and short sentences, yet withal pleasantly entertaining, and using all those arts which for centuries have made it such a favourite in the polite society of Europe. But, at the same time, we mark its boundless, well-nigh incomprehensible capriciousness, its superficial frivolity, which only calculates on sensations suited to the times, and gracefully waives the most difficult problems; we mark its entire want of earnest moral consciousness, of real scientific perception, of thorough and conscientious historical investigation, and, worse than all, the piquant flippancy (pleasing, alas! to too many) which does not hesitate to clothe the most holy Figure in history in the garb of a social democrat of modern France, nor to change the most sacred life into—a *novel.*

This book is the first part of a larger work;[1] it was written on the occasion of a journey to Phœnicia and the Holy Land. "I wrote down a sketch of it hurriedly enough in a Maronite hut, with five or six books around me. . . . The striking agreement between the descriptions of the New Testament and the places which lay around me; the wonderful harmony between the ideal portrait of the Gospels and the landscape which served as its frame—all these things were a kind of revelation to me. I seemed to have a fifth gospel before me, mutilated and torn, but still legible; and from that hour, under the guidance of Matthew and Mark, I saw, instead of that abstract being whose existence one can scarce help questioning, a genuine but wondrously beautiful human figure full of life and motion. . . . I fixed this picture, which appeared to my spirit, with a few hasty strokes, and what grew from it is this story" (*vide* Introduction).

This explains to us the whole character of the book. On a well-drawn background of Syrian landscapes, Renan sketches the picture of Christ, not in philosophical abstractions, but with the fresh colours of life; not floating in mythical mists, but with sharply defined features. Unlike the figure drawn by Strauss, which is constantly shrinking up under the mono-

[1] "Histoire des origines du Christianisme." Since then there have appeared the second part, "Les Apôtres," and the third, "St. Paul."

tonous action of the critical dissecting knife, till at last the operator complains that of few great men do we know so little as of Christ;—unlike this, here we see flesh and blood, life and development. Indeed, there is a certain warmth of feeling for the beauties of the King whom yet he seeks to dethrone. Nowhere do we breathe the close air of the study, but always the fresh breezes of an inspiriting journey. But then this vivid freshness is so dearly bought, that we could wish the lamp of study had not been wanting in that Maronite hut (and afterwards too!), and that the clever Frenchman had not so often tried to cover his want of thorough investigation by fanciful ideas and brilliant superficiality. For the "fifth gospel" from which he borrows is (as we shall soon see) not only the ocular instruction obtained on the scene of the occurrences, but to a considerably greater extent his *imagination*, which appears to have blossomed so luxuriantly under the rays of the Eastern sun, that it plays its possessor one trick after another, and finally changes him from a historian into a *novelist*.

Renan, too, sees in Jesus *nothing more than a man*. He intends to draw a "wondrously beautiful," yet "genuinely human," portrait, to the exclusion of all supernatural factors. We shall see whether he succeeds in both these respects, or whether the all too great humanity does not spoil the wondrous beauty, and make ugly stains in it. As Strauss makes use of the myth to get rid of the supernatural, so Renan uses the cognate conception of the *legend*. His views are expressed in the sentence, that "the life of Christ, as the evangelists relate it, is essentially historical, but *in no way supernatural*." The Gospels are "essentially" genuine writings, composed by apostles or their disciples in the course of the first century. Even the Gospel of St. John Renan supposes probably to have been written by an intimate disciple of his, and quite in his spirit. But for all that, in them the real history of Christ is throughout *distorted by legends*, and adorned by the traditions of the wonder-loving disciples. Moreover, these four "legendary biographers flagrantly contradict each other" (Introduction, p. xliv); "they are full of errors and of nonsense" (p. 450). The questions which we asked above,—whether the fabrication of such legends is in accordance with the otherwise conscientious and sober character of the disciples, and with the behaviour of their opponents who do not dispute the miracles,—none of them trouble Renan; his historical conscience is far above such scruples. We are merely told that tradition at that time was utterly unconcerned as to an exact record of what had happened; since "the spirit was everything, the letter nothing" to these primitive historians,—just as though no one could have had any interest in obtaining certain and exact information about the words and works of Christ (cf. Luke i. 4).

But from this mass of legends and apocryphal miracles the real history of Christ may still be extracted by means of a bold historical criticism. How, then, does it now appear?

Jesus, the son of Joseph and Mary, was born in Nazareth, not in Bethlehem, nor of the lineage of David. He grew up in poor circumstances, and notwithstanding his unusually rich gifts, he remained under the influence of the narrow views common to his people. Thus he believed in Satan, in demons, in miracles, and had no knowledge whatever of the "inflexibility of all nature's laws" (*vide* Introduction). In his youth he even showed some inclination to the uncouth and narrow-minded fanaticism of the Pharisees. "Probably," however, he learned from the mild Rabbi Hillel (who lived from 110 B.C. to 10 A.D.). In addition to the Old Testament, he "probably" read many of the apocryphal writings; and the visions of Daniel especially fixed themselves in his mind. This constant "probability" at the very outset shows that Renan is writing history only in hypotheses.

Renan divides the *public life* of Christ into three periods.[1] The first and most beautiful was "*the period of pure moral teaching*," of the tranquil Galilean life. There, from the blue skies of Galilee, from the beauties of nature, and from his own heart, Jesus extracts a consciousness of God such as no one before or after him has ever had, and he begins to preach about the heavenly Father whom he has found. "God is our Father, and all men are brethren." This was at that time the purport of his preaching. He announced a kingdom of God "which we must create in ourselves through uprightness of the will and poetry of the heart." In the Sermon on

[1] Cf. Luthardt, *ubi sup.* p. 25 et ss.; Uhlhorn, *ubi sup.* p. 15 et ss.

the Mount, "that most beautiful code of a perfect life which ever moralist drew up," we may recognise the main features of this divine kingdom: a worship built upon purity of heart and brotherly love to men; a religion without priests and outward ceremonies, entirely depending on the imitation of God and the immediate communion of conscience with the heavenly Father. The later realistic conception of the kingdom of God is an obscuration of this then pure idea. At that time, too, Jesus did not as yet perform any miracles. Had he died during this period, his idea would have remained purer. But it is one thing to conceive a great idea, and another to give it practical effect. In order to attain success, every idea must sacrifice something, for none ever yet went forth unstained from the great struggle of life. "*In order to make that which is good successful among men, less pure ways are necessary.*"[1] Without miracles the gospel could not have conquered the world. Here we see the fundamental desideratum of Renan's historical theory; it leaves no room for the moral consciousness. A little fraud is absolutely necessary in order to succeed. And so Christ was obliged to come down more and more from his ideal heights, till at length he fell into the slough of deception as soon as he endeavoured to realize his ideal.

With this we enter on the *second period* of his work, that of *intoxicated Galilean enthusiasm,* brought in by the unfavourable influence of John the Baptist's austere spirit on the milder soul of Jesus. He now adopts the Messianic belief of his nation, and begins to think more highly of his own person. In the energetic flight of his will he believes himself to be almighty, the reformer of the universe. He now preaches the kingdom of heaven, which he *himself* brings; his fundamental idea changes to that of an entire overthrow of the existing order of things, a moral revolution by which even sickness and death should be banished, but not through sanguinary political means. The kingdom of God was to be realized in a peaceable manner by men amongst men. He

[1] "Pour faire réussir le bien parmi les hommes, des voies moins pures sont nécessaires." See, too, how Renan in his "St. Paul" (1869) makes the apostle on several occasions take his refuge in jugglery, because "the contact with reality always defiles."

gathers around his person a circle of "childlike" disciples, of publicans, and especially of women and Magdalens, "who in his society discovered an easy means of becoming honest again." Thus he passes through the country riding on a gentle mule along the lovely shores of the Sea of Galilee, surrounded by applauding multitudes, with young fishermen as his enthusiastic friends, women and children in his train. It is "a constant festival," an uninterrupted intoxication, a heavenly rural wedding feast. "The new religion is in many respects a movement amongst women and children."

This lovely but visionary idyll is followed by the fatal *third period,* that of the *dark fanatical conflict* with the Pharisees and ecclesiastical rulers. In order to attack the citadel of Judaism, Jesus changes his place of action from Galilee to Judea and *Jerusalem.* In view of the temple with its priests and slaughterings, he seizes the cleansing scourge. This act loosened the last bond which bound him to the Jewish faith, and tightened the knot of enmity between him and the rulers. He and his provincials had made but small impression on the smooth and polished floor of the capital. All the more does this want of success inflame his zeal. The preacher of morals turns into a violent revolutionary, and apocalyptic enthusiast. Now he is the Messiah appeared in person, who will abolish the law and found his kingdom on the ruins of the present age. He speaks of his second coming in the clouds of heaven, makes the angels of God his servants to execute judgment on the world, and pronounces the belief in his person as Son of God in a superhuman sense the fundamental law of his kingdom. His natural meekness changes into a sharp and dictatorial manner which can bear no contradiction. Indeed, at times his ill-temper towards all resistance betrays him into inexplicable and seemingly absurd actions, as, *e.g.*, his curse against the fig-tree.

At that time the first *legendary germs* began to collect even around the living person of Christ. Because the Messiah was generally supposed to be the Son of David, Christ let himself be called so; at first unwillingly, because he well knew that he was not descended from him, but afterwards he found pleasure in the title. Thence proceed the legends of his lineage and his birth in Bethlehem. But above all, he now puts on the *appearance of miraculous power*, and in general becomes less particular in the choice of ways and means. True, even earlier than this he may have given an impulse to the formation of miraculous legends; for one of his most constant and deep-seated convictions was, that through faith and prayer a man could obtain full power over nature. Resting upon this conviction, he obtained that extraordinary power over men's minds which soon led them to attribute to his miraculous power every remarkable case of recovery from sickness, or awakening from apparent death, that happened in his neighbourhood. Fame multiplied the number of these occurrences immensely. For, on the whole, there are but few different kinds of miracles related in the Gospels; they are merely repetitions of one and the same pattern. Jesus, however, in all probability never performed real miracles; for in all cases (though Renan himself can only cite *two !*) in which scientific researches have been made as to ostensible miracles, they have been found to be baseless. Renan expresses himself more cautiously than Strauss: "We do not say that a miracle is impossible, but only that as yet none has ever been confirmed;" but in reality he means the same. But many circumstances seem to indicate that it was not till a later period, and against his will, that Jesus became a miracle-worker (pp. 265, 270). He had no choice. Miracles were universally considered an indispensable proof of a divine mission. He allowed himself, compelled by this unconquerable prejudice of the multitude, to assume the appearance of miraculous power, and in some cases really did succeed in producing improvement in the condition of physical or mental sufferers by means of his moral influence, and at other times cured those who fancied themselves possessed, by falling in with their monomania. In other cases, however, miracles were simply fathered upon him by the superstition of his contemporaries or the enthusiastic fancy of his followers. At length his miracles became *intentional frauds.* This was especially the case with the illusion practised at the *raising of Lazarus*, who was laid in the grave alive, in order that he might issue forth at the call of Jesus. "Tired of the cold reception with which the kingdom of God had met in the capital, the friends of Christ were desirous of a great miracle, in order that they might strike a heavy blow at the unbelief of Jerusalem. Lazarus and his two sisters undertook the chief part in this fraud." And Christ, who knew of it, joined in the comedy! "We must keep in mind that in this impure town, with its dull, oppressive atmosphere, Jesus was no longer the same. *His conscience had,* through the fault of men, not his own, *lost something of its original purity.*" The town had exercised a *demoralizing* influence upon him! Well it was that death soon plucked him out of the fatal meshes of a rôle which was no longer practicable.

But this death of his atoned for his momentary aberrations. Renan closes the life of Christ with the last sigh on the cross. The resurrection is unhistorical. The empty grave and the imaginary vision which appeared to the excited Mary Magdalene gave the impetus to this legend. Only the enthusiasm of love raised Jesus to the elevation of the Godhead. "Divine power of love"—thus Renan concludes with solemn, piously sounding pathos—"sacred moments, in which the passion of a hallucinated woman gave the world a risen God!"[1]

This is the sad and downward path of the life of Christ according to Renan. What is particularly repulsive in his description is the constant *mixture* of admiration and blasphemy, of approbation and detraction. But though *this* defilement of our Lord's life may raise our indignation, we are utterly disgusted when we look at the important and ambiguous part in it which Renan assigns to *the women.* Here we see only too distinctly that the writer borrows his colours from the society amongst which he moves, and for whom his novel is calculated. The young Galilean, "of ravishing beauty" and amiableness, captivated women's hearts. His words and looks penetrated their inmost soul. Women of dubious morality are not wanting. These "fair creatures" (belles créatures) having received a strong impression from him, now emulate each other in proofs of grateful love. True, Renan does not think of accusing Christ Himself of anything wrong. But still he thinks it possible that "in that dark hour in Gethsemane, Jesus thought not only of the clear

[1] "Moments sacrés, ou la passion d'une hallucinée donne au monde un Dieu resuscité!" (cf. Lect. VII.)

brooks in his native land, but also of the Galilean girls, whose love he renounced, in order to live only for his vocation!!"

We turn away in disgust. Even a rationalist like A. Coquerel wrote to Renan: "I beg you to expunge from your book an intolerably odious phrase—that about the 'fair creatures.' . . . In the name of good taste, and of the highest and most delicate rules of decency, do speak of them with more dignified gravity!"[1] Before this we have had occasion to complain of arbitrary treatment of history by the anti-miraculous critics of the life of Christ; but here we have worse than that—the morbid abortions of an imagination corrupted by the air of Paris.

Nevertheless we will give a quiet investigation to these statements of Renan. In these three periods of the life of Christ we really have a genuine human—one might even say French—development, but only at the cost of *openly giving up His sinlessness.* According to the Gospels (cf. Luke ii. 49 with John xvii.), Jesus *rises* from step to step in the development of His divine consciousness and the proof of His obedience even to death; according to Renan, He constantly *sinks lower* both in spiritual knowledge and in moral purpose and practice. In the Christ of the Gospels we are astonished at the constancy of His character, and the *uniformity* of His moral dignity. Renan goes so far in "developing" his Christ, that he at last is "no longer himself!" The sublime moral teacher, with his pure ideas, becomes an amiable but unpractical enthusiast, who as yet knows little of the world; the innocent enthusiast changes into a fanatic revolutionist, a dark prophet who only hears in his dreams the trumpet of judgment; and he at last turns into a deceiver, at first against his will, making one dishonest concession after another to the spirit of the age; then into a Jesuit, who thinks that the end sanctifies any means, and who is not even ashamed of a comedian's tricks!

[1] In the people's edition several offensive things were really eliminated. But in Renan's "St. Paul" (1869) he again assigns an important part to the Greek women, and makes the apostle entertain the warmest feelings towards his beautiful and faithful devotees, "amongst whom he appears even to have formed a more intimate connection with Lydia, though he may not have taken her with him on his travels!!"

Moral teacher, enthusiast, fanatic and deceiver, of what do these three stages of life remind us? Doubtless the *Koran* at once occurs to all of us. And verily Renan is naïve enough openly to confess that "*the life of Mohammed* supplied him with the idea of these periods" (cf. the Introd.). He has merely made the little mistake of *confounding the true Prophet with the false one!!* Who can wonder, after this, that Renan should have drawn a distorted caricature instead of a true historical picture?

Here, as in the case of Strauss and Schenkel, we see a just retribution. In the character of Christ, deity and humanity form an inseparable personal unity, and whoever, in depicting Him, excludes the divine factor, *cannot justly treat the human nature of Christ,* for he cannot depict it without bringing in shadows which would make Him quite incompetent to be the Redeemer of the world. Renan promises to show us a "wondrously beautiful" human character. But when we think of his Christ at the grave of Lazarus, how much of this beauty remains? Renan's account gives us the impression that he is *unwilling* to include these moral stains in the picture of Christ. He would willingly represent Him as more pure, if this were possible. But through his acknowledgment that our Gospels are essentially genuine apostolic writings, he is compelled to take for genuine historical tradition much that Strauss simply throws overboard as mythical. What other choice has Renan, since he denies the Godhead of Christ and the existence of the miraculous, than to ascribe these elements in the Gospels to visionary enthusiasm, or, if that will not suffice, to deceit?[1] It is of no use to try, as Renan does, to excuse these impure means which he supposes Jesus to employ by saying that this was the only way for Him to attain His object, that in this world "nothing great was ever accomplished without resting on a legend;" it is of no use to transfer the guilt from Jesus to "men who want to be de-

[1] "The case of Renan is highly instructive, as showing what a man must come to who concedes the historical character of the Gospels even merely in their fundamental features (and this every one must do, or else give himself up to an arbitrary disregard of all science), and yet refuses to acknowledge Jesus as the God-man. Such an one may get a mere man, but assuredly not a morally pure one, or a pattern of true humanity; his mere man must necessarily be a visionary and a deceiver" (Uhlhorn, *ubi sup.* p. 25).

ceived." For every man who still has a *moral consciousness* must feel that *whoever is capable of employing such means is not competent to release mankind from sin and error, and morally regenerate it;* or, on the other hand, that if such influences really did proceed from Christ, He must have been different to what Renan represents Him.

When any one can do such despite to history and its records as to impute moral faults to Christ, this fundamentally false view of the centre must dislocate the whole history which is grouped around it. He who makes Christ develope morally downwards instead of divinely upwards, is capable, ay, is compelled, to turn all else upside down. And this is actually the case in the work before us. The death of Christ is a redemption for himself, from the difficulties of his impracticable rôle, instead of a redemption for us; in fact, the whole work of Christ, instead of being accomplished step by step up to the last word, "It is finished," is less accomplished the longer it is carried on, till at length it becomes absolutely "impracticable." The resurrection, or the disciples' belief in it, instead of being a divine release from all doubts and conflicts, is rather the occasion of endless errors and enthusiastic lies. Christianity itself, this manly religion of self-denial and self-conquest, becomes a "movement amongst women and children;" and the whole history of the world and the Church, instead of being founded on divinely certain facts, rests on the hallucinations of a nervously-affected woman!!

Truly the historical difficulties and psychological impossibilities in Renan's view of the life of Christ are far more numerous than in that of Strauss. For Renan does not delay the formation of legends till after the death of Christ, but boldly includes it in His life. He who said "I am the Truth," must Himself stand and see how falsehood grows up around Him and be silent, nay, even help! Moreover, the way in which Renan treats the Gospels is far *more arbitrary* than the method either of Strauss or Schenkel; which is all the more inexcusable, inasmuch as Renan considers these writings to be essentially genuine.[1] Often a piece is taken as

[1] This arbitrary dealing is only equalled by Renan's *exegetical incapacity*. Of this he gives some perfectly astounding proofs. *E.g.* the parable of the rich man and Lazarus he explains thus: "The rich man is in hell because he is

true down to the smallest detail, when another close by (merely from an aversion to the supernatural) is declared to be a legend. And not only this, but the various passages are shuffled together like a pack of cards, *without the least regard to chronology* or the plan of the evangelists, and then put together again according to a self-invented chronology. Renan is bold enough *to fabricate an entire period in Christ's ministry about which not one of the Gospels tells anything.* According to all four Gospels (and even according to Strauss, Schenkel, and Keim), Christ meets with the Baptist before the beginning of His public ministry. But Renan transfers this meeting to the beginning of the *second* period, and represents it as preceded by the first period of pure moral teaching, which, however, he fills up with words and works of Jesus which are related by all the Gospels as taking place after that meeting (as the Sermon on the Mount, etc.). According to all the four Gospels, the first disciples are called by the Lord at the beginning of His ministry; according to Renan, this circle is not formed till the second period. All four evangelists relate miracles of our Lord from the very beginning of His public appearance; according to Renan, it is at a much later period that He permits Himself to be forced by popular pressure to assume the character of a miracle-worker. Is this the method of a conscientious historian?

In addition to this, Renan everywhere *unblushingly lets his fancy paint and speak for him;* and in the most frivolous manner brings in details about which he knows nothing whatever, in order to give his story more freshness and vividness. As soon as the picture of Christ threatens to become too lean and insignificant, by reason of the denial of all that is miraculous, Renan knows how to supply what is lacking from his imagination. We learn things that are entirely new to us, and for which

rich,—because he dines well whilst others before his door are dining ill." For this reason Luke is supposed to be "an excited democrat and Ebionite, *i.e.* most hostile to property, and persuaded that the vengeance of the poor would soon come." His Gospel has a "communistic tendency!" Here again we see how modern French conditions of life are dated back to the beginning of the Christian era. From Matt. xxii. 1–14 Renan concludes "that pure Ebionism—*i.e.* the doctrine that the poor are to be saved, and their kingdom is coming—was the doctrine of Christ!" Renan does not seem to have a notion that this parable applies to the rejection of the Jews and the calling of Christ's Church from amongst the Gentiles.

we should be most grateful if they were not entirely imaginary. Renan can tell us all about the teachers of Christ; the books that He read in His young days; His youthful tendency to zealotism; His sisters, who Renan knows were married in Nazareth; about the children of Peter; about Judas, who "most likely" led a harmless life on his estate of Hakeldama, etc., etc. On the other hand, what the Gospels know and tell, he often ignores or thinks he knows better. Thus, in contradiction to the Gospels, he knows that the family of David was entirely extinct at the time of Christ's birth. According to the Gospels, Jesus travels on foot, so that He becomes "wearied with the journey" (John iv. 6); but Renan knows that in His progress through Galilee He "used a mule. Every *now and then* the disciples would display around his person a rustic pomp, at the expense of their own clothes, which served the purpose of carpets. They laid them on the mule which bore him, or spread them before him on the earth." All this Renan's imagination extracts from Matt. xxi. 7, 8, with such slight changes as making the ass into a mule, converting the incident which took place *once* in *Jerusalem* into an oft-repeated *habit* in *Galilee,* and making the disciples spread their garments on the road, which in ver. 8 is done only by the *people.* He also knows that Jesus, who was pleased with the "straightforward and lively character of Peter, sometimes condescended to *smile* at his very decided ways." . . . "A naïve doubt was sometimes raised amongst the disciples, but Jesus with a smile or a look silenced the objection." Where else are we told about Jesus smiling? The wife of Pilate, Renan supposes, perhaps saw the "gentle Galilean from a window of the palace, which looked out on to the heights of the temple." (But according to Josephus the palace lay on the hill of Zion, in the upper town, so that this outlook was not possible.) All this sounds as lifelike as if Renan himself had been an eye-witness of the events, and yet it is mere vapour and false paint applied to real events. How grand, when compared with this sensational depiction, is the terse and chaste style, the holy gravity of the Gospels!

After this we cannot wonder that Renan should put words into the mouth of Christ which He never spoke; *e.g.* that the law was abolished, whereas He plainly said, "I am not come to destroy the law, but to fulfil it." Christ said, "Destroy [ye] this temple, and in three days I will raise it up" (John ii. 19); and the *false* witnesses changed this into: "I am able to destroy the temple of God, and to build it again in three days" (Matt. xxvi. 60, 61; Mark xiv. 57-59); but this does not prevent Renan from assuring us that "Jesus really pronounced these fatal words."

Respected hearers, can a book which professes to be *history* be more full of weak points and blunders? The same question, as in the case of Strauss and Schenkel, returns to us with redoubled force: *Is a man like this capable of writing history?*—one who draws on his imagination in the way we have seen, who brings in an entirely new chronology of his own, taken from elsewhere; one who, to judge by the solecisms we have cited,[1] has not even carefully examined the passages in question; one who paints Christ and His times in the colours of the present Parisian world;—can any confidence be placed in him? And yet the present generation, from excess of criticism, has become so uncritical as to go by hundreds of thousands (I am not exaggerating) to hear the history of all histories from a man who has laid himself open to so many charges! If one who were writing the life of Luther or Napoleon thus gave the reins to his fancy, we should expunge his name from the list of historians and place him among the *novelists;* and this we must do to Renan. But at the source of history, if anywhere, only history should be written, and not novels.

A *novel*—this is the only true title of his book with its constant mixture of truth and fiction, of historical fragments and subjective imagination. The effeminate, unhealthy, morbid tone of the modern French novel, with its utter want of moral consciousness, permeates the whole work. Hence the peculiarly *tentative style,* with its constantly-recurring "probably"—"most likely"—"to all appearance"—"well-nigh,"[2]

[1] One of the most flagrant amongst the many not mentioned is the schoolboy's error of confounding Hellenes (Greeks) and Hellenists (Greek-speaking Jews).

[2] Renan is inexhaustible in such phrases as, "Il faut supposer—on est tenté de croire—il semble—il parait—probablement—peut-être—on dit—à ce que l'on croit—je soupçonne—qui sait—si je puis le dire," etc.

which are not wanting in any important passages, and betray an involuntary distrust of his imaginative hypothesis. Like most modern *beaux esprits,* Renan always uses gentle approximations. A real *colour* is too rough and painful to sensitive eyes, so we always have *shadings.* It is only consistent of Renan finally to shade over the cardinal difference between the colours of all human acts, *i.e.* to efface the distinction between good and evil, and to represent even that which is best and most beneficent as always mixed with evil. This brings us to the *fundamental error of his standpoint: the pantheizing negation of the supernatural,* and consequently *the absence of moral feeling.* Renan's God is not the God of Scripture, the free personal Creator of the world. This is shown, not only by many pantheistic sentences in his book, some of which he puts into Christ's mouth, but also by other utterances [1] in which he declares his leaning to Hegel. He does not attribute self-consciousness to God, but only a progressive development in His self-knowledge from the stone and the plant upwards to Buddha and Christ.[2] We must not let ourselves be deceived as to this by the religious warmth of tone in his *Vie de Jésus.* But what does he mean by continuing to talk of a heavenly Father? If Jesus did so, then even He could not have attained to the "pure idea," *i.e.* the pantheistic conception of God.

This false fundamental view may explain to us the surprising *obscuration of moral consciousness* which strikes us in such sentences as these: that for the success of what is good "less pure ways are necessary;"—"the best cause is only won by ill means; we must accept men as they are, with all their illusions, and thus endeavour to work upon them; France would not be what it is (probably not!) if it had not for a thousand years believed in the flask of holy oil at Rheims; when we with our scrupulous regard for truth have accomplished what the heroes did by their deceptions, then, and not till then, shall we have a right to blame them: the only

[1] Cf. Renan's letter to Bertholet, *Revue des deux Mondes,* 1863; also Uhlhorn, *ubi sup.* p. 28.

[2] He considers God to be "le lieu de l'ideal, le principe vivant du bien," etc. "La thèse fondamentale de toute notre théologie" is the axiom that "Dieu est immanent, non seulement dans l'ensemble de l'univers, mais dans chacun des êtres qui le composent" (*ubi sup.*).

culprit in such cases is mankind, who wants to be cheated." Instead of destroying the delusions of mankind, we are merely to let them be, and to use them cleverly, cheat those who want to be cheated, and not shun false paint and ill means in order to attain our end! Here we see the democrat turn into a *Jesuit*. But these are the morals of Parisian circles—the truly French confusion between momentary, outward success, and real, durable, though slowly progressing moral welfare and blessing. And these are the moral sentiments of one who wishes to reduce Christianity to its purely moral basis while doing away with all dogmas. Here we may learn what sort of morals we may expect to result from this process. For Renan does not only give theory, he immediately *carries his maxims into practice* in his book. He knows the illusions of the public with whom he has to deal, and chooses its weak side, the love of novels, in order to attain great success. We see that he is *wanting in that very quality which is most important for the exegete and for the historian, viz. moral conscientiousness.* Not only—like Strauss—does he not believe in an absolute moral perfection, but *not even in the power of pure truth.* He thinks that it must always be assisted by some false paint and deception; whereas we all know that the whole history of the world, but still more that of God's kingdom, is one long proof that the *truth is strong and invincible in proportion as it is pure and unadulterated.* The more unadorned it is, the more durable—though not always speedy—are its effects, and every admixture of falsehood and fraud weakens it and threatens its life.[1] But a view of the world which is so corrupt as to deny this can only be pitied, not combated! . . .

And now, "what think ye of Christ," and what of His anti-miraculous biographers? Perhaps some of my hearers may have thought the judgment passed on them (which, however, is one with that of the greatest critics) somewhat hard. Those who think so, I would merely ask one question: Do you

[1] "Truth needs no colour with his colour fix'd;
Beauty no pencil, beauty's truth to lay;
But best is best, if never intermix'd."
Shakspeare, Sonnet ci.

know what accusation is brought by those who deny the Godhead of Christ against us who confess and defend it, ay, and against the whole Church? *In virtue of this denial they practically accuse us of idolatry,* and of a continuous most aggravated offence against the majesty of God, because we worship Jesus who is a mere man. They accuse Christ Himself at least of caring worse for His Church than Mohammed did for his. For whereas the latter taught and recorded in writing the exclusive Unity of the Godhead so clearly that it is well-nigh impossible for his followers to become idolaters, Christ spoke so *ambiguously* in many discourses about His unique and superhuman relation to God, that His disciples and His Church not only were able, but were almost compelled, to fall into deep idolatry! Why did He not speak more clearly in order to preclude this great evil? More than this. By the assertion that Christ was not the Son of God (in a superhuman sense), our opponents (though they will not confess it) affirm that the sentence passed on Him, because of blasphemy, was the justest verdict ever pronounced! *Nothing but His true and real divinity can save Him from the accusation of blasphemy, and us from the charge of idolatry!*

This, then, without mincing the matter, is the issue between us and our opponents. Who can be angry with us for not allowing this slur to be cast upon our Lord, upon the goodly host of His followers, and upon ourselves; or who chide us for rebutting such a charge with all our energy? How can preachers of tolerance be so devoid of understanding as to demand that we should give the right hand of fellowship to these opponents, and acknowledge the justification of their standpoint in the Christian Church, whilst they declare the central truth of our belief, as it has hitherto stood, to be a deception?

Here stands our Lord Jesus Christ, and around Him His accusers, and "their witness agreeth not together" in many points, neither in their treatment of the Gospels as historical records, nor in their apprehension of passages taken singly. Let us now comprise in a few sentences what is common to them as a body, and compare it with our old confession of belief in Christ. You will then see at once the depth of the chasm which separates us:—

THE CHURCH.	THE ANTI-MIRACULISTS.
I believe in Jesus Christ.	I believe in Jesus, who allowed himself to be called Christ (or Messiah).
The only-begotten Son of God.	The (illegitimate) son of Joseph the carpenter.
Our Lord.	Our brother, who himself was not quite free from sin and error.
Who was conceived by the Holy Ghost.	Who was naturally begotten and conceived.
Born of the Virgin Mary.	Born of Mary, the wife (?).
Suffered under Pontius Pilate.	Who (merely on account of his resistance to the rulers) suffered under Pontius Pilate.
Was crucified, dead, and buried.	Was crucified, dead, and probably "hastily interred in some dishonourable burying-place."
He descended into hell.	(?)
The third day He rose again from the dead.	Remained in death, and did not rise again, but was only in after years believed to have done so.
He ascended into heaven.	Whose body decayed in the grave, whilst his spirit was raised to heaven, if indeed there be such a thing as immortality and eternal bliss.
And sitteth on the right hand of God the Father Almighty.	(?)
From thence He shall come to judge the quick and the dead.	Who also spoke of his second coming—which was either visionary or else intended impersonally—and of his judging the world, which was undue self-exaltation.

If any one is suited by this non-miraculous Christ, we demand of him, with Strauss, that he should cease to speak of Him as the "Redeemer." If he is a clergyman, let him no longer read prayers to Christ in the Church or at the grave, and let him be honourable and straightforward enough to give his new religion a *new name.* He who no longer believes in Christ as the divine, sinless, and holy Redeemer, *no longer stands within the pale of Christianity,* though he may still hold on to a few tatters of Christian morals. For the Christian religion is, and remains, nought else than the belief in the redemption accomplished by Christ the Son of God. This doctrinal foundation, which was laid by Christ and His apostles, cannot be given up by the Christian Church to all ages without giving up herself. In so saying, we lift up no stones against those who have thus radically broken with the belief of the Church; in matters of faith and conscience we abhor all measures of force as wrong and hurtful to the cause of Christ; we would allow to every man the fullest freedom to investigate for himself, and decide freely for or against our old

Christian faith. But if this decision fall out against it, we demand an open and honourable breach, and protest aloud against those who notwithstanding proclaim as *Christianity*—ay, and even as a higher, purer form of Christianity—that which deals a death-blow at the heart of the Christian faith. And while, as a matter of course, we do battle for this central truth, we feel that we have a right to do so, not only because we have experienced the power of the truth in our own hearts, but also *because of the scientific weakness and untenableness of our opponents' position.*

Looking back upon the way which we have gone, and passing by all details, we may comprehend the weak points in the anti-miraculous accounts of the life of Christ under the following heads:—

1. Their authors are *devoid of that true historical perception* which does not make its own subjective axioms the criterion of what is historically possible, but which lets the records say what they do say, and weighs their truth according to the historical effects which the events related in them have had and are still having. Instead of this, we find that both Rationalism of every sort and Mythicism *exhibit a boundless caprice in their treatment of the records;* the former in its exposition of them, the latter in the way it cuts them down, *i.e.* both in their elimination of the supernatural element. The standard of possibility which they apply to all that is contained in these records is their own unproved (and unprovable because false) presupposition that the miraculous is impossible. Whence their right to apply this standard? Certainly not from Him who has said, "My ways are not your ways," but solely from their own good pleasure. And what else is this, if we examine it closely, than a *tremendous presumption?* They alone, at least as regards their anti-miraculous axioms, are absolutely free from error: whatever militates against these cannot have happened. *History must be suited to their tastes, instead of their learning from history, and widening the narrowness of their own ideas to suit the greatness of divine actions.* Is this historical perception or presumption? Whoever approaches the treatment of a difficult historical problem without a humble desire for instruction, will be sure to produce an abortion; above all, in the treatment of a subject

which should never be approached otherwise than with the feeling, "Put off thy shoes from off thy feet, for the place whereon thou standest is holy ground."

2. *Our opponents do not explain what most needs explanation,* viz. *the existence of the Christian Church,* with its wonderful historical development, its moral influence, the spiritual and temporal blessings which it has brought to nations and individuals. Let any impartial person look at that very natural human demagogue of Schenkel's, or at that Galilean Rabbi of Strauss', who finally is guilty of "undue self-exaltation," or at that enthusiast and deceiver of Renan's who is constantly sinking deeper in the mire ; and then let him say whether any of these characters will afford a sufficient explanation of such far-reaching and mighty events ? No ! must be the answer—none but the Christ of the Gospels, the only-begotten Son of God, is great and mighty enough for us to attach such results to His holy name ! *The very existence of the Church is in itself the strongest proof for the truth of the gospel history.* By its fruits the truth may be known to this day. *Error may propagate itself, but only for a time.* The undiminished—nay, the ever-increasing—power of the gospel after the lapse of 1800 years, is proof enough that its contents are not legends and myths, but eternal truths.

3. *These accounts do not explain to us the Person of Christ,* notwithstanding—or rather because of—its depression to the level of natural human development. The issue on this question is simple. Here is a series of discourses and actions which the four Gospels attribute to Christ (even taking into account merely what is common to all, and undisputed). But no ordinary man can have said and done, or pretended to do, these things, without laying himself open to the reproach of arrogance, self-exaltation, fanaticism, and fraud. Hence the anti-miraculists are absolutely compelled to question Christ's sinlessness and freedom from error. Their merely human Christ no longer represents true, *i.e.* pure, humanity. Here, too, on the other hand, is the Christian Church, *i.e.* a world-wide series of wholesome moral influences which proceeded *from this Person.* How can both these things be reconciled ? They are a complete enigma. For if Jesus acted and spoke as a deceiver, then the moral effects of His teaching

are inconceivable. But since these effects are indubitably certain, it follows that Christ cannot have been a visionary or a deceiver, nor can He have acted as such. But if He truly spoke and actually did what is related, then He was no mere man, but the Son of God.

4. *They do not even explain to us whence the Christ imaged forth in the Gospels originated.* How came Galilean fishermen to invent an ideal of moral and spiritual majesty such as has never been attained in history, poetry, or philosophy, if it did not walk before them in person? All endeavours to explain this by means of myths and legends, later inventions and exaggerations, accord neither with the character of that age, nor with the spirit and style of the Gospels, nor with the testimony of confessedly genuine Pauline epistles, nor with the character of the primitive Christian Church, nor yet with the behaviour of its opponents.

5. *Not one of these accounts in the least satisfies the needs of the heart,* which, above all, the gospel is assuredly intended to meet. He who yearns after help and consolation, peace and freedom, for a burdened conscience, an aching heart, or a restless doubting spirit, cannot look for this from a Jesus who has ceased to be the Saviour of the world.

6. *Every one of these accounts is based upon a false conception of God,* either deistic or pantheistic. Together with their negation of the miraculous, they deny the free, living, personal God and Creator. Their whole tendency is to do away with Christ as *the* great Witness for a supernatural world, and to "disable" His testimony against the modern naturalistic views. In so doing they lose the Father as well as the Son; or more correctly, because they will not know the Father, they cannot know the Son.

However, we may learn something from all our opponents, even from these. Fundamentally false though their anti-miraculous standpoint may be, yet they contain certain *elements of truth,* just as the cognate systems of Deism and Pantheism. Does not the applause with which they were received proceed partly from the fact that the Church has not, as yet, given to the world an entirely correct representation of the life of Christ? True, here below the Church will never fully see through the great divine mystery of His Person; what the apostles did not succeed in will scarcely be accomplished by men of our own day. A perfect representation of Christ can only be expected by one who does not believe that we know in part. Nevertheless, since these late disputes, certain theologians have truly pointed out that the Church has proceeded in too *one-sided and dogmatic* a manner in her delineations of the Person of Christ.[1] It cannot be denied that there is a considerable gulf between the portrait of Christ in the Gospels and that of our dogmatic writings. In the latter we often miss the living historical reality of the Saviour. What with the great stress laid on the two separate factors, His humanity and His divinity, we have *lost the living unity of the Person*, the human and historical element in Christ; His learning obedience in constant and free self-surrender to His Father's will has been neglected as against His divine nature.

At this point of her doctrinal development the Church has still much to learn with regard to the great Christological problem of the present day,—a problem so great and difficult that it will never be more than approximately solved. Yet we shall constantly approach towards its final solution, if only we do not forget, on the one hand, that the genuinely human does not stand in absolute antithesis to the divine, but is intimately related to it; whereas, on the other hand, in a race degenerated through sin, this true humanity cannot be fully brought out except by a fresh engrafting of the divine. The true, the perfectly beautiful, humanity of Christ is so far from being annihilated by His divinity, that it is only the latter which completes and guarantees the former.[2]

Let us therefore beware of sacrificing the divine nature of Christ to His humanity, and of removing the stumbling-block of His God-manhood at the expense of His supernatural glory. This dangerous extreme will best be avoided by constantly allowing the perfect *sinlessness*, the unique moral dignity of Christ, to work upon our hearts and consciences. In view of this, the more earnestly a man feels his sin, the more deeply will he be convinced that the divine Sonship of Christ far transcends all natural humanity. And finally, let us cast

[1] Cf. Luthardt, *ubi sup.* pp. 11 et ss.

[2] Witness the perfectly beautiful humanity of Christ, combined with His no less perfect divinity, in the Gospel ot St. John.

into the scale the fact that this same divine Christ of the Gospels at this day is still *approving* Himself to the souls of men as the One who of God is made unto us wisdom and righteousness, sanctification and redemption. This, we know in our inmost hearts, is no delusion of fable or fancy ; and this drives us to the conclusion, that the historical portrait given by the evangelists of the Son of God is safe against all attacks.

Jesus Christ is not only, as many at the present day would have it, a great *Question;* He is far rather the *Divine Answer* to all human questions and complaints. If we look at Him merely as a Question, He becomes more and more unintelligible. Let us rather strive to understand Him as the Answer to that most vital question of our hearts : Who shall save me from sin and death ? Then shall we soon learn to believe and confess, "Thou art Christ, the Son of the living God !"

SEVENTH LECTURE.

MODERN DENIALS OF THE RESURRECTION OF CHRIST.

THE discussion of this question is, as it were, the final test of all that has gone before. What I have hitherto been seeking to establish was the belief in the supernatural, in the miraculous power of the living God as manifested in His being and His revelations, and especially in the history of His Son upon earth. All these miracles culminate in the resurrection of Christ. If this be established as true, then all else stands firm; if it be a legend, then little more can be saved. Therefore the investigation of this fact is peculiarly adapted to serve as a test for the results which we have hitherto attained. For the dogma of the resurrection is *the proof of all other dogmas, the foundation of our Christian life and hope, the soul of the entire apostolic preaching, the corner-stone on which the Christian Church is built.*

We will *first* make ourselves acquainted with the views and statements of our anti-miraculous opponents; *after this* we shall proceed to investigate the historical testimonies—especially that of Paul—and the arguments of those who reject them; and *finally*, we shall inquire whether the denials of the resurrection are not contradicted by certain indubitable facts and circumstances.

I.—ANTI-MIRACULOUS THEORIES.

Not a few among those who deny the *bodily* resurrection of Christ seek to diminish the importance of the question by representing it as non-essential to our faith, and "the corporeal element" as of no special significance. What matter, they say, whether His body again issued from the grave, if only the Spirit of Christ continue to work in those who are His? "The risen One is the exalted and glorified Christ the Lord who is the Spirit; He who lives in His Church."[1] Thus we find many surreptitiously changing the resurrection of Christ's body into something quite different, whilst outwardly keeping up a show of adherence to the letter of this Article, by preaching and speaking of a "spiritual resurrection and glorification." This miserably confuses the whole issue. Whoever denies a bodily resurrection should be honest enough no longer to speak of resurrection at all.[2] *Resurrection does not refer to the spirit,* the continued existence of which Scripture takes as a matter of course, *but only to the body, and its issuing forth alive from the grave.* Only that can rise again which has before been laid down in the grave, and that is only the body, not the spirit. Let us then have done with these ambiguities.

But according to Scripture, the body of Christ was a sinless body, broken only for the sins of the world. Hence His death was freely undertaken (John x. 18) by One who, as the Son of God, possessed life in Himself, and had received from His Father power to lay down His life and to take it again (John v. 26, ii. 19, x. 17 ff.). The question therefore is, whether by the raising up of this His body, Christ really was "*declared to be the Son of God*" (Rom. i. 4), and His most important self-testimonies confirmed or not; whether He was indeed "crowned with glory and honour" (Heb. ii. 9), or whether, forsaken of God, He merely died on the cross? We must decide whether His death was accepted by God as an *atoning death* for us or not; or, in other words, whether *the work of redemption was indeed accomplished.* On the resurrection of Christ depends our hope that this work will be fully accomplished in each of us, first inwardly, but at length outwardly too, when the last enemy is destroyed in the *general resurrection* (Rom. vi. 8; 1 Cor. xv. 2). This shows the importance of the question under consideration. A birth divine and human; a perfectly sinless obedience; a world-redeeming death and passion; a resurrection by which death was overcome; followed by exaltation at the right hand of

[1] Schenkel, *Charakterbild Jesu*, p. 233.

[2] Thus, Vögelin confesses, "It would be more correct, instead of always speaking of the *resurrection* of Christ, to mention only His *continued existence* amongst us" (*Die Geschichte Jesu*, p. 111).

the Father and the mission of the Spirit,—all these things are firmly connected parts of one and the same work of redemption. Take but one link out of this chain, and the whole falls to pieces. The resurrection is the beginning of Christ's exaltation, and therefore the most important and indispensable link which connects His temporal work on earth with His eternal work in heaven. It is necessary, no less for the perfection of the person than for the completion of the work of the God-man; it is no less the source of our living faith than the firm foundation for our hope of coming glory and perfection.

It is only if we take our stand on this fundamental view that we can understand the apostle when he says: "If Christ be not risen, then is our preaching vain, and your faith is also vain; . . . ye are yet in your sins: then they also which are fallen asleep in Christ are perished" (1 Cor. xv. 14–18). If any one attaches weight to this testimony of St. Paul, he ought not to deny that the resurrection of Christ must remain the Shibboleth of our Christian faith, as it was from the beginning the centre of the apostolic preaching (Acts i. 22, ii. 31 ff.). How can Schenkel, in contradiction to such a testimony, maintain that "the Apostle Paul himself pronounced a faith which rests only on the *outward* fact of a *bodily* resurrection of Christ to be entirely worthless"?[1] What does St. Paul—in our case as in that of our Lord—mean when he speaks of resurrection, if not a bodily rising again? In the passage cited (vers. 33–54) he constantly mentions the resurrection-*body*: "How are the dead raised up? and with what body do they come? . . . This corruptible must put on incorruption, and this mortal must put on immortality." Against whom is St. Paul writing in this entire chapter, if not against the doubters of a *bodily* resurrection? And we are told that he pronounced the faith in this outward fact to be entirely worthless: he who makes the truth of his preaching, the

[1] *Charakterbild Jesu*, p. 223. To support this, Schenkel appeals to 2 Cor. v. 16, "Though we have known Christ *after the flesh*, yet now henceforth know we Him no more;" but this passage does not in the least confirm his view. For St. Paul only means that he no longer lays any value upon having known Christ "after the flesh," *i.e.* outwardly as a natural man, since he has now become acquainted with Him as the risen and glorified One. The meaning or importance of the resurrection-body is not touched upon at all.

certainty of our faith, our redemption from sin, and our hope of life, dependent on this fact! It is impossible to speak more distinctly than St. Paul does here. But nothing is clear to those who are *determined* to doubt and cavil. Moreover, unbelief has an interest, for reasons which are easy to discover, in not acknowledging any one article of our faith as of fundamental importance for the whole. For then it is all the easier to shake and undermine one after another. Hence the numerous attempts to diminish the importance of the resurrection, or to transfer it from the corporeal into the spiritual region, and by these means to make this article of faith somewhat more palatable to the miracle-fearing minds of our age.

This tendency to ignore the importance of the body proceeds from a general lack of insight into the scriptural philosophy of nature and of spirit. Those who do so are *entirely wanting in any profound apprehension of the process of salvation,* by which, according to Scripture, God is carrying on the world towards its consummation. This process must extend to the corporeal world as well as to the spiritual. For the victory of divine love over all the powers of sin and death would *not be complete* if the body of man were not once to be released from the bonds of death, and raised into that glorious condition for which God has originally destined it. Like all other terrestrial bodies, it is intended one day to be entirely penetrated by the spirit, to be translated into the glorious liberty of the children of God, and thus to be transformed in light inwardly and outwardly (Rom. viii. 21–23; Phil. iii. 21; 2 Cor. iv. 10, etc.). And how otherwise could this world-renewing process be begun than by the resurrection and transformation of that one Body over which death had no power—the sinless body of Christ the second Adam, in whom all are to be made alive (1 Cor. xv. 22 et ss.)? In His resurrection "the consummation of the world is anticipated." As in the nether world Christ broke the bonds of spiritual death, so in His resurrection He destroyed the organic power of death in the earthly creation, and impregnated it (as an organism—hence the dead bodies of the saints appear in Matt. xxvii. 52 and 53) with new and divine vital forces: just as in the heart the life-blood is prepared afresh, and from it flows forth into all the limbs. The resurrection power coming from Christ, through the medium of His word and sacraments, tends mainly to the sanctification and renewing of the sinner (Rom. v. 10; Eph. ii. 5, 6; 1 Pet. i. 3); and thus interpenetrates, first, the spiritual nature of man, planting within those who are regenerate a germ for the resurrection of the body (Rom. viii. 11). Then the spiritual life of Christ breaks forth into a manifestation in the visible world, by revivifying the bodies of those who are sanctified (in the first resurrection, 1 Cor. xv. 23; John v. 25–29; Rev. xx. 5, 6). In the succeeding general resurrection—an act of Christ's power which extends to the *whole* of the corporeal world, and introduces the great mundane catastrophe (Rev. xx. 11–13)—as well as in the formation of a new heaven and a new earth, this grand and gradually progressive process of the world's renewal has its fitting consummation. It is God's will that His glory should dwell in His whole creation, that He may be all in all (1 Cor. xv. 28; Rev. xxi. 3 et ss.). In this respect we must indorse the sentiment of Oetinger, that "corporeity is the end of God's ways."

This profound connection between the resurrection of Christ and the renewal of the whole world, is overlooked by our opponents in a spirit that is as unbiblical as it is unphilosophical. They have no comprehension for that great promise, "Behold, I make *all things new*" (Rev. xxi. 5), nor yet for the holy necessity of its fulfilment.

All the more are we ready to acknowledge the just perception of Strauss (who in this respect sees further than Keim [1])

[1] *Der geschichtliche Christus*, third edition, p. 104. We say this at the risk of Keim's classing us amongst "the zealots of the letter," as he has done with Güder (p. 135) on account of his instructive book, *The Actuality of Christ's Resurrection and its Opponents*. Keim is of opinion that "we cannot—as Schleiermacher long since proved—bind down the Christian faith to an isolated historical account, related with so many contradictions, and of so difficult and variable interpretation." Against this we would remark, that we do not consider the resurrection of Christ to be a mere "account," but also the intrinsically necessary conclusion of all that had gone before, and the starting-point of all that followed in the work of redemption. Nor is this "an isolated account related with many contradictions," but rather one which is vouched for by many witnesses, and *in the main* unanimously testified; an account which, like every miracle, is historically difficult to explain, but by no means, according to the plain meaning of the words, "of variable interpretation." The appeal to Schleiermacher, who, in respect of the resurrection, unaccountably maintained that most unfortunate theory of apparent death (*vide* below), is by no means happy. In this case Schleiermacher only showed "that one cannot remain on his standpoint."

in assigning to the resurrection its full importance; calling it as he does, "the centre of the centre, the real heart of Christianity as it has been until now," and saying that, "as regards the resurrection of Christ, it can scarcely be doubted that with it the truth of Christianity stands or falls. Does not the Apostle Paul say, 'If Christ be not risen, then is our preaching vain,' etc.? (1 Cor. xv. 14–17.) This apostolic saying cannot be explained away."[1] Indeed, Strauss acknowledges that this question is the real *test of his standpoint:* "We here stand on the decisive spot where, in face of the records which tell of the miraculous resurrection of Christ, we must either confess the insufficiency of all natural historical explanations of the life of Christ, *i.e.* give up our entire undertaking; or we must pledge ourselves to explain the purport of those records, viz. the belief in the resurrection of Christ, without having recourse to a corresponding miraculous fact."[2] Most true. This is the point at which it must be decided, more palpably than anywhere else, who is in the right, Strauss or the Church, the anti-miraculists or the miracle-believers.

Strauss has shown greater keenness of perception in this matter even than Baur, who, strange to say, seems to think that he can evade this fundamental question. He expresses himself in a strangely ambiguous manner. "What the resurrection *per se* is, it does not lie within the bounds of historical research to determine."[3] Our research has only to bear in mind that, *for the belief of the disciples,* the resurrection of Christ was incontestably certain. "No analysis can penetrate into the inward spiritual process in the disciples' consciousness by which their unbelief at the death of Christ afterwards changed into a belief in His resurrection. . . . For the disciples the resurrection was as real as any historical fact —whatever may have been the medium of this persuasion." In this way Baur quickly passes by the chief question, how this new belief can have originated in the disciples. The resurrection is supposed to be the declaration of a firm belief, that the person of Christ had not only not perished, but by death was raised to its absolute importance—expressed in the form of an external event.

[1] *Die Halben und die Ganzen,* pp. 125–127. [2] *Leben Jesu,* p. 288.
[3] *Das Christenthum der ersten drei Jahrhunderte,* p. 39.

Thus we see that Baur rests the whole development of the Christian Church, not on the objective fact of Christ's resurrection, but on the subjective belief of His disciples in it; not on Christ Himself, but on His disciples; not on a *divine act*, but on a certain inexplicable *condition of human consciousness.* Instead of the fact, we have a fiction, *i.e.* the mere conception of a fact, which may or may not have a real objective foundation. Well might Strauss blame this ambiguity. "Baur," says he, "at least verbally, *evaded the burning question.* For his words sound as if it were impossible to ascertain historically, nor were even a matter of historical research, whether the resurrection of Christ was an outward (natural or miraculous) event, or whether it only took place in the belief of the disciples. But assuredly Baur had settled in his own mind that it was by no means the former, *i.e.* an outward occurrence of any sort, and therefore he must necessarily conclude that it was the latter, *i.e.* a mere idea" (*ubi sup.* p. 228). And, indeed, we are strangely impressed, but not at all convinced, by the way in which this historian,—who examines every portion of Church history with such exactitude, and asks not merely what was believed to have occurred, but what really happened,—instead of examining into the reality of this fact to which all the apostles appeal, and on which the Christian Church is founded, simply contents himself with knowing that it was believed in! This can only be done by an idealistic philosopher, to whom history in general is nothing but a process of consciousness.

Before this Baur had remarked: "Between the death of Christ and his resurrection there lies so thick and impenetrable a darkness, that after the connection has been so violently torn and so wonderfully restored, we seem to be placed on a new theatre of history." This is perfectly true: the resurrection of Christ turned over a new leaf in the history of the world, and prepared a new soil for its development. But does "a new theatre of history" originate from a mere idea? Would not the formation of this divine idea, this belief, "from which depends the entire weight of a movement so world-wide as that of Christianity, without the corresponding fact, be a miracle as great and far greater" than the resurrection itself? Of such a theory assuredly we may say: "In any case it does not help us to attain to a historical and philosophical comprehension of Christianity."[1] According to Scripture, the apostles founded the Church on a fact. Here we have a foundation-stone. Baur founds it on a breach in the historical connection which is enveloped in enigmatic darkness, *i.e.* upon a gap. No wonder, then, that his historical construction of the building is hollow.

Many others, however, have in the most various ways endeavoured positively to show how this belief could arise in the disciples *in a natural manner.* On the one hand, the reality of Christ's *death* was denied, and reduced to a mere *trance,* so that the resurrection would be the perfectly natural *recovery from a deep swoon.* On the other hand, the reality of our Saviour's death was confessed, but the *resurrection* as an *outward* fact denied, and the origin of the belief in it attributed to *visions* experienced by the disciples.

The former of these hypotheses, that of *apparent death,* was employed by the old *Rationalists,* and more recently by Schleiermacher in his *Life of Christ.* We might remind the upholders of this theory, of the blood and water which flowed from our Saviour's opened side. However, we will let the physiologists dispute whether this symptom is a sure test of death or not. This theory is contradicted in the first place by *the unanimous voice of Scripture in all its parts, which in a hundred passages represents the death of Christ as real.* We see this throughout the Old Testament, from the promised coming of the Serpent's Destroyer, whose heel shall be bruised (Gen. iii. 15), down to such prophecies as these: "Thou hast brought me into the dust of death" (Ps. xxii. 15); "He was cut off out of the land of the living" (Isa. liii. 8); "They shall look upon me whom thay have pierced" (Zech. xii. 12, 10). And far more clearly even do we see it throughout the New Testament,—in our Lord's numerous predictions of His own redeeming death (Matt. xvi. 21, xx. 28, etc.),—in the exact descriptions of His death by all four evangelists, according to whom He really *died,* or breathed out His spirit (ἐξέπνευσε), and commended it into the hands of His Father (Matt. xxvii. 50; Mark xv. 37; Luke xxiii. 46; John xix. 30, 33),—in the apostolic testimonies of St. Peter and St. Paul, both in the

[1] Landerer, *Worte der Erinnerung an F. C. v. Baur,* p. 71.

Acts (ii. 24–32, x. 39, xiii. 28–30, 34 et ss., etc.) and in the Epistles (Rom. v. 6–10; 1 Cor. xv. 3; 1 Pet. iii. 18, etc.),—in the Revelation of St. John, where "the First-begotten of the dead" testifies of Himself, "*I . . . was dead*, and behold I am alive for evermore, and have the keys of hell and of death" (i. 5, 18, ii. 8). Again, this theory is contradicted by the divine and human necessity of Christ's death as the ground of our *reconciliation* with God. How could this death, foreshadowed by all the sacrifices of the Old Testament, be imagined as a *sacrificial death*, if Christ did not actually *expire?* And once more, this theory is contradicted by the parallel, though contradistinctive, relation in which the death of Christ is placed to His resurrection; as also by the way in which our translation from the condition of death into new life is connected with the resurrection of Christ as its pattern and principle (Rom. iv. 24, 25, vi. 3 et ss., viii. 10 et ss., xiv. 9; 1 Cor. xv. 3 et ss.; 2 Cor. v. 14 et ss., etc.).

But apart from all these considerations, there is one simple question which entirely upsets this contrivance of the rationalists. *How could the pitiable appearance of one who was just recovering from deadly wounds give rise to such a sudden and enthusiastic belief in the resurrection of death's conqueror?* Strauss has dealt a deadly blow to Rationalism by pointing this out in his trenchant way.[1] "One who had thus crept forth half dead from the grave, and crawled about a sickly patient, who had need of medical and surgical assistance, of nursing and strengthening, but who notwithstanding finally succumbed to his sufferings, could never have given the disciples the impression that he was the conqueror over the grave and death, and the prince of life. Such a recovery could only have weakened, or at best given a pathetic tinge to the impression which he had made upon them by his life and death; but it cannot possibly have changed their sorrow into ecstasy, and raised their reverence into worship." Schleiermacher defends his strange view by the argument that real death had never been known to take place without decomposition supervening; as if the shedding of Christ's blood and His death were not adequate for our redemption without ensuing corruption, the absence of which is sufficiently

[1] *Leben Jesu*, p. 298.

accounted for by the epithet "Thy Holy One" in Ps. xvi. 10 and Acts ii. 31. Schleiermacher's supposition, that Jesus afterwards lived for a time with the disciples, and then retired into entire solitude for his second death, will scarcely obtain fresh acceptation for this exploded hypothesis; for even then the apparent death would be followed by the infinite disenchantment of real decease.[1] Hence the modern opponents of the resurrection have not ventured to recur to this hypothesis, according to which *God would have founded His kingdom on a misunderstanding*,[2]—and the words of our old creed are still valid, "who was crucified, *dead*, and buried."

At present, the second of the theories which we have mentioned is in vogue among our opponents; *i.e.* they suppose the belief in the resurrection to have *arisen from visions*. This is the distinctly expressed theory of Strauss and Renan; while with Schenkel, who as usual stops half way, it is difficult to say what theory he really adopts. It would be scarce worth while to follow out the various modifications of his views, were it not that from him we learn an instructive lesson as to how the opponents of the biblical doctrine turn and twist and cover their movements with a cloud of phrases, in order, on the one hand, to remove the miraculous, and on the other, to escape the reproach of radical unbelief.

Schenkel rejects the miraculous revivification of our Lord's earthly body; he rejects the supposition of apparent death; ay, he even rejects the "visionary hypothesis." In chap. xxix. of his *Sketch of Christ's Character* (under the ambiguous heading, "The Glorification") he considers three facts to be indubitable: first, "that in the early morning of the first day of the week which followed the crucifixion, the grave of Jesus was found empty;" second, "that the apostles and other members of the apostolic community were convinced that they had seen Jesus since his crucifixion;" and last, "that the appearances of Christ which the Gospels relate as taking place after his death were essentially of the same character as that which the Apostle Paul experienced on his way to Damascus" (p. 231). And St. Paul himself, in Gal. i. 16, designates "his vision mainly

[1] *Vide* Schleiermacher, *Leben Jesu*, pp. 443 et ss., and 500 et ss. Against this theory, cf. Keim, *ubi sup.* pp. 132 et ss.

[2] Cf. also Kahnis, *Die Auferstehung Jesu als geschichtliche Thatsache.*

as an inward revelation of Christ." "The risen One is, therefore, the glorified and transfigured Christ, the Lord who is the Spirit" (p. 232).

The two first of these facts are universally acknowledged. But the third is no "fact;" it is merely a conjecture, which leaves it an entirely open question whether that appearance of Christ near Damascus was merely an inward revelation or an outward and objective one as well, and whether Gal. i. 16 is a sufficient proof for the former of these suppositions; indeed, whether this occurrence really does at all belong to the same category as the appearances of the risen Christ in the Gospels. This question will come before us presently; meanwhile "a *mainly* inward revelation" is of no use, as we must postulate *either* an external *or* an internal event.

If, however, he denies the bodily resurrection of Christ, and pronounces that which the Bible maintains to be of supreme importance to be utterly worthless, how does Schenkel explain the belief in the resurrection? He says that the Church at Jerusalem regarded the fact, that the grave of Jesus was found empty, as a miracle of divine omnipotence, and supposed that "it had taken place by the help of angels. Hence the first tradition of an angelic appearance, which was supported by the utterances of deeply-excited women" (p. 231). The feelings of love, of hope, and of trust were again awakened. "Here, too, women led the way. They believed that in the place where Christ's body had lain they had seen celestial beings. This was followed by ecstatic conditions, the consequence of deeply shaken feminine soul-life" (p. 226). It seems strange after this that Schenkel should reject Renan's supposition of morbid hallucinations. But what really happened? Did Christ in any way again approach His people? We are merely told that "his appearances were so many manifestations of his likeness, which till then had been so much obscured in the hearts of those who believed in him. He proved himself in them to be the ever-living One" (p. 233).

Apparently Schenkel feels that indefinite phrases such as these are mere evasions, and not explanations of the matter in question. For in another place[1] he endeavours to give us

[1] *Allgemeine Kirchliche Zeitschrift*, 1865, No. 5, pp. 289-384.

more precise information. Here he tells us that the appearances of the risen Christ were "real manifestations of his personality, which had issued forth from death living and glorified." This sounds almost orthodox, only that the more indefinite expression "personality" is substituted for "body." For, he continues, the corpse remained in the grave, or was removed from it in a manner which we cannot now determine; only the spirit issued forth alive (just as if *the spirit* had ever been laid in the grave !) and surrounded itself with some fresh body, "because the life of the human personality absolutely needs some (outward) organ for its manifestation." Was it, then, a kind of spiritual apparition through the medium of this new "organ," and in any case without the old body ? No, it was not this, but a "real though mysterious self-revelation of Christ's personality which had come forth from death living and imperishable," and which was of such a nature "that the disciples received the impression of having actually seen Jesus." Instead of an explanation, a fresh enigma is here presented to us. Who can extract any clear idea from this cloud of words, which seems to affirm everything, and yet is intended to deny everything ? If the body of Christ remained dead, then it is a glaring abuse of biblical language, ay, verbal "forgery" (Strauss), still to speak of Him as "risen from the dead."

Here we are met by Schenkel with a strange objection: "If Christ had returned among men after his crucifixion in the same earthly and corporeal form as before,[1] why did he not show himself to his Jewish judges and to the Roman procurator? Why did he not appear in the streets of Jerusalem before the people who had been so basely deceived as to his person ? Why did he not by his mere appearance inspire courage in his frightened followers everywhere, and utterly defeat his malignant enemies ?"[2] Why ? Because God's ways are far more wise and holy than our short-sightedness would expect. Why did our Lord always refuse to give a sign from heaven ? Why did He not at the very beginning hold an audible conversation with His Father up to heaven, in order

[1] This is nowhere maintained in the Scriptures ; for, according to them, the resurrection was the beginning of the transformation of His earthly body, which transformation was completed at His ascension.

[2] *Charakterbild Jesu*, p. 233.

publicly and irrefutably to prove His divine mission, to stop the mouths of all doubters and adversaries, and make it easy for every one to believe in Him? Why did He not come down from the cross to prove His divine Sonship? Had it been told us that Christ did, as Schenkel would have had Him, *make a public show of Himself* before His enemies, then we should have great reason to doubt the veracity of the records which contained such a statement. For this would be entirely out of keeping with all His other miracles, as well as with His character and work. That He did *not* do so, speaks for the credibility of His reappearance. Miracles may facilitate faith, but must never compel it. This objection of Schenkel's entirely ignores the moral character of true faith, which must depend upon a man's free decision. Would Christ's kingdom any longer be a kingdom of faith, if it were founded upon the fact that the risen Saviour had been seen and touched *by all—i.e.* upon a miracle which had become a *public gazing-stock?* And did Jerusalem still deserve this? Had not the people, when demanding the crucifixion of Jesus, passed sentence of death upon themselves? After Christ's entry into Jerusalem, the respite of grace for Israel had hurried to its close. With His crucifixion, Israel, as a nation, was condemned to death. Only individuals could still be saved. And Schenkel would demand a further respite for the most hardened enemies of Christ; nay, even a compulsion to believe! No; henceforth the risen Saviour could only appear, "not to all the people, but unto witnesses chosen before of God" (Acts x. 41), as a reward for their measure of faith in still following Him even when shamefully put to death. Henceforth it was ordained by "the foolishness of God," which is "wiser than men," that "by the foolishness of preaching they that *believe*" should be saved; and now Israel and the whole world, with all their wise men and scribes, had to learn from the poor fishermen to whom the manifestations of this wondrous divine victory over death had been vouchsafed.

But though Schenkel may not be a strict upholder of the "visionary theory," Renan openly professes his adherence to it. We have already seen that he regards Mary Magdalene as the creative authoress of the resurrection belief. For an explanation of "the strange rumours which spread amongst the disciples in consequence of the grave being found empty," we are referred to his work on the Apostles. This has since then appeared, and in the first chapter we are told as follows:—

"Though Jesus often spoke of resurrection and a new life, yet he never distinctly said that he should rise again in this flesh,"—just as if His repeated announcements that the Son of man should be killed and rise again the third day could have been understood by His disciples in any other sense than that of a bodily resurrection from the grave (cf. Matt. xii. 40, xvii. 9, 23, xx. 19, xxvi. 32, Mark viii. 31, ix. 9, 10, 31, x. 34, Luke ix. 22, xviii. 33). All the passages which contradict Renan's notion are disposed of by the remark, that "after a certain time had elapsed, much importance was attached to Christ's predicting his resurrection." This is the old critical artifice, to reject as spurious that portion of the records which contradicts one's presuppositions. Christ must be told what He may and what He may not have spoken.

Further on Renan cannot help confessing that "several of the Master's words *might* be understood in the sense of his again issuing from the grave." He then describes to us the state of mind in which a belief in the resurrection might arise. "Enoch and Elijah had not tasted death. The belief began to gain ground that even the patriarchs and other Old Testament worthies of the first rank had not really died, and that their bodies were alive in their graves at Hebron." How does Renan know this? It is simply a piece of his lively Oriental imagination which plays such an important part in his *Vie de Jésus.* In Acts ii. 29, Peter says of David, "He is both dead and buried, and his sepulchre is with us unto this day;" and he mentions this as a well-known fact, doubted by no one. Nor can Renan adduce a single authority for this wild assertion. But let us hear him further. "The same thing must happen to Jesus as has happened to all men (?) who had riveted the attention of their contemporaries. The world, accustomed to invest them with superhuman powers, cannot believe that they have succumbed to the hard law of death. Heroes do not die. This honoured Master had lived too profoundly amongst his followers for them not to maintain after his death that he would always live. The day after his burial was full of such thoughts as these. The women, especially in spirit, overwhelmed him with their tenderest caresses (only hear the Parisian !). Their thoughts cannot for a moment forsake this beloved friend: surely the angels must be surrounding him, and veiling their countenances with his grave-clothes. . . . The little company of Christians on that day accomplished the true miracle; they raised up Jesus *in their hearts* by the mighty love which they bore to him. They resolved that Jesus should not die. The love of these passionately-moved souls was indeed stronger than death."

According to the unanimous testimony of all the records, the reports or manifestations of Christ's resurrection *profoundly startled* both the women and the disciples, and so *suddenly broke in upon their sorrowful brooding*, that at first they *would not believe* them (Mark xvi. 11, 13 et ss.; Luke xxiv. 22 et ss.). According to Renan, they were *made way for* by the expectations of the disciples; nay, even *produced by them through a heroic resolution ! !*

Mary Magdalene played a most important part in this matter. "We must follow her step by step, for during one hour of that day she carried within her all the workings of the Christian consciousness. Her testimony decided the faith of the future." But how may we explain the appearances of Christ amongst the assembled disciples? Whilst they are sitting together, probably "something like a light breath passes over the faces of the assembly. At such decisive hours a breath of air, a rattling window, a chance murmur, may decide the belief of nations for centuries." The disciples hear the word "Peace." There was no longer any doubt; Christ is present!

Thus it is that Renan explains the belief in the resurrection. Hallucinations of a visionary woman, a breath of air, a rattling window, a chance murmur; these are his last resorts. Windy hypotheses in good sooth! Did ever unbelief give a more flagrant proof of its inability to afford a natural explanation of divine facts than this? Woe be to us if a breath of air may at any time chain us and our posterity for centuries to a momentous error from which there is no escape, especially if we happen to be in an excited frame of mind! How thoroughly must one who can thus speak have given up all belief even in a *moral* harmony of the world, to say nothing of a holy providence! Unbelief delivers mankind's choicest treasures, all its moral religious convictions, to the mercy of the merest chance; and here we see in glaring colours *how deeply, in consequence of this, it degrades man, and how shamefully it defiles his moral dignity.* And yet unbelief behaves as though it were going to help man to attain his full dignity.

A far more notable upholder of the "visionary" hypothesis meets us in the person of Strauss. He extends the myth as far back as Gethsemane, though it is not easy to imagine how it should have occurred to any one to invent such a spiritual struggle; for these myths are surely intended to exalt Christ, whereas the scene in the garden shows Him in His deepest abasement. As is his wont, Strauss begins the investigation by gathering together all the variations and contradictions of the different narratives, in order to deduce therefrom "the insufficiency of the evangelical accounts." He will not acknowledge any other witness as credible than *Paul,* who in 1 Cor. xv. only says that the revived Saviour "appeared" to the apostles, *i.e.* "they *believed* that they visibly perceived him. But he does not tell us what reasons they had for regarding the appearance as something real, and even as their crucified Master himself. Indeed, it is doubtful whether Paul ever inquired after such reasons" (*Leben Jesu,* p. 290). "We do not possess any deposition of an eye-witness about these appearances" (p. 291; since the Gospels are not apostolic). Only the *appearance of Christ before Damascus,* which is referred to by St. Paul in 1 Cor. xv. 8 and ix. 1, is related to us by an eye-witness, and that "very briefly" (p. 301); for the thrice-told story in the Acts has only the value of a "third-class testimony," on account of the spuriousness and uncertainty of this record. True, from that testimony of St. Paul about himself, short as it is, this much is evident, "that he imagined the exalted Christ to be *really and wonderfully* present, and considered the appearance fully objective" (p. 302). Notwithstanding, there is "nothing to prevent us from being of a different opinion in this matter, and considering the appearance as simply *subjective,* an event of his *inward soul-life.*" Moreover, we may safely do this, as "certain over-strained conditions of the soul were nothing uncommon with Paul," and many traits in him make us suspect that he had "a nervous constitution," which probably kept him subject to convulsions, or perhaps epileptic fits! Only Strauss forgets that the visions and revelations of which Paul speaks (2 Cor. xii. 1 et ss.) belong only to his *Christian* life, and not to his career as a Jew and a Pharisee, which closed with that first and greatest vision of Christ before Damascus.

It is evident, then, that the clear and certain meaning of that testimony points to an actual outward appearance of Christ. Nevertheless, it was merely an inward occurrence, and St. Paul must have deceived himself, since, with regard to visions in general, he was not sober and dependable enough; indeed, we may almost say, not a responsible agent. Another, too, of Strauss' manœuvres is worthy of notice, viz. the way in which he changes what St. Paul evidently considers an incontestable objective fact (1 Cor. xv. 3 ff.) into the tradition of a subjective *belief* that the Lord had been seen, and that merely because St. Paul does not enumerate the reasons which induced the disciples to consider this appearance as something objective. Does Strauss think that the apostle in this short sketch ought to have made provision for the doubts of every future sceptic? Surely the absence of all such reasons rather tends to show that the disciples had so little doubt as to the reality of Christ's appearance, that it never occurred to them to give further reasons for their belief in what they had seen and experienced.

Having by *coups de force* such as these endeavoured to give colour to his supposition that the vision of Christ before Damascus was merely inward, Strauss proceeds from this to draw "regressive conclusions as to the origin of the belief in Christ's resurrection." The appearances of Christ to the elder disciples were of intrinsically the same character. "They, too, were merely internal events, which might easily appear to the persons concerned as outward and sensuous perceptions, but by us must be comprehended as *inward facts resulting from an excitement of the emotional life, i.e.* as *visions*" (p. 304). "The endeavour of the disciples after the death of Christ must have been to include the attribute of vicarious suffering, of violent but expiatory death, in their conception of the Messiah." Such a death which was undergone for all, could only be the entrance into the Messianic glory—a transition to a new and higher life. And did not the Old Testament contain prophecies of the Holy One whom God would not suffer to see corruption,—of the Servant of God who should be taken away out of the land of the living, and yet see long life? But "from the Jewish standpoint, the soul without the body is a mere shadow" (p. 307). How else, therefore, could they imagine the soul of Christ to be exalted to His Father in heaven otherwise than by the reviving of His body? Hence their notion of His resurrection.

Some of the narratives about the appearance of the risen Christ may well make us "conjecture that the excitement of the disciples after the sudden death of Jesus, and their imagination which was constantly employed in renewing his picture, caused them to see a reappearance of their Master in any unknown person who met them under enigmatical circumstances, and made a special impression upon them" (p. 308). How is it that other mourners, whose imagination is also much occupied with the picture of their dear and suddenly departed ones, do not often suffer under a similar deception? But even Strauss remarks of the first occasions on which Christ appeared to single individuals, that "it is scarce likely that they were of this description." How were they? "The expression of Mark, that he appeared first to Mary Magdalene, from whom he had cast out seven devils, gives much food for thought. With a woman thus constituted in mind and body, there was no great step between inward excitement and a vision." The case of Paul and the (legendary) vision of Peter (Acts x.), show us that mental conditions of this kind were not rare even in the case of men of that period, and of simple culture. We may therefore well "suppose that during the days which followed the death of Jesus, there was among his followers a general frame of mind, an intensification of the emotional and nervous life, which would compensate for any want of disposition on the part of an individual" (p. 309). But how can we conceive that the belief in the resurrection should have arisen so early as the *third day?* Does not the mental revulsion from which the visions of Christ are supposed to have proceeded, need a longer space of time for its development? Certainly; but Paul only says that Jesus *rose* on the third day, not that he *appeared* at the same time (pp. 310, 311).

We must therefore suppose the matter to have taken place thus: "After the crucifixion of Jesus, his disciples, in their first panic, fled back to their homes in Galilee. There, in the regions which they had so often traversed with him, they were constantly aroused to recall anew his picture. The longer period which in this way elapsed would give time for the revolution in the feelings of the disciples" (pp. 315, 316). And here, then, the visions took place. True, this is contradicted by the Gospels, which all mention the first appearances of the risen Saviour as taking place in *Jerusalem and its neighbourhood;* and even Matthew, who tells of the angel commanding the disciples to come into Galilee, immediately afterwards relates how Jesus appeared to women from Jerusalem. But "there never was a thing so utterly superfluous as this first appearance of Christ in Matthew; it is a later interpolation into the narrative on which Matthew founded his story of the resurrection" (p. 314). For it was not until afterwards that the manifestation of the resurrection was transferred to Jerusalem and the third day, in order that "death might only have a short-lived power over the crucified Messiah" (p. 315).

This is the view of Strauss. He uses the same violence towards the records in carrying through his hypothesis as in making way for it. What he really offers as an explanation of the belief in the resurrection, amounts merely to powerful imagination, excitement of the nervous life, intensified emotions, and visions resulting therefrom.

For a historical demonstration of the actuality of Christ's resurrection, Strauss demands a double proof: *first,* it must be shown that the *direct* testimonies to the reality of this fact should meet all the requirements of historical testimonies; *second,* it must be proved that without the occurrence in question, other events which are historically certain could not have taken place.[1] Well, we think that *these two things may be proved: the historical credibility of our testimonies, and the impossibility of explaining certain indubitable facts,*—such as the belief of the disciples in Christ's resurrection; the sudden revolution in their consciousness, their preaching, and the Church thereby gathered and founded on this belief; but

[1] *Die Halben u. die Ganzen,* p. 125; cf. *Leben Jesu,* p. 289.

especially the sudden conversion of St. Paul,—*without having recourse to the resurrection as a fact,* and not a mere vision. We will now proceed to consider the *historical testimonies,*—first, that of the *Gospels,* then that of *St. Paul* (especially his vision of Christ before Damascus),—and we shall see whether the enemies of these records are right, or whether their credibility fulfils the first half of Strauss' demand.

II.—THE HISTORICAL TESTIMONIES.

Strauss demands that these should be direct testimonies, proceeding from eye-witnesses. Now, according to his presuppositions, the only book of the New Testament which could possibly have proceeded from an apostle is the *Revelation of St. John;* and this book, he says, "does not go beyond the general belief that Jesus had been killed, and was now alive again and immortal" (p. 298). Is this correct? The contradiction which this proposition contains shows how untenable such an interpretation of the passages in question must be. For only that can live *again* which was before dead; but this was not the case with the immortal spirit of Christ, only with His body. If, then, the Book of Revelation teach that Christ is living again, it witnesses to His resurrection. But it does so even directly. In chap. i. 5, Christ is called "the First-begotten of the dead." This certainly cannot mean the first of those who lived immortal after death, for there were enough such before Christ; it must mean the first among the dead who again came to life, and who, because He had broken the power of death, has become the source of new life for all who have died, *i.e.* the first risen One, who is the resurrection and the life for all others. In the same manner, chap. ii. 8—"which was dead and lived" (ἔζησεν)—mentions both, dying and coming to life, equally as *historical* facts, and must be understood in the same way. What our Lord says in i. 18, "I have the keys of hell and of death," *i.e.* power over death and the kingdom of the dead, would not be fully true if a part of Christ, viz. His body, had remained in the bondage of death. Here, then, we have (especially in ii. 8) an historical testimony from an apostle for the resurrection of Christ's body, which can be overlooked only by a most superficial exegesis.

Strauss will not acknowledge the Gospels as direct testimonies, because none of them was written by an apostle or eye-witness of the life of Christ. But we have already seen that even the most negative critics in our day grant that they belong to the apostolic age, when there must at least have been many such eye-witnesses living. Moreover, it should be borne in mind that the Gospel of St. John declares itself to have been written by an eye-witness (xix. 35, xxi. 24), and would therefore, if genuine, abundantly fulfil Strauss' first postulate. But its genuineness is maintained even by such critics as Schleiermacher, Credner, Lachmann, Ewald, Hase, and Ritschl, to say nothing of more orthodox men, such as Gaussen, Hengstenberg, Tischendorf, Riggenbach, Oosterzee, and many others. Time and space would fail us to go into this question here. Only to one thing I would draw your attention. Notice the extraordinary *vividness in St. John's narrative of the resurrection*, and see how, in a multitude of minute and delicate details, it bears *the impress of personal experience* (*e.g.* the way in which Peter and John go together to the grave; the description of the interior; the bearing of Mary Magdalene, etc.). None but an eye-witness can have described the event with such original freshness and vividness. In fact, their *exactness in isolated details* speaks strongly for the authenticity of these narratives; the more so, the more numerous the appearances which they relate as vouchsafed to different persons, and under different circumstances.

Here Strauss (like his predecessor, the author of the *Wolfenbüttel Fragments*) meets us with a second objection, viz. the variations and *contradictions* in the narratives of the resurrection. We will not deny that there may be certain differences and inexactnesses of statement in the gospel accounts. But are these really important and irreconcilable contradictions, casting suspicion on the great fact itself? Let us see.

Even in the *succession of Christ's appearances* there are supposed to be serious differences. According to Mark xvi. 9, He appears first to Mary Magdalene; according to Matt. xxviii. 9, to her and the "other Mary" together; and according to St. Paul's account in 1 Cor. xv. 5, to Cephas (Peter). But does any one of these pledge himself to relate *all* the appearances of the risen Saviour? Strauss himself confesses that this is not the case (p. 292). Does not each one choose from the rich treasure of tradition this or that appearance first, so that they supplement, but do not contradict one another? If, *e.g.*, Matthew, in relating what happened to the women on the Easter morning, blends into one several traits which according to the other evangelists are separate, is this so very important a difference? If we compare the gospel narratives with that of St. Paul, we see ten appearances of Christ, which probably took place in the following order: (1) Mary Magdalene sees the Lord first, on coming to the grave the second time (Mark xvi. 9; John xx. 16), after having told Peter and John that the stone is rolled away, and the grave empty. (2) The other women, Mary the mother of James, and Salome, having heard the angel's joyful message, hurry back in fear and great joy, whereupon the Lord meets them (Matt. xxviii. 9, 10). (3) He also appears in the course of the same day to Peter (Luke xxiv. 34; 1 Cor. xv. 5); (4) in the evening, to two disciples on their way to Emmaus (Luke xxiv. 15 et ss.); (5) and after this to the ten apostles (without Thomas) assembled in Jerusalem (Luke xxiv. 36–44; John xx. 19 et ss). (6) On the Sunday following, He appears to the apostles, with Thomas (John xx. 26 et ss.). All these appearances took place in *Jerusalem and the neighbourhood*, shortly after the resurrection. Then come those between Passover and Pentecost, when the pilgrims to the former feast had returned to *Galilee*, viz.: (7) at the Lake of Tiberias (John xxi. 1 et ss.) to seven disciples; (8) the great manifestation on a mountain in Galilee to all the disciples (Matt. xxviii. 16 ff.; Mark xvi. 15–18; Luke xxiv. 45–49), and probably at the same time to the 500 mentioned in 1 Cor. xv. 6; (9) the special appearance accorded to James the brother of the Lord (1 Cor. xv. 7), when, perhaps, the disciples were exhorted to return earlier than usual to keep the feast of Pentecost at Jerusalem. (10) The final appearance is that to the apostles on the Mount of Olives, which concluded with the ascension (Mark xvi. 19; Luke xxiv. 50 et ss.; Acts i. 4–12).[1]

In this manner the various appearances, although not fully enumerated in any one record, may be brought together.

[1] The same order has been observed by Greiner in his book on *The resurrection of Jesus Christ from the dead;* Carlsruhe (1869).

Strauss objects to this, first, that John, xxi. 14, mentions the appearance at the Sea of Tiberias as being the third (instead of the seventh); and secondly, that John does not count in the appearance before the 500. The former difficulty is easily explained by the fact that St. John is here only reckoning the appearances among *assembled disciples*, of which only two (the fifth and sixth) had gone before. The latter objection is futile, since Christ did not appear to the 500 till later (the eighth time), while Strauss himself confesses that St. John does not say that the appearance at the Sea of Tiberias was the last (p. 292). St. Paul too, in 1 Cor. xv., does not wish to give a judicial protocol ot all our Lord's appearances, but only to show the number of witnesses, and their authority, and therefore leaves out the women.

But we are told that there are far greater contradictions in respect of the *duration* and the *locality* of these appearances. True, all the evangelists and St. Paul agree that Christ rose again on the third day (p. 313). But the length of time during which His appearances took place is fixed in Acts i. 3 at forty days, whereas Luke connects the last words of the Lord immediately with His appearance to the disciples on the evening of Easter Sunday, so that scarce a day would seem to have elapsed between the resurrection and the ascension, and there would have been no time for the appearances in Galilee. Moreover, if, according to Luke xxiv. 29, Jesus commanded the disciples to remain in Jerusalem until they were endowed with power from on high, He cannot, as Matthew relates, have directed them to Galilee on the morning of His resurrection (p. 293).

This apparent contradiction, however, is very simply explained. Had we only the narrative of St. Luke, we should certainly have thought that Jesus ascended to heaven on the first day after the resurrection. But how often do the evangelists bring together sayings of Christ which were in point of time separated by weeks and months! This is the case here with St. Luke. He evidently collated the most important of our Lord's last utterances, without regard to differences of time, and so blends together sayings which the other evangelists, and he himself in Acts i., give separately in chronological order. If (as was done by us above) Luke xxiv

36–43 or 44 be taken to apply to the fifth appearance of our Lord, and vers. 45–49 as spoken at His eighth appearance in Galilee, then all is clear; for then ver. 49 contains a direction for the disciples who are in Galilee (or perhaps already returned to Jerusalem) to wait for the blessing of Pentecost at Jerusalem. This direction was not therefore given, as Strauss would have it, "on the resurrection day," but after the journey of the disciples to Galilee, so that all appearance of a contradiction to Matt. xxviii. 7 and 10 is removed.

But again, it is objected that Matthew and Mark gravely contradict themselves, because on the one hand they make Jesus appear in *Jerusalem* on Easter morning to the women, but on the other hand they relate how the angels and our Lord Himself direct the disciples to go to *Galilee* that they may see Him there. "If Jesus had indicated to the disciples that Galilee was the place where they should see him, we cannot conceive what should have moved him to show himself to them on the same day in Jerusalem" (p. 293). How strange if, immediately after the direction to go to Galilee, "Jesus himself should step into the women's way! What reason could he have had for so quickly giving up the plan which he had only just proclaimed through an angel?" (pp. 313, 314.)

A pitiable objection this, in good sooth, and quite characteristic of the heartless ways of one who is utterly unable to transport himself into the conditions and times whose historian he lays claim to be. Only look at the difference between the first appearances in and about Jerusalem, and that latter one on the mountain in Galilee. In the former, the Lord appears quite unexpectedly and suddenly, and soon disappears again; to the latter, He had bid the whole body of disciples, and doubtless remained longer in their midst. This was the chief manifestation, in which He openly asserts His participation in the government of the world, institutes baptism, commands that the gospel should be preached in all the world, and promises ever to be with His people. Far from this longer and more detailed manifestation excluding the first more fleeting appearances in Jerusalem, the latter were rather a necessary and fitting preparation for the former—not an alteration of His original plan. And must not *love* have driven Jesus to dry the tears of His followers as soon as possible, and to change their deep sorrow into the joyous assurance of victory? Could He, might He pass by His disciples, so bowed down through grief, without giving them a single word of comfort from His lips? Could He wait so long with the ocular proof of His victory till His disciples were all assembled in Galilee, after the close of the feast (to terminate which they remain those eight days longer in Jerusalem)? Nothing was more natural than that He should appear to them there. Had He *not* done so, we should have reason to be perplexed.

As it is, all these events succeed each other in a way which is not only explicable, but necessary. First come the passing manifestations in Jerusalem, intended to re-establish the crushed hopes of the disciples; then a pause of eight days, during which they have time to recall the former promises of the Lord, that He would rise again, and especially to recognise His terrible death in the light of the Old Testament prophecies as a holy necessity, as a wise and merciful decree of God (Luke xxiv. 26, 44–46). Then, after they had reached this standpoint, when their shaken faith was again confirmed and deepened, come the longer communications, the last revelations and grand directions as to their calling, first in Galilee, then on the Mount of Olives, which once was the scene of the Saviour's deepest humiliation, but now witnesses His exaltation and entrance into glory.

Would that our negative critics, before trying to master Scripture with their hair-splitting logic, only took the trouble to meditate a little on the wisdom and beauty of God's ways which are depicted therein!

But Strauss himself has confessed that, in order to make the origin of his visions conceivable, he needs a longer period between the death of Jesus and the conviction that He had risen than three days. Hence his frantic efforts to do away with the appearances at Jerusalem by any means; because, if true (even subjectively), they would cut the ground from under his feet.

Strauss asks why the disciples, if they knew of the resurrection of Jesus so early as the third day, waited to announce it till the fiftieth? He will not accept the answer given by the Acts, "that they had to wait for the Holy Ghost," because he is of opinion that the feast of Pentecost was fixed upon as the day when the Spirit was poured out, "not for historical, but for dogmatic reasons" (p. 313). Against this we remark: first, that it was not only after (Acts i. 4 et ss.), but also before His resurrection, that Jesus commanded His disciples to wait for the Comforter; secondly, that after the deep trial of their faith through the death of Christ, the disciples naturally enough had need of some time to compose themselves, and prepare for their coming vocation as witnesses of the cross; and third, that to endeavour to persuade the Christian Church that the historical miracle of Pentecost did not take place, is as reasonable as it would be to argue with a living man that he never had a birthday.

This is how the matter stands with the so-called "contradictions" in the Gospel histories of the resurrection. If we look at them closely, they dwindle down to incompletenesses and inaccuracies. And even granting their non-agreement in all details, is not *the cardinal fact clearly and quite unanimously* related by them? Do they not *all* say that Jesus rose again the third day, and appeared in Jerusalem to His disciples? What matters it much *to whom* He first appeared, so long as the cardinal point *that* He appeared is a certainty? Faith depends not on the letter of Scripture, but upon the essential substance of the facts recorded in it. And this essential substance is manifested, not only by the agreements, but even "by the differences themselves; for these are signs of the extraordinary effect which the resurrection produced amongst the disciples," and which has taken an individual shape in each of the narrators. Even a critic like Lessing remarks: "It cannot possibly be otherwise than that each of several witnesses seeing the same thing at the same time, and in the same place, should hear and see, and therefore relate it differently, for the attention of each one is differently directed." Thus the events of the resurrection appear "fixed in indelible memories, which were variously and yet harmoniously shaped according to the standpoint of the different disciples. In these records there is fixed for ever *the startled joy of the Church* at the great news of the resurrection. Here, as in a festal choir, though the voices seem at times to be confused, isolated, or contrary, yet they all are pursuing one theme in full, grand, and blissful harmony. We may clearly see the rich unity of the one resurrection history amid all its details." (Lange, *ubi sup.* p. 441.)

Indeed, we may well say that *the differences in these accounts exclude all idea of an intention to deceive.* If the evangelists had been consciously inventing, the simplest prudence would have made them avoid all traces of difference in their accounts.

Another, and a special proof of their historical veracity, is *the way in which they make our Lord appear.* Were they legends that had arisen from the visions of enthusiasts, they would certainly have represented the Lord quite differently, probably in all the blaze of heavenly glory, as He might be expected according to Dan. vii. 13, 14, x. 5, 6.[1] But in these accounts the risen Christ, with all His dignity, appears in such unpretending humanity, in such a natural state of transition between human lowliness and divine glory, that this utter absence of all extravagance is a striking testimony to the truth of that which is thus related.

But how can this be? Is not the way in which Christ still appears in His body just the most enigmatical part of the whole matter? And, indeed, the most offence of all has perhaps been taken at *the nature of the resurrection body.* It has been said that the Gospel accounts lead to quite contradictory notions as to the quality of Christ's bodily life during those forty days. At one time He allows Himself to be felt and touched, eats and drinks, showing Himself to be capable of taking bodily nourishment even though He may not need it: at another time His bodily substance would appear to be supersensuous; it is not bound down to the limits of space; He comes through shut doors, and suddenly vanishes again; He can even assume different shapes (Mark xvi. 12). What contradictions! our opponents triumphantly exclaim. "A body which can be felt cannot pass through shut doors, and *vice versa* a body which without hindrance passes through boards cannot have bones, nor a stomach to digest bread and broiled fish" (Strauss, p. 295).

Ever since the date of the *Wolfenbüttel Fragments* this con-

[1] Compare the visions of the Anabaptists in Münster at the time of the Reformation.

tradiction has been urged in disproof of the truth of the resurrection. But it rather speaks *for* it. For how should only *one* evangelist, to say nothing of all together, have made a description to all appearance so contradictory and utterly unheard of, unless it necessarily followed from the nature of the case? Would not an invented story betray itself too glaringly in this matter? Evidently it was only because the evangelists considered the truth of the resurrection to be beyond all question that they could venture to add to this great miracle such strange appearances of their risen Master. That they did so, proves their good conscience in the matter.

Like every primal generation, the nature of the resurrection body of Him who was "the First-fruits of them that slept" must remain a mystery. We cannot form any clear conception of the process by which the corpse of Christ was transmuted into a glorified body, nor can we understand the nature of the latter. We can only recall to our minds that heavy water is changed into light vapour, or dark flint into transparent glass, by heat; or that the caterpillar which slowly crawls along the ground, at length grows into an airy butterfly. And thus the glorified body of Christ was not altered as regards its fundamental components; it was *the same body*, with the marks of the nails and the wound in its side, but in a new *spiritual form of existence, and therefore standing under other laws.*[1] It therefore appears—until the ascension, when its transformation was completed—as an elementary, earthly, material body; but its elements are no longer bound by space, and it can go here or there, make itself visible or invisible —in fact, shape itself outwardly according to the internal will. And this is possible, because the body is *spiritualized through and through;* it has become an adequate expression of the spirit, and its willing instrument. The body no longer opposes its own laws (of space, gravitation, motion, etc.) to the volitions of the spirit; it does not hinder nor limit them, but implicitly obeys. All strife is at an end. If the spirit will to transport itself to any place, it can do so together with the body; the body no longer hinders it, for it is saturated with vital force and immortality. This is what the Scriptures (1

[1] Cf. Steinmeyer, *Die Auferstehungsgeschichte des Herrn* (1871), pp. 120 et ss.

Cor. xv. 44–46) call a "spiritual body" (σῶμα πνευματικὸν) in contradistinction to the "natural body" (σ. ψυχικὸν).

In this resurrection body the Lord stands during those forty days, as it were, on the boundary line of both worlds; He bears the impress of this as well as a future state of existence. It is therefore no contradiction—as Strauss would have it—that this body sometimes manifested the force of repulsion (when touched), and at other times not (when penetrating through closed doors); for it could do so or not, according to the will of the spirit. Doors could not keep out that which is in a *spiritual* state of existence. Since all matter, too, is well known to be porous, it can form no absolute barrier for the spirit. We cannot wonder, moreover, that this body, being formed from the same essential elements as the former earthly one, should be capable of eating food (Luke xxiv. 43; Acts x. 41), though not needing it, especially as the same thing is mentioned in the case of angels (Gen. xviii. 8). Our Lord does not "digest" this food, as Strauss coarsely puts it, but He assimilates it in some way or other, and transmutes it into His spiritual form of existence, so that it cannot hinder Him from disappearing. For we must not forget that it is not earthly matter *per se* which is incapable of being developed into a spiritual state of existence, but only the defilement which cleaves to it in our fallen condition that prevents this. *The terrestrial body as such is destined to be spiritualized;* but if this is its destiny, it must also possess the *capability.* This shows us at the same time the reason why the sinless body of Christ could be immediately transmuted. Its purity was the possibility of its transformation.

In this manner we see that the enigma of our Lord's resurrection body, with its wondrous appearances, no longer contains any inexplicable contradiction. And after what we have said, it will be evident that the Gospel narratives of the resurrection may be looked upon without suspicion, either by reason of their differences from one another, or of their special purport.

But even supposing that from some cause or other the testimony of the four Gospels were not valid, still we have another witness for the truth of the resurrection, whose testimony no criticism can invalidate, viz. the Apostle *Paul.*

Were he to stand quite alone, he would afford a perfect and adequate refutation of all arguments against the Church's doctrine of the resurrection, as well as of the visionary hypothesis. This is evident, partly from his testimony, partly from his personal history.

First, let us listen to his testimony. In Romans vi. 4, the expression, " Christ was raised up from the dead by the glory of the Father," cannot be reconciled with the "visionary theory" of the resurrection; for the latter is here represented as a consequence of the objective mighty working of God, not of subjective action of the human nerves and imagination. Those of our opponents who acknowledge the Epistle to the Ephesians to have been written by St. Paul, we would refer to chap. i. 19, 20 of the same, which speaks of "the working of His mighty power, which He (the Father of glory, ver. 17) wrought in Christ when He raised Him from the dead" (cf. Phil. iii. 21). But St. Paul's chief testimony, every word of which breathes a firm and joyous conviction of its truth, is contained in 1 Cor. xv.: " For I delivered unto you first of all that which I also received, how that Christ died for our sins according to the Scriptures, and that He was buried, and *that He rose again the third day according to the Scriptures; and that He was seen of Cephas, then of the twelve. After that He was seen of above five hundred brethren at once, of whom the greater part remain unto this present, but some are fallen asleep. After that, He was seen of James, then of all the apostles, and last of all He was seen of me.* . . . Therefore, whether it were I or they, so we preach, and so ye believed. Now, if Christ be preached that He rose from the dead, how say some among you that there is no resurrection of the dead?"

In these terse and clear words, the force of which is involuntarily felt even by the present opponents of the resurrection, there is contained a *double* testimony. First, St. Paul here witnesses to many appearances that were vouchsafed to other disciples, in a way which (as we showed) is perfectly consonant with the Gospel accounts, and in the language of an historical record which Strauss in vain endeavours to represent as a mere tradition of the subjective belief that the Lord had been seen. The value of this testimony cannot be lessened by Strauss' arbitrary objection, that it is doubtful whether St. Paul ever inquired closely into the reasons which the apostles had for believing in a real resurrection. How incomprehensible that a Pharisee, theoretically and practically intimate with all the statutes of Judaism, and a much feared enemy of the Christians, should suddenly have adopted this new faith, thereby changing all his former religious convictions, without assuring himself of the truth of those facts on which his new faith was founded! How incomprehensible that this man should have preached before Jews and Greeks about the crucified and risen Jesus, and entered into many a discussion on the subject with their wise men, without having inquired closely into the objective proofs for the truth of his own doctrine! This testimony to the appearances of Christ amongst the apostles retains its full historical value.

It is important to notice that St. Paul, in ver. 6, appeals for a confirmation of what he says *to witnesses who were still living.* Now any ordinary writer who should appeal for a verification of his statements to living witnesses would, for the sake of his literary honour, be sure to employ the utmost caution. And shall we suppose that a man like St. Paul, writing to the Church in such a world-renowned city as Corinth, and relating a fact on which he rests the whole Christian faith, should appeal to well-known witnesses without being sure of their veracity? Clearly this is a moral impossibility.[1]

In the second place, St. Paul appears as eye-witness to an appearance of the risen Christ which was vouchsafed to himself: "Last of all, He was seen of me also." Every one is agreed that this refers to the *appearance before Damascus,* which was the turning-point of his life. How are we to regard this: as an inward or as an outward event? Since St. Paul places this experience of his in the same category as the manifestations accorded to the other apostles, and speaks of it in precisely the same terms, it is evident that if it be a merely inward occurrence, suspicion must be cast upon the other manifestations of our Lord; whereas, if it can only be conceived of as an external event, this will be a strong argument in favour of our Lord's other appearances being externally objective—*i.e.* it will militate greatly against the "visionary hypothesis."

[1] Cf. Kahnis, *ubi sup.*

In the Acts of the Apostles we have a threefold minute history of St. Paul's conversion, chap. ix. 1–30, xxii. 1–21, xxii. 4–23; and in both the latter passages it is St. Paul himself who is relating his own history. Strauss himself confesses that this threefold narrative "sounds quite as if it had been an outward sensuous phenomenon" (p. 299). In all three accounts, too, the main points are clearly and conformably stated:—the visible appearance of a light which cast Paul to the ground and blinded him for some days; the voice, "Saul, Saul, why persecutest thou me?" and the answer, "I am Jesus, whom thou persecutest;" the direction to go to Damascus, and the transformation of Saul, under the hands of Ananias, into a soldier of Christ. But critics have laboured much over the small variations in these accounts. Baur [1] seeks to explain them by referring them to the "pragmatism" of the writer, who alters the narrative in each different connection according to his purpose in bringing it in there. This paltry criticism has been well met by the remark,[2] that a historian who purposely contradicts himself for pragmatic reasons must indeed be a strange fool. And if this same historian promises in the introduction to his Gospel to write so that we might know "the certainty of those things wherein" we have been instructed, and then, from sharp-witted pragmatism, turns so important an event as the conversion of St. Paul, first this way, then that, common sense can scarcely help thinking him a liar.

But what do these differences consist of? First, the communication which in chaps. ix. and xxii. is made by the Lord through Ananias, is immediately attached to the words of Christ Himself in chap. xxvi. This simply shows that the narrative in chap. xxvi. is condensed in comparison with the others, and this Baur himself afterwards confesses. Again, in chap. ix. 7 the companions of Paul hear without seeing; in

[1] *Der Apostel Paulus*, chap. iii.; and *Kirchengeschichte der drei ersten Jahrhunderte*, vol. i. p. 45 et ss.

[2] Cf. Beyschlag's excellent articles on "The conversion of the Apostle Paul," in *Studien u. Kritiken*, 1864, Part II. pp. 197 et ss.; and on "The visionary hypothesis and its most recent defence" (against Holsten), *ibid.* 1870, Parts I. and II. Also Schulze on "The testimony of the Apostle Paul to the resurrection of our Lord," in *Beweis des Glaubens*, 1866, p. 33 et ss.; and Grenier, *ubi sup.* p. 73 et ss.

chap. xxii. 9, they see without hearing. Formally considered, this is, of course, a contradiction; but it is perfectly explained if we consider that the companions of Saul only received a *general* sensuous impression of that which was visible and audible, *i.e.* the light and the sound, without either clearly seeing the figure or distinguishing the words spoken by the voice. Only we must not lay the stress upon "they heard" and "they heard not," but upon the words "of Him that spake to me." They heard the sound of a voice, but they did not hear the articulated words which were spoken to Saul (just as in John xii. 28, 29). Nor must we forget that by "hear" St. Paul sometimes means "understand" (cf. 1 Cor. xiv. 2). And what shall we say, finally, when the sharp eyes of our critics discover the flagrant discrepancy that in chap. ix. 7 the companions of Saul "stand speechless," in xxii. 9 "are afraid," and in xxvi. 14 fall to the earth with him? Is it not a perfect farce, for the sake of such differences, to refuse to believe records which in the main perfectly confirm one another? What liberties do critics take with the biblical writings which they would never think of in the case of profane historians! Such conduct was long ago condemned by that patriarch of critics, Lessing, who says, "If Livy, and Dionysius, and Polybius, and Tacitus are so generously treated by us that we do not rack them for every single syllable, why should we not act in the same way towards Matthew, and Mark, and Luke, and John?"

If we account for these small differences by referring them to the different historical records of which St. Luke made use, and which he did not wish to assimilate down to the last letter, then this is an excellent testimony to his conscientiousness as a historian. Then, too, that which is unanimously recorded by all three authorities gains greatly in verification. Now their unanimous testimony is this, that Christ appeared to Saul *externally and objectively; not merely inwardly in a vision.* But if the upholders of the latter view argue that Saul's companions neither saw nor heard this heavenly vision, we must correct this statement to the effect that they did not see and hear it *distinctly;* but they did receive a very strong external impression, for they stood speechless, fearing, and fell to the earth. That they did not understand what was immediately clear to Saul, is comprehensible from the nature of the glorified body, which shares the power of the spirit to reveal itself to one person and remain wholly or partially unperceived by others, according to circumstances.

When Baur goes on to stamp the part played by Ananias as a myth, we cannot help asking how the legend came to fix on a person so little known as Ananias, and why it did not rather make the Holy Ghost descend straight from heaven on St. Paul, as on the other apostles? Baur tries to explain this by the supposition that the writer wished to recommend St. Paul to the Jewish Christian party by connecting his conversion with a Jewish Christian. This is only an effect of Baur's black view of the primitive Christian era, which makes him everywhere look out for traces of an abrupt opposition between Jewish and Gentile Christians,—between followers of Peter and of Paul,—so that he often does not hesitate to represent the most artless narrative as an intentional fabrication or a didactic lie.

But putting aside the Acts, and considering only the direct testimony of St. Paul himself, it cannot be denied that the passages in his epistles which refer to that event can only mean an external, bodily appearance of Christ, and not a mere internal vision. Take, *e.g.*, the words of 1 Cor. xv. 8, "Last of all, He was *seen by me* also," and of 1 Cor. ix. 1, "Am I not an apostle? have I not *seen* our Lord Jesus Christ?" Strauss acknowledges this testimony as proving, in conjunction with the Acts, that he was persuaded that he had seen Christ, and even heard words from Him (p. 301); but he tries to take away the point of it by saying that at other times as well St. Paul "thought he had heard words from a higher world." True, in 2 Cor. xii. 1 et ss. the apostle speaks of visions and revelations which he had (proceeding, however, *from God*, and not from the action of his own nerves merely). But it is evident that this passage does not refer to the revelation before Damascus, which took place much earlier, and in quite a different manner; for here St. Paul is "caught up into paradise," and in the other case Christ appeared to him on earth. This very passage (2 Cor. xii.), then, shows that *when St. Paul is speaking of visions, he expresses himself quite peculiarly;* he describes himself as "caught up," and does not know whether he is "in the body or out of the body." So that even if the apostle did have visions, yet it is evident that he was perfectly well able to distinguish between what he saw in this condition, and what he perceived with his senses ; and that he should have deceived himself so as to confound an internal with an external occurrence, is out of the question. In the passages where St. Paul speaks of his having seen Christ, he gives not the slightest hint that this seeing was other than the natural sensuous process; whereas elsewhere he makes a sharp distinction between seeing in spirit and in body.[1]

Our opponents, therefore, have no right to place the appearance near Damascus in the same category with the later visions of St. Paul. Strauss entirely overlooks the fact, that in 1 Cor. xv. 8 he designates the manifestation of the risen Saviour which was vouchsafed to him as the "*last of all.*" None of his later visions or revelations can be classed with it, because they were of an entirely different kind. The appearance at Damascus was unique in his memory, and he could only class it with those vouchsafed to the other apostles. If, then, it was similar to these, and dissimilar to the later ones, it was *no mere vision, but an external occurrence,* in which the Lord became bodily visible.

The same thing necessarily follows from the context of these passages. In 1 Cor. xv. the apostle wishes to remove doubts as to the resurrection, by pointing to the resurrection of Christ as an established fact, since the apostles, many brethren, and last of all, he himself, had seen Him after it. Now this seeing could only be a proof of the resurrection if it was *outward and ocular,* and cannot be intended otherwise. Further on St. Paul seeks to demonstrate from the same fact the nature of the resurrection *body,* which would be meaningless if the risen Lord had not appeared in bodily form. So, too, with 1 Cor. ix. 1. Against those who maintained that he was no real apostle, and not called by the Lord, he upholds his apostleship by an appeal to his having personally met Christ. But the apostles based their authority on their personal intercourse with Christ, and their vocation by Him as witnesses of His resurrection. Thus the apostolic consciousness of St. Paul

[1] The former is attributed to the πνεῦμα as the highest faculty of intuition ; the latter to the νοῦς, *i.e.* the intellect which receives impressions from the senses.

depends on this very point, that he had seen the Saviour bodily, and not merely in a vision (like Stephen, Ananias, and others, who were not apostles).

What is the result of our investigation? *In an incontestably genuine epistle we have found an eye-witness to the fact of Christ's resurrection; St. Paul with his bodily eyes beheld the risen Lord.* Against such clear testimonies it is of little use for our opponents to appeal to Gal. i. 15, 16, "It pleased God . . . to reveal His Son *in me*," though Strauss gathers from these words that Paul laid the chief stress in this matter upon the inward revelation (p. 302); and Schenkel, on account of this passage, considers the manifestation of Christ to the apostle to have been "mainly internal." For though these words doubtless apply primarily to the scene before Damascus, yet they have a more general meaning too, and include the subsequent divine enlightenments, especially the gift of the Holy Ghost after Ananias had laid on his hands. St. Paul is here reviewing his whole life in the light of the divine act of grace which called him to be the apostle of the Gentiles. It is self-evident that this must have had an inward effect upon his heart, which, by divine enlightenment, underwent the great change through which he attained to the knowledge and discipleship of Christ. But this does not exclude the external appearance; on the contrary, the internal event was only the necessary consequence of the external one.

We submit, however, that it is not only an exegetical, but also a *psychological impossibility*, to comprehend the vision before Damascus as a merely internal event taking place in the apostle's mind. Our opponents cannot explain to us the sudden and total revolution in St. Paul's moral and religious conviction as a purely natural mental process. The attempt to do so has brought them into the greatest straits, so that their leader, Baur, after all his efforts, at length confessed himself fairly beaten. The most zealous defender of this theory at the present time is Baur's sagacious follower, Holsten.[1] But his writings clearly betray that the critical school is driven to this explanation, not by unbiassed exegetical researches, but only by

[1] "Die Christusvision des Apostels Paulus," in Hilgenfeld's *Zeitschrift für wissenschaftliche Theologie*, 1861, Part III. pp. 224–284. Against it, cf. Beyschlag, *ubi sup.*; also Krauss, *Lehre von der Offenbarung*, pp. 267 et ss.

its *pantheistic presuppositions.* "Criticism," he says, "must endeavour to comprehend this vision as an internal psychological act of Paul's own spirit, because it is subject to the law of finite causalities and the immanent development of the human spirit." Behold the cloven hoof! It is not the insufficiency or inadequacy of the records, nor is it their isolated discrepancies, that give offence; but it is the *fact* of Christ's bodily resurrection and actual appearance which is great and strong enough to overthrow all the pantheistic and deistic views of these critics. This fact must be got rid of at any cost, because it threatens the supremacy of the law of immanent development; or, in other words, because the pantheistic standpoint will not allow of anything supernatural. Here, again, we see how this so-called "historical criticism" is "in reality dogmatic or philosophical, having for its first principle the dogma of Pantheism." Furthermore, we see what it must cost to do away with the fact under consideration. If it be only an immanent psychological act,—and yet St. Paul speaks of it as a sure external fact, on which thenceforth he based his existence and his intellect, his faith and hope, his testimony and his work,—then he laboured under a *self-deception which rendered his whole life and preaching a mere illusion.* This Holsten candidly confesses. He grants that criticism must declare the actual basis of St. Paul's gospel to be a delusion, *i.e.* it converts the most notable witness and martyr for the truth into an apostle of error! This, and no less, is the price which must be paid for the denial of the fact in question.

What, then, we ask in astonishment, can the reasons be which give the critical school courage to attempt such a hazardous feat? Baur in his later writings endeavours to account for this sudden change in the convictions of St. Paul by supposing that the narrow-minded, one-sided pharisaical Judaism must at length have worn itself out by going to extremes, and then have changed into the contrary. The great achievement of Christ's death all at once made a mighty impression on the mind of Saul. How else can he have overcome his Jewish hatred to Christianity than by the involuntary impulse of his spirit, which drove him to meditate on that death? In his mind, which was accustomed to more profound thought, the idea—so intolerable to a Jew—of a crucified Messiah changed into the contrary, when he considered that that which was most opposed to the sensuous consciousness might, after all, be true in its deepest inward essence. But how does Baur know that Saul was occupied with the thought of Christ's death just at that time? If he ever were so, from his standpoint he could only regard it as a divine judgment. And why is the apostle—at other times so truthful and open—here silent as to the doubts which at that time arose in his mind respecting the correctness of his pharisaical standpoint? And even had a presentiment of the truth of Christianity at that time arisen of its own accord in his understanding, there was still a long distance between the thought and the practical resolve, which would assuredly have taken up much time. Is it usual that one should break thus radically with his past life, and entirely give up convictions hitherto so deeply rooted and notably acted out, and that he should suddenly go over so decidedly to the opposite standpoint;—and all this as a result of spontaneous mental action, without any external solicitation or influence? Would not this be without parallel? Later on, Baur felt that this was a psychological monstrosity; for in his last work he designates the conversion of St. Paul a "wonder," a mysterious secret, "which no analysis, either psychological or dialectic, can clear up." By this he does not mean that it is a miracle in our sense of the word, but still he confesses the inadequacy of all attempts at a natural psychological explanation.

This, then, is another portion of *the unexplained and inexplicable residuum of miraculous facts*, which proves the futility of all anti-miraculous theories as to the origin of Christianity.

Nor do the explanations of Baur's disciples make the matter clearer. Holsten tells us that visionary seeing is only a reproductive action: only that which lives in the mind as an image or conception can thus appear. The vision adds to those elements which already exist in the spirit a sensuous objectiveness, by exciting the nervous life, which thus makes the image appear sensibly to the outward eye. This is confirmed by physiologists. "We may assert, that if any higher or lower order of being is to appear to us subjectively in this manner, it must first be conceived and imagined, and thus impressed upon the senses."[1] Therefore Saul, if he experienced merely a natural ecstatic vision, without a supernatural divine communication, must in some way or other have received into his mind beforehand that which he afterwards saw. But even Strauss confesses that this effect could not have been produced by "the excitement into which the fanatical upholder of Jewish traditions had been brought by the threatening advances of Christianity;" for, "from such emotions a vision of Moses or Elias would have been far more likely to result than an image of Christ" (p. 303). He therefore lays especial stress on the probability that in his pharisaical self-righteousness Saul had found no enduring satisfaction. While as a ready dialectician he disputed with the Christians, or when he broke into their meetings to hale them to prison, and saw not only their sincerity, but also their tranquil peace and quiet joy in suffering, which put to shame the peaceless and joyless fanaticism of their persecutor,—his present convictions must have been shaken day by day. Could it be an erroneous teacher who had such followers? We must not therefore "wonder if sometimes, in seasons of dejection and inward distress, he put to himself the question, "Who is in the right after all;—thou, or the crucified Galilean whom these people adore?" When he had once come thus far, his bodily and mental peculiarity would easily result in an ecstasy, in which that very Christ, whom he had hitherto persecuted so passionately, would appear to him in all the glory of which His followers spoke, showing him the wrongness and futility of his course, and calling him to enter His service (pp. 303 and 304).

This is the explanation which Strauss gives of St. Paul's conversion. But neither the Acts nor the Epistles tell us anything about "seasons of dejection" or of disputations with the Christians; whereas St. Paul clearly states that he had received the gospel of no man, neither was taught it, but by the revelation of Jesus Christ (Gal. i. 12). These writings say nothing of the image of the risen Saviour which lived in Saul *before* that scene, or of a faith in Jesus which had already taken root in his heart. On the contrary, they bear witness

[1] Joh. Müller, *Ueber die phantastischen Gesichtserscheinungen*, p. 62 et ss.

to the fact that he continued to rage in his blind zeal until the Saviour met him, and that this meeting *moved and astonished him to the highest degree, not that it was internally prepared*, and then of necessity resulted from the workings of his mind. They do not as much as hint that he was in any inward uncertainty as to his conduct up to that time, nor even that the same knowledge had dawned upon him as upon Gamaliel (Acts v. 38, 39): "If this work . . . be of God, ye cannot overthrow it." The words "Saul, Saul, why persecutest thou me?" point, not to inward doubts, but to fanatical hatred and zeal; as he himself, too, witnesses (Gal. i. 13, 14). The psychological precondition for a vision, which can only be reproductive, is wanting in St. Paul. For his mind contained just the very opposite of what the vision is supposed to have reproduced and objectivized. Moreover, if his condition is supposed to have been that of internal doubt, it is well to remember that, *in the New Testament, visions are never accorded to doubters or enemies of the gospel, but only to believers when in ecstasy.*

And how about St. Paul's bodily constitution? was it such as would be conducive to a vision? The origin of visions in all those men who have experienced them, shows that the visionary, although he may be of sound mind, is invariably suffering from overstrained nerves, fever, congestion, or some sort of bodily ailment.[1] Hence the "visionary hypothesis" has to support itself with other new and strange hypotheses as to the bodily constitution of St. Paul. The "thorn in the flesh" (2 Cor. xii. 1) is interpreted by Strauss to mean "convulsive, and perhaps *epileptic* (!) fits;" and he, as well as Holsten, concludes therefrom that St. Paul was of a "nervous temperament." This conjecture is as ridiculous as it is undignified, in the case of a man who was not only of such sound and clear intellect, but also capable of such constant and severe bodily

[1] Witness Mohammed and his morbid tendency to sensual indulgence in later years (Sprenger, *Leben u. Lehre des Mohammed*, i. 209); Swedenborg and his unhappy attachment to young Polhem (Sprenger, *ubi sup.* p. 276); the Maid of Orleans and her frequent fasts, combined with a regular diet similar to that of a strictly observed Lent (Hase, *Neue Propheten*, p. 88 et ss.); and the visions of the bookseller Nicolai, in the year 1791, "when the usual bleeding and leeches on account of hæmorrhoids were omitted" (Joh. Müller, *Phantastische Gesichtserscheinungen*, pp. 77 et ss.). Cf. Krauss, *ubi sup.* pp. 274 et ss.

exertion (consider the exhausting apostolic labour by day and the work of his trade by night, Acts xviii. 3, xx. 34; 1 Cor. iv. 12), and who went on his way with unbroken vigour after undergoing the most rigorous hardships and persecutions (1 Cor. iv. 11; 2 Cor. xi. 23–28). Surely such a man does not give one the impression of a feeble, nervous epileptic. Since his conversion, the apostle feels free and strong in the Lord; shall we suppose that this effect was produced by a sickness, by an epileptic fit, or nervous convulsions? Holsten draws our attention to the fact that our actual knowledge of the outer world is in no way increased by a vision. Was not St. Paul's knowledge extended by that occurrence? Was he not enlightened with new and fruitful truths respecting himself and the world around and above him? From the scientific investigations respecting visions, Lotze draws the following true conclusion: "No notable new wisdom has as yet proceeded from the mouth of somnambulists or the dreams of ecstatics and visionaries."[1] Can we say the same of that appearance of Christ before Damascus, in view of the immeasurable new and wholesome effects which the conversion of St. Paul had on the history of the Church and the world?

We come to the conclusion that the scene before Damascus is *wanting in the chief characteristics of a vision.* There is neither the *physical precondition* in the person concerned which marks its *reproductive* character, nor the *constitutional precondition* which pertains to its *pathologically morbid* nature. The critics use the most arbitrary means to make way for this theory, adapting history to their own fancy in spite of the clearest testimonies. Again do they expect us to believe marvels far more inconceivable than the external miracles related by Scripture; and again our former maxim is confirmed, that those who seek to escape the miraculous fall into absurdities.

Every explanation of the appearance near Damascus as a merely internal event, labours under the fundamental mistake, that it must refer the conversion of St. Paul to the spontaneous activity of his own spirit, whereas *at first he could not but be passive and receptive,* in order afterwards to attain to a living activity in Christ. *Not until he had been apprehended by Christ*

[1] *Medizinische Psychologie,* p. 489.

Jesus could he press forward towards the new mark, seeking to apprehend it himself (Phil. iii. 12). It was not he who had chosen Christ, but Christ who had chosen and ordained him, that he should go and bring forth much fruit (John xv. 16 ; Rom. i. 1 ; Gal. i. 15). Thenceforth he knows and designates himself as an apostle of Jesus Christ, not by his own will, but "by the will of God" (2 Cor. i. 1); called "not of men, neither by man, but by Jesus Christ, and God the Father, who raised Him from the dead" (Gal. i. 1).

We shall see further on, that in the construction of primitive Christianity, as attempted by the critical school, we always have *a beginning without a beginning,* because everything is already existing beforehand. The same is the case with all subjective explanations of the manifestation vouchsafed to St. Paul. They are obliged to suppose that a belief in Christ existed in him before he believed, and an image of Christ, such as could only be formed afterwards, before Christ appeared to him: they make him be converted while he was still a Pharisee raging against the Christians. All these attempts are defeated by their psychological inconceivableness far more than by the difficulty of explaining the impression on the senses without an external appearance of Christ.

We revert to the issue before raised. Does the appearance of our Lord to St. Paul speak for or against the attempt to explain all His other appearances as visions, and thus to deny the reality of the resurrection? May we not safely say that the endeavour of Strauss to employ the internal nature of this event as a handle to reduce all the other manifestations related in the Gospels to mere subjective phenomena, recoils upon himself? *Just as the appearance of the risen Saviour to St. Paul before Damascus can only be conceived as external and bodily, so all the other manifestations enumerated by him in* 1 *Cor. xv. must be regarded in like manner.* But even were the former subjective, the converse would not follow with certainty, viz. that all the manifestations vouchsafed to the older apostles were so too.[1] Moreover, in comparing both, we should not overlook the distinction, that before Damascus the body of our Lord (about which, however, nothing is said)

[1] This is correctly stated by Weizsäcker, *Untersuchungen über d. evangelische Geschichte*, p. 570. Cf. Keim, *Der geschichtliche Christus*, p. 137.

was long since *fully* glorified (hence the blinding light); whereas, when appearing before the ascension, it was in a transitional state.

But St. Paul is not merely an immediate eye-witness of the resurrection; he also testifies to it with his person *and history. In his sudden transformation, and in his entire subsequent life-work,* he appears as an incomparably energetic and joyous witness and martyr for the Christian faith, who constantly refers his preaching to an immediate vocation by Christ. *He himself is one long living proof for the objective fact that the risen Saviour appeared before Damascus.*

This leads us from the historical credibility of our records —which was the first part of the proof demanded by Strauss —to the *second,* viz. *that certain indubitable events cannot be explained without having recourse to the fact of the resurrection.*

III.—COLLAPSE OF THE "VISIONARY" HYPOTHESIS IN CONSEQUENCE OF INDUBITABLE CIRCUMSTANCES AND FACTS.

Besides the *conversion and history of St. Paul* already alluded to, there is a series of other facts, all of which no less demand the bodily resurrection of Christ as a necessary precondition. Such are the *belief of the disciples,* and their unanimous testimony that the resurrection took place *on the third day;* the actual *disappearance of the body of Jesus* out of the grave; the entire *revolution in the disciples' state of mind* after the risen Saviour had appeared to them; and last but not least, the *world-wide effects* proceeding from the resurrection. Let us consider these a little more closely.

The belief of the disciples in the bodily resurrection of our Lord is confessed by the critical school; and this fact *cannot be explained as the result of a mere vision.* If we picture to ourselves the condition and consciousness of the disciples at that time, we must first ask, *how*—unless their Master actually issued forth from the grave—*could the idea of the resurrection occur to them?* They believed, we are told, in the Messiahship of Christ, and in His victorious existence after death. But why should this belief take the shape of a fact so utterly *unheard of,* as that He should shortly come forth again from the grave? It has been shown that at that time the belief in the resurrection of the dead at the last judgment was current among the Jews; but the notion of the resurrection of a dead man, who leaves his grave in a body already transformed long before the judgment-day, was as little thought of by the contemporaries of Christ (cf. John xi. 24) as by any of the Old Testament writers. This idea was so foreign to the disciples, as well as to the Jewish world in general, that had they had visions of Christ, their only conclusion could have been that His soul was living in heavenly glory; but never that the Master who had died before their eyes had gone forth from the grave again alive. *Their belief in the resurrection was to all intents and purposes quite a new belief.* "The Messianic expectations of the Jews contained no idea corresponding to it."[1] But since it is undeniable that from their first public appearance the apostles preached of their Lord, who had not only been received up into heaven, but who had also risen again in body, we ask, how was this new element introduced into their view of the Messiah unless a fact of their indubitable experience convinced them of it? Strauss confesses that the Pharisees believed only in a resurrection at the last day, but adds, "There was no difficulty, from the standpoint of Jewish thought at that time, in supposing that the resurrection of some particularly holy man might take place earlier in an isolated instance" (pp. 303, 304). The artifice of supposing an exception in this one case will not help Strauss to get over this inconvenient difficulty.

Moreover, we ask, whence did the disciples obtain the notion of a *glorified body?* On other occasions when the dead were raised, something quite different took place, viz. a return to the present *mortal* body, but not a transformation of this mortal flesh into a *glorified* body. Besides, our critics maintain that these raisings of the dead were myths or deceptions, and therefore cannot have been the source of this belief. The same is the case with the history of our Lord's transfiguration, which Strauss derives from the opinion of the Jewish Christians, that Moses was a type of Christ (pp. 516 et ss.). "The belief in the rapture and heavenly life of Enoch, Elijah, or Moses, was rather a hindrance than otherwise to the applica-

[1] Weizsäcker, *ubi sup.* p. 574.

tion of such notions to a man of the present age, especially one who had been seen to die" (Weizsäcker, *ubi sup.*). Whence, then, could the idea of a glorified body, with these apparently irreconcilable attributes of sudden disappearance and palpableness, proceed? Our opponents have not as yet answered even these preliminary questions.

With regard to the psychical possibility of visions, hallucinations, or phantasms, medical science teaches us,[1] that in consequence of a strong excitement of the imagination, and of the cerebral activity thereby caused, the organs of sense may be affected in such a manner as to make the subject believe that it hears or sees an external object corresponding to the internal impression thus produced. There are impressions on the senses—proceeding entirely from internal causes, without any corresponding external object—by which the nerves of sense are affected precisely in the same manner as by an external perception; the person who has such impressions errs only in referring the image produced by them to some outward cause. However, these visionaries themselves do not always consider the image they see to be objective realities. But though self-deception in consequence of a vision is not impossible, yet it must be remembered that a vision is always caused, in part at least, by some abnormal condition of the body. And *how soon must a subjective image of this kind vanish before any attempt at definite personal intercourse*, accompanied by *conversation* and *touch!*

Some upholders of the "visionary" hypothesis, without giving up the subjective character of these appearances, are willing to grant that influences without or from above—"a personal working of the departed spirit of Christ upon His disciples"—may have helped to produce them. Is this any more conceivable than an appearance of the risen Saviour Himself? Or is a vision thus magically produced within the disciples more comprehensible than the resurrection? Are not words and sounds (if they do not proceed from an illusion), without an actual appearance, more marvellous than the appearance itself? Do such explanations carry us a step beyond the miraculous? They are but one more proof of

[1] Cf. among others, Joh. Müller, *Lehrbuch der Physiologie*, vol. ii. pp. 563 et ss.

Rothe's maxim, that "without miracles the divine revelation must infallibly degenerate into magic."

Our opponents are compelled further to suppose that the passionate imagination of the disciples stretched out its feelers after their indispensable Master. Instead of this, we see that on each occasion He appears to His followers *quite unexpectedly;* so much so, that at first they will not believe, and He has to rebuke their unbelief. From this it is clear that they were not prepared for the immediate reappearance of Jesus, especially in the shape of a resurrection from the dead. *Here the psychological precondition of visions is wanting.* The deep dejection on account of their Master's shameful death could scarcely give wings to a new and joyous faith. We see the poor shepherdless sheep in fear of the Jews, in doubts and conflicts respecting their Messianic hopes, in perplexity as to the future. These are not the frames of mind from which ecstatic visions might be expected to proceed, but rather the contrary. For in other parts of the New Testament we see visions come upon those who are seeking for a deeper knowledge of God by means of tranquil contemplation, still communion, firm faith, and earnest prayer and fasting.

And finally, the mental and physical impossibility of visions by *so many people at once.* Critics may talk of a chain of spiritual sympathy which can bind down whole assemblies at once. But in the New Testament, visions presuppose a certain moral and religious effort and frame of mind in the individual who has them, and cannot be shown to be "infectious." In this case, too, there would always be one who began and drew the others after him; whereas, in various appearances of our Lord, many, ay hundreds, *at once and simultaneously* perceived Him. We do not deny that science can tell us of cases in which visions were seen by whole assemblies at once; but where this is the case, it has always been accompanied by a *morbid* excitement of the mental life, as well as by a morbid bodily condition, especially by nervous affections. Now even if one or several of the disciples had been in this morbid state, we should by no means be justified in concluding that *all* were so. They were surely men of most varied temperament and constitution. And yet one after another is supposed to have fallen into this morbid condition; not only the excited women, but even Peter, that strong and hardy fisherman who was assuredly as far from nervousness as any one,—James,—the two on their way to Emmaus, and so on down to the sober doubting Thomas,—ay, all eleven *at once*, and even *more than five hundred brethren together.* All of these are supposed suddenly to have fallen into the same self-deception, and that, be it remarked, at the most different times and places, and during the most varied occupations (mourning by the grave, in conversation by the wayside, in the confidential circle of friends, at work on the lake), in which their *frames of mind must assuredly have been very varied,* and their internal tendency to visions most uneven. This latter point especially is important in considering the psychological possibility of such simultaneous visions.

And could they all of them have agreed to announce these visions to the world as bodily appearances of the risen Christ? Or had they done so, could it have been pure self-deception and not intentional deceit? Surely some one or other of them must afterwards seriously have asked himself whether the image that he had seen was a reality. Schleiermacher says most truly: "Whoever supposes that the disciples deceived themselves and mistook the internal for the external, accuses them of such mental weakness as must invalidate their entire testimony concerning Christ, and make it appear as though Christ Himself, when He chose such witnesses, did not know what was in man (John ii. 25). Or if He Himself had willed and ordained that they should mistake inward appearances for outward perceptions, He would have been the author of error, and all moral ideas would be confounded if this were compatible with His high dignity."

Here we must again refer to *the great distinction between the appearances of the risen Saviour and the real visions related in the New Testament.* How entirely different was the vision of dying Stephen, who saw Jesus in *heaven,* and not upon earth! how different the vision of St. Peter, who was "in a trance" (Acts x. 10), and did not see Jesus at all! how different the ecstatic condition in which the early Christians spoke in different tongues, but did not see anything! how different, as we saw, the visionary trance of St. Paul! (2 Cor. xii.) The "visions of the Lord" mentioned here are not "brought into any connection whatever with appearances of the risen Christ" (Keim), either by St. Paul or by his opponents. If, then, the New Testament writers well know what visions and ecstatic conditions are, why do they always depict the appearances of Christ quite differently? why do they never say of the disciples, to whom these were vouchsafed, that they "fell into a trance"? Clearly, because the early Church considered those appearances as distinct and separate from the later visions.

Hence it is not possible to assume that those later visions were a continuation of the first appearances of Christ. But if the latter soon ceased, a new difficulty arises for the visionary hypothesis (cf. Keim, *ubi sup.* pp. 136 et ss.). *Why should these visions of Christ have lasted only for a few weeks and no longer?* "If the visions passed like electric shocks through rank and file, through the twelve and the five hundred; if they continued day by day and week by week; then psychological science would teach us to expect an uninterrupted communication of these impulses,—a continuous intensification of mutual infection in the great vibrating body,—an indolent life of visionary self-gratification in imaginary intercourse with the indispensable Master; but not a diminution, stoppage, and transition to healthy energy." The enigma would remain to be solved, *how the Church could so quickly sober down from her visionary condition;* since thus much at least is certain, that she by no means boasted herself of continued appearances of her risen Lord.

From all this we see how little the belief of the disciples in the resurrection can be explained by means of visions, and how little likelihood, or even possibility there is, psychologically speaking, in their case for the development of visionary conditions of mind or body. But there are still more important circumstances which cannot be explained except by the fact of Christ's bodily resurrection.

We have seen that all the biblical accounts agree in stating that the Lord arose "*on the third day.*" Strauss himself feels (p. 316) that it is hard to assign an unhistorical origin to this definite date. For it cannot be denied that the resurrection must from the very beginning have been regarded by the disciples as an event which took place on the third day; for we find in the *Christian observance of Sunday* a liturgical fruit of this belief, and one which can be proved to have been extant as early as the apostolic age. Hence the visions, too, must have begun on the third day. Strauss is well aware that *the development of a visionary condition absolutely demands a much longer space of time than a day and a half*, after which short period the violent death of Jesus was in fresh remembrance. So he tries, as we saw, to get out of the difficulty by saying that St. Paul tells us that Christ rose on the third day, but not that He *appeared* then. But the two cannot be separated. How could the disciples know that Jesus rose on the third day if He did not then appear to them, or seem to do so? Had the visions, as Strauss maintains, not begun till later on in Galilee, what reason could the disciples have had for fixing the third day as the date of the resurrection? It could not have been in order that Christ's former prophecy might be fulfilled, for Strauss does not recognise prophecies. And assuredly they would have been far more likely to change the prophecy according to its fulfilment than *vice versa*. In these straits Strauss has recourse to a desperate evasion. He says that the third day "would seem in a measure to have been the *proverbial* designation of a short time, meaning that a matter should be carried through without impediment" (p. 317), *i.e.* it means "after some time." This is a discovery for which Strauss may claim the sole credit, since there is no trace of it either in the Old or New Testament. For Hosea vi. 2 is a typical prophecy which was fulfilled, or began to be fulfilled, in the resurrection of Christ on the third day; and in Luke xiii. 32, the true rendering is not "the third day *I shall be perfected*," but, "the third day *I shall finish*," viz. my work in this region, and is to be taken literally.

Such subterfuges are vain. Even a critic like Hilgenfeld has lately confessed that the one distinct and unanimous testimony for "the third day" is, for the reasons above stated, of itself sufficient to overthrow the visionary hypothesis. We have already seen how untenable and arbitrary are the attempts of Strauss, by means of wresting the biblical accounts, to show that the first appearances of the risen Saviour took place in Galilee. If the testimony for the third day is sure, then it is clear that the belief in the resurrection could only have arisen *at Jerusalem,* and that the first appearances must have taken place there. For it is self-evident that the disciples could not have been in Galilee as early as the third day, even had the intervening day not been a Sabbath. Therefore Strauss supposes the disciples to have been in Jerusalem on that day.

But if Jerusalem became the cradle of belief in the resurrection so soon after the death of Christ, *what would have been easier for the enemies,* when this was announced as a fact to the people, *than to confute the apostles by exhuming the corpse of their Master?*

This is another great difficulty which lies in the way of our opponents: *What became of the body of Jesus? The visionary hypothesis cannot explain the fact of the empty grave,* which even Schenkel acknowledges as undeniable. Strauss is of opinion that when, at the feast of Pentecost, Christ was announced as having risen, neither His followers nor the Jews probably knew any longer which was the place of His burial, nor would they, on account of their horror of corpses, feel inclined to search after the body. "Jesus had perhaps been hastily interred, along with others who had suffered capital punishment, in some dishonourable spot; and when the apostles after a considerable time appeared with the announcement that he had risen, it must have been difficult for their opponents to produce his corpse in a condition recognisable enough to afford proofs against them" (p. 312). If the resurrection, we answer, had been only a visionary deception, the evangelists would certainly have been obliged to take care that Jesus should appear to have been buried in some unknown spot, in order that a search should be difficult. But what do they relate? That Jesus was *openly and honourably* buried in a place *quite near to Golgotha,* well known not only to the disciples, but to the Jewish councillors and the Roman magistrates; and even that the Sanhedrim had the grave sealed, and put a watch before it, so that the burial-place of "the king of the Jews" must doubtless have been known throughout the town. Shall we then, it has been well said, suppose that *none of Christ's followers,* not even the possessor of the garden, *was so distrustful or curious as to go to look at the grave himself,* when the women told of the appearance of Jesus?

Shall we imagine that *no one out of the great number of His enemies was prudent enough to examine the tomb,* and have the corpse, which assuredly would have still been in some degree recognisable even after weeks, brought out, since it must have been of the utmost importance to them openly to convict Christ's followers of a falsehood; while, as regards their horror of corpses, there were doubtless enough Gentile menials in Jerusalem whom they could have employed? Instead of this, we are told that they preferred to confess the fact of the grave being found empty, in order to saddle the disciples with the accusation of stealing the corpse! The "criticism" which can make such statements as these, itself needs criticising very much.

Others have thought to evade the question by supposing that some unknown adorer of Christ took away the corpse without the knowledge of the apostles,—thus basing this world-wide and world-ruling belief on an accident or a fraud! Are not such fancies as these signs that our critics are in despair; that, in the consciousness of having exhausted all their sagacity in textual criticism, in psychology, and philosophy, on the vain attempt to overturn the rock of our Christian faith, they are now reduced to substituting the windiest hypotheses for the historical testimonies which they reject? The empty, open tomb, with its loud question: Where is His body? puts all their attempts to shame.

Add to all these grounds for the reality of our Lord's resurrection the last and weightiest, viz. *the immeasurable effect exercised by this belief on the disciples and on the world.* Take, first of all, the *sudden revolution in the frame of mind and in the behaviour of the disciples,* which can no more be explained as the result of visions in their case than in that of St. Paul. Before the resurrection we see the disciples so fearful; they scatter when the Master is bound; the most courageous of them denies his Lord before a servant-girl; only secretly do they dare to meet with "doors shut for fear of the Jews;"—and afterwards, though holding their lives in their hands, they step forward so fearlessly before the whole nation, before the judges and murderers of their Master, and preach His resurrection with a joyousness that cannot be intimidated by any threats or ill-usage. Beforehand, they are so shaken and broken down by the sudden death of their Messiah, that their hope in Him as the Redeemer of Israel is vanished, their own future and that of their faith enveloped in impenetrable darkness; and suddenly a light of hope is kindled in them which even the most violent storm of persecution cannot extinguish. All at once they are clearly conscious of their vocation; an intrepid, joyous faith, a holy zeal, a consciousness of victory, fills their hearts, and impels them to go to Jews and Gentiles to conquer the world for their Master, and upholds and comforts them in tribulation and death. And this new faith finds an entrance everywhere; only becomes stronger and more firmly rooted through opposition and persecution; can be damped by no power, either of the sword or of science; in a stupendous revolution it conquers the world, and regenerates it morally and spiritually; it embodies itself in a living and growing Church which has penetrated to all nations, and already lasted for eighteen centuries. *Are we, then, to believe that the impulse to these immeasurable effects proceeded from visions and nervous convulsions;* from the visionary or epileptic constitution of hysterical women and weak-nerved men; that the disciples derived the clear knowledge of their extensive task from a fleeting vision; that the light of the Christian Church, the sobriety and truth of its spirit, and the earnestness of its moral energy, came from over-excited nerves; ay, that *the moral regeneration of the world proceeding therefrom had its origin in error and self-deception?* Are we to believe that the great Fact which has afforded a sufficient explanation of the history of the Church and the development of the world up to this present moment, in the end dwindles down to the phantoms of a diseased imagination or "la passion d'une hallucinée"? Believe that who will; call it what you please, only not rational or natural; and be sure that it will never stand before the judgment-seat of *history* or of *conscience.*

No; *the enormous weight of these historical effects produced by the belief in the resurrection, must crush every effort to derive it from anything but the fact that Jesus Christ, the great Redeemer of the world, actually did burst the bonds of death by rising on that Easter morning.* Who is unacquainted with the law of the sufficing reason? In view of the facts enumerated, we must say that, if anywhere, this law is lost sight of in the visionary hypothesis. Proceeding, as it does, from a desperate desire to get rid of the miraculous at any price, this theory shares the fate which we have seen pertains to every such undertaking. Wishing to do away with the supernatural, it falls into the unnatural, unhistorical, irrational. For eighteen hundred years Christ's body, the Church, has been living and conquering; and should her Head not be fully living, but half remained in death? Of a truth, unbelief believes what is most incredible.

What, then, is *the result of our investigation?* It is this: that both the proofs demanded by Strauss to substantiate the fact of the resurrection are *most fully furnished*, viz. *the historical credibility of the records*, and *the necessity of this event in order to explain other indubitably certain facts.* The historical testimonies for the resurrection as an outward fact are firmly established; they are equal to anything which may be demanded of a sure record of ancient times; and, as regards the Epistles of St. Paul, they are unimpugned by any criticism, nor can they possibly be interpreted as mere internal events. And a series of indubitable events subsequent to the death of Christ,—facts of spiritual and external experience in the history of the apostles; indeed, the entire development of the Christian Church,—all these form an inexplicable enigma without the fact of the resurrection.

On the other hand, the task that Strauss has set himself—to make us comprehend the belief in the resurrection without miracles, or else to give up his entire undertaking as a failure—has in no case been accomplished without open violence and arbitrariness. *His explanatory attempts, as well as those of all other anti-miraculous critics, are entangled in an endless chain of enigmas and difficulties.* Difficulties *exegetical:* there is the clear testimony of St. Paul, and the great distinction made by New Testament writers between the description of visions and the narratives of our Lord's appearances. Difficulties *psychological:* all likelihood is wanting for the supposition that so many and such differently constituted persons should, even by hundreds at a time, have been simultaneously predisposed to see visions; there is the sudden and thorough change in the disciples' frame of mind, especially, too, the sudden conversion of St. Paul; and finally, the speedy cessation of our Lord's appearances. Difficulties *dogmatical:* arising from the question, Whence should the idea of an isolated individual resurrection, hitherto foreign to their belief, arise in the minds of the disciples? Difficulties *chronological:* unanimous historical evidence points to "the third day," and this leaves no space for the gradual development of visions, or for the translocation of the first appearances to Galilee. Difficulties *topographical:* there, in a well-known spot, stands the empty tomb, with its loud question, Where is the body? which neither Jew nor Roman attempts to answer, though investigation would have been easy. Difficulties *historical:* there is the firm and immovable belief of the disciples in their Lord's resurrection, their preaching so full of victorious joy and martyr's courage, which not even their most bitter enemies dare on this point to gainsay; there is the Christian Sunday, a continual celebration of the first Easter victory; there is the Christian Church, founded and victoriously growing on the rock of her belief in the crucified and risen Saviour. And finally, difficulties *moral:* there is the entire moral regeneration of the world which proceeded from the preaching of the apostles; there we see the kingdom of truth coming, and are told to believe, as has been well said, that at first it was false, afterwards it constantly became more true, and at length "developed" into the sublimest truth!

The critic is not yet born who could overcome all these obstacles. Where the supernatural so palpably intrudes into history as in the resurrection of Christ, reason would be far more prudent, humbly and thankfully to mount this rock which "stands as the mountain of God," and thus continuously to increase her range of vision, than to expose one weak point after another by making futile efforts to undermine it.

A word to my readers! After the foregoing investigation, I may well utter the conclusion, that if any one among you imagines himself to be justified in his unbelief by the criticism of Strauss or Baur, he is greatly deceived. In his earlier days (when still a believer in the Bible), Baur once said, "As assuredly as the origin of the Christian Church can only be accounted for by a firm belief in the risen Saviour, so certain is it that this belief in its turn could rest upon no other ground than that of the historical truth of Christ's resurrection;"[1] nor did all the labours of Baur's later years suffice to overthrow this position.

But in addition to these more negative grounds of defence, consider, too, the *positive counterproofs of the necessity of the resurrection,*—this most comforting and hope-inspiring fact in the whole history of humanity; proofs which are not only of a historical, but also of a dogmatic nature. They proceed, as we hinted at the outset, from the nature of Christ's *Person*. As the sinless and holy Son of God, He could not see corruption; death could not bind Him continuously, since He had life in Himself; and in laying down His life He manifested Himself as eternal Love, which must live eternally because itself is life. They proceed from the *omnipotence and justice of the divine government,* which would have been annihilated had it left the Holy One of God—in whose crucifixion sin and the power of darkness had celebrated their greatest triumph—to corrupt in the grave; had it not crowned Him, who for our sakes was forsaken on the cross, with glory and honour. They proceed from the *work of Christ,* the crown of which would be wanting unless through His resurrection He confirmed His death as being a sacrifice for us, and not for Himself, and thereby overcame the last enemy—even death. They proceed from the *presence of the Holy Ghost,* whom Christ imparts, and sends in consequence of His resurrection and ascension (John xv. 26, xx. 22; Acts ii. 33); and from the personal experience of believers, who through that same Holy Ghost constantly experience the sanctifying and beatific influences of the Saviour's resurrection-life (Rom. vi. 4; Col. ii. 12 et ss., iii. 1 et ss.; 1 Pet. i. 3); because the Lord is not only the risen One, but also the Resurrection and the Life (John xi. 25). They proceed from the *internal coherence in the history of God's kingdom,*—for with the resurrection of Christ the second spiritual period of man's history begins, which will be fully realized at the end of this age,—and hence, too, from the *idea of the world's consummation;* the resurrection and transformation of Christ being the divine pledge of that general resurrection and transformation in which, as its aim and end, the history of mankind, as well as that of nature, is eventually to be merged, when this earthly sphere shall be transformed into a heavenly. Con-

[1] Bengel's *Archiv für Theologie*, vol. ii. part 3, p. 715.

sider, I pray you, all these grounds together, and then I think that the question of the resurrection on which your whole belief and your whole hope depends, will no longer cause you doubts.

The enemies of Jesus once placed a watch at His grave, that the body might not be stolen. Now, we ourselves stand before His empty tomb, to guard it with these arguments, and with the experimental proof of His resurrection-power working in our hearts, that none may again bury the Lord of glory.

Now if the resurrection be an established fact, we must remember that, according to Strauss' own confession, his entire undertaking is a failure, and the inadequacy of the purely natural human view of the life of Christ is proved (p. 288). For if this great central miracle of the resurrection stand firm, so does all that precedes and follows it: the miraculous deeds of Christ, the truth of His redeeming death, His ascension and the outpouring of the Holy Ghost; yes, even His miraculous birth and divine Sonship; for if the consummation of His life were such a miracle, may we not fairly conclude that its beginning was also miraculous? By raising Christ from the dead, God Himself has testified and confirmed that He is what the Church has ever maintained and worshipped—His only-begotten Son. Thus our belief in Him is, in every essential particular, shielded against the attacks of criticism and mythicism, and those words remain true in which the Lord has comprehended the entire miraculous history of His Church: "Fear not; I am the First and the Last: I am He that liveth, and was dead; and, behold, I am alive for evermore" (Rev. i. 17 and 18).

EIGHTH LECTURE.

THE MODERN CRITICAL THEORY OF PRIMITIVE CHRISTIANITY.

IN the preceding Lecture we adduced the origin of the Christian Church, and the moral regeneration of the world which sprang therefrom, as a principal argument for the reality of our Lord's resurrection. But what if the formation of Christianity, its life and its doctrines, should prove to be merely the natural historical result of a necessary process of development? Clearly, if this, the greatest phenomenon in the world's history, can be shown to be a merely natural link in the chain of events, then the miraculous and all supernatural revelations from God are absolutely eliminated from the history of mankind. The *Tübingen critical school* has led the van in this last and most comprehensive attempt, made under an inward compulsion by modern criticism, to exclude God from history. For as long as men could not help regarding Christianity, at least in respect of its *doctrine*, as lying beyond all analogies of human wisdom, it was in itself, in the uniqueness of its spiritual purport, an actual proof for the truth of supernatural revelation,—an immediate attestation of its Founder's divinity. Nor was it then of much use to quarrel about the external history and its miraculous or natural origin. Only if the fundamental and essential ideas of Christianity can be fully connected with natural and human factors already extant, and shown to be their intrinsically necessary development, would the battle be thoroughly and once for all decided in favour of the modern anti-miraculous view of history. For this reason the chiet efforts of the critical school have been directed towards the elucidation of primitive Christianity and its internal formation, towards the proof of a connection between its doctrines and the elements of spiritual culture which were already extant, and especially towards the investigation of its records.

Our entire research into the existence of the supernatural and of the miraculous can, therefore, only be completed by an examination of the modern critical theory as to primitive Christianity. We have gained a firm foothold for this undertaking by our discussion of the resurrection,—as being the most decisive epoch in the history of Christianity, the corner-stone on which the entire edifice of Christian teaching was erected,—and also by our consideration of St. Paul's conversion. If our opponents should, nevertheless, succeed in eliminating the supernatural element from the growth of doctrine in the apostolic age, we should find it difficult to retain this factor even in the Person of Christ. If, on the contrary, we can prove to them that it is absolutely impossible to explain the origin and growth of Christianity from merely natural and historical sources, without acknowledging the interference of a *supernatural* factor, then they can have no rational ground for denying the miraculous in general, but will be compelled to acknowledge the interposition of supernatural divine powers in all periods of the world's history.

But there is another reason yet why the discussion of this question should form the conclusion of our investigations. Of all modern opponents of our old faith, we now stand before the greatest, whom hitherto we have only mentioned cursorily. Writing as he did, only for the learned world, his name is less known to the public at large than those of Strauss, Renan, and others, but it will remain inscribed in the history of modern theology when that of many others, now known to every one, will have long since been effaced. Dr. Ferdinand Christian von Baur, professor of theology at Tübingen (died 2d December 1860), was one of the greatest, if not the greatest, theological scholar of this century; after the death of Neander, the most notable historian of the Church and her doctrines, not only in Germany, but in the world; the most indefatigable of investigators, especially as regards the history of primitive Christianity, in the elucidation of which he has deserved well of theology. He stands a head and shoulders above all other modern opponents of the miraculous. From him they all learn and draw their supplies; they are fain to appropriate the fruits of his enormous diligence if they wish not merely to beat the air, but methodically to storm the citadel of our Christian faith. Strauss himself, in the presence of this man, confesses his backwardness: "I expected," says he, "with the presumption of youth, to storm the fortress by a single assault; but it remained for my greater master to undertake a scientific siege, before which its walls must fall."

And, in truth, if human power, human diligence and acuteness, could ever bring about the overthrow of our faith, this man would have accomplished it. But our present theology is daily becoming more convinced that he was incompetent to this task, and that, in spite of all his unutterable exertions, he did not succeed in proving the merely natural origin of Christianity. This is one of the surest signs that the rock upon which our faith is founded is absolutely indestructible. To impress you with this conviction is the last aim of these lectures.

For this purpose, we will *first* make ourselves acquainted with the principles of Baur and his school, and their representation of primitive Christianity thereupon founded; and *second*, we will endeavour to give a critique of their theory.

I.—THE PRINCIPLES OF THE TUEBINGEN SCHOOL.

Baur once blamed Strauss for venturing to write a critique of the gospel history without a preceding critical investigation of the Gospels; and we ourselves have seen that Strauss passes over this point too lightly, even in his new edition of the *Life of Christ.* It is this gap which the Tübingen School endeavours to fill up. The weak point of Strauss is the strong point with these critics, or at least that to which they devote their chief attention. Their maxim is, that we must recur from the criticism of history to *that of the historical writings.* No certain conclusions as to the history of the life of Christ, or the origin of the Christian Church, can be arrived at until we have discovered by whom, under what influences, and with what tendency the different books of the New Testament were written. Thus the chief importance of the Tübingen School—*i.e.* of Baur and his followers, Schwegler, R. Köstlin, Zeller, Hilgenfeld, Holsten, etc.—lies in the *critical investiga-*

tion into the origin of the New Testament, and the history of the apostolic and post-apostolic age, with its peculiarly constituted parties.

In order to comprehend the motive principle of these investigations, we must remember that the zenith of this school's development coincides with that of the Hegelian philosophy at Tübingen. *The whole of Baur's conception of history is accordingly pervaded by the Hegelian philosophy.* Though he may gradually have overcome much of its onesidedness, he was to the last governed by its fundamental idea, viz. the immanence of God and the world, according to which the relation of the divine and human spirit must be conceived as essential unity, not as personal distinction and intercourse.[1] God does not live and reign above the world and its changes; He is only realized in and with it, and the history of the world is the process of absolute Being, which developes with an iron necessity according to natural laws. All that appears in nature and history is a revelation of the eternal Idea. But the latter is never fully realized in a single individual, only in the general development taken as a whole. The individual, as such, always stands in a certain contradictory relation to the universal Idea, negatives it, and must therefore itself be negatived. This eternally restless and aimless process is the continuous negation of a negation in which one phenomenon always calls forth the next, so that each can be connected with the preceding one and explained from it. In this monotonous path the world's history, and likewise the history of the Church, as of all religious development, is ever marching on.

With this fundamental view, Baur could not but consider the doctrines "of an eternally self-perfected personality of God, of a spontaneous creation of the world, of sin and moral perversion originating from the freedom of man, of man's personal immortality, as imperfect notions of religious belief. But above all he must, if consistent, *reject the doctrines of a truly supernatural revelation, and of a miraculous, unique union*

[1] Not until later, when Baur's historical principles had been long since settled, did he appear to recognise the personality of God somewhat more fully; when, *e.g.*, he says: "If God be truly conceived as a Spirit, then either He must be as such immediately personal, or else it is not evident what the attribute of personality can contribute to the conception of God as the absolute Being."

of God and man in Christ, and of sinless perfection in the historical Christ as the Redeemer and Saviour of the world. These he must transmute into the idea of the essential unity of the divine and human spirit, and of a continuous, necessary reconciliation and union of both, which must be principally accomplished by the moral self-development of man."[1]

From this it is evident that, on the standpoint of Baur, *the miraculous is impossible.* Everything takes place in a necessary natural development, in which one phenomenon begets another, and in which, therefore, nothing can form an absolutely new beginning (which is the nature of a miracle, *vide* p. 293), but all is only the result of germs and causes already extant. Not even *Christianity* may form any exception to this absolutely valid law. It must therefore allow of being *included as a historical phenomenon in the universal development of the world,* by being considered as a period in the general development of religious consciousness. It had no miraculous beginning, nor has there appeared in Christ any absolutely new principle which could have been the sudden and unmediated commencement of a new development. *Christianity is only the natural unity of all pre-Christian schools of thought,* "the ripe fruit of all the higher longings that had hitherto stirred amongst all branches of the great human family."[2] Baur will not acknowledge any other view of history as entirely unbiassed, or *"free from presuppositions"* as he likes to call it. For him a strictly scientific research is only that which excludes all supernatural interference of God in history, and seeks to derive every phenomenon from purely natural causes. Hence to this day the peculiar fashion, prevalent amongst the opponents of all positive belief, of acknowledging as "*scientific*" only those theories which tend to deny the supernatural, and of accusing all others of being "biassed by dogmatic presuppositions" and "unscientific:" as if a belief in the supernatural must exclude strict logic, and did not rather improve it; as if it darkened our rational knowledge, and did not rather enlighten and extend it.

Baur maintained these anti-miraculous principles to the last.

[1] Landerer, *Worte der Erinnerung an F. C. v. Baur*, p. 38. Cf. this pamphlet also for the following pages.

[2] Strauss, *Leben Jesu*, p. 167.

"Whoever," he writes,[1] "can see in the incarnation of the Son of God nothing but an absolute miracle, must thereby give up all historical connection. The miraculous is an absolute beginning; and the more this beginning is the precondition of all that follows, the more must the whole series of phenomena which belong to the region of Christianity bear the impress of the same miraculous character. If at the first point the historical continuity is rent asunder, then a similar interruption is possible at every succeeding stage. It is, therefore, very natural that historical investigation should, in its own interest, seek to *include the miracle of the absolute beginning in the one historical connection, and dissolve it as far as possible into its natural elements.*" Similarly he remarks in another passage:[2] "It is undeniable that *the tendency of historical consideration* must be *to bring down the supernatural and miraculous,* which constitutes the specific character (?) of Christianity, *to an absolute minimum;* nor can it, from its very nature, have any other tendency. Its task is to investigate what has happened in the connection of its causes and effects; but the miraculous, in its absolute sense, destroys the natural connection." So only that can be historical investigation which tries to get rid of the miraculous as far as possible. But what if the miraculous itself were historical?

Thus Baur from the outset declares war against the miraculous; but he employs a peculiar method in getting rid of it. We have already seen how, for this purpose, the Rationalists make use of the "natural," *i.e.* unnatural explanation of isolated miracles: how Strauss and Renan class miracles in general under the head of legends and fabrications. Baur, on the other hand, does not engage in many skirmishes about isolated miracles; though, where he does so, he assumes either that they were legends of unintentional origin, or still oftener, didactic fabrications. His chief endeavour is to divest the *phenomenon of Christianity as a whole* of its miraculous character; and this he does by deriving the elements of the Christian religion as much as possible from conceptions and ideas already extant in Judaism and heathenism, and by connecting them with these, as though they were the products of a natural

[1] *Das Christenthum der ersten drei Jahrhunderte,* 2d ed. p. 1.
[2] *Die Tübinger Schule,* p. 14.

development. The substance of history, as extracted by his criticism,—but often, too, invented by it,—is of its own accord to show the superfluousness and impossibility of miracles. The means by which he seeks to eliminate the miraculous, is, in short, *the demonstration of historical analogies and points of contact* between the pre-Christian and the Christian view of the world and of God.

How, then, does Baur discover these? He looks for certain views which are common on the one hand to the nature of Christianity, and on the other to the general character of that age. "The more decidedly such common points of connection appear, the clearer is the light which they cast upon the historical origin of Christianity itself."[1] Such, *e.g.*, is the idea of *universalism.* This was derived by Christianity from the world-wide Roman empire. "In its universalism Christianity stood upon the same level to which the Roman State had raised itself by its world-wide monarchy. . . . The universalism of Christianity never could have penetrated into the general consciousness of the nations had not the way been prepared for it by political universalism. In its essence, Christian universalism is the general form of consciousness to which the development of mankind up to the appearance of Christianity had attained."

Christianity became the absolute religion on account of its *purely spiritual character,* since it is more free from all that is merely outward and sensuous than any other religion, and more deeply founded on the principles of moral consciousness, knowing no other worship of God than that which takes place in spirit and in truth. The specific pre-eminence of Christianity in its character as the absolute religion, is based upon the fact, that in it man becomes conscious of himself as a moral subject. "That which exalts Christianity, as against all other belief, to the dignity of the absolute religion, is in the last instance nothing but the purely moral character of its facts (?), doctrines, and requirements."[2] This aspect of Christianity is connected with the *Greek philosophy,* through which, since the

[1] *Das Christenthum der ersten drei Jahrhunderte,* pp. 2–22.

[2] *Die Tübinger Schule u. ihre Stellung zur Gegenwart* (2d ed. pp. 30 et ss.). Cf. with what follows, Beckh, "Die Tübinger historische Schule," in the *Zeitschrift für Protestantismus u. Kirche* for March and April 1864.

time of Socrates, men had become acquainted with the conception of the *subject.* The philosophy of Plato, more especially, is very nearly related to Christianity, even in its ideal groundwork. His doctrines respecting a Creator of the world, the immortality of the soul, the essential affinity between man and God, of man's need of communion with God,—the way in which he recognises the dependence of man on a higher world, from which alone he can receive instruction as to divine things,—all these are so many points of contact with Christianity. Other tendencies of thought, at least negatively, paved the way for Christianity, since by their errors or onesidedness they called forth a revulsion of the religious consciousness in the opposite direction. Thus, *e.g.*, the haughty self-contentment of the Stoic formed as great a contrast to Christianity as did the voluptuousness of the Epicurean to Christian self-denial. The more onesided the *subjective* character of philosophy in the sceptical systems which despaired of attaining to any certainty of truth, the more must the necessity of an *objective* foundation for the truth become clear to men. There naturally followed a revulsion of consciousness from the subjective to the objective, from philosophy to religion, from mere speculation to the belief in actual revelations of God.

But the chief factor to which attention must be directed in considering the origin of Christianity is *Judaism.* Christianity is nothing but *Judaism spiritualized.* And this spiritualization of Judaism was made way for in the Old Testament by the prophets. Their writings "already contain the elements of a religion which only needed to be brought into a more general form of consciousness in order to become Christianity." As for the national impress and the particularism of the Jewish religion which is opposed to Christianity, it had broken through these bounds in the *religious philosophy of Alexandria*—this Hellenic Judaism—by the *allegorical interpretation* of the Old Testament. In this way a means had been discovered of extending at pleasure the scope of the Old Testament, and hence there originated "a more universal form of the religious consciousness which already possessed something of the spirit of Christianity." . . . "In fact, we constantly find germs of Christianity wherever Judaism or heathendom returns within itself. As often as this happens, a more universal and self-dependent form of religious consciousness is in process of development." The ascetic aspect of Christianity finally, its renunciation of the possessions and pleasures of this life, and its separation from the world, stand in close relationship with the sects of the Therapeutes and Essenes, who withdrew from the corruption of the world into still communities, where, with all things in common, they lived the most simple and laborious life, apart from all worldly delights.

In this manner Baur arrives at the conclusion that the germs of a new creation lay dormant in the dissolution of the old world, and only needed to be centred in one focus in order to raise the religious consciousness to the level of Christianity. *Christianity, therefore, is only the natural unity of all these elements.* "It contains nothing which is not conditioned by a preceding series of causes and effects; nothing which had not long before been prepared in different ways; nothing which had not already been vindicated either as a result of rational thought, or as a need of the human heart, or as a requirement of the moral consciousness."[1] But that these existing elements of a new religious growth "should converge in one special point, and in this one special individual, this is the wonder in the origin of Christianity which no historical reflection can further analyse."

According to Baur, the true kernel of Christianity appears in all those points on which Jesus insisted when He appeared as the *Reformer of the Jewish religion.* The pure elements of this religion formed the motive principle of His religious work. He did not come to destroy, but to fulfil; and the law was fulfilled by Him, inasmuch as He recurred from the merely outward ceremonial service to the internal disposition. The tendency of the most important of Christ's didactic discourses was to refer man back to himself, to call his attention to all that may be learned from the wants of his moral nature.

[1] *Das Christenthum der ersten* 3 *Jahrhunderte*, p. 21. Further on he adds, somewhat ambiguously, that the Christian doctrines would doubtless have been relegated into the ranks of so many other sayings of the wise men of old, which have long since been forgotten, "had they not in the mouth of the Founder become *words of eternal life*" (pp. 35, 36). We have already seen (p. 389) that Strauss in like manner refers the true humanitarian tendency in Christ to a Hellenic origin, and considers His purely spiritual and moral conception of God as an Old Testament heirloom.

"All that belongs to the truly moral purport of Christ's teachings, as contained in the Sermon on the Mount, the parables, etc.,—his doctrine as to the kingdom of God, the conditions of its membership whereby man is placed in a truly moral relation to God;—all this constitutes the intrinsic essence of Christianity and its substantial centre" (*Die Tübinger Schule*, p. 30). In those didactic discourses we find a system of religious truth which imparts to Christianity the *character of the purest rational religion.* "What should there be supernatural in the fact that the eternal verities of reason were once pronounced in such a way that they only needed to be pronounced in order to ensure their universal acknowledgment?" True, even the most rational verities of religion will not meet with general acceptance if they are not supported by the weight of a great personality. But there is every reason to believe that Jesus was just such an extraordinary personality, intellectually gifted in the highest degree, and morally grand. That, however, which gives His person the highest, its absolute significance, is only that in Him "first this free conception of the relation between God and man was cleared from all impurity, entered into the living consciousness of man, and found there its truest and most immediate expression" (*ubi sup.*).

In the miracles of Christ, and in the form that they have taken in tradition, we can only see an effect of the wonderful influence of Christ upon His contemporaries. No sooner had He made Himself conspicuous than men saw in Him the long-expected Saviour. The question is, whether Jesus was at once firmly convinced of His Messianic mission, or whether this idea only gradually gained ground in Him. We shall presently see that Baur does not sufficiently explain to us how Jesus came to declare Himself to be the Messiah. Decidedly as He asserted the conviction of His Messianic mission, He was exceedingly reserved as to the political expectations of His people, and held entirely aloof from them, for He only wished to work by a spiritual reformation. Early in His career He had become convinced that the sacrifice of His life was necessary to the realization of His idea. After a lengthy stay in Galilee, He went to Jerusalem, in order to bring about the crisis which ended in His death. The heads of His nation condemned Him, under the influence of the correct presentiment that He had brought on the end of the old faith. His death cut off the last possibility of identifying the Messiah, whom He claimed to be, with the Jewish Messiah, who was to have erected another kingdom of David. Not until then did the Messianic idea which He had enunciated stand forth in all its purity, and now it could not but become the principle of a new religion different from Judaism. Christianity, therefore, gained its world-wide importance through the death of Jesus. His *resurrection* is merely the declaration, put in the form of a fact, that His person not only did not perish, but was even raised by death to the dignity which pertained to Him as being the living exponent of the new spiritual religion. "What the resurrection *per se* is," says Baur, with peculiar caution, "it does not lie within the province of historical research to determine" (cf. p. 453). The conviction that His resurrection was an absolute necessity forced itself upon the disciples, and *for their consciousness* it was a firm fact. Church history, therefore, has for its starting-point, not the objective fact of the resurrection, but the *belief of the disciples* in it. This belief was the commencement of the Christian Church.

Thus primitive Christianity, according to Baur, is a form of the development of Judaism, to which, however, all the other more spiritual elements of that age contributed. In virtue of the urgent efforts which He directed towards promoting an internal and spiritual perception of the law, Christ became the author of a religious and moral reformation of Judaism; but in all this He was a mere man, nor did He exceed the limits of what was purely natural either in His person or His work. And thus, moreover, He was regarded during the primitive Christian age. The first Christians were Jews, only they believed in a Messiah who had already appeared, without, however, ascribing to Him divine attributes. In this belief their entire doctrine consisted. To substantiate this, Baur appeals to the Ebionites, a party of Jewish Christians who held to the law of Moses, and denied the birth of Jesus from the Virgin, declaring Him to be a mere man. Primitive Christianity was, in fact, nothing but Ebionitism,—*i.e.* a Jewish sect which afterwards developed into the universal Church,—not, however, because it successively drew conclusion after conclusion from its chief tenet that Jesus was the Messiah, but only because it was gradually compelled to drop one piece of the old Judaism after another.[1] For these primitive Christians had as yet no idea that the kingdom of God was to be extended beyond the boundaries of Israel. The Jewish-Christian party was predominant as far down as the beginning of the second century; but before this *another more free and universalist school* had separated from it, chiefly through the teaching and work of the Apostle Paul. This body held Christianity to be the universal religion, released itself from the bondage of the law, and directed its attention chiefly to the heathen. Hence it gradually became the more numerous, and later on the dominant party. Amongst its members *a higher* conception of Christ—of His pre-existence, His unity with the Father, His Godhead—was gradually developed during the course of the second century.

The chief representatives of the former party are St. Peter and St. James; that of the latter, St. Paul. According to Baur, the entire history of primitive Christianity is ruled by this opposition between *Petrinism* and *Paulinism*, or between Jewish Christians and Gentile Christians. There are traces of it in the New Testament. In Gal. ii. we read of a dispute between St. Peter and St. Paul as to the relative positions of the Jewish and Gentile Christians. In 1 Cor. i. we read of parties in the Corinthian Church who called themselves by the names of Paul, Apollos, Kephas, and Christ. In the Epistle of St. James we find a legal Jew setting up works as against mere faith. In course of time, however, men sought to *mediate* between these two opposites, and to reconcile them. All the books of the New Testament owe their origin either to one or other of these parties, or to an attempt at mediation between them.

For what follows from this view of primitive Christianity with respect to the genuineness of the books of the New Testament? First, that *the books in which we find the doctrine of the Godhead of Christ already developed cannot have been composed till the second century.* For the Apostolic Church, and even St. Paul, had no such high conception of Christ. And second, that only those writings which distinctly express that opposition, *i.e.* which are either decisively Petrine or entirely Pauline, can be *genuine;* whereas those in which the edge of

[1] Cf. Schwegler, *Das nachapostolische Zeitalter*, i. p. 107.

this opposition is already blunted, and which are evidently trying to mediate between the two tendencies, must belong to that later age in which men were working at the reconciliation of both parties. It is presupposed that all the writings of primitive Christianity—those of the New Testament not excepted—must have a *tendency* to exalt either the Jewish-Christian party of St. Peter, or the Gentile-Christian following of St. Paul, or else to reconcile both. From this characteristic of the Gospels we may explain their legendary miraculous contents. The more distinct the tendency of a gospel, the less can it be considered a reliable record. The more developed the doctrine of Christ's person, and the more conciliatory the tone of a book towards both parties, the more surely may we place it in a later age.

In accordance with these principles, Baur considers that *only five books of the New Testament are undoubtedly genuine and apostolic,* viz. one book of a Jewish-Christian tendency, the *Revelation of St. John,* and four Epistles which represent the Pauline or Gentile-Christian tendency in its original form, one to the *Romans*, two to the *Corinthians,* and one to the *Galatians;* whereas those to the Ephesians, Colossians, and Philippians have too high a view of Christ's person, and the others bear other traces of later origin. Of the Gospels, that of *St. Matthew* is the most authentic documental record, because it betrays least party tendency. Whilst this is Jewish-Christian, that of *St. Luke* is Pauline-universalist, that of *St. Mark* mediatory. The latest of all, chiefly on account of its highly developed philosophical Christology, is the Gospel of *St. John,* which some unknown person wrote after 160.[1] The book which most clearly betrays a tendency to reconcile the Pauline and the Petrine school is the *Acts of the Apostles,* especially because in chap. xv. it tells of the agreement between St. Peter and St. Paul in their resolution not to force the Gentile Christians to observe the Mosaic law,—a narrative which, no doubt, is diametrically opposed to Baur's entire conception of primitive Christianity, and must therefore be declared to be unhistorical.

These are, in short, the views of Baur (somewhat modified

[1] Cf., however, the concessions since then made by the critical school in regard to the age of the Gospels, as already stated.

by his school, which at present has its chief seats in Switzerland, France, and Holland) with respect to the origin of Christianity, more especially of the New Testament. At present we cannot follow this criticism into details as to the origin of the single books. Here we are concerned only with the fundamental views of the school in general, inasmuch as it represents the greatest and most extensive attempt to do away with the supernatural element in the origin of Christianity. In order to see whether this attempt has succeeded, we will now proceed to examine successively the *principles* of the school, its attempt *to connect Christianity with pre-Christian systems of thought,* its conception of the person and the consciousness of Christ, the important position which it assigns to the Apostle Paul in the history of the primitive Church, and finally, the antitheses, the intensification and reconcilement of which is supposed to have fixed the character of the entire apostolic and post-apostolic age.

II.—CRITIQUE AND REFUTATION OF THIS THEORY.

This school arrogates to its criticism a purely historical character. It claims to have approached the investigation of the Christian records without any other than a historical interest, and to have studied primitive Christianity in the unbiassed spirit of true science, which *allows of no presuppositions.* Is this, I ask, even psychologically possible? Can any one approach the investigation of a subject which so deeply affects our own life as does Christianity, without any presuppositions whatsoever? Must there not be some self-delusion in this matter? A corpse may be dissected without sympathy, and merely in the interests of science, but never a living body. Only that which does not in the least affect us can be investigated entirely in an unbiassed spirit, and merely in the general interests of science. Even Strauss has raised this objection against Baur. "With all due respect," he remarks (*Leben Jesu,* p. 13), "for what the learned gentlemen say, I must still confess that I consider what they lay claim to an impossibility; nor, even were it possible, would it seem to me praiseworthy. True, the man who writes about the rulers of

Nineveh, or the Egyptian Pharaohs, may do so merely in the interests of history. But Christianity is such a living power, and the question as to how it originated is fraught with such momentous issues for the present day, that the investigator must be destitute of all sense if he should feel none but a historical interest in it."

But this "absence of presupposition" is not only a psychological delusion,—it is belied by the principles of the Tübingen School. In reality the investigations of this school are not "purely historical," but governed throughout by the *philosophical axioms* of Pantheism: they are *not free from presuppositions;* on the contrary, *as regards the chief question,* viz. the possibility of the supernatural, they are *previously decided.* Baur maintains from the outset that the really historical and essential substance of Christianity can only be that which does not transcend our natural human standards, and which can be linked to other similar historical phenomena. Hence his constant endeavour to reduce the supernatural events which are recorded to merely natural dimensions. Their historical element must be purely natural. And why? Because, according to his Hegelian views, an immediate divine interposition in the course of history is impossible. What is this but approaching the investigation with a presupposition, whereby the main point is already decided? For surely the most important question with respect to the origin of Christianity is *whether its supernatural beginning, as related in Scripture, is historical or not?* By adopting such strongly biassed principles, and yet claiming for them a purely scientific and historical character, Baur lays himself open to the charge of *begging the question,* just as Strauss also does. *According to Scripture, all history, both of creation and redemption, begins with miracles; according to Baur, where miracles begin, history ends.* He ought then to have proved to us that the miraculous itself cannot be historical. And since he did not do so, this fundamental principle of his is a mere presupposition. True, Baur tries to assign the nature of the records as the reason for his denial of the miraculous. But this is only a veil for the true reason, which lies in his Hegelian views. And this denial is fatal to his whole system.

Thus we see that the *absence of presuppositions,* of which

this school vaunts itself so much, is in reality the *greatest possible assumption ;* that its apparently purely historical principles include the philosophical axiom that the miraculous is impossible ; and that its historical criticism is in truth dogmatical, having for its fundamental article the dogma of Pantheism. From this we may easily comprehend the motives for the attempt to *link Christianity entirely to pre-Christian systems of thought.*

Baur would be quite right in so doing if it were only we men, *i.e.* purely natural factors, which constitute history. But the greatest factor of all is the divine factor, which is supernatural, and therefore inexplicable, but none the less historical. The divine deeds, *i.e.* the miracles, are absolute beginnings which appear as something entirely new, and can therefore *never* be completely linked to the old which already exists, or *sufficiently* explained from preceding events. But in their character of absolute beginnings they are not only ordinary history, but history in its most exalted sense; they constitute the basis, the landmarks, and the internal mainspring of all historical development. No wonder, then, that Baur's attempt has signally failed.

In seeking for analogies to Christianity, Baur takes the essential nature of the latter as consisting in its universalism, its pure spirituality and genuine morality. But I have already endeavoured to show you (*vide* pp. 37–39) that these elements by no means constitute the specific nature of Christianity, which consists, above all, in our having entered into a new relation to God, not merely by recurring to our own moral consciousness, but through certain historical facts and through a distinct historical personage, viz. *Christ.* Baur constantly emphasizes only one aspect of the historical development; and by treating it as the essential one, he loses sight of the real essence and heart's core of Christianity, which is none other than the person of Christ. If Christianity be nothing but the purest rational religion, which, upon closer inspection, dwindles down to a religionless morality, how poor and meagre is its essence, though we may exalt its moral truths ever so highly! What an unmeaning phrase is it when Baur declares that the principle which makes Christianity the absolute religion is this, " that man becomes conscious of himself as a moral subject!" Is this the new, the distinctive essence of Christianity? Even our first parents, I trow, had attained to the elevation of this standpoint when, in their consciousness of being moral subjects, they were ashamed and hid themselves. Baur's definitions, therefore, do not in the least touch the specifically new elements of Christianity; nor can they do so, since for his standpoint there is nothing new, but everything necessarily follows from what has gone before. Hence, too, the points of contact so laboriously discovered are valueless, since they do not concern the root of the matter.

But they do not even sufficiently explain what Baur intends them to. What an infinite difference is there between the universalism of the Roman empire and that of Christianity!—the former resting upon the power of the sword, built up by forcible conquests, and moreover very far from being actually universal; the latter founded upon the idea of a physical, moral, and religious affinity between all men, their common descent from the first Adam, and their common redemption through the second Adam.[1] What a difference is there between a dialogue of Plato's and the Sermon on the Mount; between the strugglings of Greek speculation and the holy divine peace of our Saviour's consciousness; between the confession of Socrates, that "he knew only this, that he knew nothing," and the testimony of Him who not only knew Himself to be in full possession of the truth, but could even say, "I *am* the Truth;" between the moral fluctuations and errors even of the noblest Greek, and the sinless perfection of that One, who for this reason can attach the salvation of the world to His sole person!

And what a difference, again, is there between the asceticism of the Essenes, who shunned the world and renounced its society, and Christ's free and open intercourse with the world, prompted by His love, which was seeking lost humanity! What a *contrast*, in fact, "between the painful narrow-mindedness of Essene morality and the freedom peculiar to the spirit

[1] It should be remembered that only in the Holy Scriptures, *i.e.* on the ground of revelation, do we find the idea that all men are descended from one pair (Gen. x. 32; Acts xvii. 26). Compare this with the belief of Hellenic heathenism, that their nation was born from the soil, and the contempt resulting therefrom for all that was foreign.

and word of Jesus! In the one case, man laboriously toiling at length to place himself in the true relationship to God; in the other, full and blissful harmony with the heavenly Father in the walk and word of Christ;"—in the one case, self-isolation; in the other, intercourse even with publicans and sinners;—in the one case, secret doings; in the other, our Saviour's command to preach upon the house-tops, etc. The most recent investigations on the subject of Essenism have irrefutably proved that, in spite of isolated points of contact, "the doctrine of Jesus as compared with Essenism, both as a whole and in detail, shows less of agreement than of difference. The spirit of both is originally distinct." [1]

Moreover, how can it be historically proved that Hellenic culture and philosophy, or Alexandrine Judaism which was permeated by these, or even Essenism, had a direct influence upon the views of Christ, who was "not from below but from above," and who spoke as His Father had taught Him, not according to the doctrines of men? (John viii. 23, 28.) Impossible; for "Christianity is an entirely independent formation, which came into existence without any connection whatever with these phenomena. They had no influence whatever on Jesus, and on the circle in which His cause at first developed" (Weizsäcker, *ubi sup.*). To this Strauss objects (*Leben Jesu*, p. 165), that "though the circumstances which were the originating causes of Christianity may be no longer known to us, this by no means proves that such causes did not exist! But, we answer, so long as our opponents cannot show any sufficient natural cause for these effects, it is evident that no one can dispute our right to suppose that they had a *supernatural* cause; and this all the more, inasmuch as such a cause in fact explains everything, whereas those merely natural influences explain nothing, since their difference from Christianity is always greater than their affinity to it.

We might even go a step further in our proof for the existence of supernatural factors in history, and say: If

[1] Keim, *Der geschichtliche Christus*, 3d ed. p. 15; *Jesu von Nazara*, i. pp. 282 et ss., 306; Köstlin, "Jesus gegenüber den Parteien seines Volks," in Gelzer's *Protestantische Monatsblätter* for December 1865, pp. 363 et ss.; Kleinert, *Jesus im Verhältniss zu den Parteien seiner Zeit*, 1865; Weizsäcker, *Untersuchungen über die evangelische Geschichte*, p. 418.

primitive Christianity is nothing but a development of *Judaism, whence, then, does the latter come?* Baur does not give this question a consideration. But since Judaism claims to be a supernaturally revealed religion, and is so according to Christian views, this investigation would assuredly have been most fitting as a test of his historical principles, which aim at assigning a natural cause for everything. True, the futility of his undertaking would have become patent at the very outset. For even the old covenant, with its doctrine and history, cannot possibly be explained as the fruit of a merely natural development. Whilst all the nations of the old world are under the curse of nature-worship, we find Israel alone adoring the one *supramundane* God. Whilst all the nations of the old world, "with backward longings after a vanished golden age, live hopelessly onwards into the ever-deteriorating future," Israel alone looks hopefully forward to a future golden age of salvation. How is this? Can it be that this religion, with those prophecies which are to be miraculously fulfilled, are a *natural* product of the popular spirit of Israel, which for so long a time rebelled against them, and needed a thousand years of the heaviest divine chastisements at last to get rid of its natural tendency to idolatry, and which even then appropriated rather the husk than the kernel of these promises? Even in this preliminary question the historical principles of the critical school are found wanting.

The truth that underlies these deductions of Baur, which it was his merit to bring to light, is simply this, that the spiritual tendencies which he regards as the generating causes of Christianity really were preparations and connecting links for it; that they made way for its reception and spread, and hence attained an influence on the development of the Church which is not to be underrated. Not until the world was historically prepared by those elements of its outward and inward development, did Christianity enter it: "In the fulness of the time (when the time was fulfilled) God sent His Son" (Gal. iv. 4). But are we to conclude that because Christianity had its natural preparations and conditions, it is therefore essentially nothing but the natural unity of these historical conditions? *In this case the preparations for a matter are simply confounded with the generative cause of the matter itself;* and this is a fallacy which can only be perpetrated by the Hegelian view of history, with its aversion to the miraculous. When Christianity is once in existence, like every other original phenomenon, it resembles the egg of Columbus, and may easily be comprehended in its intrinsic truth and its grand simplicity, as the goal towards which the preceding development in many ways was distinctly tending. But for all that it remains an *original* production, a truly creative, specifically new and world-regenerating principle, which *carries the sufficing cause of its existence in itself alone.* It is not, nor ever will be, possible to compare the incomparable. Critics may draw parallels as they will in every direction between pre-Christian and Christian truths, and search after the elements preparatory for Christianity; yet always the specific and characteristic principle of Christianity will be wanting: the idea of the unity of God and man is foreign to the pre-Christian world. St. Paul's feeling for universal history can well discern those preparatory elements in their dispersion through the divine plan of education; but he would never grant that the principle of Christitianity itself could result from the "weak and beggarly elements of this world" (Gal. iv. 3, 9); it could only come in by a *divine act,* the sending of God's Son.

Baur says: "What long since in various ways was the goal of all rational efforts, and of necessity forced itself upon the consciousness of man as its essential purport," at length found its natural expression in Christianity. St. Paul says: "Eye hath not seen, nor ear heard, *neither have entered into the heart of man,* the things which God hath prepared for them that love Him: but God hath revealed them unto us by His Spirit" (1 Cor. ii. 9, 10). Baur himself seems at length to have felt that in the face of this truth all attempts at a natural derivation are insufficient; for he says: "That the elements of a new religious development, which *per se* were already extant, should have concentrated themselves in the generation of a new life at one particular point and in one special individual,—this is the wonder in the history of the origin of Christianity which no historical reflection can further analyse." And still more would this seem to be the case, when he tells us in another place that he too "acknowledges a certain supernatural character and a divine principle working in an especial manner" in Christianity, only not an absolute miracle which should exclude all natural mediation.

But we have already seen that real miracles do not absolutely exclude natural mediation; on the contrary, that they often are linked to that which is already extant. And this was the case with the miraculous entrance of Christianity into history. That there was *tinder* enough laid ready we willingly acknowledge, and thank the man who has pointed it out to us in detail. But as long as we do not recognise the lightning spark of a supernatural vital principle as having actually touched the inert mass, we can never understand the fire which suddenly burst forth and set the whole ancient world in flames;—we shall grope in the dark as long as we seek its origin below and not above.

Moreover, the attempt to deny the creative action of God in the origin of Christianity, and to reduce the supernatural to the co-operation of merely natural factors, likewise involves *the greatest historical difficulties and absurdities. If the world at that time, we ask, was pregnant with the new spiritual religion, why did she so remorselessly persecute her own offspring?* How was it that all nations did not hail it with applause, and rejoice in the new acquisition? How was it that Jews, Greeks and Romans, especially the great and wise men of the world, for three centuries carried on the most embittered warfare against Christianity with all the available resources of their religion, their statesmanship, their culture, and science; and all this in utter blindness, without seeing, what it was left for Baur to discover, that they were raging against that which was related to their own flesh and blood, and had emanated from it by natural development? Roman universalism rages against its Christian counterpart with fire and sword. The cultivated Greek calls St. Paul a babbler. The thoughtful Roman designates Christianity—this natural fruit of all past culture—as an *odium generis humani*, hated and abhorred by the whole world. How can this be explained from the standpoint of the Tübingen School? Here, if anywhere, our Lord's words are applicable: "*If ye were of the world, the world would love his own*,"—had Christianity been a natural outflow of the spirit of the age, that age must straightway have received it,—" but because ye are not of the world, but I have chosen you out of the world, therefore the world hateth you" (John xv. 19). Here we find an explanation of this hatred. The Tübingen School can give us none.

We obtain just as little satisfaction when we ask to be enlightened as to the Person of Christ and His characteristic consciousness. In this matter the historical school is very cautious and reserved; and it is not without cause that Strauss reproaches Baur with asking, "not what Jesus really did or said, but what the narrators make him do and say: thus he busies himself with the Gospels, but leaves the Lord out of the question." However, we have already seen that thus much is evident, that Baur admits as the historical purport of the life of Christ nothing but a career entirely devoid of miracles, and likewise in His Person only such moral perfection as shall not exceed the measure of natural humanity. In order to carry out his views, the Tübingen critic is compelled to reduce all that is supernatural in the discourses of Christ to mere natural truths, and to change divine revelations into natural conditions of human moral consciousness. It is self-evident that the most arbitrary means must be used in order everywhere to prove the "purely moral" character of this doctrine, and especially that the *importance of Christ's Person for the new redemption that had now appeared* must be entirely ignored. Hence the passages in which salvation appears linked to this particular Person, and which cannot possibly be applied to the mere generality of a moral relationship, must be attributed to the conceptions of a later age, which influenced the pseudo-evangelist. What shall we say, *e.g.*, when Baur explains the beatitudes to the effect that they express "the still undeveloped pure sense of a need for redemption"? Just as if the pure sense of hunger contained in itself all the reality of its appeasing! Everything must be already extant, so that we may not have to acknowledge anything absolutely new or supernatural. Even Baur's example plainly shows that all attempts to give a natural explanation of the supernatural must lead to unnatural or at least ambiguous expedients.

If the essential substance of the self-consciousness of Christ consisted merely in general principles of human morality, then we find the same historical difficulties, *the same unexplained and inexplicable residuum,* which, as we have already seen, form an insurmountable barrier for all the anti-miraculous accounts of the life of Christ. They amount to these two questions: *How could these simple moral maxims bring about that universal revolution in the religious life and thought of the whole world?* And again, *If Jesus was conscious of being a merely natural man, how could the belief in His Messiahship arise either in Himself or His disciples?* Here Baur shows himself a true Hegelian. The Messiahship of Christ became a firmly established fact of His consciousness after others had "intuitively seen" in Him the Messiah. And how so? The universally moral and purely spiritual substance of the consciousness of Christ needed a distinct *form,* in order that "through the medium of Jewish national consciousness it might be able to expand into universal consciousness."[1] And this concrete form was the Messianic idea. Now, because the substance of Christ's consciousness was universal, but its form was affected with the partiality of Judaism, therefore the personality of Jesus is to be considered "in the light of a contradiction—as a developing process"—and an inward conflict, in which "the two opposing elements are related to each other as substance to form, as idea to reality, as universal humanity to Jewish nationality, as divine sublimity to human limitation." In answer to this monstrous conception, it has well been pointed out,[2] that the effectiveness in the character and work of great men always consisted, not in a dualism, but in a *harmonious* unison between substance and form; and that classical natures have always been entire, complete, and self-contained ones (cf. pp. 367 et ss.). And how inconceivable is the way in which Baur rends asunder form and substance of the self-consciousness, as though the form suddenly appeared and enveloped the substance, instead of each being generated in and with the other! But if the form be original, that is to say, if the Messianic idea belong to the essential and original substance of the self-consciousness of Christ, how can this be reduced to mere human dimensions? It is the old story; the Hegelian must always have two aspects or factors in order to evolve from their unity and diversity the needful categories of position and negation, idea and reality, etc. etc., as reels on which to

[1] *Die Tübinger Schule,* 2d ed. pp. 30 et ss.

[2] Cf. Beckh, *ubi sup.*

spin the threads of historical development. How useless these are, even from a psychological point of view, we have here seen.

Just as little, on the other hand, is the *belief of the disciples* explained. How came the Messianic idea to be applied to Christ if He was a mere man and did no miracles? Whence the entire origin of the new religion if it had no particular *facts*, but only general moral discourses for its foundation? "If a religion do not begin with an original fact, it cannot begin at all," says Schleiermacher (*Reden über die Religion*); "for there must be some common reason for the sake of which a certain religious element is especially emphasized, and this reason can only consist in a fact." Whence arose the belief of the disciples in the divine Sonship of Christ? And if it were a mere idea, a later conception, whence its transmutation into facts in the shape of so many miraculous narratives? Whence—as we have already asked, without receiving a satisfactory answer—the belief of the disciples in the resurrection of Christ, if this was not a fact? Whence St. Paul's testimony to it, even in the Epistles which Baur recognises as genuine? Whence the *sudden inward change in Saul* if the risen Saviour did not meet him in the way to Damascus? We have seen that it is impossible to explain away this event as a merely *inward* vision. Baur is here in great straits, and feels what a large unexplained residuum is left after all his attempts at natural explanations. Hence the confession in his last book, that the conversion of St. Paul was a "wonder," and that "no analysis, either psychological or dialectic, can clear up the mystery of that act in which God revealed His Son in Paul."

Finally, we come to Baur's theory, that it was St. Paul who liberated Christianity from the limitations of Judaism and raised it to the dignity of the universal religion; because in him first "the principle of Christianity became purely and absolutely predominant" (*Der Apostel Paulus*, p. 512). If, then, he was in fact the founder of Christianity as a world-wide power, *how comes he constantly to refer all his teaching and all his knowledge to the crucified and risen Christ?* ("I determined not to know anything among you, save Jesus Christ and Him crucified," 1 Cor. ii. 2.) Whence his plain declaration, "We preach *not ourselves, but Christ Jesus the*

Lord" (2 Cor. iv. 5); and that, "Other foundation can no man lay than that *is laid*, which is Jesus Christ"? (1 Cor. iii. 11.) How can we account for his testimony that he had become what he was only through Christ, and had only begun his new course after having been apprehended by Him? (Phil. iii. 7–14, iv. 13.) How is it that he constantly puts back his own personality behind that of Christ, that He only may be preached (Phil i. 18), and is ever looking forward to the day of Christ? Surely the apostle who (Gal. i. 8) pronounces even an angel from heaven accursed if he preach any other gospel than that of Christ, would have declined the honour of being regarded as the inventor of a new Christianity; nay, rather would have indignantly repelled the reproach of having disfigured, or at least essentially altered, the gospel of Christ by his doctrine. *What, then, is St. Paul without Christ?* Why are we now *Christians* and not *Paulinists?* And why did not the apostles and primitive Christians, if they were nothing but Jews, not remain such?

Clearly, the chief motive which impels Baur to refer as much as possible of primitive Christianity to the authorship of St. Paul, is again only his *aversion to the miraculous.* For in him he has a purely human actor, and has no need, step by step, to explain away the supernatural element which shines forth so strongly in the person and work of Christ. The more he can put upon St. Paul, the less remains for Christ, and the easier is it to draw Him into the current of universal human development. Even Renan remarks on this subject: "Since we know infinitely more of Paul than of the twelve; since we possess his authentic writings and original records, we make him of the first importance, almost more than Jesus. This is a mistake. Nothing can be more false than the fashionable notion of our day, that Paul was the author of Christianity. The true founder of Christianity was Jesus."[1]

[1] *The Apostles*, p. 3. We do not, however, for a moment mean to compare this miserable production of Renan's with the investigations of Baur, which will ever continue to be of the greatest scientific value. For Renan immediately proceeds to exhibit his utter incapacity for historical insight into the real nature of primitive Christianity, by adding: "St. Paul cannot be compared either with Jesus or his immediate disciples (not even with the apostles then!). The *first places* (after Jesus) must be reserved for those great companions of Jesus, and

In view of all these unsolved difficulties, one can hardly escape the conclusion, that *the "construction" of history by the critical school makes historical enigmas instead of explaining them.* This is confirmed by Baur's account of the *apostolic age and its antitheses.*

If primitive Christianity was only a species of Judaism, its historical development presents a series of insoluble enigmas. This will become evident from a consideration of the two fundamental suppositions on which Baur's entire criticism rests, viz. that a sharp *rivalry existed between the Petrine and the Pauline party,* and that the primitive Christians did not believe in the Godhead of Christ.

We first consider the former of these suppositions. Did this antithesis between Jewish and Gentile Christianity really govern the whole Church? If this was the case, that is to say, if the development of primitive Christianity consisted of a struggle between contraries, which were for long engaged in an irreconcilable conflict, and did not coalesce until towards the latter part of the second century, then it is an enigma that they should ever have coalesced at all. Had so important a difference of principles existed within the apostolic Church, *it must assuredly have separated into two distinct parties,* which would never again have united. The Petrine party would always have appealed to St. Peter, the Pauline to St. Paul, just as to this day, three centuries and a half since the Reformation, the Lutherans appeal to Luther, and the Calvinists to Calvin, although their doctrinal differences as to the presence of Christ in the sacrament, etc., are far less important than was the matter in dispute between St. Peter and St. Paul, viz. whether the Jews who became Christians should be compelled to be circumcised, and therefore to keep the whole law, or not. *History often teaches us that what was originally one, may separate into various parts* (as, *e.g.*, the Baptists and the Methodists have split into various distinct denominations), *but not* vice versa, *that communities which were originally separated* by

those passionately moved and faithful women (*amies*) who, in spite of death, believed on him!!" Assuredly Baur's theory is grand compared with such nonsense as this, according to which Mary Magdalene is greater, and has done more for Christianity, than the apostle of the Gentiles!

reason of the different principles of their founders *should afterwards coalesce into one body.*

It was perfectly natural and necessary that Jews and Gentiles who were converted to Christianity could not all at once discard the influences of their past history, and that some time must elapse before they could stand on equal terms with each other. It was also very natural that differences should occur in the apostolic treatment of the Gentiles. Nor is this at all concealed by the Acts and Epistles.[1] But *distinctions are not antitheses,*[2] and there are weighty testimonies contained in the New Testament which go to prove that these distinctions were amicably *adjusted in brotherly unity* as early as the apostolic age. In Acts xv. the whole assembly at Jerusalem, consisting of Peter and Paul, together with James and all the other apostles and elders, agree together "to lay no greater burden" upon the Gentiles who were baptized by requiring them to keep the law of Moses. Baur gets over this difficulty by declaring the Acts to be a spurious book, written with the intention of mediating between the opposed parties. But he cannot get rid of the passage (ii. 9) in the confessedly genuine Epistle to the Galatians, where St. Paul says that James, Peter, and John, *i.e.* the heads of the Jewish-Christian party, "when they perceived the grace that was given unto me, gave to me and Barnabas the right hands of fellowship, that we should go unto the heathen and they unto the circumcision." Does this betoken rivalry, or brotherly unity? True, St. Paul is obliged severely to reprove St. Peter, because at Antioch he

[1] Cf. especially Gal. ii. 12, which tells how St. Peter allows himself to be moved for a time to deny his former intercourse with the Gentiles by the arrival of "certain that came from James," *i.e.* legal Jewish Christians from the church at Jerusalem.

[2] Not even the simply practical teaching of St. James's Epistle exhibits a fundamentally different conception of Christianity from that of St. Paul. The conviction is becoming more and more widespread, that St. James, having other opponents, was obliged to emphasize a different aspect of the Christian life to that principally described by St. Paul in his doctrine of justification, but that both of them clearly distinguish between the inward reconciliation with God by His grace through faith (attainment of the righteousness which is by faith), and the outward verification of this faith by means of decisive proofs (works). The difference lies *in the language* used by each, inasmuch as what St. Paul usually designates as "being saved" (σώζεσθαι, *e.g.* Eph. ii. 8), is expressed by St. James in the word which St. Paul generally applies to the first act of the Christian course (to be justified, δικαιοῦσθαι).

hypocritically gave himself the appearance of one who avoided intercourse with the Gentiles, whereas he had long since carried it on. But St. Paul evidently speaks of him as one who was hitherto of the same opinion with himself, and had now become untrue to his convictions; and for this very reason St. Peter could not answer him. St. Paul says (Gal. ii. 14 and 18), "If thou, being a Jew, livest after the manner of Gentiles, and not as do the Jews, why compellest thou the Gentiles to live as do the Jews? . . . For if I build again the things which I destroyed, I make myself a transgressor." These words evidently presuppose that *at first* St. Peter took up *the same position in regard to the Jews as St. Paul,* and that only in this single instance, from a fear of man which he more than once evinces, he weakly gave way to the Jewish Christians who had come from James, and inconsistently withdrew from intercourse with the Gentiles. But on two previous occasions (Acts xi. 4 et ss. and xv. 7 et ss.), he had openly defended this intercourse, and maintained the equality of Jews and Gentiles in virtue of the one faith.

We willingly admit that the opinion of the oldest Jewish-Christian churches, and of their leaders, St. Peter and St. James, may have undergone various *modifications.* For clearly the position which for some time seems to have been taken up by St. Peter, that the Jewish Christians were to keep the law, whereas the Gentiles were freed from it, was undecided, if not confused. It may be that, after the apostolic council related in Acts xv., a certain reaction was brought about by the strictly legal party, so that many repented of the concession made to their Gentile brethren, and that this caused a wavering in the behaviour of Peter and James. For we have indications elsewhere of a variety of parties amongst the Jewish Christians, whereas there is not a trace in the whole New Testament of sects properly so called, *i.e.* of ecclesiastical schisms, nor yet of a heretical Jewish Christianity. But, on the supposition that these different tendencies existed, the behaviour of the Jewish apostles as related in Gal. ii. may very well be reconciled with the position taken up by them in Acts xv.[1] These very fluctuations prove that there was *no*

[1] See the convincing demonstration of this by Lechler, *Das apostolische u. nachapostolische Zeitalter.*

fundamental contradiction between them and St. Paul, and that *it is false to represent the senior apostles as occupying an entirely Jewish standpoint.* For how could they then have formally acknowledged St. Paul as the apostle of the Gentiles, endowed with apostolic gifts, and in consideration of this have given him "the right hand of fellowship"? Surely this would have been mean hypocrisy. And how could they have *quietly looked on* whilst St. Paul converted the heathen in a way so at variance with their convictions? And St. Paul himself, too, who on other occasions (as *e.g.* in the Epistle to the Galatians) opposed the extreme Judaists so vigorously, would assuredly not have been silent had the other apostles been essentially on a level with them. And how could this inimical rivalry be reconciled with the *influence of the Holy Ghost,* who was to lead the apostles into all truth? Or, as the critical school does not acknowledge His action, we ask how, on the same supposition, can we explain the *constant communion* which St. Paul kept up with the church at Jerusalem, and the faithful care for their wants which he ceaselessly exercised by frequent *collections for Jerusalem amongst the Gentile Christian churches?* (Gal. ii. 10; Rom. x. 25 et ss.; 1 Cor. xvi.; 2 Cor. viii. and ix.; Acts xi. 29, 30, xii. 25.) When we see the Gentile Christians in Antioch, Macedonia, Greece, ministering joyfully, and often "beyond their power" (2 Cor. viii. 2–4), to the wants of the church in Judæa, does this betoken fundamental differences, or brotherly love and unity?

Jewish and Gentile Christianity are two forms of the same spirit which supplement each other; they make up a unity which soon enough was definitely exhibited in the persons of the chief apostles, though after certain fluctuations. *Nor does the question as to the treatment of Gentile Christians constitute an original and fundamental contrariety within the apostolic circle; they are essentially unanimous upon the subject. Only St. Paul and the Gentile-Christian party made more rapid progress in the direction of a free universalism than did the Jewish Christians,* especially St. James and the church in Jerusalem, which, as long as the temple stood (in which Christ Himself had taught), continued to pray there, and to take part in the Mosaic worship. It was therefore quite another thing for them to tear themselves away from Judaism than for the Gentile Christians, who had no temple and no Jewish history to look back upon. Hence *the development of primitive Christianity progressed not in contrarieties, but in steps:*[1] whilst one part soon went forward more quickly, the other slower one tenaciously clung to a lower step, until at length, through the destruction of Jerusalem and the annihilation of the temple, even the blindest eyes were opened.

The *first stage* in the development of primitive Christianity may be considered to extend from the feast of Pentecost down to the persecution to which Stephen fell victim. At this time the great body of the Church consisted of baptized Jews. Doubtless, however, there were among these many Hellenists (Greek Jews, called in the Authorized Version "Grecians," Acts vi. 1); even the seven almoners (*ibid.*) all having Greek names. During this first period the opposition against the Pharisees, then the ruling Jewish party, had developed most vigorously within the Church, as we see from the speech of Stephen. Even at this stage Christianity is by no means merely a form of Judaism. Baur admits that the first Christians recognised Jesus as the Messiah. In conjunction with this, we must believe that all the wondrous fulness which to the Jew lay in the idea of the Messiah was transferred to Him. This one point, the belief in the Messiah who had already appeared, was sufficient to make the disciples in every respect different from ordinary Jews. The Messianic expectation was the culminating point of their religious consciousness as Jews; and if an alteration took place in this climax, then their religious consciousness must have undergone an essential change in every way. Baur himself admits that by their acknowledgment of Jesus as the Messiah, even after His death on the cross, they had substantially broken through the limitations of Judaism,—an admission, however, which he does not care to follow out. A church that has been baptized by the *Spirit*, in the name of the *triune* God, and which, to the great annoyance of the Jews, confesses a *crucified* Messiah, is assuredly no longer a mere development of Judaism, but something specifically new.

[1] Thus the First Epistle of St. Peter clearly indicates a *progress* in his standpoint. Even that of St. James is no longer specifically Judaistic.

The germs, too, of a catholic conception of the Church were not wanting amongst the first Jewish Christians: on the contrary, they showed great vigour from the very beginning, though afterwards for a time somewhat pushed into the background. This can only be denied by those who reject the history of the *feast of Pentecost*, related in Acts ii., as without historical foundation. Even on this the day of her institution the Christian Church shows herself as a *missionary Church*, which is commissioned to proclaim the great deeds of God to all nations (Acts ii. 9–11). Wherefore should not the idea that the kingdom of God was to be extended far beyond the boundaries of Israel have been introduced before the appearance of St. Paul? Had not our Lord commanded the eleven, and that long before the conversion of St. Paul, "Go ye and teach all nations"? Indeed, from the very beginning He had spoken of them as "the salt of the *earth*" and "the light of the *world*" (Matt. v. 13 and 14); He had told them that He had other sheep who were not of this fold (John xv.); He had testified to the Jews that men should "come from the east and from the west, from the north and from the south, and sit down in the kingdom of God" (Matt. viii. 11; Luke xiii. 29); indeed, He had even roundly declared to them that the kingdom of God should be taken from them and given to the Gentiles (Matt. xxi. 43, etc.). Did not all this clearly enough indicate *the world-embracing nature of the kingdom of God?* Had He not even gone amongst Samaritans and into heathen borderlands (Matt. iv. 15, xv. 21), although He was primarily sent only to the lost sheep of the house of Israel? Could not such conduct on the part of their Master have implanted germs of a wider idea of the divine kingdom in the hearts of the first disciples? Nay, more. Had not long since innumerable sayings of the prophets predicted the reception of the heathen into the kingdom of God? (Micah iv. 1–4; Isa. ii. 2–4, xix. 18–25, lx.–lxvi. etc.; Ps. xxii. 28 et ss., lxxxvii. xcvi. xcvii. etc.; cf. Luke ii. 32, Matt. ii. 1 et ss., xii. 21.) Are we to suppose that all these were lost upon the first Jewish Christians? By whom else were they to be fulfilled than by the Messiah and His kingdom? and Him they believed to have come. Not only is the idea of a universal kingdom of God older than St. Paul, but even than the Roman empire to which Baur wishes to bind it down. This idea is a necessary consequence of Monotheism, and, like it, has sprung up on the soil of divine revelation.

Thus we see that the germs of Christian universalism were extant from the very outset. But the apostles had received the command to begin their preaching at Jerusalem (Luke xxiv. 47 ; Acts i. 8), and it was therefore necessary that they should first fulfil their mission for Israel.

The *second stage* includes the period from the death of Stephen to the appearance of St. Paul. Foreigners are admitted to the Church ; many *Samaritans* believe through the preaching of St. Philip; St. Peter baptizes the Roman *Cornelius* and his house after he had been convinced by the vision of the clean and unclean animals (Acts x. 11 et ss.), that "in every nation he that feareth God and worketh righteousness is accepted with Him;" the gospel penetrates to Antioch, from which place the name of Christian is spread abroad. In this period the Church became aware that the Gentiles were *now already* called to share in Christ's salvation, and that without becoming Jews by circumcision.

In the *third stage* we see the Church acting out this conviction with more and more decision, and endeavouring to develope her unity and self-dependence by reconciling her internal differences. The chief part in this work was reserved for the spirit that rose from the ashes of Stephen. *St. Paul* looks at the distinction between the Old and the New Covenant rather as one of *kind* than one of *degree*, as the other apostles at first conceived it. He considers this difference in the light of an *antithesis*, and contrasts Christ with Moses, as being the new and the only way to the fulfilment of the law,—indeed, as "the end of the law." He teaches clearly and pointedly that salvation is now to be found in the gospel of Jesus Christ alone, and not in the law; and that because this salvation is granted only *through grace*, it is destined for the Gentiles as well as the Jews, although it must first be proclaimed to the latter (Acts xiii. 46). Here, then, the *full universalist standpoint* of Christianity was attained.

This view of primitive Christianity has been successfully defended against Baur by our present historical and exegetical theology; and you can easily see how naturally everything is here developed. True, no development can take place without the *tension* and reconciliation of contrarieties. This is the truth of Baur's fundamental axiom. But it is not fair to exaggerate the differences, and still less to introduce *dissensions of later date* into the apostolic age. Now Baur is guilty of so doing, for he has simply transferred the party divisions of the *second* century back to the *first*. This is a fundamental error both in his views as to primitive Christianity and in his criticism of the New Testament writings. After the death of the leading apostles, followed by the destruction of Jerusalem and the erection of a Romish colony (Ælia Capitolina) in its place, Jewish Christianity lost its original pre-eminence, and was gradually separated from the current of development. Then, and not till then, did it begin to fall into heresy and separate itself from the Catholic Church, whereupon it soon split into different sects through the influence of the extreme party mentioned in Acts xv. 5, Gal. ii. 4. But during the lifetime of the apostles, the milder party of Jewish Christians had been in the ascendant (Acts xv. 22 et ss.), and had come to an agreement on the principal question, viz. the position of Gentile Christians with respect to the law.[1] A breach amongst the apostles on account of this matter would assuredly have exercised a most paralysing influence on the development of Christianity. But instead of this, we find that, when they leave the scene, the Church had already grown so strong that the subsequent separation of Jewish sects was unable perceptibly to impede the universal progress of Christianity.

History everywhere teaches us that each great new truth needs some time before it can make its way and scatter the old prejudices. In this case, moreover, the emancipation from the Jewish law must needs be all the more gradual, inasmuch as the new religion was also the *fulfilment of the old one.* If we keep this in mind, we shall perfectly well be able to comprehend the development of the primitive Christian Church; nor will there be any need for us to rend asunder into hostile parties that pious company, for whom the Lord Himself had prayed that they might be one, even as He was one with the Father.

We come to the *second axiom* of Baur's criticism, which

[1] Cf. the article on "Ebionites" in Herzog's *Realencyclopädie*, iii. pp. 621 et ss.

maintains that the *primitive Christians did not believe in the Godhead of Christ,* and that therefore all those writings in the New Testament which contain this doctrine in a highly developed form are *eo ipso* spurious, and of post-apostolic origin. To this we answer, that *even those five books which Baur acknowledges as genuine* (Romans, 1st and 2d Corinthians, Galatians, and Revelation), *and not only those which he supposes to have originated at a later period* (Ephesians, Philippians, Colossians, and especially the Gospel of St. John), *contain a conception of Christ which lifts Him entirely above the level of a mere man, and places Him in a perfectly unique relationship to God.* It is impossible to set up an impassable barrier between the Christology of the former and that of the latter set of writings, or to prove that the latter represent an essentially new, and therefore later standpoint. This is proved, in the *first place,* by all the predicates applied to Christ in the unimpugned epistles: "the Son of God" (Rom. i. 3 and 4); the "one Lord, by whom are all things" (1 Cor. viii. 6); the "spiritual Rock" which followed Israel through the wilderness, and hence existed before His incarnation (1 Cor. x. 4); "the Lord from heaven" (1 Cor. xv. 47); "the Lord of glory" (1 Cor. ii. 8); "the Image of God" (2 Cor. iv. 4); He "in whom" God was (2 Cor. v. 19); whom "God sent in the likeness of sinful flesh" (Rom. viii. 3); the Ruler of the world, under whose feet God hath put all things (1 Cor. xv. 25–27); the Judge of the world before whose judgment-seat we must all appear (2 Cor. v. 10; Rom. xiv. 10); yea, "who is *over all, God* blessed for ever" (Rom. ix. 5; cf. p. 249). Again, it is proved by the way in which these writings everywhere represent Christ as the risen and exalted Lord, as the centre of salvation for the whole world, and hence as One who is higher than men ("not of men, but by Jesus Christ," Gal. i. 1), while placing Him in a uniquely close relationship to God (2 Cor. xiii. 13; 1 Cor. xii. 4–6; Rom. xi. 36; cf. pp. 255 et ss.). And finally, even the Book of Revelation points to the same conclusion, with its representation of the divine majesty of Him who is "Alpha and Omega," the "First and the Last," the living One who hath "the keys of hell and death" (i. 8–18), the "Word of God" (xix. 13), who is worshipped by the saints (v. 11–14, etc.). Can any one who has considered all this believe that St. Paul and St. John, the indubitable authors of these writings, held an inferior view of Christ's person, or believed Him to be a mere man?

And is there such a great gulf between these views and the doctrine of Christ's person as contained in the later epistles? No; for their doctrinal tenets may be traced, either as germs, or even word for word, in the five earliest books. Compare, for instance, the following passages:—2 Cor. iv. 4, "Who is the image of God," and Col. i. 15, "Who is the image of the invisible God" (also Heb. i. 3); 2 Cor. v. 19, "God was in Christ," and Col. ii. 9, "In Him dwelleth all the fulness of the Godhead bodily" (also 1 Tim. iii. 16); 2 Cor. viii. 9, "Who, though He was rich, yet for your sakes He became poor," and Phil. ii. 6, "Who, being in the form of God, thought it not robbery to be equal with God, but made Himself of no reputation;" Rom. viii. 3, "God sent His Son in the likeness of sinful flesh," and Phil. ii. 7, He "took upon Him the form of a servant, and was made in the likeness of men;" 1 Cor. viii. 6, "One Lord Jesus Christ, by whom are all things, and we by Him," and Col. i. 16, "By Him were all things created," etc. (cf. Eph. iii. 9 and John i. 3); Rom. ix. 5, "over all, God blessed for ever," and Heb. i. 8 and 9, "Unto the Son He saith, Thy throne, O God, is for ever and ever" (also Tit. ii. 13); Rev. i. 5, "the First-begotten of the dead," and Col. i. 18, "Who is the Beginning, the First-born from the dead" (also Acts xxvi. 23); Rev. xix. 13, "His name is called, The Word of God," and John i. 1 et ss., "The Word was with God," etc.; 1 Cor. ii. 8, "Lord of glory," and Col. i. 27, "Christ, the hope of glory" (also Acts iii. 15); and numerous other passages.[1]

Is it possible, I ask, in the face of these parallels to maintain that essentially different views of our Lord's person are taken in the unimpugned writings and in the others? No; the distinction is merely this, that the former in most cases merely *hint* at what the others purposely *discuss* in all its bearings. This may be very simply explained from the fact,

[1] As, *e.g.*, 1 Cor. i. 24, 30, with Col. ii. 3; 1 Cor. viii. 9 with 1 Thess. iii. 13, v. 23, 24; 1 Cor. x. 4 with John viii. 58; Col. i. 17, Eph. i. 4, 2 Tim. i. 9, 1 Cor. xii. 4–6, with Eph. iv. 4–6; 2 Cor. xiii. 13 with 1 Pet. i. 1, 2; Rev. i. 4, 5, with Matt. xxviii. 19.

that in course of time the growth of heresies made it increasingly necessary to treat the doctrine of the person of Christ more in detail, and that the apostles themselves had gradually to *grow* in their knowledge of Him.

The case is similar as regards the relationship of *St. John's Gospel* to the three preceding ones. Because it surrounds Jesus with the eternal glory of His divine Sonship, and emphasizes His pre-existence, therefore its Christology is supposed to be specifically different from that of the Synoptics, and a sure proof of its later origin. But it is impossible to deny that even the three first Gospels contain a far higher than merely human view of Jesus; they, too, ascribe to Him so many superhuman, nay, divine attributes and works, that we cannot in this respect make a fundamental distinction between their teaching and that of the fourth Gospel. Passing by the history of His conception through the Holy Ghost, of His baptism, His miracles, His transfiguration, resurrection, and ascension, we would point especially to the relation in which Christ places His person *to the Old Covenant* ("But *I say* unto you," Matt. v.: His representation of Himself as the Fulfiller of the law; as greater than the temple, as Lord of the Sabbath, as Forgiver of sins, etc.; cf. pp. 246 et ss.), as also *to the world,* in which He alone can relieve the weary and heavy laden, whose future Judge He represents Himself to be, to whom is committed all power in heaven and in earth (cf. *ubi sup.* and Matt. xxviii. 18). But above all, Christ, even in the Synoptics, represents *God as His Father* in a unique sense (cf. p. 246), whom no one knows but the Son, and who alone knows the Son;[1] so that in the baptismal command (Matt. xxviii. 19) He may insert His own name between that of the Father and the Holy Ghost as one of equal dignity. In all this we cannot but recognise a distinct premonition of St. John's Christology exhibiting the germs of the doctrine explicitly taught in the fourth Gospel,—germs, too, which presuppose the pre-existence of Christ as maintained by St. John. The critical school is here labouring under the same optical

[1] Cf. Matt. xi. 27*a* and John iii. 35, xiii. 3; Luke x. 22, Matt. xi. 27*b*, and John vi. 46, xvii. 25, xiv. 6 et ss., xv. 21; Matt. xxviii. 18 and John xvii. 2; Matt. xxviii. 20 and John xiv. 18; even John x. 30 and Matt. x. 37, etc.

illusion as we pointed out in the case of Strauss. Because the higher knowledge of Christ only gradually developed in the Church, it supposes that the Church must have evolved these higher elements from her own consciousness, or borrowed them from Hellenistic philosophy.

Moreover, we would point out what peculiar and evidently untenable conclusions result from this hypothesis, that the great majority of the New Testament writings originated in the endeavour to mediate between the Petrine and the Pauline party, and were therefore composed by unknown authors in the second century. Even the tendency which these writings are supposed to betray is by no means demonstrable, not even in the Acts; indeed, it is so little proven, that every new critic discovers a fresh "tendency." Were we to enter upon an analysis of the various writings, we might thus even dispute the presuppositions of this criticism. But apart from this, how very strange it would be if not a single apostle out of all the eleven had left behind him any writings, with the exception of the one Revelation of St. John, which does not even categorically affirm its own authenticity! How inconceivable that this immense though gradual revolution from the most narrow-minded Jewish primitive Christianity to Pauline universalism, which changed a Jewish sect into the Christian Church universal, should have been guided *entirely by the works of anonymous writers,* who concealed their names under the cloak of apostolic authority, without one of their contemporaries remarking, or at least thinking it worth his while to make a note of the pious fraud! Unknown authors write the Gospels, more especially the "mediating" Gospel of St. Mark and the "sublime" Gospel of St. John; an unknown personage composes the "conciliatory" Acts; unknown forgers fabricate the Epistles to the Ephesians, Philippians, Colossians, Thessalonians, the Epistles of St. Peter, St. John, St. James, and St. Jude! In fact, the entire movement through which Christianity became itself is brought about by unknown persons. Every trace has vanished even of the "great nameless One," as Baur styles the author of the fourth Gospel. The apostles live in the *first* century, but they attain their reputation as writers during the *second* through the services of others. There, *men* appear, but without writings; here, *writings* come to light, but without men! How unnatural thus to tear asunder the men and their writings![1]

In other cases we invariably find that an age which is fertile in literary productions is followed by a conservative period, in which the productions of the foregoing are collected and digested,—first the classical, then the post-classical period. Here we should have exactly the reverse,—the first century conservative, in the main keeping to Judaism, with scarcely any productions; the second century progressive and fertile in great, but alas! unknown writers. *But does the second century in other respects bear the impress of a productive classical period of literature?* On the contrary: its undoubted products breathe a spirit which bears the same relation to that of the New Testament writings as does the tenor of a post-classical age to that of the preceding classical. *Did these writings, especially the Gospel of St. John, belong to "unknown" authors, they would be a perfectly inexplicable phenomenon* as compared with all the other products of that period. It has been well said, that it were no less absurd to ascribe the most inspiriting writings of Luther to the spiritless period of the Thirty Years' War, than to transfer the Gospel of St. John to the middle of the second century. For, notwithstanding their warm Christian life, the writings of the second century evince such a remarkable dearth of new ideas, that one plainly sees how, after the spiritual flood-tide of the first century, the ebb had set in.[2] Hence, as we have seen, negative critics have been compelled again to raise the age of the Gospels, and to place them in the apostolic age, between 50 and 100 A.D.

All this compels us to assert that *the fundamental views of*

[1] Cf. "Baur u. die Tübinger Schule," in Herzog's *Realencyclopädie*, xx. pp. 762 et ss. Hence Ritschl, too, considers the Gospel of St. John as genuine, "because the denial of its authenticity is a source of far greater difficulties than its acknowledgment."

[2] Compare, *e.g.*, the clear and sober-minded spirit of the New Testament epistles, or the quiet sublimity of the Gospel of St. John, with the *Epistles of Ignatius*, the enthusiasm of which degenerates into a well-nigh fanatic desire for martyrdom; or with the *Pastor of Hermas*, and the value ascribed by him to ascetic rigour; or with the *epistles* written (in the first century) by *Clement of Rome*, which tell the fable of the Phœnix as a fact; or again, with the *Epistle of Barnabas*, which delights in insipid allegories, and gives the most absurd typical interpretations of the Old Testament, justifying Neander's remark, that "here we encounter quite another spirit than that of an apostolic man."—*Eccl. History*, i. 3, p. 1100.

Baur entirely confuse and overturn the history of primitive Christianity and its records. Having rejected the miraculous beginning of Christianity for the sake of his philosophical presuppositions, Baur is fated constantly to see his "purely historical commencement" melt away beneath his touch. It is *a beginning without a beginning;* everything is already extant. Principles of thought which already exist are concentrated in Christ. He only introduces them into the consciousness of men, as the principle of a purely spiritual and perfectly moral religion. But by mixing up this principle with the Messianic idea He brings about His death, and with this the first beginning has failed. The essential essence of Christianity is no longer developed in connection with its Founder. Now Christianity has need of a new historical beginning, and this is furnished by the belief of the disciples in the *resurrection, i.e.* not by a fact, but merely by the notion of a fact. But since the disciples confine themselves to the exclusive national element of Christ's consciousness, this beginning also threatens to subside in the sand; Christianity is mere *Ebionitism,* and remains essentially on the Judaistic standpoint. At length the real beginning of Christianity appears in St. Paul, who, in the involuntary impulse of his dialectic consciousness, gains the day in favour of Christian universalism. But this truly Christian Pauline beginning is in danger of perishing through Petrine opposition. Happily there appears (or rather does not appear) in the middle of the second century the author of the fourth Gospel, "the great nameless One," with his free "composition guided only by the idea," but not in the least historical. Here, at last, is the final beginning, after which we cannot conceive any other, although Baur, if he were consistent, ought to maintain that pure Christianity (*i.e.* morals without dogma) was only discovered by the modern age.

Here once more we see how the "natural explanation" of Christianity accumulates enigmas instead of solving them. Aversion to the miraculous *must* and ever will be punished in this way. It denies the existence of a specifically divine factor in Christ, which is the sole thing that can make the historical origin of Christianity and its immense effects conceivable, and degrades the superhuman form of One "upon whose shoulder is the government," and who alone can have been the primary cause of so great a movement. Thus it is that the anti-miraculists are compelled, in order to explain these events, to postulate reasons which crumble away on examination, because they are utterly insufficient to sustain the weight of such a gigantic superstructure. Having degraded the supernatural to the level of the natural, they are fain to intensify the latter supernaturally, by ascribing to it forces and effects which it cannot possibly have, nor ever has had.

The failure of this attempt is quite analogous to that of modern natural science in its endeavours to break down as much as possible the original firm barriers between the various species and genera of plants and animals, and finally to prove the origin of man from the species next below him without the influence of a higher principle. Darwin, and still more the materialistic members of his school, are aiming at the same end in the region of natural science, as Baur and his followers in that of history. Both of them bring confusion into history. Both of them convert orderly development into a chaos of strife and enmity. Both of them, especially, are desirous to eliminate the miraculous as far as possible, by proving that all intervals bridge themselves over naturally. And both cannot attain their end for the same reason: because they overlook the fact that nature as well as *history often moves forward in leaps; i.e.* although its progress is constantly mediated, yet this often takes place through such imperceptible transitions that the leap is concealed from our eyes. Now we must maintain, and that on specifically *moral* grounds, that every heroic deed, as the fruit of a moral resolve, is something new and original, which cannot be entirely derived from what preceded it. Much more, then, must we derive the doings of Him who is the primal Cause of all that has ever taken place, *not from the past*, but from His *supramundane* essence. In other words, we must believe it to be a miracle; and therefore we may not deny its supernatural interposition in history, whereby new beginnings are brought about, if we are not to lose the last key to the comprehension of the most important historical phenomena. Rothe will ever be in the right as against the anti-miraculists, when he thus addresses them: "Look to yourselves, and see whether you can interpret history without miracles,—whether you can put them aside and yet give a pragmatic explanation of established historical results, the key to which we who believe in miracles already possess. I, for my part, assuredly do not believe in miracles from dogmatic cupidity, but in the *interests of history*, because I cannot dispense with them as *historical explanations* of certain indubitable historical facts. *I do not find that they make rents in history; but, on the contrary, that by their aid alone am I able to get over its gaping chasms.*"

Certainly the supernatural origin of Christianity in its divine aspect is not to be explained: We who believe in the Bible, from the outset renounce any such pretensions. But we do make bold to prove that the "natural" beginning offered to us in its stead by the critical school and the Rationalists—or, indeed, any other attempt at a natural explanation—is *far more incomprehensible;* that it results in far greater enigmas, and must therefore necessarily fail. According to our view of the matter, the beginning itself, *i.e.* the Divine Sonship of Christ, is an enigma, but all the rest is fully comprehensible, and may be deduced from it in the most simple, natural, and rational manner. The critical school, on the contrary, give us what is apparently a natural beginning, but really none at all: everywhere and nowhere; melting under our touch; and making all that follows one great incomprehensible riddle. That this is in fact the dilemma, may be proved by a recent utterance of Professor Zeller's [1] (one of the few perfectly faithful and consistent followers of Baur). According to him, the essence of Christianity is not fully represented in its primitive form, but "everywhere, if you will, or nowhere:" it can only be known fully from the sum-total of its historical phenomena, but least of all from its dogmas, which are constantly changing, and must do so, since they are merely subjective (?). So Christianity is nothing but a portion of the world's history, the substance of which is perpetually changing, whose real essence can only be determined when once the drama of history is played out, and of which we never can say what it *is*, but only what it *has been!* What a comfortless idea, that would lead us to despair of all objective truth! The entire gain from the history of the Christian dogma during eighteen hundred years has dwindled down to zero. Though Baur does not openly

[1] In *Vorträge u. Abhandlungen geschichtlichen Inhalts.*

confess it, yet this is, in fact, the logical sequence of his views. For, supposing his moral philosophical conception of Christianity to be correct, what that is permanent has its long development really added to the general ethical principles of the Sermon on the Mount, if it is, properly speaking, only our own age—shall we say, since Kant?—that has returned to this pure conception of Christianity? But if, during this long period, the Christian faith has really made no true progress, nor in any way substantially enriched itself, could we then expect much from its future development, or entertain any hope of a happy *destination?*[1] *No; for as soon as the divine origin of Christianity is done away with, its final aim is also extinguished:* these two poles are inseparable. Since it is "everywhere and nowhere," it has neither beginning nor end, and hence no true development, no real history. A development that results in nothing is merely apparent. Thus we arrive at the logical sequence of Pantheism (cf. p. 207), that there is no *being*, but only a *becoming;* and hence, since there is no real being, the becoming also must be only apparent. Is not this a comfortless view?

Here we see what is the final fate of every mere moral conception of Christianity. Instead of affording a permanent incitement to man's moral vigour, it ends (though we say this without in the least wishing to derogate from the intense moral earnestness with which Baur struggled after truth) in *a world-view which thoroughly paralyses all his moral and intellectual energy.* For why should we exert ourselves if we can hope for no real results?

If we wish to escape these sad consequences, then—in view of the real and historical character of the miraculous—we must take heart and *enlarge the narrowness of our logical conceptions to meet the greatness of divine deeds,* instead of endeavouring to cramp the latter to suit our small conceptions and reducing them to mere vanishing magnitudes just as it pleases us. He who takes the latter course *cannot help turning history upside down,* as we have seen that Strauss and Baur do. They suppose the miraculous facts to have been produced by the belief in the Messianic dignity of Christ,

[1] Cf. Uhlhorn's article on the Tübingen School in the *Jahrbücher für deutsche Theologie*, vol. iii. pp. 316–327.

whereas this belief *could* only spring from the miraculous facts. They suppose, again, that the resurrection arose from the belief of the disciples, whereas the latter *could* only have taken its rise from the fact of the resurrection. They suppose, moreover, that St. Paul introduced Christ, *i.e.* Christianity, into the world's history, whereas St. Paul was called, borne, and guided by Christ till he became a character of mark in the world's history. This is what I call turning history upside down. And what is the origin of this strange undertaking? Nothing but the *philosophical presuppositions and the aversion to miracles* with which this school approaches history. Very many of the critics of our day fall into the *fundamental error of mistaking their philosophical and speculative treatment of Scripture for historical criticism.* Consciously or unconsciously, they allow their philosophical doubts, their unbiblical conception of God, or their enmity towards the miraculous, to decide even on purely historical questions, and thereby *bring confusion into the whole.* Against this practice it has been truly remarked, that "only the man whose religious convictions are founded upon Scripture is capable of criticising it in an entirely unbiassed spirit. In the case of a man of any other convictions, his disagreement with the substance of Scripture must play him constant tricks even in matters purely formal and historical." That very thing which Baur thought to be the strength of critical science, viz. the Hegelian view of the world and of history, is its weakness; this was the barrier which cramped the struggles of his mighty spirit, and prevented him from arriving at solid results.[1] Truly it is a tragic spectacle to see such a gigantic intellect wrestling with iron diligence to attain that which in itself is unattainable, a pure impossibility; and this especially because it exhibits not so much the error of the individual as the fault of his age,—that age ruled by a onesided, idealistic philosophy, in consequence of which so many of the first minds of our century—even a

[1] Cf. Landerer (*ubi sup.* pp. 76, 77), who on p. 67 utters over the grave of his departed colleague the following noteworthy sentiment: "It would be the greatest injustice to class Baur with the worthless and frivolous rabble of those who — without the intellectual power of following his deductions — merely adopt the negative and sceptical portion of his results, in order to use them as a fig leaf wherewithal to cover their own moral shame and intellectual hollowness."

Schleiermacher—in their grandest achievements fell "victims to the limitations of this particular standpoint."

With a correct presentiment of this inevitable issue, which probably the master of this school himself experienced, his followers have since, in part, like Schwégler and Köstlin, given up theology entirely; partly, like Ritschl, approached the standpoint of revealed religion; partly, as we have seen, at least made a series of important concessions with respect to the criticism of the New Testament writings. Thus the number of those who represent Baur's standpoint whole and entire is, at least among German theologians, very small. In Tübingen there is now no longer any Tübingen School. . . .

In conclusion, a request to my readers.

And, first of all, to those who are *believers.* Let me beg you *not to place all doubters indiscriminately in one class.* Some of them seek *in order to find.* These we must never despair of: God gives success to the upright. Others, however, seek *in order to lose,* and to cast away one article after another of the old faith; they diligently gather together specious arguments in favour of the unbelief which suits them; they have soon settled the question, mostly without any great inward conflicts, and are then inaccessible to all arguments, so that, as a rule, not human words, but only divine deeds, can set their heart and head right once more. In such cases the Christian's rule will be to strive less *against* them with human arguments than *for* them before God, with the weapons of his Christian priesthood. As against such opponents, the best argument, and that most likely to make an impression, is the *actual proof of a Christian moral life.* And while we lament that in our day so many are shaking at the foundations of our faith, let us not forget to take to ourselves *a share of the blame.* The most convincing proof for the great deeds of God, such as the resurrection, does not consist, nor ever has consisted, in words; but it is now as it was eighteen hundred years ago, *the living Church itself,* in which the risen Lord is dwelling and working, which counts all things for loss that she "may know Him and the power of His resurrection." So long as through our fault this spiritual life is lacking, there will never be any scarcity of doubters and deniers of our faith.

On the other hand, let me beg our *doubting opponents* to investigate religious questions, not merely with the head and with the narrow standard of our logical conceptions, but at the same time, nay, even beforehand, with the heart and conscience, whilst carefully following up the traces which are indicated to them by the weaker or stronger promptings of their innermost needs. Let me beg them to try themselves, and see whether it is not only that in us which is low and mean that is against Christ, whereas all that is great and noble is for Him. Let me beg them not to allow themselves to be blinded by the hollow though high-sounding phrases of so many journals and other writings, which, instead of promoting real knowledge, infinitely hinder it; or by the catch-words of those who know very well what they do not want, but not what they do want, and what positive result is to remain after all their negations. Let me beg them not to begin by accounting their doubts a sign of *strength*, whereas they are the very contrary. As in the case of the first doubter in paradise, so to this day doubt in its innermost nature is a wrong compliance, a weakness, a cowardly dread of ventures and difficulties; whereas the innermost source of faith is the courage which bravely seizes and stedfastly holds to that which is invisible. "A sceptic," says J. A. Bengel, the great commentator on the New Testament, "is like a traveller who should refuse to cross a puddle or to step over a twig, till all were smoothed down and filled up. Who would think such a man wise? Faith takes up all that it can get, and marches bravely onward; unbelief is the direct opposite of this. In studying the Bible, we must do like the courier who hurries over pools and hillocks the nearest way to his destination, and does not first seek to level every clod. That which is difficult at last comes of its own accord. The most important controversies are those which a man finds in his own heart." But these latter, we add, point us to the place where Thomas, the doubter even amongst the apostles, had to learn his faith. Only *in the wounds of Christ* can we learn by faith the truth which shall make us free. There only does unbelief, even to this day, learn to surrender and humbly confess: "My Lord and my God!" He who will not seek for the truth there will never find it. All that we can do for the sceptics of the present day is to make the way there as easy for them as may be, in order that the sign of Jonah, given by our buried and risen Lord, may be to them a rock of salvation and not of offence.

All my readers together I would remind of that word: "Every way of a man is right in his own eyes; but the Lord pondereth the hearts" (Prov. xxi. 2). Whether we build, or whether we pull down, to his own Master each one of us standeth or falleth. Let us "prove all things, and hold fast that which is good;" and let us, even though we may have our own secular calling, expend some labour on this probation. That alone for which we have striven and suffered with all our might, with labour and pains, is really ours: an honourably conquered conviction, a real possession. Only in so doing do we fulfil the apostolic injunction, "Let every one be *fully persuaded* in his own mind."

My task has only been to scatter here, in hope, some of those arguments for the truth which I have found to be tenable. The rest I must leave to my readers, and to the Lord of the harvest.

THE END.

www.ingramcontent.com/pod-product-compliance
Lightning Source LLC
LaVergne TN
LVHW021234110826
845150LV00002B/336

* 9 7 8 1 4 2 5 5 6 2 2 6 7 *

MODERN DOUBT

AND

CHRISTIAN BELIEF

A Series of Apologetic Lectures addressed to
Earnest Seekers after Truth.

BY
THEODORE CHRISTLIEB, D.D.,
UNIVERSITY PREACHER AND PROFESSOR OF THEOLOGY AT BONN.

TRANSLATED, WITH THE AUTHOR'S SANCTION, CHIEFLY BY
THE REV. H. U. WEITBRECHT, PH.D.
AND EDITED BY
THE REV. T. L. KINGSBURY, M.A.,
VICAR OF EASTON ROYAL, AND RURAL DEAN.

NEW YORK:
Scribner, Armstrong & Co.,
1874.

EDITOR'S NOTE.

THE following translation is in part the work of Mr. G. H. VENABLES (translator of Schmid's *Biblical Theology of the New Testament*), and in greater measure that of the REV. H. U. WEITBRECHT—the four last Lectures, and the last section *(B)* of Lecture IV. (from page 266), having been translated by him. Mr. WEITBRECHT, who has just received Deacon's orders in the diocese of Chester, studied for some years in Germany, and being the author's brother-in-law and former pupil, has throughout been favored with PROFESSOR CHRISTLIEB'S special sanction and assistance, which have also been extended to other parts of the work. For the objects mainly kept in view in successive portions of this important Treatise, and for some changes made in the present translation, which may almost be regarded as a third edition of the original work, the reader is referred to the author's own account of them in the following Preface. In addition to what is there said, the reader's attention may also be invited to the valuable Exposition of the Scriptural Doctrine of the Trinity in Section *A* (pages 244–265) of the Fourth Lecture.

T. L. K.